The Politics of Heritage in Indonesia

This study offers a new approach to the history of sites, archaeology, and heritage formation in Asia, at both the local and the trans-regional levels. Starting at Hindu–Buddhist, Chinese, Islamic, colonial, and prehistoric heritage sites in Indonesia, the focus is on people's encounters and the knowledge exchange taking place across colonial and post-colonial regimes. Objects are followed as they move from their site of origin to other locations, such as the Buddhist statues from Borobudur temple, which were gifted to King Chulalongkorn of Siam. The ways in which the meaning of these objects transformed as they moved away to other sites reveal their role in parallel processes of heritage formation outside Indonesia. Calling attention to the power of the material remains of the past, Marieke Bloembergen and Martijn Eickhoff explore questions of knowledge production, the relationship between heritage and violence, and the role of sites and objects in the creation of national histories.

MARIEKE BLOEMBERGEN is senior researcher at the Royal Netherlands Institute of Southeast Asian and Caribbean Studies (KITLV) and Professor in Archival and Postcolonial Studies at Leiden University. She has published on the politics and mobility of knowledge in colonial and post-colonial Indonesia, through the lens of policing and violence, material culture, and heritage practices within inter-Asian and transnational contexts.

MARTIJN EICKHOFF is senior researcher at NIOD Institute for War, Holocaust and Genocide Studies, and Professor in Archaeology and Heritage of War and Mass Violence at the University of Groningen. He has published widely on the relation between archaeology, politics, heritage formation, and mass violence, in Asia and Europe during the nineteenth and twentieth centuries.

ASIAN CONNECTIONS

Asian Connections is a major series of ambitious works that look beyond the traditional templates of area, regional or national studies to consider the trans-regional phenomena which have connected and influenced various parts of Asia through time. The series will focus on empirically grounded work exploring circulations, connections, convergences and comparisons within and beyond Asia. Themes of particular interest include transport and communication, mercantile networks and trade, migration, religious connections, urban history, environmental history, oceanic history, the spread of language and ideas, and political alliances. The series aims to build new ways of understanding fundamental concepts, such as modernity, pluralism or capitalism, from the experience of Asian societies. It is hoped that this conceptual framework will facilitate connections across fields of knowledge and bridge historical perspectives with contemporary concerns.

The Politics of Heritage in Indonesia

A Cultural History

Marieke Bloembergen

Royal Netherlands Institute of Southeast Asian and Caribbean Studies (KITLV) and Leiden University

Martijn Eickhoff

NIOD Institute for War, Holocaust and Genocide Studies, and University of Groningen

CAMBRIDGE
UNIVERSITY PRESS

University Printing House, Cambridge CB2 8BS, United Kingdom

One Liberty Plaza, 20th Floor, New York, NY 10006, USA

477 Williamstown Road, Port Melbourne, VIC 3207, Australia

314–321, 3rd Floor, Plot 3, Splendor Forum, Jasola District Centre, New Delhi – 110025, India

79 Anson Road, #06–04/06, Singapore 079906

Cambridge University Press is part of the University of Cambridge.

It furthers the University's mission by disseminating knowledge in the pursuit of education, learning, and research at the highest international levels of excellence.

www.cambridge.org
Information on this title: www.cambridge.org/9781108499026
DOI: 10.1017/9781108614757

First published 2020

Printed in the United Kingdom by TJ International Ltd. Padstow, Cornwall

A catalogue record for this publication is available from the British Library.

ISBN 978-1-108-49902-6 Hardback

Contents

List of Figures — *page* vi
Preface and Acknowledgements — ix
List of Abbreviations — xiv

Introduction: Towards a Mobile History of Heritage Formation in Asia — 1

1. Site Interventions, Knowledge Networks, and Changing Loyalties on Java, 1800–1850s — 22
2. Exchange, Protection, and the Social Life of Java's Antiquities, 1860s–1910s — 61
3. Great Sacred Majapahit: Biographies of a Javanese Site in the Nineteenth Century — 97
4. Greater Majapahit: the Makings of a Proto-Indonesian Site across Decolonisation, 1900s–1950s — 129
5. The Prehistoric Cultures and Historic Past of South Sumatra on the Move — 164
6. Resurrecting Siva, Expanding Local Pasts: Centralisation and the Forces of Imagination across War and Regime Change, 1920s–1950s — 194
7. Fragility, Losing, and Anxieties over Loss: Difficult Pasts in Wider Asian and Global Contexts — 234

Epilogue: Heritage Sites, Difficult Histories, and 'Hidden Forces' in Post-Colonial Indonesia — 267

Bibliography — 282
Index — 314

Figures

0.1 The north-east corner of the basement of Borobudur, including a depiction of a painter in action, painting by H.N. Sieburgh, 1837. National Museum of World Cultures, Leiden, RV-37.643. *page* 2

0.2 The *gamelan* from Banten, in the National Museum in Jakarta. Photograph by Martijn Eickhoff, 25-2-2016. 13

1.1 'Buddha receiving offerings'. Drawing by Javanese draughtsman Adiwarna, who also made drawing of the reliefs of Borobudur. Reproduced from John Crawfurd, *History of the Indian Archipelago: containing an account of the manners, arts, languages, religions, institutions, and commerce of its inhabitants* Vol II (Edinburgh: Constable, 1820). 30

1.2 'Visit of Ario Danuningrat, the *regent* of Magelang, to Borobudur', pencil drawing by H.N. Sieburgh, 1837. National Museum of World Cultures, Leiden, RV-37-903-14. 44

1.3 Model of the old mosque of Demak on display at the old site museum. Photograph by Marieke Bloembergen, Demak, 21-1-2009. 58

2.1 Visit of king Chulalongkorn, his wife and his company to Borobudur, here, posing with Isaac Groneman eighth from left and some Dutch and Javanese officials, at the *Passangrahan* (rest house) on the site. Leiden University Library, KITLV 9890. 62

2.2 Two pages from the Guestbook at Borobudur with a drawing, made in August 1895, of the stone guard-statue located next to Borobudur, which king Chulalongkorn would bring to Bangkok a year later. It was crossed through, probably as a comment on this act, after July 1896. From 'Gastenboek Boro-Boedhoer, 1894–1896', Leiden University Library, KITLV Collections, archive Indisch Wetenschappelijk Instituut (IWI), inv. nr H 1790, 105b. 66

2.3 The garden of the Resident's quarters at Magelang, with its collection of Hindu-Buddhist statues, and a view on the Vulcano Sumbing. Drawing by F. Junghuhn, ca. 1853–1855. Leiden University Library, KITLV 50H2. 68

2.4 The Dutch colonial section at the world exhibition in Paris in 1900: an enlarged replica of the Buddhist eighth-century temple Candi Sari in Central Java; below, and in the forefront, reliefs of Borobudur, all plaster casts. Source: Ludovic Baschet, *Le panorama: exposition universelle 1900* (Paris: Librairie d'Art). Leiden University Library. 90

2.5 The Indian section, gallery 9 – 'Buddhism' – at the Victoria and Albert Museum, 1937. Victoria and Albert Museum, London, Image nr. 2017JV3717. 94

3.1 Plan of Majapahit's antiquities in 1887, by R. D. M. Verbeek (1887), working from a plan of 1810–1815 by W. Wardenaar. Reproduced from *Tijdschrift voor Indische taal-, land- en volkenkunde* 33 (1890), 14. Leiden University Library. 109

3.2 Badjang Ratoe, a temple Entrance at the Majapahit site. Supporting pillars are visible, late nineteenth century. Photographer unknown. Leiden University Library, KITLV 106718. 115

4.1 Antiquities Museum in Modjokerto, founded by Kromodjojo Adinegoro IV, the regent of Modjokero, picture taken between 1913–1930. Museum of World Cultures, Tropical Museum Amsterdam, TM 10026878. 134

4.2.a Statue still kept today in the Archaeological Museum in Trowulan, described by F.M. Schnitger in 1932 as potentially 'a portrait of Gadjah Mada. The most powerful face, which looks at us from Javanese history', in *Nederlandsch-Indië. Oud en Nieuw* (1932) 16: 10. Leiden University Library. 154

4.2.b Cover of Muhammad Yamin's biography of *Gadjah Mada. Pahlawan persatoean Noesantara*. Djakarta: Balai Poestaka, 1948'. Leiden University Library. 155

5.1 'Roemah bari' or the Museum in Palembang'. Leiden University Library, KITLV 1273. 168

5.2 Painted stone from a stone grave in Pasemah. *Jaarboek Koninklijk Bataviaasch Genootschap van Kunsten en Wetenschappen*. V (1938) z.p. Leiden University Library. 181

5.3 'The Srivijaya-dance', from Roeslan Abdulgani, *Indonesia: unique in contrast, culture and change (country, people transition, and future)* (s.l.: Ministry of Information, 1951), 110. Leiden University Library. 193

6.1 Inauguration of the Siva temple at Prambanan, 20-12-1953. Leiden University Library, KITLV 167178. 195
6.2 The Siva temple in Prambanan with Japanese flag. Picture taken by Minoru Sakata (1942–1944). By the courtesy of Joe Takeba, Nagoya City Art Museum and Takashi Sakata. 206
6.3 General Soedirman with Indonesian Republican army parading in front of Borobudur, circa 1948. From *Illustrations of the revolution 1945–1950: from a unitary state to a unitary state*. Djakarta: Ministery of Information, 1954. Leiden University Library. 209
6.4 Old stones and statues found in the ricefields, and honoured in a small temple, the pura Arjuna Metapa, and as 'national heritage', at the border of Bedulu and Pejeng, Bali. Photograph Marieke Bloembergen, 5-9-2009. 215
6.5 'The Chinese vase, here in the centre, in Halmaheira' (picture from ca. 1936). Source of this picture: Jan Fontein, 'Het verzamelen van Aziatische kunst in de twintigste eeuw', Aziatische Kunst 23(3): 2–17, there 12. Photographer unknown. Leiden University Library. 229
7.1 Map showing the spread of Buddhist culture and art from India and China to Southeast Asia. Reprinted from *UNESCO Courier* IX–6 (June 1956). 237
7.2 Rabindranath Tagore at Borobudur with his beloved reliefs, September 1927. Leiden University Library, KITLV 17755. 240
7.3 Excavation of the hidden foot by Furusawa Yasujiro, 1943, photograph Ogawa Seiyo. Source of this picture: Daigoro Chihara, *Buseki Borobudur* (Tokyo: Harashobo, 1969). Tokyo Research Institute for Cultural Properties (NIRCP). 248
7.4 Queen Juliana and Prince Bernhard pose at Borobudur together with Mrs. Isriati Moenadi and Mr. Moenadi, the governor of Central Java. 1971. Photo: Joost Evers. National Archives The Hague / [ANEFO], CC0. 262
8.1 'Great Mosque of Demak with election posters, 1955', photograph Claire Holt. New York Public Library, Jerome Robbins Dance Division, Claire Holt Collection, image 1112675. 268
8.2 The Gadjah Mada statue at the Pendopo Agung in Trowulan. Photograph by Marieke Bloembergen, 15-9-2009. 271

Preface and Acknowledgements

> [T]hose who renew or improve old and sacred buildings will either die or go mad soon afterwards.[1]

With these words, in 1840, Sosrodiningrat, an adviser to the Javanese royal court of Sunan Pakubuwono VII in Surakarta in the Netherlands Indies, is said to have responded to plans to restore the fifteenth-century mosque of Demak in Central Java. This examination of the politics of heritage in colonial and post-colonial Indonesia contains a *mobile* history of such practices of heritage formation that unfold from sites such as the mosque in Demak. The meaning of Sosrodiningrat's mosque of 1840, of course, has changed over time to people inside and outside Indonesia. Located in a country with a majority Muslim population since at least the sixteenth century, the mosque of Demak also provides the perspective of an outsider. It is situated in a heritage landscape where the eighth-century Buddhist shrine Borobudur and the ninth-century Hindu temple complex Prambanan, both listed as World Heritage Sites, dominate as the most famous monuments in Indonesia. Why, how, and for whom such heritage histories develop, and what this reveals about the ways people in colonial and post-colonial times have engaged with history, experienced the world, and related to the future, are the questions that have guided us in our research.

Writing about the politics and mobility of heritage means becoming complicit. While pursuing our enquiry, we often thought that Sosrodiningrat's words might apply not only to those who like to 'renew or improve old and sacred buildings', but also to those who study this phenomenon. We were the ones who decided whose perspectives to follow as sites and objects originating from Indonesia transformed, gained new meanings, and came to play a role in heritage politics. We have tried to be transparent in our choices. Following Marcel Mauss' insightful theorising on 'the gift', we have focused on

[1] Sosrodiningrat, adviser to Sunan Paku Buwono VII, quoted in Diary, Christiaan Jacobus van der Vlis, 7 October 1840, Leiden University Library, Special Collections Koninklijk Instituut voor Taal-, Land- en Volkenkunde (hereafter KITLV) Collections, Collection van der Vlis, inv. DH 341 'Dagboek gehouden te Soerakarta, 1840–1842'.

exchange, and the mechanisms of reciprocity and interdependency, to provide insight into the political dynamics of cultural heritage formation. With this book, therefore, we offer a new, mobile approach to the cultural-political history of archaeology and heritage formation in Asia. We show how heritage politics create differences in various ways, for various people, and in various places. We also suggest that these politics are open to change when questioned, inside Indonesia and outside, in other worlds that have somehow become connected to Indonesian heritage.

We are grateful to the many individuals and institutions, in the Netherlands, Indonesia, Japan, Thailand, Singapore, Malaysia, the United Kingdom, France, Austria, Germany, and the United States, that have supported us in various ways. The base of support was larger than we can mention here, but we would like to thank explicitly the following people and institutions, by following more or less the order of our sites of research.

In the Netherlands, conversations with Heather Sutherland, going back to 2007, formed the germ from which we developed our first ideas, and the sites-centred approach for our project, leading to what we intend to be a more inclusive, Indonesia-centred way to study the politics and social impact of heritage formation in colonial and post-colonial times. Crucial, next, was the larger research programme 'Sites, Bodies and Stories' (SBS), supported by the Netherlands Scientific Organization (NWO), 2008–2012. SBS was a collaborative programme between various institutes in the Netherlands (Free University, the Royal Netherlands Institute of Southeast Asian and Caribbean Studies (KITLV), the NIOD Institute of War and Holocaust Studies) and Indonesia (Eijkman Institute in Jakarta and Gadjah Mada University (Universitas Gadjah Mada, UGM) in Yogyakarta), providing the best possible base for our research to flourish. It was led, in an exemplary inclusive way, by Susan Legêne from the Free University who brought along expertise and colleagues from what is now the Museum of World Cultures, then the Tropical Museum in Amsterdam, and from the University of Amsterdam (Universiteit van Amsterdam, UvA). Alongside Legêne, we thank all colleagues who worked in this programme, whether as co-ordinator, post-doc or PhD researcher, assistant, or in a flanking supportive role for their inspiration and input in various ways: Inajati Adrisijanti, Sadiah Boonstra, Caroline Drieënhuizen, Mahirta Ita, Sri Margana, Sangkot Marzuki, Uji Nugroho, Bambang Purwanto, Remco Raben, Peter Romijn, Henk Schulte Nordholt, Tular Sumedi, Claudia Surjadjaja, Fenneke Sysling, Daud Aris Tanudirjo, Pim Westerkamp, Erik Willems, and Henrietta Lidchi. The academic staff of the archaeology and history departments of UGM have been extremely supportive. In 2010 and 2011 they gave us the opportunity to co-organise the MA workshops 'Archaeology and Heritage in Indonesia', which opened up a unique space for discussion, knowledge exchange, and inspiration. We have furthermore immensely profited from the sphere of academic comradeship and inspiration at the two institutes that hosted our research, and where we are now based as senior researchers, Marieke at KITLV in Leiden and Martijn at NIOD in Amsterdam.

During our research, the staff members of the various archives and libraries that we consulted in Europe and Asia, all listed in the Bibliography, have helped us immensely with all our queries. Next there are the numerous informants at the sites of heritage that were objects of our research, who helped us in finding local (oral and written) histories; some wished to remain anonymous, and others are mentioned by name in this book. We thank them all here, along with those who in the very final stage of this book provided assistance in getting the visual material for this book in good shape and in good time. Notably, also in a late stage of our research, Nico van Horn pointed out to us the existence and location of Borobudur's guestbook of the 1890s, a treasure source for this book.

At the multiple sites of our research, we have been helped by various other institutes and individuals in special ways. At the Museum Nasional in Jakarta we – and our many questions about this unique museum – were welcomed warmly by Ni Lu Putu Chandra Dewi, Retno Moerdiano, Ekowati Sundari, Dhyanti Soekarno, and Destrika. We had the same experience at the Puslit Arkenas (National Research Centre for Archaeology) where we had an inspiring and motivating conversation with Truman Simanjuntak. Henri Chambert-Loir, Arlo Griffiths, and the staff of the École française d'Extrême-Orient (EFEO) in Jakarta provided us with a homely and inspiring base, and generously led us to treasures and colleagues inside and outside Indonesia who could help us further with our queries. Didi Kwartanada, also based in Jakarta, gave us valuable advice for our research on Chinese archaeology and heritage.

In Demak, Zainal and Linda provided a perfect home and starting point for our insightful interviews with Haji Abdul Fatah, Bazuki, Mas Duti, and ibu Nunuk (all from the mosque's Taq'mir) and Haji Alin Sukianto (from the mosque's administration). At Borobudur, and in relation to Borobudur in Jakarta, various parties gave us their time and insights to help us understand the complicated local, national, and global/UNESCO (United Nations Educational, Scientific and Cultural Organization) engagements with an officially dead monument that clearly lives. We thank, among many others: Sucoro, Jack Prayono, Ariswata Soetomo, Soeparno, Banthe Vayyna (of Mendut monastery), Marsia Sutopo, Pujo Purnomo, Agus Canny, Masanori, and Yasuhiro Iwasaki. In Surabaya, Dede Oetomo was a helpful guide to Majapahit New Order histories. In Trowulan our research profited from the support of the staff of Balai Pelestarian Peninggalan Purbakala (BP3), in particular Widodo, Pak Sento, ibu Rizki and Pak Tego, and from the museum's staff, in particular Abdul Rozak, Yanti and Nurika. We thank them all.

Outside Java, in Palembang, Jambi and Pagaralam our project was generously supported by Agus Widi Atmoko from the BP3 in Jambi, Aryandini Novita and Nurhadi Rangkuti from Balai Arkeologi in Palembang, and Khairani Al Hudayah and Bambang Gunawan from the Pusat Pariwisata in Pagaralam. Abdul Haviz and Muhammen Kurniawan, living in Muarajambi, and Koriaty Ridwan, living in Palembang, gave us very relevant 'heritage' tours. Ravando Lie did preparatory research as a project assistant. In Semarang, important information and help was provided by Donny Danardono and Tjahjono Rahardjo from the Universitas Katolik Soegijapranata, Widjajanti Dharmowijono from the Yayasan Budaya Widya Mitra, the heritage activist Widya Wijayanti, and, last but not least, Daniel Tangkilisan. In Bali, scientific staff at Udayana University and the Balai Arkeologi in Denpasar, and at the BP3 and Museum Arca in Bedulu, temple caretakers (*pemangku*), informants, and friends gave us their time and histories, which helped us understand some of the local politics and idiosyncrasies of sacred sites and heritage formation in colonial and post-colonial Bali. We thank, among others, I Gusti Ngurah Anom, Gusti Mangku Agung (*pura* Samuan Tiga), I Wayan Ardika, Cokorde Gde Rai, Degung Santikarma, Dewa, Susi Johnston, Kadè, I Ketut Ardhana, Oka Astawa, Setiawan Ketut, PW, Roro Sawita, Suarbhawa, and I Wayan Patram.

We are very grateful to those archaeologists and heritage officials from older generations who allowed us to interview them and who shared their life stories and experiences in Indonesian heritage politics with us: R. P. Soejono, Inajati Adrisijanti, Endang Sri Hardiati, Timbul Haryono, I Made Sutaba, Anak Agung Gde Oka Astawa, I Gusti Ngurah Anom, and Mundardjito.

Outside Indonesia, during several visits to Singapore we received valuable information from John N. Miksic and Jan van der Putten. For our research in Bangkok, chasing the Javanese gifts that King Chulalongkorn brought along, and their local histories, we thank, first, Peter Skilling (for leading us to some of the crucial sites), and Chalong Suntarawanitch and Anuk Pitukthanin (Pooh), at Chulalongkorn University, who were our first guides at the site. Pooh became our research assisant in Bangkok and located important source material. Extremely helpful for our queries were also Rujaya Abhakorn (then at SPAFA, Asian Regional Centre for Archaeology and Fine Arts), Francois Larigarde and Nicolas Revire (then at EFEO Bangkok), Penpan Jarernparn (then at the National Museum, Bangkok), and Indonesian monk Dihan (then at Wat Bowonnit). Pooh and Han ten Brummelhuis (UvA) translated Thai source material.

In Japan where we explored the place of the Indonesian past in the Greater East Asia Co-Prosperity Sphere and looked for traces of the Japanese Borobudur excavation in 1943, we were generously supported by Akira Matsui and Akiko Tashiro from the Nara National Research Institute for

Cultural Properties (Nara NRICP) and by Yoko Futagami and Katsura Sato from the Tokyo National Research Institute for Cultural Properties (Tokyo NRICP). We thank Masuro Ijiri, at the Enzan Memorial Art Museum in Himeji, and his daughter Yuko Ijiri, then in Leiden, for providing us with insightful histories on Susume Ijiri. We thank Matthi Forrer for leading us to them, Peter Post for his valuable advice with regard to the Japanese heritage infrastructure, NIOD intern Sjir Worms for his preparatory research, Eveline Buchheim and Takashi Sakata for providing us with unique visual documentation, and Kuniko Forrer and Hoko Horii for their translations of some important Japanese texts.

Apart from the international meetings we had in the framework of our SBS project, hosted at UGM in Yogyakarta – the 'Sites, Bodies and Stories' workshop of August 2009 and the 'Sites, Bodies and Stories' conference of January 2011 – in the course of our project we have presented case studies at several international workshops where inspiring discussions with colleague-participants formed our thinking as well. We mention in particular those held at the German Historical Institute in London in 2010, thanking Indra Sengupta, at the Excellence Cluster Topoi in Berlin in 2010, thanking Gisela Eberhardt and Fabian Link, at Heidelberg University in 2011, thanking Michael Falser, at the University of Cologne in 2010, and at the Centre d'Histoire de Sciences Po in Paris in 2012, thanking Jakob Vogel, and at the Goethe University Frankfurt in 2013, thanking Fabian Link.

Several colleagues commented on earlier drafts of some of the chapters of this book; we thank in particular Henk Schulte Nordholt and David Kloos for their helpful critical remarks. Andrew Gebhardt and Femke Jacobs did amazing work in the final editing. We, of course, take full responsibility for the text that follows.

Abbreviations

AKS	Arsip Keresidenan Semarang (Residential Archive of Semarang)
ANRI	Arsip Nasional Republik Indonesia (National Archives of the Indonesian Republic)
AOK	Archief van het Ministerie voor Algemeene oorlogvoering van het Koninkrijk (Archive of the Department of Warfare of the Kingdom, in the National Archives, The Hague)
AS	Algemeene Secretarie (General Secretary of the Dutch Colonial Government)
ASEAN	Association of Southeast Asian Nations
AZ	Archief van het ministerie van Algemeene zaken (Archive of the Department of General Affairs, in the National Archives, The Hague)
BEFEO	*Bulletin de l'École française d'Extrême-Orient*
BKI	*Bijdragen tot de Taal-, Land- en Volkenkunde* (*Journal of the Humanities and Social Sciences of Southeast Asia and Oceania*)
BMGN	*BMGN – Low Countries Historical Review*
BP3	Badan Pelestarian Peninggalan Purbakala (Regional Conservation Department)
Bt	Gouvernementsbesluit (Governmental Resolution)
DIR	Directing Board
EFEO	École française d'Extrême-Orient
HBS	Hogere Burgerschool (Higher Secondary School)
ITB	Institut Teknologi Bandung (Technological Institute, Bandung)
IWI	Indisch Wetenschappelijk Instituut
JAS	*Journal of Asian Studies*
JCICC	Japan Center for International Cooperation in Conservation
JICA	Japan International Cooperation Agency
JRAS	*Journal of the Royal Asiatic Society*
KBG	Koninklijk Bataviaasch Genootschap (Royal Batavian Society of Arts and Sciences)
KIT	Koninklijk Instituut voor de Tropen (Royal Tropical Institute)

KITLV	Koninklijk Instituut voor Taal-, Land- en Volkenkunde (Royal Netherlands Institute of Southeast Asian and Caribbean Studies)
KMP	Kabinet van de Minister President
KNAW	Koninklijke Nederlandse Akademie van Wetenschappen (Royal Netherlands Academy of Arts and Sciences)
MAS	*Modern Asian Studies*
MvK	Ministerie van Koloniën (Ministry of Colonies)
NA	Nationaal Archief (National Archives, The Hague)
NAB	National Archives, Bangkok
NAI	Nederlands Architectuurinstituut (Netherlands Institute of Architecture, Rotterdam)
OPI	Office of Public Information, UNESCO
OV	*Oudheidkundig Verslag* (various years)
R&A	Registry and Archives of the Victoria and Albert Museum, London
ROC	*Rapport van de commissie in Nederlandsch-Indië voor oudheidkundig onderzoek op Java en Madoera; Uitgegeven voor rekening van het Bataviaasch Genootschap van Kunsten en Wetenschappen* (Reports of the Commission in the Netherlands Indies for Archaeological Research
SOAS	School of Oriental and African Studies, London
STOVIA	School tot Opleiding van Inlandsche Artsen (School for the Education of Native Physicians)
TKNAG	*Tijdschrift van het koninklijk Nederlandsch Aardrijkskundig Genootschap*
UGM	Universitas Gadjah Mada (Gadjah Mada University), Yogyakarta
UNESCO	United Nations Educational, Scientific and Cultural Organization
UvA	Universiteit van Amsterdam (University of Amsterdam)
V&A	Victoria and Albert Museum, London
VOC	Vereenigde Oostindische Compagnie (Dutch East India Company)

Introduction: Towards a Mobile History of Heritage Formation in Asia

> What you are regarding as a gift is a problem for you to solve.[1]

In 1838, a solitary Chinese man visited the giant Buddhist temple Borobudur, in Central Java – more than a thousand years old – and stopped to contemplate one of the reliefs. He returned often, took books, and studied and compared the Buddhist reliefs of the temple. He made drawings and notes. But the one relief that caught his attention did not directly concern the Buddha: it showed a Chinese junk.[2] Likewise enthralled by the temple, the romantic Dutch painter H. N. Sieburgh saw the Chinese visitor, whom he viewed as a true lover of antiquity. One starry night at Borobudur, Sieburgh had been entranced by the sublime temple, and longed to understand it. He called it a 'world monument',[3] as though anticipating future appropriations of the temple (Figure 0.1). But the Chinese visitor may have come to other interpretations. Was the man contemplating an alternative past world, perhaps, situating the temple in wider and older Javanese–Chinese–Buddhist connections?

Borobudur, the largest Buddhist shrine in the world, was named a World Heritage Site by UNESCO in 1991, and is today one of Asia's major sites of (local and foreign) mass tourism – like Angkor Wat in Cambodia or Bodh Gaya in India. All were ruins rediscovered in the nineteenth century and, under colonial and post-colonial regimes, transformed into majestic heritage-cum-pilgrimage sites. This study of the politics of heritage in Indonesia contains a *mobile* history of heritage that unfolds from sites such as Borobudur. Our Chinese visitor – about whom we know little more than that he was a butcher by profession and that he took books to Borobudur – and Sieburgh play tiny but meaningful roles in this history. Here, they illustrate how sites that contain material remains of an ancient past can powerfully excite the imagination and curiosity of visitors, neighbours, and guardians. Through histories, exchange,

[1] Ludwig Wittgenstein, *Culture and value*, transl. Peter Winch (Chicago: University of Chicago Press, 1984), 43.

[2] H. N. Sieburgh, *Beschrijving van Brahmansche Oudheden op het eiland Java*, Manuscript, boek 1, p. 63, in Museum Volkenkunde, Leiden, inv. nr NL-LdnRMV_A03_068.

[3] Ibid., boek 1, p. 61. All translations from the original Dutch, Malay, Indonesian or French are by the authors, unless noted otherwise.

Figure 0.1 The north–east corner of the basement of Borobudur, painting by H.N. Sieburgh, 1837.

and selective identification, sites are also political. The ambiguities, variety, and selectivity of personal identifications with sites become palpable on location, where various interested people and parties interact.

In 1838, when the Chinese man and Sieburgh came to admire Borobudur, the temple had only recently been made accessible for a public beyond the local population. This was made possible by the interventions of two successive (British and Dutch) colonial administrations in the previous two decades. Built around 800 CE under the Sailendra dynasty that ruled over much of Java, Borobudur had gone out of use when, in the tenth century, the centre of power moved to the east of Java; over time it was overtaken by vegetation. Borobudur's second public life, attracting growing attention, began in the early nineteenth century.[4] This was, notably, when the majority of the

[4] A series of catastrophic eruptions and damaging earthquakes may have played a role in this move of the centre of power from Central to East Java. See Jan Wisseman Christie, 'Under the volcano: stabilizing the early Javanese state in an unstable environment', in David Henley and Henk Schulte Nordholt (eds.), *Environment, trade and society in Southeast Asia: a* longue durée *perspective* (Leiden: Brill, 2015), 46–61.

population in Java, in a process that started in the late fifteenth century, had converted to Islam. In 1814, during the British interregnum, and on the order of the Lieutenant-General T. S. Raffles, Javanese workers cleared the temple of vegetation. This took 200 workers one and a half months.[5] In the subsequent decades, further details of the temple's ornaments and reliefs would be made visible through further cleaning works. After the devastating Java War (1825–1830) the temple's galleries and reliefs could be contemplated by curious visitors like the Chinese visitor, Sieburgh, and soon many more, including Javanese Muslims. We know a lot about Raffles' commemorated rediscovery of the site, but almost nothing of Borobudur's solitary Chinese visitor of 1838. What we do know is that the Chinese visitor carried, along with books, his own frames of knowledge, thinking, and beliefs, to identify with the temple. What he saw as important and meaningful was perhaps facilitated by state-supported archaeological interventions, but not imposed on him.

This book offers a new, mobile approach to the cultural-political history of archaeology and heritage formation in Asia, through the case of colonial and post-colonial Indonesia. We focus on the mobility of heritage and try to understand heritage formation in Asia as a multi-sited phenomenon that involves, but also goes beyond, the interests of states and heritage institutions, as well as people across state borders. We follow the concerns of local subjects and elites, of artists and tourists, of scholars and pilgrims, of state-centred archaeology and transnational cultural associations, and of global politics. To be able to combine these perspectives and understand their relations and frictions in colonial and post-colonial situations, we follow a dual approach that is both site-centred and mobile. Beginning from sites such as Borobudur and other historical remains in Indonesia, we explore, from the early nineteenth century to the late twentieth century, encounters and exchanges between various key actors, and between various forms of historical knowledge developing on site.[6] We aim to understand how various actors from within and beyond the state have contributed to heritage awareness, and to heritage formation as a process that is not exclusively related to state formation. Next, we follow the journeys of site-related objects, along with the site's visitors, to places elsewhere in the world, in order to understand their role in alternative, parallel processes of

[5] John Miksic, *Borobudur: golden tales of the Buddhas* (Boston: Shambhala, 1990), 17.

[6] For comparable site-related approaches towards Hindu and Buddhist sites elsewhere in Asia, see Alan Trevithick, 'British archaeologists, Hindu abbots, and Burmese Buddhists: the Mahabodhi temple at Bodh Gaya, 1811–1877', *Modern Asian Studies* (hereafter *MAS*) 33:3 (1999), 635–656; Alan Trevithick, *The revival of Buddhist pilgrimage at Bodh Gaya (1811–1949): Anagarika Dharmapala and the Mahabodhi temple* (Delhi: Motilal Banarsidass, 2006); Upinder Singh, 'Exile and return: the reinvention of Buddhism and Buddhist sites in modern India', *Journal of South Asian Studies* 26:2 (2010), 193–217; David Geary, 'Rebuilding the navel of the earth: Buddhist pilgrimage and transnational religious networks', *MAS* 48:3 (2013), 645–692.

heritage formation. This double approach, both site-centred and mobile, enables us to explore the political impact of exchange at multiple sites based in or originating from Indonesia. In this way we gauge the various and changing hierarchies in which heritage takes shape, is contemplated, and excludes groups of people over time.

Emphasising that culture is also political, we aim to provide insight into the relationship between heritage and violence, and into the political and religious dimensions of heritage formation. Why, when, where, and for whom do certain forms of knowledge production concerning historical sites come to dominate, at the cost of others? Why can apparently conflicting stories and engagements with sites develop in parallel? What are the effects of violent destruction, war, and regime change? Why do even unseen, hidden, or difficult histories matter at sites often framed as the frozen past of a homogeneous nation? And how can these histories still be detected and probed for their significance?

In the past two decades, it has become a common trope that heritage 'is' nothing in itself, but concerns a politically informed process of becoming.[7] Heritage formation takes place only when people consciously start relating to the 'remains of the past' as something meaningful to keep for the future. These processes of individual or communal heritage engagements are never neutral, and can unfold without much friction. But when heritage becomes the object of formal religious, moral, or political uses, and is being legitimised by historical investigation, exhibition practices, and conservation politics, it can become sensitive, as people start to actively intervene, wishing to claim, (re)define, and transform the site.[8] In this context, the importance of the more recent 'performative turn' in critical heritage studies, which explores what people actually do and experience at heritage sites, cannot be underestimated, as it helps in dismantling the perception of heritage as a primarily material phenomenon.[9] However, our mobile-cum-site-centred research goes further, and has led us to question the predicament of critical heritage studies as well as the practice of archaeological resource management, both of which today proliferate as sound

[7] Laurajane Smith, *Uses of heritage* (London and New York: Routledge, 2006).

[8] For the first wave (mostly comprising historians and characterised by a nationally oriented approach) and the second wave (which included social scientists as well and is characterised by a global multi-centred approach) in heritage studies, see David Lowenthal, *The heritage crusade and the spoils of history* (Cambridge: Cambridge University Press, 1998); Marie Louise Stig Sørensen and John Carman, 'Heritage studies: an outline', in Marie Louise Stig Sørensen and John Carman (eds.), *Heritage studies: methods and approaches* (London: Routledge, 2009), 11–28; Rodney Harrison, *Heritage: critical approaches* (London and New York: Routledge, 2013), 95–113. On the specialised field of heritage formation in (Southeast) Asia, see Michael Hitchcock, Victor King, and Michael Parnwell (eds.), *Heritage tourism in Southeast Asia* (Honolulu: University of Hawai'i Press, 2010); Patrick Daly and Tim Winter, *Routledge handbook of heritage in Asia* (London and New York: Routledge, 2012).

[9] Smith, *Uses of heritage*, 3.

solutions for the political challenge of heritage formation.[10] We argue that there is no solution for this problem, especially if we continue thinking and acting within the framework and techniques of heritage politics, which are top-down and exclusive. And even if inclusiveness is the goal, who has the authority to define the 'stakeholders' and 'communities' as the rightful heirs of a site?

This book arrives at a moment when both inside and outside academia there is an acute concern about, and journalistic interest in, the fragility of ancient civilisational sites in the context of war, religious intolerance, violent regime change, natural disasters, and national and international heritage politics. This concern has been triggered by, on the one hand, a booming competition between local communities and state governments for the recognition and status of a UNESCO World Heritage Site.[11] On the other hand, the cases of looting and iconoclasm that have shocked the world – the Taliban blowing up the giant Buddhas of Bamyan (2001) or IS selling artefacts and destroying sites such as Palmyra in Syria (2015) – have enforced mechanisms of othering Islam worldwide, but have not raised much critical self-reflection about comparable examples of destruction and looting taking place in the context of European (and American) religious and colonial histories.[12] However, despite many examples of iconoclasm in world history, the material remains of the past nonetheless can outlive regimes, performing new functions for the new parties or states taking over. Moreover, when historical sites are destroyed, they can continue to exist in the minds of people – either in the various ways they engage(d) with such sites or for the reasons these sites became destroyed.

Borobudur is not our only case. We also investigate other 'ideal types' of sites in Indonesia and their transformation into heritage, and their becoming part of various forms of knowledge, understanding, exclusion, and destruction across regime changes. Next to a number of ancient Buddhist and Hindu sites which are still meaningful as heritage sites in Indonesia today, we also explore the role of Islamic, Balinese, prehistoric, Chinese, and colonial sites and royal palaces in the dynamics of heritage and knowledge production. We aim to

[10] Laurajane Smith and Gary Campbell, '2012 Association of Critical Heritage Studies manifesto', presented at inaugural meeting of Association of Critical Heritage Studies (ASCHS), University of Gothenburg, 2012; see www.criticalheritagestudies.org/history/ (10 March 2017); Smith, *Uses of heritage*; John Carman, *Archaeological resource management: an international perspective* (Cambridge: Cambridge University Press, 2015). For an alternative anthropological approach problematising the study and practices of heritage, and focusing on gentrification and corruption, see Michael Herzfeld, 'Engagement, gentrification and the neoliberal hijacking of history', *Current Anthropology*, 51:2 (2010), 259–267.

[11] Lynn Meskell, *A future in ruins: UNESCO, world heritage, and the dream of peace* (Oxford: Oxford University Press, 2018); Lynn Meskell, 'Transacting UNESCO world heritage: gifts and exchanges on a global stage', *Social Anthropology/Anthropologie Sociale* 23:1 (2015), 3–21.

[12] However, from an academic perspective, see Astrid Swenson and Peter Mandler (eds.), *From plunder to preservation: Britain and the heritage of empire c. 1800–1940* (Oxford: Oxford University Press, 2013).

avoid 'colonial determinism'.[13] Although we do not deny the importance of identifying and discussing the colonial legacies in post-colonial heritage formation in contemporary Indonesia, we have come to realise that this alone does not capture the dynamics of heritage formation and knowledge production concerning sites in Asia. The Chinese visitor to Borobudur in 1838 is a case in point. He delivers only one of many alternative perspectives that we try to tie into our analysis, for the archaeological sites under study here, like other sites in former colonial empires, are not exclusively defined by colonialism, even if colonial relations have played a crucial role in their current shape. All along, however, more visitors have become attracted to and involved in Indonesian heritage sites, opening multi-layered relationships of exchange and interdependence.

Exchange, *Lieux de mémoire,* and the Political Dynamics of Heritage Formation

Marcel Mauss' notion of 'the gift' – i.e., 'the obligation to give is explainable because this act causes the obligation to return the gift' – is crucial for understanding the political dynamics of cultural heritage formation at the local, national, and global levels.[14] Also, because the act of giving involves one party identifying as the owner or possessor, conferring a gift bears directly on the question of 'heritage for whom?' Heritage formation, moreover, is to a large extent about morality, paternalism, and (presumed) responsibilities, about giving, taking, and restitution, and thus, as Mauss showed, about reciprocity and moral obligations. The site-centred exchanges that we explore in this book show how this mechanism works.

From the start, 'exchange' was a part of our research in the 'Sites, Bodies, and Stories' project, an inter-institutional collaboration between Indonesian and Dutch historians, archaeologists, and anthropologists, who investigated cultural heritage formation in Indonesia and the Netherlands in colonial and post-colonial times.[15] Between the members, and with informants at different locations, exchange of various forms of knowledge, reciprocal misunderstanding, and learning took place. We also searched for site-related knowledge

[13] Susan Legêne and Henk Schulte Nordholt, 'Introduction: imagining heritage and heritage as imagined history', in Susan Legêne, Bambang Purwanto, and Henk Schulte Nordholt (eds.), *Sites, bodies and stories: imagining Indonesian history* (Singapore: NUS Press, 2015), 8–9.

[14] Marcel Mauss, *The gift: the form and reason for exchange in archaic societies*, transl. W. D. Halls (New York and London: W. W. Norton, 1990); Marieke Bloembergen and Martijn Eickhoff, 'Exchange and the protection of Java's antiquities: a transnational approach to the problem of heritage in colonial Java', *Journal of Asian Studies* (hereafter *JAS*) 72:4 (2013) 1–24.

[15] Legêne and Schulte Nordholt, 'Introduction'. For general information about the 'Sites, Bodies and Stories' project, see www.ghhpw.com/sbs.php (accessed 18 March 2017).

outside the framework of academia and heritage institutions in the Netherlands and Indonesia, as well as in Thailand, Malaysia, the United Kingdom, France, Germany, and Austria. Against that background we decided not to use the concept 'shared heritage'. That concept has been developed to overcome the problem of (former) colonial hierarchies and surpass (post-)colonial sensitivities when academics or heritage organisations in the former colonised and colonising countries collaborate.[16] The concept looks noble, but it is problematic as it implies that the selected forms of 'shared heritage' can be valued, conserved, etc., only within the framework of two post-colonial states, thereby denying uncomfortable power relations and conflicting interests. Moreover, 'shared heritage' glosses over the very local, supra-local and transnational dimensions of heritage, precisely those processes of identification that go beyond the boundaries of states and empire,[17] but that are crucial in this book.

Consciously and emphatically, sites are for us starting points and analytical tools to explore the political dynamics of heritage formation at multiple locations, and across borders of communities and states. Whereas histories that focus on biographies (leading archaeologists, discoverers), institutions (museums, learned societies), monument regulations/acts (colonial, Indonesian, UNESCO), or research fields (archaeology, ethnography) tend to merge self-evidently with national perspectives, sites open views to alternative contexts as well, since they relate to spaces that transgress the formal state boundaries.[18] With our site-centred approach we thus build on, but also complicate, the highly influential analytical tool of *lieux de mémoire*, introduced by the French historian Pierre Nora.[19] In his *lieux de mémoire* project, which inspired comparable programmes worldwide, Nora initiated a method to study the emergence and workings of memory in the nineteenth and twentieth centuries by tracing specific

[16] For examples, see Intan Mardiana Napitupulu, S. Engelsman, and E. W. Veen, 'The director's foreword', in Endang Sri Hardiati and Pieter Ter Keurs (eds.), *Indonesia: the discovery of the past* (Amsterdam: KIT Publishers, 2005), 6; Cynthia Scott, 'Sharing the divisions of the colonial past: an assessment of the Netherlands–Indonesia shared cultural heritage project, 2003–2006', *International Journal of Heritage Studies*, 20:2 (2014), 81–195.

[17] Martijn Eickhoff and Marieke Bloembergen, 'Travelling far on "rather short legs": company-furniture on the move and the problem of shared heritage', *IIAS Newsletter* 59 (2012). See www.iias.nl/the-newsletter/article/travelling-far-rather-short-legs-company-furniture-move-and-problem-shared (accessed 28 October 2015).

[18] For a comparable study of trans-Asian and intercolonial interests in archaeological sites located in Siam and French Indochina, see Maurizio Peleggi, 'Royal antiquarianism: European Orientalism and the production of archaeological knowledge in Siam', in Srilata Ravi, Mario Rutten, and Beng-Lan Goh (eds.), *Asia in Europe, Europe in Asia* (Leiden and Singapore: International Institute for Asian Studies, 2004), 133–161.

[19] Pierre Nora (ed.) *Les lieux de mémoire*, vols. I–VII (Paris: Gallimard, 1984–1992). Compare with Indra Sengupta, 'Locating *lieux de mémoire:* a (post)colonial perspective', in Indra Sengupta (ed.), *Memory, history and colonialism: engaging with Pierre Nora in colonial and postcolonial contexts*, *Bulletin, German Historical Institute London* Suppl. 1 (2009), 1–8.

lieux to which (groups of) people in the national states-in-progress related for mainly historic reasons.[20] Nora and his colleagues came to focus on how these *lieux* have played a role in people's identifications with national states in Europe. In doing so, the *lieux de mémoire* programme(s) tended to ignore the possibility that there are *lieux* with liaisons to people – living within the borders of the country – who do not necessarily identify with the nation. But it may as well be argued that people may identify with sites outside their homeland, in what they consider a foreign state.[21] Our concept of sites is therefore broader than the national idea of *lieux de mémoire*, because we recognise these sites as centres of multiple spaces by themselves. Sites help us to think beyond the obvious boundaries of empire and nation-state without ignoring these boundaries.[22]

Sites in Transnational Perspective

When material traces of the past are identified as archaeological sites and become heritage, they form new spots on new maps that give historical depth to contemporary geographical and political imaginations. While these sites convey multiple historical, religious, and moral messages as they are found, the transformation to an archaeological site and the subsequent interventions – which we discuss in this book – link them to scientific, (art-)historical, and governmental concerns. This happened to the many ruins that European civil servants, military men, and travellers during the nineteenth century encountered – or in their own perception, and through colonial authority, 'discovered' – in South and Southeast Asia, whether within or outside the framework of colonial empires. Borobudur became a colonial archaeological site in 1814,

[20] Emil Brix (ed.), *Memoria Austria*, vols. I–III (Vienna: Verlag für Geschichte und Politik, 2004–2005); Étienne François and Hagen Schultze (eds.), *Deutsche Erinnerungsorte*, vols. I–III (Munich: Verlag C. H. Beck, 2001–2002); Mario Isnenghi (ed.), *I luoghi della memoria*, vols. I–III (Rome: Laterza, 1996–1997); Jo Tollebeek (ed.), *België, een parcours van herinnering*, vols. I–II (Amsterdam: Bert Bakker, 2008); H. L. Wesseling, *Plaatsen van herinnering*, vols. I–IV (Amsterdam: Bert Bakker, 2005–2006).

[21] These identifications recall Nora's use of the concept of 'milieu de mémoire', which according to Nora disappeared in Europe over the course of nineteenth and early twentieth centuries. However, we think that people's transnational identification with sites, with moral or religious motives as binding factors, is not restricted to the early modern period and deserves to be investigated for modern times and present-day Europe as well. For an example of the way the concept of 'milieu de mémoire' can be used when analysing contemporary heritage politics in India, see Tapati Guha-Thakurta, *Monuments, objects, histories: institutions of art in colonial and postcolonial India* (New York: Columbia University Press, 2004), 268–303.

[22] Thus we follow subaltern historian Dipesh Chakrabarty, who argues that the categories of European thought (including the concept of historicising) are simultaneously both indispensable and inadequate when writing about the non-European world. He stresses, therefore, the importance of questioning the structure of narratives and of making them heterogeneous by including multiple perspectives, ambivalences, and contradictions. See Dipesh Chakrabarty, *Provincializing Europe: post-colonial thought and difference*, revised edn (Princeton: Princeton University Press, 2008), 17, 43, and 45–46.

when Raffles ordered its uncovering and cleaning, thereby generating new supra-local, academic, and governmental interests.

But precisely because archaeological sites are 'localised', and because of their previous and subsequent histories, their religious connotations, their moral messages, and their social-economic or touristic functions, they are the centre of multiple geographies.[23] These do not necessarily overlap with the imperial and national boundaries in which these sites, in the course of the nineteenth and twentieth centuries, were selected and transformed through several stages of (re)appropriation: 'discovering', excavating, cleaning, restoring, conserving, circumscribing with a gate, musealising, and nominating as official national or world heritage. Against the background of this constant (re)appreciation and (re)appropriation we study heritage formation as a phenomenon that takes place within the context of various forms of knowledge production, at multiple levels and locations. Sites and objects – through texts, as images, as copies and in 'real' pieces, as souvenirs, as parts of exchanges, gifts, and thefts, or in the context of national or international exhibitions – cross orders and borders. In different forms they play a role in alternative heritage politics, which are not necessarily based in national and colonial state formations, and have coexisted in parallel worlds that have had centres other than Europe-based empires.[24] This realisation also helps us to better understand how, as Frederick Cooper has stressed, the colonial state had to deal with structures that 'complicate the relationship of ruler and ruled, of insider and outsider'.[25]

With our consciousness of the relation between culture and power, we owe a debt to, and engage critically with, Benedict Anderson's ground-breaking and highly influential *Imagined communities* (1991). Anderson identified the connection between an 'archaeological push' around 1900 in Southeast Asia and (post-)colonial nationalism. Preoccupied by nationalism and state formation, he argued that the newly founded archaeological services of that time, like the one in Batavia (set up in 1913), created regalia and tools of legitimation for the colonial state by transforming ruins into monuments. Through endless display

23 Compare with Alan Lester, 'Imperial circuits and networks: geographies of the British Empire', *History Compass* 4:1 (2006), 135; Tim Harper and Sunil S. Amrith, 'Sites of Asian interaction: an introduction', in Tim Harper (ed.), *Sites of Asian interaction: ideas, networks and mobility*, Special Issue, *MAS* 46 (2012), 249–257.

24 Compare with George W. Stocking Jnr, *Objects and others: essays on museums and material culture* (Madison: University of Wisconsin Press, 1985); S. Legêne, 'Powerful ideas: museums, empire utopias and connected worlds', in R. Omar, B. Ndhlovu, L. Gibson, and S. Vawda (eds.), *Museums and the idea of historical progress* (Cape Town: IZIKO Museums Publications, 2014), 15–30; Donald S. Lopez, *Curators of the Buddha: the study of Buddhism under colonialism* (Chicago: University of Chicago Press, 1995); Arjun Appadurai, *The social life of things: commodities in cultural perspective* (Cambridge: Cambridge University Press, 1985).

25 Frederick Cooper, *Colonialism in question: theory, knowledge, history* (Berkeley: University of California Press, 2005), 48–53.

and reproduction, these monuments were transformed into recognisable signs, connecting subjects of the (post-)colonial state to visions of great national pasts.[26] With this important insight in mind, we argue, first, that if we want to understand the dynamics of archaeology, heritage formation, and knowledge production in Asia, we need to go further back, to the first half of the nineteenth century when a series of violent colonial regime changes, war, and infrastructural developments deeply intervened in local society. Second, with our site-centred approach, we aim, moreover, to go beyond the role and engagements of the state. Broadening Anderson's state-centred framework, we follow local, transnational, and global interactions with sites at the ground level, in multiple, intercolonial and inter-Asian contexts, towards a new mobile history of archaeology and heritage formation in Asia.

Our approach is part of a transnational trend in Asian studies (and the social sciences and humanities in general), where scholars of different periods seek to investigate religious engagements of groups of people in Asia, for example, or the imaginations of Asian identities that developed beyond the borders of modern (post-)colonial states. Historians such as Susan Bayly and Engseng Ho have shown how, for that aim, ancient religious sites and burial places can greatly aid insight: they can connect to people and histories outside the national boundaries in which they are located and 'bend diasporic journeys'.[27] Comparably, Susan Bayly, in her work on the Greater India Society, addresses the heuristic value of religious sites, such as the tomb shrine and pilgrimage site of the Islamic saint Shahul Amir in southern India, because they 'bear witness to the capacity of South Asians to forge fluid but enduringly supra-local solidarities which could both exploit and transcend the circumstances of colonialism'.[28] Unlike Bayly or Ho, it is not so much the people and their

[26] Benedict Anderson, *Imagined communities: reflections on the origin and spread of nationalism*, revised edn (London and New York: Verso, 1991), 155–185.

[27] Engseng Ho, *The graves of Tarim: genealogy and mobility across the Indian Ocean* (Berkeley: University of California Press, 2006), xxv. On Islamic grave pilgrimage, or *keramat*, from an inter-Asian perspective, see Sumit Mandal, 'Popular sites of prayer, transoceanic migration, and cultural diversity: exploring the significance of keramat in Southeast Asia', *MAS* 46:2 (2012), 355–372; Terenjit Sevea, '*Keramat*s running amok', in Michael Laffan (ed.), *Belonging across the Bay of Bengal: religious rites, colonial migrations, national rights* (London: Bloomsbury, 2017), 57–72. See also Henri Chambert-Loir, 'Saints and ancestors: the cult of Muslim saints in Java', in Henri Chambert-Loir and Anthony Reid (eds.), *The potent dead: ancestors, saints and heroes in contemporary Indonesia* (Crows Nest: Allen & Unwin; Honolulu: University of Hawai'i Press, 2002), 132–141; James J. Fox, 'Ziarah visits to the tombs of the wali, the founders of Islam on Java', in M. C. Ricklefs (ed.), *Islam in the Indonesian context* (Clayton: Centre of Southeast Asian Studies, Monash University, 1991), 19–39.

[28] Susan Bayly, 'Imagining "Greater India": French and Indian visions of colonialism in the Indic mode', *MAS* 38:3 (2004), 704. For other studies on transnational imaginations of the region, see for example Timothy P. Barnard (ed.), *Contesting Malayness: Malay identity across borders* (Singapore: Singapore University Press, 2004); A. Gupta, 'The song of the non-aligned world: transnational identities and the reinscription of space in late capitalism', in Steven Vertovec and Robin Cohen (eds.), *Migration, diasporas and transnationalism* (Northampton: Edward Elgar,

travels via sites that we follow in this book; instead, we try to understand how sites, through interventions at the sites and through the sites' travels, connect – or exclude – people, not only in Asia but also in Europe and beyond.[29] As we deliberately focus on sites that (have) developed into official heritage, we are, moreover, able to analyse the related mechanisms of inclusion and exclusion and the role cultural hierarchies play in this. Such sites not only connect multiple parties, but they are in the course of time also sanctified and privileged – by the nation-state and by local and global heritage agencies.

The colonial and post-colonial state in development represent, in this book, therefore only one party among many, be it an influential one. However, even state-supported Archaeological Services, whether from the Dutch regime (1913–1942), or its Japanese (1942–1945) and Indonesian successors (from 1946 onwards), were not always the strong institutions that Anderson presumed. For one thing, official state-supported heritage policies (always in development and in discussion) and actual heritage practices on location did not always match. These policies were formed by various individuals and experts, who all developed their own – not necessarily overlapping – queries, ideals, and principles regarding research and conservation practices at sites. Heritage politics were also influenced by developments on location.

Moreover, from the late nineteenth century, the central query of archaeology in the colonies became, and remained for a long time, the reconstruction of dynastic histories and prehistoric civilisations, and the definition of sequences of periods – always from an evolutionary perspective. Archaeologists followed this query by classifying objects, and by comparing and connecting these with findings elsewhere, and, in some cases, with living 'prehistoric' or other 'higher' cultures (such as Hindu Bali) known from ethnographic research in the Netherlands Indies and elsewhere.[30] Remarkably, although the

1999), 503–519; John Ingleson (ed.), *Regionalism, subregionalism and APEC* (Clayton: Monash Asia Institute, 1997); Sven Saaler and J. Victor Koschmann (eds.), *Pan-Asianism in modern Japanese history: colonialism, regionalism and borders* (London: Routledge, 2007). For an enlightening overview of India-centred pan-Asianisms, see Carolien Stolte and Harald Fischer-Tiné, 'Imagining Asia in India: nationalism and internationionalism (ca. 1905–1940)', *Comparative Studies in Society and History* 54:1 (2012), 65–92.

29 Bloembergen and Eickhoff, 'Exchange and the protection of Java's antiquities'.

30 Daud Aris Tanudirjo, 'Theoretical trends in Indonesian archaeology', in Peter J. Ucko (ed.), *Theory in archaeology: a world perspective* (London: Routledge, 1995), 61–75; Daud Ali, 'Connected histories? Regional historiography and theories of cultural contact between early South and Southeast Asia', in R. Michael Feener and Terenjit Sevea (eds.), *Islamic connections: Muslim societies in South and Southeast Asia* (Singapore: ISEAS, 2009), 1–24; Marieke Bloembergen and Martijn Eickhoff, 'The colonial archaeological hero reconsidered: postcolonial perspectives on the "discovery" of pre-historic Indonesia', in Gisela Eberhardt and Fabian Link (eds.), *Historiographical approaches to past archaeological research* (Berlin:

Archaeological Service's work in the period between the two world wars was indeed a state-legitimising activity, the research and fieldwork of archaeology transcended the boundaries of nation-states and empires, because scholars were all interested in connections.[31] They explored past inter-Asian relations between the islands of the Netherlands Indies archipelago and tried to figure out the origins and directions of cultural transfer. Precisely in these queries about ancient cultural 'connections' lay another explanation for the essential weakness of successive Archaeological Services in colonial and post-colonial Indonesia. As we shall see throughout this book, such queries about (past) inter-Asian connections were shared by scholars, pan-Asian nationalist elites, and pilgrims based in mainland Asia. These queries also formed the core of the expansionist ideology of imperialist Japan during the Second World War. These actors also developed interest in sites located in the archipelago as part of 'their' ancient civilisation too, causing potential problems regarding the question of practical ownership at location, and thus implicating direct or indirect acts of violence. Following our site-centred method, we need to explain further how this relationship between heritage and violence worked in Netherlands Indies colonial and post-colonial situations, by starting from an object.

Violence, Regime Change, and Heritage Formation in the Netherlands Indies

Violence and heritage formation are strongly connected, yet it is not always visible how. An object as marvellous as the 'Banten Gamelan', in the Museum Nasional in Jakarta, can illustrate this. This set of bronze musical instruments, with its beautifully carved wooden frames painted red and gold, is one of the highlights of the museum (Figure 0.2).[32] Today, as part of the ethnographic collection, it represents West Java. A text informs us where the *gamelan* came from – it 'belonged to the Sultanate of Banten' – but not how it got into the museum.[33] Nor do we learn anything about the history of this sultanate, which in the sixteenth and seventeenth centuries was a centre of Islam and one of the

Edition Topoi, 2015), 133–164. For earlier overviews, see R. von Heine-Geldern, 'Prehistoric research in the Netherlands Indies', in Pieter Honig and Frans Verdoorn (eds.), *Science and scientists in the Netherlands Indies* (New York: Board for the Netherlands Indies, Surinam and Curaçao, 1945), 129–167; R. P. Soejono, 'The history of prehistoric research in Indonesia to 1950', *Asian Perspectives* 12 (1969), 69–91.

[31] Compare Ali, 'Connected histories?'

[32] See www.museumnasional.or.id/collections/etnografi/gamelan_suka_rame.html (accessed 15 June 2015). The objects have the inventory numbers 1243–1256.

[33] Visit to the Museum Nasional, M. Eickhoff, 3 January 2015. Compare with the description of the 'Banten Crown' in Hari Budiarti, 'Heirlooms of an archipelago', in Retno Sulistianingsih Sitowati and John N. Miksic (eds.), *Icons of art: National Museum Jakarta* (Jakarta: BAB Publishing, 2006), 146.

Figure 0.2 The *gamelan* from Banten, in the National Museum in Jakarta, 2016.

biggest trade centres in Asia.[34] Based on further research, we know, however, that the *gamelan* came to the museum, then the Batavian Society of Arts and Sciences, in 1832. That was directly after the almost complete destruction – like a modern Carthage – of the sultanate's *kraton* (palace) by colonial forces, which happened in clashes under changing colonial regimes, first in 1808–1813, and again in 1832.

To the west of Jakarta, the site of 'Banten', from which the Banten Gamelan originated, in the late nineteenth century became an object of (state-supported) heritage formation, as a site of early sixteenth-century colonial conquest and blossoming trade with the Vereenigde Oostindische Compagnie (Dutch East India Company, VOC). Today it is maintained, and further explored, in the light of a continuous history of devout Islam, and cosmopolitan entrepreneurial spirit and strength, tracing back to the old sultanate of Bantam. Except for the ruins of the *kraton*, there is no clear reference to the years and circumstances of its destruction in the first half of the nineteenth century. In the site's museum, which opened in 1985, the Dutch are just one of the many trading partners of this ancient sultanate. Ironically, in the Netherlands there is

[34] For histories following this perspective, see the classics: J. C. van Leur, *Indonesian trade and society: essays in Asian social and economic history* (The Hague and Bandung: Van Hoeve, 1955); Anthony Reid, *Southeast Asia in the age of commerce 1450–1680*, vol. I, *The land below the winds* (New Haven: Yale University Press, 1988).

a parallel and mirroring history of heritage formation and polishing away of violence. In this, 'Bantam', represented by the arrival of the De Houtman brothers in 1596, figures exclusively as the beginning of another peaceful and cosmopolitan success story, in this case of adventurous, entrepreneurial, and (later) ethical Dutch colonialism.[35]

The fates of the site and the *gamelan* of Banten illustrate how heritage formation (at multiple locations), whether intentionally or not, is stimulated by violence taking place at a certain site, and erases memories of the violence involved. In the history of archaeology and heritage formation in colonial Indonesia, the *kraton* – palaces of kings and princes, representing the bases of local power – are a case in point. Following the destruction by the colonial army of the *kraton* of the Balinese king Tjakranegara in Lombok in 1894, the looting of ancient manuscripts and objects was both a form of booty and an official act of caretaking and heritage formation. Likewise, during the destruction of the palaces of the South Balinese kings in the colonial military expeditions of 1906 and 1911 – following their *puputan* (a self-killing out of perseverance)[36] – objects were 'saved' that can now be admired in museums in the Netherlands and Indonesia.

In the history of heritage formation and destruction in colonial and post-colonial Indonesia, two developments seem to contrast with the fate of palaces. First, next to destroying palaces in the nineteenth century, colonial parties developed a growing positive interest in the study and maintenance of material remains of the pre-Islamic, Hindu–Buddhist past: temples, statues, inscriptions, and manuscripts. These material remains, accordingly, provided the first object of state-supported colonial explorations, measurements, cleaning, care, and conservation in order to save them for future generations that define the act of heritage formation. Second, Islamic sites – mosques and sacred graves in particular – were often respected or left to the care of the local population, even in times of violent conflict or war. The mosque in Banda Aceh, destroyed by the Dutch colonial army during the Aceh war, is an interesting exception. However, the colonial government replaced that mosque with a completely new one, in the orientalist style that was fashionable at that time, as a means of regaining consent.[37] In Banten, on the other hand, when

[35] Marieke Bloembergen and Martijn Eickhoff, 'Re-embarking for "Banten", the sultanate that never really surrendered', in Marjet Derks, Martijn Eickhoff, Remco Ensel, and Floris Meens (eds.), *What's left behind: the* lieux de mémoire *of Europe beyond Europe* (Nijmegen: Vantilt, 2015), 140–148. A recent nostalgic re-enactment of Dutch colonialism portrayed as entrepreneurial cosmopolitanism was the exhibition 'Asia in Amsterdam: the culture of luxury in the Golden Age', in the Rijksmuseum, from 17 October 2015 to 17 January 2016.

[36] For a discussion of the interpretation of the Balinese *puputan*, see Margaret Wiener, *Visible and invisible realms: power, magic, and colonial conquest in Bali* (Chicago: University of Chicago Press, 1995), 325–328.

[37] Gunawan Tjahjono, *Indonesian heritage-architecture* (Singapore: Archipelago Press, 1998), 81–82.

Governor-General H. W. Daendels (in office 1808–11), after conquering the *kraton* in 1808, ordered its destruction, he officially excluded the great mosque and sacred graves of the sultans from the demolition works.[38] These seemingly contradictory policies towards historical remains of local religion and local power seem to have been following *raison d'état*. This brings us to a final important motive that we explore throughout the book, albeit again from multiple perspectives: the role of, and attitudes towards, religion in archaeology and heritage formation.

Sites and Religion

An important question that triggered our research project was how and why, in Indonesia – with its predominant Muslim population since the late sixteenth century, today the world's largest – Hindu and Buddhist temple sites have become the distinct national sites, internationally highlighted and further legitimised by the World Heritage distinction of UNESCO, as well as by mass tourism. As our study will demonstrate, individuals and groups from various backgrounds and creeds took interest in ancient sites whether or not these were still in use for religious purposes. Insightful are the travels and experiences of the Dutch Protestant vicar Baron J. R. van Hoëvell at the mosque of Demak in 1848 (discussed in Chapter 1), or those of the Siamese Buddhist king Chulalongkorn at Borobudur in 1896 (discussed in Chapter 2). Sometimes such visitors' engagements took the form of pilgrimages and could lead to resacralisation of sites, while sometimes they were also guided by professional (archaeological) concerns. Sometimes, the creed of the one visitor was of no direct relevance to the (other) religious histories of a site. Nonetheless, as we will show, all visits could lead to contemplations of the sacredness of ancient sites.

Borobudur, with its apparent capacity to enamour people, plays a special role in this but cannot exclusively explain why the official archaeological heritage sites in Indonesia have remained remarkably neutral. Today, this image of neutrality is also supported by the Indonesian government's official heritage policy, which, by categorising archaeological sites as 'dead sites' (Borobudur, Prambanan) and 'living sites' (the mosque of Demak, temples in Bali), defines if and how visitors may use the site for religious purposes. Nonetheless, despite certain imposed restrictions, until today various religious practices play a role at 'living' as well as 'dead' sites in Indonesia.[39]

[38] E. B. Kielstra, 'Het Bantamsch Sultanaat', *Onze Eeuw* 10 (1916), 102–103; J. A. van der Chijs, 'Oud-Bantam', *Tijdschrift voor Indische Taal-, Land- en Volkenkunde* 26 (1881), 39.

[39] According to Article 21 of Law 1992, 5, concerning cultural properties, Borobudur falls under the category of 'dead monument': 'Items of cultural property which at the time of their discovery are no longer used in the manner for which they were originally intended are

Relating to these concerns of religion and neutrality, one question threads through this book: to what extent, why, and how, have Hindu–Buddhist sites in Islamic Java (and wider (post-)colonial Indonesia) been prioritised since the nineteenth century in the field of archaeological knowledge production and heritage formation – as is commonly assumed. An interesting case discussed in Chapter 1 seems to defy that assumption. It involves the restoration of the late fifteenth-century mosque of Demak, in fact an intrusive renovation, which took place in 1842–1848. It was this Islamic site (not, as is commonly believed, Borobudur) that generated the first restoration officially supported by the colonial state. The great mosque of Demak was, apart from being used for daily Islamic prayer, notably also recognised as important Javanese heritage by various royal elites in Java and Madura, who participated in the restoration. This mid-nineteenth-century collaborative heritage project defies one of the explanations recently brought forward for the remarkable absence of Indonesian Islam in Islamic and Asian art collections of prestigious museums across the world – including in the Netherlands – namely, that this was the result of conscious blindness, or the political disregard of a colonial state preferring to show neutrality towards Islam.[40]

Critical Heritage Studies

This book also engages with recent developments in critical heritage studies. This field of research explicitly aims to deal with a colonial past and colonial legacies, and uses post-colonial theory in order to question how colonial interpretations and knowledge function as a 'regime of truth and power', in the past and the present.[41] Generally, archaeology has played a crucial role in this field since the mid 1980s, and historical studies of colonial archaeology have led to an increased understanding of the role of the 'science of the spade'

prohibited from being brought into use again' (Undang-Undang Republik Indonesia nomor 5 tahun 1992 tentang Benda Cagar Budaya, pasal 38). In 2010 this was slightly adjusted and 'liberated' in article 87 of Law 2010, 11: 'Items of cultural property which at the time of their discovery are no longer used in the manner for which they were originally intended are permitted to be used for *kepentingan tertentu* [specified needs]' (Undang-Undang Republik Indonesia nomor 11 tahun 2010 tentang Cagar Budaya, pasal 87).

40 Mirjam Shatanawi, *Islam at the Tropenmuseum* (Arnhem: LM Publishers, 2014), 38–41. See also unpublished discussion papers by Remco Raben and by Marieke Bloembergen during the debate 'Islam disregarded?', Tropical Museum, Amsterdam, 3 October 2014. On the display of South and Southeast Asian art in the Rijksmuseum in Amsterdam, and lack of representation of Islam there, see Marieke Bloembergen and Martijn Eickhoff, 'Een klein land dat de wereld bestormt: het nieuwe Rijksmuseum en het Nederlandse koloniale verleden', *BMGN* 129:1 (2014), 156–169. See also Chiara Formichi, 'Islamic studies or Asian studies? Islam in Southeast Asia', *Muslim World* 106 (2016), 696–718.

41 See Ricardo Roque and Kim A. Wagner, 'Introduction: engaging colonial knowledge', in Ricardo Roque and Kim A. Wagner (eds.), *Engaging colonial knowledge: reading European archives in world history* (Basingstoke: Palgrave Macmillan, 2011), 17–23.

in the interactions between Western nations and the societies they colonised in the modern period.[42]

In critical heritage studies a strong dichotomy can be traced between the colonial and the colonised. One example is Laurajane Smith's *Uses of heritage* (2006), now a highly influential standard textbook for this critical approach. Smith, focusing primarily on the twentieth century, has identified what she calls an 'authorised heritage discourse (AHD)' that developed from the West to and towards the rest of the world, that explains and determines the course of heritage politics worldwide, and that also has unifying effects. In that context she identifies and criticises an intrinsic and problematic connection between archaeology and heritage discourse, by stressing how archaeological academic standards became, to a large extent, the norm for defining heritage in the outer European world.[43] Around the same time, Daly and Winter (in 2012) reflected in a similar way upon the generalising 'heritage culture' in Asia. Their solution is to explore local contestations of the dominant discourse. This approach provides fresh new insights into these local perspectives, but still confirms the thinking in terms of a dominant dichotomy. It neglects far more complex ambiguous engagements with sites, which can overlap, or develop in parallel, indicating that heritage awareness is also a product of local histories.[44]

In the end, Smith, Winter, and Daly do take the field of heritage studies further by addressing the multiple perspectives, local varieties, and contestations within global heritage politics. However, their framework of 'contestation' makes it difficult to estimate the influence sites can exercise on numerous individuals and parties that engage with these sites beyond the perspectives and directives of states and heritage agencies such as UNESCO. As a result, these studies seem to overlook how worldwide, and over a much longer time frame, throughout colonial and post-colonial times, multiple exchanges between various parties were pivotal for developing concepts of heritage. All along, other knowledge engagements and ways of understanding have developed, which also shape heritage sites. As the biographies of Indonesia-based sites in this book show, there were several political power relations and hierarchies at work, but

[42] Bruce G. Trigger, 'Alternative archaeologies: nationalist, colonialist, imperialist', *Man: the Journal of the Royal Anthropological Institute* 19:3 (1984), 355–370; Bruce G. Trigger, *A history of archaeological thought* (Cambridge: Cambridge University Press, 1989), 110–147; O. Moro-Abadía, 'The history of archaeology as a colonial discourse', *Bulletin of the History of Archaeology* 16:2 (2006), 4–17; Margarita Díaz-Andreu, *A world history of nineteenth-century archaeology: nationalism, colonialism, and the past* (Oxford: Oxford University Press, 2007).

[43] Smith, *Uses of heritage*, 19–21. Compare with Smith and Campbell, '2012 Association of Critical Heritage Studies manifesto'; and with J. Chan et al., 'Heritage beyond the boundaries: a manifesto', *IIAS Newsletter* 69 (2014), 22–23. See www.iias.asia/the-newsletter/article/heritage-beyond-boundaries-manifesto (accessed 8 August 2019).

[44] Patrick Daly and Tim Winter, 'Heritage in Asia: converging forces, conflicting values', in Daly and Winter (eds.), *Routledge handbook of heritage in Asia*, 1–35.

recognising these should not lead to essentialist dichotomies between the West and the rest of the world.[45] Inspiration can be found in studies of heritage in Indonesia that direct their focus on local traditions and local concepts of heritage such as '*pusaka*'.[46] However, the problem still remains that indigenous and Western heritage traditions cannot be treated as isolated, fixed cultural practices, existing side by side. Interacting and changing in relationships of exchange, these traditions were *both* part of complex cultural and political dynamics on a much wider scale – and both often had violent and religious dimensions.

Narrative Structure

This book has a large scope, in space and in time, yet the Indonesian sites and objects (which travel to places elsewhere in the world) determine the histories we follow of different people, memories, narratives, and uses of the past, and how these connect. Throughout this book, sites and site-related objects are, thus, lenses to explore the multiple perspectives and knowledge exchanges concerning the various material remains of the past based in Indonesia, within and beyond limiting forces of states in development. In order to connect the various site-related histories in one, multi-layered analysis, we have, moreover, developed a chronological and site-thematic narrative which enables us to explore, from the early nineteenth century and during regime changes, the multiple contexts and *longue durée* of sites transforming into heritage, well into the present time.

In the first three chapters of the book, situated in the nineteenth century, and starting from Hindu–Buddhist and Islamic sites in Java, focusing on site visits and encounters, we show how – despite early efforts at site appropriation and heritage control, war, modernising infrastructural interventions, and the epistemic violence of archaeological and philological 'pushes' at the end of the nineteenth century – sites remained relatively open for including many different memories, stories, engagements, and forms of knowledge seeking. The awareness of differences of knowledge forms brought about by encounters at sites did not necessarily cause deep problems, nor were the hierarchies of knowledge being fixed. In Chapter 1 we explore the encounters between European antiquarian-collectors and Javanese elites in search of knowledge,

[45] Compare with M. Bloembergen and M. Eickhoff, 'Critical heritage studies and the importance of studying histories of heritage formation', *IIAS Newsletter* 70 (2015), 46.

[46] Pauline Lunsingh Scheurleer, 'Collecting Javanese antiquities: the appropriation of a newly discovered Hindu-Buddhist civilisation', in Pieter ter Keurs (ed.), *Colonial collections revisited* (Leiden: Research School CNWS, 2007), 71. Compare with C. Kreps, 'The idea of "pusaka" as an indigenous form of cultural heritage preservation', in Fiona Kerlogue (ed.), *Performing objects: museums, material culture and performance in Southeast Asia* (London: Horniman Museum and Gardens, 2004), 1–14; Hélene Njoto, 'L'invention du patrimoine indonésien', in Remy Madinier (ed.), *Indonésie contemporaine* (Paris: Les Indes Savantes, 2016), 416–423.

as they miscommunicate or exchange knowledge at Hindu–Buddhist sites that were being rediscovered, cleaned, and documented between 1800 and the 1850s. Next, we move to the huge restoration of the mosque of Demak in the years 1842–1848, the first that was officially supported by the colonial government. It shows how various networks of knowledge, interests, and administrative and military power came together at one site, and kept the balance in fragile post-(Java) War times. All along we show how throughout, the hierarchies of knowledge were not fixed, and how knowledge exchange helped alter old loyalties or forge new ones in the context of the violent regime changes of the early nineteenth century.

Via the visit of King Chulalongkorn to Borobudur in 1896 we analyse, in Chapter 2, the exchanges of knowledge and objects taking place there, and follow Borobudur statues travelling as gifts to Siam along with the king, where they transformed into objects of popular Buddhism and legitimation of Siam's Buddhist dynasty. Thanks to the uncovered treasure of a guestbook of Borobudur, kept between 1888 and 1898, and the diary of a Javanese nobleman, we can, moreover, broaden the social scope of Borobudur with site impressions of a growing number of visitors to Borobudur, from as far away as the United States and Australia, but also – and mostly – from Java. In Chapter 3, then, we focus on the various encounters, objects, texts and stories collecting relating to the (thirteenth–fifteenth century) Majapahit site in East Java during the long nineteenth century. What makes the Majapahit site distinct from others discussed in this book is that in the twentieth century it transformed into a central heritage site of the post-colonial Indonesian state. The politics of Majapahit as a material site and spiritual symbol, we argue, were, however, of a multiple nature and had started already in the early nineteenth century.

In the next three chapters, situated in the twentieth century, we return to many of the sites we have introduced in the part of our book dedicated to the nineteenth century. In Chapter 4, we again focus on Majapahit and analyse how it became a proto-national site through local and centralising nationalist site interventions, despite the lack of evidence, and despite criticism from philological, Islamic, and communist voices. But in Chapter 5 we also broaden the scope towards Sumatra (analysing the research of Sriviyaja and the prehistoric Pasemah area). In Chapter 6 we study the makings of Chinese and Balinese sacred objects into heritage, against the background of the state-supported reconstruction of the Siva temple at Prambanan, across regime changes. Throughout these three chapters we explore the relation between stronger centralisation, and likewise the strengthening of local heritage dynamics. We also gauge the impact of the Pacific War and of decolonisation: on colonial and post-colonial heritage politics, and on long-term foreign interests, such as the Japanese and Indian engagements with sites located in Indonesia.

For the twentieth century we see, once again, that sites remained open to alternative, multi-vocal engagements – coming from local, national, and transnational perspectives. This observation also points to the essential fragility and weakness of sites as, comparably, their self-acclaimed owners can lose control more easily than they think, through the whims of history or in the eyes of new beholders. To explore this essential fragility of sites, we return in the final chapter to Borobudur, beginning in the 1920s and 1930s, focusing on 'foreign' (Japanese, Indian, Dutch, and UNESCO) perspectives across decolonisation, to explore the role of losing and anxiety over loss in heritage dynamics. Thereby our mobile analysis of heritage formation extends beyond Indonesia.

In the Epilogue, we re-evaluate the related problems of heritage and violence, and of heritage and religion, which we explore throughout the book for the colonial and early independence periods. Here we move to more recent times, and look first at the relation between sites, heritage dynamics, and the taboos and silences concerning the difficult past of 1965 in Indonesia, and second to the question of Indonesian Islam, and its implicit absence in heritage politics, both at the global level and in the Indonesian context. In light of violent heritage conflicts concerning religious-cum-heritage sites in colonial and contemporary India, it might seem remarkable that, in predominantly Islamic Indonesia, a Buddhist and a Hindu shrine remain the most important national monuments without much dispute. Yet, as we argue, one of the explanations may be that they were and are being (re)made in exchange of knowledge, and exchange of partial self-acclaimed ownership at different levels (religious, economic, scholarly, spiritual, universalising). The fate of these sites may therefore precisely make clear how a history of sites and heritage in Asia needs to be studied from a mobile, interactive approach if we want to understand not only the making and keeping of heritage sites, but also their potential leniency and openness to changing meanings, and inclusion.

By exploring the *longue durée* biographies of Indonesia-based sites and travelling objects, and by situating these in the contexts of various forms of knowledge production, we intended to bring out marginalised perspectives in heritage, history, and memory making in Indonesia. However, we have noticed that this approach, ironically, creates its own, alternative margins. Yet we hope this book shows how sites and objects over time and space, and up to today, have influenced how people look at the world, in more complex ways than one can find in museums, art-historical studies, or formal heritage politics. The complex, mobile, history of sites and objects matters, not only as it is defined and reflected by the (violent) politics of exchange and changing hierarchies at local and global levels, but also by desires, beliefs, curiosity, storytelling, and story-gathering that deeply mattered to the people involved – whether these were following acknowledged historical truth and official art-historical criteria of the time, or not. We hope that this book, and our approach, inspires further research into other possible perspectives and narratives of mobile histories of heritage in Asia.

What should become clear from this book is how ancient sites and objects, *despite* heritage formation and dominant national histories, have the capacity to include. They also trigger historical narratives and engagements of people that do not necessarily have to conflict.[47] Considered with that background, heritage formation is just one powerful form or technique of knowledge production. However, because of its potential to petrify the past, and because of its tendency to place sites and site-related objects behind a gate or in a museum's glass box, this may be the most difficult form of knowledge to change when people want to or need to.

[47] Compare Lynn Meskell, 'Introduction: archaeology matters', in Lynn Meskell (ed.), *Archaeology under fire: nationalism, politics and heritage in the eastern Mediterranean and Middle East* (London: Routledge, 1998), 8.

1 Site Interventions, Knowledge Networks, and Changing Loyalties on Java, 1800–1850s

> [T]hey bring offers to some of these idols.[1]
>
> [I]t is more important to the Javanese to visit the old temple before it falls into decay than to see the new temple being built.[2]

In 1804, Nicolaus Engelhard (1761–1831), governor of Java's North-east Coast, visited the Singasari temple, a thirteenth-century Hindu–Buddhist temple near Malang (East Java) that Dutch surveyors had rediscovered only a year earlier.[3] A new collector in the field with a growing awareness of enlightened status and taste, Engelhard took six giant statues of Java's Hindu–Buddhist pantheon from inside the temple to his residential garden, 'De Vrijheid' (Freedom) in Semarang. They would never return to the temple. In the 1810s, three of them came to the Netherlands. Mirroring this (in)famous destruction, decades later hundreds of emissaries (comprising Javanese lower elites, administrators, clerics, hajis, and workmen) would descend on another ancient site in nearby Demak. In July 1842 the courts of Central Java and Madura sent them to restore the Great Mosque of Demak, a precious heirloom of the courts. That same month, Demak was flooded by Muslim pilgrims, anxious to pray at the mosque and the holy graves nearby before the site was closed for restoration. This would be the first site of an ancient, pre-colonial past in the Netherlands Indies to be restored with support of the Dutch colonial government, in co-ordination with local parties in Java and Madura.

This chapter sets out to explore the nature, politics, and idiosyncrasies of heritage engagements in early nineteenth-century Java. Where Engelhard's dealings with Javanese antiquities took place under changing Dutch, Napoleonic, British, and again Dutch regimes within two decades of the

1 Nicolaus Engelhard watching ritual practices at Hindu–Buddhist antiquities in Java, in 1802, quoted in N. J. Krom, 'Engelhard over de Javaansche oudheden', *Bijdragen tot de Taal-, Land- en Volkenkunde* (hereafter *BKI*) 76 (1929), 440.

2 Resident of Semarang to governor-general, 21 October 1842, in Arsip Nasional Republik Indonesia (hereafter ANRI), Arsip Keresidenan Semarang (hereafter AKS), inv. nr 4361.

3 Some parts of this chapter were first published as M. Bloembergen and M. Eickhoff, 'A wind of change on Java's ruined temples: archaeological activities, imperial circuits and heritage awareness in Java and the Netherlands (1800–1850)', *BMGN* 128:1 (2013), 81–104.

nineteenth century (1797–1816), plans for the restoration of Demak's Great Mosque developed in the decade following the devastating Java War (1825–1830). The chapter focuses on the dynamics of archaeological interests, heritage awareness, and changing political status and loyalties in the context of these various violent regime changes, and of the knowledge networks developing all along at local and global levels. Reflecting Benedict Anderson's point regarding the connection between an 'archaeological push' around 1900 in Southeast Asia and (post-)colonial state formation, the Hindu–Buddhist temples of Java became 'regalia' of the late colonial and post-colonial Indonesian state.[4] But to understand the dynamics of cultural heritage politics in (post-) colonial situations, we need to go further back in time and do more. Our multiple-sites-centred approach and our focus on 'site interventions' help us to show how European and indigenous concepts and engagements with archaeological sites developed in parallel, interacted, and together contributed to the development of heritage awareness and multiple political loyalties in, of, and beyond the modern colonial state.

We focus on two 'site interventions' on Java between 1800 and 1850. We begin by exploring the new site visits and the various forms of knowledge gathering at various (Hindu–Buddhist, royal, Islamic) sites carried out by individual actors and companies composed (mostly) of men – who were British, Indo-Dutch, Dutch, Javanese, and Chinese-Javanese. Connected to various local and global knowledge networks, these individuals help us to understand how and why 'archaeology' during the first half of the nineteenth century, and across regime changes and wars, became meaningful to many in the colony, the metropole, and elsewhere. Our chronological analysis enables us to show how the end of the *ancien régime* and the following wars and regime changes stimulated a new focus on the past and, with regard to Java, especially on a particular – Hindu–Buddhist – past. All along, such individual site interventions disseminated news about sites, which generated the new interest from still more people. This was especially the case for Borobudur, which in the 1820s and 1830s gradually became more visible due to further cleaning work, performed by local Javanese. By the 1840s, Borobodur attracted Javanese and Chinese visitors alike and, indeed, the temple got crowded during Lebaran, the end of the Islamic fasting celebration. In the final part of our chapter we focus on the restoration of the Great Mosque of Demak in 1842–1848, the first *restoration* – involving a complete destruction and renewal – of a Javanese 'antiquity' supported by the colonial government. It also sheds light on our query regarding why, and to what extent, a late colonial state came to prioritise

[4] Anderson, *Imagined communities*, 155–185, esp. 184.

the study and care of Hindu–Buddhist antiquities, and suggests that Islamic objects may have been left to the care of local owners, largely out of fear.[5]

Statues, Local Stories, and Enlightened Status around 1800

Two years before Engelhard stole the Hindu–Buddhist statues for his garden, as governor of Java's North-east Coast he visited the ruins of the Hindu temple complex Prambanan (850 CE), Kota Gede (a *kraton* and royal graveyard of the Mataram kingdom dating from around 1700), and the royal *pasanggrahan* (retreat) Gimbirowati.[6] After the installation of the Batavian Republic in the Netherlands in 1795, the liquidation of the VOC in 1798 and the failed British invasion in Java of 1800, the political situation on the island was unstable. Engelhard sought to resolve problems – so-called *differentien* – with the royal rulers in Central Java, Sunan Pakubuwana IV in Solo (in office 1788–1820), and Sultan Hamengkubuwana II in Yogyakarta (in office, 1792–1812).[7] From there, he made trips to the nearby sites, which apparently triggered his archaeological interests further. In this context, he began collecting statues from Java's ancient past for his residence's garden in Semarang.[8] In 1805 he ordered lieutenant engineer H. C. Cornelius, who was in charge of the construction of a fortress in Klaten (Central Java), to clean the temples of the Prambanan complex, measure them, and draw their ground plan. This was probably the first instance of temple-ruin reconstruction in Java.[9]

Engelhard's 1802 visit to the three sites near Yogyakarta was not part of the official diplomatic programme. He travelled to Prambanan on a Friday, which he referred to as 'the Sabbath of the Mohammedans';[10] locals served as his guides. Intrigued by a local story that a giant had built the temples, Engelhard visited the burial site of a giant in a graveyard near the *kraton* of Pleret.[11] The

5 This is the central tenet in Shatanawi, *Islam at the Tropenmuseum*. See also the debate 'A history of disregard: a debate on Islam, Indonesia and collecting practices at the Tropenmuseum', Amsterdam, 2 October 2014.

6 The authors thank Sri Margana (UGM) for identifying these locations (5 April 2011).

7 Dagregister van den reis van de Gouverneur Nicolaus Engelhard naar Sourakarta en Djogjakarta, 1802, ANRI, Arsip Keresidenan Yogyakarta 17241891 inv. nr 348 (hereafter Dagregister Engelhard ANRI). For Engelhard, see F. de Haan, 'De Historie van een Oudgast', *Tijdschrift voor Indische Taal-, Land- en Volkenkunde* 18 (1901), 195–225; J. H. M. Kommers, *Besturen in een onbekende wereld: het Europese binnenlandse bestuur in Nederlands-Indië: 1800–1830. Een antropologische studie* I (Meppel: Krips Repro, 1979), 70–74. See also Amrit Gomperts, Arnoud Haag, and Peter Carey, 'Mapping Majapahit: Wardenaar's archaeological survey at Trowulan in 1815', *Indonesia* 93:1 (2012), 177–196.

8 N. Chutiwongs, 'Çandi Singasari – a recent study', in E. A. Bacus, I. C. Glover, and P. D. Sharrock (eds.), *Interpreting Southeast Asia's past: monument, image and text* (Singapore: NUS Press, 2008), 101.

9 A. J. Bernet Kempers, *Herstel in eigen waarde: monumentenzorg in Indonesië* (Zutphen: De Walburg Pers, 1978), 29.

10 'Vrijdag den 20e Augustus', p. 129, Dagregister Engelhard ANRI.

11 'Woensdag den 18e Augustus', p. 122, Dagregister Engelhard ANRI.

story, as Engelhard understood it, referred to a princess named Lara Jonggrang, and it offered an explanation for the ruined buildings, particularly the nearby Buddhist site of 'thousand temples', Candi Sewu, and the large statue of Durga (Siva's consort) at Prambanan.[12] Modern archaeologists dismiss this local myth, although contemporary Indonesian guides often refer to the site as 'Lara Jonggrang'.[13] In the story, Bandung Bandawasa asked Princess Lara Jonggrang to marry him. Rather than refusing outright, she conditioned her acceptance on a complex of a thousand temples and statues being built overnight. When he appeared to be succeeding with the help of giants and dark spirits, she made the cocks crow earlier to insist that dawn had already come. Bandung Bandawasa cursed the princess, who turned to stone, and the temples remained unfinished.[14] Engelhard also refers to a Dutch belief that giants built the temple, reminiscent of the early modern European account of megalithic graves, which references the pre-Flood Old Testament world where giants figure,[15] though he did not believe such explanations, considering himself an enlightened man. In fact, Engelhard presumed the builders of magnificent antiquities were not Javanese but 'foreign'; he also believed these antiquities held no importance to local Javanese, claiming they 'do not honour [the temple ruins] although they bring offers to some of these idols, without being able to explain why'.[16] This contempt seems curious coming from someone who chiselled his name into the statues at *pasanggrahan* (guesthouse) Gimbirowati, a place of retreat and meditation for Sultan Amangkurat I. But it is consistent with Engelhard's theft of statues, which according to an account of British lieutenant-colonel Alexander Adams, drove inhabitants near the Singasari temple to secret precious historical objects into the jungle to prevent further removals.[17]

[12] Today it is located in the northern chamber of the main temple of Siva on the Prambanan site, which was restored and reconstructed in the twentieth century (see Chapter 6)

[13] See the Festschrift for the archaeologist I Gusti Ngurah Anom, on the occasion of his departure from the Balai Pelestarian Peninggalan Purbakala (BP3) of Central Java (at the Prambanan site) in which Bandawasa is now associated with the various methods and objects of restoration and reconstruction directed by the BP3. The first chapter tells the story of *bandung* Bandawas in poetry: Sumijati Atmosudiro, *Bandung Bandawasa di masa kini; Kisah Balik Megahnya hasil pemugaran Benda Cagar Budaya* (Plaosan: BP3 Wilayah Jawa Tenggah; Kementeri Kebudayaan dan Parawisata, 2003).

[14] Lunsingh Scheurleer, 'Collecting Javanese antiquities', 79. Compare with Carel Frederik Winter, 'Oudheidkunde: oorsprong van oudheden te Brambanan', *Tijdschrift voor Neêrlandsch Indië* 2:1 (1839), 469–471.

[15] Jan Albert Bakker, *Megalithic research in the Netherlands, 1547–1911: from 'giant's beds' and 'Pillars of Hercules' to accurate investigations* (Leiden: Sidestone Press, 2010), 33.

[16] Krom, 'Engelhard over de Javaansche oudheden', 440.

[17] Sarah Tiffin, 'Raffles and the barometer of civilisation: images and descriptions of ruined candis in *The History of Java*', *Journal of the Royal Asiatic Society* (hereafter *JRAS*) Series 3 18:3 (2008), 357.

What can we make of these early European interventions and perceptions of Java's temple ruins? With regard to temple ruins in Asia, little research has yet been done for the early nineteenth century.[18] An important question here is if and how European perceptions changed in an Asian context, for the past they became aware of was not their own.

Regime Change, Knowledge Gathering, and Changing Loyalties

Following the Netherlands' revolutionary period, intrusive regime changes and military invasions did not have an immediate impact on the new archaeological and reconstructive engagements in Java. Ongoing archaeological activities such as cleaning, drawing, and mapping, in fact, made these sites more visible and accessible.[19] But the appointment of Louis Bonaparte as king in 1806 (ruling over the Netherlands) did have a disruptive impact on the already unstable Dutch possessions in Asia. This also led to diverse forms of knowledge seeking and multiple appropriations of the sites, changing under the subsequent regimes. In 1807 Bonaparte appointed Marshal Herman W. Daendels governor-general, who introduced a policy of centralisation and began infrastructure works with the notorious Grote Postweg, crossing the length of Java, made by service labour. When the Kingdom of Holland was incorporated into France in 1810, Daendels returned to Holland. In June–September 1811 British–Indian forces under Governor-General Lord Minto invaded Java and defeated the Franco-Dutch troops. Minto claimed Java for the British government and, in Minto's anticipation of the need for research in languages, geography, history, religion, and administrative statistics, the British expedition came to include orientalists.[20] Thomas S. Raffles, the colonial administrator and expert in Malay, became lieutenant-governor, ruling

[18] A few recent publications reflect important exceptions and a growing interest; see Roy Jordaan, 'Nicolaus Engelhard and Thomas Stanford Raffles: brethren in Javanese antiquities', *Indonesia* 101 (April 2016), 39–66; Sarah Tiffin, *Southeast Asia in ruins: art and empire in the early nineteenth century* (Singapore: National University of Singapore Press, Royal Asiatic Society of Great Britain and Ireland, 2016); Sarah Tiffin, 'Java's ruined candis and the British picturesque ideal', *Bulletin of SOAS* 72:3 (2009), 525–558. Compare with Lunsingh Scheurleer, 'Collecting Javanese antiquities'. See also, for a factual approach to early archaeological research in nineteenth-century (eastern) Java, Gomperts, Haag, and Carey, 'Mapping Majapahit: Wardenaar's archaeological survey at Trowulan in 1815'. On early nineteenth century British archaeology in Sri Lanka, see Sujit Sivasundaram, 'Buddhist kingship, archaeology and historical narratives in Sri Lanka, 1750–1850', *Past & Present* 197:1 (2007), 111–142.

[19] For a recent discussion on the historiography on this period and the continuities in colonial ideology and policy, see Alicia Schrikker, 'Restoration in Java, a review', *BMGN* 130:4 (2015), 132–144.

[20] Holger Hoock, *Empires of the imagination: politics, war, and the arts in the British world, 1750–1850* (London: Profile Books, 2010), 324.

Java as part of the British Empire. Raffles continued to build up and reorganise colonial bureaucracy. He also used military force to establish British power: in June 1812 British–Indian troops conquered the *kraton* of Yogyakarta. Here too, destruction went hand in hand with heritage formation, as army officers looted many ancient manuscripts (and much correspondence) that would become a key collection in the British Museum, now the British Library in London.[21] The situation changed again in 1813 when the Netherlands became a kingdom with the family of Stadtholders (who had governed until 1795) as the royal family; Java was returned to the control of the Netherlands under the terms of the Anglo-Dutch Treaty of 1814.[22]

Against this unstable background, as Central Javanese kingdoms also jockeyed for power, Java's material remains of the past – sites – drew more attention. Local and colonial parties used them not only to study and reconstruct pasts, but to change, (re-)establish, and enhance status and potential loyalties, as well as for spiritual empowerment. Some of the dynamics of knowledge seeking and reappropriation can be framed, as art historian Holger Hoock has done, in Raffles' imperial-enlightened policy and plans for a centralised land revenue system grounded in sound socio-cultural and statistical knowledge.[23] Obviously, to get such information, interactions with local informants were crucial.[24] And Dutch orientalists spurred interest in historical remains among these informants, elites, and village heads alike. But the various archaeological activities at sites during the British period were also triggered by earlier interventions, and stirred by motives that did not always overlap with those of British, imperial, and orientalist enquiry. These illustrate how antiquities were, as well, pilgrimage sites providing access to spiritual power,

21 Peter Carey (ed.), *The British in Java, 1811–1816: a Javanese account* (London: Oxford University Press for the British Academy, 1992), Introduction.

22 Peter Carey, *The power of prophecy: Prince Dipanagara and the end of an old order in Java, 1785–1855* (Leiden: KITLV Press, 2007), xiii; Peter Carey, 'The Sepoy conspiracy of 1815 in Java', *BKI* 133:2/3 (1977), 294–322.

23 Hoock, *Empires of the imagination*, 324, 327.

24 This observation reflects an important shift in the historiography on colonial knowledge production, which goes back to the 1990s, and intended to give agency (back) to local informants, as well as showing their influence in selection and prioritising of knowledge. On this shift, for South Asian history, see (recently), Harald Fischer-Tiné, *Shyamji Krishnavarma: Sanskrit, sociology and anti-imperialism* (New Delhi: Routledge, 2014), xvii–xviii. Compare, on colonial knowledge production, translators and informants in the Netherlands Indies, Tony Day and Craig J. Reynolds, 'Cosmologies, truth regimes, and the state in Southeast Asia', *MAS* 34:1 (2000), 1–55; Heather Sutherland, 'Treacherous translators and improvident paupers: perception and practice in Dutch Makassar, eighteenth and nineteenth centuries', *Journal of the Economic and Social History of the Orient* 53:1–2 (2010), 319–356; Andreas Weber, 'Sprache im "Zwischenraum": Adriaan David Cornets de Groot (1804–1829) als multilingualer Grenzgänger im zentraljavanischeschen Surakarta', in Mark Häberlein and Alexander Keese (eds.), *Sprachgrenzen – Sprachkontakte – kulturelle Vermittler: Kommunikation zwischen Europäern und Außereuropäern (16.–20. Jahrhundert)* (Stuttgart: Franz Steiner Verlag, 2010), 223–243.

where people could present objects for offering. Sites, thus, could be used to build up various local, transnational, and transcendental loyalties, to influence them in the context of multiple, unstable power relations.

Raffles assigned the Scot Lieutenant-Colonel Colin Mackenzie (1754–1821) to head a commission to investigate land tenure conditions in Java.[25] As a history enthusiast, Mackenzie rose from the rank of army engineer to that of colonel in British India as he surveyed Mysore (south-west India) between 1799 and 1809, where he developed expertise in the study of Jainist antiquities and ancient inscriptions (to understand land revenue systems) and collected a massive amount of ancient coins, discussing his findings in *Asiatick Researches*.[26] In Central Java, during one of his commissioned explorations concerning land tenure, Mackenzie and his corps of Madras engineers tried to make a short excursion to Prambanan 'to make some enquiries of the Sites of the ancient capital [adding in a footnote "one of the capitals called Majapahit"][27] and some other objects of curiosity', but had to postpone extensive investigations. Later, in his report to Raffles, Mackenzie remarked that the site belonged 'to the earlier colonists of the island', implying colonists of an Indian civilisation whom he and his Madras engineers probably recognised as such. The team made sketches of some of the sites' 'interesting monuments' (including the nearby eighth-century Buddhist Candi (temple) Sari);[28] Mackenzie wrote 'a description of the remains of this ancient capital', which he would send separately and later publish.[29]

In December 1812, six months after the terrifying British attack on the *kraton* of Yogyakarta, at which Mackenzie was present, and which led to the fall of Hamengkubuwono II, the supportive new sultan, Hamengkubuwono III (in office, 1812–1814), visited the sites of Prambanan and the nearby eighth-

[25] John S. Bastin, *The native policies of Sir Stamford Raffles in Java and Sumatra: an economic interpretation* (Oxford: At the Clarendon Press, 1957).

[26] Hoock, *Empires of the imagination*, 316, 471. Nicolas Dirks, 'Guiltless spoliations: picturesque beauty, colonial knowledge, and Colin Mackenzie's survey of India', in Catherine B. Asher and Thomas R. Metcalf (eds.), *Perceptions of South Asia's visual past* (New Delhi: American Institute of Indian Studies, 1994), 211–232. See also Guha-Thakurta, *Monuments, objects, histories*, 11; Charles Allen, *The Buddha and the sahibs: the men who discovered India's lost religion* (London: John Murray, 2002).

[27] 'Military report journal of Lieutenant C. Mackenzie of the Madras engineers in Java. From October 1811 to June 1813. With an appendix. (Fort William, 4 December 1813), British Library, Mss EUR F148/47. The association with the thirteenth–fourteenth-century kingdom Majapahit based in East Java is erroneous but may refer to the spread of 'local' memory regarding Majapahit – which we will discuss in Chapter 3.

[28] 'Antiquities of Prambana. Drawings illustrative of a description of the Ancient ruins at prambana in Java. Taken on the spot in January 1812. Respectfully presented to the right honourable the Earl of Minto (under whose auspices the journey was undertaken) by his lordships much obliged & most obedient servant Colin Mackenzie, Calcutta, 9th December 1812', British Library, Mss EUR F148/47.

[29] 'Military report journal of Lieutenant C. Mackenzie of the Madras engineers in Java. From October 1811 to June 1813. With an appendix. (Fort William, 4 December 1813)', British Library, Mss EUR F148/47.

century Buddhist temple Sewu. He did so at the invitation of the linguist and self-taught historian John Crawfurd, by that time Resident of Yogyakarta. The sultan's visit to the sites of Prambanan and Sewu figures in the Babad Bedhah ing Ngayogyakarta ('Chronicle of the fall of Yogyakarta'), written in 1812–1814, by an uncle of the sultan, Pangeran Arya Panular (c. 1772–1826).[30] Panular joined the sultan in his trip to the sites, together with a big party, consisting of the British secretary of the Yogyakarta Residency, the British commander and the major of the military garrison, the Chinese captain Tan Jin Sing, royal relatives, court *priyayi* (Javanese nobility), and *prajurit* (*kraton* soldiers). The sultan travelled by carriage, together with Crawfurd, the garrison commander and the Chinese captain; the others followed on horseback.[31] This was not merely leisure and knowledge seeking, but a masquerade of power relations, too – an early 'heritage performance'.

At Prambanan, after taking refreshments offered by Crawfurd, the party immediately went to see the statue of Lara Jonggrang inside the northern chamber of the main temple. Panular, in addition, meaningfully and erroneously mentions the figure of 'Patih Gadjahmada' next to Lara Jonggrang.[32] Watching the statues, the sultan assigned one of his other uncles, Pangeran Kusumayuda, to make a drawing of Lara Jonggrang and the adjacent figures. There was a jocular familiarity between Crawfurd and the party; perhaps as a sign of the good relationships between the sultan and Crawfurd, some of these drawings of antiquities, signed by Adiwarna, would end up in Crawfurd's *History of the Indian Archipelago* (1820). There Crawfurd praised the sketches 'from a Native of Java, having the merit of being drawn with minute fidelity', and mentioned the artist by name (Figure 1.1).[33] By contrast, in his Javanese archaeological travel diary published in the *Verhandelingen van het Bataviaasch Genootschap* (1814), Mackenzie spoke only of an unnamed 'China-man' who helped him organise his visits to the Prambanan site.[34]

[30] This *babad* is introduced, transliterated, and translated in summary by Carey (ed.), *The British in Java,* 136–138 and 320–322. Details on the text and Panular are from Carey's introduction. We also gratefully make use of Carey's translation and the summary of the relevant passages in Canto XXXIII.

[31] Carey, *The British in Java,* 137.

[32] Carey concludes this must have been the demon described by Raffles as 'Dewth Mahikusor'. While the demon-like figure Panular refers to has no relationship to the fourteenth-century *patih* and builder of the Majapahit empire Gajah Madah, the fact that Panular thinks it must reflect Gajah Mada points to a particular site-related historical awareness that we will address in the next chapter. See Carey, *The British in Java,* 137 and 338.

[33] John Crawfurd, *History of the Indian Archipelago: containing an account of the manners, arts, languages, religions, institutions, and commerce of its inhabitants* (Edinburgh: Constable, 1820), vi.

[34] Colin Mackenzie, 'Narrative of a Journey to examine the Remains of an Ancient City and Temples at Brambana in Java', *Verhandelingen van het Bataviaasch Genootschap der Kunsten en Wetenschappen* 7 (1814), 1, 7, 16, 28, and 43.

Figure 1.1 'Buddha receiving offerings'. Drawing by Adiwarna, 1820.

The sultan's trip to the sites was related to the reconstructive archaeological activities that had been taking place at the site, which also may have stirred new 'collecting' (like those of Engelhard) by local elites, for ambiguous reasons of status and spiritual concerns. Carrying away statues to preserve them could be part of that. Historian and Javanologist Peter Carey has pointed to evidence that some princes in Yogyakarta took statues from various Hindu and Buddhist temples around Yogyakarta to decorate their *dalem* (palace, retreat). But perhaps they also did this to 'save' them or assemble spiritual power. During the British military invasion in Yogyakarta, Sultan Hamengkubuwono II ordered two statues at the Prambanan site to be moved to the nearby 'bridge across the kali [river] Opak'.[35] Also, when the site of temple remains near Kalasan was used to build a stockade, Chinese inhabitants nearby moved Buddhist statues to an adjacent graveyard. They buried the statues that were too heavy to remove.[36] The moving of objects, here, in comparison to Engelhard's actions at Candi Singasari, seems to have been driven more by a sense of insecurity and care for ancient spirits than coveting new status.

35 Carey, 'Sepoy conspiracy', 301–302 and 316 n. 55. On the British invasion near that site, see Carey, *The British in Java*, 427 n. 138. For the relationship between early nineteenth-century archaeological practices and reanimated site-related historical interests of Javanese elites, see Merle C. Ricklefs, *Polarising Javanese society: Islamic and other visions, c. 1830–1930* (Leiden: KITLV Press, 2007).

36 J. D.P., 'Journal of an excursion to the native provinces in Java in the year of 1828, during the war with Dipo Negoro', *Journal of the Indian Archipelago and Eastern Asia* 7 (1853), 368.

That Hindu–Buddhist statues could amplify status and spiritual power in insecure times became very clear to Sunan Pakubuwono IV (1788–1820) in 1815, when he briefly associated with conspiring sepoys (Indian soldiers) of the (British) Light Infantry Battalion in Surakarta. On Raffles' orders, this battalion, which contained many high-caste Hindu landowners from Bengal, had been kept as garrison at the Central Javanese courts after the invasion of the *kraton* of Yogyakarta. In late 1815, leading figures of this garrison began preparing a conspiracy against the British. This conspiracy was pre-empted but, for the kind of archaeological interventions we explore here, the sepoys' preparations for it are all the more interesting. The sepoys managed to involve high members of the Surakarta court in their plot, including the younger brother of the sunan, Pangeran Mangkubumi and, through him, the sunan himself. For this they used the language of the Hindu–Buddhist imagery, which they encountered and recognised in Central Java's landscape. One of the leading conspirers (Dhaukul Singh) flattered the sunan; approaching the *kraton* with an image of Rama in his hand, he told him: 'if you are a descendant of a worshipper of the great Rama, then you are my master'.[37] Another (Ripaul Singh) pleased the sunan and his wife by giving dance and gymnastic performances in the private apartments of the *kraton*. The sunan gave him luxury goods in return. A third (Corporal Mata Deen), who was the master of the garrison's Hindu religious ceremonies, and who spoke good Malay, fired the sunan's fascination for Indian religious practices. In conversations with the sunan they would emphasise that 'Java had a special Hindu heritage which . . . should be once again revitalised'. As Raffles would later summarise to one of his colonels: 'the Sepoys always pointed out that Java was the land of Brama. This they would say was the country in which their gods took delight; this must be the country described in their sacred books and not Hindustan . . . and that it was a sin and a shame that the land of Brama should remain in the hand of infidels.'[38]

While members of the court in Yogyakarta apparently did not support the sepoys in any notable way, in Surakarta the sunan became highly interested in the sepoys' religious rituals. He lent them Hindu statues from the court collection and provided money for the decoration and lighting of the statues. He also attended some of the ceremonies inside the fort, 'usually alone and disguised as a common Javanese, but sometimes also accompanied by members of his family' – later arriving in his carriage, and received by Mata Deen and Dhaugkul Singh.[39] This, again, was another 'heritage performance' in which various fragile power relations were being renegotiated – eventually to the

[37] Carey, 'Sepoy conspiracy', 301, based on a report to Raffles, by the British Resident in Surakarta, Major J. M. Johnson (1813–1816).

[38] Raffles, to Col. Burslem, 16 January 1816, quoted in Carey, 'Sepoy conspiracy', 301.

[39] Ibid., 302.

complete loss of power of both parties. While the sunan may have anticipated the re-establishment of Surakarta supremacy in Central Java, and the sepoys Bengali rule in Java, or a return to Bengal, none of this materialised. When it became clear that the conspiracy was doomed to fail, as the British were already aware of it and were investigating the plans, the sunan withdrew to preserve his position.[40] But he was enriched with new knowledge of spiritual power and a much wider world connected to Java's Hindu–Buddhist statues.

How Java's ruined temple sites, as centres of new forms of attention and knowledge gathering, also attracted Javanese elites in and around the princely courts, can be gauged from a Javanese source of a very peculiar, encyclopaedic character, the *Serat Centhini*: a generative compendium of knowledge of more than 3,500 pages written in the form of a poetic travelogue. It was composed in metric verses by a team of poets and clergymen at the court of Surakarta, who started compiling it in 1814 – around the same time that Sunan Pakubuwana IV allied with the sepoys – on the initiative of one of the sunan's sons, Pangeran Amangkurat III (who would succeed his father as Pakubuwana V, 1820–1823).[41] While the *Serat Centhini* compiles and addresses various aspects of Javanese life and knowledge, Java's antiquities are part of the stories. These travel stories show the writers' awareness and use of various local and new ways of knowledge gathering concerning sites.[42]

The *Serat Centhini* follows the travels of several (elite-born) characters on Java, Mas Cabolang and Sehk Amongraga being the most important. By travelling, they also historicise sites and landscapes.[43] Their journeys lead them to historical sites and ruins of temples, including Prambanan, Borobudur, and Mendut. In one of the journeys, probably around 1820, a group of friends climb Borobudur terrace by terrace, gallery by gallery, studying and describing the statues and reliefs. They recognise all sorts of figures: a cart drawn by an elephant and driven by 'a king, or at least a prominent person' 'because he is sheltered by an umbrella'; a person riding on an elephant; a man with wings; all kinds of animals, flowers, houses, and

40 Ibid., 312.

41 On the modern encyclopedic nature of the *Serat Centhini*, see Tony Day and Will Derks, 'Narrating knowledge: reflections on the encyclopedic impulse in literary texts from Indonesian and Malay worlds', *BKI* 155:3 (1999), 309–341; and on this, in relation to various competing forms of knowledge gathering at the time in Java (including Mackenzie's), see Day and Reynolds, 'Cosmologies, truth regimes, and the state'. See also Soebardi, 'Santri-religious elements reflected in the book of Tjentini', *BKI* 127 (1971), 331–349; Benedict R. O'G. Anderson, *Language and power: exploring political cultures in Indonesia* (Ithaca: Cornell University Press, 1990), 271–298. A transcription of the *Serat Centhini* was first published in Javanese script in 1909.

42 The Indonesian archaeologist Soekmono recognised the value of the *Serat Centhini* as an interesting local source for archaeological and art-historical research. See Soekmono, 'Serat Centhini and the rejected Buddha from the main stupa of Borobudur', in Marijke J. Klokke and Karel R. van Kooij (eds.), *Fruits of inspiration: studies in honour of Prof. J. G. de Casparis* (Groningen: Forsten, 2001), 474–485.

43 Day and Reynolds, 'Cosmologies, truth regimes and the state', 29.

mountains. They find the figures arranged 'like *wayang* characters', but also wonder what they mean. On the fourth terrace, while it is getting dark, they decide to stay overnight. After sunrise, they climb further to the top of the temple, where they encounter, in the large *stupa* ('a big stone cage'), a big statue, which they describe as 'uncompleted'. All in all, they find what they see incomprehensible, questioning 'the will of the sculptor'. But they also mention that all of this dates back to the 'Buda period'.[44]

In another episode, Mas Cabolang and his company arrive at the ruins of Prambanan in a well-described mountainous landscape.[45] From a woman in the village they learn the name of the site. She takes them to the village head, who, delighted, shows them around the temple. As during the visit at Borobudur, the travellers minutely describe what they see, and here the text refers to another Javanese source, the *Serat Rama*, to explain a Ramayana relief on one of the temples. After their visit, the friends return to the home of the village head, where they join dinner. Mas Cabolang then asks about 'the story' of the temples, since he has heard two versions and wants to know which one is correct. The village head treats his guests to his version of the Lara Jonggrang story, which, as Tony Day and Craig Reynolds nicely summarise, 'lasts several hundred verses and a night of pleasurable listening'.[46] The village head embedded the story of Lara Jonggrang in a history of concrete (but partly imaginary) local kingdoms – Pengging and Prambanan – and their competing kings.[47] Thereby he gave his public, Mas Cabolang and his friends, as well as the readers of the *Serat Centhini*, narrative anchors to reimagine the temple as part and parcel of the local historical landscape.

Regulation, Competition, and Popularisation of Antiquarian Care

During the regime changes of the early nineteenth century, Java's Hindu–Buddhist antiquities became part of a colonial political reform programme: first under the British, and then, after the Napoleonic Wars, under a restored Dutch regime, and in the context of a modernising Dutch colonial state. As discussed above, however, during this same period, Javanese elites

[44] For the *Serat Centhini* and the visit to Borobudur, see Soekmono, 'Serat Centhini and the rejected Buddha'. For the word 'Bude'/ Buda, as referring to a broader complex of pre-Islamic (or non-Islamic) set of beliefs in Java, see Nancy Florida, *Writing the past, inscribing the future: history as prophecy in colonial Java* (Durham and London: Duke University Press, 1995), 325; Ricklefs, *Polarising Javanese society*, 177–179.

[45] This description is based on the summarised translation by Day and Reynolds, in Day and Reynolds, 'Cosmologies, truth regimes and the state', 34–35.

[46] Ibid., 35.

[47] For a summary of the story of the village head, in English, see Soewito Sentoso, *The Centhini story: the Javanese journey of life* (Singapore: Marshall Cavendish International (Asia) Prive limited, 2006), 122–123.

reappropriated the Javanese Hindu–Buddhist antiquities. Also, Java's ancient Hindu–Buddhist sites began to earn fame outside Java, not only among a reading elite-public in Europe, but importantly, as we shall see in Chapter 2, also in wider Asia. This was partly due to the publication of Raffles' *History of Java* in 1817, his two-volume magnum opus based on information on the history, antiquities, and population of Java, which several British, Dutch, Javanese, and Indian men (in)directly instructed by Raffles, had gathered.[48] Volume II included a description of these informants' encounters with and research at various temple sites, thirteen drawings, and three reconstructions. This work spread the fame of Java's Hindu–Buddhist antiquities and helped generate wider, international interest in the sites – in Europe, Asia, and the Americas.[49] These local and global interests in Java's antiquities would, after 1815, develop parallel to, compete with, and undermine a growing awareness among cultural and political elites in the Indies and the Netherlands, that archaeological care in the colony should be a priority of the state, out of self-legitimation. International competition in archaeological research and care – and exchange of knowledge – had already begun, however, under the British regime.

In the archaeological section of his *History of Java*, Raffles emphasised that before the British arrival on Java the antiquities of Java had not drawn much attention. Numerous remains either lay buried under rubbish in the ruined temples or were only partially examined. As an explanation, he referred to the Dutch devotion to commerce that was too exclusive to allow any interest in this subject. At the same time, according to Raffles, there was a narrow-minded Dutch policy that denied antiquarians from other nations the opportunity to conduct research in Java.[50] The Javanese people did not care, either, he contended: 'The indifference of the natives has been as great as that of their conquerors.'[51] Thus the Javanese temples in Raffles' *History of Java* also demonstrated the 'real' British concern.

In nineteenth-century Dutch sources, as well as later historical overviews about archaeology in the Netherlands Indies, a recurring theme is that Raffles 'embezzled' the 'Dutch' archaeological activities of Engelhard, and used insights provided by Engelhard and Cornelius in his *History of Java* without giving them credit.[52] F. G. Valck (1799–1842) – Resident of Yogyakarta at the end of his life, a self-taught scholar of Javanese culture, and a fervent collector of Javanese antiquities – for example, argued in 1840 that, in research, 'the

[48] T. S. Raffles, *The History of Java*, I–II (London: Black, Parbury and Allen, 1817).

[49] 'Raffle's History of Java', *De Curaçaosche Courant,* 16 September 1820.

[50] Raffles, *The History of Java*, II, 5–6. [51] Ibid., 6.

[52] Nicolaas Johannes Krom, *De Sumatraansche periode der Javaansche peschiedenis. Rede uitgesproken bij zijn ambtsaanvaarding als buitengewoon hoogleraar aan de Rijksuniversiteit te Leiden, op 3 december 1919* (Leiden: Brill, 1919), 4–5; Gerret Pieter Rouffaer, 'Monumentale kunst op Java', *De Gids* 4:9 (1901) part II, 234; H. Groot, *Van Batavia naar Weltevreden: het Bataviaasch Genootschap van Kunsten en Wetenschappen, 1778–1867* (Leiden: KITLV Uitgeverij, 2009), 175–177.

English' had merely followed the footsteps of Engelhard and that Raffles had used Engelhard's work to add lustre to his own publication.[53] This discussion, telling as it is for British–Dutch competition in appropriation of knowledge and care of Javanese antiquities, deviates from the argument we wish to emphasise in this book. Where this discussion is part of a teleological nation-state-centred discourse within the historiography of archaeology, it blinds us to the fact that Raffles' work, although not presented as such, was the result of knowledge exchange under changing, uncertain regimes: between various British, Dutch, Indian, Chinese, and Javanese men, at multiple sites, during various moments, and within various, changing hierarchies, resulting in various forms of knowledge concerning the sites – knowledge that transformed further while travelling along multiple networks and, at some time, gathered, generalised, and compiled by key figures of the network then, and by key institutions.[54]

For ensuring institutional continuities of archaeological knowledge gathering in Java, 1813 was an important year as it witnessed the 'reanimation' (as one of Raffles' biographers wrote) of the Batavian Society of Arts and Sciences, the learned society that had been founded in Batavia in 1778.[55] In his inaugural address to the society's Dutch, and now also British, members, Raffles was polite and optimistic. As president of the society, he praised its history and explained its recent decline as being the result of the war that 'has desolated the finest countries in Europe'. He foresaw a 'revival of the institution' under his own government. He also praised the archaeological work on the island conducted during his own rule, pointing, in particular, to Mackenzie's Java-based and previous India-based explorations.[56] By that time, one of the new members of the Batavian Society, John Crawfurd, the above-mentioned Resident in Yogyakarta, had also started studying archaeological sites and objects of this area, with Javanese assistance. His 1820 publication *History of the Indian Archipelago* would further spread the fame of Java's Hindu–Buddhist antiquities, and became a helpful guide and

[53] F. G. Valck, 'Oudheidkunde: gedachten over de Ruïnen van de Hindoesche godsdienst, welke op Java voorkomen', *Tijdschrift voor Neêrland's Indie* 3:1 (1840), 189.

[54] This argument that early nineteenth-century colonial knowledge production was an interactive, haphazard, and dynamic process, involving various local actors, goes against the view of the political scientist and historian Farish A. Noor, who, in his keynote address at the 'Imagining Asia(s)' conference at ISEAS in Singapore, 11–12 October 2016, titled 'A knowledge that kills: knowing Asia, arresting Asia', portrayed Raffles' work as the mighty and 'killing' product of one single authoritarian man. Compare with Farish A. Noor, *The discursive construction of Southeast Asia in nineteenth-century colonial-capitalist discourse* (Amsterdam: Amsterdam University Press, 2016).

[55] Demetrius C. Boulger, *The Life of Sir Stamford Raffles* (London: Marshall and Son, 1897), 177; Groot, *Van Batavia,* 157–184.

[56] Thomas S. Raffles, 'A Discourse delivered at a Meeting of the Society of Arts and Sciences in Batavia, on the Twenty-fourth day of April 1813, being the Anniversary of the Institute', *Verhandelingen van het Bataviaasch Genootschap der Kunsten en Wetenschappen* 7 (1814), 3, 14, and 34. See also Groot, *Van Batavia*, 173–174.

reference work for subsequent Dutch seekers for archaeological knowledge on Java. But it was only Mackenzie's name that Raffles mentioned.

Of all the British and Dutch experts Raffles had recruited to collect archaeological information on the island, Mackenzie seemed, indeed, to have been a key figure in activating and (re)connecting an island-wide network, consisting of a loose association of uneven exchange partners, sharing an interest in archaeological knowledge gathering. Some of this loose network could also be traced back to older networks of the Batavian Society, some to already connected, court-based, and Javanese elites' knowledge circles.[57] Since his assignment as surveyor of statistics on land tenure in 1812 and his visit to Prambanan, Mackenzie had continued collecting archaeological information on the island. He travelled through Java accompanied by a group of Dutch engineers, including Cornelius, who had been Engelhard's assistant, and a team of Asian draughtsmen, some of whom had been trained in India. There was also one unnamed Javanese elite informant.[58] Whereas Mackenzie made detailed notes, his team was responsible for measuring and drawing the temples. It was not easy for Mackenzie to find reliable informants and translators.[59] He developed an archaeological questionnaire (in English, French, and Dutch), which he sent to potential informants on the island, and he successfully made contact with Javanese aristocracy, showing interest in their history, customs, and literature.[60]

The distribution of Mackenzie's archaeological questionnaire was not merely a scholarly activity but also an act of legitimation of the British government on the island.[61] Answering it, as did Engelhard, for example, meant showing loyalty to the new government and, as such, the questionnaire helped build up a supportive network for this same government. In that way, under the British regime (and its successors) archaeology became part of

[57] Apart from Mackenzie, Raffles had recruited several other British and Dutch experts who collected archaeological information all around the island: Colonel Adams, Captain G. Baker, Major M. Johnson, J. C. Lawrence, T. Horsfield, H. C. Cornelis and J. W. B. Wardenaar. See N. J. Krom, *Inleiding tot de Hindoe-Javaansche kunst* I ('s-Gravenhage: Nijhoff, 1920), 6. Compare with Charles O. Blagden, *Catalogue of manuscripts in European languages belonging to the library of the India Office,* Vol. I, *The Mackenzie Collections,* Part 1, *The 1822 Collection and the Private Collection* (London: Oxford University Press, 1916), 61.

[58] Blagden, *Mackenzie Collections 1*, 25; Day and Reynolds, 'Cosmologies, truth regimes and the state'.

[59] On this, see also Blagden, *Mackenzie Collections 1*; Donald E. Weatherbee, 'Raffles' sources for traditional Javanese historiography and the Mackenzie collection', *Indonesia* 26 (October 1978), 63–93; Day and Reynolds, 'Cosmologies, truth regimes and the state', 25–29.

[60] For this questionnaire, see Krom, 'Engelhard over de Javaansche oudheden', 435–448. For Mackenzie's collecting activities on Java, see Seda Kouznetsova, 'Colin Mackenzie as collector of Javanese manuscripts and Manuscript BL MSS JAV. 29', *Indonesia and the Malay World* 36:106 (2008), 375–394.

[61] For Raffles, the 'degenerate Javan', and the Dutch 'tyranny' on Java, see Tiffin, 'Raffles and the Barometer of Civilisation', 345, 355, and 359.

a political reform programme: conducting archaeological investigations became a means to support – in this case – Raffles' governmental reorganisations, to criticise former Dutch misrule, to create connections, and thereby emphasise hierarchies of knowledge, also with regard to the local population. Javanese sites with temple ruins became, in this context, an obligation of good governance; this is how and why Raffles came to explain their decay not only by a supposed 'degeneration' of Javanese society, but also by the misrule of the Dutch VOC.[62] In this light, the new regime began conserving temples – removing the vegetation was the first step – to symbolise a new enlightened government that recognised that it had more than just commercial commitments. At the same time, British nationalist-imperial objectives were never far away. In 1813, Mackenzie, pleading in a letter to Raffles for the 'preservation' of archaeological sites, reasoned: 'it might at some future day call to remembrance an event that will be always deemed interesting to the [British] Nation at large, the incorporation of Java in the British empire'.[63]

For self-proclaimed 'enlightened' men such as Raffles and Mackenzie, archaeological activities had a moral dimension and, as such, were strongly connected to the legitimacy of the British Empire. In that light, it was undesirable for them to show earlier Dutch initiatives in the field. The difference between the drawing 'View of the ruins of a Bramin temple at Brambanan' made by Cornelius in 1807, and the plate 'The large temple at Brambanan' made by William Daniell, based on Cornelius' drawing and printed in *History of Java* of 1817, can serve as a good example. In the original drawings Cornelius depicted how three Dutch ensigns measured the temple – in fact the Sewu temple, located near the Prambanan temple site – with the help of Javanese workers who were removing vegetation. The engraving in Raffles' book does not show these activities. It depicts the ruined temple full of vegetation with a small Javanese staff standing and sitting next to it.[64] As such it represents, as Sarah Tiffin rightly concluded, primarily a romantic-exotic place full of passivity and decay.[65] The same phenomenon can be observed with regard to Engelhard's archaeological activities. Raffles admired Engelhard's collection of statues in Semarang, which to him revealed 'several very beautiful subjects in stone', but he also stressed that Engelhard, while collecting and carrying away statues, had ruined the Singasari temple.[66]

[62] Raffles, *The History of Java*, II, 6.

[63] Mackenzie to Raffles, 14 April 1813, British Library, London, Colonial Office, Mss Eur F 148/47, 1.

[64] John S. Bastin and Pauline Rohatgi, *Prints of Southeast Asia in the India Office Library: the East India Company in Malaysia and Indonesia 1786–1824* (London: Her Majesty's Stationery Office, 1979), 168.

[65] Tiffin, 'Java's ruined candis', 553 and 558.

[66] Raffles, *The History of Java*, II, 41 and 55.

These examples demonstrate how the idea of archaeological care stimulated British self-legitimation and pride: by disconnecting the buildings and statues from the Dutch and Javanese people who, in Raffles' eyes, had long neglected them. Comparable mechanisms of appropriation can be seen on the level of interpretation. Raffles' suggestion that in the past Java had been 'colonised from different parts of the continent of Asia' pointed to a connection between Java and the Asian continent.[67] It offered an alternative space to value this past, which to a large extent was part of the British Empire. By appropriating Javanese antiquities, Raffles could support that Greater British view of a local past. On his departure from Java in 1815, Raffles would take away the Javanese antiquities that he had gathered. While Raffles' Javanese antiquities travelled first to the Indian Museum in Calcutta (founded in 1814), and then to London – where some are still on display in the British Museum – (British) India became the context par excellence in which to interpret the Javanese past.[68]

After Java returned to the control of the Netherlands under the Anglo-Dutch treaty, a new Dutch colonial government took over. Antiquities now also became part of governmental policies. In 1819, a governmental regulation put inhabitants of the villages Boemi Segoro and Boro Boemen in charge – by way of unpaid service but freed from the obligation to pay land revenue – of guarding, under the direction of the *regent* of Magelang, Borobudur and Candi Mendut and keeping the temples clean.[69] Through such an assignment, local parties – such as the *regent*, lower Javanese administrators, and villagers, as well as the leading Resident of Kedu (also posted in Magelang) – became further engaged with these sites and their fate. The assignment in itself seems to indicate that the government officially came to recognise these sites as remains of an old 'civilisation', to be preserved for the future – but this might be an anachronism, as the description is based on an 1863 summary. Yet we do know that, in 1822, Governor-General G. van der Capellen indeed took a general step towards archaeological care, and tasked an archaeological commission in Java to 'search, collect, and store' antiquities and prevent the plundering of archaeological sites. However, not much is known of the activities of this commission.[70] Notably, the assignment referred exclusively to the plundering

[67] Raffles, *The History of Java*, II, 63.

[68] In the British Museum, these objects now contribute to a perspective related to 'the history of humanity' and are presented as 'objects which previous civilisations have left behind them, often accidentally, as prisms through which we can explore past worlds and the lives of the men and women who lived in them'. In this way, the colonial dimension of collecting these objects is concealed. See Neil MacGregor, *A history of the world in 100 objects* (London: Penguin Books, 2012).

[69] Gouvernementsbesluit (governmental resolution, hereafter Bt) 1 October 1819, 22, summarised by the Resident of Kedoe, to the *regent* of Magelang, 16 March 1863, ANRI, Algemeene Secretarie (General Secretary, hereafter AS), Bt 15 January 1864, 43.

[70] For the decision of 11 June 1822, see ANRI, Koninklijk Bataviaasch Genootschap Directing Board (hereafter KBG DIR) 0022.

of archaeological sites by Chinese and Javanese.[71] How Engelhard or Raffles 'collected' statues, apparently, was a different story.

Part of the reason that the first archaeological commission in the Indies seems to have been forgotten is that the restoration of Dutch colonial rule, which involved an absorbing and intrusive centralised land revenue policy, would soon be disrupted by the calamitous Java War of 1825–1830. This war started out as a social-religious rebellion against the Dutch, led by Prince Dipanagara (1785–1855), a grandson of Sultan Pakubuwana II, who as self-proclaimed *ratu adil* (righteous king) found many followers in his quest to restore traditional Javanese power. The war involved a large part of the (impoverished) countryside in Java and, towards the end of the war, shifting elite loyalties, from the side of Dipanagara to the Dutch.[72] During the war, in which a Dutch army manned by Javanese fought against Javanese, about 200,000 Javanese died, one-quarter of the cultivated area was damaged, and many properties were destroyed. In 1830, Dipanagara's weakened troops were crushed, and Dipanagara, misled by the Dutch, ended up in custody in far-away Celebes. Among those who died on the Dutch side during the Java War was the same *regent* of Magelang who in the late 1810s had taken a strong interest in Borobudur, and who was responsible for the villagers cleaning and protecting the site in the early 1820s. His grave would become, in the words of the later Resident of Kedu, as sacred as Candi Borobudur and Mendut to the population in that region, to be cared for and protected along the same lines.[73]

The end of the war in Java coincided with the Belgian Revolution of 1830 in Europe, which had consequences for the Dutch: the Dutch Kingdom lost Belgium, but gained undisputed control over Java. The Javanese Central Kingdoms, which had been almost sovereign principalities, from then onwards had to adjust to their subordinate position.[74] A new phase of colonial rule started with the introduction of the 'cultivation system', a system of cultivated land revenue based on forced labour. Nonetheless, it was during this first long turbulent period (1815–1830) that both on Java and in the Netherlands the first effective state initiatives were developed to safeguard archaeological sites and objects in Java, and to connect the two parts of the kingdom more strongly through colonial archaeological collecting. Java's antiquities formed the binding tool.

[71] ANRI, AS, Bt 24 July 1823, nr 7. See also Groot, *Van Batavia,* 192, 261–262, and 444.

[72] For recent interpretations of the Java War, see Peter Carey, *Destiny: the life of Prince Diponegoro of Yogyakarta 1785–1855* (Oxford: Peter Lang, 2014); Schrikker, 'Restoration in Java'.

[73] Resident of Kedoe, 16 January 1863, to governor-general, in ANRI, Bt 15 January 1864, 43.

[74] J. A. Somers, *Nederlandsch-Indië: staatkundige ontwikkelingen binnen een koloniale relatie* (Zutphen: Walburg Pers, 2005), 81–106; Carey, *The power of prophecy*, 261–343.

In 1815 the three immense statues which Engelhard had carried away from Candi Singasari, representing the goddesses Bhairava, Ganesha, and Siva, got packed for a journey to the Kingdom of the Netherlands, as a present to the newly installed King Willem I. Engelhard had decided on this gesture after he had met C. G. C. Reinwardt, who in that same year, as head of the Natuurkundige Commissie (Commission for Physical and Natural Historical Research), had travelled from the Netherlands to Java to collect objects of natural history for the king. Following the example of Engelhard, the Assistant Resident of Malang, D. Monnereau, gave away another token from the Singasari temple, the similarly impressive statue of Prajnaparamita, to be presented to the new king, Willem I, as well.[75] These statues arrived in Amsterdam in 1819 and were first placed in the garden of the Royal Dutch Institute of Sciences, Literature, and Fine Arts, set up by Louis Bonaparte in 1808,[76] but would later be integrated in the collection of the newly founded Museum of Antiquities in Leiden (established in 1818). In 1903 they moved to Leiden's National Museum of Ethnography, today the National Museum of World Cultures, where all of them except the Prajnaparamita (which returned to Indonesia in the 1970s) are still on display.

These stone gifts originating from Candi Singasari, the Royal Institute, the Natuurkundige Commissie, and the Museum of Antiquities all fed into the new institutionalised dynamics of collecting and exchange, which came into being in the Netherlands, and created potential continuity with regard to archaeological research, both in the Netherlands and in the colonies. Significantly, in 1818 King Willem I appointed Caspar J. C. Reuvens as the Netherlands' first professor of archaeology at Leiden University; in the same year Reuvens also became the director of the new Museum of Antiquities in Leiden. Combining both functions and with the financial support of the new state, Reuvens began collecting antiquities on a scale the Netherlands had not witnessed before. This included the acquisition of statues from the ancient Roman and Greek (so-called classical) world, Egypt, and the Netherlands Indies.[77] In that framework, in 1824 the three giant statues Engelhard had collected from Candi

[75] Rita Wassing-Visser, *Koninklijke geschenken uit Indonesië: historische banden met het Huis Oranje-Nassau (1600–1938)* (Zwolle: Waanders, 1995), 54–55 and 58–59. On the Natuurkundige Commissie's mission to the Netherlands Indies in general, see Andreas Weber, *Hybrid ambitions: science, governance, and empire in the career of Caspar G. C. Reinwardt (1773–1854)* (Leiden: Leiden University Press, 2012).

[76] Casper J. C. *Reuvens, Verhandeling over drie groote steenen beelden in den jare 1819 uit Java naar den Nederlanden overgezonden (1824): gedenkschriften in de hedendaagsche talen van der derde klasse van het Koninklijk Nederlandsch Instituut van Wetenschappen, Letterkunde en Schone Kunsten. Deel III* (Amsterdam: Pieper & Ipenbuur, 1826), i-vii and 1–223.

[77] For Reuvens, see Ruurd B. Halbertsma, *Scholars, travellers and trade: the pioneer years of the National Museum of Antiquities in Leiden, 1818–1840* (London: Routledge, 2003); Mirjam Hoijtink, *Exhibiting the past: Caspar Reuvens and the museums of antiquities in Europe, 1800–1840* (Turnhout: Brepols, 2012).

Singasari became central figures in an essay of Reuvens, his first one on Javanese statues, written for the *Verhandelingen* of the Royal Institute. In that article Reuvens also took a position in the Dutch–British archaeological rivalry with regard to the Javanese past and reproached the British for disparaging the Dutch initiatives in this field. He argued, for example, that Raffles apparently had a very low opinion of Engelhard since he left the latter's archaeological work unmentioned.[78] At the same time Reuvens acknowledged that Raffles himself had contributed to the knowledge of Javanese antiquity as well, concluding: 'being members of a commonwealth of science, we must not judge according to national lines and show these writers our gratitude'.[79]

In 1832, two years after the end of the Java War when the Dutch position on the island seemed secure, Reuvens again showed his commitment to Javanese antiquities. In that year he sent a memorandum to the high colonial administrator Jean Chrétien Baud, who was about to become governor-general in the Indies, in which he pleaded for measures to protect archaeological sites and objects. He wrote: 'There seems to be a feeling on Java that these monuments are communal property and that everyone, especially the higher civil servants, can take away what they like.'[80] It is not known on which sources Reuvens based this view. He must have heard about the case of a Dutch gentleman in Salatiga who destroyed a statue of Ganesha near his home after his bankruptcy.[81] As far as we know, it is the first act of iconoclasm reported by colonial sources. Reuvens reasoned that the government could not solve this problem.[82] He suggested therefore that private owners should make drawings of objects and measure the shape of temples in detail. A society, according to Reuvens, would be the best way to support this project.[83] He was apparently not aware that an archaeological commission on Java had already existed from 1822. When we compare the justification of the assignment of that commission with Reuvens' explanation, it is remarkable that the former referred exclusively to the plundering of archaeological sites by Chinese and native people, and did not refer to civil servants, which Reuvens did.[84] However, Reuvens' suggestion in

78 Raffles, *The History of Java*, II, 41; Reuvens, *Verhandeling*, 11.
79 Reuvens, *Verhandeling*, 13.
80 Memorie ter bevordering der Javaansche Oudheid-Kunde, 29 August 1832, ANRI, KBG DIR 0093.
81 This anecdote in mentioned in a letter from C. Leemans, curator at the Museum of Antiquities, to the Minister of the Interior (Willem A. Baron Schimmelpenninck van der Oye), 2 April 1842, in ANRI, AS, Bt 17 August 1842 nr II.
82 Memorie ter bevordering der Javaansche Oudheid-Kunde, 29 August 1832, ANRI, KBG DIR 0093.
83 Ibid. See also Groot, *Van Batavia*, 261–263. Compare with Brenda Deen Schildgen, *Heritage or heresy: preservation and destruction of religious art and architecture in Europe* (New York: Palgrave Macmillan, 2008), 121–132.
84 ANRI, AS, Bt 24 July 1823, nr 7. See also Groot, *Van Batavia,* 192, 261–262, and 444.

1832 that taking care of archaeological sites and objects should and could be primarily a state-regulated civil obligation did not have any effect, either.[85]

The year 1840 saw a radical change of policy, with Governor-General C. S. W. van Hogendorp commissioning a new archaeological regulation. It was the result of an intervention by Baud, who had become minister for the colonies in The Hague. Baud knew of the visit to Java of the French archaeologist Ernest De Sancigny and therefore advised taking measures. The regulation of 1840 officially forbade the export of antiquities from Java without the permission of the governor-general, and it obliged local authorities to make an inventory of the antiquities in their region.[86] Following this regulation, in 1842 the government assigned the Batavian Society to collect data from the regional authorities in Java, and to invite them to send archaeological objects to the society, on the basis of the lists compiled in 1840 – however, with one important restriction: objects and statues should not be transported if the local population cared for them. Apart from those, once the collected objects arrived in Batavia they would become part of the museum of the Batavian Society and as such become 'national property'.[87]

This use of the category 'national property' implies that the care for archaeological sites at that moment was officially transformed from a state-regulated civil responsibility to an obligation of the – internally expanding – colonial state itself that aimed to prevent interference from other colonial powers. By defining archaeological objects in Java as 'national property', the spatial geography of the newly founded Kingdom of the Netherlands was enlarged and archaeological activities gained a moral component. The Dutch colonial authorities certainly recognised that there were also local Javanese appropriations, and they were prepared to respect these, but not as the heart of the matter. This notion of the Dutch colonial state as the caretaker of the remains of (what they saw as) a magnificent Javanese past is an early expression of modern state-related heritage awareness. Thus, in the 1840s, we argue, Java's antiquities transformed into a national obligation of the Dutch colonial state. This, however, did not mean that this state became fully in charge. Alternative site engagements, and interests in care, had been developing all along.

[85] It might have been too much in line with the social criticism he had formulated earlier in the Netherlands. There he spoke repeatedly, and without much effect, of the decline of cultural life and the dominance of a mercantile spirit, which could only be stopped by a good classical education and state investments in archaeology. Compare with Martijn Eickhoff, 'Archeologisch erfgoed: een onbeheersbaar concept', in Frans Grijzenhout (ed.), *Erfgoed; de geschiedenis van een begrip* (Amsterdam: Amsterdam University Press, 2007), 237–238.

[86] Groot, *Van Batavia*, 308.

[87] ANRI, KBG DIR 1509, Bt 3 December 1842, nr 18. See also Groot, *Van Batavia,* 310.

The Power of Sites in Weak States

In 1828 the deeply spiritual Sunan Pakubuwana VI (r. 1823–1840) of Solo visited the sacred mountain *gunung* Tidhal, south of Magelang. He was in search of spiritual power – much needed in times of the devastating Java War.[88] He also went to contemplate at nearby Borobudur. After the first unearthing operation under Raffles in 1814, between 1818 and 1822, the temple was further cleaned. As a result, by the time Pakubuwana VI arrived, its shape and ground plan had become more visible, possibly because the villagers of Boemi Segoro and Boro Boemen who had been assigned to keep Borobudur performed this work.

Though it was still not completely cleaned, by 1822 the sight of Borobudur nevertheless whetted people's desire to see more of it, and inspired them to work. In 1835 and 1836, C. L. Hartmann, posted in nearby Magelang as Resident of Kedu, carried out several clearance works on his own initiative, probably again with the help of local workers gathered by the *regent* of Magelang.[89] While the temple thus became increasingly visible and accessible, it attracted more and more individuals. Through their eyes we see some of the diverse and multiple interests that connected various people to Java's Hindu–Buddhist temple sites, interests that did not necessarily serve the new Dutch colonial state.

Among the new visitors to Borobudur was the Dutch artist Hubertus N. Sieburgh (1799–1842), who gave us the intriguing impression of his encounter with the temple and with one of its (Chinese) visitors with whom we opened this monograph. But, like the Chinese man, Sieburgh also felt empowered by the temple in an idiosyncratic way that had little to do with pride of state care. Sieburgh was the first artist from the Netherlands who went to Java, on his own initiative, just to visit the ruined temples of Java – which he had learned about through the images that by now had spread around the world.[90] His aim was to make what he called 'pittoresque' travels. During his stay on Java, from 1836 until his early death in 1842, he painted the main corpus of temples and other ruined buildings that at that time were known to exist. These were paintings in the romantic style without any intention to give a precise documentation of the site itself. For example, one temple – the Candi Lumbung near the Prambanan complex – was painted as a moonlit scene. In some exceptional cases he included

[88] Carey, *The British in Java*, 454 n. 263.

[89] Bernet Kempers, *Herstel in eigen waarde*, 68; Soekmono, 'Serat Centhini and the rejected Buddha', 481.

[90] Marie-Odette Scalliet, 'Natuurtonelen en taferelen van Oost-Indië: Europese schilders in Oost-Indië in de negentiende eeuw', in J. H. van Brakel et al. (eds.) *Indië omlijst: vier eeuwen schilderkunst in Nederlands-Indië* (Amsterdam: KIT; Wijk en Aalburg: Picture Publishers, 1998), 39–89.

Figure 1.2 'Visit of Ario Danuningrat, the *regent* of Magelang, to Borobudur', pencil drawing by H.N. Sieburgh, 1837.

people in his work. His painting of Candi Papak near the Singosari complex showed a fire with people standing next to it; and in 1839 Sieburgh made a drawing on the occasion of the visit of the *regent* of Magelang, Ario Danuningrat, to Borobudur, the place where Sieburgh was staying for three months (Figure 1.2).[91]

It took Sieburgh a lot of effort to organise his trips on the island as he needed official approval to travel through Java.[92] Local people helped him through the jungle while the Javanese village heads supplied him with food.[93] During his travels Sieburgh began writing a book on the antiquities of Java.[94] The 420-page manuscript contains descriptions of the sites as well as Sieburgh's experiences and observations on location, and shows Sieburgh as a romanticist. He recounts a harrowing night at Borobudur, where in the darkness the Fates appeared.[95] This terrifyingly sublime experience made him question the

[91] Jean Victor de Bruijn, *H. N. Sieburgh en zijn beteekenis voor de Javaansche oudheidkunde* (Leiden: Luctor et Emergo, 1937), 12–35.
[92] For this approbation, see ANRI, AS, Bt 26 June 1837, nr 13.
[93] Conrad Leemans, 'H. N. Sieburgh en zijne oudheidkundige onderzoekingen in de binnenlanden van Java', *Algemeene Konst- en Letterbode* 2 (1846), 306.
[94] Sieburgh, *Beschrijving van Brahmansche Oudheden op het eiland Java*, boek 1.
[95] Ibid., 112–113.

value of his own life and long for academic knowledge. Generally to Sieburgh, when he visited the archaeological sites of Java, the Dutch nation was far away; Borobudur, in his words, was a 'world monument'.[96] Sieburgh also observed other visitors, and wrote disapprovingly that some of them just 'came, saw, and went'. He admired those visitors, like the Chinese butcher, who took notice of what they saw, and who studied the reliefs by comparing them, making notes, and drawing. According to Sieburgh, the Chinese man was the 'real lover of antiquity'.[97]

Sieburgh's activities, experiences, and observations show how the ruined temple sites from Java connected a diversity of people for many different reasons. At that time, the new Dutch colonial state seemed only one of many interested parties. Although in the 1840s the colonial state developed some initiatives, there was no 'archaeological' state monopoly yet. Thus, when the Dutch prince Hendrik travelled in Java in 1837, Java's ruined temples could be operated as diplomatic tools in the hands of both the colonial government and the Javanese princely rulers. After an audience with Sunan Pakubuwono VII in Surakarta, Prince Hendrik visited the 'tantric' Candi Sukuh accompanied by the crown prince of the Mangkunegaran court, Pangeran Adipati Ario Prang Wedono. During his trip the prince also visited other sites: the Majapahit site in Trowulan (East Java), Prambanan, the Hindu temples at Dieng, Borobudur, and the nearby Buddhist temple Mendut (rediscovered in 1834). Much had changed since the time of Engelhard: a visit to the sites had become part of an official diplomatic programme run by local and governmental parties. At Candi Mendut, moreover, there was a guestbook for Prince Hendrik to sign, and the prince knew of the existence of most of the other sites thanks to Raffles' *History of Java*.[98]

Meanwhile, some of Java's recaptured temple sites, being further cleaned and explored by government-supported initiatives, resumed as pilgrimage sites not exclusively for artists, princes, and elites. At least, this was the case for Borobudur. Assigned by the Dutch colonial government to draw the reliefs of Borobudur (1849–1853), the military topographer F. C. Wilsen noted the site's popularity: 'Every day people come, from the remote districts Banjoemaas, Djokjokerta, Soerakarta and from elsewhere, to visit the monument or to honour the Buddha statues of the highest terrace with offerings.'[99] Visitors

[96] Ibid., 61. [97] Ibid.

[98] For travels of Prince Hendrik de Zeevaarder (or Prince Henry of the Netherlands) to the Netherlands Indies in 1836–1837, see Wassing-Visser, *Koninklijke geschenken uit Indonesië*, 64–86. Compare with Katrientje Huyssen van Kattendijke-Frank, *Met prins Hendrik naar de Oost: de reis van W. J. C. Huyssen van Kattendijke naar Nederlands-Indië, 1836–1838* (Zutphen: Walburg Pers, 2004).

[99] Frans C. Wilsen, 'Boro Boedoer', *Tijdschrift voor Indische Taal-, Land- en Volkenkunde 1* (1853), 285.

brought offerings of incense and flowers presented on banana leaves to one of the two 'Buddha statues' near the eastern entrance, or the big 'unfinished' Buddha statue, which was then still in the Upper Stupa.[100] Sometimes they coloured the Buddha statues with yellow powder. They were seeking, as Wilsen learned, to prevent illness or showing gratitude for a healthy birth. For Wilsen all this was a sign 'that the people still believe in a helping hand that arises from Boro Bodoer'. Since in his eyes, this did not relate to their present Islamic belief, he found their behaviour 'silly' ('onnoozel'). However, he immediately revised this remark, comparing it with Catholic devotion towards statues in Europe.[101]

That Borobudur was far from 'dead' Wilsen realised all the more strongly after *puasa*, the Muslim fasting period, when he saw the temple transformed in order to host a true popular feast ('een waar volksfeest'). During New Moon:

> the young and the old, men and women, especially children, natives and Chinese people, from all sides stream to Borobudur.
>
> Galleries and terraces get crowded, and the otherwise so lonely Buddha sees himself surrounded by a continuously growing mass of people, who wander around, cheerfully bantering or shivering; who admire the reliefs, on which they recognise so many objects and images familiar to them; who bring offerings and set off fireworks . . . as if the era has returned, in which the Buddha filled the hearts [of the people] and was seated high on his throne full of majesty and glory.[102]

In trying to capture the meaning of all this, Wilsen's conclusion was threefold. First, typically, he inferred from this that the Javanese had never fully converted to Islam: 'the bulk of the [Javanese] nation lives today much closer to polytheism than the belief in the one and only true God and his Prophet'.[103] Second, Borobudur in the past should have been an important pilgrimage site, the call of which remained alive among Javanese from generation to generation; and, third, the Javanese recognised as their own the tools, weapons, musical instruments, and dances depicted on the reliefs, and the names of the gods as figuring in the *wayang* stories. While Wilsen himself concluded from the physiognomy of the people depicted in the reliefs that the temple must have been built by people from Bengal, the activities at Borobudur convinced him that time and again the temple was being appropriated and reappropriated by local Javanese inhabitants – even to such an extent that they

[100] For the history of the transportation of this statue, the so-called unfinished Buddha, from the *stupa* to the shades of one of the Kenari trees nearby, see Chapter 2. On earlier possible travels of the statue, from elsewhere to the *stupa*, and contemporary discussions of its meaning, see Soekmono, 'Serat Centhini and the rejected Buddha'.

[101] Wilsen, 'Boro Boedoer', 286–288. [102] Ibid., 287. [103] Ibid., 288.

carried away Buddha heads from Borobudur to their own village.[104] Whether it was in the ways Wilsen suggested or not, Borobudur, by the 1840s, clearly had become a site of significance and attraction, to many more people than a few archaeologically interested, enlightened orientalist-cum-administrators and Javanese elites. More widely known, it attracted visitors from diverse social and ethnic backgrounds, including Javanese Muslims.

The Problem of the Great Mosque of Demak: a Restoration Driven by Anxieties

There was, in terms of fame and wide appeal, at least one other ancient site in Java's historical landscape that competed in value and meaning with Borobudur: the Great Mosque of Demak. Around the same time that Borobudur opened up to a widening world, it was this important site of Islamic worship that, in the history of heritage formation in Indonesia, became the first object of government-supported restoration. This restoration involved the responsibility and support of multiple local parties. Here, we can reconstruct this history due to a unique archival 'working' file of the colonial state, which included correspondence with the various local parties interested in the restoration, kept in the Indonesian National Archives in Jakarta. In addition, there is an important Javanese source, composed at the court of Pakubuwono VII in Surakarta, describing the restoration's history – first hand, according to Nancy Florida – the *Serat nalika bangun Masjid ing Demak* ('When the Demak Mosque was [re]built', inscribed in 1885–1886). For that source, we follow Florida's (brief) summary and interpretation.[105]

Built in the late fifteenth century at the west side of the central square (*alun alun)* in what is now a provincial town on the north coast of Java, the Great Mosque of Demak is still recognised today as Indonesia's oldest mosque. It goes back to the first Islamic kingdom on Java, and its first ruler, Raden Fatah. Fatah, accordingly, had it raised during the decline of the nearby Hindu kingdom of Majapahit in East Java (thirteenth–fifteenth centuries; see Chapters 3 and 4) ruled by his father, before he went on to defeat that kingdom. Local lore and Javanese historical traditions (the *babad*) have it that Demak's Great Mosque was built by the nine saints (the *wali songo*) who brought Islam to Indonesia. In the nineteenth century, such traditions also spoke of eight

[104] Ibid., 287–291.

[105] *Serat Nalika Bangun Masjid ing Demak* (composed Surakarta, author unknown; inscribed Surakarta, 1885–1886), MS. SP 203 Ra; SMP KS 81B. See Florida, *Writing the past, inscribing the future*, 323–325. Florida's summary of that source fits, with regard to the Surakartan court's perspective, particularly well with what we can infer from the correspondence in ANRI. In the following we will make grateful use of the (short) excerpt she translated.

saints.[106] The eight large pillars in the main hall in particular are believed to be raised by the *wali*, and therefore considered sacred, especially the one erected by Sunan Kalijaga. To Muslims from Java, a pilgrimage to the mosque of Demak could equal what the *hajj* to Mecca is to the whole Islamic world. These pilgrims would also visit the sacred graves of the first rulers of Demak located next to the mosque, and Sunan Kalijaga's grave in nearby Kadilangu.[107]

To the Javanese rulers of Mataram, and their descendants, the Great Mosque of Demak was (and is) extremely important to Java's heritage – to be saved and maintained at all costs.[108] Maintenance of the mosque, at least as we know now for the nineteenth century, was a shared responsibility of the central Javanese courts and the local *regenten* (heads, Javanese aristocracy) who claimed lineage to the Mataram kingdom. We may call this a form of local heritage awareness and heritage politics, which had developed, at least as a local ideal, at multiple locations with parties claiming more or less direct lineage, when the colonial state slowly began to display interest in Java's material remains of the past. Notably, by that time the mosque, a sacred inheritance of Java, stood on colonial governmental grounds. As we saw, on the other hand, the pre-Islamic, Hindu, and Buddhist antiquities attracted the earliest and most positive attention from European visitors and leading actors in the field of archaeology and 'care'. However, it was not the ruins Borobudur and Prambanan, now world-famous as World Heritage Sites, but the Great Mosque of Demak that would become object of the first official restoration project.

The restoration of the Mosque of Demak was, in fact, an almost complete renewal, which makes it all the more curious, considering its sacred aura. As the restoration took place with the proactive support of the colonial state, the case seems to defy one of the explanations recently brought forward for the remarkable absence of Indonesian Islam in both 'Asian art' studies and exhibitions, as well as in Islamic studies and Islamic art exhibitions. Where the first type of studies and exhibitions focus on Hindu–Buddhist art, the latter are Islamic but Middle East-centred, stretching from Spain in the west to Mughal

[106] On these traditions, see Fox, 'Ziarah visits to the tombs of the wali'. Today, at Demak, information leaflets circulating at the site (on the mosque's history) recount how nine saints, together with Raden Fatah were responsible for the building of the mosque. See for example *Masjid Agung Demak. Sebuah karya besar peninggalan wali. Cikal bakal berdirinya kerajaan Islam* (Demak: Pertamina, 2000) (collected at the mosque of Demak by M. Bloembergen during visits to Demak, 2–6 February 2011 and 6 July 2012).

[107] Prijohoetomo, 'De betekenis van Demak voor den Islam', *Nederlandsch Indië Oud en Nieuw* 13 (1928–1929), 262. On this practice of grave pilgrimage, or *keramat*, from an inter-Asian perspective, see Mandal, 'Popular sites of prayer, transoceanic migration, and cultural diversity'; Sevea, '*Keramats* running amok'. See also Chambert-Loir, 'Saints and ancestors'.

[108] Florida, *Writing the past, inscribing the future*, 319–351, in particular, 320–323. See for a mention of Demak as the main *pusaka* of Java in Javanese sources, the Dutch translation of the Babad Tanah Djawi: Willem L. Olthof, *Babad Tanah Jawi: de prozaversie van Ngabèhi Kertapradja* (Dordrecht: Floris, 1987), 31 and 313.

India in the east, ignoring – further east – Malaysia and Southeast Asia, where, even counting Indonesia alone, the largest Muslim population of the world lives.[109] Some scholars have argued that blindness to Indonesian Islam was the result of the conscious political disregard of the colonial state.[110] Yet the restoration of the Great Mosque of Demak seems to show a different, concerned attitude, partly inspired by the anxieties of local religious leaders, and a foreign occupier. This case may help us to understand how various knowledge networks and power structures of the colonial state-in-development came together at one site, what specific meanings were attached to it (by whom and for whom), how these meanings were exchanged between the various parties, and thus how site interventions and heritage politics shaped various hierarchies and loyalties to, and beyond, the colonial state. It also makes clear how, to a state-in-development aware of the feebleness of its legitimacy, a monopoly in heritage politics was both urgent and sensitive.

Saving Java's Great Mosque: 'Our Heritage'[111]

'You, I order to Demak
To attend to the disassembly of
The *pusaka* Grand Mosque
For it is to be rebuilt
Grandpa general, who is in charge
[and/or: who had the idea in the first place]
Asks for our blessings
Go ye to Semarang
And I grant for the Mosque's [restoration] expense
Three thousand rupiah.[112]

[109] See the recently opened permanent exhibitions of Islamic art at the Louvre in Paris (2012) and the Metropolitan Museum in New York (2014). Compare, for example, Barbara Brend, *Islamic art* (Cambridge, MA: Harvard University Press, 1991). Asian art museums in Australia seem to deviate from this trend of having a blind spot for Islam in Southeast Asia. See in particular J. Bennett, *Crescent moon: Islamic art and civilization in Southeast Asia* (Seattle: University of Washington Press, 2016).

[110] Shatanawi, *Islam at the Tropenmuseum*, 38–41. This argument, as disputed by Marieke Bloembergen and Remco Raben during the debate 'Islam disregarded?' Tropical Museum, Amsterdam, 3 October 2014, seems to gloss over both the complexities of Islam in Indonesia and the sensitivities of the colonial state which the case described in this chapter makes clear. On the exclusion of the Islamic worlds of Southeast Asia in the field of Islamic studies, but also briefly discussing this trend in the museum world, see Formichi, 'Islamic studies or Asian studies?', 699–703.

[111] 'Ons erfstuk' as phrased by Sunan Pakubuwana VII, in a letter of 8 November 1841, to refer to the Mosque of Demak, in the Dutch translation by J. A. Wilkens (the Javanese original is missing from the file), ANRI, AKS, inv. nr 4361.

[112] Florida's translation of an excerpt of the *Serat Nalika Bangun Masjid ing Demak*, in Florida, *Writing the past, inscribing the future*, 323–324.

In August 1840, the Resident of Semarang, G. L. Baud – a nephew of J. C. Baud, the previous governor-general (1832–1834) and then minister of colonies (1840–1848) – approached the Netherlands Indies government in Buitenzorg with the worrisome news that the Great Mosque of Demak, 'the first Mohammedan temple built on Java', was sagging so much on its feeble structure that it was about to collapse. The Islamic 'priests and clergy' ('priesters en geestelijken', clerics) in Demak (he gave no names) in charge of the daily care of the building had convinced him that, if a collapse took place, 'the thinking of the Mohammedan people' was such that they would consider this to be 'a proof that this temple was not sufficiently taken care of', and that soon rumours would spread 'about war and the destruction or change of the Mohammedan belief, under the population of the whole of Java'.[113] The clerics were convinced that this could be prevented by 'a complete renewal' of the building of the mosque, with the condition that this would take place with the consent and material support of the courts of Surakarta and Yogyakarta. The Resident suggested, in addition, that the sultans of Madura and Sumenep could be included in the plan as well.[114]

Baud's confidential letter marked the beginning of one and a half years of negotiations between various parties in Java and Madura, and the government. Matters of dispute were whether the restoration could take place at all, whether it could or should be a complete renewal, and – as the work took place (1842–1848) – how it should be organised and financed. Obviously, while different interests and forms of meaning-giving were at stake, it seems that all parties came to agree on the significance of two stories connected to the building. Whether they considered this 'truth' or not was not an issue: one story concerned the antiquity (or age) of the mosque as the oldest of Java, and the other that it had been built by the nine saints. These two stories mattered and made the mosque a precious case to care about and to keep for the future. The restoration of the great mosque thus reveals how coexisting forms of heritage awareness interacted in and contributed to local and state-centred dynamics of heritage politics.

In the early phase one additional story complicated and obstructed decision making. Within court circles in Yogyakarta and Surakarta the story went that, according to prophecies, this special mosque would collapse by itself after 400 years, crumbling on the holy graves located near the mosque.[115] According to

[113] Confidential letter from Resident of Semarang (Baud), to governor-general, 27 August 1840, ANRI, AKS, inv. nr 4361.

[114] Confidential letter from Resident of Semarang (Baud), to governor-general, 27 August 1840, ANRI, AKS, inv. nr 4361.

[115] Confidential letter, from Resident of Semarang to governor-general, 26 February 1841, reporting on a meeting with 'the most important clergymen in Demak', including Pangeran Wedyoe, who informed him about the history of the mosque, ANRI, AKS, inv. nr 4631.

the Dutch antiquarian C. J. van der Vlis, living in Surakarta at that time, the sunan's *rijksbestuurder* (government representative), Raden Adipati Sosrodiningrat, performing as the sunan's main adviser in this matter, had added 'that those who renew or improve old and sacred buildings will either die or go mad soon afterwards'.[116] From such perspectives, any interference was unwanted. On the other hand, the colonial government held to the guideline that, when it came to internal Islamic affairs within indigenous society, it should show interest and consideration, but stay aloof as much as possible, on behalf of peace and order. But on neither side were voices unanimous about the lines to follow, and opinions changed. Resident Baud, persuasive and himself convinced about the urgency of this matter, remained persistent. In October 1840, the whole enterprise seemed to collapse: both Sunan Paku Buwono VII (r. 1830–1858) and Sultan Hamengku Buwono V (r. 1823–1826; 1828–1855) were against the complete renewal of the mosque, and the Residents of Yogyakarta and Surakarta reported that the case should be closed because it concerned indigenous religious affairs.[117] Baud would not leave it there. It helped him that, by contrast, the sultans of Madura and Sumenep, Tjakra Adiningrat, and Abdurrachman Pakunataningrat I supported renovation.[118]

The subsequent discussion for and against renewal of the mosque not only reveals the different (and changing) meanings and interests attached to the Great Mosque, but also reflects the ambiguous and changing hierarchies between the various parties engaged in it. From the conflicting reactions from the courts in Yogyakarta and Surakarta versus those in Madura and Sumenep, Baud initially and condescendingly concluded that this demonstrated 'how little one can trust what natives bring forward as arguments'. Assuming authority to decide who was right, he argued that the sultan of Sumenep, Abdurrachman Pakunataningrat, known as an 'honest and educated native', would be the best to give informed written advice.[119] In the meantime, Baud went to Demak to reconsult the local clerics, who confirmed the prophecy about the mosque's collapse, but nonetheless pleaded for renovation. In Madura, the sultan argued that, indeed, 'it would go against the traditions and the feelings of the Mohammedan people, if the old temple of Demak were to be demolished,

[116] Diary, Van der Vlis, 7 October 1840, Leiden University Library, Special Collections, KITLV Collections, Collection van der Vlis, inv. DH 341 'Dagboek gehouden te Soerakarta, 1840–1842'.

[117] Resident of Surakarta, to governor-general, 10 October 1840, and to Resident of Yogyakarta, 7 October 1840, sent as attachments to the letter of general secretary to Resident of Semarang, 28 October 1840, ANRI, AKS, inv. nr 4361.

[118] Resident of Surabaya to governor-general, 7 October 1840, sent as an attachment to the letter of general secretary to Resident of Semarang, 28 October 1840, in ANRI, AKS, inv. nr 4361.

[119] Confidential letter from Resident of Semarang to governor-general, 6 November 1840, AKS, inv. nr 4361.

precisely because it was built, 300 years ago, by the Saints (Walies)'. But, considering that 'the old temple of Demak is in a dilapidated state, and in order to prevent accidents', it should be repaired.[120]

Thus buttressed in his conviction, Baud presumed that he had gathered enough ammunition for his colleagues in Surakarta and Yogyakarta to get the required consent and support from the courts there. However, he again met with resistance. In letters of March 1841 accompanying those of the sultan and the sunan, the Residents of Yogyakarta and Surakarta expressed their hope that Baud would leave this matter. Taking the perspective of the Central Javanese courts, they reasoned that, in deciding the fate of the mosque, 'the wish of the *susuhunan* and the sultan, as well as of their staff of administrators and clerics', should obviously carry more weight than 'the feelings' of the sultans of Madura (an island separate from Java) or 'the wishes' of the clerics of Demak – especially here, in an exclusively religious case in which the government had never before interfered.[121] To Baud, it was state interests, not religion, that mattered, however. In a long, indignant letter to the governor-general, he re-emphasised, with arguments of governance, that the collapse of the mosque could cause social unrest, and renovation was 'much desirable and very opportune', namely 'to reassure peace and contentment' among the population. Mosque renovation was in the state's interest. In this light, the Residents of Yogyakarta and Surakarta should have understood that the consultation of the sunan and sultan was meant to be 'pro forma', and 'to assure the Priests here' who attached importance to the consent of the Central Javanese courts.[122]

Baud managed to convince the reluctant Residents of Surakarta and Yogyakarta to try again, by turning upside down and questioning the arguments 'against' that had been put forward by them. One of these concerned whether it would make sense to compare practices in Mecca, as there appeared to be a sense of awareness among the clerics, *priyayi*, sunan, and sultan at the courts of Central Java that in Mecca restoration of the mosque and the grave of the Prophet Muhammad were common. Another one was the rumour that in the past the court in Surakarta had taken steps to prevent the decay of the mosque of Demak. Baud also emphasised the motives of the clerics in Demak, who were in favour of renewal because 'the collapse of the temple would have to be understood as being the result of a lack of interest and care for the religion', and that 'demolishing and renewal could take place, as long as all the building material of the old temple that had not perished would be used'.[123]

[120] Assistant Resident of Madura (Boeton den Groll) to Resident of Surabaya, 4 January 1841, ANRI, AKS, inv. nr 1688.

[121] Quoted in confidential letter from Resident of Semarang to governor-general, 23 April 1841, ANRI, AKS, inv. nr 4361.

[122] Confidential letter from Resident of Semarang to governor-general, 23 April 1841, ANRI, AKS, inv. nr 4361.

[123] Resident of Surakarta, J. F. T. Meijer, to sunan, 23 October 1841, ANRI, AKS, inv. nr 4361.

The outcome was that both the sultan and the sunan now agreed to 'renewal', on condition that old material would be reused as far as possible. The sultan added the condition that any old material that turned out to be unusable in the mosque's repair would be preserved in the new mosque or buried. The sunan subtly distanced himself from any responsibility for the decision to reconstruct (and thus from its anticipated failure), calling it the wish of the government. But he left no doubt of whose 'heritage' was at stake:

> It is my urgent prayer that the supreme Deity may protect the wish of grandfather [the governor-general][124] so that the restoration of our heirloom, the Great Temple of Demak, may succeed. I also pray that it will be blessed by the Prophet Muhammad and that it will earn the approval of all Walies, who once built the Great temple, and who today are buried on Java. May the Walies provide welfare to all those who participate in this job.[125]

Changing Performative Hierarchies, in a Delicate Landscape

Work on the Great Mosque of Demak started on 3 July 1842, in the fifth month of the Javanese calendar, Jumadilawal. The clerics in charge had chosen this period with care, since according to 'tradition', the mosque was built in this month.[126] From the third week of July, all parties involved, from the courts of Central Java and Madura to the *regent* of Semarang, had sent their emissaries (*priyayi*, lower administrators, clerics, hajis) to attend to the works, as well as labourers to be involved. The sultan sent two of his *wedono*, thirteen lower *bupati*, sixty-five *mantri*, seven esteemed Islamic leaders from Yogyakarta and several villages, and ten clerics of lower rank.[127] The sunan sent a comparable variety and number of emissaries, including a village cleric.[128] In addition to these emissaries, moreover, a large number of 'strangers from all over Java' streamed into the town, on to the site of the mosque. Reporting on the peopling of Demak in October 1842, the Resident of Semarang explained to the governor-general: 'it is more important to the Javanese to visit the old temple before it falls into decay than to see the new temple being built'. This, he continued, also explained why 'before the demolition' of

[124] Colonial administrative hierarchical regulations required that the indigenous leaders addressed their Dutch superiors in the Binnenlands Bestuur (Colonial Administration) with the term 'father' and the governor-general with 'grandfather'.

[125] Sunan Paku Buwana VII to Resident of Surakarta, translation by J. A. Wilken, ANRI, AKS, inv. nr 4361.

[126] Governmental Resolution, 31 March 1842, Q (secret), ANRI, AKS, inv. nr 4361.

[127] Resident of Yogyakarta to Resident of Semarang, 15 July 1842, ANRI, AKS, inv. nr 4361.

[128] Pakubuwono VII to Resident of Surakarta, 24 June 1842, ANRI, AKS, inv. nr 4361.

the building, the biggest donations and offerings came from these visitors, in total mounting up to 4,000 or 5,000 guilders.[129]

Against the background of the recently resolved Java War and a concern for the fragilities in the new balance of power, it was not so much the crowd of pilgrims from the Javanese Muslim world gathering in Demak, but especially the presence of the representatives from the courts of Central Java, and the large donations of money from these courts, that in the course of the work in Demak would start to worry the government. However, in the initial stage, when the organisation was set up, these anxieties were subordinated to diplomacy: the government seemed to be more concerned to ensure that things would be arranged according to local hierarchies and presumed sensitivities.

The royal and clerical parties from Central Java and Madura had a performative function in Demak, illustrating the importance of the mosque of Demak to the various Javanese parties, and re-emphasising the various hierarchies – between Javanese *priyayi* elites and their subjects, and among Javanese elites themselves. At the request of the *regent* of Demak (Raden Toemenggoeng Ario Adinegoro), the government had confirmed by resolution that the sultans of Yogyakarta, Sumenep, and Madura and the sunan of Surakarta would, during the works, have representatives on site, and that the *regent* and clerics from Semarang would participate in the renovation of the temple – the latter with the argument that both Demak and Semarang had been responsible for the daily maintenance of the mosque. The visible presence of the Central Javanese courts in Demak, in addition, served as a proof that the princely rulers who descended directly from the Kingdom of Mataram consented with the renovation of the mosque. They were also meant to stimulate the collection of financial donations from the Islamic population in Demak and Semarang as well as in the court cities needed for the reconstruction work.

The organisation of the work on the mosque of Demak would soon reveal the various sensitivities and ambiguities in the power relations between the colonial government and local elites, and among local elites themselves. According to the ways colonial administration was organised, and because this concerned 'indigenous affairs', the management of the work was in the hands of the *pangreh praja* (the indigenous administration, here, the *regenten*) and the clerics of Demak and Semarang – and these all fell under the supervision of the Resident of Semarang, on behalf of the government. For the restoration of a mostly teak wooden construction, the government allowed the felling, for free, of trees from the governmental woodland, located in the district Singen Lor, to be provided in the form of paid village labour.[130] The costs for other

[129] Resident of Semarang to governor-general, 21 October 1842, ANRI, AKS, inv. nr 4361.

[130] Paid village labour mentioned in Resident of Semarang to *regent* of Semarang, 15 April 1842, O; the specific location of the woods is in *regent* of Semarang to Resident of Semarang, 1 July 1842, ANRI, AKS, inv. nr 4361.

building material and labour would be covered by donations from the represented courts, elites, and their Islamic subjects (it was formulated more broadly as 'the Muhammadan population'); moreover, at the suggestion of the Resident of Semarang, the government would provide an additional 5,000 guilders. On this latter point, however, the governor-general hesitated as to whether this was really necessary since as a rule 'the government should not intervene in such works more than needed to reveal that it was concerned, in order to preserve peace and order, and that in general the population would have to carry out the labour'.[131]

The governor-general authorised the Resident to order the start of the work and to provide further financing if necessary, on condition of governmental approval. Labour fell mostly under the responsibility of, and was provided by, the population (and a number of *kerbau* (water buffalos)) that fell under the *regenten* of Demak and Semarang, with the division key of one-third on behalf of Semarang, two-thirds on behalf of Demak.[132] For a while, the courts of Solo and Yogyakarta sent their labourers as well.[133] Around July 1842, at the request of the *regent* and the clerics of Demak, who had become worried about the dangers in the demolition works and rebuilding of the Great Mosque, 'European expertise' was called in. This led to colonial governance further moving away from the principle of 'religious neutrality' and getting actively involved in the renewal of the most ancient and sacred mosque of Java, represented by a Dutch civil engineer of the colonial department of Hydraulic Works (Waterstaat). Toean Fabriek (Mister Factory), as the *regent* referred to him, would be temporarily attached to this project as technical adviser in the demolition of the mosque. He would supervise and sign the monthly overviews of man- and *kerbau*-power, materiel, and financing of the project.[134]

While the demolition work evolved slowly, the colonial government came to realise that this site intervention, which involved so many parties with powerful authority among the local population, was quite delicate. The ostensible presence of representatives from the courts of Solo and Yogyakarta, and the amount by which they supported the restoration – or the performative power of these courts –transformed, in the eyes of colonial administration, from something diplomatically needful into something worrisome that challenged the balance of power. Thus, by September 1842, the Resident of Semarang assigned the Assistant Resident of Semarang and the *controleur* (colonial

131 Governmental Resolution, 31 March 1842, Q (secret), ANRI, AKS, inv. nr 4361.

132 Governmental Resolution, 31 March 1842, Q (secret), ANRI, AKS, inv. nr 4361.

133 *Controleur* van der Poel to Resident of Semarang, 28 September 1842, in ANRI, AKS, inv. nr 4361.

134 Administrative measure, Resident of Semarang, 6 July 1842, and *regent* of Demak to Resident of Semarang, 7 July 1842, ANRI, AKS, inv. nr 4361.

administrator) to keep a watchful eye on socio-political developments in Demak.

What had started to worry the colonial authorities was that so many Javanese pilgrims, representatives, and workers sent from the Central Javanese courts in one town might expose the financial and material input of the courts, thus stoking unwanted loyalties and strengthening local power. Therefore, in September 1842 the governmental secretary asked the Resident of Semarang to find out, diplomatically, how much money was still needed to finalise the works, in the hope that further financial support from the courts could be prevented; and to enquire in secret about the relationship between the representatives and workers from the courts, and the local population, and about the meanings the local population attached to the presence of these courts in town, as well as to their considerable material input in the renovation of the Great Mosque.[135] To a certain extent, the resulting report reassured the colonial authorities, as the Resident informed the governor-general that 'the representatives of both courts were behaving quietly and calmly, remaining aloof, and that they had more reasons to be annoyed by the austerity and cool attitude of the *regent* [of Demak] than that they exercised influence over the local population'.[136]

Still, with the Java War fresh in their mind, the colonial authorities tried to keep a watchful eye on all the roads that led from the courts in Central Java, to the restoration works in Demak. This resulted in extra information during these years on the roads, nodal points, and widening engagement with and knowledge dissemination on the state of the Great Mosque in Demak. Thus, we can follow, for example, on 17 November 1842, the *priyayi* Raden Toemenggoeng Kartodipoera and Raden Ngabehi Resonegoro from Surakarta, assigned by the sunan to attend to the restoration works and to report about the proceedings, setting off for Demak. Kartodipoera's report to the sunan reveals how much the colonial state tried to keep this whole enterprise under surveillance. As they were crossing Central Java, the two *priyayi* had to report to the colonial military or administrative units they passed: to the commander of the military fort in Boyolalie, to the Assistant Resident at Salatiga, to the commander of the fort in Goenarang, and to the Assistant Resident of Semarang. This journey is probably just an example of the route that the representatives of the courts of Solo and Yogyakarta had to follow to get to Demak. It reached into the heart of the area in which only fifteen years before bloody fights had taken place between governmental troops (manned by Javanese as well, and sometimes directed by

135 Governmental secretary to Resident of Semarang, 23 September 1842, ANRI, AKS, inv. nr 4361.

136 Secret letter from Resident of Semarang to governor-general, 21 October 1842, ANRI, AKS, inv. nr 4361.

Javanese allies who had defected) and the Javanese troops of Prince Dipanagara.

In the end the government followed the advice of the Resident of Yogyakarta, who worried that the rulers of Yogyakarta and Surakarta 'would raise in esteem in the eyes of the population not only the subjects of the courts, but also those outside, living on governmental grounds; that, because of that, they [the Javanese rulers] would regain influence, the more so because they would be seen as the material benefactors providing the means to rebuild the temple',[137] and this, the Resident reasoned, should be prevented at all costs. Moreover, the gathering of so many emissaries from 'the lands of Djocjacarta and Soerakarta, amongst whom there were many who once had fought under Diponegoro, and on whom we should have a watchful eye, these emissaries would have the opportunity to bond, not only amongst each other, but also with those of the governmental population who once were below the [Central Javanese rulers], and plot a conspiracy'.[138]

Thus, whereas initially the colonial authorities considered the restoration of the mosque a state interest, they now feared that this enterprise would turn against the state. And therefore, the government, by official resolution of 26 November 1842, ordered the Residents of Yogyakarta, Surakarta, and Surabaya, to convince the rulers of Yogyakarta, Surakarta, Sumenep, and Madura, to stop their funding of the restoration work, and to call home their emissaries. From January 1843, the courts of Yogyakarta and Surakarta stopped sending emissaries until the works were due to be finished in 1847. These would involve the complete demolition of the wooden mosque, and the near-replacement of the building partly in wood and partly in brick (the walls and some of the less sacred pillars), and with a stone tile floor.[139]

How the sacred wooden pillars were restored or if they were replaced at that time is unknown. This may have suited keepers and users of the mosque very well. Today this big, intrusive, nineteenth-century restoration is not explained at the site, nor is it within Indonesia-based archaeological circles – even though one can draw conclusions about it from the old wooden model and from a painted reconstruction of the pre-1842 mosque on display at the site museum (Figure 1.3).[140] Whatever the original mosque had been worth before the renovation, it was the site of the building and the ground on which it stood that mattered to a widening Islamic world. Even more so, the mosque and its restoration had become compelling to people of a variety of faiths.

[137] Bt 26 November 1842, M, ANRI, AKS, inv. nr 4361.

[138] Bt 26 November 1842, M, ANRI, AKS, inv. nr 4361.

[139] Resident of Surakarta to Resident of Semarang, 14 January 1843, and Resident of Semarang to *regent* of Demak, 24 January 1843, ANRI, AKS, inv. nr 4361.

[140] Last visited by Marieke Bloembergen in July 2012 when a new prestigious site museum to replace the old one was under construction.

Figure 1.3 Model of the old mosque of Demak on display at the old site museum in Demak, 2009.

Site-Seeing beyond Faiths and Traditions

Intriguingly, some of the first European visitors to pay serious historical interest in the mosque of Demak in the nineteenth century were believers from another creed.[141] In 1847, the Protestant vicar and antiquarian chair of the Batavian Society, W. R. Baron van Hoëvell, visited the Demak mosque after a brief formal meeting with the *regent* of Demak, Ario Adinegoro. While partly commissioned by his church, Van Hoëvell intended to collect 'a treasure' of linguistic, ethnographic, and archaeological knowledge – whether in the form of stories or objects – for the Batavian Society in his three-month journey across Java and Madura.[142] (In Chapter 3 we follow him further eastward to the site of 'Majapahit'.)

141 On the Christian influence on respectively French and German academic traditions of orientalism, compare Urs App, *The birth of orientalism* (Philadelphia: University of Pennsylvania Press, 2010); Suzanne L. Marchand, *German orientalism in the age of empire: religion, race and scholarship* (Cambridge: Cambridge University Press, 2009).

142 Wolter R. van Hoëvell, *Reis over Java, Madura en Bali in het midden van 1847*, Part I (Amsterdam: P. N. van Kampen, 1849), foreword.

Five years later, attracted by the same historical and sacred aura of the site, Van Hoëvell's colleague from the Batavian Society, Protestant vicar and antiquarian S. A. Buddingh, followed exactly the same trail as Van Hoëvell. Buddingh more or less recounted the same histories as Van Hoëvell, whose accounts were in turn mostly recapitulations of Crawfurd's *History of the Indian Archipelago*.[143] Buddingh, like Van Hoëvell, paid a courtesy call to the *regent* of Demak, Tjondro Negoro (who had succeeded Ario Adinegoro in 1851). Buddingh found Tjondro Negoro 'the most civilised head, of all civilised Javanese heads': he gave his children a 'completely European education'; besides Javanese and Malay, his sons spoke 'nederduitsch', French, and English; his wife and daughters did 'ladies' needlework [dames-handwerken]'. This visit must also have made an impression on Tjondro Negoro's children and may have been an example to at least one of them, his eldest son Ario Adipati Tjondronegoro.

Tjondronegoro the younger would become known as one of the first Javanese modern, site-seeing travel writers who followed older Javanese and new European examples of learning by travelling. R. M. Tjondronegoro V, who would become *regent* of Kudus (1858–1880) and Brebes (1880–1885), published his travels in Java under the pseudonym of Poerwolelono. Dwelling on the new Javanese encyclopaedic travel traditions like the *Serat Centhini*, and on Western forms of the individualist modern travel account, he was the first to publish in this genre in Javanese.[144] Tjondronegoro was an example of the Javanese *priyayi* generation who – inspired by colonial modernising in schooling, infrastructure, and experiencing the world – tried cultural innovation while building on Javanese traditions.[145] Perhaps telling for Poerwolelono's interest in alternative ways to gather knowledge, whether about the past or the present, but also emphasising his status in colonial scientific society, is that in 1870 he became a member of the Batavian Society, followed by membership in the Koninklijk Instituut voor Taal-, Land- en Volkenkunde van Nederlandsch-Indië

143 S. A. Buddingh, *Neêrlands-Oost-Indië; Reizen … gedaan gedurende het tijdvak van 1852–1857*, 3 vols., 2nd edn (Amsterdam: Van Kesteren & Zoon, 1867), 165.

144 See, for an introduction to Tjondronegoro's travel account, with a short biography, and a Dutch translation of the complete Javanese text, Judith E. Bosnak, Frans X. Koot, and Revo A. G. Soekatno, *Op reis met een Javaanse edelman: een levendig portret van koloniaal Java in de negentiende eeuw (1860–1875). De reizen van radèn mas arjo Poerwolelono* (Zutphen: Walburg Pers, 2013), 9–13. For a less complete French translation, but with an important introduction that emphasises Purwelolono's modern look at the world around him, see Marcel Boneff, *Pérégrinations javanaises: les voyages de R. M. A. Purwa Lelana. Une vision de Java au XIXe siècle (c. 1860–1875)* (Paris: Ed. De la Maison des sciences de l'homme, 1986). Compare with Ricklefs, *Polarising Javanese society,* 144–145.

145 Compare John Pemberton, *On the subject of 'Java'* (Ithaca: Cornell University Press 1994); Kenji Tsuchiya, 'Javanology and the age of Ranggawarsita: an introduction to nineteenth-century Javanese culture', *Reading Southeast Asia* (Ithaca: Cornell University Press, 1990), 75–108.

(Royal Netherlands Institute of Linguistics, Geography and Ethnography of the Netherlands Indies, KITLV) in 1879.

Tjondronegoro's activities in and around the mosque of Demak differ slightly from those of Van Hoëvell and Buddingh, but his writing resembles theirs in the detailed, rational, and distanced way in which he describes the mosque and the setting of the graves. And Tjondronegoro's journal is an intriguing mixture of pilgrimage and leisure site-seeing as he visits the office of the *regent* of Demak, a place he must have known, but which he describes with the distance of the travel writer: 'a European house, but there is a Javanese *pendopo*, painted white and covered with leaf gold'.[146]

Hold this picture for a moment in your mind. This Javanese image of status, the *regent* of Demak's home with a European flair, seems the perfect closing frame for a chapter that began with a European symbol of status, Engelhard's European-style residency garden featuring a Javanese Hindu–Buddhist statue.

[146] Bosnak, Koot, and Soekatno, *Op reis met een Javaanse edelman*, 161.

2 Exchange, Protection, and the Social Life of Java's Antiquities, 1860s–1910s

On 1 July 1896, a distinctive company climbed the stairs of Borobudur. Among the visitors were a few Dutch and Javanese officials and the Dutch physician-cum-amateur archaeologist Isaac Groneman, who was the honorary chairman of the Archaeological Society in Yogyakarta (founded in 1885).[1] They accompanied their distinguished guests: King Chulalongkorn of Siam and his wife, who were followed by members of the royal family, among whom were his (half-)brothers Prince Damrong Rajanubhap and Prince Sommot (Figure 2.1). They visited the galleries of the multi-storeyed temple, and the king studied many details of the relief panels. Finally, the king climbed to the upper terrace, where he presented a floral offering to the Buddha statue in the highest *stupa* and prayed.[2]

As happened elsewhere in Asia at rediscovered ancient religious sites, in late nineteenth-century Java practices of archaeology and heritage formation came to interact, overlap, or develop in parallel with those of pilgrimage, tourism, and diplomacy.[3] All these site-centred activities entailed experiences and forms of knowledge production, which – whether or not in exchange – contributed to the further transformation of sites. Borobudur, as a major Buddhist shrine in a world that had become predominantly Muslim since the late sixteenth century, is but one peculiar example that brought these various interests together, coming from within and outside the Netherlands Indies.

[1] The parts of this chapter focusing on Chulalongkorn's visit and travels of site-related objects to Siam, Europe, and back were first published as Bloembergen and Eickhoff, 'Exchange and the protection of Java's antiquities'.

[2] Chulalongkorn, *Itinéraire d'un voyage à Java en 1896*, compiled and edited by Chanatip Kesavadhana (Paris: Association Archipel, 1993), 114–121; *De Locomotief*, 6 July 1896; Report by A. J. Quarles de Quarles, 17 December 1896, in National Archives, The Hague (hereafter NA), Ministerie van Koloniën (Ministry of Colonies, hereafter MvK), V 3 November 1896, X 18.

[3] On resacralization of sites in India, see Trevithick, 'British archaeologists, Hindu abbots, and Burmese Buddhists'; Trevithick, *The revival of Buddhist pilgrimage at Bodh Gaya*; Singh, 'Exile and return'; David Geary, 'Rebuilding the navel of the earth: Buddhist pilgrimage and transnational religious networks, *MAS* 48:3 (2013), 645–692. Compare Marieke Bloembergen, 'Borobudur in "the light of Asia": scholars, pilgrims and knowledge networks of Greater India, 1920s–1970s', in Laffan (ed.), *Belonging across the Bay of Bengal*, 35–56.

Figure 2.1 Visit of king Chulalongkorn, his wife and his company to Borobudur, 1896.

King Chulalongkorn toured Java on an unofficial mission to explore technological, political, and cultural matters in the Dutch colony, and to establish direct political relations, thereby stressing his position as a reforming head of an independent kingdom. Though he does not explicitly state his purpose in his travel diary, Chulalongkorn suggests he was on a pilgrimage to Java's Buddhist sites as the highest representative of the Buddhist order of Siam.[4] Most of the other men present did not have comparable religious motives. The Europeans among them might have associated Asian temple ruins in general with decay, despotism, and decadence. This particular temple, however, manifested to them primarily the grand civilisation of a far-away Buddhist past on a predominantly Islamic island, as well as a unique work of art. They also were aware of the

[4] Chulalongkorn, *Itinéraire d'un voyage*. The (incomplete) French translation that we mainly use in this paper is based on the version that Chulalongkorn's eldest son published in 1923. We thank Patcharawy Tunprawat (Bangkok, 1 March 2011) and Peter Skilling (e-mail, March 2011) for their generous help in consulting the more complete Thai original of this diary as well. Note that denominator Theravadin for the Buddhist order in Siam is not used in the contemporary sources around this event, as this term was not then in use. See Peter Skilling, 'Theravada in history', *Pacific World* 11 (2009), 61–94.

'discovery' by Raffles and of subsequent Dutch-colonial documentation work on the site, and of the lavish publications on Borobudur illustrated with lithographs and collections of photographs that had been published since the 1850s. With regard to the dealings with Buddhist shrines by Buddhists elsewhere in Asia, Groneman, moreover, had observed Buddhist praying practices before, at the Kelani temple in Colombo. Expecting a comparable ritual, and in consultation with the highest Dutch civil administrator (present as well), the Resident of Kedu, he therefore had arranged for frangipani flowers to be waiting for Chulalongkorn at the highest terrace – to be used as an offering to the Buddha statue in the main *stupa*.[5] Thus a 'staged praying' of a Siamese Buddhist king, with Sinhalese Buddhist prayer as a model, was the first official instance of Buddhist practices at Borobudur in its modern life, and a meaningful moment of resacralisation.[6]

Meaningfully, while climbing the temple with his Dutch and Javanese hosts, Chulalongkorn exchanged Buddhist knowledge for material gifts – that is, statues and reliefs from Borobudur, which he took back home to Bangkok. Chulalongkorn's pilgrimage-cum-diplomatic tour thus stands as a remarkable episode of site-damaging in the historiography of (post-)colonial Indonesian archaeological care, and Borobudur in particular.[7] But it does also fit with a growing worldwide interest in Borobudur.

In this chapter, we situate Borobudur and other Hindu–Buddhist material remains of the past in Java in these widening knowledge networks and growing interests from inside and outside Java, which also stimulated the colonial state to institutionalise archaeological care and protection. The chapter centres around our analysis of the visits of King Chulalongkorn to Borobudur (in 1896 and 1901), and the exchange of knowledge and Hindu–Buddhist site-related objects that took place during his travel through Java and back to Bangkok. Thanks to a Borobudur guestbook kept from 1888 to 1898, we provide further insight into the background and site impressions of a growing number of visitors from Europe, the United States, and Australia, but also (and mostly) from Java, and their impressions, beliefs, and sense of humour regarding site-seeing in general, and Borobudur in particular. We also analyse how, despite efforts at centralising and state control of antiquities, objects from Borobudur, Prambanan, and other Java-based temples were given away, sold, and copied, travelling to other locations: not only with Chulalongkorn to Siam, but also, in the context of world exhibitions, to France, the Netherlands, and the UK, and subsequently back to Java. Thus, we can see

[5] Isaac Groneman, 'Een Boeddhistischen-koning op den Borobudoer', *Tijdschrift voor de Indische Taal-, Land- en Volkenkunde* 39 (1897), 367–378.

[6] Compare Bloembergen, 'Borobudur in "the light of Asia"', 39.

[7] Miksic refers to this episode as an example of 'official indifference to Borobudur's fate'; see Miksic, *Borobudur*, 3.

how Java-based Hindu–Buddhist sites came to play a role in various forms of heritage formation and knowledge production, at multiple locations, which referred to Greater British Indian, Greater Siamese, Greater Dutch, and Greater Javanese geographies, establishing through exchange, and re-rating, the new economic, moral, and political value of ancient things.

The Social Life of a Temple: Borobudur's Aesthetics, Guests, and Guestbooks

Interest in Borobudur grew and developed further after the first official grand assignments to study and portray the temple. Adolph Shaeffer's 1844 daguerrotypes and Wilkens' drawings (1849–1853) published by Leemans in 1873, were followed by lithographs of drawings by Sieburgh and others in books and journals published in the Indies, the Netherlands, and France. Lavishly illustrated decorative albums circulated, with the famous photographs by Isidore van Kinsbergen (1863) and, later, those of Sultan Hamengkubuwono VII's Christian court photographer Kassian Cephas (who photographed Prambanan in 1889, as well as Borobudur's briefly uncovered 'hidden foot' in 1890–1891).[8] All along, the (somewhat reluctant) government, the (eager) Batavian Society, and/or private parties sought to gain control over research and protection. That is a useful context in which to understand the range of visitors and their impressions, as well as the 'temple' guestbooks, one of which turned up in a Leiden-based archive.

Prince Hendrik signed the guestbook of Mendut in 1837, so it seems reasonable to suppose that nearby Borobudur had one, too. The guestbook we found covers the period 1888–1898 and reflects several important site interventions at and around Borobudur.[9] It was probably the Yogyakarta-based Archaeological Society that initiated the book. This society arose in the context of one important intervention at Borobudur, when the Dutch railway engineer

[8] See, on the popularisation of Borobudur through the spread of engravings, photographs, and lavish photo albums, 1840s–1890s, Gerda Theuns-de Boer, 'The distribution of Van Kinsbergen's oeuvre: decorative albums, engravings and world exhibitions', in Gerda Theuns-de Boer and Saskia Asser (eds.), *Isidore van Kinsbergen: fotopionier en theatermaker in Nederlands-Indië/photo pioneer and theater maker in the Dutch East Indies* (Leiden: KITLV Press; Amsterdam: Huis Marseille, 2005), 124–142; Saskia Asser, '"A capable and experienced photographer": Van Kinsbergen and the artistic traditions of his time', in Theuns-de Boer and Asser (eds.), *Isidore van Kinsbergen*, 86–124. On Cephas, see Claude Guillot, 'Un example d' assimilation à Java: le photograph Kassian Céphas', *Archipel* 22 (1981), 55–73; G. J. Knaap and Yudhi Soerjoadmodjo, *Cephas, Yogyakarta: photography in service of the sultan* (Leiden: KITLV Press, 1999).

[9] 'Gastenboek Boro-Boedhoer, 1888–1894' and 'Gastenboek Boro-Boedhoer, 1894–1896', Leiden University Library, Special Collections, KITLV Collections, archive Indisch Wetenschappelijk Instituut (hereafter IWI), inv. nr H 1790, 105a and 105b. We thank Nico van Horn, the former curator of the KITLV archival collections, who pointed us to the whereabouts of this source, 6 November 2015.

J. W. IJzerman, initiator and first chair of the society – during excavation works – encountered what is now famously known as the 'hidden foot' of the temple: an extra terrace and wall with reliefs covered by soil.[10] In 1890–1891, Cephas photographed all 160 of them, for which, under the supervision of *controleur* W. Meyer, the wall was being uncovered and recovered again, part by part, as those responsible worried that otherwise the temple would collapse.

The connection between the guestbook and the Archaeological Society is also reflected by the fact that the society's honorary chair, the self-taught archaeologist Groneman, who would write the first brief guide to Borobudur (in 1898), from 1896 onwards figures often in its pages, as a special, knowledgeable guide for special (not all) visitors. The book, organised with the headings 'Date', 'Name and status of the visitor', 'Coming from', 'Travelling to' and 'Remarks', mentions the background of the visitors, along with social life and hierarchies at the temple, which sometimes reflect colonial society. The absence of non-elite Javanese visitors (Europeans are by far the majority) in the book displays an intriguing mechanism of exclusion: possibly they could not write or more likely were considered less remarkable 'visitors'. King Chulalongkorn, on the other hand, was apparently too remarkable: he is not in the guestbook either. Nevertheless, this special visitor left his mark when he chiselled his name in the inner wall of the main *stupa* after making his prayer and offerings to the so-called unfinished Buddha. Curiously, by way of a 'Remark', someone crossed through a drawing made by another visitor in August 1895 of the stone guard statue that Chulalongkorn would take to Bangkok in 1896 – suggesting a criticism of this removal (Figure 2.2).

One of the Javanese *priyayi* who signed the guestbook several times was Kassian Cephas, Yogyakarta's court photographer, who came to shoot the reliefs of the hidden foot. For his first visit, he stayed three months.[11] Another *priyayi* signed on 1 July 1894, for himself and his wife: Tjondronegoro, or Poerwolelono, *regent* of Kudus, later Brebes. He left no comments, perhaps because this was – at least – his second visit to the temple. In the second edition of his travel reports, Tjondronegoro had already written extensively about his first encounter of the sight as well as the building and excavation histories of the

[10] Only in 1931 did the French Sanskritist Sylvain Lévi, connecting the images to Tibetan texts, provide evidence that these reliefs depicted in carved images the content of the Indian text *Karmawibhanggha*, showing earthly life and the lessons of karma, or the laws of cause and effect. See Sylvain Lévi, *Mahakharmavibhangga: la grande classification des actes* (Paris: Ernest Leroux, 1932); Nicolaas J. Krom, *Het karmawibhanggha op Borobudur* (Amsterdam: KNAW, 1933); Jan Fontein, *The law of cause and effect in ancient Java* (Amsterdam: KNAW, 1989). Cephas' photographs were reproduced in Part II of the Borobudur monograph by Krom and Van Erp; see N. J. Krom and T. van Erp, *Beschrijving van Barabudur, Part II, Bouwkundige beschrijving en een aanvulling op deel I door N. J. Krom* ('s-Gravenhage: Nijhoff, 1931).

[11] On 1 October 1891. On 21 October 1891 Cephas returned and signed again, now in the company of J. Broers, the residential secretary, and I. J. van Oosterzee Jnr, Adjunct Inspector-General, from Batavia.

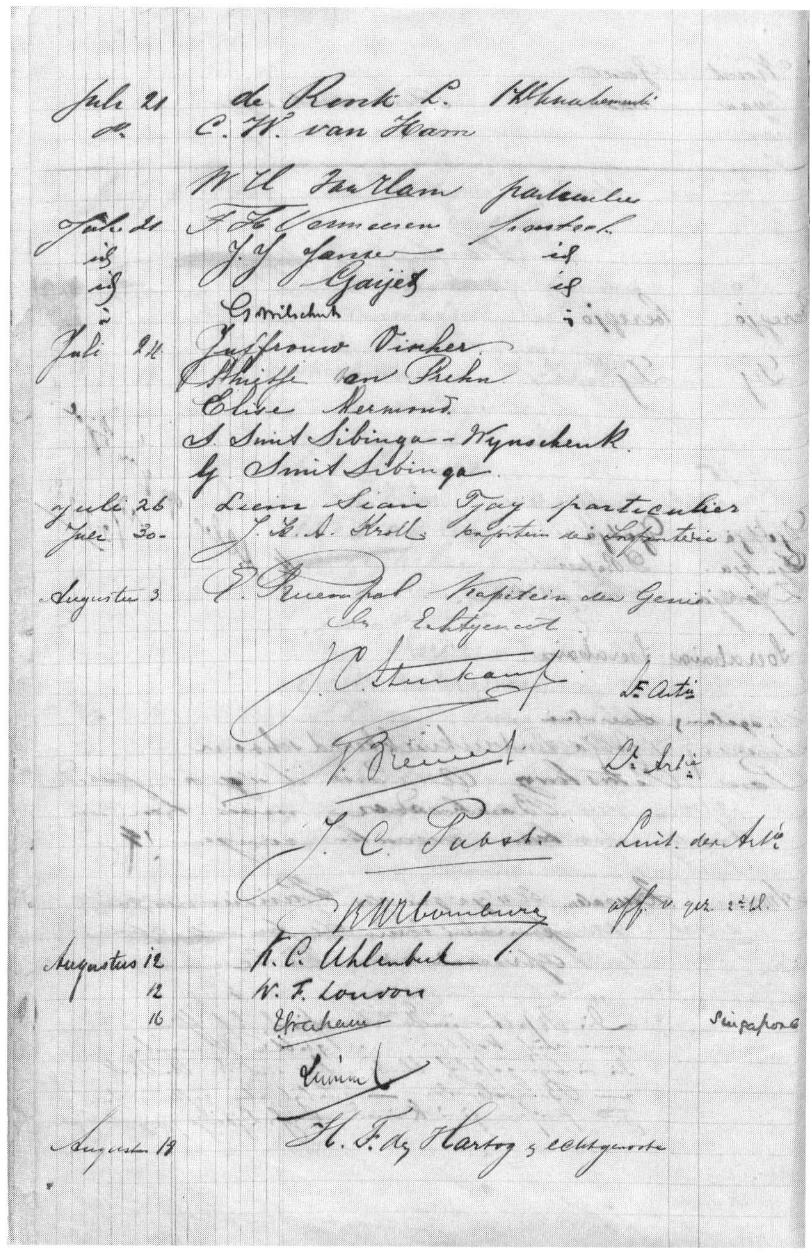

Figure 2.2 Two pages from the Guestbook at Borobudur, August 1895.

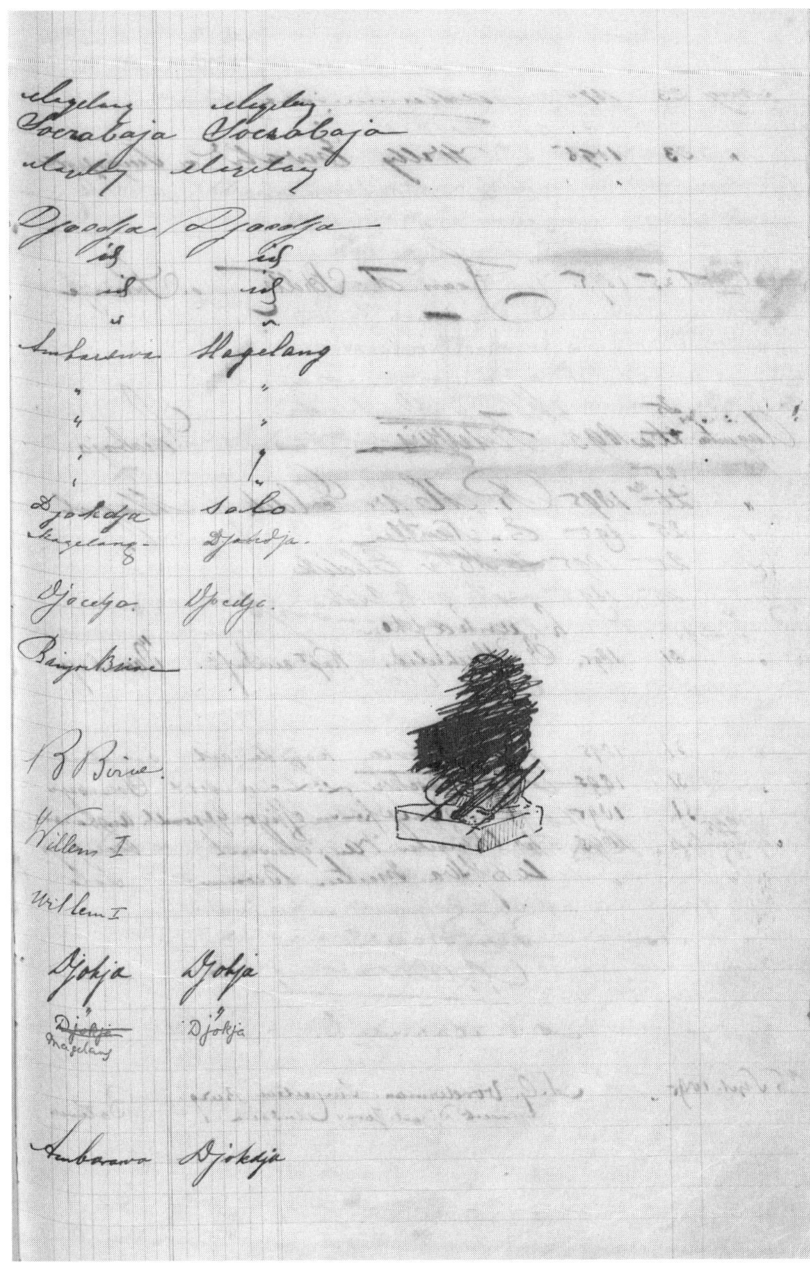

Figure 2.2 (cont).

temple. These in-depth impressions of Tjondronegoro are worth pausing over, for they show the diplomatic way for a Javanese nobleman to access the temple and the stories it had, and his reflections provide insight on the temple in the context of the modernising changes he encountered – both with regard to the ongoing uncovering of Java's past, and to construction of new buildings and infrastructural interventions. He wrote as a discerning analyst of buildings, a pious modernist Muslim, a paternalist head of lower-status Javanese, and as a scholar.

A Javanese Nobleman's Modernist Impressions

Before Tjondronegoro went to see Borobodur, he spent several days visiting the house of the *regent* of Magelang. The modern layout intrigued him: it included the *regent*'s quarters (half traditional Javanese *pendopo*, half living and guest rooms) plus two other modern stone buildings, one used as 'Soos' (clubhouse) for Europeans, the other as a hotel. Next he visited the house of the Resident, where – famously depicted in contrasting ways by Nicolaas Pieneman (in 1830–1835) and Raden Saleh (in 1857) – Dipanagara was tricked into surrender. Tjondronegoro admired both the modern building and the location, with stunning views of a ravine, and in the distance Sumbing mountain, woods, villages, and rice fields (Figure 2.3). He did not mention Dipanagara's

Figure 2.3 The garden of the Resident's quarters at Magelang, drawing by F. Junghuhn, ca. 1853–1855.

humiliation at this site, nor did he say anything about the Hindu–Buddhist statues assembled in the garden.[12]

The next day Tjondronegoro set off for Borobudur, via the main road to Yogyakarta. He already knew, or had just learned in Magelang, that it had once been called 'Temple of the Buddhas' or 'Tjandi Poro Boedo', because it contained 'an immense number of stone images of the Buddha'. But he was not prepared for what he saw. Awestruck, he tried to apprehend the dimensions of the temple. Then, as in Demak, he detailed information about the kind and size of the stones (sandstone) used and the layered structure of the temple, as well as describing images on some of the reliefs, which depicted a carriage pulled by elephants and driven by an important man protected by a parasol; men riding horses and elephants; a sailboat; and land and sea animals. On the top, he noticed that the four entrance roads leading to Borobudur overlapped exactly with the four directions indicated by the compass. He concluded that the builders of that time must have had advanced tools.[13] At the foot of the temple, Tjondronegoro found rows of statues, some with tiger and elephant heads, whose damage he deplored ('People here think that they were defaced during the time when the Javanese turned to Islam, to make sure that people would no longer idolise these statues'). Considering the temple's immensity and beauty with so many reliefs and statues, Tjondronegoro concluded that he needed more time at Borobudur.

Next, he went to nearby Mendut, which he describes as a tall, pointed building. In contrast to Borobudur, he noticed, you could enter it, 'like a house or a mosque'. Inside, Tjondronegoro faced a twenty-foot-high statue cut from a single stone, flanked by two smaller statues. The place reminded him of 'a Chinese temple', and Tjondronegoro believed it must have been used for prayer. He also recognised it as being made from the same sandstone as Borobudur, and noticed that the three statues 'are called Trimoerti'. The roof of the temple surprised him, as it was made of stones stacked on top of one another, without any support. On the outside, the walls were covered with reliefs 'like Borobudur'.[14]

Most tellingly regarding heritage consciousness, Tjondronegoro referred to the two temples as 'monuments' and 'buildings of our ancestors'.[15] And he reflected on the stories he had heard about their rediscovery in his own time, on the reasons why and under what circumstances they had become buried by earth 'so that they looked like hills'. In his retelling of the story of their rediscovery, Tjondronegoro immediately pointed to the relation between heritage and violence. Borobudur had been rediscovered, 'when the English took Yogyakarta'; Mendut had been rediscovered 'after the Dipanagara War'.

[12] Bosnak, Koot, and Soekatno, *Op reis met een Javaanse edelman*, 13, 244–246. The fact that Tjondronegoro did mention the earthquake means that these travel observations, perhaps also regarding Borobudur, are not from 1858 – when Tjondronegoro originally made his four travels across Java – but dating from the time when he, as *regent* of Kudus, made official journeys.

[13] Ibid., 247. [14] Ibid., 248–249. [15] Ibid., 249.

Furthermore, Tjondronegoro reflected on the building histories and past uses of the two temples, and developed an interesting theory. Based on the way such stone buildings must have been constructed, he argued that these temples never had time to be used because of the pre-emptive arrival of Islam.[16] And now that he had seen 'these two buildings of our ancestors', Borobudur and Mendut reflected not only a change in religion, but also a profound loss of knowledge and ability among Javanese. Tjondronegoro knew of no contemporary people with the capacity to construct such buildings, or who possessed such knowledge. Even as he recognised the sweep of history, he lamented and even disparaged contemporary Javanese:

> They are circumcised and say they adhere to Islam. But they do not really appreciate their belief, because in daily life they still follow old traditions of polytheism. I am saying this because until today they honour trees and huge stones by bringing offerings in the form of flowers, creams, candies and the like. And not only people who do not really know Islam do this, but also people who are very knowledgeable of their religion. According to Islam such behaviour is forbidden, because it is comparable to idolatry.[17]

Tjondronegoro thus performed the role of a paternalist *priyayi*, who followed a strict modernist line in Islam that, in the context of the popularising *hajj* to Mecca, had been developing more and more strongly in Java since the early nineteenth century.[18] He blended this belief with the attitude of a modern historian and member of the scientific Batavian Society. Perhaps informed by the historical methods taking shape in Europe and the developing scholarly knowledge around the temple, Tjondronegoro expressed his regret that no 'witnesses' could be consulted regarding the construction and the builders of the two temples: no sources, no dates for the beginning and end of construction, no names of the architects, builders, or even kings. 'This is why, at this moment, nobody knows the history of these two monuments.' Concluding his site-seeing report, he felt certain that if such testimony and evidence existed, the ensuing understanding would prompt 'a surge of visitors' to Borobudur.[19]

Impressions of a Guestbook: 'a Surge of Visitors' and the Banalisation of Borobudur

If Borobodur's guestbook makes one thing clear, it is to confirm Tjondronegoro's forecast of an upsurge of visitors.[20] But it is unlikely they

[16] Ibid. [17] Ibid.

[18] Ricklefs, *Polarising Javanese society*; Michael F. Laffan, *Islamic nationhood and colonial Indonesia: the Umma below the winds* (London: Routledge Curzon, 2003).

[19] Bosnak, Koot, and Soekatno, *Op reis met een Javaanse edelman*, 249.

[20] The following is based on a systematic, qualitative analysis of 'Gastenboek Boro-Boedhoer, 1888–1894' and 'Gastenboek Boro-Boedhoer, 1894–1896' in Leiden University Library, Special Collections, KITLV Collections, archive IWI, inv. nr H 1790, 105a and 105b.

were driven by knowledge and understanding of the temple's history. Averaging between one and ten visitors per day, some arrived in groups, but most came in couples, as friends, as family, or as brothers-in-arms. Many military men visited, including, fresh from the ongoing Aceh War, Lieutenant-Colonel H. Colijn, who would become prime minister of the Netherlands. Large groups came for special occasions, such as the opening of the bridge Progo-Brojonolan, on 22 October 1893, which brought thirty-one people to Borobudur. Some visits, like Cephas' and Tjondronegoro's, were most surely driven by scholarly and historical interests: language official A. Wilkens came from Surakarta with his wife (1 June 1888); self-taught scholar G. P. Rouffaer (10 December 1889), Arabist C. Snouck Hurgronje (17 February 1891), ethnographers C. M. Pleyte (13 November 1894), and Herman ten Kate (20 September 1897, accompanied by Groneman) also signed the book. Others came with educational and contemplative motives. Some Protestant missionaries stand out: Pa (Johannes) and Ma van der Steur, from the Oranje-Nassau institute for orphaned and delinquent Indonesian youths in Magelang, brought along their pupils for an extended visit, from 28 January to 3 February 1895. Pa and Ma van der Steur were deeply impressed, but not religiously conquered, by Borobodur, though it did inspire Pa van der Steur, and Father Tydeman as well, to write long poems in praise of God. The majority of visitors, however, came as tourists seeking leisure.

Visitors who signed the book came from the higher and intermediate ranks of local, colonial society, and a globalising world: princes, princesses, and barons, administrators and scholars, educated people in a private capacity, missionaries, military men – all with the means to travel (even long distances) or located nearby. The military almost all came in small groups, sometimes accompanying young women. Women were, overall, well represented, as wives, mothers, daughters, and female friends. Most visitors came from Java, the majority being European, some Chinese and Javanese, and only one or two identifiably Eurasian. In two periods[21] among the fifteen Javanese *priyayi* visiting, were, in addition to Cephas and Tjondronegoro, the *regent* of Magelang (Danoekoesomo) (25 February 1891),[22] the *regent* of Blora (27 June 1894), and the *regent* of Madioen (1 July 1894). Most of the at least seventeen Chinese visitors came in groups of three or four. Kwee Ang Kie, a Chinese major in Magelang, brought along his family. A large number of other visitors, counted for the same period, came from distant countries besides

[21] Numbers counted here are based on a systematic check for the periods 1 December 1888 to 1 October 1889 (book I); and from 27 June 1894 to 9 May 1895 (book II), and, in addition, random checks, while leafing through the books for the remaining periods.

[22] He was probably part of an inspection team in the framework of the photographing, uncovering, and recovering of Borobudur's hidden foot. This team consisted additionally of J. A. Arment, Resident of Kedu, L. E. Dam, and H. A. de Groot, *controleur* of Probolinggo.

the Netherlands: England (10), Scotland (3), France (8), Germany (7), Austria-Hungary (4), Spain (5), Belgium (1)), the United States (15), Brazil (1), Australia (7), and New Zealand (1). Many were on their way to further spots – travelling from Britain or the United States to India, from Australia to Hong Kong, or from France to Colombo – or going home in the opposite direction.

Not all visitors wrote comments, but most did, ranging from very short impressions – of the temple or of the nearby 'hotel' (the *passagrahan*) – to paragraph-long observations, poems, and a few drawings. These could be serious and emotional comments on the temple and its surroundings, but the majority, and as people do today, made silly jokes – about the temple, as well as other visitors and their comments – which sometimes show an awareness of the temple's religious meaning. Together all these comments provide a glimpse of social relations in colonial society, what people did at the temple, and thus how the temple was appropriated by multiple strands of this society. Also, we see how the temple could stir various sentiments: of complete relaxation and leisure, deep excitement, religious awareness, and, in reaction to that, also existing anti-religious sentiments. Some examples and impressions follow.

Many of the comments concerned not the temple, but the visitors themselves and their (male or female) 'others'. Thus, on 26 February 1888 a married couple from Ngandjoek (East Java), recommended ladies to wear 'alpino petten' (Alpine berets, referring to then-trendy mountain climbing in the Swiss Alps), when climbing 'the temple of the gods'. One used the pejorative term for Eurasians: 'Echt Liplaps!' ('Typical for creole people!').[23] A group of visitors from Magelang, perhaps well meant, likewise expressed a condescending attitude to the largest and oldest population group living on the island. 'We admire the travelling and patience of our little Javanese', on 11 September 1899. This prompted a 'Very smart!' from another visitor.

While only a few Javanese signed the book, they entered it in other ways. On 17 August 1890, a sigh came from two officers second class from Magelang: 'What surprises me the most is that the Javanese man who lives in the surrounding knows the least about the meaning of Boroboedoer.' And, eight years later, a special Javanese visitor, trying to make Borobudur a source of income, attracts attention: Groneman, who on 2 and 3 July 1898 accompanied the Assistant Resident for Native Affairs from Celebes during his visits to the temple, warned the other visitors about a beggar: 'A well-dressed Javanese man, rather young, who follows the visitors, asks them for a fee, pretending that he belongs to the *pasangrahan* [which functioned as repose and starting point to the temple], and that he is assigned to keep the ruin clean.'

[23] Liplap, in Malay, means literally 'layered (in multiple colours)'.

Some of the comments seem to reflect class distinction, as well as humorous animosity between social classes. Thus, when the cosmopolitan Prince and Princess Schcrbatoff, travelling from St Petersburg, visiting the temple on 27 February 1890, gave as their only 'Remark' 'hotel très comfortable', and the French industrial and deputy Koechling-Schwartz, on 1 February 1893 likewise found himself 'très surpris' to find such a good hotel here, this prompted a reaction: 'très spirituel. Décidement M. Koechling Schwartz le Baraboudour ne vous a pas fait d'impressions.'

A number of the visitors commented in the guestbook with childish or corny jokes referring to bodily functions that seem familiar today. One remarked: 'The perfect spot to recover from malaria or intestinal disorders'. Two female friends from Yogyakarta and Kasoeran complained about the heat, rhyming in Dutch and Malay: 'Heerlijk, frisch! Jammer dat er geen pantjoeran is!' (Lovely, fresh! A pity that there is no pool'). Theirs got a rhyme in return, from someone who had at least an inkling of what the temple was about: 'Mandie dan in de pis van een boedist' ('Wash yourself then in the piss of a Buddhist'). Another reacted to an infantry captain from Magelang who wondered if there was a swimming pool nearby, with: 'Waarachtig. Verzuip je maar in het nirvana' ('Really. Drown yourself in the nirvana').[24]

While some, often military men, confined their bodily references to beer ('Bier auf eis!' on 14 August 1890; 'A nice pot of beer', 24 August 1890), others were merely puerile, suggesting they spent their time at Borobudur goofing around. A group of friends from Yogyakarta rhymes: 'Voor ieder zonder kunstgenot heeft Boroboedoer wis geen smoel. Slechts minnaars van antiquiteiten kunnen aangenaam daar de uren slijten' ('For anyone without artistic taste, Borobudur has no face. Only lovers of antiquities will spend pleasant hours at the temple'), triggering a slightly vulgar response: 'Die dit liedje heeft gedicht, kan wel poepen zonder licht' ('The person who has rhymed this song can poop without light').

Some leisure travellers likened Borobudur to glamorous sites they were familiar with. One visitor (on 21 July 1895), pretending to be the French actress Sarah Bernhardt, wrote, 'A Paris il n'y a pas de Baraboedoer mais bien un moulin rouge.' Raden Mas Toemenggoeng Tjokro Negoro, *regent* of Blora (on 27 June 1894), compared it to the recently installed railway lines and trains connecting Solo, Semarang, and Yogakarta to Surabaya: 'Soengoe bagoes kareta api ... tetapi Lebih bagoes Boroboedhoer!!!!! Maar sama enak' (So beautiful a train ... But more beautiful Borobudur!!!!! But, all the same nice'). Others simply gush with enthusiasm: 'prachtig' (beautiful), 'elegant-prachtig' (elegantly beautiful), 'grootsch' (majestic), 'alles

[24] Two ladies from Djocja (Yogyakarta) and Kasoeran, 29 June 1890; J. Broos, captain of infantry, 3 July 1890.

schitterend' (everything fabulous). Two Australian travellers wrote 'Unapproachable & Sublime. Beats the "Taj" in British India.'[25]

Some expressed concern for the decay of the temple and supported the colonial government's steps to 'honour' it with financial support ('berbagai onkos') for its maintenance, while others urged more, including three low-ranking *priyayi* travelling to Solo from Ngadiredjo. 'How much Borobudur surprises the heart; but even more surprising is how the government has already invested in honouring this temple. Surely the government is wise.'[26] A certain Harloff, a 'private person' from Semarang on his way to Candi Mendut, writing seven years earlier (before the photograph of the hidden foot), was impressed by the temple and its builders, but more cynical about its contemporary maintenance: 'A giant in decay. I admire the energy and ambitions of the old Hindus, less so that of the government.' Someone reacted: 'What do you want. That the government paints the B.B. green?', which another visitor crossed through and added: 'Coward!' and 'Surely a public servant.'[27]

The most pensive comments were of religious reflection. Seemingly serious and devout visitors scribbled lengthy streams of thought, sometimes even preaching in rhyme. Others would mock or tease these preachers, often parodying their style. Thus, Borobudur, via the guestbook, became a forum for airing and criticising religion(s) and religious feelings. Far from expressing concern over a non-Christian site, some devout visitors marvelled at Borobudur and its natural surroundings. A. W. Hurst Boram of the British and Foreign Bible Society in Magelang, on 12 May 1895, enthused about 'the capabilities of the Javanese people, and, if belief in such a noble man causes them to rear [raise] such edifices to his glory what would true belief in the true God Christ cause them to do for His glory? – Humbly follow His works.' Another visitor disparaged: 'Don't talk such nonsense.' At the end of January 1895, missionaries Pa and Ma van der Steur arrived with twenty of their pupils. The students, perhaps asked to comment, were laconic: 'none' ('gene') (twice), 'pleasant' ('prettig') (three times), 'very nice' ('Heel mooi') (six times), 'beautiful' ('prachtig'), 'very beautiful' ('Heel prachtig'), and '(very) beautiful work' ('(Heel) prachtig gewerkt') (six times). But Pa and Ma van der Steur were verbose and didactic. On the first day (28 January 1895), Pa rued Borobudur's state of decay, which to him was symbolic of Java, the Dutch nation, Dutch citizenship, and Christianity:

> At the foot of Borobudur we see and deplore Java's decay. Every Dutchman should ask himself, at this foot, seriously: did I, as a member of the Dutch nation, have anything in my power to fight the noticeable decay and bring new energy. Every *Christian* should

[25] M. O. and L. MacGregor, from Melbourne, on the way to Hong Kong, 30 September 1895.

[26] Poerbodipoero, Soerokartiko, and Amongsoebroto, all lower administrators, from Ngadiredjo, travelling to Solo, 18 May 1895.

[27] Harloff, private person from Semarang, with Candi Mendut as next stop, 1 July 1888; anonymous reaction on same day.

ask himself did I bring by word and example the lessons of the Lord, who does not found temples to honour God, because of the temples of the heart which he creates to become the House of the Holy Spirit; moreover he has to ask 'Is my heart such a temple?'

Referring to the Old Testament, Isaiah 54, Van der Steur continued:

> If the impressively beautiful nature inspires many hearts to go to Him who said:
> 'Mountains will move, and hills will be shaken, but my faithful love will never move' then his prayer has been heard.

'Did Janus ask himself these questions?' was the comment of one visitor on the same day, and: 'Approved of by the First and Second Chamber, and ratified by HM the Queen-regent', added another.

S. M. ('Ma') van der Steur confesses her admiration for the man-made temple, but the magnificent view from Borobudur's top confirmed her belief in the one and only God:

> mankind's hands created a wonderful piece of art here, and yet, when we stand at the top of the temple, we see how that which is made by man, no matter how beautiful, cannot compete with the creation of the Lord. Oh Lord, how great are Thy works, so deep are Thy thoughts.[28]

Other followers show impatience or contempt for the preachers, like the anonymous: 'L. S. Mister v. d. Steur is kindly asked to cut his moving prose out of this guest book and to keep his mouth shut'; 'That is *right*.'[29] And Borobudur raised doubts among believers regarding the comparison of religions and religious reform.[30] After exploring Borobudur extensively over two days under Groneman's guidance, J. Kremer wrote 'this is a very sombre monument. How is it possible that people think that Christianity, with all its optimism, has anything to do with Buddhism?'[31] A similarly dubious vicar from Magelang, G. Jonckbloedt, on 11 January 1895, quoted Heinrich Heine: 'Wir begreifen die Ruinen nicht eher als bis wir selbst Ruinen sind' ('We do not fathom the ruins until we are ruins ourselves'). On the other hand, some expressed exaltation and felt Borobudur spoke directly to them. On the day before Christmas 1894, William and Ethel J. Marshall from Edinburgh exclaimed '"Sermons in stones" Wonderful!'

28 S. M. van der Steur, 3 February 1895. 29 Anonymous, 3 February 1895.

30 On the role of Buddhism in Christian reform movements in the nineteenth century, see among others Philip Almond, *The British discovery of Buddhism* (Cambridge: Cambridge University Press, 1988); Heinrich Dumoulin, *Christianity meets Buddhism* (La Salle, IL: Open Court Publishing Company, 1974); Marchand, *German orientalism in the age of empire*; Marcel Poorthuis and Theo Salemink, 'Christelijke omgang met het boeddhisme in Nederland', *Tijdschrift voor Nederlandse Kerkgeschiedenis* 12:4 (2009), 137–150.

31 J. Kremer, entries 3 and 4 August 1895.

Royal Buddhist Reform, Travelling Sites, and (Dis)connecting Heritage Awareness

When King Chulalongkorn visited Borobudur between 30 June and 3 July 1896, he did not sign the temple's guestbook, but he did take away reliefs and statues home to Bangkok – under Groneman's guidance, whose expertise, in turn, fit in the growing international curiosity about Buddhism. When composer Alberto Friedenthal toured the temple, 'climbed down from Nirvana', as he noted in the guestbook, and immersed in 'the teachings of the noble Siddharta Gathama',[32] he was clearly aware of a renewed popular enthusiasm for Buddhism in Asia, well into India, and to some extent in the West as well. Friedenthal may have been attracted to Buddhism by reading (about) the bestseller *The Light of Asia* (1879) by Sir Edwin Arnold, an exalted poem on the life of the Buddha, which promoted Buddhism in Europe and the United States. Recent scholarly research on this 'globalising' revival has highlighted the crucial role of monks such as Anagarika Dharmapala in Lanka, of the American T. S. Olcott and other members of the international Theosophical Society (founded in New York in 1875, but headquartered in India from 1883), and of the reformist Buddhist King Chulalongkorn as motors of the Buddhist revival in Asia.[33] They all helped shape what is now referred to as the Theravadan Buddhist world. Archaeological rediscovery of and care for ancient Buddhist sites (such as Bodh Gaya in north India, where the Buddha found enlightenment) were both inspired by and helped further stimulate the Buddhist revival. This is the key context of King Chulalongkorn's pilgrimage to Borobudur.

This modernist reformer of an independent kingdom among colonised states, some of which had Buddhists as a majority among their subjects, came not merely as the head of the Buddhist order of Siam, a position with both religious and political power.[34] He also appealed to broader cultural values, such as

[32] Alberto Friedenthal, 28 September 1895.

[33] Trevithick, 'British archaeologists, Hindu abbots, and Burmese Buddhists'; Trevithick, *The revival of Buddhist pilgrimage at Bodh Gaya*; Allen, *The Buddha and the sahibs*; Anne M. Blackburn, *Locations of Buddhism: colonialism and modernity in Sri Lanka* (Chicago: University of Chicago Press, 2010); Anne M. Blackburn, 'Ceylonese Buddhism in colonial Singapore: new ritual spaces and specialists, 1895–1935', Asia Research Institute Working Paper Series 184 (Singapore: Asia Research Institute, National University of Singapore, 2012); Singh, 'Exile and return'; Geary, 'Rebuilding the navel of the earth'. On Buddhism in Europe and the United States, see Almond, *The British discovery of Buddhism*; Rick Fields, *How the Swans came to the lake: a narrative history of Buddhism in America*, 3rd edn, revised and updated (Boston and London: Sambbhala, 1992 [1st edition, 1981]); Laurence Cox, *Buddhism and Ireland: from the Celts to the counter-culture* (Sheffield: Equinox, 2013); Martin Bauman, 'Global Buddhism: developmental periods, regional histories, and a new analytical perspective', *Journal of Global Buddhism* 2 (2001), 1–43.

[34] Compare with Sraman Mukherjee: 'Relics, ruins, and temple building: archaeological heritage and the construction of the Dharmarajika Vihara, Calcutta', in Nayanjot Lahiri and Upinder Singh (eds.), *Buddhism in Asia: revival and reinvention* (New Delhi: Manohar, 2016), 147–190.

ancient gift-giving practices, in which relics of the Buddha circulated.[35] This was how he could become a persuasive authority on Borobudur, as Groneman, his self-taught European host, observed. By education and experience as a Buddhist king, Chulalongkorn was familiar with Buddhist and Hindu temple constructions. He had read Raffles' classic *The History of Java* (1817), but was also well versed in the more recent production of Buddhist (*pali*) knowledge by Western scholars, and was an important supporter of the Pali Text Society (set up in Ceylon in 1881, by the former civil servant-turned-*pali* scholar T. W. Rhys Davids) that connected these scholars and promoted their work.[36] Moreover, like his father King Mongkut, and his half-brother Prince Damrong, Chulalongkorn had developed a particular interest in antiquities and ruined religious sites of the past for religious, scholarly, and political reasons. Registering museums and archaeological excavation projects in neighbouring colonised regions of South and Southeast Asia, and especially watching foreign engagements with Angkor and other Khmer antiquities in Siemreap – the province at the border of French Cambodia that was Siamese until 1907 – must have all strengthened Chulalongkorn and his brothers' awareness of the value of ruins and cultural heritage to various parties. As Maurizio Peleggi has argued, they became good for legitimising lineages of the Chakri dynasty and of Greater Siam, at home and abroad.[37] But this kind of political calculation during Chulalongkorn's encounter with Borobudur cannot be assumed.

Borobudur inspired awe and fascination in Chulalongkorn, as he inspected galleries, registered and counted the Buddha statues, and guessed at figures and tales about the Buddha in his (previous) lives on the reliefs. He noticed that the palaces on these reliefs resembled those in Siam, and echoing Tjondronegoro, noted in his diary 'that the people in the past must have known the history [of the Buddha] in detail, much better than we do now'.[38] Members of his retinue photographed (details of) the site, and the king held long discussions with Groneman on the temple's meaning and history, deeply impressing his hosts.

The king appeared quite knowledgeable about the 'speaking' stones of Borobudur, and dazzled his hosts with his interpretations that differed from those of Dutch and foreign orientalists, who by contrast did not much impress him.[39] In fact, he even instructed Groneman and the rest of the party (erroneously) that Borobudur could not have been created by 'Mahayanist

[35] Sraman Mukherjee, 'Relics in transition: material mediations in changing worlds', *Ars Orientalis* 48 (2018), 20–42; Anne M. Blackburn, 'Buddha-relics in the lives of southern Asian polities', *Numen* 57 (2010), 318–340; John S. Strong, *Relics of the Buddha* (Princeton: Princeton University Press, 2004).

[36] Patric Jory, 'Thai and Western Buddhist scholarship in the age of colonialism: King Chulalongkorn redefines the Jatakas', *JAS* 61:3 (2002), 891–918.

[37] Peleggi, 'Royal antiquarianism'. [38] Chulalongkorn, *Itinéraire d'un voyage à Java*, 116.

[39] *De Locomotief*, 6 July 1896; Report, A. J. Quarles de Quarles, 17 December 1896, NA, MvK, V 3 November 1896, X 18.

Buddhism' ('coming from northern Buddhist regions'), but by 'Hinayanist Buddism' ('coming from southern Buddhist regions') like the temples in Siam. But he also pointed out that the different meditative postures of the Buddha statues of Borobudur represented the historic figure of the Buddha – not, despite Groneman's erroneous conviction, a transposition of the sun.[40]

The fact that a learned Buddhist king from Siam, who himself was not sure of all the meanings, overruled a self-taught Dutch orientalist in his interpretations of the Borobudur indicates that with regard to this temple site the hierarchies of knowledge were – still – flexible.[41] The exchange of interpretations on Borobudur's meanings between Chulalongkorn and Groneman would be, moreover, one – and not the first – of a series of material and immaterial exchanges related to Buddhist and Hindu temple art on Java, between King Chulalongkorn and Dutch colonial and local Javanese parties. The beginning of these exchanges might be traced to Chulalongkorn's first visit to Java in 1871, when he offered the citizens of the colonial capital Batavia a statue of the white elephant – from Siam – that still stands in front of the National Museum in Jakarta, formerly the museum of the Royal Batavian Society of Arts and Sciences.

The cumulative nature of these and subsequent material and immaterial gifts bring to mind Marcel Mauss' influential observation, cited earlier, that 'the obligation to give is explainable because this act causes the obligation to return the gift'. Put another way, gifts create and legitimise interdependent relationships.[42] As King Chulalongkorn's visit to Borobudur highlights, Mauss' theory can help us understand how the political dynamics of heritage formation worked at the local, trans-Asian, and global levels. Gifts and exchanges may even be crucial to these dynamics. Also, because in the act of giving, the person who gives presents himself (or herself) as the owner, the question of whose heritage this is bore directly on the men investigating Borobudur in 1896.

[40] Groneman, 'Een Boeddhistischen-koning op den Borobudoer', 368–369; Chulalongkorn, *Itinéraire d'un voyage à Java*, 108, 118–119; *De Locomotief*, 6 July 1896; Report, A. J. Quarles de Quarles, 17 December 1896, NA, MvK, V 3 November 1896, X 18; Isaac Groneman, *Boeddhistische tempelbouwvallen in de Praga-vallei: de Tjandi's Barabadoer, Mendoet en Pawon* (Semarang: Van Dorp, 1907), 17 and 19.

[41] See, however, the Javanologist J. Brandes, at that time an established linguistic administrator in Batavia, who was trained at Leiden University. In letters to Groneman on 21 June and 1 August 1896 Brandes disputed Groneman's new ideas on Borobudur, inspired by Chulalongkorn; dismissed the idea to carry out, at the invitation of the king, further research in Siam; and refrained from commenting on an essay-in-the-making by Groneman: 'Because I do not see myself in a position to contradict the king on this point, especially since I have not created the occasion to do so.' See Jan L. A. Brandes, *Eenige uiteenzettingen* (Batavia: Albrecht & Co., 1902), 23–27.

[42] Mauss, *The gift*, 1.

Gifted Gifts

The day before his sojourn to Borobudur, Chulalongkorn had extensively explored the Prambanan temple ruins, a few kilometres east of Yogyakarta. In a way this Hindu temple, dating from the ninth century, was very topical, since it had only recently been the subject of an archaeological intervention. In 1892–1893, using the framework of the young Archaeological Society, Groneman had initiated and directed an excavation at the site, a project that also involved members of the court of Sultan Hamengkubuwono VII, including his now-famous photographer Cephas. Hamengkubuwono VII, the Dutch government, and a local scientific society in the Netherlands together provided the funds for these excavation works. The Prambanan excavation team uncovered temple structures, reliefs, and statues in the niches of the three main buildings of the Prambanan site, the Hindu temples dedicated to Vishnu, Brahma, and Siva. Some of the findings, to Groneman's satisfaction, 'rivalled the famous statues of the old Greek architects in truth and beauty', and surpassed what he had seen of Hindu temples elsewhere in Java, Ceylon, and India. The excavation had attracted the curiosity of Javanese Muslim visitors, some even travelling from outside Central Java to see the results. In the eyes of the surprised Groneman, these visitors were, apparently, the rightful inheritors, or so he believed.[43] Now the Archaeological Society, and Groneman, who liked to perform as expert host to foreign statesmen and scholars at Java's Hindu–Buddhist sites, could proudly introduce the excavated treasure to a wise and charming Buddhist king, Chulalongkorn.

It was during Chulalongkorn's inspection of the Prambanan remains that the two leading figures of the Archaeological Society, the head R. M. E. Raaf and the honorary head Groneman, became so impressed by the king's knowledge of Hindu and Buddhist monuments. They also toured nearby temples Candi Kalasan and Candi Sari, after which they lionised Chulalongkorn with speeches in English by Raaf and Groneman, and with two gifts: an honorary membership of the Archaeological Society and the published report on the Prambanan excavations by Groneman and Cephas, which included Cephas' photographic impression of the uncovered ruins, luxuriously folded in a large casing. Chulalongkorn accepted these gestures gratefully, invited anyone who was interested to consult him on the Buddhist tradition in Siam, and donated 200 guilders to the Archaeological Society.[44]

The next day Chulalongkorn travelled to Magelang, and spent three days in the area instead of one as planned, during which he also visited other Buddhist and Hindu Javanese temple sites nearby, deeply admired the giant Buddhist

[43] Isaac Groneman, *Tjandi Parambanan op Midden-Java, na de Ontgraving: met lichtdrukken van Cephas* (Leiden: Brill, 1893), 3, 8.

[44] *De Locomotief*, 30 June 1896; Chulalongkorn, *Itinéraire d'un voyage à Java*, 108–114.

images in the Mendut temple (early ninth century), and expressed his worries about their decay.[45] The king concluded his visit to Borobudur with two gestures, with definite consequences for the temple. After giving another flower offering and praying to the Buddha in the main *stupa*, he marked his signature in the inner wall of this *stupa*, with the royal order that this should be engraved in gold.[46] Then, with the formal consent previously given to him by Governor-General C. H. A. van der Wijck, he carefully selected some real tokens of Borobudur to take home to Bangkok.[47]

It was quite a shipment, including among other things five Buddha statues, an unclear number of 'speaking stones' or fragments of the reliefs of the first gallery (depicting episodes of the Jataka, on the previous lives of the Buddha), two lions, a *kala* head, and a large guardian statue near the temple – the one that had been pictured and crossed out in the guestbook, and which local lore believed to represent Borobudur's architect.[48] As the story goes, Chulalongkorn returned home with 'eight cartloads' of sculpture.[49] This load, however, included a number of reliefs from Prambanan, depicting episodes from the Ramayana – probably selected by Chulalongkorn from the *gouvernementsloods* (an improvised governmental storage, located at the Resident's premises, for stone statues from archaeological sites in the residence of Yogyakarta), again with formal consent of the governor-general;[50] and statues from the Singasari temple in eastern Java, which Chulalongkorn visited later in his journey. There, Chulalongkorn had selected a small and a giant Ganesha statue – the latter larger than the huge Ganesha from Singasari, which the Netherlands Indies' government, through 'the gift' of Engelhard, had shipped to the Netherlands in 1819 (and is now on display in the National Museum of World Cultures in Leiden). On the role of the Netherlands Indies'

45 Report, A. J. Quarles de Quarles, 17 December 1896, NA, MvK, V 3 November 1896, X 18.

46 Chulalongkorn, *Itinéraire d'un voyage à Java*, 376. The Dutch engineer Theodoor van Erp, responsible for the first overall conservation of Borobudur in 1907–1911, removed the signature – also out of indignation about the whole transaction. See N. J. Krom, *Beschrijving van Barabudur, Part I, Archaeologische beschrijving* ('s-Gravenhage: Nijhoff, 1920), 38, 40, and 45.

47 Chulalongkorn, *Itinéraire d'un voyage à Java*, 17, 68; Theodoor van Erp, 'Eenige mededelingen betreffende de beelden en fragmenten van Boroboedoer in 1896 geschonken aan de Koning van Siam', *BKI* 73:1 (1917), 285–310.

48 Krom and Van Erp, *Beschrijving van Barabudur, Part II*, 18–19.

49 The precise number and kind of antiquarian gifts Chulalongkorn took home are unclear. Compare the relatively modest overview of Van Erp (who refers to 'eight cartloads'), in Van Erp, 'Eenige mededelingen', 20, with Krom, *Beschrijving van Barabudur, Part I*, 22 and 38–40; Krom and van Erp, *Beschrijving van Barabudur, Part II*, 38; Miksic, *Borobudur*, 30. For a recent Indonesian inventory, based on Van Erp's investigations, which we discuss below, see Utama Ferdinandus, 'Arca-arca dan Relief pada Masa Hindu Jawa di Museum Bangkok', in Edi Sedyawati, Ingrid H. E. Pojoh, Supratikno Rahardjo, and R. Soekmono (eds.), *Monumen: karya persembahan untuk Prof. Dr. R. Soekmono* (Depok: Fakultas Sastra Universitas Indonesia, 1990), 78–101.

50 Governor-general to Resident of Yogyakarta, 17 July 1896, ANRI, AS, Bt 16 October 1896, 21.

government in the Singasari gifts (both currently on display in the National Museum in Bangkok), stories contradict each other.[51] But surely other antiquarian gifts took place without the formal consent of the central government, gifts from local parties – colonial civil servants, representatives of the Javanese administrative elite, and Javanese princes? Among the latter was Prince Mangkunegara VI (r. 1896–1916) in Solo, who offered Chulalongkorn four Buddha statues from his collection, supposedly originating from Candi Plaosan.[52]

It is beyond the scope of this chapter to dwell on the number and choice of all of the individual objects and considerations for the exchanges, but a closer look at Dutch and Siamese sources, as well as at what we can find of these 'gifts' in Bangkok, reveals some of the possible motives and selection criteria that guided Chulalongkorn at Borobudur. They also expose the ambiguous role of Dutch colonials, both officially and informally, in this exchange, and the lack of control of the central government over local diplomatic exchanges, and thus power politics. They also reveal the multiple, contradictory, and sometimes overlapping appreciations of the temple by Siamese and Dutch colonial parties. While Chulalongkorn regarded the temple at once as a living sacred Buddhist site, as a source of history, as a source of Buddhist learning, and for reform at home, Dutch parties, mainly responsible for the exchange at the time, considered the site a unique artwork from a past Buddhist civilisation, as a source of (religious) history, and, apparently, as a diplomatic tool. And later, when all was done, other Dutch caretakers saw the temple as a living sacred site as well, since they considered it 'desecrated' by having lost 'unique' elements to the Siamese king.[53]

The Dutch engineer Theodoor van Erp, who under the Netherlands Indies' government would assume responsibility for the first overall restoration of Borobudur in 1907–1911, investigated this episode during his preparatory

[51] See the conflicting versions of the self-taught Indologists J. Knebel and G. P. Rouffaer in J. L. A. Brandes, *Beschrijving van Tjandi Singasari; en de Wolkentooneelen van Panataran* ('s-Gravenhage: Nijhoff; Batavia: Albrecht, 1908), 53 and 83. According to Knebel, these were gifts from local officials, 'with the formal consent of the government'; according to Rouffaer, the transactions happened 'against the will of the governor-general'. Van Erp follows Rouffaer's version.

[52] These may relate to the statues taken by princes – of Yogyakarta, however – in the context of the early nineteenth-century cleaning explorations under British rule that Carey is referring to; see Peter Carey, 'Sepoy conspiracy', *BKI*, 301–302 and 316 n. 55; see also Chapter 1 of this book. See also Chulalongkorn, *Itinéraire d'un voyage à Java*, 142–143. Chulalongkorn had the statues placed at the four corners of the library (Phra Mondop) of the Wat Pra Keoh. In 1982, they were replaced by copies, and the originals were moved to the museum of Wat Pra Keoh; they were still on display there in March 2011. See M. C. Subhadradis Diskul, *History of the Temple of the Emerald Buddha* (Bangkok: Bureau of the Royal Household, 1980), 31–32.

[53] See especially Krom, who refers to this episode as 'tempelschennis' (desecration of the temple) and 'one of the most sordid episodes in the history of Borobudur': Krom, *Beschrijving van Barabudur, Part I*, 38.

work with growing indignation. He explored the governmental archives and interviewed Javanese eyewitnesses who had helped to carry the stones away from Borubudur. Precisely what the governor-general consented to give to Chulalongkorn, when the king visited him after his arrival in Java, remains unclear. But the correspondence between the Netherlands Indies' government and the local administration in Yogyakarta and Magelang (Kedu) convinced Van Erp that Governor-General van der Wijck had merely agreed to Chulalongkorn taking only one Buddha image from Borobudur, 'if possible'.[54] But the governor-general later tried to withdraw this gesture, first with the argument, ignored by Van Erp, to the Resident of Kedu, 'that it would be very difficult to transport a statue from this temple ruin'. Van Erp was more charmed with the governor-general's subsequent insistence that the Resident of Kedu should take care 'Not to give a statue [from Borobudur], of which the loss would harm the *kunstwaarde* [art value] of the temple'.[55] However, Chulalongkorn had set his eyes on Borobudur, and he had impressed his hosts. The result was that the Resident proposed, in a telegram to the governor-general, the following:

> The king of Siam wishes [to receive] from Borobudur five Buddha statues in different postures, two lions, and some ornaments, as well as the only available *raksasa* [the guardian statue], posting in front of the *pasangrahan*; of all the other objects he would like, numerous samples are available. By agreeing with this request the art value will not be harmed. Politely request decision.

The governor-general acquiesced, telegraphing that he had 'no objection to agreeing to the demands of the king regarding Buddha statues'.[56]

This correspondence, interesting for many reasons, indicates that diverse appreciations of the uniqueness of the objects connected to Borobudur were at stake, and may partly explain the exchange. The fact that Borobudur had so many Buddha images for each of several different postures may have played a role in Chulalongkorn's choices. It seems to explain the casualness of his selecting Buddha statues at Borobudur, in comparison to how he valued the one and only Buddha statue in the nearby Candi Mendut. That giant seated Buddha, which was accompanied by two similarly giant Bodhisattvas, had impressed Chulalongkorn most of all. According to Groneman, the king observed that there was only one comparable Buddha statue in Siam but it was much more damaged. His half-brother Damrong, who was present as well, called the

54 Van Erp, 'Eenige mededelingen', 19.

55 Telegram, 10 June 1896, quoted in both Van Erp, 'Eenige mededelingen', and Krom, *Beschrijving van Barabudur, Part I*, 38. This telegram and the previous one of the same date, bringing up the more practical objection, are in ANRI, AS, Bt 16 October 1896, 21.

56 Letter, 4 July 1896, quoted in both Van Erp, 'Eenige mededelingen', and Krom, *Beschrijving van Barabudur, Part I*, 38. This letter and the consent of the governor-general of 5 July 1896 are in ANRI, AS, Bt 16 October 1896, 21.

Mendut Buddha 'priceless'.[57] In his diary, Chulalongkorn remarked that he found the statues in Mendut so beautiful that if he could take them home he would build a temple for them – but that he would not because they were sacred and because they belonged to the Javanese people.

As we see in Bangkok today, Chulalongkorn chose five of the postures of the Buddha, that is five of the six postures that can actually be found at Borobudur – four of them (*bumisparsa mudrai* (touching the earth), *vara mudra* (giving), *dyana mudra* (meditating), *abaya mudra* (eliminating fear)) were each represented ninety-two times at the four lower levels on each side of the temple, and the fifth posture, *vitarka mudra* (preaching), was represented sixty-four times on the highest gallery. Chulalongkorn left untouched the Buddha statues in the *stupa* on the circular terraces around the central *stupa*, seated in a preaching posture, as he did with the 'unfinished Buddha' in the main *stupa*. Possibly these were too sacred and too firmly allocated to the most sacred parts of the temple, in the eyes both of the king and of his hosts.

In Siam the Javanese statues, arriving as diplomatic gifts to the king and as pilgrims' souvenirs, embarked on their new status, soon transforming into trophies of the antiquarian interest of the royal Chakri dynasty of Siam, and as we shall see below, as gifts, or objects for popular Buddhist worship, which the king granted to the people, in the way Peleggi described, 'as the king of the Siamese, rather than the king of Siam'.[58] As such, the Javanese antiquities could play their particular role in the royal elites' conservative-reformist politics of nation-building and social control, and thus in legitimising their vision of Greater Siam.[59]

To celebrate their arrival, King Chulalongkorn first displayed the Javanese antiquities in front of the royal palace in Bangkok and invited hundreds of Buddhist priests.[60] Borobudur's Buddha statues then found a new 'shelter' in the Wat Phra Keo (the temple of the Emerald Buddha and monastery attached to the royal palace) in Bangkok. King Vajiravudh (Rama VI, r. 1910–1925), Chulalongkorn's son and successor (Chulalongkorn died in 1910) transferred them to other important temples in Bangkok. He enshrined four of them in the niches of the new *chedi*, which

[57] Groneman, 'Een Boeddhistischen-koning op den Borobudoer', 377–378.

[58] Maurizio Peleggi, *Lords of things: the fashioning of the Siamese monarchy's modern image* (Honolulu: University of Hawai'i Press, 2002), 9.

[59] On the Siamese royal family's elite investments in cultural and political reform and royal historical legitimation, see ibid.; Peleggi, 'Royal antiquarianism'; Jory, 'Thai and Western Buddhist scholarship'. For a recent, more locally contextualised perspective, assessing the (limited) effects (of the royal reform policies) on monastic education, see Justin Thomas McDaniel, *Gathering leaves and lifting words: histories of Buddhist monastic education in Laos and Thailand* (Seattle: University of Washington Press, 2008), 92–116.

[60] Jacob A. N. Patijn, 'Over den Boroboedoer', *Tijdschrift van Nederlandsch-Indië* Tweede nieuwe Serie 5 (1901), 386–389.

he had erected at Wat Rachathiwat, the monastery where Chulalongkorn's father and precursor, King Rama IV (Mongkut, r. 1851–1868), had resided when he was a monk. He had the fifth one placed at the Wat Boworniwet, the site of another important royal monastery (where King Mongkut had stayed as well) and monastic university.[61] Other pieces were kept in the park of the royal palace. Some of these objects, including the giant Ganesha of Candi Singasari, and the temple guardian of Borobudur, moved in 1926 to the Royal National Museum, to be exhibited in modern fashion for the public. This happened after two scholarly men had inventoried and reorganised this museum's collection: Chulalongkorn's half-brother Prince Damrong and the French archaeologist George Coedès who, once again, added to the colonial scholarly motive in this multi-sited and multidimensional story of heritage formation.

Restricted Restitution and Missing Links

As gifts, most of the Javanese antiquities today are still enshrined and on display in Thailand. The important exceptions may illustrate the topical relevance and importance of these Javanese antiquities in Thailand, and explain the diplomatic attitude which the Dutch colonial (heritage) authorities and their post-colonial successors chose to take, despite amazement and sometimes regret about the original gifts, expressed by insiders and outsiders alike.

In 1926, while inventorying the royal collection together with Coedès, Prince Damrong consented to let some of the Javanese antiquities return to their place of origin in exchange for others. Three of the Ramayana reliefs of Prambanan temple (out of the four Chulalongkorn had brought home) could travel back to Java, where the Netherlands Indies' Archaeological Service (set up in 1913) could use them for one of the service's major projects at the time: the reconstruction of the Siva temple at Prambanan, which began in earnest in the late 1920s. Van Erp, still very much engaged with this history of gift giving and return, provided a preliminary interpretation as to what made this restricted restitution possible, which today still sounds plausible. According to Van Erp, it was thanks to the (in his view fortunate) combination of three people: the charismatic (and immense) Dutch colonial archaeologist P. V. van Stein Callenfels, who visited Bangkok in September 1926 and tried his diplomatic talents,[62] the 'powerful co-operation of George Coedès', who intermediated, and Prince Damrong, former minister of interior administration and head of the

[61] Subhadradis Diskul, *History of the Temple*, 31–32.

[62] For Van Stein Callenfels, see Bloembergen and Eickhoff, 'The colonial archaeological hero reconsidered'.

Royal Council, who provided a strong hand in the self-legitimising cultural reform politics of the royal Siamese elite.[63]

As becomes clear from his official report, Prince Damrong agreed with the return of three reliefs of the Prambanan complex, depicting fragments of the Ramayana story (which he referred to as Ramakien, the Siamese derivation of the Ramayana), in exchange for three alternative antiquities, proposed by the Netherlands Indies' Archaeological Service.[64] What can be added to Van Erp's findings is that archaeologist F. D. K. Bosch, then head of the Netherlands Indies' Archaeological Service, may have diplomatically prepared this restricted restitution. In 1926, during restoration activities at the Singasari temple in East Java, the Archaeological Service encountered a fragment of stone that belonged to the giant Ganesha statue, which Chulalongkorn had brought to Bangkok in 1896. Bosch advised the Netherlands Indies' government to grant the missing fragment of Ganesha to the king of Siam as an acknowledgement of their highest esteem to the royal house of Siam. While not explicitly referring to the reconstruction plans for Prambanan, Bosch conjectured that this gesture might help to make the king of Siam inclined to show his gratefulness 'in a way that could become of use for future archaeological activities in the Netherlands Indies'.[65]

And, thus, most of the Ramayana reliefs of Prambanan were able to return from their thirty-year 'exile', as Van Erp put it. But the mere wish to get back the splendid Buddhas and lions of Borobudur was understandably impossible. Prince Damrong conceded – diplomatically – that for personal and scholarly reasons he would have preferred that those were also to return to their provenance. But he excluded a general restitution of the Javanese objects, explaining that he was powerless against the devotion of the king and the people in Siam to 'Chulalongkorn's gifts to the nation'.[66] Van Stein Callenfels, who was impressed by Damrong's story of the new power of the Javanese antiquities, connecting the people to the king of Siam, wrote to Van Erp what he had heard and seen of this in Bangkok:

[63] Theodoor van Erp, 'Nog eens de Hindoe-Javaansche beelden in Bangkok', *BKI* 83:1 (1027), 503–513.

[64] Prince Damrong, on 10 November 1926, informed Jao Praya Mahitor, head of the Office of the Royal Secretary, of the return of the three stones: National Archives, Bangkok (hereafter NAB), M-R7B/22.11/15. We thank Han ten Brummelhuis for his translation of this letter. In March 2011, the National Museum in Bangkok had seven stone Javanese images on display that referred to an exchange with 'Thai objects' in 1927.

[65] Bosch to the director of Education, Religion and Industry, 22 May 1926, ANRI, AS, Bt 21 June 1926, 4.

[66] Van Erp, 'Nog eens de Hindoe-Javaansche beelden'; Prince Damrong to Jao Praya Mahitor, 10 November 1926, NAB, M-R7B/22.11/15. See also Damrong's diary of his third trip to Java in 1934, published by his sister in 1937. We thank Anuk Pitukthanin, who collected and translated these sources for us.

> The old king was already much beloved during his life and is now on his way to becoming a saint – or, rather, he already is. I saw long processions of pilgrims, among them Buddhist monks, moving towards his equestrian statue in front of the throne hall. The [Javanese] statues are considered to be his gifts to the nation, and they share in his sanctity.[67]

To convince his readers, and perhaps himself, Van Erp added that Coedès also emphasised that 'the holiness of Chulalongkorn's gifts to the nation' should not be taken as a hollow phrase, but as 'living reality'.[68]

In other words, since Chulalongkorn's death in 1910, the Javanese antiquities had officially become part of a popular Buddhist cult that supposedly legitimised the royal elite of the Chakri dynasty, and thereby Greater Buddhist Siam. Recent studies on the royal antiquarian interest in Siam and on the King Chulalongkorn cult in Thailand in the 1990s point to the fact that Prince Damrong, as an active antiquarian, and religious political reformer, was one of the architects of this cult.[69] This does not, however, remove the fact that, from royal and popular Siamese perspectives, the Javanese antiquities were in the right place, relocalised as objects of Siamese popular Buddhist cult and heritage.

To Van Erp all this loss was very painful. Two decades earlier, while working on the restoration of Borobudur and investigating this history for the first time, his learned colleagues of the Batavian Society had tried to persuade him that these losses from the temple were gifts to the king – and not 'theft', as he called it. Nevertheless, in 1923 Van Erp still described this history as the 'kidnapping' of precious pieces from Borobudur.[70] Writing in 1927 and probably relieved by the restitution of the Prambanan reliefs, Van Erp seemed to empathise with local Siamese engagements with Borobudur's treasures. But he also expressed continuous regret by speculating that these precious pieces were 'once . . . presented to the temple, and in the honour of which once a marvellous consecration took place'. By imagining the same Buddha statues as an original popular gift by Javanese people to the temple, one in the distant past, he implicitly obliged the Dutch colonial authorities, who in his view had been so careless with their diplomatic antiquarian gestures to Chulalongkorn in 1896, to 'return' something to the temples and to make good.[71] This was a clear sign of supra-local heritage awareness – the

[67] Quoted in Van Erp, 'Nog eens de Hindoe-Javaansche beelden', 512–513. [68] Ibid., 513.

[69] Peleggi, *Lords of things*; Peleggi, 'Royal antiquarianism'; Irene Stengs, *Worshipping the great moderniser: King Chulalongkorn, patron saint of the Thai middle class* (Singapore: NUS Press, 2009), 84–91.

[70] Theodoor van Erp, 'Hindu-Javaansche Beelden, thans te Bangkok', *BKI* 79:1 (1923), 429; Van Erp, 'Nog eens de Hindoe-Javaansche beelden', 513. For the Batavian Society's reaction to Van Erp's first report, see ANRI, KBG DIR 1006. This report, intended for King Chulalongkorn, was published in 1917 (Van Erp, 'Eenige mededelingen').

[71] Van Erp, 'Nog eens de Hindoe-Javaansche beelden', 513.

wish to keep something of the past for the future as a national obligation – that by then had strongly developed in the Netherlands Indies – and at the level of the colonial state.

A Dutch Moral Obligation

So much for the 'official indifference to Borobudur's fate', as the Southeast Asia archaeologist John Miksic summarised this Siamese episode in the travels of the collection under study here.[72] He was referring to the apparent absence of modern heritage awareness in the Netherlands Indies at the time.

Indeed, apart from a few cynical reactions in the Netherlands Indies' press, the 1896 Dutch gift from Borobudur to King Chulalongkorn passed by unnoticed.[73] But three years later Dutch newspapers, first in the Netherlands Indies and then in the Netherlands, began referring to the 'gifts' as aggressive demolition of the Borobudur, kindly supported by the generous Dutch government, and thus as an outrageous scandal.[74] The ambiguity of this moral indignation becomes clear when we look at the three giant statues from Candi Singasari, which had been sent to the Netherlands in 1819 as a gift to King William I, and kept there, with the official consent of the Netherlands Indies government. This well-known displacement of unique Javanese statues, which the Dutch civil servant Nicolaus Engelhard had carried away from their original shrines in Singasari's tower temple (and which included the Ganesha statue mentioned above), until then had caused no controversy at all.

As to the Javanese antiquarian gifts to the king of Siam, public indignation did eventually arise. The former Indies journalist J. F. Scheltema, who had worked for the then-critical Indies dailies *De Locomotief* and the *Bataviaasch Nieuwsblad*, called the whole episode 'the most disastrous year for Borobodur'. On discovering that Borobudur and Prambanan reliefs, some of which depicted monkeys, were kept in Bangkok, he denounced those responsible for the gift-giving:

> if there be anything in the dogma of Karma, which provides for our sins being visited on us in lives to come, that their least punishment might be their transformation, when called to new birth, into monkeys abandoned to ceaseless squabbles over their kanari-nuts (honours, dignities, preferment with big salaries, fat pensions,

[72] Miksic, *Borobudur*, 30. [73] *De Locomotief*, 10 July 1896.

[74] *Soerabajasche Courant*, 17 June 1899; *Nieuwe Rotterdamsche Courant*, 15 August 1899, NA, MvK, V 28 November 1899, 6. See also the discussion between J. A. N. Patijn, Groneman and J. F. Niermeijer in *Kroniek*, 13 October 1900, *Tijdschrift van Nederlandsch-Indië*, 1900, 317, and *Soerabajasch Handelsblad*, 1 December 1900. See also J. F. Scheltema, *Monumental Java* (London: Macmillan, 1912), 235 and 243–246.

etc.), clawing one another with their sharp nails, to find at last that all the shells are empty.[75]

These were all also cynical reactions to the news that the core of the Dutch colonial entry to the World Exhibition in Paris would consist of Buddhist and Hindu monumental remains of Java, parading as precious art to be protected. The whole issue contributed to a serious discussion in the Netherlands, focusing on the question of whether the Dutch government should invest in the restoration of the temple.

The discussion of heritage politics in the Netherlands Indies took place in the context of the lobby for monumental care in the Netherlands that proceeded slowly and not really effectively from the 1870s under the guidance of Victor de Stuers,[76] who worked as head of the newly created governmental Department of Arts and Sciences of the Ministry of the Interior during the scandal around the gifts to Chulalongkorn. Alarmed by the indignation about Borobudur's losses in the Indies, De Stuers tried to influence colonial monumental care, but mostly just irritated the Department of the Ministry of Colonies. Another context was provided by the activities of the organising committee for the Dutch colonial entry to the World Exhibition in Paris in 1900, which aimed to put the Buddhist and Hindu monumental remains of Java in the spotlight. The director of that project, J. W. IJzerman, used this Dutch colonial mission to Paris for his archaeological lobby: to establish private and governmental financial support for monumental care in the Indies.[77]

The civil engineer IJzerman, responsible for the construction of a modest railway network in Central Java, and who had detected and uncovered the hidden foot of Borobudur, was one of the founders and a former president of Yogyakarta's Archaeological Society in 1885. At the time of Chulalongkorn's visit, IJzerman was working in Sumatra. IJzerman advised Minister of Colonies J. T. Cremer, whom he knew from the time Cremer was a tobacco entrepreneur in Deli (Sumatra), to let the upheaval around the gifts to Chulalongkorn rest. Although nobody made the arguments explicit, for diplomatic reasons it seemed better not to sour relations between Siam and the Netherlands, and – after all – a gift was a gift. Moreover, considering the parade of Dutch colonial antiquities in Paris, it was not really the right time to attract attention to Dutch blundering in colonial monumental care. Against that background, it seems understandable that IJzerman advised the minister, instead of enquiring further in Siam, to focus on the future maintenance and also restoration of Buddhist and Hindu antiquities in the Indies.

75 Scheltema, *Monumental Java*, 245.
76 Jos Perry, *Ons fatsoen als natie: Victor de Stuers 1843–1916* (Amsterdam: Sun, 2004).
77 Jan W. IJzerman, 'Over Boro-boedoer', *TKNAG* Tweede Serie 16 (1899), 307–348, 391; *Nieuwe Rotterdamsche Courant*, 15 August 1899.

There was thus a subtle but meaningful shift in attitudes in the Netherlands and the Netherlands Indies: from apparent indifference to the state of these monumental remains, to explicit heritage awareness (this was 'our' Indies heritage) caused by the combined and conflicting notions of 'demolition', 'protection', and 'musealisation'. The result was, in comparison to the earlier initiatives of antiquities care on paper of the 1840s and the restoration of the mosque of Demak (1840–1848), a general attention to the maintenance of Hindu and Buddhist remains – first and foremost, Borobudur – and the wish to restore them in order to keep them for the future. While the restoration of Demak's Great Mosque was triggered, mainly, by various parties' not necessarily overlapping concerns for the Islamic faith, keeping the *local* balance of power and fear for *local* unrest, now international diplomatic interests were at stake as well, displayed by influential governmental and private parties in the modern colonial state-in-development. At this stage, Java's Hindu–Buddhist temple remains gained a new value that made them fit for imperial propaganda.

Greater Holland

The centrepiece of the Netherlands' entry at the 1900 Paris Exhibition was a plaster cast replica of the Buddhist temple Candi Sari, surrounded by plaster casts of Borobudur and other temple art from Java.[78] The moulds for this Javanese temple show were made on location in Java, the casts in Holland. By way of a finishing touch, the organisers also produced a mould and cast of a great treasure in the National Ethnographic Museum in Leiden: the thirteenth-century Singasari statue of Prajnaparamita, then and now referred to as the Mona Lisa of Java. This goddess personified the perfection of wisdom. This statue, transported to the Netherlands in 1822 as a gift to King William I and restituted to Indonesia in 1977, was thought to be a portrayal of Ken Dedes, the first queen of the pre-Islamic Singasari dynasty that ruled in East Java in the thirteenth century. In Paris, this Dutch crown jewel awaited eager viewers in the core of the Dutch pavilion, Candi Sari (Figure 2.4).

This was the first Dutch entry to a World Exhibition that was officially and financially supported by the Dutch government. The choice to flaunt such a sophisticated colonial spectacle (there was no Dutch national pavilion at the famous Rue de nations) represented a new colonial sense of pride and energy in the Netherlands. This new colonial zeal was fuelled by Dutch

[78] On the political significance and reception of 'Candi Sari' at the World Exhibition in Paris, see Marieke Bloembergen, *Colonial spectacles: the Netherlands and the Dutch East Indies at the World Exhibitions, 1880–1931* (Singapore: Singapore University Press, 2006), 164–219. This paragraph is partly based on that chapter.

Figure 2.4 The Dutch colonial section at the world exhibition in Paris in 1900.

military victories in Lombok and Aceh as well as the idea of a Dutch ethical mission in the colony, which would be officially launched as the Ethical Policy in 1901.[79] Both motives were inspired by the intrusive military, along with administrative and technological expansion taking place in the colony from the last decade of the nineteenth century, in which most of the members of the Dutch colonial committee responsible for this choice had participated, including IJzerman. Apart from promoting systematic conservation politics in the Netherlands Indies, and thereby legitimising the Dutch colonial government as the successor, explorer, and custodian of past high civilisations, the Javanese antiquities had another topical relevance: the push of archaeological interest in Asia, Africa, and Europe. In Paris, Candi Sari would ultimately have to withstand comparison with the reproduction of the antique tombs from Carthage in the Tunisian section, and with temples from Indochina in the French colonial section. At least Candi Sari was older than the Pagoda of Phnom Penh, which, not coincidentally, was also on display in Paris.

[79] Ibid., 170–173.

With this apotheosis of Buddhist and Hindu Javanese temple art, its organisers meant to teach important lessons about the origin and nature of civilisation in general and about the Netherlands in particular: the Netherlands as a sophisticated and modern colonial empire, guardian of an honourable civilisation to which, indirectly via India, all great European civilisations could be traced. Because of the novelty of Javanese Hindu and Buddhist art in Europe as well as for the spirit and religious world view that seemed to permeate it, the Dutch colonial pavilion attracted much admiration from Europe's cultural elite. During the exhibition, the organisers presented and sold the plaster casts from the pavilion, partly by auction to private visitors before the exhibition had to be packed away,[80] and partly directly, to the Museum of Antiquities in the Netherlands (Leiden) and to the Musée indochinois du Trocadéro in Paris. Implicitly, these antiquities were branded 'Made by the Dutch Empire'. In this way, the casting and reproduction of this colonised other's past meant defining and representing modern Dutch identity.

After the World Exhibition closed, the organisers had to demolish most of Candi Sari and return what was left to the Netherlands for auction. However, with the Dutch state as official owner, the plaster casts and moulds remained useful to stress the importance of the Netherlands Indies for the Netherlands, during exhibition tours abroad, and at home for a mainly Dutch public. An important Dutch 'local' stage in the history of this peculiar collection of plaster casts would be the Colonial Institute in Amsterdam, the ultimate keeper of the moulds. Founded in 1910 by organisers of the Dutch colonial entry in Paris (including IJzerman), the institute aimed 'to instil in the world some respect for the small country that embraces such a vast area of activity in East and West and that can maintain itself with honour in that area'.[81] In the institute's Ethnographic Museum, the plaster casts of the Buddhist and Hindu–Javanese temple art came to be used in different ways: as eye-catchers next to the main entrance, as part of the ethnographic exhibition, more or less fixed in an evolutionary story, as precious treasures in the so-called temple room, and as ornaments, bricked in the wall of the central hall. In this way, the institute reduced this highly esteemed old 'civilisation' to *couleur-locale*, thereby contributing to the stereotyping of the Javanese indigenous culture as one mystical Buddhist–Hindu culture, and thus giving an awkward blend to contemporary Indonesian Islam. The casts were, however, also meaningful ornaments in a Dutch and European context: they defined and represented Dutch identity, as a small but esteemed culture-loving, modern empire.

[80] For details on the auction, providing insight into the multiple values of images of Hindu–Buddhist deities in Europe, see *Nieuws van den Dag voor Nederlandsch-Indië,* 26 September 1900.

[81] *Koloniaal Weekblad*, 15 December 1910, quoted in Bloembergen, *Colonial spectacles*, 266.

The First Order: to Greater Java and back to Greater Siam

In February 1938, Prince Mangkunegara VII of Solo (Central Java), a passionate researcher and collector of the Buddhist and Hindu Javanese antiquities, ordered a copy of the Prajnaparamita at the Colonial Institute. He had seen a bronze copy of this statue in the Colonial Institute a year before, when he visited the Netherlands for the marriage of Princess Juliana to Bernard von Lippe-Biesterfeld. Originally he had wanted it in bronze.[82] For unknown but likely economic reasons, he changed his mind and ordered a copy in the much cheaper Hartguss, or white cement. The general secretary at the Colonial Institute, J. C. Lamster, replied to the prince that the institute naturally would take care of his request. Moreover, the costs would be restricted to the transport of the cement beauty, since the board of curators of the institute would see it as an honour if Prince Mangkunegara would accept the copy as a gift.[83]

There is an irony in this exchange of 'wisdom' and honour: by requesting a copy of the statue, Mangkunegara VII seemed to accept the fact that the 'real' Prajnaparamita, originating from East Java and from Java's past, remained in the Netherlands. If we interpret this colonial dealing in antiquities as a form of interdependency, thus as an event by which Mangkunegara VII enhanced his own status within the Dutch colonial empire, the prince followed a longer tradition of cultural diplomacy conducted by his family at the Mangkunegaran *kraton* in Solo. Through cultural knowledge and gifts, they could confirm formal relations with private and official persons who showed interest in Java's Hindu and Buddhist past and in the temple remains from that past, of which so many were located in the neighbourhood of Solo. More than forty years earlier, in July 1896, the father of Mangkunegara VII, Mangkunegara VI, provided such a diplomatic gesture by presenting four antique stone Buddha images (with unclear provenance, but now ascribed to Candi Plaosan) to a very special guest who visited him at his *kraton* that year, King Chulalongkorn. During his tour through Java, King Chulalongkorn had made no secret of his special interest in the Buddhist antiquities in Java, and Mangkunegara VI was one of many who paid the king honour with gifts from their private collections of antiquities and even from actual temple sites from Java. But this particular gift was, as it were, an exchange between peers, or so it was in the eyes of King Chulalongkorn, who in his travel diary described Mangkunegara VI almost as

[82] Secretary of the Colonial Institute, M. C. Lamster, to Mangkunegara VII, 1 March 1937, with pencil annotations by Mangkunegara VII, Arsip Mangkunegara, Solo, Correspondence Mankunegara VII, inv. nr K70.

[83] Mangkunegara VII to Colonial Institute, 7 February 1938, and Colonial Institute to Mangkunegara VII, Royal Tropical Institute in Amsterdam (hereafter KIT), archive of the Colonial Institute, inv. nr 4401.

a soulmate, a wise and honourable prince of his age, and a man of the same sensibility and taste.[84]

In 1896, for Mangkuncgara VI, this gift of the four Buddha images may have been a moment of empowerment. While the colonial state had reduced his palace, like the ones of the three other principalities in Central Java, to a dependent princedom that functioned as colonial administrator, he still could play a superior role in the context of the growing antiquarian and archaeological curiosity, expressed by different parties in the colony over the course of the nineteenth century. This curiosity was directed to a past to which the local royal families might relate their genealogy and their moral/religious affinities and expertise.[85]

The Second Order: Greater India, Greater Britain

In 1914, Stanley Clarke, deputy keeper of the Indian Section of the Victoria and Albert Museum in London (V&A), learning that the Colonial Institute had kept moulds of the relief panels of the Borobodur, had to exhibit much more patience than Mankunegara VII, when he eagerly ordered copies of six well-chosen relief panels. With this request Clarke aimed to meet 'one of the most pressing needs' of the museum: to fill the deficiencies in the Indian Section Collections. He defended this purchase to the advisory council of the museum with the information that Borobudur, to be regarded as 'the Parthenon of Asia', 'was built by Indian Buddhist immigrants from the Saka Kingdom of Sarahstra . . . the great reliefs represent scenes in the life of Gautama Buddha'.[86] But Clarke came away empty-handed. The board of the Colonial Institute informed him that, while they kept the moulds and casts, they could not dispose yet of an installation for plasterwork, since they were constructing a new building for their institute. If the V&A could wait a few years, then the Colonial Institute would be happy to propose a transaction. This answer caused much annoyance at the V&A. In the eyes of its director it was unreasonable that the rest of the world should be deprived of getting casts of existing moulds for 'a few years [!] merely because the Colonial Institute in Amsterdam has plans for a new building'.[87]

In subsequent correspondence, eight years after the end of the First World War, and half a year after the final supply of the plaster casts, J. C. van Eerde, the curator of the Ethnographic Museum of the Colonial Institute, explained to Clarke that the colour of the original stone in which the reliefs were carved

[84] Chulalongkorn, *Itinéraire d'un voyage*, 142–3.

[85] Compare Tsuchiya, 'Javanology and the age of Ranggawarsita'; Pemberton, *On the subject of 'Java'*.

[86] V&A, Registry and Archives (hereafter R&A), MA/1/A520, V&A minute paper, 7 March 1914.

[87] V&A, R&A, MA/1/250, Colonial Institute to Director, V&A, 19 May 1914; Minute papers, Director, V&A, to Stanley Clarke, 29 May 1914.

Figure 2.5 The Indian section, gallery 9 – 'Buddhism' – at the Victoria and Albert Museum, 1937.

'is grey, just like the figures of the ancient Javanese sculptures in the Raffles collection in the British Museum'.[88] Thereby Van Eerde completed the circle: to learn about the original Borobudur, you did not need to go that far if you were in London. You merely had to visit the 'Gallery of Indian Religions' in the British Museum, where two heads of Borobudur Buddha statues, brought to England by Raffles, showed the real colour of Borobudur. The new plaster casts of the Borobudur reliefs, although painted in a different shade of red-grey, gained a similar place in the Victoria and Albert Museum: in the 'Indian Section', in Room 9, dedicated to 'Buddhism', as examples of the peaceful diffusion of Indian Buddhist religion and temple art, to the other regions of Southeast Asia (Figure 2.5). In that story, and in this British context, they illustrated the greatness of the old Indian Buddhist civilisation, and thus contributed to the idea of Greater India, the jewel in the British crown.

[88] V&A, R&A, MA/1/250, Van Eerde to Stanley Clarke, after July 1926.

The Ambiguities of Sites

In light of Mauss' principle of gift and reciprocal obligation as a driving force behind the local, transnational, and global dynamics of heritage formation, the transfer of Borobudur's plaster casts from Amsterdam to London shows us transnational imperial competition at the institutional level, between an old and a young metropolitan tool of imperial propaganda. By the time of this transfer, the V&A (and thus London) performed as the British centre; for that reason, it may have regarded itself as superior.[89] The Colonial Institute in Amsterdam may have seen that differently. That institute represented a small empire that could not afford real sweeping political gestures, only symbolic ones, as in Paris in 1900. But the Colonial Institute could play a dominant role in this transaction as the permanent keeper (and the Dutch government as the owner) of the moulds of the splendid Borobudur that had become of intense interest to so many different parties in Europe, Asia, and beyond.

The interdependency between the Colonial Institute and Mangkunegara VII explains why the Javanese prince could get his Hartguss copy for free (but not the bronze, and he had to pay for the transport costs) but the Victoria and Albert Museum could not. This difference in the exchange value of the Javanese antiquities clarifies what made these transactions colonial, and how they defined the Dutch Empire. The different conditions of these transfers show how Dutch entrepreneurs and colonial officials came to see care for Javanese antiquities as a Dutch ethical responsibility, part of the Ethical Policy that the Dutch government launched around 1900. But they could neither enact nor legitimise this responsibility without the collaboration and antiquarian interests of local Javanese princes or elites that articulated a (historical and moral) liaison to these antiquities as well – like Mangkunegara VII, or Mangkunegara VI in 1896, although this prince may have regarded his gifts to Chulalongkorn as an equal exchange between royal parties.

By exchanging Javanese Buddhist antiquities for Siam-centred Buddhist knowledge, King Chulalongkorn created a new future for the Javanese antiquities as objects of Buddhist culture, royal antiquarian interest, and political legitimisation in Siam. On the other hand, the various local and central parties in Java with whom Chulalongkorn had these antiquarian transactions (the colonial government, the Archaeological Society, local colonial civil servants, and princes), by giving the antiquities to the king, saw themselves as owners. These multiple Javanese and colonial ownerships, and the apparently automatic character of the gifts, also indicate that in colonial Java at the very local level

89 Tim Barringer, 'The South Kensington Museum and the colonial project', in Tim Barringer and Tom Flynn (eds.), *Colonialism and the object: empire, material culture and the museum* (London: Routledge, 1998), 11–28.

the notions of material heritage and of its ownership were at that time very diffuse and not in the least controlled by the colonial state-in-progress.

This ambiguous situation concerning archaeological heritage politics in the Netherlands Indies would partly change with the creation of the Colonial Archaeological Commission, and its successor, the Colonial Archaeological Service, respectively in 1901 and in 1913. By setting the terms and objects of heritage policy in the Netherlands Indies, and by creating the means, this prioritised governmental institution would play a significant role in the development of archaeological research and conservation politics in colonial and post-colonial Indonesia. However, the state legitimising heritage politics never excluded the very local, 'foreign', and global interests. Although self-evident to some, these diverse interests were not necessarily visible at the site. Remarkable archaeological interventions, like the visit of a Siamese Buddhist king, the taking of statues, casts, and plasters, or the restoration of a ruined temple in decay, were needed to make them visible.

The coexistence of different relations to Javanese antiquities as heritage around 1900 was only temporarily and superficially unproblematic. The absence of real competing territorial claims among the powers involved can only partly explain this situation. Moreover, the balance would soon change as a result of the development of Indonesian nationalism. After 1900, a group of Indonesian regionalists and nationalists, becoming further aware of the value of local temple remains for the historical imagination – partly via the World Exhibition, and partly via colonial archaeological knowledge provided in texts, books, maps, and excavations – started to highlight 'their own' past and roots, consciously connecting the greatness of a Hindu past civilisation to a powerful Indonesian national future. As we shall see, these new involvements with Buddhist and Hindu sites in Java and Sumatra occurred simultaneously with Greater Asian interests emanating from India and Japan. The site of the ancient Majapahit empire was, in these many regards, a problematic site, but meaningful to Java long before it became the scene of such modern archaeological interventions.

3 Great Sacred Majapahit: Biographies of a Javanese Site in the Nineteenth Century

> People told me that all objects originated from Modjopahit; that doesn't mean that that is true; for ... it is a common truth that Javanese are inclined to presume that everything old in the west comes from Padjajaran, and in the east from Modjopahit.[1]

On 3 September 1970, a significant gift revealed how much old 'things' mattered to Dutch and Indonesian parties and how they could function to ease a difficult decolonisation process. During a gala dinner at the royal residence, Huis ten Bosch, in The Hague, Queen Juliana of the Netherlands 'returned' to President Soeharto of Indonesia a fourteenth-century Javanese manuscript on palm leaves as 'a gift to the Indonesian people'.[2] The precious object, preserved in a leather etui and tin cover, had been stored in the Leiden University Library since the early twentieth century. It was (then) the only existing copy of the Old Javanese panegyrical poem *Nagarakrtagama* ('The kingdom ordered by holy tradition'), written in 1365 by the Buddhist poet and court official Mpu Prapanca, in honour of King Rajasanagara (Hayam Wuruk) of the eastern Javanese Hindu–Buddhist kingdom of Majapahit. Now more often referred to as *Désawarnana* ('The description of the regions', the title Prapanca used), the poem offered a unique contemporary's view of court life, law, culture, and parts of the realm under Hayam Wuruk's reign (1350–1365), when the Majapahit empire was at its zenith of wealth, territorial scope, and influence. Briefed by philologists in Leiden and diplomats in Jakarta, Queen Juliana and Dutch politicians at the ceremony understood that this object had 'almost sacred meaning to Indonesia'.[3] 'Many Indonesian People', as a Dutch press release

[1] Jan F. G. Brumund, *Bijdragen tot de kennis van het Hindoeïsme op Java*, Verhandelingen van het Bataviaasch Genootschap van Kunsten en Wetenschappen 33 (Batavia: Lange, 1868), 183.

[2] *Nederlandse Staatscourant*, 4 September 1970, nr 170; 9 September 1970, nr 171, as referred to in Ministry of Foreign Affairs to the Embassy in Jakarta, 22 September 1970, NA 2.05.313, Code archive of the Ministry of Foreign Affairs, 1965–1974, inv. nr 2700.

[3] Prime Minister Piet de Jong to F. J. F. M. van Thiel (chair of the Tweede Kamer), 9 July 1969, NA 2.05.188, Archives of the Dutch Embassy in Indonesia, 1962–1974, inv. nr 863.

explained, 'see this old kingdom [Majapahit] as the predecessor of modern Indonesia.'[4] By also fulfilling a personal wish of President Soeharto, the Dutch government made a strong diplomatic gesture, not least because it figured powerfully in both parties' imaginations.

The ceremony at the royal residence in The Hague is one of several dramatic transactions regarding the site of the capital of the Majapahit empire, located in Trowulan in East Java, that are central to this chapter. These transactions have taken place at the site since the early nineteenth century, and concern site-related stories, texts, and objects. They help us to understand the development of the Majapahit site, and *Nagarakrtagama* as a contemporary source depicting its greatness, into the major regalia of the post-colonial state of Indonesia. But the transactions we look at in this chapter, which focuses on the nineteenth century, enacted between individuals and groups from in and beyond (post-) colonial Indonesia and the Netherlands, also reveal other engagements with the site's histories and spirits. They took place, moreover, at several locations, and for reasons that did not necessarily overlap with the interests of professionalising (state) archaeology and national heritage politics. During encounters – at the site or with regard to site-related objects – these individuals and groups exchanged knowledge, sometimes in reciprocal misunderstanding, and always in various, changing hierarchies.

What makes the Majapahit site distinct from others discussed in this book is that it transformed in the twentieth century into a proto-national heritage site of the post-colonial Indonesian state, representing the powerful spirit, scope, and core of a Greater Indonesia, and the site of the inception of Java's conversion to Islam. From there it would develop in the pre-colonial Indonesian nation-state. The special meaning of *Nagarakrtagama* for this site comes from the fact that, in nineteenth-century colonial Java, no direct literary sources concerning the domain and history of the kingdom of Majapahit were known until this text was relocated in 1894, in the context of a colonial war. This was, as we will discuss at more length in the final part of this chapter, when the Dutch government philologist, Jan Laurens Andries Brandes (1857–1905), acknowledged the value during a military expedition to Lombok (1894), and took this fourteenth-century text from the eighteenth-century *kraton* of Cakra Nĕgara. While Balinese nobility had been aware of the manuscript – because of their interest in the old connections between Majapahit and the Balinese royal courts[5] – Brandes'

[4] 'Suatu naskah jang unik diserahkan kepada Indonesia', a one-page typescript of a published text (with a photograph of palm leaves), probably the article in *Nederlandse Staatscourant* (n. 1) describing the gesture as a 'gift', and explaining the meaning for Indonesians, content, form and material of the manuscript; sent together with Indonesian translations of the speeches by the queen and president by the Dutch ambassador in Jakarta to Minister of Foreign Affairs J. Luns, 21 October 1970, NA 2.05.313, Code archive of the Ministry of Foreign Affairs, 1962–1974.

[5] Theodore Pigeaud remarks that this *Nagarakrtagama* manuscript had already drawn the attention of a Balinese reader and that this reader had made notes on the *lontar* (palm-leaf) manuscript,

'rescue operation', as it is still understood among philologists and Javanese historians, was considered a milestone. Only in the 1880s did scholars become more seriously interested and develop tools to read Old Javanese and to study the world it came from. The *Nagarakrtagama,* then, relates in a unique way to the site and the history of its making in the twentieth century. The direct connection – of the site's author and his eyewitness account of the kingdom at the acme of its power – is what gave it so much prestige, to the effect of gaining mythical and sacred proportions of state regalia in Indonesia up to today.[6] To archaeological explorers who aimed to identify and reconstruct the heart of the kingdom of Majapahit, *Nagarakrtagama* became what the *Iliad* was for the site of ancient Greek Troy to Heinrich Schliemann.

We argue that the dynamics of knowledge production about – and heritage formation of – Majapahit were multifarious, and started much earlier than is usually considered.[7] 'Majapahit', as relating to a once major kingdom that ruled over Java in a faraway past, was part of popular memory on Java and Bali, and of local politics of history and legitimation, before any foreign interest in the ruins of this site was triggered; and the interests in the site were further stimulated partly because of these retraceable local histories.[8] As with other sites, local informants mattered: visitors to Majapahit's ruins in eastern Java who came from outside the region, whether they were foreign or Javanese, never gained further epistemological access to the site of Majapahit without the assistance and information provided by the local (European and Javanese) administration or by local village heads.[9] To make sense of what they saw,

next to passages concerning the island of Bali and the description of a court festival in Majapahit; see Theodore G. Th. Pigeaud, *Java in the fourteenth century: a study in cultural history. The Nāgara-Kĕrtāgama by Rakawi, Prapañca of Majapahit, 1365 AD, vol. I, Javanese texts in transcription*, Translation series, Koninklijk Instituut voor Taal-, Land- en Volkenkunde 4:1 (The Hague: Nijhoff, 1960), xi–xii.

6 For this it does not matter that the text itself was an old copy of the original. This copy, after the defeat of the Majapahit empire, must have travelled to Lombok along with some of the remaining royal elites. See Stuart O. Robson, *Deśawarnana (Nāgarakrtāgama), by Mpu prapañca*, transl. from the Javanese, Verhandelingen van het Koninklijk Instituut voor Taal-, Land- en Volkenkunde 169 (Leiden: KITLV Press, 1995).

7 See especially Anthony Reid and David Marr (eds.), *Perceptions of the past in Southeast Asia* (Singapore: Heinemann, 1979); Jacques Leclerc, 'Sentiment national et revendication territorial en Indonésie', *La Pensée* 169 (1973), 57–69; Jacques Leclerc, 'La circonscription: remarques sur l'idéologie du territoire nationale en Indonésie', *Culture et Développement* 7:2 (1975), 283–317, republished in Françoise Cayrac-Blanchard, Stéphane Dovert, and Frédéric Durand (eds.), *Indonésie: un demi-siècle de construction nationale* (Paris: Harmattan, 2000), 15–48; Michael Wood, *Official history in modern Indonesia: New Order perceptions and counterviews* (Leiden: Brill, 2005).

8 S. Supomo, 'The image of Majapahit in later Javanese and Indonesian writing', in Reid and Marr (eds.), *Perceptions of the past*, 171–185; Ricklefs, *Polarising Javanese society*, 109; Gomperts, Haag and Carey, 'Mapping Majapahit'; Amrit Gomperts, Arnoud Haag and Peter Carey, 'The sage who divided Java in 1052: Maclaine Pont's excavation of Mpu Bharada's hermitage-cemetery at Lĕmah Tulis in 1925', *BKI* 168:1 (2012), 1–25.

9 For the relevant shift in historiography concerning colonial knowledge production, translators, and informants in the Netherlands Indies and India, we refer to our Chapter 1, n. 24.

visitors to the Majapahit site collected – whether systematically or not – local lore or 'tjerita' (*cerita,* stories) as Buddingh called them in 1867.[10] Their descriptions, biased and prejudiced as they may be, thus provide insight into the ways various individuals, of local, Dutch colonial, or foreign origin, engaged with the site and with particular site-based objects within various and changing hierarchies. In keeping with Mauss, they also show that site-related transactions (like the gathering of knowledge and objects) served to create new loyalties, gain status, or strengthen existing ties.

It is remarkable that these various queries, and engagements with the site coexisted, converged, (mis)communicated, or interacted for quite a long time without insurmountable problems. Certainly, the Majapahit site had complications: since the nineteenth century, stories about the fall of the Hindu–Buddhist Majapahit empire and the ruinous state of its remains have shaped historical interpretations of Java's early conversion to Islam. Relevant to the queries for historical knowledge at the site were the ancient Islamic graves, like the Muslim grave of Putri Campa (one of several in Indonesia) cared for by Islamic guards in Trowulan or the graves at nearby Troloyo, and attracting pilgrims.[11] Was the conversion to Islam violent or peaceful, was Islam native or foreign to Java, and how did it relate to the material remains of the Hindu–Buddhist past? Local histories (like those provided by the *babad*) and scholarly interpretations conflicted.[12] In that regard, the site was probably as problematic and open for contestation in the nineteenth century as it would be in the twentieth. To what extent did state-supported archaeology and heritage formation, regime change, and decolonisation affect the ongoing local and external engagements with this site? What powers were ascribed to the site by institutions and individuals from outside and inside the area to include or exclude others? Let us look at the biographies of this site as it transformed into an official heritage site. Starting

10 Buddingh, *Neêrlands-Oost-Indië; Reizen*, 2nd edn.

11 Louis Charles Damais was the first to suggest that these pointed to the existence of a Muslim community within the Majapahit empire; see Louis Charles Damais, 'Etudes javanaises VII: les tombes musulmanes datées de Tralaya', *Bulletin de l'École française d'Extrême-Orient* (hereafter *BEFEO*) 48:2 (1957), 353–416. Compare with M. C. Ricklefs, *Mystic synthesis in Java: a history of Islamization from the fourteenth to the early nineteenth century* (Norwalk: East Bridge, 2006), 11–15.

12 On conflicting versions of the *Babad Tanah Djawi,* see Merle Ricklefs, 'A consideration of three versions of the "Babad tanah Djawi", with experts on the fall of Madjapahit', *Bulletin of the School of Oriental and African Studies, University of London* 35:2 (1972), 285–315. As pointed out therein by Ricklefs (p. 286), H. J. de Graaf and Th. Pigeaud were among the first Dutch historians/Javanologists who tried to see that period of early Islamisation on its own merit, and not, like Krom, as 'the decline and fall' of the great Hindu–Buddhist epoch. See H. J. de Graaf and Theodore G. Th. Pigeaud, *De eerste moslimse vorstendommen op Java: studiën over de staatkundige geschiedenis van de 15de en 16de eeuw* ('s-Gravenhage: Nijhoff, 1974); Theodore G. Th. Pigeaud, *Islamic states in Java 1500–1700: eight Dutch books and articles by H. J. de Graaf*, Verhandelingen van het Koninklijk Instituut voor Taal-, Landen Volkenkunde 70 (The Hague: Nijhoff, 1976).

from the site as it is today, we will return to focus on the multiple locations and makings of this particular Majapahit site in the nineteenth century; in Chapter 4, we continue the analysis of its transformation in the twentieth century.

A Multi-sited Site of Memory: Local Stories, Loss, and Loyalties

Nagarakrtagama relates in a unique way to the court of Majapahit, the polity that ruled over Java in the thirteenth and fourteenth centuries. Located near Trowulan (about 90 minutes' drive south of Surabaya), the site stretches over an area of about 90 square kilometres and centres around a museum dating from colonial times but rebuilt, reorganised, and renamed several times since the 1980s. Following a recent excavation scandal (that involved government-supported parties), the museum is now called the Majapahit museum. Scattered over the area are ruined remains relating to the kingdom's royal compounds – including a gate (Gapura Wringin Lawang) and a large tank (*Kolam Segaran*) – and religious domains, like the sacred graves, supposedly dating from the beginning and the end of the Majapahit empire, and several ruined temples. Apart from the graves, which have been sites of pilgrimage throughout the nineteenth century, most of these remains were excavated, cleaned, restored and/or partly reconstructed in the first decades of the twentieth century.

During the New Order regime of President Soeharto (1967–1998), a boost of new archaeological research took place, partly funded by the Ford Foundation. The work included the field school in 'settlement archaeology', under the direction of the Athens- and US-trained Indonesian archaeologist Mundardjito, and then Indonesia-based American archaeologist John Miksic, who was trained at Cornell University.[13] In the aftermath of the prestigious Save Borobudur campaign within the framework of UNESCO, restorations and reconstructions were carried out between 1990 and 1998, under the Department of Education and Culture's Heritage Directorate, led by the Balinese archaeologist I Gusti Ngurah Anom.[14] In addition, there is the remarkable Pendopo Agung, an open hall

[13] In 1991 the Indonesian Field School of Archaeology (IFSA) was founded by the Pusat Penelitian Arkeologi Nasional, with support of the Ford Foundation. This school collaborated with archaeologists from the Balai Arkeologi and Universitas Gadjah Mada in Yogyakarta and from Universitas Indonesia in Jakarta, and with guest teachers (young archaeologists from all over Indonesia). The site of Trowulan became their working field and training site: interview, Marieke Bloembergen with Mundardjito, Jakarta, 25 June 2012. See also John N. Miksic, 'Survei permukaan Trowulan dalam rangka IFSA, Juni 1991/Recent research at Trowulan: implications for early urbanizations in Indonesia', in Hasan Muarif Ambary, et al. (eds.), *Pertemuan Ilmiah Arkeologi* (Jakarta: Pusat Penelitian Arkeologi Nasional, 1994), 357–367.

[14] I Gusti Ngurah Anom (1943–) learned the techniques of reconstruction, as developed by Vincent van Romondt, who directed the reconstruction of the Siva temple in the 1930s and early 1950s (see Chapter 5). Anom found his informants – former 'stone seekers' during the

construction, initiated and built by East Java's Army Division Brawijaya (named after Majapahit's last king), which we discuss in the Epilogue. It was inaugurated shortly after the coming to power of Soeharto that followed the pre-empted coup of 30 September 1965, and the subsequent anti-communist repression and massacres of (alleged) communists.[15] For historical reasons, but also telling for the importance of this area in the framework of state-centred heritage politics, the regional conservation department for East Java, the Balai Pelestarian Peninggalan Purbakala (BP3), is located in Trowulan, not (the provincial capital) Surabaya.[16]

Although archaeologists and formal heritage politics had not designated the Trowulan area a site in the early nineteenth century, it nevertheless existed on multiple mental (historical, moral, and spiritual) maps due to its Hindu–Buddhist material remains. In fact, it was identified as the core of the Majapahit empire; its existence and former power were undisputed. As for the history of the fall of this empire, the 'classical' Javanese tradition and circulating stories also explained the presence of Hindu–Buddhist temple ruins, and the rise of Islam. Based on various written Javanese traditions, the historian Merle C. Ricklefs has summarised the story of Brawijaya, the last king of Majapahit, and his descendants, as follows. As a Buda (the Javanese word referring to Hindu–Buddhist), Brawijaya married a Muslim Chinese princess (to which the above-mentioned grave of the princess of Campa refers), whom he sent away to Sumatra. Their son Raden Patah, born and raised as a Muslim in Palembang, returned to his father in Java. The king recognised his son, and gave him the land that was later to be known as Demak, the first Islamic state in Java. Raden Patah would rule over Demak, as its first sultan. In 1487–1489 he gathered a coalition of the Islamic states located in the north-east of Java, and with them raided and conquered Majapahit, bringing this empire to an

colonial times – when he worked at the regional archaeological service in Prambanan in the 1960s: interview, Marieke Bloembergen with I Gusti Ngurah Anom, Saba, 8 June 2012. See also Sumijati Atmosudiro, *Bandung Bandawas di masa kini; Kisah Balik Megahnya hasil pemugaran Benda Cagar Budaya* (Klaten, Plaosan: BP3 Wilayah Jawa Tenggah; Kementeri Kebudayaan dan Parawisata, 2003).

15 Wood, *Official history in modern Indonesia.*

16 Majapahit also remains an extremely important site for Indonesia's political elites, as shown by the new activities in the area by Hashim Djojohadikusumo – brother of the presidential candidate Prabowo – who has set up a Majapahit Society (Mandala Majapahit), and invests in archaeological research: *Tempo.co*, 14 June 2014. See https://nasional.tempo.co/read/584988/hashim-djojohadikusumo-dirikan-mandala-majapahit (accessed 5 August 2019); and *detikNews*, 5 December 2014, 'Bangun Mandala majapahit di UGM, Hashim: Keluarga kami keturunan Majapahit', https://news.detik.com/berita/d-2769011/bangun-mandala-majapahit-di-ugm-hashim-keluarga-kami-keturunan-majapahit (accessed 22 May 2017). The regional government, moreover, is said to invest in the reconstruction of houses of the Majapahit era: 'Ratusan rumah akand jadi kampong Majapahit', *Tempo*, 21 January 2014. See www.tempo.co/read/news/2014/01/22/058547182/Ratusan-Rumah-Akan-Jadi-Kampung-Majapahit- (accessed 9 May 2017).

end.[17] In the meantime, what remained of Majapahit royal rule was being continued in Bali, by Hayam Wuruk's marshal Gajah Mada's conquest of 1343; and by the exile of royal elites to Bali when the Majapahit empire fell in decay after Raden Patah's conquest, bringing along some of the empire's chronicles – including *Nagarakrtagama*.[18]

Javanese court chronicles or *babad* (literally meaning 'clearing' or 'purifying'), compiled centuries after the fall of Majapahit, entailed efforts to relate the genealogy of the Islamic kingdoms – that after the fall of Majapahit (in 1478 or 1527) ruled over (parts of) Java – to Majapahit's last powerful king, Brawijaya. These kingdoms developed from Majapahit's successor, the kingdom of Demak, to the rulers of Mataram in the last quarter of the sixteenth century. These *babad*, as well as some of the *pusaka* like old *kris* (daggers) kept in custody of the *kraton* in Solo and Yogyakarta, and supposedly dating from Majapahit times, legitimised subsequent kingdoms on the grounds of continuity and hereditary succession.[19] In response to Raffles' and Mackenzie's enquiries, the *babad* were partly transcribed and translated, further studied, and, in the course of the nineteenth century, disseminated via new (Javanese, Malay, and Dutch) journals and scholarly publications.

These stories of legitimation belonging to the domain of elites, princes, and *priyayi* circulated further, as *babad* were sung to an extended audience, and later, in the twentieth century, popularised in *ketoprak* (folk drama) performances.[20] The *pusaka* said to originate from Majapahit, kept in the *kraton* of the princely courts in Central Java, also reached wider audiences. They were used for ceremonial processions, which drew a wider public, and which confirmed the continuity of royal power – both to Javanese subjects and, importantly after the Java War, to the colonial administration. Thus, the Dutch antiquarian C. J. van der Vlis observed in Solo in 1840 how certain Majapahit

[17] Ricklefs, *Polarising Javanese society*, 177–178. See also Ricklefs, '"Babad tanah Djawi"'.

[18] Robson, *Deśawarnana (Nāgarakrtāgama) by Mpu Prapañca*, 4.

[19] On these legitimising meanings of the *babad*, see B. J. O. Schrieke, 'Breuk en continuïteit in de Javaanse geschiedschrijving', in *Gedenkboek uitgegeven ter gelegenheid van het vijf en twintig jarig bestaan van het rechtswetenschappelijk hoger onderwijs in Indonesië op 28 oktober 1948* (Groningen: Wolters, 1949); Supomo, 'The image of Majapahit', 174–175. On the *babad* and the fall of Majapahit, see Ricklefs, '"Babad tanah Djawi"'; on the Majapahit *kris* in Solo, see Diary, Van der Vlis, June 1841, Leiden University Library, Special Collections, KITLV Collections, Collection van der Vlis, inv. DH 341, 'Dagboek gehouden te Soerakarta, 1840–1842'.

[20] Florida, *Writing the past, inscribing the future*, 10–17. On performative traditions of Javanese texts, see Bernhard Arps, *Tembang in two traditions: performance and interpretation of Javanese literature* (London: School of Oriental and African Studies, 1992); Supomo, 'The image of Majapahit', 181, speaks in general terms about the popularising of Majapahit from the *babad* until the popular performance tradition *ketoprak*, a creation of Solonese court officials in the early twentieth century. On the popularising of Majapahit in twentieth-century performing arts, see Matthew Cohen, *Inventing the performing arts: modernity and tradition in colonial Indonesia* (Honolulu: University of Hawai'í Press, 2016), 163–166.

pusaka (an old *kris* and a spear) kept at the *kraton* of Susuhunan Pakubuwono VII of Solo, were honoured in public. The objects were deeply worshipped, treated to weekly offerings of rice and related dishes (every Friday), and not to be touched without a respectful *sembah* (polite greeting with slight bow, and closed hands held before the head). The *susuhunan* carried them with great ceremony during his official audiences with the Resident, and on the occasion of accession;[21] the *pusaka* also came out in public during traditional Javanese feasts, such as the Garebeg Maloed Dal (celebrating the birthday of the Prophet Muhammad). The court of the sultanate in Yogyakarta likewise had Majapahit *pusaka*, two spears, which were used for comparable occasions. According to *babad* traditions, as later scholars found out, the most important spear, called Kjahi Agĕng Plèrèd, was made from a sacred *kris*, named the 'bradjah seng-koeh', and believed to be the penis transformed into metal of Sèh Moelånå Maribi, a noble man (*wong tåpå*) from the times of Majapahit, who accordingly had played a role in the rise of the Mataram dynasty. Thus the spear symbolised the connection between Mataram and Majapahit, as well as the power and (male) potency of the once unified Javanese empire. This was emphasised by the high honour the sultan expressed to this spear. When he carried it in public it was always shaded by the *songsong gilap* (the golden parasol), an honour allowed only to kings of the same or higher rank.[22]

As the Majapahit empire had exercised political, economic, and religious influence all over Java, scholars have counted at least 242 religious domains relating to the empire across the Javanese countryside.[23] Thus, in the early nineteenth century, not only in Trowulan but also far away in Central Java, local informants (the village head) would connect specific statues to histories of (wars with) Majapahit – as Van der Vlis discovered in a village near Solo in 1841. Van der Vlis encountered a huge stone statue of a squatting man, in the village of Kloeroehang, near Tawang Mangoe. It held, on the left, with its right hand, weapons, while the left hand rested on the man's chest. From the description given to him, Van der Vlis understood this was a temple guard.[24]

[21] Diary, Van der Vlis, 10 May 1841, Leiden University Library, Special Collections, KITLV Collections, Collection van der Vlis, inv. DH 341, 'Dagboek gehouden te Soerakarta, 1840–1842'.

[22] W. F. Stutterheim, *De kraton van Majapahit*, Verhandelingen van het Koninklijk Instituut voor de Taal-, Land- en Volkenkunde van Nederlandsch-Indië 7 ('s-Gravenhage: Nijhoff, 1948), 33–34; J. Groneman, *De Garĕbĕg te Ngajogyåkartå* ('s-Gravenhage: Nijhoff, 1895).

[23] Robert W. Hefner, *Hindu Javanese: Tengger tradition and Islam* (Princeton: Princeton University Press, 1985), 27; Theodore G. Th. Pigeaud, *Java in the fourteenth century: a study in cultural history. The Nāgara-Kĕrtāgama by Rakawi, Prapañca of Majapahit, 1365 AD, IV, Commentaries and recapitulation*, Translation series / Koninklijk Instituut voor Taal-, Land- en Volkenkunde 4:4 (The Hague: Nijhoff, 1962), 479.

[24] Diary, Van der Vlis, June 1841, Leiden University Library, Special Collections, KITLV Collections, Collection van der Vlis, inv. DH 341, 'Dagboek gehouden te Soerakarta, 1840–1842'.

These scattered objects and their stories must have contributed to the widespread fame of the power of Majapahit, and the location of its throne in East Java. Raffles, who saw the Majapahit site in 1815, tellingly referred to it as 'the pride of Java' (and nonetheless probably took a statue).[25]

Early 'Foreign' Interventions: Truth or There

The first signs of more structural foreign interest in the Majapahit site relate to the British invasion and subsequent British regime, where knowledge gathering, in the context of violent overtaking of power, became part of the new colonial empire's interest in centralising revenue, rule, and enlightened scholarly and political overview.[26] Both Dutch and British imperial interests make it possible to trace early nineteenth-century local engagements with the site. It was in the British Empire's framework, when Raffles, after receiving some preliminary reports, in 1815 sent the Eurasian captain engineer J. W. B. Wardenaar (1785–1869) to eastern Java, to depict, draw, and map the site of Majapahit. Wardenaar's visit represents one meaningful intervention within the above-mentioned existing engagements with the site, from which we can start following the dynamics of knowledge production, exchange and (re)signification between local forms of knowledge and foreign queries.[27]

In 2012 the Javanologists and archaeologists Amrith Gomperts, Arnoud Haag, and Peter Carey emphasised the importance of Wardenaar's findings, presented in a report and a map, for today's archaeology in Trowulan. Wardenaar's findings, they argue, showed the truth – or his map pointed to geometrical 'faithfulness' and 'accuracy', and his report with its details on the various ruins on the site reflected 'reliability' for further archaeological research.[28] Here we are not so much interested in 'truth' but, following Mauss, in the exchanges of forms of knowledge between foreign and local interpretations of the site, taking place 'there' at the site; and in the kind of loyalties and interdependencies resulting from those exchanges. Following our

25 Raffles, *The History of Java*, II, 54–55: 'I observed near the former site of *Majapáhit* two images of *Ganésa*, and some other mutilated deities of the Hindu mythology. Near the tank was the figure represented in one of the plates, partly human and partly of the form of a bird.' See illustration ibid., 45.

26 Hoock, *Empires of the imagination*, 324.

27 On Wardenaar's work at and on Majapahit, see Gomperts, Haag and Carey, 'Mapping Majapahit'.

28 Ibid., 179 and 192. Although these three authors likewise concentrated on nineteenth-century local oral traditions, partly retraceable via these foreign visitors' reports, their aim is to show that, with the help of Wardenaar's map and notes and the GPS techniques now available, it is possible to locate Majapahit's *kraton* and the infrastructure of the kingdom. See also Amrith Gomperts, Arnoud Haag and Peter Carey, 'Stutterheim's enigma: the mystery of his mapping of the Majapahit kraton at Trowulan in 1941', *BKI* 164:4 (2008), 411–430; Gomperts, Haag and Carey, 'The sage who divided Majapahit in 1052'.

site-centred approach, and through alternative reading of site-related objects and sources, we focus on (what is being said about) contemporary uses and meaning giving to these sites, by local inhabitants and (European and Javanese) visitors from outside. In that way we can see how 'Majapahit' located complex, multi-layered and multi-centred political, moral, scholarly, and spiritual engagements, which gave this site its own dynamics.

As Ricklefs has explained, foreigners visiting the Majapahit site in the early nineteenth century noticed that, to local inhabitants, the area was full of historical significance. Certain material remains that today are key to the Majapahit site near Trowulan, were guarded by priests, received offerings (incense and flowers), or generated fear because of a belief in their supernatural potency.[29] Based on nineteenth-century site observations of what he coined Hindu–Javanese 'art', Krom concluded that 'People on location remained aware that here and nowhere else once was [the glorious kingdom of] Majapahit.'[30] Moreover, it seems that excavation at the site did not start with European interventions, as the British lieutenant H. G. Jourdan would notice in 1813.

Jourdan, appointed by Raffles as Resident of Djapan (today's Mojokerto) and Wirosobo in East Java, was probably the first person representing the British interregnum to visit the site of Majapahit, as Gomperts, Haag, and Carey have pointed out. This was when he, within the British Empire's overall programme of knowledge gathering (among other purposes, for revenue collecting), had to survey the area in April 1813 – months before the British troops took Surabaya (in August 1813). He noted the location and ruined site of 'Majapahit, the ancient capital of the eastern empire', immediately realising a heroic task for the British: 'the site is now overrun with a thick bamboo jungle and few traces of this once extensive city are now to be discovered'.[31] But he also observed that 'idols, which prove that the art of sculpture had attained some degree of perfection, have been dug up at different times near the spot. The natives retain a kind of superstitious reverence for these relics, which they are unable to explain but do not attempt to conceal. They regard the idols as representations of evil genies whose favour it is necessary to conciliate.'[32]

[29] See Ricklefs, *Polarising Javanese society,* 109. Lunsingh Scheurleer gives more examples of the 'topical' meaning of sacred-site-related objects in Java and Javanese popular uses of these objects during the nineteenth century. She relates this to *agama kejawen* (literally, Javanese religion or a syncretic Islamic belief system which integrates older Hindu–Buddhist and animistic practices believed to be typically Javanese). See Lunsingh Scheurleer, 'Collecting Javanese antiquities', 77–84.

[30] Nicolaas J. Krom, *Inleiding tot de Hindoe-Javaansche kunst* ('s-Gravenhage: Nijhoff, 1923), II, 175.

[31] Quoted in Gomperts, Haag, and Carey, 'Mapping Majapahit', 178; Hoock, *Empires of the imagination*, 315–349.

[32] Quoted in Gomperts, Haag, and Carey, 'Mapping Majapahit', 178; from Lt H. G. Jourdan, manuscript, 'Report on Djapan and Wirosobo', 28 April 1813, British Library, London, India Office Library & Records, Mackenzie Private collection 21, pt 10, p. 355.

Such observations through the eyes of foreign visitors about practices of digging up statues and the religious care of graves make clear that the Majapahit site was not just a ruin. To local inhabitants the place was full of spirits to be respected, and Islamic graves to be worshipped (*keramat*), and thus to them the site was very much alive, with various interconnected religious dimensions.

Interestingly, the early foreign (or non-local) visitors in search of historical knowledge had already followed the track, and the key markers of the site – the Gapura Wringing Lawang (the gate), the Kolam Seragan (the large tank), and the sacred graves – that today still feature as such in Trowulan, in the BP3's guidebooks, in the local museum, and at the site. Visitors used these markers to envision the size, reach, and outlook of the original site. Yet, while the twentieth-century visitors – scholars and Indonesian nationalists alike – seemed to develop a keen interest in the rise and growth of this empire, nineteenth-century visitors were predominantly inspired by the theme of decay.

The site expeditions under Raffles, which included Jourdan's visit, the circulating questionnaires by Mackenzie already discussed, and the visit by the military engineer Wardenaar in 1815, may have helped to disseminate detailed knowledge about the site's infrastructure, and thereby its canonisation.[33] In August 1815, Raffles ordered Wardenaar to survey the antiquities of Majapahit, and draw the above-mentioned map of the area marking key structures and adding notes that together identified various objects scattered in the teak woods around Trowulan. Javanese being Wardenaar's mother-language, he must have gathered very detailed information for this map from the local population.[34] This detailed map, now recognised as very accurate by specialists, did not gain a place in Raffles' *History of Java*, nor did Raffles make much use of Wardenaar's drawings. Wardenaar, however, kept a simpler map and drawings as well at his home in Surabaya. He maintained a lively interest in the area's antiquities after working as a land-revenue collector in the area for the Dutch colonial administration after the British retreat. Vicar-cum-antiquarians Wolter Robert van Höevell in the late 1840s and Jan Frederic Gerrit Brumund in the early 1850s registered and admired a number of Majapahit objects in Wardenaar's estate.[35]

[33] Alternatively, according to Gomperts, Haag, and Carey, in 'Mapping Majapahit', Wardenaar's work is important because he may actually have located the remains of the *kraton* of Majapahit.

[34] Ibid.

[35] See Van Hoëvell, *Reis over Java, Madura en Bali*, Part I, 209. See also J. F. G. Brumund, 'Iets over steenen voorwerpen van verschillend gebruik uit den Hindoe-tijd op Java gevonden', in *Indiana: verzameling van stukken van onderscheidenen aard, over landen, volken, oudheden en geschiedenis van den Indischen archipel*, 2nd part (Amsterdam: P. N. van Kampen, 1854), 111.

Wardenaar was an important informant for some British and later Dutch officials and antiquarians (such as Brumund and the painter Sieburgh), who were interested in the area or antiquities in general or in Majapahit in particular. Among those visitors was also Van Hoëvell, by then chair of the Batavian Society, who used some of Wardenaar's drawings in the publication of his travels. After Wardenaar died, in 1879, his son donated the map and notes to the Batavian Society where, despite the society's growing interest in antiquities, Wardenaar's documents were temporarily lost. A decade later Brandes, the linguist and secretary of the board of the Batavian Society, found them sewn into the minutes of the society. The geologist R. D. M. (Rogier) Verbeek later noted that Wardenaar's map was 'the oldest document we have on Majapahit's capital'.[36]

Wardenaar's map, notes, and memory may have thus provided an important framework for those nineteenth-century foreign visitors who needed orientation at the site and for the further canonisation of the site (Figure 3.1). As a transmitter, Wardenaar exemplifies how archaeological knowledge was useful for the creation of new bonds of loyalty, status, and interdependency under changing regimes. With a Javanese mother and knowledge of the local language, Wardenaar had easier direct access to local knowledge traditions than the British visitors or Van Höevell, and contributed to scholarly knowledge networks supported by the Batavian Society under the British and Dutch colonial regimes.

Joko Dolok: a Legitimising Journey

Most of the objects Wardenaar listed and mapped in 1815 are main attractions at the Majapahit site in Trowulan today. Soon after Wardenaar's visit, however, a remarkable one disappeared from the site and showed up in Surabaya: a colossal Buddhist statue, commonly known as 'Joko Dolok' (fat guy). It has a Sanskrit inscription on its base, and is now recognised by scholars as portraying a Buddhist monk, possibly King Krtanagara, the last ruler of the East Javanese Singasari kingdom (thirteenth century) that preceded Majapahit.[37] The question of how this statue was transported, from where,

[36] R. D. M. Verbeek, 'De Oudheden van Madjapahit in 1815 en in 1887, met een kaartje', *Tijdschrift voor Indische Taal-, Land- en Volkenkunde* 33 (1890), 14. Raffles' copy of the map, as Gomperts, Haag, and Carey, 'Mapping Majapahit', discovered, can be found in the Drake collection of the British Museum, registration nr 1939.0311, Inventory number: 0.5.36. Mrs J. H. Drake was a great-great-niece of Thomas Stanford Raffles.

[37] Different stories have been compiled on the meaning of the name Joko Dolok. Compare Natasha Reichle, *Violence and serenity: late Buddhist sculpture from Indonesia* (Honolulu: University of Hawai'i Press, 2007), 23–49; Gomperts, Haag, and Carey, 'Mapping Majapahit', 187–188. See also A. C. Broeshart, J. R. van Diessen and R. G. Gill, *Surabaya: beeld van een stad* (Purmerend: Asia Maior, 1997), 12: 'literally fat guy'. There the authors suggest that there

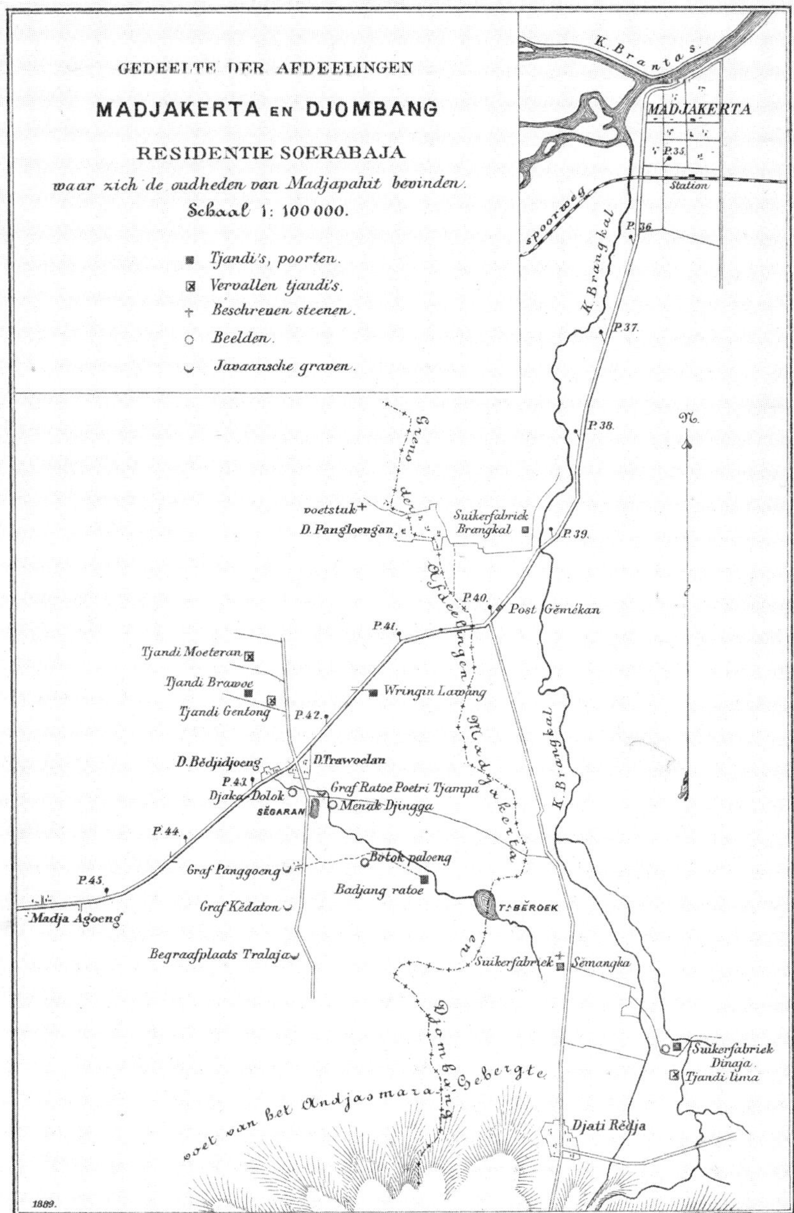

Figure 3.1 Plan of Majapahit's antiquities in 1887, by R. D. M. Verbeek (1887), working from a plan of 1810–1815 by W. Wardenaar.

and under what circumstances had been the object of incidental queries in the nineteenth century. But these queries did not lead to Joko Dolok's return to Trowulan, and today spiritual seekers visit it in a small park in Surabaya, Taman Apsari. What the nineteenth-century queries about the statue's provenance do show, however, is how knowledge (maps, travelling objects, etc) could serve to create or deepen loyalties and to strengthen status and authority under new regimes in many ways.

Only two years after Wardenaar depicted Joko Dolok at the site and after the British regime had departed the then new Dutch Resident of Surabaya, A. M. T. de Salis (1786–1834), ordered the immense statue moved from the Majapahit site to the *alun alun* in front of the Residency in Surabaya. This furthered local elite interest. Little is known (or reported) about the circumstances and motives of the removal and transport of this statue. There has been some discussion about the precise location from where the statue was taken, but today archaeologists believe they know its place of origin.[38] The stories that circulated at the time are revealing. When the painter Sieburgh visited East Java in 1836 and drew the ruin of Candi Rimbi in Jombang, a village head averred that during his youth he had helped to carry the statue from one of this candi's niches. Sieburgh remained sceptical: he found Joko Dolok far too big to fit in either of Candi Rimbi's niches.[39] The *regent* of Surabaya, Pandji Tjogro Negro, learned that Joko Dolok had been removed from the Majapahit site 'from Kendang-Gadjah to the south of the old city Madjapahit' when the Batavian Society sought the statue for its museum.[40]

As for the motives of Resident de Salis' intervention in 1817, we speculate that the transport may primarily have served a new Dutch colonial (or the restoration of an old) regime that sought improved public standing by displaying care for local archaeological heritage.[41] Whether true or not, about half

has probably been a mixing up of sounds, in which case earlier people referred to the sculpture as Djogo Dolok. This means something like 'guardian of trees'. In the latter book there is a picture of the statue without a roof.

38 Verbeek, 'De Oudheden van Madjapahit', 12. On the basis of notes from Wardenaar, Gomperts, Haag, and Carey, 'Mapping Majapahit', 187–188, have reconstructed that before 1817 the Joko Dolok statue must have been located a bit further to the north: near Trowulan, at a cemetery (dating from before Majapahit) called Lemah Tulis. It was there, when he was mapping the site, that Wardenaar encountered the statue and noted that some bases for wooden pillars gave reason to think that 'once here was a house or a small temple'.

39 Brandes followed the Candi Rimbang interpretation, but later, on the basis of Verbeek's findings, corrected this. See Sieburgh, *Beschrijving van Brahmansche Oudheden op het eiland Java*, boek 1. See also De Bruijn, *H. N. Sieburgh*, 163–165.

40 *Regent* of Surabaya, 9 September 1872, to the Resident of Surabaya, quoted in *Rapport van de commissie in Nederlandsch-Indië voor oudheidkundig onderzoek op Java en Madoera of 1907* (Batavia: Albrecht & Co.; 's-Gravenhage: M. Nijhoff, 1909) (hereafter *ROC* followed by year), 205.

41 See also Bloembergen and Eickhoff, 'A wind of change on Java's ruined temples', *BMGN* 128:1 (2013), 81–104.

a century later when the Batavian Society tried to obtain the statue for its museum, Resident van Deventer refused, noting the local uses of the statue, and cited a letter from the *regent* of Surabaya, which was read (translated into Dutch) aloud in the society's meeting of 19 November 1872.[42] Based on this report submitted by the *regent*, Resident van Deventer concurred: 'If the statue Djoko Dolok were to be carried away from the place where it stands today, it would certainly generate suffering and sorrow amongst the population, who would have nothing left to bring honour to, when needed.'[43] This would not be the last case in which a European civil servant would use local (in this case Javanese and Chinese popular) interests to oppose certain state-centred forms (in this case Batavia-centred) of heritage politics. The board of the Batavian Society decided to leave Joko Dolok in Taman Apsari, surrounded by other Hindu and Buddhist antiquities, where it still plays a modest role in local Buddhist and syncretic veneration and meditation practices, and attracts Indonesian and international tourists – and links Surabaya to the Majapahit site near Trowulan.

1850s–1890s: Site of Loss, Decay, and New Legitimations. Whose Moral Debt?

In 1847, during the journey in which Van Hoëvell visited Demak, he also toured the ruins of Majapahit, where he became overwhelmed by a sense of loss, decay, and Dutch moral obligation. The *regent* of Mojokerto, Toemenggoeng Tjondronegoro, and his son – appointed *patih* – were his companions during this trip.[44] Reflecting romantic and self-legitimising motives, some European visitors to the Majapahit ruins appreciated the artfulness in its baked brick architecture, reliefs, and statues, thereby promoting the site in wider circles and in new ways. Others saw the crumbling state of the material remains of that once great empire as the destructive outcome of Asiatic despotism and subsequent forces of Islamisation in Java, presumed to spoil local taste and arts.

Such views of decay, decline, and degeneration led to arguments legitimising the ethical colonial rulers-successors and calling on the Dutch colonial state's obligation of archaeological care. Moreover, the remains of Majapahit, though in far worse shape than Borobudur, more clearly invoked a former majestic

42 *Regent* of Surabaya, 9 September 1872 to Resident of Surabaya, quoted in *ROC 1907* (1909), 205; and *Notulen van de Algemeene en Bestuursvergaderingen van het Bataviaasch Genootschap van Kunsten en Wetenschappen*, XI (1873), 143.

43 Resident of Surabaya to Batavian Society, 3 October 1872, in *Notulen van de Algemeene en Bestuursvergaderingen van het Bataviaasch Genootschap van Kunsten en Wetenschappen*, XI (1873), 144.

44 List of *regenten* of Mojokerto, compiled by the late *regent* R. Kromo Djojo Adinegoro (1894–1916), in a letter to assistant resident R. A. Kern, 12 December 1919, Leiden University Library, Special Collections, KITLV Collections, Archive R. A. Kern, KITLV H 797, inv. nr 70.

city-state, and perhaps therefore also appealed to foreign visitors' notions of continuity. However, while Asiatic despotism, anti-Islamic sentiments, and Gibbonesque ethical and moral pondering on regime change, or the fall of empires and rise of new ones, may all seem typical of the nineteenth century's Western-centred topoi, the anti-Islamic motive in the appreciation of the Majapahit site and the fall of Majapahit was not restricted to prejudiced European visitors. By the late nineteenth century, a movement against modernist, purifying forms of Islam developing in Java would also play a role in some Javanese elite's appreciations of the site and of the histories of its fall.[45]

But there were also other local engagements with the site, ones that resembled foreign visitors' sense of loss. One such example involved the *regent* of Mojokerto, the above-mentioned Tjondronegoro, who proudly guided Van Hoëvell around the site. The stories the *regent* provided give clues to wider interests in the Majapahit site and its history. We follow this tour, which suggests the site's canonised components in the mid nineteenth century.

To put interest in the Majapahit site in further context: by the mid nineteenth century, two factors stimulated 'foreign', colonial, and local interests in the material remains of Majapahit 'in situ'. First, this was a period when scholarly and preservationist concerns about Java's antiquities (and ancient texts) grew, which, naturally, was also observed by local elites.[46] Dutch and colonial institutes pursued systematic knowledge of and care for Java's antiquities and their histories. These included Reuvens' efforts to legislate the protection of antiquities in the colony and the Batavian Society's growing interest in collecting archaeological objects, now partly supported by the 1840s regulation by which local authorities in Java became obliged to list the antiquities in their region; the Batavian Society authorised the collection of objects based on these lists.[47] Second, modernisation and visible grand infrastructural changes in East Java's landscape likely stimulated the same awareness and interest in the material remains of Majapahit. In 1847, when Van Hoëvell visited Majapahit, the landscape had changed considerably from Wardenaar's and Raffles' time – due to the growing number of sugar enterprises established in this area.[48] Some of these sugar factories would soon prove relevant for the further understanding as well as destruction of the remains of Majapahit, as apparently they used Majapahit bricks for their

[45] For this late nineteenth-century strand, among Javanese elites who were against orthodox, purifying Islamic developments in Java, see Ricklefs, *Polarising Javanese society*, 176–214.

[46] Ibid., 176–177; Bloembergen and Eickhoff, 'A wind of change'. Regarding Javanese reactions to (and uses of) the scholarly interest in ancient Javanese texts and *kraton* culture in this period, see Pemberton, *On the subject of 'Java'*; Tsuchiya, 'Javanology and the age of Ranggawarsita'.

[47] On Van Hoëvell's role in stimulating the Batavian Society's collecting policy regarding antiquities, see Groot, *Van Batavia*, 308–315.

[48] Van Hoëvell, *Reis over Java, Madura en Bali*, I.

factories and houses. The *regent* of Mojokerto, Van Hoëvell's host, was very much aware of these changes and ambiguities.

To stir Van Hoëvell's imagination about the enormous reach of the former empire, on the way from Mojokerto to Trowulan the *regent* told him that he had ordered the road from Mojokerto to Surabaya paved with bricks originating from the Majapahit ruins, and that many of the sugar factories had also used these bricks for their buildings.[49] The *regent* also gave Van Hoëvell a historical explanation for the changing name of Mojokerto, until 1838 known as Djapan, and part of Majapahit's legacy. The name 'Djapan' (meaning 'slow', 'lazy') was, accordingly, a curse by the 'sultan of Demak', the successor of the Majapahit kings, who was angry about the reluctance of the local heads of the former Majapahit empire to help build the new capital in Demak. Leaving any conclusion about the 'truth' of this to his readers, Van Hoëvell added that the 'truth' was that the local population had requested the government change the pejorative name to Mojokerto.[50]

In 1847, when Van Hoëvell journeyed across Java and Madura, and visited Majapahit, liberal criticism (of the Dutch colonial government and its exploitative Cultural System) circulated among certain colonial elites. Van Hoëvell published his travel journal only in 1849 in Amsterdam, after his expulsion from the Netherlands Indies (stirred by his fight for press freedom in the colony) and in the midst of the revolutionary movement in Europe. This, and his liberal discontent about the exploitative nature of the *Cultuurstelsel*, may have sharpened his critical tone towards 'his fatherland'. Invoking a once great empire in decay, the ruins inspired him to criticise possible Dutch exploitative rule in the Indies, which illustrates early – pre-Ethical Policy – ethical sentiments.[51]

On the site, the *regent* – possibly at the request of Van Hoëvell, who had read his classics (Raffles, Crawfurd) and was informed by Wardenaar – took Van Hoëvell to a number of the site's key attractions, including a ruined gateway, tangled in the roots of majestic *waringin* trees and filled with earth, vegetation, and stones. Van Hoëvell noted that it was built of baked bricks, stacked on top of each other without cement, and rose from a trychite foundation. He learned that it was locally known as 'Tjandi Pasar, but also referred to as "Waringin Lawang"' – the name it still carries today. The *regent* explained to Van Hoëvell that it used to carry the title 'gapoero gapi' (royal gate) and probably served as one of the most exterior gateways of the *kraton* of 'one of Majapahit's royal figures'. Later, Van Hoëvell observed that the *regent* had proudly incorporated

[49] Ibid., 174. [50] Ibid., 172–173. He erroneously translated this as 'beautiful fruit'.

[51] Maartje Janse, 'Representing distant victims: the emergence of an Ethical Movement in Dutch colonial politics, 1840–1880', *BMGN* 128:1 (2013), 53–80. On Van Hoëvell's criticism on the Cultuurstelsel, see C. Fasseur, *Kultuurstelsel en koloniale baten: de Nederlandse exploitatie van Java 1840–1860* (Leiden: Universitaire Pers, 1975).

this 'gapoera gapi' into his coat of arms. Significantly, today this restored and partly reconstructed gate is an icon of the Majapahit site – featuring on the cover of the BP3's guides, as well as on Stuart Robson's 1995 translation of the *Deśawarnana/ Nāgarakrtāgama*.[52]

Next, the *regent* took his guest to 'Tjandi Brawoe', for which Van Hoëvell had also acquired one of Wardenaar's drawings. Pondering the name, translated (by the *regent*) as 'temple of ashes', Van Hoëvell understood the temple as a sacred keeper of the ashes of royal families. Then they went to Sanggar Pamalangan, the trachyte-stone remains of a temple ('a formless pile of stones') with two statues, the first of a 'half-human/half-bird' figure, and the second a 'distorted figure, which the Javanese called Menak Jingga' (now in Trowulan's museum). The *regent* told Van Hoëvell that the Javanese believed the second figure represented the son of king of Blambangan, who came to Majapahit to ask the princess to marry him. She refused because he was too ugly and he, out of frustration and jealousy, transformed into stone. Apparently, Javanese also ridiculed the figure 'because of his foolishness' and because monkeys from the surrounding woods left their excrement on the statue.[53]

The subsequent attraction was Badjang Ratoe, a gate crowned by a Siva-head, and inside, interestingly, supported by wooden posts to prevent the building from collapsing, pointing to a previous restorative intervention (Figure 3.2). Van Hoëvell deeply admired the sculptured pillars of the gate, recognised *kala* heads, and compared the style of the building – as he did elsewhere at this site – to Balinese architecture. He learned that the *regent* did not dare to approach the gateway due to superstitions about fatal accidents faced by traditional heads who entered. They proceeded to the graves at Trowulan, where, at the grave of the princess of Campa, Van Hoëvell recounted stories (by 'Javanese writers') about this princess that are very similar to Crawfurd's.[54] Javanese stories portrayed the princess of Campa, daughter of the king of the Siamese kingdom of Campa, as one of the key people who had brought Islam to Java. When 'Browidjojo, king of Majapahit', heard about her beauty he longed for her and gained her hand. She became the most beloved of his wives and could thereby exercise enormous influence on the king. She used that influence in the interest of Islam, her family's faith, inviting two of her nephews, one of whom (Raden Rahmat) would become widely famous in Java as Sunan Ngampel. The tour

[52] Van Hoëvell, *Reis over Java, Madura en Bali* I, 174–175 and 184–185; I Made Kusumujaya, Aris Soviyani, and Wicaksono Nugroho, *Mengenal kepurbakalaan Majapahit di daerah Trowulan* (Mojokerto: BP3 Jatim, s.d. after 2001); Robson, *Deśawarnana (Nāgarakrtāgama) by Mpu Prapañca*.

[53] Van Hoëvell, *Reis over Java, Madura en Bali*, I, 176–178.

[54] Crawfurd, *History of the Indian Archipelago*, 307–332.

Figure 3.2 Badjang Ratoe, a temple Entrance at the Majapahit site, late nineteenth century.

ended at the giant pond, Segaran. From underneath a *pendopo*, Van Hoëvell admired the pond and again rued the despotic decadence and of the kings that ruled the Majapahit empire: 'What a work of giants! How generous shall the king have poured out the treasures of art and taste in this place of lust [*lustoord*], where he came to enjoy himself with his *harem*!' On the way back from Trowulan to Mojokerto, the *regent* told Van Hoëvell that he, too, lamented that everything left of Majapahit faced disappearance and destruction.[55]

The tour illustrates how both men displayed heritage awareness stirred by the sense of loss, perhaps generated by the interventions of the sugar industry and colonial economic and infrastructural development – though neither developed an urge for site salvation. But while Van Hoëvell used the site to criticise both Eastern despotism and Dutch colonial usurpation, the *regent* seemed to understand the site as a source of self-confirmation, strength, and aggrandisement.

Poerwolelono, a Modernist in Majapahit

The melancholic, self-legitimising interest of the *regent* of Mojokerto in the site, as well as Van Hoëvell's semi-scholarly travelogue, closely resemble the technical engagements of the travel writer Poerwolelono, or Tjondronegoro, the *regent* of Kudus (1858–1880), and Brebes (1880–1885), whom we followed during his travels to Demak and Borobudur and to Candi Mendut. Poerwolelono visited Majapahit during his second trip, which went from Semarang in Central Java to Surabaya in East Java. In comparison with Van Hoëvell (and later Buddingh), Poerwolelono's description of the site is remarkably concise and unromantic. Interested in the technical details – material, construction, size – of the various buildings at the site, he retells some of the local histories in a disinterested way, distancing himself from mythology or what he depicts as superstition.[56] Mostly not referring to the local names, he starts, like the *regent* of Mojokerto and Van Hoëvell, at the 'gate of the old *kraton*' (Gapura Wringin Lawang), noting the building material, the height, and cementless construction, and compares it to the *kraton* in Surakarta, and the graveyards of the *wali songo*. From there, Poerwolelono visits 'the estate of the *kraton*', where he sees 'a very big basin' ('kolam Segaran') that had been surrounded by a wall of brickwork which had collapsed. Nearby he finds the grave 'said to belong to the princess of Campa' and the statue of Ménak Djinggo 'representing the king of Blambanang, seated'. He notices that the tomb next to Princess Campa's grave is well maintained and describes it as a sacrificial site. Poerwolelono concluded that it all had once formed part of the *kraton*'s estate.

[55] Van Hoëvell, *Reis over Java, Madura en Bali*, I, 184–185.

[56] In the following, we use the Dutch translation of Poerwolelono's visit to the site from Bosnak, Koot, and Soekatno, *Op reis met een Javaanse edelman*, 132–134.

After describing some of the other buildings, Poerwolelono assesses the size of the city-state as so enormous 'you can hardly believe that here only three generations of kings of Modjopahit ruled. You would think there were more. Visitors to the ruins of Majapahit will be disappointed when they see that all of this today is one big forest, and that, apart from the ruins, there are no villages.' Like the *kraton* as a whole, visitors learned that locals believed many of the statues at the site represent historical or mythical figures. These stories, as related by Poerwolelono, the *regent* of Mojokerto, and Van Hoëvell clearly indicate that Majapahit was an active and vibrant topic among the local population long before it became a focus of modern heritage politics. Islamic priests guarded the sacred graves, such as that of the princess of Campa, as Raffles and Wardenaar had noticed. This was the case in the early twentieth century, and today this site still attracts pilgrims, especially on certain days of the Javanese calendar such as *kemis kliwon* (Thursday night). Obviously, this does not mean that such rituals of care and pilgrimage did not change over time. They developed in dialogue with external events.

The Badjang Ratoe, for example, apparently had the power to change people's 'fate' (what today we call 'career').[57] Poerwolelono himself did not dare to come close, as he explained to his readers, emphasising that local villagers had also vehemently forbidden him to do so. Almost half a century later, when J. Knebel of the recently established Archaeological Commission systematically explored the site, he still encountered the fear generated by this gate. But he did notice that inhabitants of the village of Temon (where the gate was located), had entered the site and left offerings, probably to its powerful spirits.[58]

It is intriguing, that, when Van Hoëvell considered the Badjang Ratoe gate, it had already experienced an archaeological intervention, as wooden pillars supported the inner part of the gate (see Figure 3.2). By the time Knebel saw it, a framework of iron pillars had replaced the wooden construction. He discovered that this had been done by 'a European', 'who, according to popular belief, by repairing this *cursed* building, did penance with his fortune'.[59] Unfortunately, we do not know who carried out the previous wooden effort in conservation, nor why. But it was one of the signs that Majapahit was not simply a site to deplore decay, but also a religious site, a place of worship with a flock of believers, caretakers, and a local religious infrastructure. It was a site that people wanted to experience, that demanded care, and that gained new life,

[57] Krom, *Inleiding tot de Hindoe-Javaansche kunst*, II, 190: 'an administrator cannot enter it without damaging his career, or his chances for promotion'. See also Buddingh, *Neêrlands-Oost -Indië; Reizen*, 2nd edn.

[58] J. Knebel, 'Beschrijving Hindoe-oudheden in de afdeeling Modjokerto der residentie Soerabaja', *ROC 1907* (1909), 55.

[59] Ibid.

along with the various interventions and visits it hosted. And when it became a site for more systematic archaeological research, discovery, and dissemination, it already had a conscientious public.

Awareness of Different Forms and Techniques of Knowledge Production

In 1853, what British reporter John Riggs called the 'Grand Exhibition in Batavia' opened for the public, aiming to allow Batavia and the Netherlands Indies to compete with modern nations elsewhere in the world, active in organising national arts-and-crafts exhibitions. Majapahit was categorised under the entries from East Java, Surabaya, as one of the few antiquities on display next to all other wares that emphasised the Netherlands Indies' resources, trade, and modernity. In this Majapahit subsection, Riggs saw a sample of the fruit 'Mojo', sent in from the *patih* of Mojokerto, 'Chokkro Poorbo Negoro'. This fruit, Riggs learned, played a role in the explanation of the name and the history of Majapahit. There were also *kris*, a prince's dagger, five spears, a brass axe, two plates, a porcelain jug, an earthenware ball, a lamp, a saucer, a bell, and an ivory *kris* handle – all, according to the impressed Riggs, 'dug up near the ruins of Majapahit'. He explained how 'curious' this collection of antiquities was, as it had 'belonged to a people who once held sway over a great part of Java, previous to the introduction of Mohamedanism, in about AD 1478, and thus before Europeans had doubled the Cape of Good Hope'. He left open whether these people were native or not.[60]

This display of Majapahit objects at the Grand Exhibition, small as it seems, was an important development in the biographies of the site they originated from. It reveals how individuals like the *patih* of Mojokerto came to recognise the value of the site for self-advertising to a larger public, and this on an apparently powerful site of knowledge dissemination with an – ideally – all-Indies reach. However, the Grand Exhibition closed after three months, and this short performance, remarkable as it was, has been forgotten. Still, we might consider this exhibition as part of a long-term and slow shift in which the Majapahit site transformed from a site of various knowledge encounters, into a site of new forms of knowledge, commitments, interdependencies, and contesting as well as conflicting appropriations.

Until now, we have seen no real conflicts between the different sorts of engagements that Majapahit triggered. They ranged from scholarly and travellers' romantic (art-)historical interests, lamenting decay and calling for

[60] Jonathan Rigg, 'The Grand Exhibition of Batavia', *Journal of the Indian Archipelago and Eastern Asia* 7 (1853), 283–284.

self-legitimising revival, to local historical pride, heritage awareness, and religious sentiments of deep respect, hope, and fear. However, the encounters at the site also generated *awareness* – among the various parties drawn to the site – of these different knowledge attitudes, or better, of the beliefs in different kinds of knowledge, determining relationships to the site. But with J. G. A. Pocock's theories on past relationships in mind, to what degree did this lead to conflicts and a new historical awareness about the site?[61] It seems that no dominant unified historical view on the site developed. On the other hand, all parties became aware that economic interests (sugar factories, roads) were paramount, considering that material remains of Majapahit were sacrificed to modernising industry and infrastructure, albeit not the graves.

Looking at this as an encounter of different regimes of knowledge, it is tempting to presume that visitors who engaged with the site from the Western-scientific centred perspective (which developed in the nineteenth century) would refer to these different regimes in hierarchical ways, as belonging to 'the scientific' mind versus 'the believer's' mind respectively. But intriguingly, the encounters at the site and the travels of objects that we have discussed show that the hierarchies between the different regimes of knowledge were neither clear nor fixed. However, the theme of decay, postulated among both foreign and Javanese elite circles, seemed to be the most repetitive, as well as a motive for site maintenance and salvation.

Scholarly discussions and discourse on the site developed at alternative forums, away from the site. At the site itself, other views encountered by visitors seemed to matter. The British scholars-cum-military men in the early nineteenth century observed that there were other ways of respecting statues without commenting upon these negatively. Perhaps this was because these 'other attitudes' could lead them to information they were interested in. The Resident of Surabaya recognised that the religious value which Joko Dolok had to some of the population in town, added to the political value of this statue a powerful gift that could generate further loyalty of colonised subjects. And vice versa: Javanese elites, like the *regent* of Mojokerto or Poerwolelono, may have looked with fresh eyes at the site because of the 'foreign' historical interests it generated, realising that the new knowledge about Majapahit, and foreign knowledge-gathering methods could be useful to them, and to their status. This local insight, in the value of alternative forms and methods of knowledge gathering, would be one of the sources of conflicts in mentality and cultural politics emerging in relation to the Majapahit site from the last quarter of the nineteenth century onwards – within Javanese and colonial society, and between

[61] J. G. A. Pocock, *The ancient constitution and the feudal law* (Cambridge: Cambridge University Press, 1987).

colonial societal institutions, individuals, and the state. The local awareness of different knowledge regimes and of different methods of knowledge production and uses developed in interaction with professionalising and institutionalising archaeology and philology, which represented stronger state interest.

The Javaneseness of Majapahit

With the expansion of the colonial state from the late nineteenth century, state interests in research, collecting, and maintenance regarding the antiquities at the Majapahit site grew as well – first indirectly, via the 'civic' Batavian Society, then via the Archaeological Commission (1901) and subsequent Archaeological Service (1913). But Majapahit also became meaningful to certain members of the Javanese elite as an important site of new local historical interest and legitimation. Their interest concerned the Javaneseness of (Hindu–Buddhist) Majapahit. Initially these interests of local elites and 'the state' met and supported each other, and interpretations could even overlap.

In the 1870s Majapahit became a source of potential conflict *within* Javanese society. News about archaeological research and findings on Java's pre-Islamic history, among others by the Western-trained Javanese painter and self-taught antiquarian Raden Saleh Sharif Bustaman, made a number of *priyayi* develop views on the Islamic past that differed from the *babad* traditions they knew.[62] This was an elitist reaction to a popular movement towards the purification of Islam in Java which started in the early nineteenth century and which in Indonesian historiography of Islam and nationalism has been referred to as 'modern' or 'modernist'.[63] It was also an ambiguous result of colonial indirect rule, modernisation, and Western education which sons of *priyayi,* like Poerwolelono, and later the son of the old *regent* of Mojokerto, could experience; they could now attend the new, Western-oriented *Hoofdenschool* (school for *priyayi*/district heads) in order to become professional colonial officials. This modern education partly buttressed and partly harmed their authority as traditional leaders.[64] As Ricklefs has discussed, a revisionist historical dispute

[62] Ricklefs, *Polarising Javanese society*, 176–177. As Ricklefs has shown, it was in particular news about paleontological findings near the Solo river that reached Raden Saleh, and which, in and beyond the Javanese journal *Bramartani*, stirred the discussion with regard to Java's Islamic past.

[63] Ricklefs, *Polarising Javanese society*; Taufik Abdullah, *Schools and politics: the Kaum Muda movement in West Sumatra 1927–1933* (Ithaca: ISEAP, 1971); Deliar Noer, *The modernist Muslim movement in Indonesia 1900–1942* (Singapore: Oxford University Press, 1973). For critical reflection on this, see Laffan, *Islamic nationhood and colonial Indonesia*, 7–8.

[64] Ricklefs, *Polarising Javanese society*, 180–181; Heather A. Sutherland, *The making of a bureaucratic elite: the colonial transformation of the Javanese priyayi* (Singapore: Heinemann, 1979).

about the fall of Majapahit appeared in the Javanese journal *Bramartani* and, notably in three remarkable texts, was published separately. These texts – the *Babad Kĕdiri*, the *Suluk Gatholoco*, and the *Sĕrat Dĕrmagandhul*[65] – were written and published in the 1870s (and republished, translated, and studied by colonial philologists in the 1920s). Depicting Islam as 'foreign to Java and the Javanese', they emphasised the essential Javaneseness of the Majapahit empire.[66]

Remarkably, these 1870s Javanese texts have been ignored in the historiography on Indonesian uses of the Majapahit past. That critical historiography argues that Indonesian nationalists started to identify with the Majapahit empire as a glorious national past, mainly through their reading of the colonial publications of the *Pararaton* – an important source for Majapahit's history dating from the sixteenth century – and the *Nagarakrtagama* (and their translation and dissemination in textbooks). But, as we have seen, the site and its material remains already mattered as evidence of a great past. The 1870s texts indicate that the site, probably also in reaction to the archaeological interventions, entered into new Javanese elites' forms of historical reflections. What differed here in comparison to the nationalist era, however, was the reach of the moral and political space to which the texts were linked – in the 1870s, the focus of the authors was strictly Java-centred, whereas in the 1920s the purview of the nationalist readers of *Nagarakrtagama* came to encompass the Netherlands Indies as a whole.

As becomes clear from Ricklef's translation of the *Babad Kĕdiri*, the *Suluk Gatholoco*, and the *Sĕrat Dĕrmagandhul*, the new *priyayi* authors explicitly referred to the material remains of the Majapahit empire (texts and statues) as evidence of or arguments for an advanced past, in ways historians and archaeologists would do today. One other author, in the journal *Bramartani,* rewrote the history of Java, referring to archaeological findings or material evidence (stone inscriptions, and research at Borobudur) as a progression of epochs. First the Hindus came to Java, and after that Aji Saka's people,[67] he wrote, bringing

65 A number of historical linguists, most notably Ricklefs and Drewes, have translated, discussed, and contextualised these still remarkable texts. See Ricklefs, *Polarising Javanese society*, 176–213; G. Drewes, 'The struggle between Javanism and Islam as illustrated by the Serat Dermagandul', *BKI* 122:3 (1966), 309–365.

66 Anthony Reid, 'The nationalist quest for an Indonesian past', in Reid and Marr (eds.), *Perceptions of the past*, 286 (on Soeriokoesoemo portraying Arabian Islam as a form of imperialism 'no less pernicious than the Dutch'); Jacobus J. van Miert, *Een koel hoofd en een warm hart: nationalisme, javanisme en jeugdbeweging in Nederlands-Indië, 1918–1930* (Amsterdam: De Bataafsche Leeuw, 1995).See also Chapter 4.

67 'Aji Saka's people' refers to another Javanese tradition, explaining the founding of Majapahit, in which the mythical person Adji-Saka – travelling from Mecca, via Ceylon, the coast of Coromandel, Sumatra, and Borneo – arrived in Java, where he killed the man-eater King Dewa-tjengkar and, with the alphabetic script, brought 'civilisation' to Java. The author may have been trained at the Instituut voor de Javaanse taal in Surakarta (1832–1843). This tradition, transcribed from epic poems and transformed into prose by the linguist C. F. Winter in collaboration with Javanese interlocutors, has played an important role in the education of, first, Javanese

the 'Siamese religion'. He elaborated that this was the time when people started to write inscriptions on stones, like those now in Batavia's museum or at Borobudur. Then a period followed in which 'the Arabs' introduced 'Arab religion' that employed 'magical means, ruses, and lies'.[68] To such writers, the material remains thus served as evidence of a – morally superior – past civilisation, to which they felt connected, and felt cut off by an essentially non-Javanese, foreign Islam. In that sense, there was a curious overlap with the way romanticist foreigners in the mid nineteenth century interpreted the ruins of Majapahit as the result of the destructive forces of Islam.

The 1870s texts provide alternative, revisionist views to the local (oral) versions of textual traditions we have discussed so far regarding the fall of the Majapahit empire: namely, as the Majapahit empire being *betrayed* by a *foreign* Islamic intruder, instead of a local king peacefully consenting to the new religion. They depict Raden Patah as a treacherous son who betrays his benign father; and, as Ricklefs has pointed out, they forge a link between the Dutch, bringing European learning (*budi*), and the pre-Islamic civilisation (*buda*) on Java, as a legitimising 'good'.[69] The *Babad Kĕdiri* and the *Sĕrat Dĕrmagandhul*, to which we restrict ourselves, are of particular interest here as they contain observations on material remains as historical evidence, and on the notion of heritage (in material or intangible form), in relation to defining the nature of Javaneseness.

The *Babad Kĕdiri*, written in the early 1870s and probably, as Ricklefs reasons, by Ky. Ng. Rĕksadiwirya, presents the story of the Islamisation of Java, as told by Butalocaya, the cave-dwelling king of the spirits. In the afterword, M. Sumasĕntika, a retired *wedana* (district head), confesses that he had inserted certain lies in the story 'in the interests of the elegance of the words', but adds 'all of the antiquities that are mentioned above exist'.[70] Among the material evidence he mentions is the grave of the last (Hindu) king of Majapahit, Brawijaya. He tells how this king converted to Islam despite himself and, because a king cannot change his words, has been buried (instead of burned according to Hindu tradition), at his request, at Majapahit.[71]

priyayi at this institute, and subsequent generations of teenagers in Indonesia. See Ronit Ricci, 'Reading a history of writing: heritage, religion and script change in Java', *Itinerario* 39:3 (2015), 419–435; C. F. Winter (transl.), J. J. B. Gaal and T. Roorda (eds.), *Het boek Adji Saka: oude fabelachtige geschiedenis van Java van de regering van vorst Sindoela te Galoeh tot aan de stichting van Madja-Pait door vorst Soesoeroeh* (Amsterdam: Frederick Muller, 1857).

68 Quoted in Ricklefs, *Polarising Javanese society*, 176. 69 Ibid., 179. 70 Ibid., 188.

71 As we will discuss further in the Epilogue of this book, the grave of Brawijaya, 'rediscovered' at Siti Inggil by a certain Haji Idris in 1961, and located in a new grave monument built in 1970, plays a significant role in (stories about) New Order legitimations, as well as in power seeking by individual pilgrims. Official academic archaeology in Indonesia and the BP3 in Trowulan deny that Brawijaya is buried there: interview, Marieke Bloembergen with Pak Tego, Trowulan, 14 June 2012.

Material remains demonstrate conflicting histories. And in the *Babad Kĕdiri*, we learn how the armed forces of Brawijaya's son, after they came to power, attempted to destroy 'all traces of the *Buddha* religion'.[72] The act of burning 'Buddhist texts' returns in the *Sĕrat Dĕrmagandhul*, a tale written for the opening of the head school at Probolinggo, which Ricklefs argues explains why the theme of Western learning (*budi*) is a leading motive in *Sĕrat Dĕrmagandhul.*[73] On the story of the fall of Majapahit, the main character in this story learns from his teacher and two spirits why the Javanese changed their religion. One of the spirits tells how he denounces Sunan Bonang – who according to Javanese tradition is one of the *wali* who brought Islam to Java – while seeing him vandalise a Hindu–Buddhist image. He warns Sunan Bonang that 'that was the creation of an exalted ruler, the Honoured King Jayabaya', who had been 'granted an exalted revelation, who ... knew to write down things which had not yet occurred':

> and, sir, the rules for writing
> and the rules of the Javanese in literature
> are an esteemed inheritance from the ancestors
> All believed the reports,
> Great the reverence for
> the written reports of old
> the antiquities could be examined.[74]

However, according to the *Sĕrat Dĕrmagandhul* (as in the *Babad Kĕdiri*), during the conquest of Majapahit, 'the honoured *Buda* heirlooms' are burned: 'there remained not a single one of these foundations of the *Buda* religion'.[75] Later, the fleeing Brawijaya, by now converted to Islam under his son's pressure, regrets that step. Then he gets a lesson from his companion, the spirit Sabdapalon, who reveals himself as Sĕmar – known as the wisest of the three *punokawan* (clowns), and a favourite character in the Javanese *wayang* play:

> My lord, know well,
> If you have changed your religion,
> abandoning the *Buda* religion,
> indeed weak will be your descendants in the future,
> for they will have abandoned Javaneseness
> Their Javanese-Javaneseness disappeared.[76]

Quite according to the Western-centred rules of modern, professional history, Dĕrmagandhul emphasises at the beginning of his exposé that history has been corrupted and that there are different versions of the past. The author distinguishes between true and false knowledge, stating that the first can be

[72] Quoted in, and free translation by, Ricklefs, *Polarising Javanese society*, 185.
[73] Ibid., 196 and 209. [74] Ibid., 200–201. [75] Ibid., 200–203. [76] Ibid., 206–207.

found in all the cities where schools are built (referring to colonial institutions) by joining 'the tree of knowledge' and by following the religion of the king. Those who, on the other hand, follow the religion of the *wali*, who follow the command of the sultan of Demak, 'should go to a grave ... should just be driven away'.[77] At the stage in the story when Brawijaya, in his flight, reaches Probolinggo, the writer/teacher explains that in the future, a united people of the (Netherlands) Indies will gather to learn and to become Javanese through their devotion to 'knowledge [*kawruh*]', 'proficiency in external matters', and thus '*budi*'.[78] This historical interpretation as taught to Děrmagandhul, emphasising the importance of 'Western' learning in order to be able to distinguish 'false' from 'true' history, may in one way well illustrate how local elites and (state-supported) colonial archaeology by the end of the nineteenth century came to meet and support each other. But this was an interdependent relationship which the author of *Sěrat Děrmagandhul* seems to be aware of.

Thus, while European explorers of the histories of the Majapahit site depended on local elites and caretakers to gain access to (interpretations of) the site, local elites came to use archaeological knowledge to strengthen and legitimise their position – also with regard to other, competing local elites and religious leaders.

A Philological and Archaeological Push

In November 1894, during a raid by the colonial army on the *kraton* of the Balinese king Tjakranegara in Lombok, the governmental philologist Brandes took the old manuscripts and other treasures that were kept in the *kraton*'s library. This included *Nagarakrtagama*. Thus, the official legitimation still goes, state philologist Brandes 'saved' these historical treasures from looting and fire. Considering the Javanese *priyayi's* revisionism with regard to the history of Majapahit's fall, and the new *priyayi* writers' concerns about the 'vandalisation' and loss of the texts and stone images of this kingdom, this violent rescue of *Nagarakrtagama* gains extra meaning. As it was supposed to be a key text to the disclosure of the world of the Majapahit empire, it became important to *all* parties interested in Majapahit's history and whereabouts: scholars seeking to crack the code of Old Javanese, Javanese elites seeking historical connection and legitimation for their position, and, by now, also a modern 'ethical' colonial state in a phase of expansion and development in need of legitimising continuity and in need of a civilised image.

This mission of what we may call philological violence (borrowing from Gayatri Chakravorty Spivak's 'epistemic violence') took place at Brandes'

[77] *Sěrat Děrmaghandul*, translated, cited and commented upon ibid., 196–211, here 198.
[78] Ibid., 207–208.

instigation, with the official support of the government.[79] It was part of a larger philological and archaeological push driven by the Indological department at Leiden University in the Netherlands, the Batavian Society, and the young Archaeological Society (set up in Yogyakarta in 1885) in the Netherlands Indies. This push overlapped with a literary revival within the royal courts in Central Java, as well as among some Javanese elites elsewhere.[80] The aim was to systematically reveal the world of pre-Islamic Java by decoding its language, as transmitted in manuscripts, inscriptions, and sculpture kept in royal libraries and in the Batavian Society's collection. Brandes was part and parcel of this double push. The colonial linguistic study of Old Javanese, including its literature, and of the world it came from was still a relatively young field.[81] The language was known only to Brahmans in Bali and *priyayi* intellectuals in Java, and some individual scholars were trying to master it, partly with the assistance of Javanese informants – whereas archaeology was a matter of private trial and error. A philologist by training, Brandes also experimented in archaeology. His philological work resulted in the translation and dissemination of sources and new interpretations of the social world, the founding and the royal genealogy of the Majapahit empire. For his archaeological initiatives, which would include efforts to restore Candi Mendut, Brandes would be rewarded with the position of the first chair of the Archaeological Commission in 1901.

In 1885, Brandes had arrived in the Netherlands Indies as linguistic civil servant (*taalambtenaar*) with a thorough overview of the manuscripts kept in Leiden's libraries, and assigned to study Old Javanese and other languages of the archipelago, in as far as these could serve him in his understanding of Old Javanese and the cultural history related to it.[82] This assignment included the manuscripts, the inscriptions on stones and copper plates, and other relevant sources (the *babad*, from later date and written in new Javanese) that were

[79] On Brandes' mission to Lombok, see G. P. Rouffaer, 'Herdenking aan Dr J. L. A. Brandes', in *Beschrijving van Tjandi Singasari in de residentie Pasoeroean en De wolkentoneelen van Panataran in de residentie Kediri: Archaeologisch onderzoek op Java en Madura II* ('s-Gravenhage: Martinus Nijhoff; Batavia: Albrecht & Co., 1908), i–xlvi. On epistemic violence, see Gayati Chakravarty Spivak, 'Can the subaltern speak?', in Cary Nelson and Lawrence Grossberg (eds.), *Marxism and the interpetration of culture* (Basingstoke: Macmillan Education, 1988), 271–313.

[80] Tsuchiya, 'Javanology and the age of Ranggawarsita'; Van Miert, *Een koel hoofd.*

[81] H. Kern, 'In memoriam J. L. A. Brandes', *BKI* 59:1 (1906), 2; Eugenius M. Uhlenbeck, *A critical survey of studies on the languages of Java and Madura* ('s-Gravenhage: Nijhoff, 1964), 108–112.

[82] First trained as a theologian in Amsterdam, Brandes studied languages at the Indological Department in Leiden. While his PhD thesis (1884) was on the comparative phonetics of the Malay–Polynesian language family, he tried to master Old Javanese, together with the study of Indian epigraphy: Kern, 'In memoriam J. L. A. Brandes'.

kept in the museum of the Batavian Society.[83] While thus gaining an overview of 'the field' and its textual and material sources as kept in Batavia, Brandes translated and published the *Pararaton (Ken Arok)* or the Book of Kings of Tumapĕl and of Majapahit, in 1897.[84] Krom hailed the translation as 'a new fundament' for the study of the Old Javanese past.[85] But at the time it seemed suspect, being an indirect, 'post-Majapahit' source. Hence the importance all parties attached to the *Nagarakrtagama*, as the first textual source coming from that golden age. It would stir the interest of a group of Javanese nationalists, who, when the first Dutch translation (by Kern) of a first part of *Nagarakrtagama* appeared in 1908,[86] were rallying around Boedi Oetomo ('Noble Endeavour', 1908; the Javanese cultural nationalist association set up by Javanese elites) and later in the Committee for Javanese Nationalism and its journal *Wederopbouw* (1917), aiming for Javanese awakening or Javanese cultural development.[87] Connections between cultural nationalism and colonial archaeology were clearly reflected by one of the first issues of *Wederopbouw* in 1919.[88]

It took some time, though, before the influence of the stories from the 'forgotten' *Nagarakrtagama* – albeit not forgotten by the Balinese – was disseminated more widely to the centres of cultural nationalism (Batavia, Yogyakarta, Solo). The stories did so in various translated and popularised forms: the transcription of the text into Balinese characters by Brandes in 1902,[89] the first translation into Dutch by Kern, published in series in the *Bijdragen tot de Taal-, Land- en Volkenkunde* (*BKI*) between 1908 and

[83] The results were published as a supplement to Groeneveldt's catalogue of the society's archaeological collection. See W. P. Groeneveldt and Jan L. A. Brandes, *Catalogus der Archaeologische Verzameling van het Bataviaasch Genootschap van Kunsten en Wetenschappen, met aanteekeningen omtrent de op verschillende voorwerpen voorkomende inscripties en een voorloopigen inventaris der beschreven steenen* (Batavia: Albrecht, 1887). Brandes collected further, all to gain insight in all possible relevant sources – including the *Babad*. See Kern, 'In memoriam J. L. A. Brandes', 3.

[84] J. L. A. Brandes, *Pararaton (Ken Arok). Het boek der koningen van Tumapĕl en van Majapahit: uitgegeven en toegelicht*, Verhandelingen van het Bataviaasch Genootschap van Kunsten en Wetenschappen 49:1 ('s-Gravenhage: Martinus Nijhoff; Batavia: Albrecht & Co., 1897); N. J. Krom, *Pararaton (Ken Arok). Het boek der koningen van Tumapĕl en van Majapahit: uitgegeven en toegelicht door Dr J. L. A. Brandes*, Verhandelingen van het Bataviaasch Genootschap van Kunsten en Wetenschappen 62 (second edn, edited by N. J. Krom) ('s-Gravenhage: Martinus Nijhoff; Batavia: Albrecht & Co., 1920).

[85] Krom, *Pararaton*, xiii.

[86] H. Kern, 'I. De eerste zang van den Nāgarakrĕtāgama', *BKI* 61 (1908), 395–403.

[87] Reid and Marr (eds.), *Perceptions of the past*; Van Miert, *Een koel hoofd*, 92–128.

[88] F. D. K. Bosch, 'Iets over Oost-Javaansche kunst en hare verhouding tot de Midden-Javaansche en de Balische', *Wederopbouw* 1 (1918), 54.

[89] J. Brandes, *Nâgarakrĕtâgama: lofdicht van Prapanjtja op Koning Rasadjanagara, Hajam Wuruk, van Madjapahit, uitgegeven naar het eenige daarvan bekende palmbladhandschrift aangetroffen in de puri te Tjakranagara op Lombok, Batavia*, Verhandelingen van het Bataviaasch Genootschap voor Kunsten en Wetenschappen 54:1 (Batavia: Landsdrukkerij; 's-Gravenhage: Nijhoff, 1902).

1919, corrections provided by Krom of 1919, and by Poerbatjaraka in 1924.[90] Further popularisation soon followed, first via the historical textbook by W. Fruin-Mees, which included *Nagarakrtagama* – it came out in Dutch (1919–1920) and in Malay (1921–1922) – and then via the popular Malay edition of *Nagarakrtagama*, published by the colonial government's department for popularisation-cum-propaganda, the Balai Poestaka or Volkslectuur (Readings for the People), in 1922.[91] The textbook by Fruin-Mees was especially important for stimulating the imagination, not only in words – as others have suggested – but also in pictures, as it contained clear proofs in the form of photographs from antiquities, all provided by the Archaeological Service. As we shall see in the next chapter, it is a question of how much these proofs at the site really mattered to the nationalist imagination of Majapahit.

Important for the site itself, but less understood, were the effects of archaeological professionalisation, site interventions, and heritage engagements on location. Two systematic surveys of the Majapahit site around 1900 also indicate local interest in the site. First, the geologist R. D. M. Verbeek conducted a survey in 1886–1887 on behalf of the Batavian Society[92] (and in 1891 wrote the first systematic inventory of antiquities on Java). Although this overview included Islamic graves, it sought out only 'the most important Hindu remains'.[93] Second, the newly founded Archaeological Commission

[90] This concerns the following publications by Kern, 'I. De eerste zang van den Nāgarakrĕtāgama'; 'II. Korte geschiedenis van Koning Rājasa in den Nāgarakrĕtāgama', *BKI* 61 (1908), 403–408; 'Zang V tot XII en XV tot XVII van den Nāgarakrĕtāgama', *BKI* 63 (1910), 337–367; 'Zang XVIII tot XXII van den Nāgarakrĕtāgama', *BKI* 66 (1912), 337–347; 'Zang XXIII tot XXXII van den Nāgarakrĕtāgama', *BKI* 67 (1913), 189–202; 'Zang XXXIII tot XXXVI en XXXVIII, XXXIX, L, LI van den Nāgarakrĕtāgama', *BKI* 67 (1913), 367–382; 'Zang LXXV tot LXXXIII van den Nāgarakrĕtāgama', *BKI* 69 (1914), 33–51; 'Zang LXXXIV tot XCI van den Nāgarakrĕtāgama', *BKI* 69 (1914), 297–313; *Het oud-javaansche lofdicht Nāgarakṛĕtāgama van Prapañca (1365 AD)* ('s-Gravenhage: KITLV, 1919); J. H. C. Kern, N. Krom and L. F. van Gent, *Het oud-Javaansche lofdicht Nagarakertagama* (Weltevreden: Balai Poestaka, 1922); and Poerbatjaraka, 'Aanteekeningen op de Nagarakretagama', *BKI* 80 (1924), 219.

[91] W. Fruin-Mees, *Geschiedenis van Java*, 2 vols. (Weltevreden: Commissie voor Volkslectuur, 1919–1920); W. Fruin-Mees, *Sedjarah tanah Djawah*, transl. S. M. Latif, 2 vols. (Weltevreden: Balai Poestaka, 1921–1922); Kern, Krom, and Van Gent, *Het oud-Javaansche lofdicht Nagarakertagama*.

[92] Verbeek, 'De Oudheden van Madjapahit'. This would be, in a way, a pilot of Verbeek's subsequent project, intended to make an inventory of the antiquities on the whole island of Java: R. D. M. Verbeek, *Lijst der voornaamste overblijfselen uit den Hindoetijd op Java met eene oudheidkundige kaart*, Verhandelingen van het Bataviaasch Genootschap van Kunsten en Wetenschappen 46 (Batavia: Landsdrukkerij; 's-Gravenhage: M. Nijhoff, 1891).

[93] However, interestingly, Verbeek included the graves of honoured persons, or graves that were deeply honoured by the population. He argued that these 'Obviously did not belong to the remains of the Hindu period'. Without explaining why, he merely concluded that they 'obviously' would deserve their place on an antiquarian map. See Verbeek, *Lijst der voornaamste overblijfselen,* 18.

continued this inventory, and its member Knebel conducted a follow-up survey of the antiquities in Mojokerto in 1906–1907.[94]

To gain information and assistance in exploring the site, both Verbeek and Knebel paid courtesy calls to the *regent* of Mojokerto, and they used his subordinates (in Knebel's case the *patih*) to gain access to other local informants (village heads and the *juru kunci* – guards – of sacred places). Both researchers compared their findings with earlier reports – Verbeek, notably, using the list and drawings of Wardenaar that Brandes had found in the minutes of the Batavian Society.[95] They listed statues and building structures, observed what certain people did with certain objects (including trees) and what these objects did to people, and held interviews gathering local histories. Knebel noted the *specific* kind of offerings people made to the trees, graves, and stones and gathered local histories about offerings and objects. He did this without commenting on them, albeit comparing some to other histories. Interestingly, people related objects concretely to the time of the Majapahit empire and to specific kings. Thus, for example, at Candi Brahoe (*desa* (village) Moeteran), one of the villagers who accompanied him explained that this temple had been founded by a Brawijaya, and built with brick stones without cement. The bodies of the kings Brawijaya I, II, III and IV were burned here, and their ashes were buried in the hole underneath the stone in the middle of the temple room.[96]

Relevant to the issue of the Javaneseness of this site, Knebel encountered an anti-Islamic story about the grave of Princess Campa told by its *juru kunci* Sahid. Sahid emphasised that in reality, the person buried in *desa* Trowulan was not the princess of Campa, but the last king of Majapahit, Brawijaya V, and that his real grave was located a bit more eastwards.

The surveys by Verbeek and Knebel thus reveal how local stories circulated and show ambiguous relationships with Islam and with pre-Islamic beliefs. Also, both surveys, if only because of the researchers, their methods, and the stories they collected, further stirred local interest, as we shall see.

94 Knebel, 'Beschrijving oudheden Modjokerto'.
95 Verbeek, *Lijst der voornaamste overblijfselen,* 4; Verbeek, 'De Oudheden van Madjapahit'.
96 Knebel, 'Beschrijving oudheden Modjokerto', 55.

4 Greater Majapahit: the Makings of a Proto-Indonesian Site across Decolonisation, 1900s–1950s

> In the future Indonesia will form its own bloc, namely the Central Asian bloc, consisting of Indonesia, the Philippines, Malacca, Siam, Vietnam, and Burma. This bloc could be called the Gadjahmada bloc, because Gadjah Mada once formed it in 1350. This Gadjahmada bloc will consist of a population of 120 million people, three-quarters of whom are Indonesians. It is not too big and geopolitically viable. In this way, the Indonesian people can become a locomotive in the world system.[1]

> Sites are not my problem.[2]

In 1912, as a gesture of friendship and loyalty to the colonial state, *regent* Kromodjojo Adinegoro IV presented his collection of Hindu–Buddhist statues, together with the museum building he had raised in Mojokerto, to the government as a gift. This gift reflected two decades of research and collecting in the Majapahit area. The timing seemed good, as preparations for the founding one year later of the Oudheidkundige Dienst, the Dutch Colonial Archaeological Service in Batavia, were in full swing. Krom, as head of the temporary Archaeological Commission (founded in 1901), proposed that the government honour the *regent* 'in public' for this gesture, which he found 'very valuable' and 'highly important' from archaeological and art-historical perspectives. Moreover, he argued that the collection at the site, which might eventually be enlarged with pieces

[1] Muhammad Yamin, quoted in the Dutch journal *Het Dagblad*, 1 August 1949, reacting to Philippines president Elpidio Quirino's plan to form an anti-communist bloc in Asia.

[2] The Leiden-trained Indonesian historian and lawyer Soenario (1902–1997), quoted on his use of a map of a Greater Majapahit drawn and published by anthropologist H. Otley Beyer in 1926, in an interview that took place in 1974, with the French historian Jacques Leclerc, in Leclerc, 'La circonscription', in Blanchard, Dovert and Durand (eds.), *Indonésie*, 43. For the Majapahit map drawn by Meyer, see G. Nye Steiger, H. Otley Beyer, and Conrado Benitz, *A history of the Orient* (Boston: Ginn, 1926), 179.

from elsewhere in East Java, would be the ideal centre for the study of what he referred to as 'East Javanese art'.[3]

Art with a capital A was a new, overarching stylistic appreciation of the material remains of East Java's Hindu–Buddhist past. With this categorisation, Krom followed a new academic trend in which Buddhist remains, perceived as Indian in origin, became classified as Indian 'Art'.[4] Krom's appreciation of the Hindu–Buddhist remains in Java would set the tone in the Netherlands Indies' archeological scholarly world.[5] This was a remarkable shift in scholarly valuation, as it awarded both historical and artistic value to religious objects of Java's past. But it was also exclusive, as this valuation primarily concerned products of particular, Hindu–Buddhist, non-Islamic origin. Moreover, Krom made a hierarchical distinction between earlier art forms in Central Java and a later art form, produced in East Java. The former were appreciated for their Indian origin and standard, and thus were considerd classic, while the latter were seen as more localised and characteristically Javanese – and less Indianised – and thus, implicitly in Krom's view, lesser.[6] It is unknown whether *regent* Kromodjojo Adinegoro held comparable pejorative views about East Java art during his lifelong interest in the material remains of the Majapahit past. But he surely found confirmation and legitimation for his 'gift' in scholarly as well as Indonesian nationalistic circles, bringing in his own 'local' and Javanese elitist interest.

In addition to Kromodjojo, who was born and raised in the region, the Indies-born architect and self-taught archaeologist, Henri Maclaine Pont, is another important figure who stimulated long-term local engagement with the site. While he played an activist role at the site, beginning in 1923, the Majapahit site shifted (for Indonesian nationalists) from a Greater Javanese into a Java-centred proto-Indonesian site. This implied a nationalist re-evaluation of Krom's concept of 'East Javanese art' as an expression of a purer local Javanese genius. This development does not mean, however, that the interests of the various parties engaging with the site stopped overlapping, nor that alternative local engagements (of religious, spiritual, or regionalist character) faded away. We argue in this chapter that these various and potentially conflicting interests are best understood as competing visions of the grand, pre-colonial history of the Majapahit site. We explore how and why, after

3 Krom, *Inleiding tot de Hindoe-Javaansche kunst*, II, 187; Director of Education and Religion to Raden Adipati Ario Kromo Djojo Adiningrat, *regent* of Mojokerto, 10 July 1913, ANRI, AS, Mgs. 12 August 1913, 1932.

4 Nicolaas J. Krom, 'Kort verslag van een studiereis in Voor- en Achter-Indië. I. Britsch-Indië (eerste reis)', *ROC 1910* (Batavia: Albrecht & Co.; 's-Gravenhage: M. Nijhoff, 1911), 53. On the impact of the new appreciation of Indian art in the Netherlands Indies, see Bloembergen, 'Borobudur in "the light of Asia"'.

5 See Krom, *Inleiding tot de Hindoe-Javaansche kunst*, I–III.

6 Nicolaas J. Krom, 'De oudheden van Modjokerto', *Nederlandsch-Indië. Oud en Nieuw* 1 (1916–1917), 99–106; see also Nicolaas J. Krom, 'De waardering der Hindoe-Javaansche kunst', *Nederlandsch-Indië. Oud en Nieuw* 8 (1923–1924), 178. Compare Stutterheim's critique of this view: Willem F. Stutterheim, 'Oudjavaansche kunst', *BKI* 79 (1923), 323–346.

1900, in the context of new, more systematic practices of research, translation, and collecting, and the setting up of two local museums in the region, one in Mojokerto, one in Trowulan, various layers of the local population living in and around Trowulan became further involved in (material) knowledge gathering, and in reimagining the Majapahit past through the site and its material remains.

Interestingly, while there is a rich critical historiography on the way Indonesian nationalists used 'Majapahit' to assert a grand Indonesian past, this historiography is very much Solo-, Yogyakarta- and Batavia-centred.[7] This may partly explain why, strangely, Kromodjojo is ignored in that historiography. Another reason may be that, as a co-operative *priyayi,* he was dropped from Indonesian nationalist historiography. In this chapter, we first follow him, and then focus on the architectural and archaeological social engineering activities of Maclaine Pont in the 1920s and 1930s. Both men founded an archaeological museum on location, and stimulated an interest and collaboration in collecting and reconstructing activities among the local populations. Both museums also became the object of Batavia-based colonial archaeological officials' attempts to control and centralise archaeological collecting and exhibiting practices. Against the background of these local and centralising activities, we move to the nationalist, Majapahit-centred, Greater Indonesia imaginations of the 1930s–1950s – as expressed by Muhammad Yamin in the quotation that heads this chapter.

As the Australian historian Anthony Reid and the Indonesian historian Supomo have shown, the early nationalist spokesmen of Greater Majapahit based their ideas on textbooks that summarised the recent findings of archaeological research and philological translation, such as Krom's *Hindoe-Javaansche Geschiedenis* ('Hindu–Javanese history', 1926 [1931]) and Fruin-Mees' *Geschiedenis van Java* ('History of Java', 1919–1920; translated into Malay in 1922). These spokesmen took over the state-centred, national framework of history-writing, in which Krom and Fruin-Mees themselves had remarked how coincidental it was that the domain of Majapahit overlapped with that of the Netherlands Indies.[8] We should add, however, that not only the philological transcribers and translators, but also rediscoveries, excavations, and interpretations by archaeologists and epigraphers were direct sources for the nationalist elites. Some of

[7] However, for the New Order period, see Wood, *Official history in modern Indonesia*, 81–82 and 196–207. As we argued in Chapter 3, Javanologists Gomperts, Haag, and Carey carefully reconstruct what we call site interventions. But they do so with a particular interest in the whereabouts of the *kraton*, less so in the discursive process of knowledge production and 'the construction of the site'. See for example Gomperts, Haag, and Carey, 'Stutterheim's enigma'; Gomperts, Haag, and Carey, 'Mapping Majapahit'.

[8] Supomo, 'The image of Majapahit', 181; this was pointed out earlier by Bosch, 'Iets over Oost-Javaansche kunst', and the Indonesian writer Bujung Saleh, 'De mythe als opium en zelfkennis van het volk', *Indonesië* 9: 6 (1956), 449–452.

those elites – such as Poerbatjaraka or Hoesein Djajadiningrat – were philologists and/or epigraphers themselves, and were involved in making Javanese history. Cultural congresses, moreover, were an important medium for the contribution to and dissemination of knowledge about Java's Greater Majapahit Past. Colonial scholars also directly contributed to the nationalists' journals, or their writings were republished. This growing corpus of scholarly knowledge inspired the nationalists to construct an image of Majapahit's greatness – helpfully visualised by historical maps – that came to function as inspirational predecessor and symbol of their aim: a future unified, independent nation-state.

In spatial terms, however, the nationalists' imagination extended beyond Maclaine Pont's limited research field. Likewise, their conception of Majapahit's greatness went far beyond what critical philologists such as Cornelius C. Berg (1900–1990) could take; Berg began to raise his voice in the 1930s against literal interpretations of old Javanese texts. What stirred the nationalists' imagination had less to do with archaeological research taking place at the site in Trowulan, and more to do with texts, maps, and histories that they believed demonstrated the greatness, artfulness, and reach of Majapahit. And that, perhaps, explains the power of their narrative: to them, the site itself did not seem to matter or, as the Leiden-trained lawyer, historian, and diplomat Soenario put it: 'Sites are not my problem.'[9] Not coincidentally, most of these Majapahit spokesmen were trained at the higher Dutch colonial education institutes, and, from the 1920s, were based in the Netherlands Indies' centres of cultural heritage politics: Batavia, Yogyakarta, and Solo – not Demak, or Trowulan for that matter.

The *Regent* and the Archaeological-Geneaological Sensation

Although ignored by Indonesian national historiography, Kromodjojo Adinegoro IV, son of R. A. A. Kromodjojo Adinegoro III, is still known as the great caretaker of Majapahit's heritage in the area of Trowulan. Today, his Indonesian Wikipedia page refers to him as 'bupati Majapahit'.[10] In one of his first publications – with Brill, on *wayang* traditions from the region – Kromodjojo claimed that almost all

[9] Soenario, quoted in Leclerc, 'L'circonscription', 43. See n. 2 of this chapter. Soenario was co-founder of the nationalist Perhimpunan Indonesia, and is thus considered one of the founding fathers of the Indonesian Republic. In post-independence Indonesia, he became minister of foreign affairs (1953–1955), co-organisor of the Bandung Conference (1955), and Indonesian ambassador to the UK.

[10] See http://id.wikipedia.org/wiki/RAA_Kromodjoyo_Adinegoro (accessed 5 December 2013). See also the information at the entrance of the museum in Trowulan, or newspaper clippings in the library of the BP3, such as 'R. A. A. Kromojoyo, tokoh di Balik Pelestartian kepurbakalaan. Tidak sekader lurahnya Majaphit, tapi Bupatinya Majapahit', *Jawa Pos*, 24 November 2007 (with a picture of him standing with a group of Dutchmen and -women, in front of his museum in Mojokerto).

regenten of Java descended from the last king of the Majapahit empire, Brawijaya V.[11] He would build his case based on lifelong historical, philological, and archaeological research in the region.

While growing up outside the cultural-political centres of Batavia, Yogyakarta, and Solo, Kromodjojo nonetheless became part of the scholarly scene in Java. He belonged to the generation of Javanese elites who from an early age received Western schooling, attended the new HBS (Hogere Burgerschool, Higher Secondary School (Dutch language)), and became interested in the history of the Majapahit site, which he explored further in the 1880s as *juru tulis* (writer) in Jombang (near Surabaya).[12] Aiming for systematic research, Kromodjojo read *Nagarakrtagama* and *Pararaton*, started collecting and inventorying statues and stones, and, in 1911, founded a museum in Mojokerto, the first Majapahit museum in the area (Figure 4.1). And he wrote a guideline and inventory for the study of the museum's collection, various reports about his historical, linguistic, and epigraphic researches, and an Old Javanese alphabet – some published as booklets, others in the reports of the Archaeological Service and the cultural journal *Djawa*.[13]

Though he claimed to be a direct descendant of the last great pre-colonial and pre-Islamic king Brawijaya, Kromodjojo was a faithful servant in the colonial state's *pangreh praja*.[14] He married into the local elite and enjoyed good

[11] Kromo Djojo Adinegoro, *Eene schets van de wajang poerwo en naar aanleiding hiervan het een en ander over de wajang gedek – wajang kroetjil, gamelan en gamelan melodieën – krissen en andere wapens* (Leiden: Brill, 1913); L. S. A. M. von Römer, 'Iets over het congres voor de Javaansche cultuurontwikkeling', *Wederopbouw* 1 (1918), 165–197. For a blog in which the *regent's* geneaology (or trah) goes back to Brawijaya, see http://kromojayankanoman .blogspot.nl/2012/10/serat-sara-silah-trah-kromodjayan.html (accessed 5 December 2013).

[12] Kromo Djojo Adinegoro, 'Opmerkingen aangaande de Lebaran of het Zoogenaamd Inlandsch Nieuwjaar', *OV 1923* (1923), 56; *Soerabaijasch Handelsblad*, 10 March 1934. On Kromodjojo's schooling and historical interest, see also http://id.wikipedia.org/wiki/RAA_Kr omodjoyo_Adinegoro (accessed 5 December 2013). The name of Kromodjojo is missing from the list of pupils who successfully finished HBS in those years (information from Tom van den Berge, January 2014).

[13] *Soerabaijasch Handelsblad*, 10 March1934; Kromo Djojo Adinegoro, *Eene schets van de wajang poerwo*; Kromo Djojo Adinegoro, 'Opmerkingen aangaande de Lebaran'; Kromo Djojo Adinegoro, 'Eenige opmerkingen aangaande den val van Majapahit', *OV 1915* (1915), 29–32; Kromo Djojo Adinegoro, 'Eene beknopte handleiding voor het onderzoek naar de Hindoe- en Boeddhabeelden [...] betrekking hebbend op de beelden in het museum in Modjokerto' (typescript, 1916, KITLV Collection [published 1921]); Kromo Djojo Adinegoro, *Eene beknopte handleiding voor het onderzoek naar de Hindoe- en Boeddhabeelden* (n.p., 18 February 1921); Kromo Djojo Adinegoro, *Oud Javaansche oorkonden op steen uit de afdeeling Modjokerto, opgehelderd door Raden Adipati Ario Kromodjoio Adi Negoro, Oud regent Modjokerto* (n.p., 1921); Kromo Djojo Adinegoro, 'Bijvoegsel over de opmerking aangaande de Lĕbaran, ofwel het Inlandsch nieuw jaar', *OV 1924* (1925), 76–80; Kromo Djojo Adinegoro, 'De begraafplaatsen der oude regenten van Grisee voor, tijdens en na de Compagnies tijd', *Djawa* 5 (1925), 253–254.

[14] Sutherland, *The making of a bureaucratic elite*. For Kromodjojo's support of colonial security politics, see correspondence between colonial authorities and Kromodjojo and his informants on (preventive) counter-insurgency research into religious and mystical movements in the area

Figure 4.1 Antiquities Museum in Modjokerto, picture taken between 1913–1930.

relationships with sugar barons and colonial *regenten*. The colonial government honoured him with several aristocratic titles, and made him an honorary member of the Batavian Society.[15] Obviously, such a figure aided the official colonial archaeological interest in the area, which developed in tandem with that of the *regent*, in a relationship of exchange and interdependency.[16]

In 1899, perhaps triggered by the first enquiries by Verbeek, Kromodjojo reported numerous brick remains in *desa* Sentonoredjo, in the area of Trowulan.[17] In 1913, he initiated the first excavations at the Majapahit site in

after the 'unrest' in Baron in 1907, in Leiden University Library, Special Collections, KITLV Collections, Archive G. A. J. Hazeu (adviser on Indigenous and Arab Affairs), KITLV H 1083, nrs. 62 and 95.

15 'Bij het overlijden van R. A. A. Kromodjojo-Adinegoro, oud-regent van Modjokerto', *Soerabaijasch Handelsblad*, 10 March 1934. The titles he received were Ario (1901), Adipati (1905), the prestigious right and colonial honorary code to carry the yellow parasol (1909), Officier in de Orde van Oranje Nassau (1920), and Ridder in de Orde van de Nederlandsche Leeuw (1925).

16 Marieke Bloembergen and Martijn Eickhoff, 'Conserving the past, mobilizing the Indonesian future: archaeological sites, regime change and heritage politics in Indonesia in the 1950s', *BKI* 167:4 (2011), 405–436.

17 *Oudheidkundig Verslag* 1941–1947 (Bandoeng: A. C. Nix & Co., 1949), 44–45. This site would later be explored by the pre-historian W. J. A. Willems from May to October 1941, on the order

Trowulan, based on the descriptions in the *Nagarakrtagama*, which were now more easily available, at least to him.[18] 'An excavation team' was in charge, probably consisting of villagers in service who followed the command of the *regent*. The newly founded Archaeological Service (directed by Krom) supported this enterprise and inspected the results. The first findings were assumed to be the remains of a wall. Krom and Kromodjojo decided that this was likely to be the surrounding wall of the *kraton*, and a good reference point for further systematic research. Kromodjojo's next excavation to attract the attention of the Archaeological Service was the basement of a temple, Candi Tikus, today restored and reconstructed, and reported as a feat of arms of the *regent* in all the guides for Majapahit, which the regional archaeological department has been publishing since the 1960s.

Kromodjojo's writings reveal how he studied material remains alongside the *Nagarakrtagama* and *Pararaton*, developing a historical awareness of sites and people's ritual practices. He described the chronology of Buddhist and Hindu periods, and that of rulers and their lands, and tried to connect these insights to his (mainly Islamic) present. He took an implicit position against India-centred explanations of the origins of the Hindu–Buddhist civilisation in Java. In the guidelines for the study of the statues and stones kept in his museum, he emphasised that the statues reflected a syncretic civilisation, which he called typical for Java and unthinkable in an Indian context.[19] As for the explanation for the end of the Majapahit empire, he concluded that Majapahit was not violently destroyed, but just decreased in importance due to the gradual spread of Islam, and the conversion to Islam by one part of the population, while another part moved to Tengger, Banyuwangi, and Bali.[20]

Kromodjojo combined his linguistic and historical interest with an anthropological eye for the present, seeking to understand what he came to see as the 'non-Mohammedan' legacies of Majapahit in his district.[21] Kromodjojo concluded that many sacrificial rituals being practised by the local population were a direct legacy of the Majapahit empire. Telling examples, to him, were the rituals known as *njadran*[22] (sacrifices for death). He also emphasised his own

of W. Stutterheim (then head of the Archaeological Service). Willems' research was financed by the residential council of East Java; see Gomperts, Haag, and Carey, 'Stutterheim's enigma', 419.

18 Brandes, *Nâgarakrĕtâgama*. See also Kern, *Het oud-javaansche lofdicht Nagarakrtagama van Prapanca*, previously published – between 1908 and 1919 – in the journal of the Koninklijk Instituut voor Taal-, Land- en Volkenkunde (then the Royal Institute of Linguistics and Anthropology), *Bijdragen tot de Taal-, Land- en Volkenkunde* (BKI).

19 Kromo Djojo Adinegoro, 'Eene beknopte handleiding' (typescript, 1916), 2; Kromo Djojo Adinegoro, *Eene beknopte handleiding* (n.p., 1921).

20 Kromo Djojo Adinegoro, 'Eenige opmerkingen aangaande den val van Majapahit'; Kromo Djojo Adinegoro, *Eene beknopte handleiding* (n.p., 1921), 30.

21 Kromo Djojo Adinegoro, 'Bijvoegsel over de opmerking aangaande de Lĕbaran'.

22 He was probably referring to the Javanese *sadran*, the care of graves.

role as *regent* in this kind of ritual, and that of his son who succeeded him in 1916: his son paid the *penghulu* (local chief of Islamic affairs) of Trowulan to gather the ingredients for the sacrifice-ritual, and he himself took these to one of the places indicated by the village head.[23] It is possible that Kromodjojo was actually writing about an *invented tradition* of which he himself was a motor. But whether it was invented or not, here we see how reports on site interventions can lead us to specific local engagements with sites from the lower regions of society; engagements that point to forms of care (here *njadran*) that alternate with heritage politics. In public honour and gratitude for the *regent*'s gifts of Hindu–Buddhist statues and the Mojokerto museum, the Archaeological Service made Kromodjojo honorary curator of the museum. As this apparently became a hereditary post, this gesture guaranteed continuity in the building of a museum collection and of heritage management at location.[24]

A *Priyayi* Museum, for the People

The museum in Mojokerto was dissolved around 1995, when the collection was moved to the Majapahit museum in Trowulan. The initial collection grew out of the pieces assembled haphazardly by the previous *regenten*, in front of the *regent*'s house, as encountered there by Brumund and Van Hoëvell, and was subsequently enriched by Kromojojo's acquisitions and findings, reaching as far away as the Penanggunang mountain, southeast of Mojokerto. To give an idea of the museum's content and the order of the exhibition, and to gauge its impact and meanings, we have Kromodjojo's guidelines for the study of the collection (1916 and 1921),[25] visual documentation (1918),[26] and an essay by Krom (1916).[27] The museum contained not only a collection of stone inscriptions important for the study of Java's ancient history, but also an almost complete overview of art from the plains of the Brantas river, representing remains of the first large Hindu kingdom in East Java in the eleventh century, and the subsequent Majapahit empire.[28] Objects were, according to 'Hindu'

[23] Kromo Djojo Adinegoro, 'Opmerkingen aangaande de Lebaran of het Zoogenaamd Inlandsch Nieuwjaar', 56, 59–60; Kromo Djojo Adinegoro, 'Bijvoegsel over de opmerking aangaande de Lĕbaran'.

[24] Director of the Department of Onderwijs en Eeredienst (Education and Religion) to Raden Adipati Ario Kromo Djojo Adiningrat, 10 July 1913, ANRI, AS, Mgs. 12 August 1913, 1932. The *regent*'s assignment in Bt 12 March 1915, 59, is mentioned in ANRI, AS Bt 2 December 1921, 55, when the management was handed over to his successor, Raden Toemenggoeng Kromo Adinegoro.

[25] Kromo Djojo Adinegoro, 'Eene beknopte handleiding' (typescript, 1916), 2; Kromo Djojo Adinegoro, *Eene beknopte handleiding* (n.p., 1921).

[26] Photographs, dated around 1918, kept in what is today the Museum of World Cultures, in particular the Tropenmuseum Amsterdam, formerly the Colonial Museum, and the National Ethnographic Musuem in Leiden.

[27] Krom, 'De oudheden van Modjokerto'. [28] Ibid., 100.

and 'Buddhist' religion, arranged in one central hall, and outside, around the building. Inside the building, one huge statue of Vishnu – the maintainer – seated on Garuda, posted at the end of hall, drew all attention. Above, on the wall, a portrait of the *regent* watched over everything, with a map of the region on the left. This display thus connected (as understood using Benedict Anderson's analysis of museums and maps), the *regent*, as the actual ruler, to his ancient domain.[29]

With, according to Krom, an average of 300 visitors a day, the museum facilitated various queries of local communities and scholars, as well as outside elites, which were, considering pictures of visitors offering to specific statues,[30] of a spiritual, scholarly-orientalist, and nationalist nature. It also catered to a regionalist interest, without contesting the interests of the central state. In this role, the museum demonstrates the subnational dimension of the museological landscape in Indonesia, which Anderson omitted from his theory on the relation between colonial state formation, archaeological museums, and maps.[31]

Krom, with the central museum in Batavia in mind, later expressed regret that pieces that belong together were divided between two museums,[32] but he was also pleased that a large portion of the antiquities from Majapahit found a place in Mojokerto's museum. This was important not only for scholarly interests – as the collection showed 'an excellent overview of the sculptured art from this centre of East Java, especially the Majapahit period' – but also for educational purposes. Krom conluded: 'the founder [Kromodjojo Adinegoro], who is at the same time honorary curator, has immediately understood that [the museum] should serve to stir the interest of the Javanese population in its majestic past. The crowds of visitors, and the eagerness with which they take notice of the extensive explanations next to some of the objects, prove that he was right.'[33]

The beginning of official historical propaganda for Majapahit was thus a local initiative that at this stage combined well with the central interests of the Archaeological Service. As the (art-)historical and archaeological interest in the site became more institutionalised – on location and in Batavia – soon other, private, parties got involved, adding new perspectives.

29 Anderson, *Imagined communities*, 155–185.

30 Museum of World Cultures (formerly the Colonial Museum), Amsterdam, Photographic collection, inv. nr KIT 60047222. According to the description of the photograph, the offerings took place only in the case of illness. Other pictures in this collection show people bathing in holy water for healing purposes, again indicating how sacred the natural landscape in the region and ancient objects in it were.

31 Anderson, *Imagined communities*, 155–185.

32 Krom, *Inleiding tot de Hindoe-Javaansche kunst*, II, 187.

33 Ibid., 195–196.

Architectural Social Engineering and the City-State

In 1923 Kromodjojo had a visit from Henri Maclaine Pont (1884–1972), who consulted the *regent* about his site explorations into the plan of the Majapahit empire. Maclaine Pont, an Indies-born, Dutch-trained architect, who moved in the circles of the recently founded Java Institute in Yogyakarta (1919), is famous today for his design of the Technological Institute in Bandung (Institut Teknologi Bandung, ITB, 1919), which was inspired by local architecture and building techniques.[34] As an architect he had developed a strong interest in the techniques and histories of landscapes and buildings in Java. Originally inspired by his reading of the *Pararaton* and the *Nagarakrtagama* – especially verses 8 to 12, where the poet Prapanca describes the buildings of the *kraton* – this interest included the plan and structure of the city-state Majapahit. In 1923, on a three-month mission in Surabaya for his new post as inspector-technician of the Burgerlijk Geneeskundige Dienst (Civil Medical Service), he spent his Sundays exploring what he presumed to be the site of the old centre of Majapahit. Following *Nagarakrtagama*, and what he considered an eyewitness account of Prapanca, he noticed, from the ongoing excavations since the discovery of Candi Tikus, that Kromodjojo was on the same track. Kromodjojo provided him with a map indicating the possible position of the outer wall, a map that would become Maclaine Pont's lifelong project: to reconstruct and understand the old plan of the Majapahit city-state in order to inspire social development in the area.[35]

Through this gift of the map, the architect and the *regent* became connected by their historical interest in the site. Although Maclaine Pont would dispute Kromodjojo's theories of the 'outer walls' of the kingdom, and paternalistically referred to him as 'the congenial greybeard' ('sympathieke grijzaard'), he gave him credit for making that first map.[36] Over the years, and in local memory, the *regent* and Maclaine Pont would become a strong team in regional heritage politics. From the early 1920s when Maclaine Pont arrived at the site until the *regent*'s death in 1934, the *regent* would be Maclaine Pont's crucial informant, partner, and mediator in propaganda activities in the area – although their motives may not have entirely overlapped. This differentiated collaboration, in changing hierarchies, defined the colonial character of their project.[37] Where the *regent* may have started out from an elite-centred interest in the material

[34] For Maclaine Pont, see Ben F. van Leerdam, 'Architect Henri Maclaine Pont. Een speurtocht naar het wezenlijke van de Javaanse architectuur', PhD thesis, Delft University (Delft: Eburon, 1995); Gerrit de Vries and Dorothee Segaar Höweler, *Henri Maclaine Pont: architect, controleur, archeoloog* (Rotterdam: Stichting Bonas, 2009); Gomperts, Haag, and Carey, 'The sage who divided Java in 1025'.

[35] Leerdam, *Maclaine Pont*, 6; 'De geboorte van Modjopahit', manuscript by H. Maclaine Pont, in Nederlands Architectuurinstituut (hereafter NAI), Archive Maclaine Pont, inv. nr MACL 76.

[36] Henri Maclaine Pont, 'Madjapahit: poging tot reconstructie van het Stadsplan, nagezocht op het terrein aan de hand van den Middeleeuwschen dichter Prapanca', *OV 1924* (1925), 44.

[37] Compare Cooper, *Colonialism in question*.

remains of Majapahit's past, seeking hereditary legitimation, Maclaine Pont added to that the perspectives of a Javanese 'popular genius', of city/community planning, of social engineering, and of *popular* arts, which he would soon commemorate in an archaeological museum in Trowulan.

To Maclaine Pont, the 'Majapahit' site brought together all that he cared for as a modern, ethically, and socially minded architect with a passion for (what he understood to be) popular Javanese culture. As archaeologist, and Javanologist to a certain extent, he was self-taught, but he spoke the living Javanese language. His interests in the site were part of a social and architectural query, which he shared with a generation of modern architects in the Netherlands Indies. Although the way they articulated solutions and evaluations of 'local culture' differed widely, they all sought a new architectural language, an architecture for modern urban development that suited the tropics and local styles and needs, one emphatically distinct from the neoclassical style that had dominated the nineteenth century.[38] Their quest for 'local architectural' inspiration overlapped with the query of the generation of Dutch scholars, who in the Indies in the 1920s and 1930s sought the Javanese or Indonesian roots of the Hindu–Buddhist monuments – which challenged the views of their Indian, Sanskrit-oriented teachers, and Greater India-oriented scholars from India.[39]

For a new modern colonial architecture, Maclaine Pont had found the solution in what he called the 'eigen karakter' (local character) of Javanese architectural traditions (especially the *pendopo*). To this end, he studied the reliefs of Borobudur and Prambanan, comparing them with living building constructions in Java and Sumatra.[40] Majapahit reliefs at the museum in Batavia also provided relevant building images, which taught him what he defined as the non-monumental outlook of the old Javanese city.[41] All this

[38] On the colonial architectural query and the history of colonial urban planning in the Netherlands Indies, see Huib Akihary, *Architectuur en stedebouw in Indonesië: 1870–1970* (Zutphen: Walburg Press, 1990); Pauline van Roosmalen, 'Ontwerpen aan de stad: Stedenbouw in Nederlands-Indië en Indonesië, 1905–1950', PhD thesis, Technical University (Delft: Technische Universiteit, 2008); Cor Passchier, *Building in Indonesia, 1600–1960* (Volendam: LM Publishers, 2016).

[39] Johannes G. de Casparis, 'Historical writing on Indonesia (early period)', in Daniel G. E. Hall (ed.), *Historians of South East Asia* (London: Oxford University Press, 1961), 121–164; Bloembergen, 'Borobudur in "the light of Asia"'.

[40] Leerdam, *Maclaine Pont,* 6; De Vries and Segaar Höweler, *Maclaine Pont*, 38–39. See the drawings Maclaine Pont made during his travels around Central Javanese monuments in 1914/1915 in H. Maclaine Pont, 'Beredeneerde opgave der reisschetsen, gemaakt in mei en juni 1915', *Nederlandsch-Indië Oud en Nieuw* 15:2 (1930), 45–54, 69–87. On the use of architecture and temple reliefs for historical research, see also H. Maclaine Pont, 'De historische rol van Majapahit', *Djawa* 6 (1926), 1; and H. Maclaine Pont, 'Inleiding tot het bezoek aan het emplacement en de bouwvallen van Majapahit', *Djawa* 7 (1927), 171.

[41] Henri Maclaine Pont, 'Javaansche architectuur', *Djawa* 3 (1923), 112–117 and 170, plates 22 and 23; Henri Maclaine Pont, 'De nieuwe Javaansche bouworden', *Djawa* 4 (1924), 44. Compare the description of the newly acquired relief, inv. nr 4821, and the comparable remarks

research led Maclaine Pont to the rather static conclusion that 'the ground rules of Javanese architecture are today still the same as they were in the past'.[42]

To his architectural-archaeological inquiry, Maclaine Pont added a strong ethical-paternalistic and social motive. He had come to believe that 'knowing' the building and planning techniques from the Hindu–Buddhist past could provide the solution for what he saw as architectural and social poverty in contemporary Java – which he had studied as inspector-technician of the Civil Medical Service. If he could revive the old technical knowledge among Javanese, he reasoned, this might stimulate the development of Javanese (vernacular) housing architecture and ship building in the present and future.[43] Insight into architectural changes in the past, moreover, might deepen understanding of socio-political changes in the past and present. In general, it was the idea of Majapahit as a city-empire – or Nagara, as he preferred to call it – that kept Maclaine Pont going.[44] Maclaine Pont perceived in Majapahit's plan, which he would explore – and shape – over the years, a unity in style and function that suited his interest in modern city planning. But he also saw Majapahit as the key to understanding what Javanese culture was capable of. Typically, Maclaine Pont remarked that external forces – not necessarily 'Muhammadan but Arabic' – had prevented Majapahit from fully blossoming in its late phase; and, typically as well, he called on the Dutch colonial government to take over the consolidating and unifying role played by the last king of Majapahit.[45] This is where his view on the meaning of the site partly overlapped with those of the Indonesian nationalists who evoked Majapahit to

by Kohlbrugge on the non-monumental outlook of houses on the reliefs, in *Notulen van de Algemeene en Directievergaderingen van het Bataviaasch Genootschap van Kunsten en Wetenschappen*, XCVII (1909). This same relief also served to illustrate propaganda material of the Majapahit Society: Henri Maclaine Pont and Frederik D. K. Bosch, 'Beschouwingen over Majapahit', *Indisch Bouwkundig Tijdschrift* 10 (1926), 2–18.

42 Maclaine Pont and Bosch, 'Beschouwingen over Majapahit', 4.

43 Ibid., 2, 7: 'to inspire the interest of the Javanese, for the good works from his glorious past [Om den Javaan weer te boeien, met de goede werken uit zijn glorietijd]'. See also Maclaine Pont, 'Javaansche architectuur'; Maclaine Pont, 'De nieuwe Javaansche bouworden'. See also an unpublished proposal of December 1926, by Maclaine Pont, submitted to the Batavian Society, to support a systematic survey on the state of the arts of the local building and ship-building inudustry in Java and Madura, 'Voorstel tot het houden eener enquete in zake de inlandsche bouw- en scheepsbouwambachten op Java en Madoera, 1-12-1926', ANRI, KBG DIR 1032.

44 This would become a major theme again in the 1960s, but then to guide the ideal of a unified state, under the 'Old Order' of Soekarno and the subsequent 'New Order' of Soeharto, where Maclaine Pont's map would be the guide for starting a prestigious aerial photography project. See Muhammad Yamin, *Tatanegara Madjapahit: Risalah Sapta-parwa berisi 7 djilid atau parwa, hasil penelitian ketatanegaraan Indonesia tentang dasar dan bentuk negara Nusantara bernama Madjapahit, 1293–1525*, 4 vols. (Jakarta: Prapantja, 1962). Compare Slametmuljana, *The structure of the national government of Majapahit* (Jakarta: Balai Pustaka, 1966).

45 Maclaine Pont, 'De historische rol van Majapahit', 2, 24.

inspire the Indonesian nation.[46] But they did so in Batavia and Central Java, not at the site.

Maclaine Pont's first 'Majapahit' publication was programmatic.[47] Helped by the data of Wardenaar, Verbeek, Knebel, and Kromodjojo, and with a very close reading of Prapanca's descriptions of the buildings in the kingdom, he developed a hypothesis about the layout, and especially the orientation of the city-state, which he argued heaved a bit to the left in comparison to the map provided by the *regent*. With this cartographic intervention, certain building structures (the main gate, the Seragan pont) fit in the plan of a Javanese city, which he had reconstructed based on a central Javanese *kraton*. Maclaine Pont provided a preliminary example showing how following Prapanca could lead to further insights, and he called for more systematic research. This report, and this call, would trigger a remarkable cultural society – through which, for the next two decades, Maclaine Pont gained lasting, albeit not undisputed, support for his ambitions.

The Majapahit Society, a Monstrous Alliance

On 15 April 1924 a number of engaged individuals founded the Vereeniging Majapahit (Majapahit Society), a civic organisation with private funding, to be based in Trowulan. The Archaeological Service's director Bosch, charmed by Maclaine Pont's preliminary findings, supported this initiative out of his principled interest in the 'too long unacknowledged' 'particular local art value' of the material remains of the 'Javanese middle ages' in East Java, following the 'classic' period of Central Javanese art.[48] The double aim of the Majapahit Society was to advance archaeological research on Majapahit, and to bolster knowledge about, and interest in, the ancient past (*Oudheidkunde)* of Java. In the early phase of propaganda and fund-raising – Maclaine Pont and Bosch went on a promotional lecture tour (though their relationship would eventually sour) in Surabaya, Mojokerto, Malang, Semarang, Solo, Yogyakarta, and Weltevreden – the social motive behind this was further explicated.[49] The society aimed to promote the study of Majapahit's role in the history of Java 'from a social point of view', with concrete educational aims: 'to teach again those old skills and methods, and . . . means, the design and the adornment, in which the ancient ideology which still lives amongst the

[46] Supomo, 'The image of Majapahit'.

[47] Maclaine Pont, 'Madjapahit: poging tot reconstructie van het Stadsplan', 36–75, 157–168.

[48] Bosch himself was also active in promoting the interest in Majapahit as the site 'where one of the most glorious periods of Javanese history had been reached', and a site of the arts of East Java. See, for example, Bosch, 'Iets over Oost-Javaansche kunst', 52–54.

[49] The lectures were published in 1926 by *Indisch Bouwkundig Tijdschrift*. See Maclaine Pont and Bosch, 'Beschouwingen over Majapahit'. See also *De Indische Courant*, 10 October 1925, on a lecture held by Maclaine Pont for the Soerabaiaschen Kunstkring.

people . . . to the present generation, or to use it for the good in other ways'.[50] The organisation thus refigured Majapahit as the key to understanding Javanese antiquity, and presented itself as a tool for the ethical development of Javanese culture in the present and the future.

Although we have no exact figures for the number of members of the society – one supportive newspaper reported 'around a hundred' in 1932[51] – it is important to note that this initiative managed to connect different parties not only in the region, but also in the cultural centres in Batavia and Yogyakarta/Solo.[52] Others, however, were less charmed with the initiatives developing at Trowulan from the beginning, but this may have had more to do with personal dislike than with the site in itself. In 1924, Sam Koperberg, the proactive secretary of the Java Institute, expressed his doubts to Mangkunegara VII: 'I am afraid that people make too much fuss about Majapahit and that this case is doomed to disappoint.'[53]

In 1925 Maclaine Pont settled in Trowulan to represent the Majapahit Society and start his site explorations in the region, occasionally collaborating with the service's technical inspector.[54] His aims were: to locate the remains, structure/plan, irrigation works, agrarian production, and scope of the Majapahit empire; to train the local population in recovering and reviving the old building techniques, for which he tried to gain extra support from the Batavian Society (to no avail);[55] and to set up a site museum, or field museum as Maclaine Pont referred to it, at the Trowulan site, to sort and display the results of the excavations. There was, in that sense, no formal collaboration with the museum in Mojokerto. His first building, mainly used for keeping and sorting, arose in 1926. It was soon followed by a second, with a remarkable hanging 'equilibripetal' ('seeking balance') roof construction, inspired by Javanese *pendopo* architecture. This roof covered the museum display, which officially opened to the public in 1931.[56]

[50] Undated concept letter, intended for fundraising for the society, NAI, Archive Maclaine Pont, inv. nr MACL 33.

[51] 'Modjokerto. Madjapahit', *De Indische Courant,* 22 June 1932.

[52] See the society's letter to Mangkunegara VII, offering him an honorary membership, 26 October 1924 (accepted by Mangkunegara VII on 20 December 1924), Arsip Mangkunegara, Solo, Correspondence MVII, inv. nr M 2.

[53] Sam Koperberg to Mangkunegara VII, 14 March 1924, Arsip Mangkunegara Solo, Correspondence MVII, inv. nr K 92,8.

[54] Maclaine Pont was officially affiliated to the Archaeological Service for this aim by Governmental Resolution of 6 November 1924, 610. See also 'Personalia', *OV 1924* (1925), 97; *OV 1925* (1926), 104.

[55] 'Voorstel tot het houden eener enquete in zake de inlandsche bouw- en scheepsbouwambachten op Java en Madoera, 1-12-1926', ANRI, KBG DIR 1032.

[56] Architectural experts have discussed these constructions as ingenious, highly original examples of modern colonial architecture, inspired by and suitable for local traditions and circumstances.

The society and the museum, as well as Maclaine Pont's research methods and training activities, had their impact in the region. The organisational structure connected the local administration, village heads, villagers, and sugar factories in various ways to engage with regional-nationalist archaeological research, and to repair and reconstruct artefacts.[57] Together, the institutions and Maclaine Pont's activities helped to establish certain past–present relations in connection to the Majapahit site on which subsequent local and central regimes in colonial and post-colonial times could build.[58] Maclaine Pont himself became a public figure. Because of his lectures in the region, he became known for having a vision with 'mythic proportions' – prompting him to emphasise that he was not a 'Ziener' (visionary with supernatural power).[59]

For his explorations into the structure of the Majapahit empire and the location and plan of the palace, Maclaine followed a 'topographical method', which he had derived from the recent and methodologically highly topical work of Van Stein Callenfels on East Java.[60] Referred to as 'archaeologische prospectie' in the Netherlands and 'Landesaufnahme' in Germany, this method became popular in Europe at the end of the 1920s. It entailed the exploration of patterns in material remains in relation to the surrounding landscape, in order to gain insight into a site's history and meanings, and the ethnicity of its

For an extensive analysis and pictures of the museum in development, see De Vries and Segaar-Höweler, *Maclaine Pont*, 50–53.

57 On the support of local population and sugar factories, see Henri Maclaine Pont, *Mythe, overlevering en historisch besef op Java en de merkwaardige ontwikkeling van het Museumwezen in Nederl. Indië* (Mojokerto: Oudheidkundige Vereeniging Majapahit, 1936).

58 On Majapahit architecture in New Order East Java, compare Benedict R. O'G. Anderson, 'Cartoons and monuments: the evolution of political communication under the New Order', in Anderson, *Language and power: exploring political culture in Indonesia* (Ithaca: Cornell University Press, 1990), 152–194. In recent years, probably in the context of decentralisation, the regional administration in East Java announced plans to financially support every family head living near the Majapahit site if they wanted to remodel their houses in the Majapahit style (*Joglosemar*, 3 January 2011). In 2014 it initiated plans for a 'kampong Majapahit' in Majapahit style; see www.tempo.co/read/news/2014/01/22/058547182/Ratusan-Rumah-Akan-Jadi-Kampung-Majapahit- (accessed 25 May 2017).

59 De Vries and Segaar-Höweler, *Maclaine Pont*, 48.

60 Leerdam, *Architect Henri Maclaine Pont*, 52; Henri Maclaine Pont, 'Aantekeningen bij het artikel van Dr Van Stein Callenfels: "Bijdragen tot de topografie van Oost-Java in de Middeleeuwen"', *OV 1926* (1927), 88–100; P. V. van Stein Callenfels and L. Van Vuuren, 'Bijdragen tot de topografie van de residentie Soerabaia in de 14de eeuw', *Tijdschrift van het koninklijk Nederlandsch Aardrijkskunding* (hereafter *TKNAG*) 41:2 (1924), 67–81; P. V. van Stein Callenfels, 'Bijdragen tot de topografie van Oost-Java in de Middeleeuwen II', *OV 1926* (1927), 81–87; P. V. van Stein Callenfels, 'Bijdragen tot de topographie van Java in de Middeleeuwen', in *Feestbundel uitgegeven door het Koninklijk Bataviaasch Genootschap van Kunsten en Wetenschappen bij gelegenheid van het 150-jarig bestaan 1778–1928*, vol. II (Weltevreden: Kolff & Co., 1929), 370–392. For an extensive analysis of Maclaine Pont's archaeological method and work in the region, see Gomperts, Haag, and Carey, 'The sage who divided Java in 1025'.

inhabitants.[61] In that framework, Maclaine Pont traced names of places, and of functions, in old charters, and compared these to contemporary vocabulary, and to the place names on 'Landrentekaarten' (land-tax maps), for which he consulted village heads and villagers. In an ever-growing area, he located remains of walls and terps, analysed sedimentary structures, and collected, again with local assistance, sculptures, figurines, and terracotta potsherds for the museum; and he build two extra sheds (*loodsen*) to sort the growing number of potsherds. While involving local inhabitants at the lowest level of the administrative structure in his project, Maclaine Pont slowly appropriated Majapahit as a kingdom that was a unified city-state, and a community with a social welfare plan.

By 1930, 1,233 objects were added to the collection as purchases and as gifts, and 11,980 others through excavation.[62] In that year, just before Maclaine Pont departed for a ten-month trip to Europe, he received extra funding from the Archaeological Service to dig trenches to test his hypothesis regarding the ground plan of the palace complex.[63] But this would be the last substantial gesture to come from Batavia. The Archaeological Service was not entirely convinced and was less and less tempted to support this enterprise. From 1930, in the context of the international financial crisis, and subsequent cuts in the budget of the Archaeological Service, support from the central institutions in Batavia – both the Archaeological Service and the Batavian Society – for Maclaine Pont's activities in Trowulan soon dried up. This new distance of the centralising, colonial archaeological politics from the site in the 1930s is remarkable when considering the status Majapahit would soon gain as a proto-site of the Indonesian nation.

Centralising and Local Connections to the Past

The withdrawal of government support did not disrupt work in Trowulan – on the contrary, the activities of the *regent* and Maclaine Pont had a long-lasting impact on cultural and economic politics of Majapahit, small-scale though it was. The findings during the explorations of and excavations at the site were collected in the field museum for sorting and further investigation, and put on display. In 1932, as a proof of the impact of the museum as educative tool for local society, the correspondent of the *Indische Courant*, explicitly supporting a fund-raising campaign for the Majapahit Society, emphasised its success

[61] Martijn Eickhoff, *Van het land naar de markt: 20 jaar RAAP en de vermaatschappelijking van den Nederlandse archeologie* (Amsterdam: RAAP, 2005), 13–15.

[62] See 'Begroting Oudheidkundige Dienst voor 1930', Arsip Mangkunegara VII, Solo, inv. nr P.589.

[63] 'Majapahit', *OV 1929* (1930), 17–18; 'Oudheidkundige Vereeniging Majapahit', *OV 1930* (1931), 29–37.

based on the number of visitors. Apparently, in its first year, the museum attracted little attention (137 visitors), but in the next year, in June alone, it counted 1,500 visitors, predominantly Javanese from the region. The *Indische Courant* explained this local interest by the fact that the collection at that stage (in 1932) 'already' gave 'a good overview of the lifestyles etc. of all layers of the population in bygone ages'.[64] But all this work was now about to be destroyed due to the lack of money.

One economic side effect of the excavation and collecting activities was a booming trade in Majapahit antiquities. Apparently, news spread about their value as 'local', East Javanese, popular Hindu–Buddhist art, and by late 1933 or early 1934 various antiquities from Majapahit were offered for sale in Surabaya. This worried the Archaeological Commission, the advisory committee of the Archaeological Service.[65] Since the mid 1920s this commission – which had some members of Javanese and Netherlands Indies origin, with a Dutch majority – had served as a permanent advisory body, in front of which the Archaeological Service also had to defend policies and budget priorities.[66] During a meeting of the commission in April 1934, one of its members, the architect Cosman Citroen (a citizen of Surabaya involved in the establishment of the new City Museum there) explained that a Chinese Society, recently founded in Trowulan, had started to collect antiquities, both bronzes and terracotta objects. He and Bosch, who had checked with Maclaine Pont, reassured the commission that no objects were derived from the museums in Trowulan and Mojokerto. They explained the sudden availability of Majapahit antiquities by the fact that Maclaine Pont, who used to 'buy' everything old that people found in the ground, had stopped doing so; now people continued excavating but tried to sell to other interested parties in Surabaya.[67]

This discussion about selling Majapahit antiquities reflected Director Bosch's broader worries regarding the functioning of the Monument Act-in-development (implemented in 1931), and the relation between central and local museum policies – concerns shared by his predecessor, Krom. But, with regard to Trowulan in particular, Bosch feared that the Archaeological Service had lost

[64] *De Indische Courant*, 22 June 1932.

[65] 'Notulen van de 4de vergadering van de Oudheidkundige Commissie, gehouden te Djocjacarta', 15 April 1934, Arsip Mangkunagaran VII, Solo, inv. nr P.1212. In 1934 the commission included Mangkunegara VII, R. A. A. Soemitro Poerbanegara (*regent* of Bandjarnegara, Central Java), and P. A. Soerjodiningrat (Yogyakarta, a half-brother of the sultan?). B. Schrieke was chair. The other members were architects C. Citroen and Th. Karsten, self-taught Javanologist J. L. Moens, and P. H. W. Sitsen.

[66] The commission was originally set up as an advisory tool during the 'Restoration problem' (Restauratie-kwestie) which became a topic of governmental dispute up in the 1920s (which we discuss in Chapter 5). It concerned the question whether the Siva temple at Prambanan could be reconstructed or should be kept as found.

[67] 'Notulen van de 4de vergadering van de Oudheidkundige Commissie, gehouden te Djocjacarta', 15 April 1934, Arsip Mangkunagaran VII, Solo, inv. nr P.1212.

a measure of control, in terms of both heritage management and research objectives. Bosch criticised the financial management of the Majapahit Society, the lack of reporting on a project of which the work terrain seemed to expand endlessly while the hypothesis on which the research was built – on the location, reach, and regular layout of the city – had grown 'wild'. He withdrew most of the personnel, together with the government funding.[68]

Maclaine Pont nonetheless continued his archaeological work in East Java, partly due to building assignments. Over the years, the relationship between Maclaine Pont and the Archaeological Service froze.[69] In November 1939 Maclaine Pont described the heart of the matter in a letter to his Aunt 'Tien' as complete mis-appreciation of his important work, explainable only by jealousy.[70] The unnamed potsherd-seekers mentioned in his letter point to the local backing of Maclaine Pont's ideals. He had indeed found local support – practical, but also financial and moral – in the region: from the *regentschapsraad* of Mojokerto, from the *regentschapsraad* of Djember, from the growing numbers of visitors to the museum in Trowulan,[71] from the *regentschapsraad* from Kediri, from the sugar entrepreneurs,[72] and, last but not least, from 'the' local population, as Maclaine Pont would emphasise again and again.[73] This local support, from the lower layers of society, formed the core of his defence against the efforts of the Archaeological Service to centralise museum and collecting policies in the 1930s.

In 1935, Bosch defended the structural centralisation of museum and collecting policies in the colony, during a speech at the inauguration of the Java Institute's Sonobudoyo Museum in Yogyakarta.[74] He was motivated by the Archaeological Service's efforts to adapt (and extend) the Monument Act of 1931 to local circumstances, in order to prevent looting and export of Hindu–Buddhist antiquities, and the service's ongoing efforts to register and control the collections of the various local museums. While Bosch discussed what he saw as a general problem of local museums, his talk and the location where it took place could be read as a direct criticism of *particular* museums: the one in Trowulan (the Majapahit Society's collection) and the one in

68 'Oudheidkundige Vereeniging Majapahit', *OV 1930* (1931), 29; criticism from Bosch can be found in Maclaine Pont to Bosch, 1 June 1931, NAI, Archive Maclaine Pont, inv. nr MACL 33.

69 From 1937, financial reserves for the works in Trowulan were gone, and the Archaeological Service's special funding stopped. However, Maclaine Pont continued the works by paying his three-man staff from his own resources: the rental of his house in Batavia. From 1940 the Archaeological Service resumed funding. See De Vries and Segaar Höweler, *Maclaine Pont*, 62.

70 Maclaine Pont to Tante Tien, 25 November 1939, NAI, Archive Maclaine Pont.

71 *Soerabaiasch Handelsblad*, 8 September 1939.

72 Maclaine Pont to Tante Tien, 25 November 1939, NAI, Archive Maclaine Pont.

73 Maclaine Pont, *Mythe, overlevering en historisch besef op Java*; Maclaine Pont to Tante Tien, 25 November 1939, NAI, Archive Maclaine Pont.

74 F. D. K. Bosch, 'De ontwikkeling van het Museum-Wezen in Nederlandsch-Indië', *Djawa, Tijdschrift van het Java-Instituut* 15 (1935), 209–221.

Mojokerto (the *regent*'s collection). To Bosch, these two local museums were not as important as the Sonobudoyo Museum and the Batavian Society's museum.[75] This distinction gave Maclaine Pont more reason to fervently defend his work with the argument that 'local interests' made an important difference.

Maclaine Pont found Bosch's reasoning painful, elite-centred, and short-sighted. He vented his gall in a long essay published in 1936 by the Majapahit Society – in the series Majapahitsche Dunne Boekjes ('Majapahit booklets'), which appeared very irregularly – under the attention-grabbing title 'Myth, historical legacies and historical consciousness, and the remarkable development of the museum system in the Netherlands Indies'.[76] He emphasised the Trowulan Museum's distinctions from other local museums: it was a field museum, and as such not meant to keep its collection, but to inform people about the ongoing research in the region, and as a temporary shelter. Moreover, the Trowulan field museum's collection criteria were, as Maclaine Pont believed, guided by a deep and broad interest in local society. He had two arguments: first, the museum had never tried to enrich its collection from outside the anticipated research field, and had never carried away statues that were still honoured *in situ* by the local population. This had also a methodological reason, namely to protect historical-topographical data.[77] Second, the collections in Trowulan nonetheless had been enriched by very beautiful 'specimana' that almost all came to the museum as 'gifts'. This indicated that 'the museum had become more and more well known and popular – especially among the rural population'. People were prepared to make long and exhausting journeys, he argued, to present their findings because 'to widely outstretched located communities, the name and place of Majapahit have not lost their lustre. Thus: the gift of an ancient cultural good [*cultuurbezit*], to which the owners attached much more importance than the caretaker, transformed into a gesture of piety.'[78]

To Maclaine Pont, local interest in the past – emphatically not restricted to a Hindu past – thus legitimised a historical collection on location. And to him it made no difference whether it concerned the 'middle ages' or prehistory. Maclaine Pont illustrated this point with a story of an 'old simple man' in the village of Tarik; the former had been looking for a specific place, which had been relocated for military purposes. The old man recognised the name, but informed him that this place, under that name, had been moved some kilometres further to the north. And there Maclaine Pont indeed found the remains of an older, pre-Majapahit settlement: 'And this story, including the special detail about the moving of a place, is told to me by an old village man, eleven

[75] Ibid., 214. [76] Maclaine Pont, *Mythe, overlevering en historisch besef op Java.*
[77] Ibid., 2. [78] Ibid., 3.

and a half centuries later. Is this not proof of a connection with the past?'[79] To Maclaine Pont this example was a 'symptom' that 'real connections with the past' were felt among all layers of the population in the countryside, and remain unbroken – in East Java, Central Java, and West Java. But, he argued, in East Java the historical consciousness of the population was 'STRONGER' than in many other regions. The popular historical consciousness he encountered was – using the repertoire of folklore studies – 'real' and '*eigen*' ('people's own', 'local'), even 'in the blood'. It connected 'the people' in every region with the local past and the ancient past, and with the role their region had played in the general history of the people.[80]

Studies on Maclaine Pont as the progressive architect that he was fail to recognise his contribution to racial thinking, in ways not unique for that time. Maclaine Pont believed that a (Javanese) people and a site generated a certain collective cultural and architectural tradition over its millennium-old history. And he believed that this cultural gem was unchanging and could be revived because of popular traditions and a popular will. In that sense he resembled the Indonesian elite's cultural nationalism, which developed outside this site. At the same time, it seems that more than others, Maclaine Pont emphasised the importance of collaboration at the site with the local population, appreciating their contributions as a crucial condition. Typically, one does not see this in his scholarly publications, except for his discussion with Bosch, where the local interest was his rhetorical weapon. Meanwhile, another 'local' group – Indonesian elites based in Batavia, Yogyakarta, and Solo – had become deeply interested in the great Majapahit empire as well, though perhaps less so in the site.

Majapahit in and outside Nationalist Imaginations, 1920s–1950s

In November 1934, the Solo-based Islamic journal *Adil* announced the play 'Mojopahit and Islam', to be staged in the town of Demak and performed by its inhabitants. The journal explained that Demak was the site where Raden Patah founded the first Islamic kingdom on Java. In three acts, the play would recount (Act 1) the meeting of the nine *wali* in Ampel (Surabaya). This led to (Act 2) the mission of their representatives to the king of Majapahit, Brawijaya, to ask permission to convert the people of Majapahit to Islam. Finally (Act 3), the Hindu king Giriwandojo renounces his royal power, and Raden Patah becomes king of Demak.[81] By depicting the Islamisation of Java as peaceful and

[79] Ibid., 12. [80] Ibid., 12.

[81] *Adil,* 15 November 1934, summarised in *Overzicht van de Inlandsche en Maleisch-Chineesche pers* 45 (1934), 736. This colonial weekly overview of the Chinese and Malay press in the Netherlands Indies does not mention the author. Unfortunately we have not yet traced the original issue of *Adil*.

uncontested, these inhabitants of Demak portrayed a pre-colonial Java in which Islam was endemic and a source of national pride and in which Majapahit played merely a preparatory role. They thereby took a stance against nationalist intellectuals who in the 1920s and 1930s came to see Majapahit as the forerunner of the Javanese culture and nation and, later, as a powerful unifying force for the Indonesian nation. The play in Demak, however, illustrates how Majapahit not only had a unifying allure, but also posed problems for the Indonesian nation.[82] Some disputes (such as the one present in the play 'Mojopahit and Islam') go back to the older, critical engagements from the 1880s, against modernising or purifying Islam.[83] Others coincided with what is referred to as the (nationalist) Javanese cultural awakening.

From around 1918, a number of protagonists from the Islamic party Sarekat Islam (SI, founded in 1912), like its Java-born leader Oemar Said Tjokroaminoto (1882–1934) and his brother Abi Koesno Tjokrosoejoso (1897–1968), or the Sumatra-born Abdoel Moeis (1883–1959), became notably annoyed by the emphasis on the greatness of the (temple remains of the) ancient Hindu–Buddhist times on Java. They deemed such an emphasis much too dominant at the Congress for the Development of Javanese Culture in Solo in 1918, and in the related journal, *Wederopbouw* of the Committee for Javanese Nationalism.[84] Abdoel Moeis, for example, in the Surabaya-based Sarekat Islam journal *Neratja* warned of 'the danger that cannot be underestimated' of stoking pride in an ancient Hindu past of Java. He worried that this might cause Islamic subjects to convert to Hinduism and lead to religious conflict. He argued that the reviving interest in the ancient Hindu Javanese past is part of the 'Verdeel en Heers politiek' (divide-and-rule strategy) of colonial authorities.[85] Such critical voices, while not silenced and often raised, seem to have been overpowered by a nationalistic discourse on Majapahit, much discussed by historians, that came to dominate the writing and thinking of a small but influential group of Indonesia's nationalist and cultural elite, both from Java and Sumatra.[86]

[82] Supomo, Reid, and Van Miert have analysed the disputes around the Greater Majapahit visions of the 1920s, 1930s, and 1950s, pointing to alternative views by other Indonesian intellectuals who reasoned from Islamic, Marxist, and/or modernist perspectives. See Supomo, 'The image of Majapahit', 183–184; Reid, 'The nationalist quest for an Indonesian past'; Van Miert, *Een koel hoofd*.

[83] Compare Ricklefs, *Polarising Javanese society*.

[84] See B. J. O. Schrieke, 'Nota over het Congres voor Javaansche Cultuurontwikkeling (5, 6–7–1918 in Solo)', pp. 26–28, Arsip Mankunegara VII, Mangkunegaran, Solo, inv. nr YN 1005.

[85] Abdoel Moeis, 'Bahaja jang tidak boleh dipandang ketjil', *Neratja*, 4 July 1918. See also Soepprodjo, 'Congres hal kemadjoean bangsa Djawa di Solo', *Oetoesan Hindia*, 3 July 1918.

[86] Supomo, 'The image of Majapahit'; Reid, 'The nationalist quest for an Indonesian past'; Leclerc, 'Sentiment national et revendication territoriale en Indonésie'; Leclerc, 'La circonscription'; Van Miert, *Een koel hoofd*; Wood, *Official history in modern Indonesia*.

In the writings of the generation of nationalist elites of the 1920s and 1930s, the standard story consisted of four motifs: the sense of a local/ Javanese genius and of local artistic capacities; the idea of the physical and spiritual-visionary power and administrative capacities of its leaders, especially Gajah Mada;[87] the unity and wide reach of the empire; and the role of Islam, whether as endemic or external force, whether further unifying or distorting. Against that backdrop, Javanese *priyayi* such as Soetatmo Soeriokoesoemo and Radjiman Wediodiningrat, and Sumatra-born elites, such as Sanusi Pané and Muhammad Yamin, resemble Maclaine Pont, inspired by ideas about the (Javanese) spirit, artfulness, civilisational ideas, and state power of the Majapahit empire. They focused in particular on the Majapahit praised by Prapanca, the Majapahit under Hayam Wuruk, and the Majapahit under his marshal Gajah Mada as the great unifier of an immense empire, reaching from Papua in the east, to Malacca in the west, or even to Persia and Madagascar.

Revive the Past – Soeriokoesoemo

To Soeriokoesoemo (1888–1924),[88] a member of the Pakualaman house in Yogyakarta, and one of the founders of the Comité voor de Javaansche Cultuurontwikkeling (Committee for Javanese Cultural Development, 1919), Majapahit (as the greatest unified state) and Gajah Mada (as its architect) were tools to bridge the differences between Central and West Javanese regionalists, and between Java and what he called, from a Java-centred perspective, the 'surrounding islands', and to move towards a shared ideal: 'A higher Unity, the Cultural State of Indonesia'.[89] Soeriokoesoemo was a theosophist and member of the Javanese mystical movement Selasa-Kliwon, but 'above all', as the historian Hans van Miert portrayed him, a fervent Java-centric nationalist, striving for the revival of Majapahit and its royal rule on Java.[90] In his brief essay 'Het rijk van Gadjah Mada' ('The realm of Gadjah Mada'), Soeriokoesoemo linked visions of past state formation to the founding of the first important Indonesian political parties and cultural political organisations: Boedi Oetomo, the Indische Partij, Sarekat Islam, and the Javaansche

[87] In verse 12, strophe 4, of the *Nagarakrtagama* Prapanca had described Gajah Mada's power as outstanding.

[88] On Soeriokoesoemo, *Wederopbouw*, and the Javanese nationalists' dreams of the revival of Majapahit, see Van Miert, *Een koel hoofd*, 92–128. See also Takashi Shiraishi, 'The disputes between Tjipto Mangoenkoesoemo and Soetatmo Soeriokoesoemo: Satria vs. Pandita', *Indonesia* 14 (1981), 93–108; Ruth T. McVey, 'Taman Siswa and the Indonesian National Awakening', *Indonesia* 4 (1967), 128–149.

[89] Soeriokoesoemo, 'Ons derde levensjaar', *Wederopbouw* 3:1 (1920), 1–4: 'een hoogere eenheid, de Cultuurstaat Indonesië'.

[90] Van Miert, *Een koel hoofd,* 96. Soeriokoesoemo assisted architect P. A. J. Moojen during his research into the damage to Hindu temples caused by the great earthquake in Bali of 21 January 1917 (briefly discussed in Chapter 6).

Cultuurcongres. He sketched these together as one movement towards renewal, and towards political and spiritual satisfaction. His view of Majapahit contained all the aforementioned motifs of the 1920s Javanist cultural nationalists' visions of Majapahit. The biggest effort in the past to create unity between Java and the outer islands, he reasoned, had taken place under Majapahit's chancellor Gajah Mada (literally, Giant Elephant) during the fourteenth century. This was 'the golden age of Indonesia'.[91]

Soeriokoesoemo, and some other contributors to *Wederopbouw*, through their Central Javanese *priyayi*'s culturalist perspective, tended to take an anti-Islamic stance, along the lines set out by the critical texts of the 1870s and 1880s discussed in Chapter 3. Unlike Poerwolelono, the Javanese culture in which Soeriokoesoemo took pride, and which was his inspiration for a great national Indonesian future, was a syncretic *Hindu–Buddhist* Javanese culture. To him, the architectural material remains of the past demonstrated 'the divine temple of the Javanese nation'.[92] Soeriokoesoemo and others in *Wederopbouw* tended to flesh out the great Central Javanese monuments, especially Borobudur, as the main evidence of the Javanese people's ability. At Borobudur, Soeriokoesoemo noticed that 'there, many children of the nation fulfil their daily *samadhi* [prayer]'.[93] Soemarsono, a Javanese intellectual living near Borobudur, was thrilled by the way historian Fruin-Mees had discussed the Hindu–Javanese temple building, and by how she had portrayed Borobudur – 'the triumph of Buddhism in all its magnificence' – as made by Javanese.[94] Majapahit ruins, in that sense, apparently could not spur the imagination so strongly – despite their spiritual signification on location and despite Bosch's defence of their artfulness.

In contrast to Soeriokoesoemo and other authors in *Wederopbouw*, Sanusi Pané and Muhammad Yamin, the two Sumatra-born nationalists and future writers of official Indonesian history, were directly inspired by interventions at the actual site of Majapahit, and by concrete findings on the site. They lavishly illustrated their historical writings with photographs of key temples and gates and of statues representing kings of Majapahit from the colonial Archaeological Service. Sanusi Pané's *Sedjarah Indonesia* ('History of Indonesia', first published in 1943–1945) features a stone statue unifying Siva and Vishnu, believed to be a portrayal of Kertarajasa, the founder of the Majapahit empire. The statue was then in the Museum of the Royal Batavian Society and is today held by its successor institution, the National Museum in Jakarta.[95] As the American Indonesianist Michael H. Bodden has argued, these

91 Soeriokoesoemo, 'Het rijk van Gadjah Mada', *Wederopbouw* 3:1 (1920), 6.
92 Soeriokoesoemo, 'Ons derde levensjaar', 4 ('de goddelijke Tempel van de Javaansche natie').
93 Ibid., 4. 94 Soemarsono, 'Boekbespreking', *Wederopbouw* 3:4 (1920), 83–84.
95 Sanusi Pané, *Sedjarah Indonesia*, vol. I, 4th edn (Jakarta: Balai Pustaka, 1950), 82; originally published in 1943: Sanusi Pané, *Sedjarah Indonesia* (Djakarta: Balai Poestaka, 2603 [1943]).

two writers' poetic and dramatic engagement with a glorious national past may have been intensified in the context of a more repressive milieu after the communist revolt of 1926–1927,[96] which prohibited direct nationalist speech in public. But the growing availability of material evidence of that great past also must have driven them.

Revive the Past – Muhammad Yamin and the Re-embodiment of Gajah Mada

It is difficult to overestimate how much Muhammad Yamin's (1903–1962) work on Majapahit influenced Indonesian perceptions of that past. Of equal importance was his engagement with archaeological heritage politics as minister of culture and education in the 1950s. Majapahit spoke to Yamin's imagination. As a young nationalist, he wrote the play 'Ken Angrok and Ken Dedes', about the king of the thirteenth-century Singasari empire who created unity in his kingdom, thereby laying the foundation of the great Majapahit empire, but had to die for his previous sins. It was staged on the occasion of the All Indonesia Youth Congress in Batavia in late October 1928.[97] At this congress, a milestone in Indonesian national and nationalist history, the various regional and religious youth organisations united and took the oath, the *Sumpah Pemuda*, of belonging to one fatherland, Indonesia, one nation, the Indonesian nation, with one language, Bahasa Indonesia. Yamin's play on the dramatic beginnings of the Majapahit empire gave historical legitimation to the ambitions of the nationalist youth. According to Yamin's foreword in 1950 (featuring a picture of the famous statue Prajnaparamita as Ken Dedes discussed in Chapter 1), the play was restaged thirty-nine times across Indonesia and involved *gamelan* music, singing, and the use of 'the language of unity, bahasa Indonesia'.[98]

While for this play *Nagarakrtagama* and *Pararaton* were Yamin's crucial sources of inspiration, his later work shows that he actively sought further material to bring to life Majapahit's powerful image, and assess its historical importance for a future Indonesia. Yamin's archive in the National Archives of Indonesia reveals that, at some time, he investigated and happily borrowed from the photographic archive of the Archaeological

For the original statue, see the National Museum of Indonesia, inv. nr 256/103a/2082. Its origin is ascribed to Candi Sumberjati, Blitar, eastern Java, fourteenth century.

96 Michael H. Bodden, 'Utopia and the shadow of nationalism: the plays of Sanusi Pane 1928–1940', *BKI* 153:3 (1997), 336–337.

97 Andries Teeuw, *Modern Indonesian literature* (The Hague: Nijhoff, 1979), 27; Muhammad Yamin, *Ken Arok dan Ken Dedes: Tjerita Sandiwara jang kedjadian dalam sedjarah Tumapel-Singhasari pada tahun 1227 AD* (Jakarta: Balai Pustaka, 1951), 5. The play was first published in *Pudjangga Baru*, January 1934, 209–246.

98 Teeuw, *Modern Indonesian literature*, 27.

Service to document his later historical writings.[99] These were, in chronological order, the often reprinted biography of Gajah Mada (which Yamin wrote when, during the Japanese occupation, he worked for the Japanese propaganda service Sendenhan, and which was first published in 1945); his *6000 Tahun Sang Mérah Putih* ('6000 years of the sacred red-white', the colours of the national banner, 1951); his *Lukisan Sedjarah* (a history of Indonesia and the world in images, 1956), and a historical atlas (1956) – the latter two used at teacher training schools. Apart from that, Yamin also published a seven-volume work in 1962 on the administration of the Madjapahit empire, with a foreword that praised the 'liberation' of New Guinea.[100]

The map drawn by Maclaine Pont reappeared in Yamin's *Lukisan Sedjarah*, together with photographs from the ruined remains and terracotta findings at the site.[101] And Prapanca's *Nagarakrtagama* provided the basis for a map of the Majapahit empire, 'the fatherland of the Indonesian people'. Reproduced in both *Gadjah Mada* and Yamin's historical atlas, this map overlapped with that of the independent Republik Indonesia, which included Dutch-occupied New Guinea. In *Sang Mérah Putih,* Yamin claims that the walls of the *kraton* of Majapahit were red and the floors white, proving the continuous influence of the sacred red and white colours.[102]

To illustrate the impact of Yamin's engagements with findings at the actual site of Majapahit: in a small terracotta head, excavated near Trowulan, Yamin officially recognised the face of Gajah Mada. He followed an earlier suggestion of the Indies-born, self-taught archaeologist F. M. Schnitger, who wrote on this image: 'might be a portrait of Gadjah Mada. The most powerful face, which looks at us from Javanese history' (Figure 4.2.a).[103] Yamin used it for the cover of his Gajah Mada biography (Figure 4.2.b).[104] Although he included Schnitger's note which merely suggested this *might* be Gajah Mada's portrait, Yamin placed Gajah Mada's name below the image. Later, in his *Lukisan*

[99] ANRI, Arsip Muhammad Yamin, inv. nrs. 526 'foto-foto tentang prasasti'; 561 'lukisan sjarah di lengakapi gambar-gambar patung pada masa Majapahit'; 572 'naskah tulisan berjudul "Prasasti Trowulan" salinan menurut transkripsi O.V. 1918, Bijl. K. 108-112'. The latter concerned copperplate inscriptions found by the *regent* of Mojokerto in 1918, and entailed a chronological list of kings and 'overzetplaatsen' on the order of the king of Majapahit. For the transcription, see 'Bijlage K. Oorkonden van Trawoelan', *OV 1918* (1919), 108–112; Pieter V. van Stein Callenfels, 'De vorsten van de Trawoelan. Plaat no. III', *OV 1919* (1919), 22–30.

[100] Yamin, *Tatanegara Madjapahit,* I, 5.

[101] Muhammad Yamin, *Lukisan sedjarah, jaitu risalah berisi 563 gambar, foto dll., melukisan perdjalanan sedjarah Indonésia dan sedjarah dunia untuk dipergunakan dipelbagai perguruan* (Amsterdam: Djamabtan, 1956), 12–15.

[102] Muhammad Yamin, *6000 Tahun Sang Merah-Putih* (n.p., 1953), 162.

[103] Friedrich M. Schnitger, 'Gajah Mada', *Nederlandsch-Indië. Oud en Nieuw* 16:10 (1932), 291. On this history, see also 'Salah Tafsir Wajah Gajah Mada', *Suara Karya*, 27 September 1984.

[104] Muhammad Yamin, *Gadjah Mada: Pahlawan Persatuan Nusantara*, 3rd edn (Jakarta: Balai Poestaka, 1948).

Figure 4.2.a Statue still kept today in the Archaeological Museum in Trowulan, described by F.M. Schnitger in 1932 as potentially 'a portrait of Gadjah Mada'.

Figure 4.2.b Cover of Muhammad Yamin's biography of *Gadjah Mada*.

Sedjarah he included the 'humanised' painting of the statue by the Menadonese painter Henk Ngantung titled 'Gadjah Mada' (1950).[105] Ngantung's painting was perhaps the first reproduction after the cover of Yamin's book, and tellingly, right after its first public unveiling, President Soekarno bought it and moved it to the presidential palace.[106]

In subsequent decades, the portrayal of the terracotta image on Yamin's book generated a tradition of reproductions in print, on covers of schoolbooks, in stone, and in Indonesia's public spaces, which in turn *made* this terracotta image the Gajah Mada known today, from the big muscular statue in front of the headquarters of the Indonesian Police Forces in Jakarta (Kebayoran Baru) to several comparable stone copies near Trowulan. Those from New Order times, like one from 1986, representing the military police at the Pendopo Agung in Trowulan,[107] took on a remarkable likeness to President Soeharto. But this is not the official scholarly archaeological line of thought in Indonesia. On display in the museum in Trowulan, the original terracotta image exemplifies Majapahit's society's popular art – the way Maclaine Pont would have liked to have seen it, too – and is described as a 'Celengan Figur Manusia' (money box with human face).[108]

Revive the Past – Sanusi Pané

Yamin's fellow Sumatran Sanusi Pané (1905–1968), albeit from the Batak region (Tapanuli), a poet, playwright, journalist, and later official historian, likewise engaged with Majapahit.[109] Pané's portrayal of Majapahit, disseminated through nationalist journals of the 1930s and Japanese propaganda,

105 Yamin, *Lukisan sedjarah,* 12 (image nr 25). 'Humanised' is the term used by Koperberg; see Samuel Koperberg, 'Pelukis2 Indonesia', *Mimba Indonesia* 22 (29 May 1954), 22–24.

106 On this painting, see Koperberg, 'Pelukis2 Indonesia'. During Soekarno's and Soeharto's reign, the painting was kept in the Istana Negara in Bogor. Under President Megawati, it moved to the Istana Merdeka in Jakarta, where it is now on display in the Ruang Kredensial, which is often used by the president to receive foreign guests. See 'Lukisan Karya Gadjah mada Henk Ngantung', *Sudut Istana,* 14 February 2014, www.presidenri.go.id/index.php/sudutistana/2014/02/13/190.html (accessed 18 July 2014).

107 See also the head of Gajah Mada at Jl. Gajah Mada in Trowulan. On the Pendopo Agung, conceptualised under President Soekarno in 1964, and built in 1966 to mark the New Order, see the Epilogue of this book.

108 Visits by Marieke Bloembergen to the museum, 15 September 2009, 13 June 2012.

109 On Sanusi Pané, see Keith Foulcher, 'Perceptions of modernity and the sense of the past: Indonesian poetry in the 1920s', *Indonesia* 23:2 (1977), 39–58; Susan Rodgers, 'Imagining tradition, imagining modernity: a southern Batak novel from the 1920s', *BKI* 147: 2–3 (1991), 273–297; Bodden, 'Utopia and the shadow of nationalism'; Cohen, *Inventing the performing arts*; Ethan Mark, '"Asia's" transwar lineage: nationalism, Marxism, and "Greater Asia" in an Indonesian inflection', *JAS* 65:3 (2006), 461–493. Ethan Mark is the first author to point to the importance of Sanusi Pané's Asianist ideals – Pané first identified with India, and with Tagore's thinking; during the Japanese occupation, Pané connected Indonesia to Japan.

was similarly influential. Pané joined the Partai Nasional Indonesia (PNI, the Indonesian nationalist party) and authored one of the first official Indonesian history books written by an Indonesian.[110] The book expresses views he developed during the Japanese occupation, when he – like Yamin and the future head of the Archaeological Service Soekmono – worked in the service of Japanese propaganda. Pané did this as a writer and cultural commentator for the new Japanese-sponsored journal *Asia Raya*; later (October 1942) he was head of the Pusat Kesenian Indonesia (Centre for Indonesian Arts) and, from March 1943, of the Keimin bunka shidôsho (the Centre for the Guidance of Popular Culture and Enlightenment, translated into Indonesian as Kantor Besar Poesat Kebudajaan). This institution was set up to 'improve' or 'ennoble' Indonesians and Indonesian culture ('meninggkian deradjat penduduk'), by preserving classic and traditional Indonesian arts, and by training artists. With divisions for literature, the arts, music, and theatre, its aims were threefold: to eliminate Western culture and fight its authors (American, British, and Dutch); to get to know and recognise an original 5000-year-old Asian culture as the capital to develop a Greater Asia; and to direct all its talents and capacities to win the war.[111] As Ethan Mark has shown, already before his work for the Japanese propaganda service, Sanusi Pané combined his nationalist aspirations in an intriguing way with Asianist ideals, partly fed by a theosophical education and a journey to India in 1929.[112] The Hindu–Buddhist civilisation of the Majapahit empire, exercising power, according to Prapanca, over a region that went beyond the borders of the Netherlands Indies, could serve either aim as part of a powerful Greater Indonesian and Greater Asian past.

To Sanusi Pané, Majapahit seemed to have been, in the first instance, an inspirational source for a form of romantic nationalism. His plays *Kertadjaja* (1932) and *Sandakala ning Madjapahit* ('Twilight over Majapahit', first published in *Timboel* in 1932; 1933) are both about heroes sacrificing themselves for their kingdom and people, and are both romantic nationalist appropriations

110 Pané, *Sedjarah Indonesia* (1943). In this book we have used the fourth, slightly revised edition of 1950–1951). On this work, and also on Pané's other propaganda writings during this period, in which he linked Indonesia to a Japanese Greater South Asian region and past, see Mark, '"Asia's" transwar lineage', 479–489.

111 Mark, '"Asia's" transwar lineage', 479 and 485; Helena Geertruida Spanjaard, 'Het ideaal van een moderne Indonesische schilderkunst, 1900–1995: de creatie van een nationale culturele identiteit', PhD thesis, Leiden University, 1998, 115; Sanento Yuliman Hadiwardoyo, 'Genèse de la peinture indonésienne contemporaine: le rôle de S. Sudjojono', PhD thesis, École des Hautes Études des Sciences Sociales, Paris, 1981, 115; *Keboedajaan Timoer I* (Djakarta: Kantor Besar Keimin Bunka Shidosho, Kantor Besar Poesat Kebudajaan, 2603 [1943]), 2–3. Compare *Keboedajaan Timoer II* (Djakarta: Keimin Bunka Shishodo, 2604 [1944]), 1.

112 Mark, '"Asia's" transwar lineage'. See also Cohen, *Inventing the performing arts*, 164.

of early Javanese Hindu–Buddhist history.[113] The latter play, for example, about the decline of the Majapahit empire, tells a 'lakon' (story), introduced by a Buddhist monk who calls to the 'Sjiwabuddha', about the struggle of a young *ksatriya* hero, Damar Wulan, to defend his empire in the service of his people. The monk also explains that the *lakon* is based on the *Pararaton*, *Nagarakrtagama*, *Damar Wulan*, and *Serat Kanda*.[114] In a poem published in 1931, Sanusi himself is the protagonist. He muses while he sits among the ruins of Majapahit, expressing his sadness about the tedious present, and wondering when the grandeur and beauty of 'my homeland' ('tanah airkoe') will return:[115]

> MADJAPAHIT
> Akoe mengembara seorang diri
> Antara bekas Madjapahit
> Akoe bermimpi, terkenang doeloe
> Dan teringat waktoe sekarang.
>
> O Déwata, pabila Gerang
> Akan kembali kemegahan
> Dan keindahan tanah airkoe?[116]

Sanusi Pané may have been inspired by the news about the excavations and research at the site in the Trowulan area, but we have no proof that he actually went and sat there. His theosophical formation may have influenced him in seeing Java's ancient Hindu–Buddhist sites as important sources of inspiration for his 'tanah air' (fatherland). But this took him much further than Trowulan, for Sanusi Pané went for an inspirational journey to India in 1929, to explore both Asian spiritual and nationalist matters – which raises the question of how much the site at Trowulan mattered to his historical interpretations.

Yet despite Pané's Greater Asian mindset, his *Sedjarah Indonesia*, which was used in Indonesian education until the 1960s, followed an exclusively nationalist perspective. He wrote this multi-volume work while employed as

113 See Teeuw, *Modern Indonesian literature*, 27 and 40–41; Bodden, 'Utopia and the shadow of nationalism', 341–345. Compare on the play, as performed and received, Cohen, *Inventing the performing arts*, 163–166.

114 Sanusi Pané, *Sandhyakala ning Majapahit* (Jakarta: Pustaka Jaya, 1971); reprinted from *Timboel* 7:1–6 (1932), 7–8.

115 He thus takes a pose inspired by Edward Gibbon, but also builds on the Malay traditions of poetry, the *pantun* in which melancholy is an important motif. See Teeuw, *Modern Indonesian literature*, 12. See, alternatively, Keith Foulcher, *Pujangga Baru: literature and nationalism in Indonesia, 1933–1942* (Bedford Park: Flinders University, 1980), 36. Foulcher points to the fact that the aspect of the *pantun* tradition that survived in the 1930s was 'the folk traditional view of the poet, and of the emotions approppriate to poetry. Central to the pantun's projection of its composer is a tendency towards self-pity and melancholic self-effacement.'

116 This poem (translated into French by the French epigrapher Charles-Louis Damais, and quoted in Leclerc, 'La circonscription', in Blanchard, Dovert and Durand (eds.), 30, was published in a Balai Poestaka volume from 1931; see Sanusi Pané, *Madah Kelana* (Batavia: Balai Poestaka, 1931), 35.

director of the Japanese propaganda institution, the Centre for Indonesian Arts. Much in line with Soeriokoesoemo and Yamin, he projected the origin of the Indonesian nation into the distant past, long before even the Majapahit empire, when Indonesian ancestors from 'Hindia Belakang' (Achter India, India Minor) settled in the archipelago. Pané seems to have been inspired by modern historical methods, emphasising uncertainty about the sources, critically comparing the various available sources – including statues and inscriptions – leaving space for doubt, but also following the standard narrative that *Nagarakrtagama* as a source of that time was more trustworthy than, for example, the *Babad Tanah Djawi*.[117]

The history of Majapahit is only one important step in Pané's longer framework of a national history. An anti-colonial national perspective leads the story from the arrival of the Dutch, unifying wars, working towards independence. Only in his chapters on 'religion, temples, and arts' and on the fall of the Majapahit empire does Pané mention some of the remains in Trowulan. He explains Majapahit's decline as the result of internal conflicts, the lack of a powerful centre, the taking over of the trade relationships in the Strait of Malacca by Malaka, and, finally, the blossoming of Islam. Islam, although the Demak kingdom did conquer the Majapahit empire, came into the archipelago by trade, and along with the charismatic nine *wali*. The so-called grave of Princess Campa, whether or not the story about the princess it contained was true, was evidence of that peaceful spread of Islam.[118]

Demystifying Majapahit or Decolonising Majapahit

Countering the unifying visions of Pané, Yamin, and Soeriokoesoemo, the question whether Majapahit (and the ancient Hindu–Buddhist past in general) defined 'Indonesia' had been in dispute among Indonesians in the 1910s, 1920s, and 1930s.[119] This debate revived in the 1950s. As Supomo has shown, to some Marxists, the Hindu–Buddhist past, with its feudal hierarchies, offered no model; others expressed no interest at all in the past.[120] The Sumatran poet-intellectual Sutan Takdir Alisjahbana active in the group around the Sumatra-based journal *Pujangga Baru* ('The modern poet') reasoned that 'Indonesia' was a new creation that could learn only from modern developments. He took the modernist standpoint that the past was 'dead' ('mati-sematinja')[121] and refused to recognise

[117] Sanusi Pané, *Sedjarah Indonesia*, 86, 93, 94, 96. [118] Ibid., 169–171 and 174.

[119] Supomo, 'The image of Majapahit', 183; Drewes, 'The struggle between Javanism and Islam'; Ricklefs, *Polarising Javanese society*, 176–213, 232–233; M. C. Ricklefs, *Islamisation and its opponents in Java c. 1930 to the present* (Honolulu: University of Hawai'i Press, 2012).

[120] Supomo, 'The image of Majapahit', 183–185; Reid, 'The nationalist quest for an Indonesian past', 296–298.

[121] Teeuw, *Modern Indonesian literature*, 37.

Majapahit (or Sriwijaya) as a progenitor.[122] In dispute with Sanusi Pané and Poerbatjaraka, he published articles, dismissing the importance of the past, later compiled in *Polemik Kebudajaan* ('Polemics on culture', 1948). This volume would have a huge influence on post-war intellectual debates about Indonesian culture.[123]

Meanwhile, some colonial scholars were developing alternative views on Majapahit, based on new research methods and new views regarding old sources, providing Takdir with ammunition for his negative attitude towards the past. But this new, revisionist scholarly knowledge did nothing to challenge the image of Majapahit as the Indonesian nation-state's powerful predecessor. The work of the archaeologist Willem Stutterheim helped initiate this discussion with 'The *kraton* of Majapahit' (1948), a posthumously published study that aimed to reconstruct the outlook and layout of the *kraton* and capital city of Majapahit with more advanced 'local knowledge', of, especially, the Javanese *kraton* and the Balinese *puri*.[124] Stutterheim argued that earlier scholars such as Kern had lacked enough local knowledge to grasp the picture of Majapahit when translating the *Nagarakrtagama*. He believed others, including Maclaine Pont, were too inclined to take Prapanca's poetic eulogy literally – so that the *kraton* of Majapahit took on the allure of Versailles.[125]

Stutterheim compared observations of the Majapahit empire by a contemporary outsider, the Chinese traveller Ma Huan, with his personal knowledge of palaces in Java and Bali, and a systematic reading of the relevant verses of *Nagarakrtagama,* thereby retranslating names of the buildings and open spaces, and of (royal, religious, and military) institutions and ranks mentioned. In this way, he tried to reimagine the route Prapanca took, and to see what he actually described.[126] Next, he tried to correct the image of Majapahit as suggested by the translation, partly, like Maclaine Pont, resorting to the temple reliefs of the Majapahit era that depicted houses and other

[122] Takdir Alisjahbana, quoted and translated by Supomo, 'The image of Majapahit', 183. The original source is 'Menudju masjarakat dan kebudajaan baru', in Achdiat K. Mihardja (ed.), *Polemik Kebudajaan* (Jakarta: Perpustakaan perguran kementerian P. P. dan K., 1954), 14. On Takdir Alisyahbana, the group around the journal *Pujangga Baru* (New Poet), and the polemics on Indonesian culture, see Heather Sutherland, '*Pujangga Baru*: aspects of Indonesian intellectual life in the 1930s', *Indonesia* 6 (October 1968), 106–127; Foulcher, *Pujangga Baru*; Teeuw, *Modern Indonesian literature*, 28–39; Robert E. Elson, *The idea of Indonesia: a history* (Cambridge: Cambridge University Press, 2008), 72.

[123] On the cultural debates of the 1950s, see most recently Tod Jones, *Culture, power, and authoritarianism in the Indonesian state: cultural policy across the twentieth century to the reform era* (Leiden: Brill, 2013), ch. 3 (71–111).

[124] W. F. Stutterheim, *De kraton van Majapahit*, Verhandelingen van het Koninklijk Instituut voor de Taal-, Land- en Volkenkunde van Nederlandsch-Indië 7 ('s-Gravenhage: Nijhoff, 1948). There is also a slightly revised version, not used for the publication, kept in the archives of the Bataviaasch Genootschap, ANRI. For a comparison of the two versions, see Gomperts, Haag, and Carey, 'Stutterheim's enigma'.

[125] Stutterheim, *De kraton van Majapahit*, 1–7. [126] Ibid., 7–107.

buildings probably of that time. He arrived at a much more modest image of the Majapahit *kraton* and its direct surroundings. Majapahit had, to summarise Stutterheim crudely, a simple Balinese-style palace of bricks and stones with the ground plan of a Javanese *kraton*. The site of the *kraton* covered around 1 square kilometre, and was surrounded by a high wall. In contrast to the Javanese *kraton*, the buildings within and outside this wall, although built not on the ground but on relatively high bases, were of a very modest size, and made of wood instead of stone – in styles like the *bale bale*, still found in Bali.[127] The surrounding 'city' had no outer wall. Suggesting that there was thus a certain continuity within the layout of Javanese royal cities, Stutterheim proposed investigating practices and world views regarding the Javanese *kraton* to help envision the reconstruction of Majapahit.[128]

While some scholars have situated Stutterheim's reconstruction of Majapahit in an ongoing query for the location of the kingdom's *kraton*,[129] we see this work as an exponent of a larger movement of (Dutch) scholars that started in the late 1920s and gained momentum in the 1930s, who were, intentionally or not, working towards a demystification of Majapahit – that is, developing a realistic view on Majapahit as a site and empire via strict academic source criticism of historical texts, ethnographical methods, and an eye for the historical landscape. The philologist Cornelis C. Berg, professor of Javanese at Leiden University, was one important factor in this movement. Just before and after the Second World War, he presented, based on his new theories on the value of Javanese texts as historical sources, fresh interpretations of Majapahit's history that then seemed too radical in the eyes of both Dutch and Indonesian scholars. Berg argued that the old Javanese sources *Nagarakrtagama* and *Pararaton*, as well as the *babad* and other later texts written in modern Javanese, were all the product of the same, static religious culture, and should be understood in that context.[130] *Nagarakrtagama*, Berg reasoned, should be read as a priestly text: written by a priest concerned with

[127] Ibid., 54–55 and 107–109, and concluding summary/overview on 116–118. [128] Ibid., 118.

[129] Gomperts, Haag, and Carey value Stutterheim's work because he apparently managed to trace the location of the *kraton*; they find it an enigma why he chose not to emphasise this finding, and even stated that he was not preoccupied with the question of the location of the *kraton*. See Stutterheim, *De kraton van Majapahit,* 1; Gomperts, Haag, and Carey, 'Stutterheim's enigma'. To us it seems that Stutterheim was especially interested in reconstructing the – modest – shape and outlook of the Majapahit *kraton*, more than in revealing its location.

[130] C. C. Berg, *Javaansche geschiedschrijving*, Part IIA of F. W. Stapel (ed.), *Geschiedenis van Nederlandsch-Indië*, 5 vols. (Amsterdam: Joost van den Vondel, 1938–1940), 3. For his revisionist work on old Javanese history in general, and as an introduction in English, see C. C. Berg, 'Javanese historiography: a synopsis of its evolution', in G. E. Hall (ed.), *Historians of South East Asia* (London: Oxford University Press), 13–23. On Prapanca, and other sources regarding Majapahit in particular, see C. C. Berg, 'Arya Tada en de Gajah Madah gelofte', *BKI* 98 (1939), 253–283; C. C. Berg, 'Kartanegara, de miskende empire builder', *Orientatie* (July 1950), 1–32; C. C. Berg, 'De evolutie der Javaansche geschiedschrijving', *Mededelingen der Koninklijke Nederlandse Akademie van Wetenschappen, afd. Letterkunde,*

the doctrines of a Greater Majapahit in his own time, and, with what ought to be, not what was.[131] In Berg's eyes, Prapanca, although 'highly overrated' as a historian by Krom, was more comparable to a literary magician than to a historian in the Western meaning of the term.[132] But, he later noted in a reinterpretation of Majapahit's early history, Prapanca 'probably knew what he wanted, and, as we can presume, was relatively well aware of the history of the dynasty that he served'. Berg was less complimentary about the *Pararaton*, which he called 'an artistically overrated compilation of romantic-historical stories or abstracts of stories edited around 1500 by a historian of poor capacities', and elsewhere 'clumsy'.[133]

Working from his theory, Berg came to new reconstructions of the early history of Majapahit in which, for example, the *Pararaton*'s Ken Angrok could never have existed, and in which Kertanagera – the last king of the Singaraja kingdom – was the real empire builder, rather than Hayam Wuruk or Gajah Mada of the Majapahit empire; and in which it would not make sense to speak of a continuity between the two empires.[134] Also, Berg's Majapahit, like Stutterheim's, was much smaller than was depicted by Yamin and Sanusi Pané. As far as Berg was concerned, Prapanca merely displayed his geographical knowledge; 'it has, however, an enormous cultural historical value, and we can only hope that for once it will attract attention for that reason'.[135]

Although highly esteemed for his knowledge of the languages and the sources, Berg's interpretations were not well received, neither among contemporary Dutch scholars nor their (often Dutch-trained) Indonesian colleagues. Berg was very productive, and most of his new interpretations appeared in the early 1950s, right after Indonesian independence, a time dominated by nation-building politics, for which Majapahit was a great source. Many Indonesians, then occupied with studying the past, therefore 'genuinely believed that Berg's writings . . . were written out of spite against the newborn Republic', and saw it as their duty 'to combat what they considered to be fallacies in Berg's arguments', according to Supomo.[136]

Nieuwe Reeks 14:2 (1951); C. C. Berg, 'De geschiedenis van pril Majapahit I. Het mysterie van de vier dochters van Krtanegara', *Indonesië* 4:6 (1950/1951), 481–520; C. C. Berg, 'De geschiedenis van pril Majapahit II. Achtergrond en oplossing der pril majapahitsche conflicten', *Indonesië* 5:3 (1951), 193–233; C. C. Berg, 'De Sadeng oorlog en de mythe van groot Majapahit', *Indonesië* 5:5 (1952), 385–422.

131 Supomo, 'The image of Majapahit', 184; Berg, 'De geschiedenis van pril Majapahit I', 481.

132 Berg, *Javaansche geschiedschrijving*, 14–15.

133 The first two quotations are from Berg, 'Kartanegara', 4; the third is from Berg, 'De Sadeng oorlog en de mythe van groot Majapahit', 395.

134 Berg, 'Kartanegara', 18, 28.

135 Berg, 'De Sadeng oorlog en de mythe van groot Majapahit', 413.

136 Supomo, 'The image of Majapahit', 185. For (his) references, see his own contribution to the debate: S. Supomo, 'Tugas penulis babad dan pelaksanaannja', in *Laporan ilmu pengetahuan nasional kedua 1962*, vol. VI (Jakarta: Madjelis Ilmu Pengetahuan Indonesia, 1965), 9–36;

When the epigrapher J. G. de Casparis, working in Indonesia in the 1950s, discussed Berg's theories on Singasari and Majapahit with some of his Indonesian students, they reacted with: 'of course [this is] the theory of a Dutchman'. De Casparis, briefly a staff member of the Dutch Archaeological Service before the Second World War, had become pro-Republican during the Indonesian revolution and the Dutch military aggression. In an essay on 'Historical writing on Indonesia (early period)', he defended these views of his students to his readers, who were likely to be prejudiced in the opposite direction: 'they felt it to be an attempt to minimise the greatness of a figure such as Ken Arok and of an empire such as Majapahit'. From a scientific perspective, De Casparis expressed his doubts about this attitude, but politically he understood: 'it should never be forgotten that their history means something more than just a number of academic questions'.[137]

Ironically, in 1954, a time when the authority of *Nagarakrtagama* was both disputed and sacralised, the first Indonesian translations appeared of *Nagarakrtagama* (by Slametmoeljana) and of Krom's chapter on the Hindu–Javanese time in Frederik Willem Stapel's standard *History of the Netherlands Indies* (1938–1940) (by Arif Effendi). These translations gave Indonesia precisely that greater image of Majapahit which a new generation of Indonesian intellectuals such as Bujung Saleh had begun to doubt.[138] In post-colonial, nation-building Indonesia, however, Berg had injured the authority of *Nagarakrtagama* and of Prapanca as a historian. He had downplayed the size and power of the kingdom in a period of nation building when the site and the text had gained almost sacred meaning. The power of the imagination, and the authority to decide about the imagination, however, eclipsed uncomfortable academic discussions – so much so, in fact, that (as shown in Chapter 3) *Nagarakrtagama* could perform as a potent 'gift' and mediator in Dutch–Indonesian decolonisation. This site-related text, in the end, spoke much more to the Indonesian nationalist imagination than did Majapahit, and illustrates both the power and the weakness of sites generally.

Slametmuljana, 'Adakah Prapantja sungguh pudjangga kerato?', *Bahasa dan Budaja* 1:2 (1952), 14–22; Sutjipto Wirjosuparto, 'Prapantja sebagai penulis sedjarah', *Peneltian Sedjarah* 1:1 (1960), 15–20.

137 De Casparis, 'Historical writing on Indonesia (early period)', 154 and 162. For a biographical essay, see Amrit Gomperts and Marijke J. Klokke, 'In memoriam J. G. de Casparis: 31 May 1916–19 June 2002', *BKI* 159:4 (2003), 471–487.

138 G. J. Resink, 'Uit het stof van een beeldenstorm', *Indonesië* 9 (1956), 440; Saleh, 'De mythe als opium en zelfkennis als zweep'; N. J. Krom, *Zaman Hindu, Terdjemahan Arif Effendi* (Jakarta: Pembangunan, 1954).

5 The Prehistoric Cultures and Historic Past of South Sumatra on the Move

Di kala ku merindukan keluhuran dulu kala
Kutembangkan nyanyi dari lagu Gending Sriwijaya.
(When I'm longing for the ancient nobleness
I will sing the song of Gending Sriwijaya.)[1]

'To Moechtar'[2]

In 1902 during the military expedition to Jambi (Palembang residency, South Sumatra), Dutch colonial troops 'found' an old temple in the jungle, or so it was reported briefly in the Dutch daily *Algemeen Handelsblad*. This discovery resulted in transporting four 'beautifully carved' stones to the Batavian Museum's collection in Java.[3] A curator there described the objects simply as '*makara* ornaments' – notably without mentioning the military context of their acquisition.[4]

The newspaper 'discovery' story overlooked that local inhabitants had long known of the temple, and that the transported objects already had a 'colonial' history. They had been mentioned in reports and photographed in 1877–1879, during the 'Sumatra expedition' organised by the Royal Dutch Geographical Society (Koninklijk Nederlandsch Aardrijkskundig Genootschap, KNAG). At that time the expedition team considered the stones too heavy to transport and therefore merely took photographs.[5] Remarkably, the newspaper not only fails

1 These are the first two sentences of the song 'Gending Sriwijaya'. See Margaret J. Kartomi, 'The paradoxical and nostalgic history of "Gending Sriwijaya" in South Sumatra', *Archipel* 45 (1993), 37–50.

2 Dedication in Friedrich M. Schnitger, with contributions by C. von Fürer-Haimendorf and G. L. Tichelman, with an introduction by J. N. Miksic, *Forgotten kingdoms in Sumatra* (Oxford: Oxford University Press, 1989 [1939]).

3 'Tempelsteenen uit Djambi', *Algemeen Handelsblad*, 28 February 1902.

4 *Notulen van de Algemeene en Directievergaderingen van het Bataviaasch Genootschap van Kunsten en Wetenschappen*, XV (1902), ccxv–ccxvi; C. J. Neeb, 'Het een en ander over Hindoe oudheden in het Djambische', *Tijdschrift voor Indische Taal-, Land- en Volkenkunde* 45 (1902), 120–127; J. Brandes, 'Bijschrift bij de door den heer Neeb gezonden photo's van Oudheden in het Djambische', *Tijdschrift voor Indische Taal-, Land- en Volkenkunde* 45 (1902), 128–133.

5 Photos 135 (Hindoeïstische makarakop te Djambi), 136 (Hindoeïstische makarakop te Djambi), and 137 (Hindoeïstische makarakoppen te Djambi) in D. D. Veth, *Midden-Sumatra: reizen en onderzoekingen der Sumatra-expeditie, uitgerust door het Aardrijkskundig Genootschap 1877–1879* (Leiden, 1879); A. L. van Hasselt and J. F. Snelleman, *Reizen in Midden-Sumatra*

to mention this history, but also ignores the role of local informants. In 1902 military officer C. J. Neeb reported that a local villager ('kampongbewoner') knew that the stones had been part of a *pendopo* of a certain 'Pangeran Ratoe' (which literally means 'Prince King'), where they had been used as seats.[6]

Such archaeological interventions in late colonial Sumatra may seem like marginal phenomena, especially when compared to the connected military interventions, but they were, as the newspaper article shows, essentially linked to the violent expansion of the colonial state. The first archaeological activities on Sumatra, performed in the context of the colonial state, dated from the start of the nineteenth century. But it was during the second half of the nineteenth century that the now 'archaeological' sites of South Sumatra were more systematically inventoried and appropriated in the context of historical and ethnographic descriptions, geographical expeditions, military conquest, and the establishment of governmental structures.[7] This chapter examines how South Sumatra, in particular Palembang, the Pasemah area, and Jambi, became gradually incorporated in the colonial archaeological infrastructure as it was developed in Batavia, the administrative centre of the expanding colony. It focuses on interactions during this process between state-supported 'modern' heritage concepts, local, and regional (Sumatra-based) appropriations of certain archaeological sites and objects, and the development of nationalist history writing by Sumatra-born Indonesians who also included the early past of Sumatra.

In the late colonial period, the archaeological infrastructure in the Netherlands Indies grew both more complex and more regulated. Archaeological activities were backed by the prestigious Batavian Museum, with its archaeological collection and staff. But throughout the 1920s and 1930s, new institutions such as the Archaeological Service of the Netherlands Indies (established in 1913), the Monument Act (of 1931),[8] and a network of newly founded local and regional

1877–1879, door de leden der Sumatra-expeditie, uitgerust door het Aardrijkskundige Genootschap, part I (Leiden, 1881), 244–246; C. H. Cornelissen, A. L. van Hasselt and J. F. Snelleman, *Reizen in Midden-Sumatra 1877–1879, door de leden der Sumatra-expeditie, uitgerust door het Aardrijkskundige Genootschap*, part II (Leiden, 1882), 202–204. See also Paul van der Velde, *Een Indische Liefde: P. J. Veth (1814–1895) en de inburgering van Nederlands-Indië* (Amsterdam: Balans, 2000), 229–233 and 244–259. Compare with Arnold Wentholt (ed.), *In kaart gebracht met kapmes en kompas: met het Koninklijk Nederlands Aardrijkskundig Genootschap op expeditie tussen 1873 en 1960* (Heerlen: ABP, 2003), 21–23 and 43–49; Pieter ter Keurs, 'Collecting in Central and South Sumatra', in Hardiati and Ter Keurs (eds.), *Indonesia: the discovery of the past*, 85–89.

6 The temple complex was, according to Neeb, already reported in the 1860s. See Neeb, 'Het een en ander over Hindoe oudheden in het Djambische', 120–121.

7 For the changing Sumatra policy of the colonial government in Batavia, since the Treaty of London of 1824, see Elsbeth Locher Scholten, *Sumatran sultanate and the colonial state: Jambi and the rise of Dutch imperialism 1830–1907* (Ithaca: Southeast Asia Program, Cornell University, 2004), 51–55, 92–96, 126–128, and 245–266.

8 For the Monument Act, see 'Besluit van den Gouverneur-Generaal van 13 Juni 1931 no. 19', *Staatsblad van Nederlandsch-Indië* 238 (1931).

(sometimes private) museums gave these activities a much broader social, local basis. The archaeological infrastructure was nonetheless Java-centric or, more precisely, Batavia-centric. Batavia hosted not only the central museum with the largest archaeological collection of the colony, but also the headquarters of the colonial archaeological service. The leading staff of these institutions belonged to the colonial establishment. As state archaeologists, they actively participated in programmes organised to welcome foreign guests of state, giving guided tours in the museum in Batavia or at the famous temple sites of Java.[9] They organised research expeditions all over the colony, were active in international academic networks, and were connected to the networks of privileged Javanese intellectuals who gained important but lesser positions in scholarly knowledge production and cultural politics, figures such as Hoesein Djajadiningrat and Ngabehi Poerbatjaraka. The colonial archaeologists in these networks became public figures, whose archaeological 'discoveries', excavations, and public presentations not only gained the attention of colonial newspapers, but also had a prescriptive power. As a result, their methods of excavating, their perspective on the display, export, and exchange of objects, and their ways of dealing with local society (for which ethnographic knowledge of local circumstances was considered vital) became more and more codified and seen as a crucial part of the 'heritage' policies and the moral legitimation of the modern colonial state.

This same colonial archaeological establishment critically observed how Indonesian nationalists incorporated archaeological knowledge in nationalist Indonesian interpretations of the past. However, their stance towards this development did not mean, as this chapter on Sumatra will show, that there were no contacts or moments of exchange. Colonial archaeological heritage sites and objects already had a clear, though multifaceted, function in local and regional society, long before they were incorporated in the colonial archaeological infrastructure, and they continued to have this function, now in dialogue with this infrastructure.[10] In comparison to Java, the archaeological initiatives on South Sumatra started to attract worldwide attention relatively late, only at the beginning of the twentieth century. The appeal of the archaeology in this part of the archipelago centred first on the material culture of the Stone Age (megaliths and stone axes). It provided the island with a 'new' prehistoric past and integrated the island into the discourse of the early history of mankind, in which evolution, race, and language were central categories. At the same time, archaeologists and linguists started to reconstruct a new historic past. With considerable certainty they succeeded in identifying Palembang as the capital of the Srivijaya empire (seventh–thirteenth centuries). This made South Sumatra one of the most

[9] B. D. Swanenburg, *Iwan de Verschikkelijke: leven en werken van Dr P. V. van Stein Callenfels* (Maastricht: Leiter Nypels, 1951), plates 15, 16, and 22.

[10] The colonial archaeological interventions cannot therefore be interpreted as the sole initiators of Western-style heritage formation, as Smith has argued: Smith, *Uses of heritage*, 17.

important centres of pre-colonial Southeast Asia. It gave a new, historical time-depth to the Sejarah Melayu or Malay Annals, a set of manuscripts in the Malay language that date from the fifteenth and sixteenth centuries and that deal with the history of the origin, evolution, and demise of the Malacca sultanate.[11] These new findings on the antiquity of Sumatra-based kingdoms contested Java-centric histories of the archipelago and were also integrated into the nationalist world view of a new generation of Sumatran intellectuals.[12] However, in the colonial context, paradoxically, they would also strongly contribute to the development of Batavia as the 'archaeological' centre of the Netherlands Indies.

In Sumatra, as elsewhere in the colony, archaeological practices and the related processes of heritage formation were profoundly shaped and complicated by colonial hierarchies – but not exclusively. Starting on location in South Sumatra, we follow the moves of specific prehistoric (Stone Age) and historic (Srivijaya) objects from South Sumatra (in particular Jambi and Pasemah) to Palembang, Batavia, the Netherlands, and the rest of the world (and in a few cases also back to South Sumatra) and question who made them move and for what reasons. Thus we aim to visualise the inner dynamics of the related archaeological networks and trace their role as a context for heritage formation from a local to global level. Which interdependencies were at work, which tensions evolved, and which hierarchies were established or challenged?

In order to analyse the local dimensions of the moving archaeological objects we focus in particular on the history of the municipal museum in Palembang – named 'Palembangsch Museum' but also known as 'Roemah bari' (Old House) (Figure 5.1) – and on the biography of one its most prominent supporters, Friedrich M. Schnitger. He would travel through Sumatra, the Netherlands Indies, the Netherlands, and the rest of the world, and end up as an inmate of the concentration camp Mauthausen in Austria, where he was killed in spring 1945.[13] Based on letters and publications of Sumatra-based scholars such as Schnitger who were part of the colonial archaeological networks, and a number of archaeologists belonging to the establishment in Batavia, we reconstruct diverse Sumatran perceptions and involvements. We are particularly interested in how local inhabitants – such as people living in the proximity of the

[11] For the print and translation history of these texts, see Roelof Roolvink, 'The variant versions of the Malay Annals', in Charles C. Brown and Roelof Roolvink (eds.), *Sejarah Melayu or Malay Annals* (Kuala Lumpur: Oxford University Press, 1970), xv–xxxv. See also Henk Maier, *We are playing relatives: a survey of Malay writing* (Leiden: KITLV Press, 2004), 13. Compare with H. Maier, 'We are playing relatives: Riau, the cradle of reality and hybridity', *BKI* 53:4 (1997), 679–680.

[12] Hans van Miert, 'The "land of the future": the Jong Sumatranen Bond (1917–1930) and its image of the nation', *MAS* 30:3 (1996), 591–616.

[13] 'Häftlingsnummer: 137.690, H-Kategorie: Niederlande/Schutz, Name: Martin Schnigter, eingeliefert in MH: 1945, gestorben: 23.4.1945 in Mauthausen': e-mail from Ildikó Cazan-Simányi, Museum für Völkerkunde Wien, 12 January 2012.

Figure 5.1 'Roemah bari' or the Museum in Palembang, late 1930s.

archaeological sites involved, workers, foremen, and religious leaders – engaged in the archaeological activities of South Sumatra. Whereas in Java local elites took archaeological initiatives and sometimes held leading positions as at the Majapahit site, in Sumatra they generally played a secondary role.

Geographical and Military Expeditions, Governmental Networks, and Academic Officials

From the early nineteenth century, South Sumatra experienced severe colonial violence. In 1819 and 1821 the Royal Netherlands Indies Army (KNIL) was sent to Palembang on a military mission directed against the sultanate and its sultan Mamhud Badaruddin II. In 1824, after many years of fighting and political unrest, Palembang was brought under direct Dutch colonial rule. The last sultan was exiled in Ternate and his palace was burned to the ground.[14] In the mid nineteenth century, when the colonial government in Batavia was increasingly interfering in the outer islands, the KNIL was again active in South Sumatra. Between 1851 and 1859 they attacked the so-called Palembangse Bovenlanden (Palembang highlands), which included the city of

[14] For the history of the Palembang sultanate in the years 1811–1825, see Michiel Otto Woelders, 'Het Sultanaat Palembang 1811–1825', dissertation, Leiden University ('s-Gravenhage: De Nederlandsche Boek- en Steendrukkerij V/H H. L. Smits, 1975), 1–27.

Lahat and the Pasemah highlands, in order to bring them under Dutch colonial authority. The Pasemah highlands were the last to be fully subjugated, in 1866.[15] The first military expedition to Jambi dates from 1885. The colonial military interventions in Sumatra, like those to Jambi, created new governmental structures. In 1906, a few years after the military invasions in this part of Sumatra, the colonial government incorporated Jambi into the colonial state administration, as a single Residency with its own Resident.[16]

In the nineteenth century, Dutch (self-taught) archaeological experts generally did not regard Sumatra as a place to find beautiful Hindu remains. In 1840, the antiquarian F. G. Valck, in his publication on ruined Hindu shrines on Java, described the objects from Sumatra (and also from Borneo and Malacca) as 'rawer', 'smaller', and 'imperfect'.[17] The tradition, dating at least from the eighteenth century, of transporting statues from their original place in the country site to the garden of the house of the Resident, however, also continued in South Sumatra. In 1830, A. H. von Gehren, the military commander of Palembang, for that reason transported such a statue to Palembang.[18] In the following decades a collection of statues could be found in front of the house of the Resident of Palembang, but their provenance was unknown.[19] It was certainly not exclusively a custom of colonial officials, as a few years earlier Sultan 'Mohamad Pacharoedien' had also transported statues to sit in front of his *pendopo*.[20]

The first archaeological reports on the Palembang highlands (which included Lahat and the Pasemah highlands) came from military officials such as S. Ullmann, a second lieutenant of infantry, and E. P. Tombrink, a medical officer.[21] In 1863, Tombrink sent what was to be the first large archaeological object from the region to Batavia, in order to enable 'those archaeologists who study Hinduism to see the statue themselves'.[22] Then, around the turn of the century, regional government representatives of the colonial state (District Officers H. E. D. Engelhard, C. J. Batenburg, F. J. Junius and W. Hoven, and

[15] A. N. J. Th. à Th. van der Hoop, *Megalithic remains in South-Sumatra* (Zutphen: Thieme, 1932), 3.

[16] For an overview of the residents of Palembang and Jambi, see Locher Scholten, *Sumatran sultanate,* 298–299.

[17] Valck, 'Oudheidkunde', 191. Compare with E. P. Tombrink, 'Hindoe-Monumenten in de Bovenlanden van Palembang, als bron van geschiedkundig onderzoek', *Tijdschrift voor Indische Taal-, Land- en Volkenkunde* (1870), 9–10.

[18] Tombrink, 'Hindoe-Monumenten', 38. [19] Ibid., 45.

[20] J. W. Boers, 'Oud Volksgebruik in het Rijk van Jambi', *Tijdschrift voor Neêrland's Indie* 3:1 (1840), 374; Tombrink, 'Hindoe-Monumenten', 45.

[21] L. Ullmann, 'Hindoe-Beelden in de Binnenlanden van Palembang', *Indisch Archief. Tijdschrift voor de Indiën* 1:2 (1850), 493–494; Tombrink, 'Hindoe-Monumenten', 5.

[22] Tombrink, 'Hindoe-Monumenten', 30–31. Compare with *Notulen van de Algemeene en Bestuursvergaderingen van het Bataviaasch Genootschap van Kunsten en Wetenschappen,* I (1864), 327–328.

the Resident L. C. Westenenk) developed an interest in the archaeological remains. Carved megaliths, the so-called images, were set upright and, when 'in danger of being lost' were transported to the small park near the government's office in Pageralam.[23] The tradition of transporting statues to the garden of the house of the Resident, which served a combination of representative, antiquarian, and aesthetic purposes, here acquired an additional ethical dimension. In the Colonial Archaeological Service report of 1922, Westenenk furthermore published a series of photographs of the statues from Pasemah.[24]

Subsequently, news about the archaeological remains of the Pasemah highlands reached academics in Amsterdam and Batavia. In 1929, J. C. van Eerde, director of the Ethnological Section of the Colonial Institute in Amsterdam, visited the region, and in 1930 Bosch, as head of the Colonial Archaeological Service, followed.[25] In 1931 A. N. J. Th. à Th. van der Hoop arrived in Pageralam, the capital of the region, in order to prepare his dissertation for the University of Utrecht on the 'Megalithic remains in South Sumatra'.[26] Following the colonial infrastructure in South Sumatra, which the colonial government had developed for a combination of military, administrative, and economic reasons, Van der Hoop used the concept of 'the road' for organising his work.[27] The colonial road system not only functioned as a grid within which to arrange his observations, but also as a model to offer his readers a way to verify these observations during their own travels. During his stay in Pasemah, Van der Hoop compiled, at the Archaeological Service's request, a list of remains to be placed under the protection of the Monument Act.[28] This Monument Act explicitly aimed to include the protection of movable and immovable 'monuments' dating from prehistoric times.[29] To the great regret of Van der Hoop, who in 1934 would become curator in the museum in Batavia,

[23] Engelhard in 1891 sent drawings of a statue from Tandjoeng Aro in Pasemah to Batavia. See *Notulen van de Algemeene en Bestuursvergaderingen van het Bataviaasch Genootschap van Kunsten en Wetenschappen*, 29 (1891) 37–38; L. C. Westenenk, 'De Hindoe-Oudheden in de Pasemah-Hoogvlakte (Residentie Palembang)', *OV 1922* (1922), 31–37. For the activities of Batenburg, Junius and Hoven, see Van der Hoop, *Megalithic remains*, 7.

[24] Westenenk, 'De Hindoe-Oudheden'.

[25] Van Eerde did not mention Pasemah in his travelogue. However, in Palembang he acquired military objects from 1819 and 1821, and some prehistoric objects; see J. C. van Eerde, 'Kort Verslag nopens de studiereis van den Directeur der Afdeeling Volkenkunde naar Nederlandsch-Indië (4 April–21 November 1929)', *19e Jaarverslag der Koninklijke Vereeniging 'Koloniaal Instituut'* (1929), 52 and 59–60; F. D. K. Bosch, 'Verslag van een reis door Sumatra', *OV 1930* (1931) Bijlage C, 151.

[26] A. N. J. Th. à Th. van der Hoop, *Megalitische oudheden in Zuid-Sumatra* (Zutphen: Thieme, 1932).

[27] For the development of the transportation network in Middle Sumatra and the establishment of 'colonial control', see Freek Colombijn, 'A moving history of Middle Sumatra', *MAS* 39:1 (2005), 1–38.

[28] Ibid., 6–9.

[29] 'Besluit van den Gouverneur-Generaal van 13 Juni 1931 no. 19', *Staatblad van Nederlandsch-Indië*, 238 (1931).

in the end this Monument Act was not enforced in Pasemah. As a result in the following years, other – local – colonial officials with an archaeological interest, such as C. W. P. de Bie and Schnitger, were free to excavate and sometimes even remove the archaeological objects from Pasemah.[30]

The megalithic remains of the Netherlands Indies had meanwhile become known in academic circles worldwide. The Sumatran megaliths were, however, not yet part of the corpus that in the course of the nineteenth century had been compiled on other islands of the archipelago, in particular Sumba, Timor, and Celebes, mainly by colonial explorers and missionaries. In 1927, the Dutch prehistorian A. E. Van Giffen, for example, did not mention Sumatra in his overview of megalithic culture as a worldwide phenomenon.[31] Likewise, W. J. Perry, a Manchester-based anthropologist specialising in comparative religion, did not include Sumatra in his study *The megalithic culture of Indonesia* (1918), limiting himself to the Timor region, Celebes, and Borneo. He justified this by stating that Sumatra had been influenced by 'higher civilisations'.[32] Perry's thesis that megalithic culture had originated in Egypt and from there had spread around the world, including Indonesia, would as a result interest audiences in the Netherlands Indies. Five years later he elaborated on this in *The children of the sun: a study in the early history of civilization* (1923), which now included Sumatra. Following observations from the British traveller H. O. Forbes, Perry concluded that 'stone workers' in 'Passumah Lands' came to the island 'at some unknown time in the past'.[33]

Military, government, and academic officials thus together created a body of archaeological knowledge in which places and objects from South Sumatra came to be of archaeological interest. Against this background, some local colonial officials in Palembang came to feel the need of a municipal museum, especially since the few beautiful finds from the region were often sent to the museum in Batavia, without any questioning. Another motivation was the idea of the saving, or 'salvation', of local culture that officials believed was threatened by colonial modernisation. By collecting and displaying archaeological

30 Van der Hoop to the head of the Archaeological Service, 6 May 1940, ANRI, KBG DIR 1088 1940.

31 A. E. van Giffen, *De Hunebedden in Nederland (met atlas). Deel II* (Utrecht: Oosthoek, 1927), 547–549. Compare with Martijn Eickhoff, *De oorsprong van het 'eigene': Nederlands vroegste verleden, archeologie en nationaal-socialisme* (Amsterdam: Uitgeverij Boom, 2003), 69–105.

32 W. J. Perry, *The Megalithic culture of Indonesia* (Manchester: Longmans and Green, 1918), 4.

33 W. J. Perry, *The children of the sun: a study in the early history of civilization* (London: Methuen, 1923), 41. He was referring to Henry O. Forbes, *A naturalist's wanderings in the eastern archipelago, a narrative of travel and exploration from 1878 to 1883* (London: Sampson Low, 1885), 201–204. For the reception of Perry's work in the Netherlands Indies, see 'The children of the sun', *Het nieuws van den dag voor Nederlandsch-Indië* (23 January 1925). See also A. C. Kruyt, 'Boekbespreking "The children of the sun" by W. J. Perry', *Tijdschrift voor Indische Taal-, Land en Volkenkunde* 64 (1924), 292–299.

and ethnographic objects, they hoped to revitalise waning local traditions and to counteract this development.

Roemah Bari: the Municipal Museum at Palembang

On 22 April 1933, the municipal museum at Palembang officially opened in an old wooden house gifted to the city by the Resident of Palembang, J. L. M. Swaab (Figure 5.1). This skilfully carved house originally stood in the *kampong* of Talang Pangeran, where it was the residence of the *pasirah* (local term for village head or *kampong* head). According to Swaab, the museum would make the customs of the 'people of Palembang' more widely known and thus contribute to its status. Due to the economic crisis, the official opening was kept low-profile. There were no festivities except for a small ritual welcome meal, the *sedeka* or *slametan*. Among the invitees were local leaders and the men who had been involved in the transfer of the building from the *kampong* to the city.

A Buddha statue that had been transported from the *kampong* of Bingin near Moewara Klingi[34] sat in the museum garden. The building had three rooms; one dedicated to traditional clothing (including dancing costumes for girls and a wedding dress and jewellery), another displayed models of boats used in Palembang (including original oars), and the third exhibited a collection of *kris* daggers. A special place displayed a *piagam* ('manuscript') from Palembang, which was a gift of the *demang* (district head) Raden Haji Mattjik, and a collection of small statues, donated by the colonial elite of Palembang. Most of the other objects were gifts of C. A. Pelt, a retired administrator of the oil company BPM, who had been based at Muara Enim, an oil well near Palembang.[35]

The initiators of the municipal museum of Palembang did not produce a catalogue, and there is no contemporary visual documentation, which prevents precise analysis of the museum's original contents. The Java Institute's cultural journal, *Djawa,* published some related official correspondence, which, however, does not discuss the past of city of Palembang. The published correspondence in *Djawa* points only to ethnographic objects, to illustrate the high level of the local crafts. But the journal refrains from mentioning the history of the Islamic Palembang sultanate, the long-lasting presence of a large Chinese community, and, last but not least, the prestigious link with the powerful Srivijaya empire. And neither the Sumatran Stone Age culture nor the

[34] For this statue, see L. C. Westenenk, 'De Hindoe-Javanen in Midden- en Zuid-Sumatra', *Handelingen van het Eerste Congres voor de Taal-, Land en Volkenkunde van Java; Solo, 25 en 26 December 1919* (1921), 9. Compare with Sukanti, *Koleksi Arkeologika: Museum Balaputra Dewi* (Palembang, 2010), 60 (number 04.9; Desa Bingin Jungut).

[35] 'Het Palembangsche Museum', *Djawa. Tijdschrift van het Java-Instituut* 13 (1933), 263–264.

megalithic culture of the Pasemah region are referenced. This approach seems a clear example of how ethnographic musealisation in the Netherlands Indies turned the culture and history of people defeated by the Dutch colonial army into ethnographic traditions.[36]

With that ethnographic framework, the museum in Palembang stood alongside the exhibition of arts and crafts objects from Palembang and the Pasemah area that was organised in Amsterdam in 1922 by the newly founded Zuid-Sumatra Instituut (Institute of South Sumatra), which fell under the Colonial Institute.[37] In the catalogue's introduction, District Officer Batenburg from Palembang mentioned that these traditions showed what the inhabitants of the regions 'nowadays are still able to achieve', but recalled how these same inhabitants were not interested in the beauty of the rare art objects from Palembang, often dating from the era of the sultans. Nonetheless, they were not willing to sell them, as they were family relics. Generally, they did not support the quest for these objects, although, according to Batenburg, the collecting was done partly for 'their own benefit'.[38] This all leads to the question: beyond the ethnographic scope of the municipal museum, what was known in colonial society of Palembang's history?

The History of Palembang and the 'Discovery' of Srivijaya

In early and mid nineteenth-century historical descriptions such as Protestant minister S. A. Buddingh's travelogue, the city of Palembang appears as a place with a rich and multifaceted history and culture in which the local sultanate was of pivotal importance. Buddingh distinguished between an 'old' and a 'young' history.[39] The 'old history' referred to the pre-VOC era, a dark and largely unknown history. The information available to him was based on mythical oral traditions that Major W. L. de Sturler had compiled in the 1830s.[40] According

[36] Max Lane, *Unfinished nation: Indonesia before and after Suharto* (London: Verso, 2008), 13.

[37] *Catalogus van eene verzameling van voorwerpen van kunstnijverheid uit de hoofdstad Palembang en de landstreek Pasemah Lebar* (Amsterdam: Zuid-Sumatra Instituut, 1922).The Sumatra Institute had a combined cultural and economic interest in the island; see for example G. F. de Bruyn Kops, *Overzicht van Zuid-Sumatra* (Amsterdam: Zuid-Sumatra Instituut, 1919). For this ahistorical ethnographic approach, see also the catalogue on South Sumatra of the 's Rijks Ethnografisch Museum in Leiden that appeared in 1918: H. W. Fischer, *Catalogus van 's Rijks Ethnografisch Museum Deel XII Zuid-Sumatra (Sumatra IV)* (Leiden: 's Rijks Ethnografisch Museum, 1918).

[38] C. J. Batenburg, 'Een woord vooraf', in *Catalogus van eene verzameling van voorwerpen van kunstnijverheid*.

[39] S. A. Buddingh, *Neêrlands-Oost-Indië. Reizen ... gedaan gedurende het tijdvak van 1852–1857*, 3 vols., 1st edn (Rotterdam, 1859–1861), III, 102 and 104.

[40] See W. L. de Sturler, *Bijdrage tot de kennis en rigtige beoordeling van den zedelijken, maatschappelijken en staatkundigen toestand van het Palembangsche gebied* (Groningen: Oomkens, 1855).

to these traditions, the people of Palembang were generally known as 'Maleisch'. One of its great leaders, 'Sri-Toeri-Boewana', a descendant of Alexander (Iskander) the Great, was banished in 1253 by the 'emperor' of Majapahit, and finally in 1432 the ruling king of Majapahit conquered the city. Soon afterwards the city would turn to Islam; this conversion was marked by the wedding of a member of the royal family to 'Soehoenan Rachmet', who was, according to Buddingh, an Arab missionary of Islam.[41] Buddingh related this 'young' history to the first VOC presence in the city and the era after the start of the nineteenth century, during which the colonial state was in violent conflict with the Palembang sultanate, which resulted in its fall.[42]

Buddingh further describes his visit to some sites in the city related to its multifaceted history. He mentions the house of the Resident, the mosque, a Chinese temple, the grave site of the sultans of Palembang, the ruin of the former *kraton*, an island in the Musi river where a prince from the Majapahit era was buried, and the so-called Bukit Siguntang hill, where, according to local lore, the grave of Sultan Iskander was located. It was a *kramat* or holy grave, sheltered and marked by three huge stones. Buddingh is not convinced that Alexander the Great did visit Palembang in reality, and explains the story in relation to a later Hindu immigration from India, which brought the story of Iskander to Palembang. He mentions the offerings of food, flowers, and herbs on location, as well as the presence of thousands of squirrels that were eating the offerings.[43]

In the nineteenth century Palembang was not known for its archaeological past, but in 1918 the French Indologist Georges Coedès published an article in the *Bulletin* of the EFEO regarding Palembang's ancient history, which caused a sensation. Coedès identified Palembang as the centre of the Srivijaya empire, which once covered large parts of Southeast Asia.[44] He referred to European and Asian scholars who had been and were working in this field, such as Groeneveldt and Japanese scholar J. Takakusu.[45] In the network of specialists studying Southeast Asia's early past, this insight – based on two inscriptions, among which was the Kota Kapur, and a precise reading of ancient Chinese, Tamil, and Arabic sources – was

[41] Buddingh, *Neêrlands-Oost-Indië; Reizen*, 1st edn, III, 104. [42] Ibid., 102–104.

[43] Ibid., 87, 90, and 96–97. For a comparable visit 'programme', see De Sturler, *Bijdrage tot de kennis en rigtige beoordeling*.

[44] George Coedès, 'Le Royaume de Çrîvijaya', *BEFEO* 18:6 (1918), 25–27. For Coedès, see Pierre-Yves Manguin and Mubin Sheppard (eds.), *Sriwijaya: history, religion and language of an early Malay polity. Collected studies by George Coedès and Louis-Charles Damais* (Kuala Lumpur: Malaysian Branch of the Royal Asiatic Society, 1992), viii–xv.

[45] Junjirō Takakusu, *A record of the Buddhist religion as practised in India and the Malay archipelago (AD 671–695) by I-Tsing* (Oxford: Clarendon Press, 1896).Takakusu studied with Max Müller in the 1890s, translated I Tsing's account of his seventh-century voyage to India and the Malay archipelago (1896), and represented Japan at the Orientalist Congress in Hanoi in 1902, organised by the young EFEO.

revolutionary.[46] Barely a year later, the Leiden-based archaeologist and Sanskritist J. Ph. Vogel recognised that Coedès' paper was of 'extraordinary importance for the old history of the Indian Archipelago'.[47] At the 'Eerste Congres voor de Taal-, Land en Volkenkunde van Java' (First Congress of Language, Geography and Ethnography) in Surakarta, Westenenk referred to it as the 'explorations' of Coedès. Its consequences were far-reaching. Both Palembang and Jambi, known since the end of the seventh century as the region of 'Malayur' or 'Malayu', gave name to the language that was spoken by all the people that were living in the area of the Srivijaya empire, argued Westenenk.[48]

In December 1919, Krom, in his inaugural lecture as professor in Indian archaeology at Leiden University, praised the work of Coedès as a 'discovery'. Thanks to Coedès, Krom now was able to distinguish, for the eighth and ninth centuries, a so-called Sumatran period in Javanese history. According to Krom, during these centuries Java was characterised by a cultural flourishing in which fine and impressive temples, such as Candi Kalasan, Borobudur, and Mendut were built. Krom also argued that, during this time, Java embraced Mahayana Buddhism. Following this line of reasoning he further remarked that *stupa*, like those on top of Borobudur, are very rare on Java, which was a significant observation, because during that same era similar *stupa* seemed to be relatively common in Sumatra.[49]

Only a few months later, in March 1920, the archaeologist P. V. van Stein Callenfels gave a presentation on Srivijaya during a meeting of the Algemeen Nederlandsch Verbond (General Dutch Language Association) in Surabaya.[50] He drew the conclusion that during the first millennium AD, Palembang had been the centre of a kingdom that ruled Sumatra, Malacca, Burma, Cambodia,

[46] The Kota Kapur inscription was found on the island of Bangka in 1892 by J. K. van der Meulen, a 'bestuursambtenaar' working at 'Midden'-Bangka. Kern 'published' it in 1912. He also referred to an inscription found at Wiang Sa (Thailand), 'published' by Finot in 1910. See Louis Finot, 'Inscriptions du Siam et de la Péninsule malaise (Mission Lunet de Lajonquière)', *Bulletin de la Commission archéologique de l'Indochine* (1910), 147–154; H. Kern, 'Inscriptie van Kota Kapoer', *BKI* 67 (1912), 393–400.

[47] Jean Ph. Vogel, 'Het Koninkrijk Çrîvijaya', *BKI* 75 (1919), 626. For Vogel, see Hanneke J. 't Hart-van den Muyzenberg, 'Vogel, Jean Philippe (1871–1958)', in *Biografisch Woordenboek van Nederland*, http://resources.huygens.knaw.nl/bwn1880-2000/lemmata/bwn4/vogel (accessed 24 April 2014).

[48] Westenenk, 'De Hindoe-Javanen', 2–3.

[49] He mentioned, moreover, that an indigenous movement in Java had also developed an interest in the Hindu–Javanese past as a 'foundation' of a national future. See Krom, *De Sumatraansche Periode der Javaansche geschiedenis*, 12–13 and 32. For Krom, see G. Jensma and H. de Vries, *Veranderingen in het hoger onderwijs in Nederland tussen 1815 en 1940* (Hilversum: Verloren, 1997), 302.

[50] This organisation promoted, among other things, the use of the Dutch language among the inhabitants of the Netherlands Indies; see Kees Groeneboer, 'Nederlands in den vreemde. Het Algemeen-Nederlands Verbond in Nederlands-Indië 1899–1949', *Neerlandia* 97:4 (1993), 140–144.

parts of India, and finally, after the year 775, also Java. According to Van Stein Callenfels it had been common to regard Java as a starting point for studying the antiquity of the archipelago; from Java, the consensus was that in the course of history culture had spread to the other islands. But thanks to the discovery of Coedès, the perspective had changed; Sumatra had once played an important role in history as well. Like Krom, Van Stein Callenfels directly connected the construction of the shrines of Kalasan, Borobudur, and Mendut to influence from Palembang.[51]

Looking for Srivijaya in Palembang (and Putting Traces on Display in Batavia)

According to a mid nineteenth-century report by Dutch colonial military official De Sturler, Palembang inhabitants knew the city had once hosted a great civilisation that had been supplanted by a later one.[52] We do not know to what extent this awareness extended to the early twentieth century, but Coedès' discovery would soon start to resonate. What traces were left of the old kingdom in the modern city? Could, for example, the sultanate of Palembang be linked to the Srivijaya empire?[53] As a result all archaeological findings in the expanding and modernising city potentially gained the status of additional evidence for the Coedès thesis.

In 1920 Resident L. C. Westenenk reported to Bosch, the head of the Archaeological Service in Batavia, that two stone inscriptions had been found in Palembang – the Kedukan Bukit inscription and Talang Tuwo inscription – that were comparable with the Kota Kapur inscription from Bangka. The findings caused a small sensation.[54] The inscriptions were immediately sent to the museum in Batavia and placed in the archaeological collection covering the whole of the Netherlands Indies.[55] The circumstances of the 'discovery' of the Kedukan Bukit inscription by District Officer Batenburg are known in part. For a long time the inscription had been in the possession of a local family who lived at the foot of the hill Bukit Siguntang. To them, the stone inscription had an important value: the family used it as a 'mascot' for boat races.[56] In that sense, the stone had a clear function in local society before its 'discovery'.

The colonial infrastructure activities in Palembang of the 1920s and 1930s turned out to be an important (potential) incentive for new archaeological

51 'Hindoe-Oudheden', *De Sumatra Post* (11 March 1920).

52 De Sturler, *Bijdrage tot de kennis en rigtige beoordeling*, 9.

53 According to Van Stein Callenfels, during his presentation in Surabaya, this connection was still unclear. See 'Hindoe-Oudheden', *De Sumatra Post* (11 March 1920).

54 'Hindoe-inscriptie bij Palembang', *Algemeen Handelsblad* (28 December 1920); 'Hindoe-inscriptie', *Het Nieuws van de Dag voor Nederlandsch-Indië* (19 November 1920).

55 Manguin and Sheppard, *Sriwijaya*, 46 and 48.

56 Ibid., 45 and 85.

discoveries. During his visit to Palembang in 1930, Bosch realised that in the past layers of brick had often been reused as road surfaces,[57] but during the construction work archaeological objects might also be found. For example, in 1928 the municipal construction office discovered five statues from the Srivijaya era, a stone with an inscription, and a bronze Buddha head (weighing more than 5 kg).[58] That same year the architect P. J. Perquin, who was construction engineer at the Archaeological Service, started researching the Bukit Siguntang hill after construction workers searching for bricks discovered some fragments of a statue.[59] In 1931 four bronze statues were found near the site of the sultan graves during the construction of the municipal water treatment plant. The archaeological finds of 1931, in particular, exposed the tensions that had become intrinsic to colonial archaeological network. The issue was not how the objects and the sultan graves were connected, but who was going to own the discovered objects. In line with the central museum policy in development, as we discussed in Chapter 4, Bosch wanted the statues, considering their 'great value', to be transported to the museum in Batavia, where they would be safe from fire and theft. The Batavian Museum regarded the objects as compensation for losses suffered from fire at the Paris colonial World Exhibition, which had destroyed the Dutch pavilion, including many treasures sent by the museum.[60] The mayor of Palembang wished to keep the statues in the municipal museum in Palembang.[61] But here, in contrast to the museums in Mojokerto and Trowulan, apparently the colonial hierarchies did not leave much space for discussion, and the objects were taken to Batavia.[62]

As a result, the local colonial authorities tried to improve the conditions in the municipal museum in order to meet the strict standards set by the museum in Batavia. But the secretary of the Batavian Society said a 'regional museum' could not afford such investments. The mayor of Palembang must have been disappointed: opening a local museum to display precious local archaeological finds with local ethnographic objects did not work out. In this context, the practice of making plaster casts – in 1932 the museum in Palembang received two copies of statues from the museum in Batavia – might have offered some consolation or compensation for objects lost, but here again confirmed colonial

[57] Bosch, 'Verslag van een reis door Sumatra', 154.

[58] 'Oudheden in Palembang gevonden', *De Sumatra Post* (15 August 1928).

[59] P. J. Perquin, 'Oudheidkundig Onderzoek te Palembang', *OV* (1928), Bijlage J, 123.

[60] The losses of the museum were described by Bosch and Le Roux in a gloomy article: Frederik D. K. Bosch and Charles C. F. M. le Roux, 'Wat te Parijs verloren ging', *Tijdschrift voor Indische Taal-, Land- en Volkenkunde* 71 (1931), 663–683.

[61] 'Belangrijke archaeologische vondst', *De Sumatra Post* (25 August 1931).

[62] 'Verslag over 1931', *Uitreksels uit de Oudheidkundige Verslagen over 1931–1935* (1938), 8. See also 'Aanwinsten', *Jaarboek I Koninklijk Bataviaasch Genootschap van Kunsten en Wetenschappen* (1933), 219; 'Bijschriften bij de foto's van eenige belangrijke aanwinsten der Oudheidkundige verzameling in 1932 en 1933', *Jaarboek II Koninklijk Bataviaasch Genootschap van Kunsten en Wetenschappen* (1934), 114–115.

archaeological hierarchies.[63] After all, even the making of copies was exceptional. Another special find, the Telaga Batoe inscription, decorated with serpents' heads, discovered in 1934 by the Palembang municipal construction agency, was transported to the museum in Batavia immediately, without the municipal museum receiving a plaster cast in return.[64]

Yet, being a local museum not only meant that 'important' objects from Palembang were sent to Batavia, it also implied that objects from the surrounding South Sumatran regions could be acquired for the museum in Palembang. In 1934, for example, the museum was offered a stone urn filled with more than 200 beads from Soengai Itam. The objects had been owned for some years by a private person and had now been bought by the local administrator J. D. de Roock from Lahat in order to donate them to the museum. In accordance with the Monument Act of 1931, the Archaeological Service in Batavia granted a permit for this transaction.[65] Especially in the 1930s many objects from the Pasemah highlands and Jambi were transported to Palembang. These transports confronted the colonial archaeological officials in Batavia again and again with new 'realities'. Officially, the archaeological regulations were setting the standard for the whole colony, but in South Sumatra the archaeological initiatives of local colonial officials repeatedly transgressed these central regulations. No wonder that colonial archaeological officials in Batavia such as Bosch and Van der Hoop regarded regional museums, which confronted them with the limits of centralised colonial control, as a potential problem. Bosch called the establishment of local museums an 'epidemic' and feared the lack of continuity in these initiatives in his 1935 report, but he foresaw a big challenge for these same museums. Using the argumentation of what is today referred to as salvation ethnology, he reasoned that they could counteract the cultural decline caused by modernisation and expansion of the colonial state.[66] Following this position, Van der Hoop was very critical when visiting and inspecting the museum in Palembang in 1937. Meanwhile the museum consisted of two 'adat' houses; in 1937 an extra house was added, with the financial support of 'rubberfondsen' (rubber funds), which functioned as a place for gatherings

[63] Director of Batavian Museum to mayor of Palembang, 19 December 1932, ANRI, KBG DIR 1051, Correspondence 1932.

[64] In Batavia it was given the number D 155; see Willem F. Stutterheim, 'De archeologische verzameling: lijst van aanwinsten 1935', *Jaarboek III Koninklijk Bataviaasch Genootschap van Kunsten en Wetenschappen* (1936), 198 and illustration 6. Compare with J. G. de Casparis, *Selected inscriptions from the seventh to the ninth century AD* II (Bandung: Masa Baru, 1956), 15–46; Friedrich M. Schnitger, *Oudheidkundige vondsten in Palembang* Bijlage A, *Verslag over de gevonden inscriptie's door Dr W. F. Stutterheim* (Palembang: Ebeling, 1935).

[65] J. D. de Roock to the Assistant Resident from Lahat, 11 September 1934, and Resident of Palembang to Hoofd van de Oudheidkundige Dienst, 5 October 1934, ANRI, KBG DIR 1058, Correspondence 1934.

[66] F. D. K. Bosch, 'De ontwikkeling van het Museum-Wezen in Nederlandsch-Indië', *Djawa: Tijdschrift van het Java-Instituut* 15 (1935), 209–221.

and lectures.[67] According to Van der Hoop, the houses were beautifully restored but unfit for exhibiting archaeological objects. That same year, a 'museum committee' was set up in order to (re)arrange the mutual relations between local museums and the museum in Batavia. For unknown reasons, however, 'Palembang' did not join.[68]

The Prehistoric Past of Sumatra between Palembang and Batavia

In the mid and late 1930s archaeological objects increasingly became an integral part of the collection of the municipal museum in Palembang. In 1935 the mayor of Palembang tried to get the approval of the head of the Archaeological Service for the transportation of two carved megaliths from the Pasemah area to the garden of the museum in Palembang. In general, Van der Hoop, as curator of the Batavian Museum and the specialist in this particular archaeological field, was against such transports. First, there was an academic reason; the location of the objects involved had not yet been excavated. The statues were furthermore often in good condition, so there was no urgent need to put them on display in the safe surroundings of a museum. Van der Hoop also reasoned that the general public did not value the carved stones as much as the Hindu antiquities, which made it less urgent to transport them. It is remarkable that local inhabitants do not play a noteworthy role in Van der Hoop's rationale, because he often mentions them in his dissertation. He refers to the names the local inhabitants gave to various stones, to the belief in the petrification of men and animals and the influence of Islam which leads to the demolishing of ancestor houses.[69] (As we show in Chapter 6, this would work out differently with regard to heritage politics concerning Hindu–Buddhist antiquities in Java, where Javanese elites' and cultural nationalists' interests became an argument for conservation and reconstruction on site.) From the two candidates discussed in 1935 – the Batoe Gadjah and Air Poear – Van der Hoop only gave permission for the transport of the Batoe Gadjah, reasoning that it was important because it depicted a bronze kettledrum, and provided a valuable clue for dating Pasemah culture.[70] He advised the mayor to mark the original place of the stone with a concrete pole with an inscription. Remarkably, Van der Hoop reserved the Air Poear for the Batavian Museum's collection, where it would represent Pasemah

[67] 'Museum van Palembang. Uitbreiding en Verbetering', *Algemeen Handelsblad* (27 March 1936); 'Het Palembangsche museum', *Bataviaasch Nieuwsblad* (15 April 1937).

[68] 'Concept-Notulen der vergadering van Museum Besturen', 4/5 July 1936, ANRI, KBG DIR 1068, Correspondence 1936. Compare with 'Vergadering der Museumbesturen', *Het nieuws van den dag voor Nederlandsch-Indië* (7 July 1936).

[69] Van der Hoop, *Megalithic remains*, 4–5 and 62.

[70] Ibid., 33–35. For the Air Poear, see also H. W. Vonk, 'De "batoe tatahan" bij Air Peoar (Pasemah-landen) met naschrift', *Tijdschrift voor Indische Taal-, Land- en Volkenkunde* 74:2 (1934), 296–300.

culture. In reaction, the mayor turned to regionalism, while again ignoring appropriations of ancient stones by the local population.[71]

In the mid 1930s, the archaeological activities in Palembang were strongly stimulated by the self-taught archaeologist Schnitger. Schnitger ignored Van der Hoop's advice to mark the location of the Batoe Gadjah[72] and rejected Van der Hoop's desire to acquire the Air Poear. As curator of the municipal museum in Palembang, Schnitger succeeded in putting Palembang on the archaeological map of the Netherlands Indies. He initiated archaeological activities that ranged from collecting, excavating, and publishing in academic and popular media from a local to global level. And he compiled an inventory of the museum's collection. But relations with Van der Hoop were tense. From a report in a local colonial newspaper, Van der Hoop gathered that Schnitger was ignoring the interests of the local Pasemah population[73] and had even committed desacralisation by excavating a megalith in order to photograph it and to move it to the museum in Palembang. He concluded that Schnitger, who apparently thought that the stone involved was of no importance to the local inhabitants, never gained their trust.[74] For the Resident of Palembang this accusation was sufficient to launch an investigation. The *controleur* of the Pasemah area, H. A. J. Ockers, who had accompanied Schnitger during the excavation, reconstructed the events and consulted some relevant local Sumatran leaders. It turned out that the megalith, after being excavated and photographed, was replaced in the same condition as before. According to the local district head of Aloen Doea and to the heads of the smaller communities (*marga*), the stone involved was of no importance, although they did sometimes clean it. There was thus no reason to speak of desacralisation, Ockers concluded, but he did not question if the information he gained had been shaped by colonial hierarchies and cultural misunderstandings.[75]

As an archaeologist connected to the central archaeological museum in Batavia who specialised in the archaeology of the Pasemah area, Van der Hoop played a complex double role. On the one hand, he disapproved of the transport of megaliths from the Pasemah area, but on the other hand he actively participated in acquiring objects from Pasemah for the Batavian Museum and,

[71] Telegram Burgemeester Van de Wetering, 12 November 1935; Van der Hoop to the Head of the Archaeological Service, 13 November 1935; Head of the Archaeological Service to mayor of Palembang, 23 November 1935; mayor of Palembang to the head of the Archaeological Service, 26 November 1935; 2 December 1935, all ANRI, KBG DIR 1062, Correspondence 1935.

[72] In 1937 Van der Hoop visited Sumatra and noticed that the site was not marked, see 'Verslag Dr. v.d. Hoop. Sumatra', pp. 4–5, 19 July 1937, ANRI, KBG DIR 1074, Correspondence 1937.

[73] 'Een merkwaardige Mohammedaansche grafsteen bij Pageralam', *Nieuwsblad voor de residentiën Palembang, Djambi en Banka* (27 June 1936).

[74] Van der Hoop to head of the Archaeological Service, 2 July 1936, ANRI, KBG DIR 1066, Correspondence 1936.

[75] 'Optreden F. M. Schnitger', Resident of Palembang to head of the Archaeological Service, 25 August 1936, ANRI, KBG DIR 1068 Correspondence 1936.

Figure 5.2 Painted stone from a stone grave in Pasemah, 1938.

on such occasions did not seem bothered by local interests. In 1937, he played an active role in the transportation of a part of the painted stone grave of Tandjoeng Aro that was excavated in 1932 by C. W. P. de Bie (Figure 5.2). De Bie did this on his own initiative, although he collaborated with the *controleur*. He furthermore reported his findings to the Archaeological Service, made reproductions of two of the paintings that had been discovered (which were coloured white, black, red, yellow, and grey), and published the excavation results in the *Journal of the Batavian Society*.[76] Soon afterwards the Archaeological Service officially declared the site a monument. The *controleur* of the Pasemah highlands arranged the construction of a gate with a door and a zinc roof, in order to keep 'curious people' away.[77] In 1936, according to the Resident in Lahat, people repeatedly demolished the roof, gate, and door, and the stone grave was in danger of deteriorating. Filling in the grave again was proposed as the best solution.[78]

[76] C. W. P. de Bie, 'Verslag van de ontgraving der Steenen Kamers in de doesoen Tandjoen Ara, Pasemah-Hoogvlakte', *Tijdschrift voor Indische Taal-, Land- en Volkenkunde* 72 (1932), 626–635.

[77] Ibid., 626 and 630.

[78] Assistant Resident of Lahat, Resident of Palembang, and head of Archaeological Service, 17, 23, and 29 April 1936, ANRI, KBG DIR 1065, Correspondence 1936.

A year later, Van der Hoop himself could travel to the stone grave of Tandjoeng Aro – by then an official monument – during a research trip to Sumatra. When applying for funding for this trip at the Archaeological Service he had proposed to organise the transport of the stone grave, or at least the painted part of it, to Batavia.[79] In June 1937 he re-excavated the stone grave. As the transportation of the whole grave was impossible for technical reasons, he decided to restrict himself to the transport of the painted stone that De Bie had given the number 9. After the stone was lifted, it was packed in leather and mats, put in a crate, and transported to Lahat by truck and to Batavia by boat. Aaccording to Van der Hoop, the inhabitants living in the small hamlet (*dusun*) near the site did not object. However, he felt it was important to organise a *sedekah* afterwards. The request of the inhabitants of the *dusun* to leave the grave open – they argued it was sometimes frequented by 'strangers' – was not granted by Van der Hoop because it would lead to the destruction of the other drawings.[80] After his return to Batavia, Van der Hoop wrote a revealing letter to the German palaeontologist and prehistorian G. H. R. von Koenigswald, also active in the Indies, about his proceedings. He described 'roaming all over Sumatra' and 'taking with him one stone of a painted stone cist'; local Sumatran support or appropriations were not mentioned at all. For Van der Hoop, practising archaeology clearly excited him, and restrictions were more likely technical than cultural. In that sense Van der Hoop, as well as Schnitger, whose position in the archaeological network might have been different, were very comparable in the way they practised archaeology in colonial society.[81]

In the Batavian Museum, the painted stone from Tandjoeng Aro was incorporated into the prehistoric section, where it would become one of the 'cornerstones' of Indonesian nationalist history (Figure 5.2). In 1953 the Sumatra-born Muhammad Yamin, then the Indonesian minister of education, would argue – with the rock paintings in South Sumatra as proof – that the white and red colours of the Indonesian national flag were key to a unified Indonesian people at least 4,000 years ago – as he argued (discussed in Chapter 4) for the *kraton* of Majapahit.[82] In the Museum Yearbook of 1938, the act of transporting the painted stone was legitimised solely by academic reasoning as 'a desirable measure' needed to conserve the painting.[83] Ironically, because the stone was moved, it was rescued from a deterioration process that was in the first place the result of a colonial intervention (the excavation by De Bie). In the prehistoric section of the

[79] Van der Hoop to head of Archaeological Service, 3 May 1937, ANRI, KBG DIR 1072, Correspondence 1937.

[80] 'Verslag Dr. v.d. Hoop. Sumatra', 4–5, 19 July 1937, ANRI, KBG DIR 1074, Correspondence 1937.

[81] Van der Hoop to Von Koenigswald, 28 July 1937, ANRI, KBG DIR 1074, Correspondence 1937.

[82] Yamin, *6000 Tahun Sang Mérah Putih*, Lukisan VI, 122–123.

[83] A. N. J. Th. à Th. van der Hoop, 'De praehistorische verzameling', *Jaarboek V Koninklijk Bataviaasch Genootschap van Kunsten en Wetenschappen* (1938), 67.

museum the painted stone would be connected to the new and modern knowledge of evolution of humanity and culture. Yet, surprisingly, it would soon gain an additional – national – meaning within the walls of the museum.

On the occasion of the opening of the prehistoric department in 1933, the curator, Van Stein Callenfels (in 1934 Van der Hoop would take over the position),[84] evaluated the history of collecting prehistoric objects by the Batavian Society. Discussions on the material culture of prehistoric times had started in the 1860s, following the European debate on the Swiss lake-dweller discoveries of the early 1860s.[85] Yet the objects themselves – often stone tools – were never given much attention in the museum, except for the donation of stone tools from Ede (the Netherlands) by Governor-General L. A. J. W. Sloet van de Beele in 1863.[86] This changed after the new prehistoric department opened in 1933. The objects were arranged following a story of linear advancement from Palaeolithic and Mesolithic to Neolithic times. The collection showed that during these periods there had been many connections with and migrations between different parts of Asia. It comprised old objects from the collection of the Batavian Society, and recent acquisitions purchased in Indochina and Japan or exchanged with other museums in Asia, Australia, and Europe. Over the course of time, the museum obtained other objects, via the state-sponsored excavations of the Archaeological Service, or as donations by colonial officials such as L. C. Heyting and J. A. van Beuge.[87] A year later some members of the Indonesian elite, like the *regent* of Goenoeng Kidoel and the sultan of Sepoeh, would start donating prehistoric objects as well.[88]

The first catalogue, written by Van Stein Callenfels and published in 1934, contained a small section on megaliths written by Van der Hoop. He described the Pasemah area as an important centre of megalithic culture, comparable to the 'megalithic monuments' of East Java and the stone cists of Central Java, excavated in Goenoeng Kidoel. He described as 'unique' the wall paintings of the gravestones from Pasemah in black, white, red, and yellow, and often depicting humans and buffalo.[89] In the third edition of catalogue, which

[84] A. N. J. Th. à Th. Van der Hoop, 'De praehistorische verzameling', *Jaarboek II Koninklijk Bataviaasch Genootschap van Kunsten en Wetenschappen* (1934), 63.

[85] For the discovery of the Swiss lake dwellings following the drought in the winter of 1853, see Trigger, *A history of archaeological thought*, 83–84.

[86] Pieter V. van Stein Callenfels, 'De praehistorische verzameling', *Jaarboek I Koninklijk Bataviaasch Genootschap van Kunsten en Wetenschappen* (1933), 205–215. Compare with Groot, *Van Batavia*, 478–479.

[87] Van Stein Callenfels, 'De praehistorische verzameling', *Jaarboek I* (1933), 215.

[88] Van der Hoop, 'De praehistorische verzameling', *Jaarboek II* (1934), 68.

[89] A. N. J. Th. à Th. Van der Hoop, 'De Megalithen', *Jaarboek II Koninklijk Bataviaasch Genootschap van Kunsten en Wetenschappen* (1934), 106; Pieter V. van Stein Callenfels, *Korte gids voor de praehistorische verzameling van het Koninklijk Bataviaasch Genootschap van Kunsten en Wetenschappen* (Bandoeng: Nix, 1934). Compare with A. N. J. Th. à Th. van der Hoop, 'De Praehistorie', in Stapel (ed.), *Geschiedenis van Nederlandsch Indië* I, 98–108.

appeared in 1948, Van der Hoop again mentioned the painted stone from Tandjoeng Aro; it made the Pasemah area the oldest centre of 'art from Indonesia'.[90] This is a clear example of the way colonial perspectives on archaeological objects contributed to the 'Indonesianisation' of the past.[91] Nonetheless, in the colonial cultural hierarchy, Pasemah culture would also be connected with primitivism or backwardness (Westeneck would relate the anthropomorphic megaliths to 'Negritos', and Van Stein Callenfels suggested a connection with the nose disease rhinoscleroma).[92]

Prehistoric Sumatra between Amsterdam and Switzerland

In 1919 an archaeological site near Boengamas above Palembang became a governmental nature reserve ('natuurmonument'). A few years earlier the site had been described by the 'brothers' Sarasin from Switzerland as a 'workshop for making stone implements'.[93] Between 1893 and 1896, Paul and Fritz Sarasin – cousins and lovers – had been active in studying ethnography, including stone tools in Asia, especially Ceylon and Celebes.[94] They had encountered the stone tools from Boengamas in the Völkerkunde Museum, Basel. The tools had been collected by the geologist August Tobler, who donated them to the museum in 1913.[95] According to Paul Sarasin they could be compared to those from the Danish Neolithic.[96] Following a decision by the colonial government of 1919, the one-hectare area Boengamas-Kikim was

90 A. N. J. Th. à Th. van der Hoop, *Korte Gids voor de Praehistorische Verzameling van het Koninklijk Bataviaasch Genootschap van Kunsten en Wetenschappen door P. V. van Stein Callenfels*, Edition III (Bandoeng: A. C. Nix & Co., 1948), 33. Compare with A. N. J. Th. à Th. van der Hoop, *Korte Gids voor de Praehistorische Verzameling van het Koninklijk Bataviaasch Genootschap van Kunsten en Wetenschappen door P. V. van Stein Callenfels*, Edition II (Bandoeng: Nix, 1939); A. N. J. Th. à Th. van der Hoop, *Catalogus der Praehistorische Verzameling* (Bandoeng: Nix, 1941), 317 and fig. 111.

91 For the nationalisation of the prehistoric department of the Museum of the Batavian Society, see Bloembergen and Eickhoff, 'The colonial archaeological hero', 154–155.

92 Westenenk, 'De Hindoe-Oudheden', 32; Pieter V. van Stein Callenfels, 'Naschrift', in H. N. Noosten, L. Kirschner and J. J. Th. Vos, 'Rhinoscleroom op Bali', *Geneeskundig Tijdschrift voor Nederlandsch-Indië* 74:14 (1934), 850–851. Compare with Niewenhuis, who related the absence of 'higher' culture to malaria. See A. W. Nieuwenhuis, *Körperliche und kulturelle Volksentartung in Gebieten endemischer Malaria* (Leiden: E. J. Brill, 1936), 79–82 and 86.

93 Van der Hoop, *Megalithic remains*, 42. Compare with Paul Sarasin, 'Neue lithochrone Funde im Innern von Sumatra', *Verhandelungen der Naturforschenden Gesellschaft in Basel* (1914), 107.

94 Bernard C. Schär, *Tropenliebe: schweizer Naturforscher und niederländischer Imperialismus in Südostasien um 1900* (Frankfurt am Main: Campus, 2015).See Paul Sarasin and Fritz Sarasin, *Die Steinzeit auf Ceylon. Ergebnisse naturwissenschaftlicher Forschungen auf Ceylon* (Wiesbaden: Kreidel, 1908); Paul Sarasin and Fritz Sarasin, *Materialien zur Naturgeschichte von Celebes. 5. Die Toala-Höhlen von Lamongtjong* (Wiesbaden: Kreidel, 1905).

95 Information about this donation is provided by Richard Kunz (Museum der Kulturen, Basel) 16 November 2016.

96 Sarasin, 'Neue lithochrone Funde im Innern von Sumatra', 109.

declared a reserve and gated with wooden posts,[97] though in 1931 Van der Hoop noted that the 'regulation seems to have been forgotten', and the 'railway line from Lahat to Tebingtinggi runs in a deep cutting through a corner of the reserve'.[98]

Notwithstanding this neglect on location in Sumatra, in the 1930s Sumatra became increasingly known in the Netherlands for its prehistoric past. In Amsterdam, at the Colonial Institute's Etnographic Museum, it was Sumatra that would be connected to the earliest past of mankind. Three stone tools found in 1927 in Serdang proved the existence of an old Palaeolithic culture on the island.[99] The discovery and transfer of these objects were clearly connected to both the economic exploitation of Sumatra and the idea of scientific progress. Furthermore, the intrinsic tensions in the colonial archaeological infrastructure again came to the surface: the *controleur* who discovered the objects, L. C. Heyting, a linguist and self-taught scholar of ancient Bali and Java, soon would feel offended by the claims to his finds made by 'Batavia'.

In 1924 Van Stein Callenfels publicly announced that the first Palaeolithic tool of the archipelago had been found in Batu Kemang on Sumatra's east coast; soon afterwards more comparable tools were found.[100] In 1927, while walking along a BPM pipeline at the rubber plantation Boeloe Telang, Heyting found a set of prehistoric tools,[101] and in 1928 (together with M. Kistemaker) discovered others. They planned to donate them to the Batavian Society,[102] but things worked out differently. Heyting, during a visit to Lombok, met Van Eerde who, as director of the Ethnological Section of the Colonial Institute in Amsterdam, showed interest in the objects, too. Van Eerde managed to arrange their export – with the consent of Van Stein Callenfels who, as Bosch was on leave, was acting as adjunct head of the Archaeological Service.[103] However

[97] 'Natuurmonumenten in Nederlandsch-Indië', *Indisch staatsblad* 39 (1919). Compare with 'Natuurmonumenten', *De Sumatra Post* (20 August 1919); 'Natuurmonumenten', *De Gooi- en Eemlander: nieuws- en advertentieblad* (4 December 1929).

[98] Van der Hoop, *Megalithic remains*, 42. Compare with Karel W. Dammerman, *Overzicht der Nederlandsch-Indische natuurmonumenten* (Buitenzorg: Nederlandsch-Indische Vereeniging tot Natuurbescherming, 1924); Cornelis G. G. J. van Steenis, *Album van natuurmonumenten in Nederlandsch-Indië, naar photographische opnamen van vele natuurvrienden* (Batavia: Nederlandsch-Indische Vereeniging tot Natuurbescherming, 1937).

[99] Johannes P. Kleiweg de Zwaan, *Praehistorie en anthropologie: gids in het Volkenkundig Museum* (Amsterdam: Koninklijke Vereeniging Koloniaal Instituut, 1929), 48–50. Compare with Van der Hoop, *Catalogus der Praehistorische Verzameling,* 14.

[100] Pieter V. van Stein Callenfels, 'Het eerste palaeolitische werktuig in den archipel', *OV 1924* (1924), 127 and 133.

[101] 'Uitreksel uit de Memorie van Overgave van den Controleur te Pangkalan Brandan L. C. Heyting (21 April 1927–1 Juni 1928)'; see ANRI, KBG DIR 1044, Correspondence 1931.

[102] 'Praehistorische vondsten', *De Indische Courant* (18 June 1928).

[103] J. C. van Eerde to Heyting, 20 August 1929, ANRI, KBG DIR 1044, Correspondence 1931.

during the transfer some of the objects came into, and remained in, the possession of Van Stein Callenfels in Batavia. After being informed about this transaction, Heyting began to worry that the objects would not reach the collection of the Batavian Society. For that reason, he expressed his annoyance that he had not received an official expression of gratitude from Van Stein Callenfels.[104] But according to Van Stein Callenfels, Heyting was about to smuggle the objects to the Netherlands, thus violating all legal arrangements. Moreover, as it was Van Eerde who had donated the objects, Van Stein Callenfels felt no need to thank Heyting – to the further annoyance of the latter.[105] It would take a few years before the relationship between Heyting and the Archaeological Service normalised. In 1934 – after the retirement of Van Stein Callenfels – Van der Hoop, as secretary of the Batavian Society, confirmed to Heyting that the objects given by Van Eerde to Van Stein Callenfels were indeed part of the collection of the museum in Batavia. He furthermore explained that the Monument Act of 1931 prohibited the export of stone tools, although the exchange of objects by the Batavian Society with other museums was still possible. Van der Hoop saw no offence in the transfer of the tools collected by Heyting to the museum in Amsterdam.[106] Local, Sumatra-based perspectives were clearly absent in this line of argument but, remarkably, the catalogue of the Museum in Amsterdam mentioned them. According to the physical anthropologist J. P. Kleiweg de Zwaan, local people did not know the original function of such objects and often considered them to be magic. Owning such a stone was believed to make people invulnerable in battle and bring happiness and prosperity.[107]

Schnitger and the Municipal Museum in Palembang

The municipal museum in Palembang did not have a section dedicated to the prehistoric past. Considering the limited number of objects from the Sumatran Palaeolithic past, in combination with the archaeological network that made these objects move to Batavia and Amsterdam, this comes as no surprise. But even for the historical past related to the Srivijaya era, the museum had difficulties compiling convincing displays. Palembang might once have been a powerful centre of a great kingdom and there might have been an active municipal policy to collect archaeological objects, but real proof was and remained meagre. Both Coedès and Bosch knew that areas near Palembang

104 Heytink to the head of the archaeological service, 29 November 1929, ANRI, KBG DIR 1044, Correspondence 1931.
105 Van Stein Callenfeld to Heytink, 12 December 1929, ANRI, KBG DIR 1044, Correspondence 1931.
106 Van der Hoop to Heytink, 27 December 1934, ANRI, KBG DIR 1058, Correspondence 1934.
107 Kleiweg de Zwaan, *Praehistorie en anthropologie,* 45.

held few relics, and Bosch even doubted that Palembang had been the capital city of Srivijaya.[108] On the other hand, at the same time a Dutch audience became familiar with the existence of Srivijaya via publications on the Netherlands Indies for a general public, such as the 1934 'Java' album of the chocolate company Droste.[109] Srivijaya was also an integral part of Frederik Willem Stapel's five-volume *Geschiedenis van Nederlandsch Indië* ('History of the Netherlands Indies') of 1938.[110] And, in Palembang, the local archaeological initiatives undertaken in order to find the missing evidence started to pay off.

In the mid 1930s, Schnitger led the efforts to put Palembang on the archaeological map of the Netherlands Indies and the world. He not only collected objects from the Pasemah area, but also was active in the city of Palembang itself. In 1935, in the Dutch newspaper *Algemeen Handelsblad,* Schnitger portrayed Srivijaya as a 'big and magnificent city', based on locating its remains in eastern Palembang.[111] Schnitger, who had become curator of the municipal museum in Palembang, would go on publishing his research in Netherlands Indies newspapers and in the small essay series 'Oudheidkundige vondsten in Palembang' ('Archaeological findings in Palembang').[112] A few years later he would compile these publications into a dissertation titled 'The archaeology of Hindoo Sumatra'. He obtained his doctorate in 1937 from the Völkerkunde Department of the University of Vienna, which was famous for its diffusionist approach in cultural development.[113] However, Schnitger's dissertation was very object- and

[108] George Coedès, 'Les inscriptions Malaises de Çrîvijaya', *BEFEO* 30 (1930), 30; Bosch, 'Verslag van een reis door Sumatra', 155–156. Compare with Nicolaas J. Krom, 'De heiligdommen van Palembang', *Mededeelingen der Koninklijke Nederlandsche Akademie van Wetenschappen* nr I, *Afdeeling Letterkunde* (1938), 401.

[109] Johann C. Lamster, *'Indië', gevende eene beschrijving van de inheemsche bevolking van Nederlandsch-Indië en hare beschaving* (Haarlem: Droste's Cacao- en Chocoladefabrieken, 1928), 163.

[110] Nicolaas J. Krom, 'Het Hindoe-Tijdperk', in Stapel (ed.), *Geschiedenis van Nederlandsch Indië*, I, 143–169.

[111] 'Sjriwidjaja, Groote en schitterende stad', *Algemeen Handelsblad* (04 May 1935). Compare with Friedrich M. Schnitger, *Oudheidkundige vondsten in Palembang* (Palembang: Ebeling, 1935), 3; and with Friedrich M. Schnitger, *The archaeology of Hindoo Sumatra* (Leiden, 1937), 1–2.

[112] Schnitger often published in *Nieuwsblad van Palembang*; see 'Vondst in Palembang', *De Indische Courant* (27 June 1935). See also Friedrich M. Schnitger, *Oudheidkundige vondsten in Palembang* (Palembang: Ebeling, 1935); Friedrich M. Schnitger, *Oudheidkundige vondsten in Palembang*, Bijlage A (Palembang: Ebeling, 1935); Friedrich M. Schnitger, *Oudheidkundige vondsten in Palembang*, Bijlage C (Leiden: Brill, 1936). For an overview of his publications, see J. N. Miksic, 'Introduction', in Schnitger, *Forgotten kingdoms in Sumatra*, xvi–xvii.

[113] Schnitger, *The Archaeology of Hindoo Sumatra*; Miksic, 'Introduction', x. See also Frederik Barth et al., *One discipline, four ways: British, German, French, and American anthropology. The Halle Lectures* (Chicago: University of Chicago Press, 2005).

site-centred, and did not offer a real narrative on the history of the island and its cultures. Nevertheless, in *Forgotten kingdoms in Sumatra* of 1939, which was based on the same material but written as a romantic jungle travelogue for a broader audience, he employed the familiar tropes of 'discovering archaeologists' and 'lost worlds'.[114] But, in fact, Schnitger mostly worked in an urban environment. For the municipal museum in Palembang he assisted the reconstruction of a 3.6-metre granite statue called the 'Great Buddha of Palembang', whose head had been kept separately in the Museum in Batavia. Schnitger was the first to recognise that the statue and the head belonged together.[115] In its full glory the restored statue was placed in the garden of the municipal museum.

In his writings, Schnitger repeatedly mentioned the presence of local people, local perspectives, and local support, though in condescending terms. His preface to *Forgotten kingdoms in Sumatra*, for instance, describes the Sumatran people as 'childlike'. Narrating a sojourn to the village of Muara Jambi, he refers to the local inhabitants as 'primitive and kind'.[116] But he also praises the work of the foreman and draughtsman Raden Mohammad Akib.[117] And *Forgotten kingdoms in Sumatra* is dedicated to an Indonesian named Moechtar, though Schnitger never says who this is or was, and there is no further reference to Moechtar in the book.[118] The dedication is nonetheless remarkable. Van Stein Callenfels, by contrast, whose foreman Moenaf could carry out excavations independently, never credited his work in publications.[119]

With his team of local workers, Schnitger not only researched the Srivijaya era, but also included the Islamic past of Palembang in his projects and publications. In 1935 he partly excavated and mapped the sultan graves at Geding Soera and Lemabang, and the Islamic shrine of Panembahan. According to Schnitger, Geding Soera had been a nobleman from Demak, who, after the fall of Majapahit, left for Palembang; his descendants ruled until 1823. Some of the buildings Schnitger excavated had been destroyed by the Dutch in 1659. Schnitger disliked Islamic architecture and found the Muslim graveyard at Lemabang 'tasteless'.[120]

114 Schnitger, *Forgotten kingdoms in Sumatra,* preface.

115 'De Boeddha zonder hoofd. Na 13 eeuwen gerestaureerd', *Het Nieuws van den Dag voor Nederlandsch-Indië* (19 July 1935). Compare with Schnitger, *The Archaeology of Hindoo Sumatra*, plate 1; Schnitger, *Oudheidkundige vondsten in Palembang*, Bijlage C, 4; Miksic, 'Introduction', xi.

116 Schnitger, *Forgotten kingdoms in Sumatra,* 12.

117 Schnitger, *Oudheidkundige vondsten in Palembang*, 1.

118 Schnitger, *Forgotten kingdoms in Sumatra*.

119 Bloembergen and Eickhoff, 'The colonial archaeological hero', 147–148.

120 Schnitger, *Oudheidkundige vondsten in Palembang*, Bijlage C, 1–4 and 13. Compare with Schnitger, *The Archaeology of Hindoo Sumatra*, 1–3 and plates IV–V.

What mattered most was finding additional evidence that Palembang had been the capital of the Srivijaya empire – such as the nine stones with inscriptions, including the Telaga Batoe stone. According to Schnitger they proved the existence of a shrine that had been in use between the sixth and the tenth centuries.[121] The Kedukan Bukit inscription was a key object. According to Schnitger that particular inscription was nothing less than the foundational charter of the empire.[122] However, soon the established scholars in the centre of the archaeological network would dispute this view. Willem F. Stutterheim, who at the time was working for the Archaeological Service and soon would become its director (1936–1942), wrote a report in 1935 in which he concluded that the Kedukan Bukit inscription referred to a king who had made a pilgrimage in order to conquer Srivijaya; as a result it could not be a foundational charter.[123] A few years earlier, Stutterheim had criticised the general idea of a Sumatran period in Javanese history. Based on Krom's connecting the construction of the Central Javanese temples Kalasan, Borobudur, and Mendut to influence from Palembang, Stutterheim argued for a Javanese period in Sumatran history.[124] For Schnitger, archaeological remains became even more important and in 1936 in Muara Jambi he discovered seven ruins, including a royal mausoleum, and fourteen statues, which he believed part of a great city, probably greater than Palembang. Schnitger suggested that it had either been conquered by Srivijaya, at the end of the seventh century or been the capital of Srivijaya itself.[125]

During the last part of his career Schnitger did not leave many traces in the Netherlands Indies.[126] In 1936 he left for Europe; in 1937 he defended his PhD at the University of Vienna[127] and never returned to Asia. Apparently, Schnitger, pretending he had died in battle, had floated a fantastic story about his heroic role as a pilot during the German attack on Warsaw and his being awarded an Iron Cross. The *Sumatra Post* concluded that, considering this

[121] Schnitger, *Oudheidkundige vondsten in Palembang*, Bijlage A, 5–6. In his dissertation he speaks of thirty stones; see Schnitger, *The Archaeology of Hindoo Sumatra,* 1.

[122] Schnitger, *Oudheidkundige vondsten in Palembang*, 5.

[123] 'Sanscriet inscripties. De vondsten van Schnitger', *De Indische Courant* (26 March 1935); Schnitger, *Oudheidkundige vondsten in Palembang*, Bijlage A.

[124] Willem F. Stutterheim, *A Javanese period in Sumatran history* (Surakarta: De Bliksem, 1929), 22–23.

[125] Schnitger, *The Archaeology of Hindoo Sumatra*, 5–7. Compare with Schnitger, *Forgotten kingdoms in Sumatra,* 16.

[126] In his introduction to the reprint of *Forgotten kingdoms in Sumatra* in 1989, John Miksic could as a result give no information about the way Schnitger's life ended. See Miksic, 'Introduction'.

[127] His supervisors were Oswald Menghin and Wilhelm Koppers. See 'Rigorosenakt', 'Rigorosenprotokoll', including 'Lebenslauf' F. M. Schnitger, Archiv der Universität Wien. Compare Schnitger, *The archaeology of Hindoo Sumatra.*

fantasy, Schnitger's earlier archaeological discovery stories should be read with suspicion.[128] In 1942, he contacted the SS-Ahnenerbe organisation – the research department of the SS – in Germany for support for his publications, and claimed to have information about espionage activities in the Netherlands, specifically in the Colonial Institute in Amsterdam.[129] This story turned out to be a fraud as well. As a result, in 1944 Schnitger was arrested and sent, without trial, to a concentration camp (in *Schutzhaft*, protective custody); his lack of 'pure' racial descent (his great-grandmother was Chinese) was given as an explanation for his behaviour.[130] On 23 April 1945, Schnitger died in the Mauthausen concentration camp.[131] Today he is still present in Palembang, as his name is mentioned in the explanation shield of the Arca Singa displayed in the park beside the Sultan Mahmud Badaruddin II Museum – an indication of the continuing local appropriation of his colonial archaeological work in post-colonial Palembang.

Local Culture and Srivijaya, Palembang and Indonesia

Coedès' discovery in 1918 identifying Palembang as the centre of the Srivijaya kingdom fuelled not only archaeological activities, but also the pride of Sumatran nationalists. In 1922, the medical student and self-taught specialist in Sumatran history Mohammad Amir, who was president of the Jong Sumatranen Bond, included Srivijaya in his overview of the history of the Sumatrans as a seafaring people in a speech to the organisation.[132] The Jong Sumatranen Bond – a 'co-operative' nationalist organisation founded in 1917 by Sumatran students from STOVIA (School tot Opleiding van Inlandsche Artsen – a medical school) – aimed to create unity among the Sumatran peoples by promoting their culture, Malay language, and history. It gave a platform to a generation of young, intellectual, and politically engaged Sumatrans such as Muhammad Yamin, Mohammed Hatta (later to be prime minister), and Amir.[133] In his 1922 speech Amir referred to Sumatran ships that had traded

[128] 'Een vreemde geschiedenis. Is dr F. M. Schnitger werkelijk gesneuveld bij Warschau?', *De Sumatra Post* (16 October 1939). For additional information, see Leiden University Library, Special Collections, KITLV Collections, Dossier H 814 (238) – correspondentie Tichelman–Schnitger, 11 December 1935 / 13 October 1939.

[129] 'Spionage-Bericht erstattet von Dr F. M. Schnitger', Pottenstein 22 March 1942 / 'Widerstand in Holland im Kolonialinstitut', Bundesarchiv Berlin, Ahnenerbe NS 19, 2025.

[130] 'Vermerk für SS-Standartenführer Dr. Brand', 22 May 1944, Bundesarchiv Berlin Ahnenerbe NS 19, 1826.

[131] 'Häftlingsnummer: 137.690, H-Kategorie: Niederlande/Schutz, Name: Martin Schnigter, eingeliefert in MH: 1945, gestorben: 23.4.1945 in Mauthausen', e-mail from Ildikó Cazan-Simányi, Museum für Völkerkunde Wien, 12 January 2012.

[132] Van Miert, 'The "land of the future"', 599.

[133] In 1930 it merged in the Young Indonesia (Indonesia Moeda) organisation; see ibid., 596, 604 and 615; Reid, 'The nationalist quest for an Indonesian past', 286–287.

with Malacca, Cambodia, Siam, China, and Java during the Srivijaya era. Following Krom, he furthermore stated that the Sumatrans had brought Mahayana Buddhism to Java, with the 'great' Borobudur and the 'fine' Mendut as a result.[134]

In 1925 the Jong Sumatranen Bond invited Van Stein Callenfels to one of its meetings in order to get the latest scholarly 'news' on Sriviyaja. Van Stein Callenfels would later publish his presentation in their journal, *Jong Sumatra*, where he concluded that the most famous temples in Java were the result of Sumatran influence and appealed to readers to investigate what other Javanese cultural elements were in fact of Sumatran origin.[135] A few years later in the same journal, South Sumatra would be described as 'the crown of antiquity, twinkling like a diadem in the traditions of Indonesian peoples'.[136] According to the historian H. van Miert, this 'exalted phrasing of Sumatranism' did not really compete with 'the rhetoric for Indonesian unity' because among the members of the Jong Sumatranen Bond these new insights increased the 'feeling of a common identity' as well as the 'self-confidence towards their Javanese counterpart, with its obvious past greatness'.[137]

The meaning of Srivijaya for Indonesian nationalists, whether or not born in Sumatra, remained complicated, however, in relation to Majapahit. In his famous 'Indonesia Accuses' speech of 1930 during his trial at the Bandung courthouse, Soekarno referred to both empires when he attacked colonialism and imperialism. According to Soekarno, imperialism was timeless and not restricted to the 'white races', as the history of Majapahit and Srivijaya demonstrated.[138] However, by 1945 Soekarno was emphasising that Srivijaya and Majapahit had attained not only a state of freedom (*merdeka*) but also that they were national states encompassing the whole of Indonesia. Similarly, Yamin called Srivijaya the first 'Negara Indonesia', and Majapahit the second 'Negara Indonesia'.[139]

[134] Amir, 'Iets over de Sumatranen als zeevarend volk', *Gedenk-Nummer van Jong Sumatra. Orgaan van den Jong Sumatranen Bond 1917–1922* (Weltevreden: Jong Sumatranen Bond, 1923), 38. Compare with Amir, 'Geschiedenis. Datoek Katoemanggoengan en Parapatiëh nan Sabatang', *Jong Sumatra* (September–October 1922), 5–10.

[135] Pieter V. van Stein Callenfels, 'Sumatra's beteekenis voor Prehistori en Archaeologie', *Jong Sumatra* 8 (October 1925), 3. He was elaborating on an earlier talk he gave in Surabaya, 'Hindoe-Oudheden', *De Sumatra Post* (11 March 1920). Compare with Van Miert, 'The "land of the future", 611.

[136] Van Miert, 'The "land of the future", 611. [137] Ibid.

[138] Soekarno, *Indonesia klaagt aan! Pleitrede voor den Landraad te Bandoeng op 2 December 1930* (Amsterdam: De Arbeiderspers, 1931), 9.

[139] Quoted in Pierre-Yves Manguin, 'Welcome to Bumi Sriwijaya or the building of a provincial identity in contemporary Indonesia', in Cayrac-Blanchard, Dovert, and Durand (eds.), *Indonésie*, 208.

In 2000, the archaeologist Pierre-Yves Manguin addressed the question of why, despite its obvious historiographic difficulties and the lack of convincing archaeological evidence, Srivijaya is so prominent in contemporary Palembang as a name and a historical entity. He furthermore pointed out that the better-documented Islamic Sultanate of Palembang, headed, moreover, by a national hero, is much less visible.[140] This chapter helps explain the contemporary prominence of Srivijaya in Palembang. We have discussed the way South Sumatra – in particular Palembang, the Pasemah area, and Jambi – was gradually incorporated in the colonial archaeological infrastructure, and we explored the related interactions that took place during this process between state-supported 'modern' heritage concepts, local (Sumatran) appropriations of certain archaeological sites and objects, and the developing nationalist history writing of Sumatran Indonesians that also included the early past of Sumatra. The archaeological and especially the museological initiatives in the city of colonial times were, from the start, connected to local Sumatran ethnological traditions. The ethnographic 'musealisation' in Palembang seemed to turn local culture and history into static ethnographic 'traditions'. However, the connection with Srivijaya gave these same traditions a new and extra vigour while anchoring Srivijaya in local society. A good example of this local rooting is the 'Gending Srivijaya', the song and dance created by a team of local artists and first performed in Palembang, South Sumatra, during the Japanese occupation in 1945. This group was led by a journalist who was a local government official of the Department of Information under the Japanese: Nung Cik A. R., born in 1910 in Palembang. The composer of the melody was Ahmad Dahlan Mahibat, who was born in Palembang in 1911. Whereas Nung Cik A. R. was a nationalist (a member of the Partai Nasional Indonesia), Ahmad Dahlan was not involved in party politics at all. Nung Cik A. R. had been asked to create a welcome ceremony for Mohammed Syafei, the West Sumatra-born head of the all-Sumatra Advisory Council (Chuo Sangi In) of the Japanese Sumatra Command, on his official visit to Palembang in early August 1945.[141] In subsequent years, the song remained popular, and in 1950 President Soekarno chose it as the official state music of the province.[142] The photo 'A Sriwijaya dance from Palembang' in the picture book *Indonesia: unique in contrast, culture*

[140] Ibid., 205–206. For Srivijaya as being handicapped by the obscurity of the sources, see Reid, 'The nationalist quest for an Indonesian past', 289.

[141] Kartomi, 'The paradoxical and nostalgic history'. Compare with Timothy P. Daniels, 'Imagining selves and inventing Festival Sriwijaya', *Journal of Southeast Asian Studies* 30:1 (1999), 37–38.

[142] After Soeharto took over power in 1965, it was forbidden to perform Gending Sriwijaya, because of the communist affiliation of Nung Cik A. R. The ban was lifted in 1970. See Kartomi, 'The paradoxical and nostalgic history', 41.

Figure 5.3 'The Srivijaya-dance', from Roeslan Abdulgani's, *Indonesia*, 1951.

and change (country, people transition and future) published by the Ministry of Information of the Republic of Indonesia in 1951 and dedicated to 'our many friends abroad who have given us so much help in our struggle for National Independence' only added to the ceremony's status (Figure 5.3).[143] Local culture, Srivijaya, Palembang, and the Indonesian nation had become connected as if it had never been otherwise.

[143] Roeslan Abdulgani, *Indonesia: unique in contrast, culture and change (country, people transition, and future*) (n.p.: Ministry of Information, 1951), 110.

6 Resurrecting Siva, Expanding Local Pasts: Centralisation and the Forces of Imagination across War and Regime Change, 1920s–1950s

On 20 December 1953, during a festive ceremony with more than a thousand spectators, and hundreds of children waving red and white flags, President Soekarno officially inaugurated the Siva temple, the largest temple in the ninth-century complex at Prambanan (Figure 6.1). To his mainly Muslim audience, Soekarno explained that the Siva temple stood as proof of the abilities of Indonesian people in the past, and as a promise for the modern *independent* Republic of Indonesia of the future. With the words, spoken in Dutch: 'Pick up the flame, not the ashes', he told them that it was not the stones, but the spirit of this monument that mattered. In this way, Soekarno transformed a ninth-century Hindu temple ruin into the first national monument of a young state that had a predominantly Muslim population – the largest in the world.

The Siva temple, listed as a UNESCO World Heritage Site in 1991, was a professional archaeological reconstruction, which the Dutch colonial Archaeological Service had begun in the 1910s. The method it employed was based on the principle that reconstruction is possible only as long as there are enough original elements to 'fit' an ornamental story. The French EFEO, following the Dutch example, recognised its importance and referred to it as 'anastylosis'.[1] Nonetheless, when it came to the roof of the Siva temple, a bit of conjecture was also employed. But this would not matter: speaking at the inauguration, the newly appointed minister of education and culture, Muhammad Yamin,

[1] Anastylosis, first developed in Greece, proceeds on the principle that reconstruction is possible only with the use of original elements, which by three-dimensional deduction on the site have to be replaced in their original position. The Netherlands Indies Archaeological Service – which never employed the term – was the first to develop this method in an Asian setting, by trial and error, beginning around 1900 (Candi Mendut) and more systematically after 1917 (Candi Panataran). These efforts provided a direct example for the French scholars of the EFEO in Indochina, who had been visiting Java since 1898. See F. D. K. Bosch, 'Het restaureren van Hindoe-Javaansche bouwwerken', *Djawa* 2 (1922), 8–14; Bernet Kempers, *Herstel in eigen waarde*, 93–97; Catherine Clémentin-Ojha and Pierre-Yves Manguin, *A century in Asia: the history of the École française d'Extrême Orient* (Singapore: Didier-Millet, 2001), 97.

Figure 6.1 Inauguration of the Siva temple at Prambanan, 20-12-1953.

also applauded the reconstruction as the most significant national achievement since the proclamation of Indonesian independence on 17 August 1945.[2]

Unquestionably, colonial archaeological interventions and reconstruction by trial and error at Java's remarkable Hindu–Buddhist sites had helped prepare this momentum of nation building in the history of archaeology and heritage politics in Indonesia. Soekarno's own story, told during the 1953 inauguration of the Siva temple, about the pride he felt as a child upon seeing Prambanan and Borobudur may have been apocryphal, but it is plausible. This would have been in 1909, when Theodor van Erp was in the midst of 'his' four-year restoration project at Borobudur, a project that could have attracted the interest of any

[2] See the printed version of his speech: M. Yamin, 'Tjandi Loro Djonggrang', *Budaya* 12 (1954), 7.

youngster at the time.[3] To be part of the archaeological and cultural elite's networks would matter, moreover, for gauging the potential of archaeological works and reconstruction plans. In 1918, Prince Mangkunegara VII in Solo, a passionate researcher and collector of remains of the Javanese Hindu past, grew excited upon learning that the Archaeological Service's architect and construction engineer, P. J. Perquin, had sketched 'how the Loro Jonggrang temple may have looked'. He rushed to Prambanan with his wife, urging Perquin to show him around.[4] Perquin's drawings were a milestone in the ongoing efforts of various parties in colonial Indonesia, since at least the time of Engelhard, to make sense of this site and incorporate scattered remains to restore its original shape – reconstructive imaginations and techniques in accordance with the means and norms of heritage politics at the time.[5]

Ruins have the power to trigger the imagination. But as we saw when Indonesian nationalists broadened the power and scope of the ancient Majapahit empire beyond available evidence, sites may be exploited according to the interests, whims, and fancies of various powerful parties, and to the neglect or destruction of others. Around 1900, in the context of the professionalisation of archaeology and the establishment of the colonial Archaeological Service in the Netherlands Indies, archaeological sites became priorities for state research, conservation, and reconstruction. The state-supported research and heritage politics included certain well-known sites such as Borobudur and Prambanan, but also fairly new site categories such as the Balinese, Chinese, Islamic, and colonial antiquities. State-supported site interventions, however, also triggered further interest from some other parties, such as Prince Mangkunegara VII, who would himself actively stimulate the research, restoration, and maintenance of certain sites on Java.[6]

In this chapter we use the Siva temple as the central analytical tool to explore the nature, continuities, and discontinuities of institutional heritage engagements across regime changes and war. Thereby we show how professional, state-supported archaeology led to the consolidation of certain structures and methods of heritage formation in such a way that subsequent regimes could easily take over. Along the way, we test the power and limits of sites in the growing centralisation of heritage politics, from the ethical and conservative colonial state of the 1920s and 1930s, the Japanese occupation, revolution, and

[3] For two Javanese poetic reactions to Borobudur, dedicated to J. W. Ijzerman, see Noto Soeroto, 'De Boro-Boedoer', *De geur van moeders haarwong* (Amsterdam: S. L. van Looy, 1916), 53–55.

[4] Mangkunegara VII to P. J. Perquin, 12 February 1924, Arsip Mankunegaran, Solo, Correspondence Mangkunegara VII, inv. nr P 29.

[5] On British examples, see Tiffin, *Southeast Asia in ruins*.

[6] W. F. Stutterheim, 'De oudheden-collectie van Z. H. Mangkoenagoro VII te Soerakarta', *Djawa* 17 (1937), 1–112. Mangkunegara VII, among others, encouraged the research regarding the temple sites at the Lawang mountain (especially Candi Sukuh), and supported the restoration of the ancient Javanese bathing place Jalakunda.

recolonisation war, and into the new independent Republic of Indonesia of the 1950s. In addition to the Siva temple, we explore developments at some newly recognised old sites and objects following the mandate of the service from 1913, by which archaeology and heritage politics extended other local pasts. However, while the Archaeological Service was expanding its reach, and further defining its priorities, archaeological site interventions also expanded the forces of imagination – on location and beyond. This becomes particularly clear in the second part, when we turn to Bali as a site of restoration and archaeological explorations. Here, again, heritage formation and violence went hand in hand: the first systematic efforts into archaeological research and conservation practices followed the violent military invasions early in the twentieth century, which had led to the infamous *pupatan* of the rajas of Badung (1906) and Klungkung (1908), the destruction of their palaces, and the incorporation of South Bali in the colonial state-in-development. Similarly important were the heritage measures discussed and taken after the gigantic earthquake that hit Bali on the morning of 21 January 1917. Against that background, we explore subsequent state-supported archaeological involvements in Bali in the colonial era, and gauge the legacies of colonial archaeological heritage politics in post-colonial times.

In the final part we look closely at the development of archaeology and Chinese past in the Netherlands Indies, as a backdrop of the central case of this chapter: the nationalisation and decolonisation of the Prambanan temple site. We do this in order to illustrate how research, collecting, conservation, and reconstruction activities were intimately connected to the development of social hierarchies and processes of (racial) marginalisation. During excavations undertaken at the Prambanan site, the Archaeological Service found many potsherds relating to Chinese inter-Asian trade and migration and, from 1934, started to officially collect these under the telling denomination 'Foreign Ceramics'.[7] In addition we focus on the travels and social history of a Chinese object: a porcelain vase that was produced in the fifteenth century in the Jingdezhen region. Probably soon thereafter it travelled to the North Moluccan island of Halmahera, in the context of Chinese Moluccan trade (Figure 6.5). There, in 1934, a Dutch colonial official spotted the vase as part of the interior of a house owned by a village head. After the Batavian Society bought it from the owner, and through war and decolonisation, the object became connected to the forced migration of the Dutch collector and museum official Egbert van Orsoy de Flines (1886–1964) from Indonesia to the Netherlands.[8]

[7] 'De Keramische Verzameling', *Jaarboek I 1933 Koninklijk Bataviaasch Genootschap van Kunsten en Wetenschappen* (Bandoeng: A. C. Nix & Co., 1933), 227–230.

[8] P. Lunsingh Scheurleer (ed.), *Asiatic art in the Rijksmuseum Amsterdam* (Amsterdam: Meulenhoff; Landshoff, 1985), 33. See also www.rijksmuseum.nl/nl/collectie/AK-RBK-1965–87 (accessed 3 November 2016).

We begin – and end – this chapter, however, at the Siva temple, to explore its resurrection from late colonial times, and across war and decolonisation.

Siva in Colonial Java

Of all Hindu–Buddhist temple sites in the Netherlands Indies, why the Archaeological Service decided to take up the gigantic task of reconstructing the Siva temple is not obvious – not, at least, when we take it from the state of the temple at the turn of the twentieth century. The interest may have been caused by the mere size of the site as a whole, its fame, and the connected stories about Lara Jonggran, and by paths of trial and error taken by archaeologists. While it was only at the beginning of the twentieth century that methods for archaeological research and restoration became topics of discussion and standardisation, the practice of reconstruction was nothing new in the Netherlands Indies, neither in general nor for the Siva temple in particular. As we have seen, during the nineteenth century, the larger ruined temple complex at Prambanan was the scene of several intrusive archaeological interventions. These led not only to destruction, but also to reconstruction – on paper or in paintings – and to drawings of ground plans, ruins, and statues on and near the site, contributing to the development of a 'reconstructive gaze'. In these efforts to reconstruct, European concepts of 'monumentality' mingled with local attitudes regarding the site as ancient, sacred, and connected to mythical histories. Except for the exploratory missions under the British regime, most of the nineteenth-century interventions were of local, private, and not necessarily 'professional' character. More generally, before the Archaeological Service's efforts to centralise and standardise, archaeological research, conservation, restoration, and reconstruction – whether on paper or in reality – were, in nineteenth-century Java (as elsewhere in Asia), a matter of trial and error.

In the context of an ethical-cum-expansionist colonial state seeking legitimation, the Hindu–Buddhist temple art of Java became a showcase of Dutch benign and ethical colonial policies at the World Exhibition in Paris in 1900. The awareness of decay and destruction, whether caused by natural or human factors, and raised among private and government circles, became the motor of the more systematic thinking on how to conserve and even reconstruct ruins of precolonial pasts. Dramatic episodes for the Siva temple, at least according to some contemporaries and the historiography of archaeology in the Netherlands Indies,[9] were two destructive interventions that we have discussed in Chapter 2:

[9] J. L. A. Brandes, 'De waarde van Tjandi Prambanan tegenover de andere oudheden van Java en een hartig woord over de deblayeering', *Tijdschrift voor Indische Taal-, Land- en Volkenkunde (TBG)* 47 (1904), 427–432; Bernet Kempers, *Herstel in eigen waarde*; Miksic, *Borobudur*, 30.

the cleaning and restoration works initiated and directed by Isaac Groneman (1892–1893) in the framework of the young Archaeological Society, and taking place with the support of Sultan Hamengkubuwono VII; and the visit by King Chulalongkorn to Borobudur, Prambanan, and other temples in Java (in 1896), from where Chulalongkorn took away samples of various temple sculptures, including four reliefs from the Siva temple, depicting scenes of the Ramayana epic – all with the consent of Groneman and the Archaeological Society, who believed they had colonial government support. Soon thereafter Van Erp denounced this as 'deportation'.[10] Using the metaphor of repressive politics common in the Netherlands Indies in the 1920s and 1930s, Van Erp spoke of sending into 'exile' artefacts from Hindu–Buddhist temple sites and four Ramayana reliefs from Prambanan, among other relics. With regard to Groneman's 'cleaning' of the Prambanan site, the historiography follows the ordeal of Brandes who, in 1904, as chair of the Archaeological Commission, denounced the works by Groneman and his team at Prambanan as 'archaeological murder'.[11] In Brandes' eyes, Groneman's work had forever destroyed the chance to restore the temples at Prambanan. Against the rules and practices of conservation developing at the time, which Groneman believed Brandes should have known and respected, the latter had ordered the removal of all stones that lay scattered and loose on the site – including those with ornaments – and to heap them up at the west side of the central square of the temple complex. Brandes thereby disconnected the stones, and the logics of the architecture, from the site. He did not register to which of the six temples on the site the removed stones belonged. It was particularly this 'cleaning' practice that caused the later scandal.[12]

In 1918, the architect Perquin gained modest fame as the man who had 'the courage' to bring order to the mess Groneman had left.[13] In that year, the Archaeological Service initiated cleaning works around Candi Sewu (located on the site) and excavations. Findings were put on display at the house of the administrator in charge of the survey of Prambanan. Meanwhile, Perquin enthusiastically tried to get the scattered pieces of the Siva temple together, directly on the site, without a 'proefopstelling' (test installation). The apparently disorganised reconstruction work done by Perquin and the somewhat awkward results soon evoked heated criticism within the circles of the Archaeological Service. The concerned parties then got involved in a more general and principled discussion on the issue of reconstruction. Since

[10] Van Erp, 'Nog eens de Hindoe-Javaansche beelden', 33.

[11] Brandes, 'De waarde van Tjandi Prambanan', 430. For this quote, see Bernet Kempers, *Herstel in eigen waarde,* 101. Compare with Bosch, 'Het restaureren van Hindoe-Javaansche bouwwerken'.

[12] Bernet Kempers, *Herstel in eigen waarde*, 101–106.

[13] Ibid.; Bosch, 'Het restaureren van Hindoe-Javaansche bouwwerken', 12.

elsewhere in Europe and in Asia, 'keep as found' restoration ethics dominated, the reconstruction works at Prambanan were interrupted for an official exploration of the advantages and disadvantages of reconstructing the Siva temple. Following a comparable international debate,[14] the points raised were: should the task of the service be restricted to the Dutch principle of 'keep as found' (which the first director of the Archaeological Service N. J. Krom (1913–1916) advocated) or could it also embark on reconstruction (put into practice by people such as Perquin and Brandes (at Mendut) before him, and supported by Krom's successor as head of the service, Bosch)?[15] And if the service allowed reconstruction, where should it draw the line? What if the material remains to undertake the reconstruction were not sufficient? Were deduction and fantasy allowed and, if so, to what extent?[16]

These questions were fundamental, since the answers could have immense consequences. One of the main arguments *for* reconstruction was that by this the actual form and beauty of the original monument, and its shadow, could become visible, whereas the 'authentic' ruin, with all its often negative connotations like neglect, decay, or even decadence and despotism, disappeared. Another argument – used in the Netherlands – was the utility of the 'monument' in the present. For both arguments, the questions mattered: visible for whom and useful for whom? Prominent Dutch colonial archaeologists at the time, such as Krom, Bosch, Stutterheim, and later August Bernet Kempers, were well aware that their work, resulting in the material revisualisation of the Buddhist and Hindu Indonesian past, did not fit in with the 'keep as found' restoration ethics in the Netherlands. They also knew, on the other hand, that their restoration work had inspired an Indonesian nationalist elite who identified for various reasons with these sites. The inter-Asian and international academic queries and debates concerning these material remains of Java's Hindu and Buddhist pasts – in short whether and how they originated from India, and if and how active local appropriations played a role as well – likewise dwelt on issues that touched upon (Javanese) nationalist interests. And

[14] For the debate on restoration in Dutch context, see J. A. C. Tillema, *Schetsen uit de geschiedenis van de monumentenzorg in Nederland* ('s-Gravenhage: Staatsuitgeverij, 1975); Roel Pots, *Cultuur, koningen en democraten: overheid en cultuur in Nederland* (Nijmegen: Sun, 2000). For various debates on restoration in Asian contexts, see Indra Sengupta, 'Code for the colony: John Marshall's *Conservation Manual* and monument preservation between India and Europe', in Michael Falser and Monica Juneja (eds.), *'Archaeolizing' heritage?: Transcultural entanglements between local practices and global virtual realities* (Berlin and Heidelberg: Springer Verlag, 2013), 21–37; Crispin Branfoot, 'Remaking the past: Tamil sacred landscape and temple renovations', *Bulletin of SOAS* 76:1 (2013), 21–47; Clémentin-Ojha and Manguin, *A century in Asia*, 97–98.

[15] N. J. Krom, 'Het restaureren van oude bouwwerken', *Tijdschrift voor Indische Taal-, Land- en Volkenkunde* (*TBG)*, 53 (1911), 1–15; Bosch, 'Het restaureren van Hindoe-Javaansche bouwwerken'.

[16] For a short summary of this discussion, see Bernet Kempers, *Herstel in eigen waarde*, 107–112.

it was precisely the awareness of the nationalist interest in this past which made the most influential of the colonial archaeologists active in the Indies, Bosch, clash with restoration experts from the Netherlands in the discussion that became known as the 'Restauratiekwestie' or Restoration problem (1923–1926).

The Dutch architect H. P. Berlage, world-renowned for his modern rationalist architecture, expressed the Dutch viewpoint on the colonial restoration problem most clearly. In 1923, on a journey to study architecture in the Netherlands Indies, Berlage received, via committed and influential architects and archaeologists in the Netherlands, a semi-formal commission to advise on restoration politics in the Indies. In his report, Berlage argued that the Hindu and Buddhist temples in Java 'should be approached as historical monuments'. In his view, the temple ruins had, in the present, no utility that related to their original function. During his explorations of the temples he had noticed that local inhabitants brought offerings to Hindu and Buddhist statues, but he considered these offerings expressions of an animistic belief that still existed and that had nothing to do with the old Hindu civilisation. Thus, in the present these buildings 'had no meaning any more for the spiritual life [geestesleven] of the Javanese people'. His conclusion was that these monuments were therefore not applicable for reconstruction aims, and needed only 'sympathetic conservation, a task to be fulfilled by both Europeans and Javanese'.[17]

On the other hand, as head of the colonial Archaeological Service, Bosch disputed Berlage's idea that the Hindu and Buddhist temples on Java lacked meaning for the spiritual lives of present-day Javanese. Berlage's report was for Bosch a reason to stimulate the government to form a special committee to formulate a clear policy with regard to restoration or reconstruction projects for the future. The committee was formed in negotiation with several cultural organisations, and included a minority of highly educated Javanese elites who were also involved in colonial cultural institutions such as the Royal Batavian Society and the Java Institute.[18]

The discussion of restoration politics and the arrival of Berlage in the Indies had also inspired the theme of the second conference of the Java Institute, which took place in Yogyakarta in 1924 and was dedicated to 'The value of the old Javanese monuments for Javanese culture now and in the future'. At that conference, most of the Javanese and European speakers, especially Radjiman

[17] Report, H. P. Berlage, undated (before 17 December 1923), ANRI, KBG DIR 1026.

[18] Martha A. Muussens, 'De restauratiekwestie', *Djawa* 4 (1924), 77–98; *Verslag van de commissie van advies inzake de restauratie der Hindoe-Javaansche monumenten, nopens de reconstructie van de Çiwatempel te Prambanan* (Weltevreden: Kolff, 1926), 141. Original correspondence on the restoration issue between the various parties in the Netherlands and the Netherlands Indies can be found in ANRI, KBG DIR 1026 and 1027; and in ANRI, Algemeene Secretarie, Bt 27 March 1924, 1.

Wediodiningrat and Bosch, stressed the spiritual value of these monuments – twenty years before Soekarno would say the same at his Prambanan inauguration speech.[19] In his formal reaction to Berlage, Bosch elaborated this viewpoint on the topical meaning of the Hindu and Buddhist monuments: 'The deeper meaning of [these] buildings ... lies in the awesome, ennobling, inspiring force that comes from them and that has an effect on those Javanese who are susceptible to it, that is for the moment only the most developed [Javanese].' He reproached Berlage for looking at this problem too much from a Dutch-centred perspective. While in Holland complete architectural examples of almost every epoch were available, this was not the case in Java. Therefore, Bosch, writing to the director of the Department of Education and Religion, pleaded for the Javanese cultural elite's interests in restoration politics in the Indies to be taken seriously.[20]

In line with Bosch, in 1926 the 'Restoration Committee' decided, considering 'the Javanese cultural awakening', and out of respect for the cultural and religious-philosophical values of the Hindu and Buddhist monuments on Java, that the Archeological Service should not only preserve but also reconstruct.[21] In the subsequent decade, the Dutch engineer Vincent van Romondt took over from Perquin, and with the help of Indonesian employees, developed reliable techniques of reconstruction. Local inhabitants were recruited for the crucial task of 'stone matching', a concept that became part of the professional vocabulary for anastylosis-style reconstruction within the post-colonial Indonesian Archaeological Service.[22] With this technique, for which the Dutch did not employ the concept 'anastylosis' but that of 'reconstruction', the Netherlands Indies' Archaeological Service set an influential example for the French in Indochina, particularly in Angkor.[23] Significantly, the Archaeological Service of the Netherlands Indies institutionalised specific colonial restoration ethics that differed from those followed in the Netherlands. The 'restoration problem' and its effects therefore serve as

[19] The so-called *prae-adviezen* (propositions) presented at that conference, by Bosch, Radjiman, and the architect and Majapahit expert Maclaine Pont, were published in *Djawa* 4 (1924), 121 and 167–269. The architect C. P. Wolff Schoemaker went against the consensus; claiming the Javanese were not capable of such constructions, he emphasised Indian authorship of the Hindu monuments in Java and withdrew from participation in the conference. See C. P. Wolff Schoemaker, *Aesthetiek en oorsprong der Hindoe-kunst op Java* (Semarang: Van Dorp, 1925).

[20] Ibid.

[21] 'De Hindoe-Javaansche monumenten: de arbeid der Restauraticcommissie', *Djawa* 6 (1926), 51–52; *Verslag van de commissie van advies inzake de restauratie der Hindoe-Javaansche monumenten*, 11–12. For the final report, see 'Vertrouwelijk verslag van de commissie van advies inzake de restauratie der Hindoe-Javaansche Monumenten, nopens reconstructie van de Çiwa-tempel te Prambanan', 11 December 1926, ANRI, KBG, Varia 0043.

[22] Interview, Marieke Bloembergen with I Gusti Nura Anom, Saba, 8 June 2012.

[23] Clémentin-Ojha and Manguin, *A century in Asia,* 96–97; Penny Edwards, *Cambodge: the cultivation of a nation* (Honolulu: University of Hawai'i Press, 2007), 160.

a strong argument against the statement, often brought up in the context of the critical heritage studies movement, that concepts of conservation simply travelled from Europe in a one-way direction to the rest of the world.[24]

Siva across the Japanese Occupation and Decolonisation

In the final years of Dutch colonial governance in the Indies, among the many preparatory measures to save 'heritage' in anticipation of war in the Pacific, the colonial Archaeological Service ensured that the techniques of anastylosis would be remembered, and made a film of the work at the Siva temple[25], though it turned out to be unnecessary because the Japanese regime did not radically change the Archaeological Service's aims, research focus, and activities, and the works at the Siva temple continued.[26]

Under a slightly different institutional structure and – after the internment of all Dutch civil servants in April 1942 – a new Japanese director, the Archaeological Service continued the kind of site-related conservation and construction work begun in the 1930s.[27] The Javanese engineer Soehamir, who had worked at the Archaeological Service just before the Japanese occupation, became the new executive director. In need of further archaeological and technical expertise in relation to Java's Hindu and Buddhist monuments, the Japanese authorities released a few detained Dutch archaeologists and commissioned them to continue their (now more narrowly defined) job.[28] Among them was Stutterheim, who died in September 1942 of a brain tumour, but left a 'Report on the upkeep and repairs (restoration) of Old Javanese monuments' that dealt with the problem of wartime restoration, advising the

[24] Smith, *Uses of heritage*, 19–21.

[25] This film, focusing on the restoration activities of the Archaeological Service at Borobudur and Prambanan, made in 1940 by J. H. Zindler, is kept at Beeld en Geluid Institute, Hilversum, the Netherlands (hereafter BG), Collection Rijksvoorlichtingsdienst, nr 119674.

[26] This confirms the findings of recent research on archaeology under authoritarian regimes, which indicate that regime change does not immediately lead to new forms and practices of archaeology. For a collection of relevant and comparable case studies, see Michael L. Galaty and Charles Watkinson, *Archaeology under dictatorship* (New York: Springer, 2006).

[27] This paragraph, slightly revised, is based on Bloembergen and Eickhoff, 'Conserving the past, mobilizing the Indonesian future'.

[28] Iguchi and Tokugawa argue that this initiative was spurred by the worries of Marquis Tokugawa. Tokugawa, director of the Raffles Museum in occupied Singapore after September 1942, accordingly sent to Java his predecessor at that post, the vulcanologist and geologist Prof. Tanakadate Hidezo, whom he knew from 1929 when they joined the Fourth Pacific Science Congress in Java. Tanakadate, visiting Java in 1942, then became responsible for the decision to protect all research institutions in Java and Sumatra, and for the order to return imprisoned Dutch staff to their positions. See Masatoshi Iguchi, 'Introduction about the author, the book, and the historical background', in Marquis Tokugawa, *Journeys to Java* (Bandung: ITB Press, 2004), xxxi–xxxii and 195. Compare E. J. H. Corner, 'Obituary of Prof. H. Tanakadate', *Nature* 167 (14 April 1951), 586–587; E. J. H. Corner, *The marquis: a tale of Syonan-to* (Kuala Lumpur and Hong Kong: Heinemann Asia, 1981).

continuation of works at the Siva temple alone because (among other reasons) the expertise was still there.[29]

In the first ten months after the occupation, under the military regime, the service's two offices (the main office in Batavia and the technical office at Prambanan) were cut off from each other. At the end of 1942, the Japanese regime arranged for both offices, as separate institutions, to fall under Bunkyo Kyoku (the central Department of Education) in (what was now designated) Djakarta: Kobijitu Kenkyu Sho (Djakarta's) and Buseki Fukkya Koji Jimmu Sho (Prambanan's). The first Japanese Department of Education chief was a linguist, Kayashima, and later Isyima took over. The office at Prambanan also fell under the responsibility of the sultanate in Yogyakarta. A third institution that came under the Bunkyo Kyoku and that had an interest in archaeological findings was the museum of the Royal Batavian Society, under the new name Hakubutukan, and directed by R. Kinosita.[30]

After a hiatus of almost all site-related activities shortly after the Dutch capitulation, the service resumed conservation work in Java at a *kraton* (Ratu Boko), two temples (Candi Plaosan and Banyunibo), and the grave of one of the legendary nine founders of Islam (*wali sanga*) in Java, Sunan Drajat. During this period, the reconstruction of the Siva temple remained a top priority. Reports on archaeological findings written by the Kobijitu Kenkyu Sho and sent to the Hakubutukan indicate that outside Java only privately initiated research or excavations took place. These were, however, also officially reported.[31]

Clearly, the new regime, as well as Japanese officials with a great interest in historical/archaeological matters, paid special attention to the work of the Archaeological Service and at Indonesian archaeological sites. The Japanese head of the office in Prambanan, accompanied by Soehamir, often went to check on progress at the Siva temple; he also undertook the translation into Japanese of Krom's *Inleiding tot de Hindoe-Javaansche geschiedenis* ('Introduction to Hindu-Javanese history', 1926) which was then (and now) recognised as an essential introduction to the Hindu and Buddhist past of the archipelago.[32] It is likely that this work remained an unfinished ideal.[33] These

[29] *OV 1941–1947* (1949), 49–50. [30] *OV 1948* (1950), 20–21.

[31] As far as we have collected material on this, there are several reports of found objects, offered to the museum in 1943 in ANRI, KBG DIR 1109. For the discovery of golden Buddha statues in Palembang, see Mangkunegara VII to Mrs Moens, 26 September 2602 [1942], Arsip Mangkunegaran, Solo, Correspondence Mangkunegara VII, nr M 52–5.

[32] Report by Van Romondt on the activities of the Archaeological Service during the period 1942–1945, in *OV 1941–1947* (1949), 49–50. Van Romondt had not seen the translation.

[33] Soehamir, in his report on the Archaeological Service during the Japanese occupation, mentioned that there were no publications during that period; see *OV 1948* (1950), 22 and 40. In 1984, however, a Japanese translation of Krom's chapter 'Hindoe-Javaansche tijd' was published in Stapel's standard work *Geschiedenis van Nederlandsch-Indië*, vol I. See Iwao Aryoshi, *Indonesia Kodaishi* (Nara: Tenrikyo-Doyu-Sya, 1985). This work, by Iwao Aryoshi

endeavours can partly be understood within the context of Japan's plans for the Greater East Asia Co-Prosperity Sphere as well as the propaganda about and search for a larger Asian cultural identity.[34] Personal religious interests played a role as well.

The reconstruction of the Siva temple was the only project that continued even in the chaotic period of March 1942 after the brief military struggle when the Japanese took over (Figure 6.2).[35] According to archaeologist Hideichi, the first Japanese scholar who has studied the practices and policies of Japanese archaeology in Asia during the Pacific War, the Japanese set about this reconstruction in order to gain support among the people of Indonesia; but they also intended the temple to function as a place of comfort to the souls of soldiers who had died during the war.[36] In this way, they 'converted' the temple site into both a place of Asian unity and a war monument.

Japanese interference in archaeological sites in Indonesia was reinforced by propaganda (including movies) and organised school visits to sites, especially Trowulan (for Majapahit), Borobudur, and Prambanan.[37] As part of a general Japanese policy for the training of school children *at* historical sites (a practice taken over by the Indonesian Republic during the revolution)[38], such trips brought children and their teachers from Surabaya (the SMT Surabaya), Gentengkali (the Sekolah Keradjinan dan Dagang (SKD), school of crafts and trade), and from the school for rail workers in East Java to visit the museum and the ruins at the site of Majapahit in Trowulan, 'So that they will understand how high the culture has been from our ancestors'.[39] Likewise for propaganda

(1914–1984), related to an earlier, private interest developed in wartime Java. Aryoshi studied Dutch in Leiden in 1936–1939, on behalf of the Japanese Ministry of Foreign Affairs, worked in Surabaya at the Japanese consulate in 1940, and during the Japanese occupation. After the Second World War, he retained his function as a diplomat in Asian affairs and returned to Indonesia to work, again, at the consulate general of Japan in Surabaya in 1969–1975. We thank Hoko Horii for translating for us the introduction and biography on the author of this book.

34 Mark, '"Asia's" transwar lineage'; J. Victor Koschmann, 'Asianism's ambivalent legacy', in Peter J. Katzenstein and Takashi Shiraishi (eds.), *Network power: Japan and Asia* (Ithaca and London: Cornell University Press, 1997), 83–103.

35 For Soehamir's report, see *OV 1948* (1950), 20–41.

36 Sakazume Hideichi, *Taiheiyou sensou to koukogaku* (Tokyo: Yoshikawa Kobundo, 1997). We thank Kuniko Forrer for translating the relevant paragraphs.

37 *OV 1948* (1950), 23 and 40. The Japanese Propaganda Service (Senden Bu) made a documentary on the reconstruction of the Siva temple. We have not located this film. It is not in the collection of Japanese propaganda films of the NIOD. Another film, on Field Marshal Hisaichi Terauchi's visit to Borobudur is in BG, Collection Rijksvoorlichtingsdienst, nr 2731, 'Japans Journaal' (1943).

38 Soehamir, 'Verslag van de werkzaamheden van de voormalige bouwkundige afdeling van de Oudheidkundige Dienst van 8 maart 1942 tot 19 december 1948', *OV 1948* (1950), 23.

39 NIOD site, *Soeara Asia*, 21 December 1943; *Soeara Asia*, 8 January 1944; *Soeara Asia*, 21 December 1943; *Soeara Asia*, 8 January 1944; *Pewarta Perniagaan*, 2 July 1943 (due to copyright issues the Indonesian newspapers are no longer online available on the NIOD website). On a visit to Trowulan and Mojokerto by the school for railway workers of East

Figure 6.2 The Siva temple in Prambanan with Japanese flag, 1942–1944.

purposes, at the end of 1944 and in 1945, the site of Majapahit provided the historical setting and legitimation for the public military training of the Surabaya division of the *seinendan*, the youth corps (boys from the ages of 14 to 22, set up in April 1943), of the Barisan Pelopor Soerabaia (Surabayan commando), and of the *angkatan moeda* (youth troops) – all framed by speeches of officials on the site's historical importance.[40] Intriguingly, to Soehamir's dismay, school visits in Central Java initially led to the practice of graffiti and subsequent signs prohibiting graffiti near the temple sites,[41] but in Bali school visits may have had an interesting side effect: a wider Indonesian engagement with these sites as Indonesian or as local heritage. A reorganisation of the system of guarding and surveilling archaeological sites may have had the same effect. During this period, the Japanese director made the indigenous administration responsible for reporting (twice a year) on the situation at these sites, and for cleaning and guarding them, unlike previously, when the

Java, see *Pewarta Perniagaan*, 2 July 1943. On legacies, see the guide to the Majapahit site in Trowulan: Djoko, *Trowulan: Bekas ibukota Majapahit* (Jakarta: Balai Poestaka, 1983). Djoko (1921–?), born in the area, and who would become head of the Department of Education and Culture in Jakarta in 1961–1966, started his career as a school teacher in 1942, during the Japanese period.

40 NIOD site, *Soeara Asia*, 13 and 25 November 1944.

41 *OV 1948* (1950), 23.

Archaeological Service paid guards to do so.[42] This seems an efficient way to involve people outside the official and professional sphere of heritage politics, and to familiarise them with the notion of heritage within 'Asian', 'national', or 'regional' borders.

The period of war and revolution, which followed the Indonesian declaration of independence and the capitulation of Japan, exerted a great impact on the structure, research subjects, and site-related activities of the Archaeological Service. But even with this upheaval, archaeological research, conservation, and reconstruction work continued. This indicates the legitimising power of the 'caretaking' of archaeological monuments, not only by the colonial state but also by the republic. During this period, there were in fact two Archaeological Services. One was the Djawatan Purbakala (later Dinas Purbakala), owned by the republic, and set up in Yogyakarta by the Ministry of Education and Culture in February 1946. Soehamir became the executive director, assisted by the philologist Poerbatjaraka. The other was the 'Dutch colonial' service, which after a brief period when Republican parties occupied the Museum of the Batavian Society, moved its office to Batavia, with Van Romondt as executive director until Bernet Kempers took over in 1947.

Both services tried to continue their work as far as war and civil war permitted. For the Dutch Service, formally denied access to the *candi*-rich domain of the Republic's service, this more or less meant that excavation and conservation activities moved eastwards, to a new office in Makassar (later under the charge of C. Krijgsman), and worked mainly in Celebes. They also sent investigative expeditions to Bali. The Republican service, further interested in 'Indonesian origins', extended paleontological research activities in the Sangiran river; and it continued work at Ratu Boko, among other projects. During Soehamir's tenure, it continued the reconstruction of the Siva temple – the summit of archaeological conservation skills.[43]

Of course, military clashes and the civil war took their toll on the service's prized objects around Yogyakarta: the office at Prambanan was looted after the second 'clash' between Dutch and Indonesian Republican troops, and many unpublished reports and drawings were lost – years of work. Snipers had used the scaffolding around the Siva temple as their operation base; bullets had damaged the temple; the statues of Bogem were blown up. The damage at Borobudur was limited. The nearby *pasanggrahan* was completely ruined, but this sparked site-related excavations in an area that the service had not yet touched. Looking back in 1954, Bernet Kempers lamented the losses, but the extent of the harm is unclear. The ensuing damage and destruction delayed the

[42] Ibid., 22–23. [43] *OV 1948* (1950), 24–27 and 36–37.

reconstruction of the Siva temple, but it also gave rise to new heritage concerns.[44]

Professional relationships between the two offices in 'Yogyakarta' and 'Batavia' in this period of revolution and military clashes became sensitive, and sharpened in the process of separation/detachment. For example, the Dutch Service in Batavia saw proof of the Siva's temple's growth shortly after the first military clash from a photograph sent by the Republican Service.[45] Against such strained professional communication, Republican leaders and newspapers used archaeological sites for propaganda purposes (Figure 6.3), not only for the local public but also for foreign journalists and an international (American) public.[46] One film about Borobudur and Prambanan, ironically, showed footage of the monuments accompanied by Beethoven's Fifth Symphony and a minuet by Mozart, apparently appealing to the general idea of a universal civilisation.[47]

In terms of political choices there were some personal twists. The Dutch epigrapher Johannes G. de Casparis, who had begun working for the Colonial Archaeological Service shortly before the war, exchanged archaeological information with a highly interested Soekarno during the tumultuous year of 1948, and sided with Indonesian nationalists in 1949.[48] Even when the tide turned definitely in favour of the Republic in 1949, political sensitivity remained high; looking back, Bernet Kempers realised that the way to forge collaboration with the Indonesian Archaeological Service in Yogyakarta was not (as he had done in 1949) to 'inspect', which gave the impression of paternalistic intervening/meddling in Republican affairs. Better to wait for an invitation – which happened when Republican authorities asked him to teach at UGM in 1950, a few months after the transfer of sovereignty.[49]

At the level of knowledge exchange and learning, intellectual relations improved after 1950, perhaps also because there was so much at stake. Future

[44] A. J. Bernet Kempers, 'Oudheidkundig werk in Indonesië na de oorlog', *Indonesië. Tijdschrift gewijd aan het indonesisch Cultuurgebied* 7 (1954), 491.

[45] Ibid., 487.

[46] 'Para wartawan loear negri melihat pemoeda', *Soeara Merdeka*, 9 February 1946; 'Di kaki Boroboedoer', *Kedaulatan Rakyat*, 12 March 1947; 'Borobodoer', *Pandji Ra'jat*, 1 August 1947. All three articles refer explicitly to the use of Borobudur as a special training area for the Indonesian *pemuda* fighting for the Free Indonesian Republic.

[47] Diary of F. M. van Asbeck, 4 May 1946, private archive of Elsbeth Locher-Scholten (translation, M. Bloembergen); for this movie, see BG, Collection Rijksvoorlichtingsdienst, nr 2960, camera, C. H. Breyer.

[48] Gomperts and Klokke, 'In memoriam J. G. de Casparis', 474–475.

[49] Bernet Kempers, 'Oudheidkundig werk in Indonesië na de oorlog', 492. Compare the report, 'Het oudheidkundig instituut en de verschillende deelstaten en autonome gebieden. Strikt vertrouwelijk, 16-X-'47', in which Van Romondt follows more or less the same line of argument: as long as the Republican Service remained convinced that the Dutch Service wanted to play the leading role, co-operation would never work, he argued (Leiden University Library, Special Collections, KITLV Collections, Archive Van Romondt, KITLV H 1139, 10).

Figure 6.3 General Soedirman with Indonesian Republican army parading in front of Borobudur, circa 1948.

heads of the Indonesian Archaeological Service, Soekmono and Satyawati Soeryono Soeryo (later Soeleiman), joined the staff at the office in Jakarta, and continued the studies they had begun before the war. Both finished under Bernet Kempers. With the inauguration of the Siva temple in 1953, Soekmono became the Indonesian Archaeological Service's first Indonesian director; he later became inextricably associated with the restoration of Borobudur under the auspices of UNESCO (discussed in Chapter 7).

Disaster and Restoration in Bali

Over the past four decades, scholars of Bali have sharpened our insight into the impact of the study and collection of texts and oral traditions on the makings and self-identification of Bali in colonial and post-colonial times. They have illuminated the role that administrator-orientalists, self-taught culture experts, tourists, and the Balinese themselves have played in these cultural knowledge dynamics.[50] Curiously, however, this critical tradition has left aside the role and

[50] See in particular Adrian Vickers, *Bali: a Paradise created* (Ringwood, Victoria: Penguin, 1989; 2nd edn, Tokyo: Tuttle Publishing, 2012); Henk Schulte Nordholt, 'The making of traditional Bali', *History and Anthropology* 8 (1994), 89–127; Helen Creese, 'In search of Majapahit: the transformation of Balinese identities', Centre of Southeast Asian Studies Working Paper 101 (Clayton, Victoria: Monash University, 1997); Wiener, *Visible and invisible realms*, 14–21;

impact of archaeological research and of the exchange between archaeologists and their informants. One explanation may be a predominant interest in the history of the study and use of texts and rituals to understand Balinese culture; another reason may be a lack of historical self-reflection by archaeology in and on Indonesia. In any case, it is tempting to state that Willem Stutterheim's research on Bali – and the historical interpretations he developed – within and beyond his Balinese network, had a deep impact on how in contemporary Indonesia this area and some of its sacred sites are valued and situated in the Balinese past.

However, the first official state-supported heritage interventions in Bali began earlier – in the context of disaster, violence, and destruction. The brutal incorporation of South Bali in the colonial state paved the way. This was after the invasion of the colonial army in 1904, and the *puputan* of the South Balinese nobles of the princely states of Badung (1906) and Klungkung (1908). In the course of these events Dutch military troops caused further casualties, completely destroyed the old palaces of Klungkung and Badung, and facilitated the official looting of palace antiquities – which became reserved for the museum in Batavia, and the ethnographical museum in Leiden.[51] Plans were developed to start a museum in Denpasar (Badung) for cultural preservation with a focus on archaeology and arts at the site where the *puputan* of 1906 had taken place. When the museum eventually opened in 1932, the architecture served as unifying symbol, its main buildings and walls inspired by palaces and temples typifying Bali's provinces.[52]

Next, the gigantic earthquake that hit Bali on the morning of 21 January 1917 was the immediate occasion for the colonial state to intervene in Bali, partly to restore destroyed buildings, houses, and temples. This earthquake, which was felt as far away as Surabaya in East Java, was devastating, hitting hardest in South Bali. At least 1,358 people died, 1,060 were injured, 64,000 dwellings (including a number of old palaces and 10.000 rice barns) were ruined, roads

Michel Picard, *Bali: cultural tourism and touristic culture* (Singapore: Archipelago Press, 1998).

51 Francine Brinkgreve, 'Balinese chiefs and Dutch dominion', in Hardiati and Ter Keurs (eds.), *Indonesia: the discovery of the past*, 122–145.

52 The history of the making and socio-political meanings of this archaeological *and* art museum in itself, is still in need of serious scrutiny, but falls beyond the scope of this book. For a brief official history, see *Mengenal beberapa museum di Bali* (Denpasar: Proyek Penegmbengan Permuseuman Bali, Direktorat Jenderal Kebudayaan, Departemen Pendidikan dan Kebudayaan, 1981/1982), 18–44. For brief references to this museum as a site of curatorship, collecting, and re-evaluating Balinese art in the 1930s and early 1940s, see among others, Spanjaard, 'Het ideaal van een moderne Indonesische schilderkunst', 87–88; Picard, *Bali: cultural tourism and touristic culture,* 85; Siobhan Campbell, 'Early Kamasan art in museum collections', *BKI* 170 (2014), 267, 270, and 272. On the museum's impact on the art industry in Bali, also in passing, see Adrian Vickers, *Balinese art: paintings and drawings of Bali, 1800–2010* (Tokyo: Tuttle, 2012), 172 and 213.

and bridges were damaged, and in what was immediately understood to be calamitous, 2,431 temples (*pura*) were destroyed, including what was considered to be Bali's mother-temple, Pura Besakih, on the slopes of Gunung Agung.[53] Against the background of violent conquest-cum-heritage formation, this earthquake offered the colonial government an opportunity to ground itself more firmly in South Bali, through aid. But the earthquake also offered comparable opportunities to the Balinese local rulers, who had suffered damage to their authority.

As David Stuart Fox discussed in his study of Pura Besakih, Balinese religious practices helped spur widespread restoration.[54] One early local reaction to the disaster was that it was a punishment by the gods because of people's neglect of Pura Besakih, and according to 'tradition' all Balinese – kings, priests, and ordinary people alike – shared responsibility. In the multiple systems of value emerging in the early inventory of damages, Pura Besakih's restoration therefore took priority. Various parties in Bali and Batavia negotiated multiple and ambiguous moral political concerns to establish delicate new power relations after the war. Both among Balinese rajas and their (forced) local workforce, and among the colonial parties that meddled in local restoration activities, opinions differed on how to influence the slippery and ambiguous power relations on location. And colonial restoration interests in Bali were hampered by a Java-centred or even India-centred framework of understanding Balinese culture.

Bali, as the site of a predominantly Hindu population, had fascinated foreign visitors and colonial officials-cum-scholars since at least the early nineteenth century. They believed that the Hindu culture of Bali was a continuation of old Hindu–Buddhist Java, where Islam had taken over and the royal exodus from the collapsing Majapahit empire had established this civilisation on Bali in the fourteenth century. Notably, this idea also prevailed in Bali, where Balinese sources also refer to Javanese links, and to the Balinese courts' Javanese origins.[55] Ethnographers also came to use information about old Java and old India to understand Bali's caste system, temple rituals, and cremation

[53] Stuart Fox extensively discusses the background and procedures around the restoration of Pura Besakih; see David Stuart Fox, *Pura Besakih: temple, religion and society in Bali* (Leiden: KITLV, 2002), 297–305. See also Schulte Nordholt, 'The making of traditional Bali'; G. Kemmerling, 'De aardbeving van Bali op 21 Jan. 1917', *Jaarboek van het Mijnwezen in Nederlandsch-Indië* 46 (1917), 1–49; C. Lekkerkerker, *Bali en Lombok: overzicht der litteratuur omtrent deze eilanden rond 1919* (Rijswijk: Blankwaardt en Schoonhoven, 1920), 204–205, 207.

[54] Stuart Fox, *Pura Besakih*, 297–305.

[55] For a recent, thorough historical analysis of early nineteenth-century knowledge production on Bali, which also looks at knowledge exchange on location, see Helen Creese, *Bali in the early nineteenth century: the ethnographic accounts of Pierre Dubois*, Verhandelingen van het Koninklijk Instituut voor Taal-, Land- en Volkenkunde 305 (Leiden: Brill/KITLV, 2016). See also Vickers, *Bali: a Paradise created*; Schulte Nordholt, 'The making of traditional Bali'.

practices.[56] Along with this historical and anthropological curiosity, an appreciation for Balinese arts, architecture, and stone- and woodcarving began to emerge after 1900 with the arts and crafts movements in Europe. This interest suited Western modern art tastes, and placed Balinese objects in the Dutch colonial pavilions at the World Exhibitions of 1900 (in Paris) and 1910 (in Brussels).[57] These multiple factors shaped the interventions in restoration activities of 'old' buildings as the colonial state desperately sought local legitimacy.

One might expect that the Java-centred colonial archaeological restoration ideals – which, as we have seen, were in a state of full experimentation – would not necessarily overlap with the religious needs and artistic tastes of the Balinese. However, at that time, the Archaeological Service approached antiquities that were still in use, such as mosques, Chinese *klenteng*, and Balinese temples, in a way that can be described as colonial pragmatism/paternalism: the service left the maintenance of these buildings to local religious communities, but felt free to intervene in conservation projects on technical grounds. But these quasi-lenient pragmatic principles would clash with the more principled modern architectural standards of conservation and beauty of P. A. J. Moojen when he took charge of the post-disaster restoration activities in Bali. Significantly, he was assisted by the Javanese engineer and intellectual we saw earlier in Chapter 4, Soetatmo Soeriokoesoemo, who worked as surveyor at the department of Burgerlijke Openbare Werken (Public Works, BOW), and whose Javanese-centred outlook further complicated the situation.

A self-acclaimed expert on Balinese architecture since his first visit to Bali in 1914, and by 1917 also head of the Association of Netherlands Indies' Art Circles, Moojen disagreed strongly with Bosch, then head of the Archaeological Service, on the question of whether change and modernisation were part and parcel of architectural development (Bosch), or to be countered, and restored to an imagined original, based on the architectural instructions found in ancient Balinese and Indian texts (Moojen).[58] From 1917 to 1922,

[56] Examples of scholars who used Java and India to understand Bali, or the other way around, include J. C. van Eerde, 'Hindu-Javaansche en Balische eeredienst', *BKI* 65 (1911), 1. See also Perquin, on his first archaeological mission to Bali in 1915 in *OV 1915* (1915), 61–62. He went there to gather comparative information to understand ancient Java, but also concluded that direct relationships between India and Bali had been almost non-existent, but that Bali had received its 'complete Hindu civilization from Java'. Compare A. J. Bernet Kempers, *Monumental Bali: introduction to Balinese archaeology and guide to the monuments* (Singapore: Periplus Editions, 1991), 83–84. One could here also think of the influence of the (later disputed) Indian caste expert Louis Dumont on studies on Bali, albeit in critically adapted, ways. See, for example, D. B. Miller, 'Hinduism in perspective: Bali and India compared', *Review of Indonesian and Malaysian* Affairs 18 (1984), 36–63; Leo Howe, *Hinduism and hierarchy in Bali* (Oxford: Carey, 2001).

[57] Bloembergen, *Colonial spectacles*, 294.

[58] 'Rapport der Commissie benoemd door de Directie van het Bat. Gen. van K. en W., in hare vergadering van den 9e Augustus 1917, met opdracht om een onderzoek op Bali in te stellen ter

despite differences of opinion and thanks to good connections in Batavia (including Governor-General J. P. graaf van Limburg Stirum), the government assigned Moojen to work in Bali on post-disaster restoration projects. Together with the Resident of Bali and Lombok, Moojen's job was to formulate a proposal for the classification of buildings eligible for financial support, and to direct and inform the Balinese during restoration activities for non-classified buildings, which formed the base for his subsequent activities in Bali.

Moojen's technical assistant, Soeriokoesoemo, whom we introduced in Chapter 4, was an active member of Boedi Oetomo, a theosophist, and later a member of the Volksraad (People's Council). His Java-centric views on how Balinese Hindu temples may have looked complicated restoration politics. Concerned about Soeriokoesoemo's political activities in Bali, local authorities, moreover, may have prompted his request to be retransferred to Java. In his report, Moojen did not mention any of Soeriokoesoemo's advisory activities, nor his technical work for the Bali Museum, preferring to emphasise his own role.[59] And Moojen followed what he thought were Balinese interests as he inventoried temples and palaces, and sought local leaders as 'the' representatives of Balinese communities to inform himself of local needs. He became convinced that Balinese (material and 'living') culture deserved treatment distinct from general colonial policies, and in the end even pleaded for the cultural protection of the island of Bali as a whole. Moojen's arrogant attitude began to turn people against him. In 1922 he lost the support of Van Limburg Stirum, and was removed from his position in Bali.[60] In the People's Council, Soeriokoesoemo gave a long speech on his own role contributing to the knowledge he said he had built up through his negotiations with local chiefs, regarding Balinese connections with the Besakih temple and other local traditions. He sided with Moojen's and local elites' views on what Bali, and the building up of Bali, was or should be about.[61]

beantwoording van de vraag of en zoo ja, in welken zin van Gouvernementswege maatregelen waren te treffen om bij het herstel en de wederoprichting door de jongste aardbeving verwoeste tempels, vorstenverblijven enz. de oorspronkelijke Balische kunst tegen neiging tot verbastering in bescherming te nemen', Batavia, 18 September 1917, Leiden University Library, Special Collections, KITLV Collections, Archive P. A. J. Moojen, KITLV H 1169, inv. nr 25.

59 Soeriokoesoemo to Moojen, 22 February 1919, Leiden University Library, Special Collections, KITLV Collections, Archive Moojen, KITLV H 1169, inv. nr 27; P. A. J. Moojen, *Bali: verslag en voorstellen aan de regering van Nederlandsch-Indië* (Batavia: Bond van Nederlandsch-Indische Kunstkringen en Nederlandsch-Indisch Heemschut, 1920).

60 Schulte Nordholt, 'The making of traditional Bali'. See the polemics between Resident of Bali J. T. Damsté and Moojen, fought out in the newspapers, for example: 'De reconstructie van Balische tempels', *Nieuws van den Dag* (21 March 1923) (based on an interview with Damsté, reflecting his opinions); P. A. J. Moojen, 'Tempelbouw op Bali', *Javabode*, April 1923. See also *Javabode* of 21 March 1923.

61 Typescript of question by Soetatmo Soeriokoesoemo, in the meeting of the People's Council of 19 June 1923, Leiden University Library, Special Collections, KITLV Collections, Archive Moojen, KITLV H 1169, inv. nr 26.

State-supported restoration activities after the earthquake reveal one of the two main motives for considering 'antiquities of Bali' that were still used as sacred. The first, 'intervene to prevent further loss', resulted from the idea that there were no real antiquities in Bali, since the Balinese were continuously renovating their temples, preferring the new to the old. The second, 'stay aloof', came from the observation that the Balinese, on the other hand, also deeply honoured many ancient objects as extremely sacred, not to be touched or seen except on special occasions. Both considerations – intervene and stay aloof – were vital in the second episode of state-supported archaeological involvements in Bali.

The Makings of Old Bali

Located in the valley of the Pakerisan and Petanu rivers in Gianyar, South Bali, the neighbouring villages of Pejeng and Bedulu are today known for their many antiquities. The larger area, the Pakerisan valley, which stretches from the holy spring Tirta Empul in Tampak Siring in the north to the so-called Elephant Cave (Goa Gajah) in Bedulu in the south, was recognised by UNESCO in 2012 as part of a multi-sited, Bali-centred World Heritage Site.[62] It was the core of that valley that first attracted the official interest of colonial state archaeology. This centred around Pejeng and Bedulu – the one hosting the palace of a raja with faded power, the other the important temple Samuan Tiga which, in the ancient past, had allegedly united Bali's various kingdoms and beliefs. What had raised the interest were the many old Hindu and Buddhist statues (*arca*) in the area, scattered around village temples, smaller temples in open spaces, house yard temples, and rice fields (Figure 6.4), dating from the eighth to the thirteenth centuries – thus, notably from before the Majapahit exodus. Today, most of these *arca*, as sacred objects, can still be found in the temples and open rice fields, but some of them are – still as sacred objects – in the archaeological museum in Bedulu. It is also there where in 1974 the Indonesian government established, at the official opening of the museum in its new building, the regional conservation department for East Indonesia, the Balai Pelestarian Peninggalan Purbakala (BP3) – thus in a small village, and not in Bali's capital and university city Denpasar.

[62] See: http://whc.unesco.org/en/decisions/4797 (accessed 10 July 2017). UNESCO recognised the site, notably, as a 'cultural landscape' with tangible and intangible characteristics. The Pakerisan valley is recognised as the oldest region where the traditional Balinese water management system for rice cultivation (the *subak* system) functions. This system, moreover, reflects the religious Tri Hita Karana philosophy and is part of temple culture. In all of this, the holiness of the water (of the holy rivers) plays a crucial role, hence the large number of temples and sacred statues and stones in this area.

Figure 6.4 Old stones and statues found in the ricefields, and honoured in the pura Arjuna Metapa, at the border of Bedulu and Pejeng, Bali, 2009.

Emphatically via this area, Bali officially became a field of archaeological research and heritage politics for the Dutch Colonial Archaeological Service, and thus for the colonial state. In the mid 1920s the archaeologist Willem Stutterheim visited Pejeng and Bedulu for a first systematic inventory of and research into ancient stones and statues – at his own initiative and in his free time,[63] but nonetheless officially representing the Archaeological Service as an associated staff member (*adjunct oudheidkundige*). His assignment included exploring whether an inventory of all antiquities in Bali was needed, and possible. Stutterheim's research in the Pakerisan valley took place during three trips between 1925 and 1927, resulting in a two-volume book, *Oudheden van Bali* ('Antiquities of Bali', 1929–1930) published with the Kirtya Liefrinck Society in Singaraja (North Bali).[64] This foundation was set up in 1928 on the initiative of the Resident of Bali and Lombok, L. J. J. Caron. It had its own library and aimed to promote the collection, preservation, and study of Balinese ancient texts (*lontar*), and knowledge dissemination through publications. It involved Dutch colonial scholars and a group of Balinese, mostly Brahman, intellectuals representing the various provinces of Bali. Soon the interest broadened to the study of Balinese culture in general – including inscriptions, antiquities, and religion. In this context, the Kirtya Liefrinck also became a political platform for discussion on the nature, reform, or preservation of Balinese religion.[65]

Notably, Stutterheim was not the first foreigner to come to Pejeng expressing archaeological curiosity about old objects. The oldest and most sacred object in the area, the famous gong or Moon of Pejeng, a huge kettledrum (the largest known) in the *pura* Penataran Sasih in Pejeng, had attracted attention and some intrusive inspections since the early eighteenth century, which the local villagers experienced as sacrilegious acts.[66] But apart from the Moon of Pejeng, the antiquities in the Pakerisan valley, for as far as they were noticed at all by foreigners who visited the area after the 1900s, did not receive any serious scholarly attention before Stutterheim. He was inspired by the transcription of

[63] During the 'groote vakantie' (school holiday), for he was still working as director of the Algemeen Middelbare School (AMS) in Solo. See F. D. K. Bosch, 'Oudheidkundig Verslag over het eerste en tweede kwartaal van 1927', *OV 1927* (1928), 28.

[64] W. F. Stutterheim, *Oudheden van Bali*, vol. I (Singaraja: Kirtya Liefrinck – Van der Tuuk, 1929); W. F. Stutterheim, *Oudheden van Bali*, vol. II, Platen (Singaraja: Kirtya Liefrinck – Van der Tuuk, 1930); W. F. Stutterheim, 'Verslag van den adjunct-oudheidkundige nopens zijn reis naar Bali', *OV 1925* (1926), 90–102; W. F. Stutterheim, 'Rapport van Dr W. F. Stutterheim over een reis naar Bali van 1–10 October 1926', *OV 1926* (1927), 150–155; Bosch, 'Oudheidkundig Verslag over het eerste en tweede kwartaal van 1927', *OV 1927* (1928), 28–29.

[65] *Mededeelingen van de Kirtya Liefrinck–Van der Tuuk* 1:1 (1929), v–viii; Michel Picard, 'Balinese religion in search of recognition: from *Agama Hindu Bali* to *Agama Hindu*', *BKI* 167:4 (2011), 482–510; Vickers, *Bali: a paradise created*, 2nd edn, 211–214.

[66] See Bernet Kempers, *Monumental Bali,* 81. See also, in a condescending tone, Stutterheim, *Oudheden van Bali*, vol. I, 8.

two Balinese inscriptions provided by Van der Tuuk and Brandes (1885) and a larger number of copper plates collected by Van Stein Callenfels in the 1920s, which indicated that Bali might have had a civilisational history before Majapahit's exodus, which encouraged the foundation of the Kirtya Liefrinck Society.[67]

But long before formal scholarly study began, the local population knew that the *arca* had been there since ancient times, and were therefore old, but they did not consider them historical objects. They believed the *arca* were (and are) extremely sacred – not as representations of gods, but believed to contain magic spirits, on which the well-being of the larger community depended. People would present offerings to the *arca* to prevent magical forces from being released from the stones and generating evil. This was something foreign observers clearly became aware of, and at least some of them considered it an interesting topic for research in itself.[68] Stutterheim, moreover, noticed in Pejeng – then a village of about 200 families – that people were 'proud to be in the possession of the "Moon of Bali"'. Some people believed that 'it was older than the moon', others told him it was the wheel of the moon wagon, and others proposed that it might be a piece of jewellery from the legendary giant Kebo Loewa.[69] In his official report, Stutterheim included local stories, like those about Kebo Loewa, as keys to historical truths, which had later been reinterpreted. He tried to trace them back to the relevant Balinese written traditions, like the Usana Bali – in the translation by the nineteenth-century colonial administrator and scholar R. Friederich – which describes among other things the fight of the gods against the demon king Maja Danawa, seated in Bedulu, who was infamous for his efforts to extinguish the Hindu religion on Bali.[70] Thus, as in nineteenth-century Majapahit, through the visit of Stutterheim to Pejeng, we see how various forms of historical knowledge and past attitudes intersected at one site and – in parallel, or through exchange – came to play a role in new knowledge production and heritage dynamics. Thereby, probably inspired by his Leiden teacher, the philologist and Javanologist W. H. Rasser,[71] Stutterheim consciously tried to include local histories, the historical landscape, and topical demographic data in his scholarly

[67] Stutterheim, *Oudheden van Bali*, vol. I, 8; H. N. van der Tuuk and J. L. Brandes, 'Transcriptie van vier Oud-Javaansche oorkonden gevonden op het eiland Bali', *Tijdschrift voor Indische Taal-, Land- en Volkenkunde* 30 (1885), 603–607; Pieter V. van Stein Callenfels, 'Historische gegevens uit Balische oorkonden I', *OV 1920* (1920), 40–44; Pieter V. van Stein Callenfels, 'Historische gegevens uit Balische oorkonden II', *OV 1920* (1920), 130–134; Pieter V. van Stein Callenfels, 'Historische gegevens uit Balische oorkonden III', *OV 1924* (1925), 28–35.

[68] Stutterheim, *Oudheden van Bali*, vol. I, 37, 105; W. F. Stutterheim, 'Voorlopige inventaris der Oudheden van Bali', *OV 1925* (1926), 165 (inv. nr 46).

[69] Stutterheim, *Oudheden van Bali*, vol. I, 22–23.

[70] Ibid., 20; R. Friederich, 'De Oesana Bali', *Tijdschrift voor Neerland's Indië* 9:3 (1847), 245–373.

[71] Bloembergen, 'Borobudur in "the light of Asia"'; See Berg, 'Javaansche geschiedschrijving', 9.

approach. For him it was a precondition that enabled him to make sense of the *arca* and their local meanings. For example, the relatively large number of Brahman families in Pejeng in comparison to surrounding villages convinced him that Pejeng had played an extraordinary role in the region, especially with regard to religious affairs.[72]

One may expect that formal archaeological interventions – which involve the wish to excavate, clean, investigate, and read the objects, to register them, and to conserve them, and thus to touch them – would clash with local practices of care, that is to bring offerings to prevent the spirits from being released,[73] and especially not to touch them, unless in the context of a cleaning ritual performed by a priest or *pemangku* (a lower-ranking priest and daily caretaker of a temple). But there is a commonality: an intention to 'care'. The collaboration of the local villagers in Pejeng and Bedulu when Stutterheim came to systematically register and investigate the *arca* in the mid 1920s seems interesting in this context. Stutterheim came to know the 'amazingly large storage' of *arca* mainly through the help of villagers, who would come daily to his temporary office on location to report on 'new' locations of *arca*. And, while they would not dare to touch these *arca* themselves, they let Stutterheim do so. This was 'because', Stutterheim reasoned, 'the magic forces that thus could come out would immediately attack the foreign visitor, and that was his problem, not theirs'.[74]

If we look at how Stutterheim had organised his research, then we see that other factors, particularly local power dynamics, were as important as the villagers' assistance. It mattered that the then influential local ruler Tjokorde Gde Raka Soekawati, the *punggawa* (district head) of nearby Ubud and member of the People's Council, co-initiated the inventory activities, for which Stutterheim gave him credit.[75] During his three trips to Bali, Stutterheim received similarly influential support of the village heads (*perbekel*) of Bedulu (I Wayan Limbak) and Pejeng (Tjokorde Ngoerah) through Soekawati's influence. He stayed at their quarters. In the latter case this was in the *puri* (palace) of Pejeng. Both heads mediated in getting the villagers involved. The assistance of priests and *pemangku*, finally, was needed as well, since the latter were in charge of the daily 'care' (or 'treatment', as Stutterheim called this form of care) of some of the *arca* or groups of *arca*.[76] In some special cases they, or the priests, would have to do the necessary cleaning rituals, before the archaeologist could investigate ('touch') the objects involved.

[72] Stutterheim, *Oudheden van Bali*, vol. I, 30. [73] Ibid., 27. [74] Ibid., 29–30 and 95–96.

[75] Stutterheim, 'Verslag van den adjunct-oudheidkundige nopens zijn reis naar Bali', 90. Stutterheim mentions that while W. O. J. Nieuwenkamp may have spread the news about the site that came to be known as Yeh Pulu, Soekawati had identified this site before him. Bernet Kempers also gives Soekawati the credit for initiating antiquarian research in the region. See Bernet Kempers, *Monumental Bali*, 86.

[76] Stutterheim, *Oudheden van Bali*, vol. I, 95–96 and 122.

These research practices not only indicate how local power relations facilitated research and directed Stutterheim to specific paths of past relationships, but they may have also helped to legitimise the special positions of rajas, *perbekel,* and priests grounding their authority in local society.[77] It is also meaningful in itself, however, that in this way the local communities became involved in the makings of old Bali and became aware of the particular value of other forms of knowledge of the past and other past relationships.[78] Also outside Pejeng and Ubud, the group of Balinese intellectuals around the journal *Bhawanagara*, published by the Kirtya Liefrinck, followed Stutterheim's archaeological research with interest. Under the title 'Babad toea Poelau Bali' ('The old *babad* of the island Bali'), in 1931, I Made Sweta explained to his readers that, after the publication of *Oudheden van Bali* ('Antiquities of Bali', 1929–1930), Stutterheim was now assigned 'to come to this island to take care of the remains of "ancient art". The result of this work . . . will be very satisfying.'[79]

In order to understand the long-term impact of Sutterheim's presence on Bali, we must briefly observe his methods of research and findings. With the help of villagers, Stutterheim traced, in Pejeng, Bedulu, and surrounding villages, in the *sawah* and alongside the holy rivers, 124 locations (*pura,* village temples, smaller temples, family temples, properties outside temples, rock temples, and open rice fields) registering for each location all *arca*, inscriptions, and statues he could find. These included recent findings like the clay *stupa* tablets and Buddhist statues uncovered during a landslide in the south of Pejeng in 1924, which had been moved to the *pura* Penataran Sasih, which also hosted the Moon of Pejeng.[80] Most *arca* that Stutterheim registered, however, were known never to have been moved.[81] In his inventory, published in the Archaeological Service's Reports, Stutterheim registered the finding place as well, and often mentioned the names of the householder of family temples. He categorised the *arca* in style and historical periodisation, with the help of inscriptions; by comparing with Javanese (*Nagarakrtagama*) and Balinese

[77] This points to the inescapability of how the 'local elite informant', whether a Brahman, a village head, or a raja, influences not only the perspective, but also the knowledge traditions and path of past relationships we follow as scholars. Compare Margaret Wiener on the inescapability of partiality, herself building on the teaching and information of one particular informant as well, and also on Goris and his informants: Wiener, *Visible and invisible realms,* 14–21.

[78] Compare on the awareness of different past relationships, referred to as *eling* (to commemorate) and *uning* (to know), existing together in Bali at the same time: Gregory Bateson, 'An old temple and a new myth', *Djawa* 17 (1937), 291–307; Henk Schulte Nordholt, 'Temple and authority in South Bali, 1900–1980', in H. Geertz (ed.), *State and society in Bali* (Leiden: KITLV, 1994), 137–164; Bloembergen, *Colonial spectacles*, 333–354.

[79] I Made Sweta, 'Babad toea Poelau Bali', *Bhawanagara* 1:1 (1931), 28–30.

[80] Later, the tablets moved to the Bali Museum. See W. F. Stutterheim, 'De oudheden van Pedjeng', *Djawa* 17 (1937), 441.

[81] Stutterheim, 'Voorlopige inventaris der Oudheden van Bali', 165 (inv. nr 46).

sources (*Usana Bali*) and oral traditions; and, typically for the method of these times, by reconstructing the genealogy of kingdoms. Based on all of this, Stutterheim came to the conclusion that these *arca* pointed to the existence of Hindu–Buddhist kingdoms in Bali flourishing long before the Majapahit exodus to the island. By comparing the extraordinary number of Brahman families to those in (larger) villages in the area, he reasoned that Pejeng would have played a powerful role in the region.[82]

All these findings contributed to the development of what we may call, using a scholarly term of the time, 'local genius'[83] and – a recent scholarly term – 'community-based archaeology', which, taken together, define the legacies of colonial archaeological heritage politics in Bali. Stutterheim's research in the region provided structures on which other parties after him could build. On the other hand, these structures were, in the first instance, determined by the many *arca* in the region and the local willingness to testify about them and, in some cases, move them.

Exploring 'Old Bali' across Regime Changes

During the post-colonial era, entailing a new episode of state-supported archaeological involvements in Bali, there was a clear continuity in the way local communities facilitated professional archaeological research in the Pakerisan valley. The village head of Bedulu who hosted Stutterheim, I Wayan Limbak, in subsequent decades provided a base for a range of archaeologists visiting the region after Stutterheim. The first of them was the Dutch engineer C. Krijgsman, who came to do conservation and reconstruction works in the area during the revolution era and in the post-independence 1950s, thereby representing two Archaeological Services.[84] Krijgsman noticed a remarkable interest from the local population in new excavations at archaeological sites, which, he reasoned,

82 Stutterheim, *Oudheden van Bali*, vol. I, 30.

83 The idea of 'local genius', a term which could be compared to the anthropological notion of 'local agency', developed in the context of a still dominant theorising on the 'Indianisation of the region', to emphasise the role of local inhabitants in developing a civilisation with its own local characteristics. See F. D. K. Bosch, '"Local genius" en Oudjavaansche Kunst', *Mededelingen der Koninklijke Nederlandse Academie van Wetenschappen*, Afd. Letterkunde, Nieuwe Reeks 15:1 (1952); H. G. Quaritch Wales, 'Cultural change in greater India', *JRAS* (1948), 17. Bosch and Quaritch Wales are known to have introduced the term, but the idea of a local genius was used earlier, during the 1920s and 1930s, to take a stance against Greater India perspectives. See Bloembergen, 'Borobudur in "the light of Asia"'; Kwa Chong-Guan, 'Introduction: visions of early Southeast Asia as Greater India', in *Visions of Greater India: an anthology from the Journal of the Greater India Society* (Singapore: Manohar, 2013), xv–xlvii.

84 Remembering 'Pak Krisman': interviews, Marieke Bloembergen with the Bedulu-born archaeologist Oka Ostawa, former head of the Balai Arkeologi in Denpasar, whose father also hosted Soekmono and Soejono, 16 February 2011; with *pemangku* Gusti Mangku Agung of *pura* Samuan Tiga (Bedulu), 21 February 2011, 4 June 2012.

could be explained by the organised school trips.[85] In the 1960s, Javanese archaeologists followed.[86]

Meaningfully, Krijgsman as well as Soekmono not only carried out archaeological research, but also imported to Bali principles and techniques of conservation and reconstruction of ancient sites that had been developed in Java in colonial times. President Soekarno's inauguration of the reconstructed ninth-century Siva temple at Prambanan in December 1953 spurred a 'reconstruction movement' in post-colonial Indonesia that was part of post-independence Indonesian national heritage politics. Soekarno made this event of nation building relevant for Bali as well. While stressing the spiritual importance of this monument for the whole – predominantly Muslim – nation, he emphatically addressed and invited the 'Hindu Balinese' students of the young Gadjah Mada University in Yogyakarta to come and pray – which they did, at night, after the national inauguration ceremony.[87] They were guided by Balinese priests, who had travelled from Bali especially for this occasion, to inaugurate the site as not only Indonesia's first national monument, but also a site sacred to Balinese beliefs.[88]

Although in Java Soekarno thus somehow accommodated new national Indonesian heritage politics to Balinese interests, this did not mean heritage politics would work in Bali the way they (ideally) worked in Java. In Bali, the early post-colonial Archaeological Service's professional conservation and reconstruction concerns clashed with sentiments on the ground. For instance in 1954, the local inhabitants in Kapal claimed that restoring the *pura* Sada meant meeting present-day religious needs and present-day notions of beauty. Echoing conflicts of restoration ethics during the 1917 earthquake-related rebuilding of ruined temples and palaces, the responsible Balinese in Kapal wanted restoration in the form of renewal, whereas the Archaeological Service, represented by Krijgsman, aspired to restoration to the original state. In the end, Krijgsman found that it was hard to match – let alone enforce – archaeological

[85] Bloembergen and Eickhoff, 'Conserving the past, mobilizing the Indonesian future', 424; Jef Last, 'Omzwervingen met de archeologische dienst op Bali', *Cultureel Nieuws Indonesië* (1954), 1142.

[86] Dinas Purbakala head Soekomono, and prehistorian Soejono. See Soekmono, 'Ngajah, Gotong-Rojong di Bali', *Madjalah ilmu-ilmu sastra Indonesia/Indonesian Journal of Cultural Studies* 3:1 (March 1965), 31–38. Soekmono witnessed how all members of the local community of Bedulu, including women, engaged in restoring the *pura* Samuan Tiga, integrating this into their daily life. Typically, he referred to this as 'gotong royong', concluding that this was possibly the way in which people had built the Buddhist and Hindu temples in ancient Java.

[87] See the reports in the Indonesian newspapers *Kedaulatan Rakyat*, 21 December 1953; *Kedaulatan Rakyat*, 22 December 1953; *Merdeka*, 21 December 1953; and in the Dutch journal *Cultureel Nieuws Indonesië* 36–37 (1954), 1121.

[88] For Sugriwa's own report, see I Gusti Bagus Sugriwa, 'Tjandi Prambanan', *Damai* 17 (January 1954), 5–6, 18; see also 'De Prambanan ingewijd', *Cultureel Nieuws Indonesië* 36–37 (1954), 1121 (taken from the Jakarta-based journal *De Nieuwsgier*, 23 December 1953).

principles of reconstruction with local practices of temple care and maintenance.[89]

The different notions of how to maintain old temples in Bali may also be explained in a different way: according to Balinese religious ideas, it is not necessarily the building of a temple, but the ground on which it is built, that makes the site sacred.[90] From that perspective, renovations or renewal do not make a temple less old in the eyes of the religious users and caretakers of a temple. This we learned ourselves by trial and error when in stubborn confusion we continued to ask the dates of the visibly new constructions in the old *pura* Penataran Sasih (the temple that keeps the Moon of Pejeng, and many of the *arca* Stutterheim had studied), which is today official Indonesian heritage. The answer we got was that every construction in the temple was as old as the temple.[91]

In Bali, two dramatic events caused interruptions of heritage politics in the mid 1960s: the great earthquake of 1964 and the pre-empted coup in Jakarta in 1965, followed by the massive repression of the supposed communist perpetrators and mass killings. These dramatic events, however, also provided the legitimation and need for restoration activities, literally and symbolically. In Pejeng for example, restorations and renovations at the *pura* Penataran Sasih, in 1966, on the initiative of *puri* Pejeng, were meant as a gesture of healing and self-legitimation.[92]

It was under the new president Soeharto, during the New Order, that state-supported archaeology and heritage politics in Indonesia experienced a great push.[93] Money and foreign expertise became available, and the government stimulated (re-)inventories of existing collections, excavations, and reconstruction projects, as well as building new regional museums – all emphatically in the footsteps of the UNESCO Save Borobudur campaign that started in 1974. Thus, in that same year, the informal headquarters of archaeology in Bali, located in Pejeng and Bedulu, became institutionalised. First, the

[89] Bloembergen and Eickhoff, 'Conserving the past, mobilizing the Indonesian future', 429.

[90] R. Goris, 'The temple system', in J. L. Swellengrebel (ed.), *Bali: studies in life, thought and ritual* (The Hague and Bandung: W. van Hoeve, 1960), 103.

[91] Compare Bateson, 'An old temple and a new myth'. Bateson, who was interested in the age of a specific temple, heard conflicting stories about the time it had been founded. During several visits to the *pura* Penataran Sasih, in 2009, 2011, and 2012, we enquired when certain new elements had been added. Our informants answered that these elements were old or original, even when they were visibly recently added: conversations, Marieke Bloembergen with archaeologist Oka Ostawa, at *pura* Penataran Sasih, 17 February 2011 (who denied, in response to our question, that there had been any renewals at this temple); temple guide Wayan Budyana, at *pura* Pentaran Sasih, 11 June 2012; with Gusti Mangku Agung, *pemangku* of *pura* Samuan Tiga, Bedulue, 21 February 2011 (his explanation in connection to our query concerning temple renewals was that 'the building can be renewed, not the statues').

[92] Information privded by the *pemangku* of *pura* Panataran Sasih, 18 February 2011.

[93] Compare Jones, *Culture, power, and authoritarianism in the Indonesian state*, 160–172; Wood, *Official history in modern Indonesia*.

government opened the archaeological museum – nowadays known as Gedung Arca, in its new building, strategically located on the border of Bedulu and Pejeng (the presumed centre of the old Hindu kingdom). The building also housed the regional conservation department (now known as BP3).[94] Next to that, in 1980, a regional *balai arkeologi* (centre for archaeological research) was installed in Denpasar, with a new building opened in 1985. All along, promotion of heritage awareness took place via the local and national newspapers, and on television.[95] Besides the implementation of the Indonesian Monument Act of 1992, and the development of tourism, national heritage demarcations as well as ticket offices arose at temple entrances. In the 1990s a number of remarkable temple reconstruction projects were initiated – following excavations and Buddhist findings in the 1980s – at *pura* Mengening (reconstructed as a *stupa*) and *pura* Pegulingan (reconstructed as a Javanese *candi*) – both located in the Pakerisan valley, inaugurated by the minister of education and culture in the 1990s, and today part of Bali's multi-sited World Heritage Site.

It remains uncertain the extent to which these post-colonial, state-based archaeological interventions – which have an undeniable impact on local heritage formation – are also a colonial legacy. By looking at new self-identifications, the redefinition of social relations, and the newly acquired status of certain archaeological sites, we identified a series of connected reasons that support our impression that, at least in Pejeng and Bedulu, colonial archaeology – in all its complexity and, in particular, being community-based – has had considerable long-term effects. In Pejeng and Bedulu today, archaeology seems to have become integrated into the daily life of many people, and into local socio-political power relations. Since the 1920s, a number of generations have engaged in different roles with archaeology. Since the 1970s some people play these roles *formally*: they work for the BP3 as *pegawai negeri* (government officials), in the villages, as caretakers of the temples and *arca*, or at the office of the BP3, or in the museum. Others, among them priests and village heads, some of whom are children or grandchildren of the Balinese who worked for Krijgsman, have studied archaeology and/or became professional archaeologists with degrees from Udayana University in Denpasar, elevating their status among their peers.[96] They still remember the

[94] Suaka Peninggalan Sejarah dan Purbakala Bali, later the Balai Pelestarian Peninggalan Purbakala.

[95] On Balinese history (including archaeology) in television broadcasting, see Helen Creese, 'Balinese television histories: broadcasting historical discourses in Bali', *Review of Indonesian and Malaysian Affairs* 34 (2000), 11–38.

[96] Interviews, Marieke Bloembergen with archaeologist and former head of the Balai Arkeologi in Den Pasar Anak Agung Oka Astawa (Den Pasar, 28 January 2010, and Bedulu, 18 February 2011), and with Ida Bagus Wayahan Bun, preacher (*pedanda*) and archaeologist connected to Udayana University (Pejeng, 21 February 2011).

tall 'Pak Krisman' (Krijgsman) as a sociable man who, like his predecessor Stutterheim, did great work to relocate, conserve, and restore the remains of the old, pre-Majapahit, pre-Javanese temples and kingdoms of Pejeng.

Furthermore, there is an ambiguous interdependency between priests, 'rajas' (now in high administrative positions, also in the field of heritage), and official archaeological knowledge. Priests and *pemangku* eagerly read the books written by local scholars, to comprehend the histories of 'their temple' and the *arca* they contain. But they themselves are (still) needed to perform the cleaning rituals – moving and temporarily storing the spirits – before archaeologists can study the *arca*. The highest official (the *bupati* of Gianyar) legitimises the work done, by stressing the importance of the archaeological research, and the care of local heritage, for the consolidation of local self-esteem.[97] And, last but not least, also in terms of knowledge, archaeology has been integrated into life. People know that the temples are 'bersejarah' (that they have a history/are historical), because of the *arca*. But this does not mean that academic archaeological knowledge has the monopoly on valuing and determining these sites. The *arca* have not lost their sacredness. And – speaking of the power of sites – there are still some *arca* in smaller localised family temples that are too sacred to be moved or touched. The BP3 did not manage to get permission to move these precious objects to the museum.[98] This all indicates that – despite monument acts and heritage markings, state-supported archaeological investigations and conservation projects – on the local level, neither the government nor the local archaeological state institutions are in complete control over the uses, discourse, or valuations of sites in Bali. And this was the case both in colonial and in post-colonial times.

Let us see how this worked for another 'local' heritage and research field, that of Chinese ceramics.

Chinese *Pusaka*, 'Foreign Ceramics', Japanese Interests, and Forced Migration

In 1934, the Archaeological Service initiated several 'prospection' projects in the mountains near Palembang and Jambi, in North, South, and Central Java,

97 Oka Astawa, A. A. Gde, I Made Sutaba, et al., *Pura Samuan Tiga: Bedulu Gianyar* (Bedulu: Pemerintah kabupaten Gianyar dan paruman pura Samuan Tiga, 2006). This book contains a foreword by the then governor of Gianyar, A. A. Gde Agung Bharata. The *pemangku* of *pura* Samuan Tiga had on his bookshelves several books (recent translations) by the Dutch philologist C. Hooykaas, who worked as language official in Bali in the late 1930s. These included, for example, C. Hooykaas, *Surya Sevana: dari pandita untuk pandita dan Umat Hindu*, transl. Swariyati (Surabaya: Paramita, 2004).

98 Visits, Marieke Bloembergen to family temples in Bedulu, together with Kadè, an official of the BP3, 19 February 2011.

and at the Prambanan temple site. Most of the potsherds found at Prambanan were Chinese, dating from the ninth century, and seemed comparable to those found at Samarra in Mesopotamia.[99] In 1938 a similar large-scale project was undertaken in Celebes.[100] This new method of mapping archaeological phenomena was executed by a team of trained researchers, partly consisting of local volunteers who collected fragments of ancient Chinese ceramics. They did so under the inspired leadership of the collector and self-taught expert on Chinese ceramics, Egbert van Orsoy de Flines (1886–1964) and with the support of the Archaeological Service.

Chinese porcelain or earthenware, and fragments of it, could be found all over the archipelago, as Chinese–Indonesian contacts had existed for at least two millennia, in the context of inter-Asian trade and migration. For scholars, it was an innovation to use prospection to gain insight into the history of these Chinese–Indonesian contacts.[101] However, the practice of collecting Chinese ceramics was not new. They were collected and kept in many places and used for many reasons. At the time that the Archaeological Service initiated the prospection at Prambanan, moreover, the collecting of and trade in Chinese ceramics was booming, and Orsoy de Flines' private collecting history in itself fits into that trend.[102]

In the Netherlands Indies, Chinese ceramics apparently became an object of conscious and systematic state-supported research only in the early 1930s. In these years, the Batavian Society began the collecting, study, and display of Chinese ceramics as one of its new activities. The Monument Act of 1931 explicitly included Chinese archaeological sites.[103] Then, in 1933, the Batavian Society opened a special department in its museum, displaying Chinese ceramics found in the archipelago.[104] We can understand many of

[99] E. W. van Orsoy de Flines, 'De keramische Verzameling 1934', *Jaarboek III Koninklijk Bataviaasch Genootschap van Kunsten en Wetenschappen* (1936), 210.

[100] See 'Verslag van een reis voor onderzoek en studie van de antieke Uitheems ceramiek. Voorkomende in Zuid- en Midden Celebes, van einde Maart tot begin mei 1939', Stadsarchief Amsterdam, collection 1303 (Familie de Flines), file 841. For an elaborate report on fieldwork in Java, see E. W. van Orsoy de Flines, 'Onderzoek naar en van keramische scherven in de bodem in Noordelijk Midden-Java, 1940–'42', *OV 1941–1947* (1949), 66–84.

[101] For the method, being developed in Germany in the 1920s and known as 'Landesaufnahme', and briefly discussed for the research in Trowulan in Chapter 4, see Eickhoff, *Van het land naar de markt*, 13.

[102] For a general overview of the history of collecting china, see Vimalin Rujivacharakul, 'China and china: an introduction to materiality and a history of collecting', in Vimalin Rujivacharakul (ed.), *Collecting china: the world, China, and a history of collecting* (Newark: University of Delaware Press, 2001), 15–30.

[103] Bernet Kempers, *Herstel in eigen waarde*, 223–227.

[104] In earlier years, the museum had a small collection of china on display in the so-called *bronskamer* (bronze room); see 'De keramische Verzameling', *Jaarboek I Koninklijk Bataviaasch Genootschap van Kunsten en Wetenschappen* (1933), 225.

the dynamics involved by following one of the showpieces of this collection: a porcelain flask produced in the fifteenth century in the Jingdezhen region. The museum acquired the flask in 1937 in the Moluccas, and the curator of the ceramics collection, Orsoy de Flines, praised the flask and believed that it could compete with those in the excellent collection of former Ottoman sultans, kept in the Topkapi Palace Museum in Istanbul.[105] Meaningfully, he found the art value and historical uniqueness of the new acquisition of greater importance than its ethnographical and historical features. This observation is telling for the way 'connoisseur'-collecting traditions disconnected the Chinese population in the Netherlands Indies from Chinese ceramics history. Whereas the Siva temple – almost without any problems – slowly but certainly developed into a national Indonesian site, the material culture of Chinese–Indonesian relationships, while it gained a place in the museological landscape of the Netherlands Indies, was marginalised in an effective way and with long-lasting effects.

The Netherlands Indies' history of the porcelain flask is strongly connected to the biography of Orsoy de Flines. Born in the Netherlands, as a young man Orsoy de Flines left for the Netherlands Indies to work as a bank employee and planter. He became a well-known collector of Chinese and other types of 'foreign' ceramics that, he learned, could be found everywhere: in the Indonesian soil, in the homes of the inhabitants of the archipelago, within buildings, and at antique shops. For his slowly growing collection, he founded a private museum at Ungaran (near Semarang). In 1929, he bequeathed this collection to the museum of the Batavian Society.[106] Until then the china collection of the Batavian Museum had been rather small. But in 1933 the society considered it necessary to move the collection to a permanent exhibition hall in the museum. This hall was built with the insurance money from the treasures the society had lost in the fire that burned down the Dutch colonial pavilion in Paris in June 1931.[107] Out of gratitude for his 'gift', but also because of the expertise Orsoy de Flines had displayed in dating and identifying ceramics, the society appointed him curator of the new ceramics department of the museum. In his new official function, Orsoy de Flines continued his collecting activities with the support of the Archaeological Service, while members of the service repeatedly contacted him to identify and 'date' potsherds they found during excavations. The Batavian Museum's collection began to grow substantially. In 1937, it consisted of seventy displays with porcelain and earthenware from Japan, Siam, Cambodia, Persia, Arabia, and

[105] E. W. van Orsoy de Flines, 'De Keramische Verzameling', *Jaarboek IV Koninklijk Bataviaasch Genootschap van Kunsten en Wetenschappen* (1937), 175.

[106] 'Belangrijke schenking aan het museum', *Het Nieuws van de Dag voor Nederlands-Indie* (10 December 1929).

[107] 'De keramische Verzameling', *Jaarboek I* (1933), 226–227.

Western Europe.[108] Postcards depicting showpieces of the collection were for sale whereas in the exhibition room, wall maps showed the origin and spread of the collected objects.[109]

At the museum, remarkably, Orsoy de Flines developed a clear collection plan in which the art value was not the first point of interest:

> To bring together a collection that as much as possible contains all those types and shapes that from earliest periods until the seventeenth century were imported in the archipelago, including plain pottery for daily use as well as finer pieces and showpieces . . . when judging the collection it is not in the first place the artistic value, but the ethnographic and the historical value that counts.[110]

Surely, not only foreign collectors or colonial elites appreciated the museum's collecting of Chinese ceramics. According to Orsoy de Flines, 'indigenous visitors' showed much interest in the collection.[111] He was also informed about the way local or 'Indisch-Chinese' (meaning Peranakan Chinese) owners kept their pieces of pottery in their homes. They treated such pieces, often sacral family pieces, as *pusaka* (best translated as 'heirlooms'). The heirs of such a *pusaka* believed that these had protective powers. Therefore, as we saw in Bali with the *arca*, these objects could count on special care, as Orsoy de Flines noticed. The Chinese *pusaka* were often kept inside homes: 'below the bed', 'hanging under the roof', 'on the roof', 'in bamboo crates', or 'stored away in a clothing box'. To display them in all their splendour (*pronk*), a typical Dutch way of treating precious objects in order to show wealth or taste, was uncommon, according to Orsoy de Flines.[112] However, in the context of a flourishing global trade in Chinese ceramics, he became concerned that in the Netherlands Indies, and among both Indonesian and Peranakan Chinese owners, the economic value of the object came to outweigh traditional values: 'the respect of the fear for good or bad influence of the *pusaka* disappears quickly'.[113]

This brings us back to 'our' special fifteenth-century Chinese flask, which had found its way from China, probably via trade in the fifteenth century, to the North Moluccan island of Halmahera, and there had lived the life of such a family *pusaka* – until the Batavian Museum acquired it in 1937. Orsoy de Flines had expressed particular worries with regard to *pusaka* transforming into trade objects in the Moluccas. He knew that the inhabitants of these islands, due to early Chinese contact, often owned porcelain objects that dated from the

[108] E. W. v. Orsoy de Flines, 'De keramische Verzameling', *Jaarboek V Koninklijk Bataviaasch Genootschap van Kunsten en Wetenschappen* (1938), 159.

[109] Orsoy de Flines, 'De Keramische Verzameling', *Jaarboek IV* (1937), 174.

[110] 'De Keramische Verzameling', *Jaarboek I* (1933), 227–228. [111] Ibid., 225.

[112] E. W. van Orsoy de Flines, 'Vroeg Ming en pre-Ming blauw-wit chineesch porselein in Nederlandsch-Indië', *Maandblad voor Beeldende Kunsten* 15 (1938), 342–344.

[113] Ibid., 268.

fifteenth century. But he also knew that, there, people stored these objects in a different way from the way he had seen in Java. In the Moluccas, people used these objects during family festivities and afterwards put them away in covered pits behind their houses. As a result, Orsoy de Flines feared, it might happen that cattle got stuck in these pits with damaging effects for the porcelain treasures.[114] But what worried him most in the Moluccas were the rivals on his – and the Batavian Museum's – market: Japanese traders who tried to buy pieces for Japanese collectors. Bitter and suspicious, he wrote: 'the so-called Japanese fishers are everywhere in our archipelago'.[115]

In 1937 Orsoy de Flines arranged for the colonial administration in the Moluccas to prevent export of porcelain objects to Japan. Colonial officials on location were asked to register and photograph precious objects, and request that owners avoid dealing with Japanese traders unless someone from the colonial administration was present. If someone sought to sell a vase, they would try to acquire it for the museum in Batavia. This arrangement, which Orsoy de Flines phrased as a policy of salvation, is a good example of the interaction of indigenous, Japanese, and colonial heritage notions, with unmistakably competitive and patronising dimensions.[116] As soon as this arrangement led to the acquisition of a *pusaka*/Chinese object for the museum, Dutch colonial circles responded enthusiastically. They did so, for example, in 1937 when, due to the mediation of Dr H. Schneider, a medical officer, based in Ternate, the museum obtained the fifteenth-century flask that originated from the Jingdeshen region in China, but had become a family *pusaka* in Halmaheira (Figure 6.5).[117]

The colonial sources – year reports, official correspondence, publications – do not tell us much about the involvement of Chinese people in the collecting practices of Orsoy de Flines. In his 1933 annual report, however, he does mention the 'Indisch Chinese' who keep Chinese ceramics at home.[118] One year later he mentions beautiful donations from 'Indisch Chinese' living in Palembang, the Riau islands, South Celebes, East and South Borneo, Banka, Belitung, and Banten. Collecting china from the soil of the Netherlands Indies, and in particular the discovery of Han ceramics, made it clear to Orsoy de Flines that Chinese had been present in the archipelago since the first century.[119] But in the second half of the 1930s the number of these acquisitions decreased considerably due to the economic crisis.[120] The cultural capital that had previously been acquired by the Indonesian Chinese via donating family

114 Ibid., 344. 115 Ibid., 271.

116 Orsoy de Flines, 'De keramische Verzameling', *Jaarboek IV* (1937), 175.

117 Orsoy de Flines, 'Vroeg Ming en pre-Ming blauw-wit chineesch porselein', 270. Compare with Jan Fontein, 'Het verzamelen van Aziatische kunst in de twintigste eeuw', *Aziatische Kunst* 23:3 (1993), 12.

118 'De keramische Verzameling', *Jaarboek I* (1933), 225.

119 Van Orsoy de Flines, 'De Keramische Verzameling 1934', *Jaarboek III* (1936), 207 and 209.

120 Van Orsoy de Flines, 'De keramische Verzameling', *Jaarboek V* (1938), 160.

Figure 6.5 Chinese vase from Halmaheira, circa 1936.

pieces to the museum had obviously become less valuable. They now wanted money for their heirlooms.

Given the Japanese desire for Chinese porcelain, the Japanese occupation of the Netherlands Indies worried Orsoy de Flines. Paradoxically his porcelain expertise enabled him to stay and work in the museum much longer than his colleagues.[121] However, in September 1943 he was interned as well.[122] Half a year after the end of the Pacific War, but now in the context of the Indonesian revolution and Dutch recolonisation, in January 1946, Orsoy de Flines returned to Batavia/Jakarta and learned that the museum was in the hands of Indonesian nationalists.[123] Apparently they appreciated his expertise, for they offered him the keys to the ceramics room. Orsoy de Flines noted that some pieces had been moved or damaged, but nothing was missing. But the displays now had Japanese explanations. There were also some new acquisitions. He learned that farmers

[121] 'De Keramische Verzameling. 1941 tot eind Februari 1942', *Jaarboek IX 1 Jan. 1941–31 Dec. 1947. Koninklijk Bataviaasch Genootschap van Kunsten en Wetenschappen* (1948), 111.

[122] In the report Van der Hoop wrote about the meeting of the Batavian Society of 23 May 1947, in ANRI, KBG DIR 1105, he explains that Orsoy de Flines was interned in September 1943. Van der Hoop also mentions that Orsoy de Flines, during the work under Japanese direction, lived in the museum for a time.

[123] 'De Keramische Verzameling. Maart 1942 tot eind December 1947', *Jaarboek 00* (1900), 120.

had found these objects and donated them to the museum, which was then under Japanese control.[124] We do not know what the general message was of the reorganised collection. Yet we can presume that the collection of foreign, predominantly Asian ceramics suited very much the Japanese view of one Greater Asia that had rediscovered its unity and identity under Japanese guidance.

Deviating from this Japanese Greater Asia perspective, Orsoy de Flines followed a clear Indonesian-nationalist perspective in the Dutch-language catalogue of the collection of 1949, writing in the preface:

> Where museums in Europe, America, and other parts of the world that aim to display a complete overview of Chinese and Japanese ceramics, can rely on the art trade to acquire missing types, this procedure is impossible for the Batavian Museum. What comes from abroad, and as a result has not been ancestral property of Indonesians, or what has not been excavated in the archipelago cannot be purchased. The reason for this is that the collection should be of use for historical research on Indonesia.[125]

Remarkably, the Peranakan or 'Indisch Chinese' are absent in this explanation and justification of the museum's collection policy, despite their pre-war donations of Chinese ceramics to the museum. Categorised as foreign ceramics from Indonesian soil, the collections seem to function to connect (and date) the different archaeological and historical cultures of the Indonesian archipelago. But the catalogue at the same time ignores the history of Chinese trade connections and of Chinese migration and settling in the archipelago. This approach, in which the ceramics are not regarded as Chinese–Indonesian heritage, would determine the perspective on the collection for a long time, also in post-colonial times: Orsoy de Flines' catalogue was translated into English and reprinted in 1969, 1972, and 1975.[126] Orsoy de Flines' perspective obviously fitted very well into the Indonesian ideas of a national past, in which the Chinese minority, in all its diversity, became marginalised, as early as during Soekarno's rule but especially after the violent regime change of 1965.[127]

Meanwhile, the journey of the fifteenth-century porcelain flask again resumed, as it now travelled to the Netherlands. This happened in the context of post-colonial tensions between Indonesia and the Netherlands, which in December 1957 reached a climax as a result of the dispute over New Guinea,

124 Ibid.

125 E. W. van Orsoy de Flines, *Gids voor de Keramische Verzameling (Uitheemse Keramiek). Koninklijk Bataviaasch Genootschap van Kunsten en Wetenschappen* (Nix: Batavia, 1949), 3.

126 E. W. van Orsoy de Flines, *Guide to the ceramic collection (foreign ceramics)* (Djakarta: Museum Pusat Djakarta, 1969); E. W. van Orsoy de Flines, *Guide to the ceramic collection (foreign ceramics)* (Jakarta: Museum Pusat Jakarta, 1975).

127 Following this tradition, a 2001 catalogue of the collection asked rhetorically: 'Why are these non-Indonesian ceramics exhibited?' See *Koleksi Keramik Museum Nasional* (Departemen Kebudayaan dan Pariwisata Direktorat Jenderal Sejarah dan Purbakala Museum Nasional, 2001).

then still Dutch territory. The situation escalated following Indonesia's defeat in the UN General Assembly in an attempt to pass a resolution in favour of Indonesia's claim to this territory. As a result, that same month, all Dutch residents in Indonesia were forced to leave or apply for Indonesian citizenship. Until that time, Orsoy de Flines, considering his affective relation with 'his' china collection, had lived in a relatively privileged position. When the Dutch government formally recognised Indonesian independence in 1949, he had obtained a verbal agreement from the new Indonesian Museum management (led by Hoesein Djajadiningrat) that he could continue to live *in* the museum (he inhabited a small room there), an arrangement that had started under the Japanese occupation; and that his collection, according to his own will and gesture of 1932, would be bequeathed to the museum after his death. But in December 1957 Orsoy de Flines had to leave. The story goes that the Indonesian authorities told him that he had to leave the next day by boat, and that he had only one night to choose some objects from his own collection to take along. In order to keep the collection 'intact', Orsoy de Flines chose the flask from Jingdezhen/Halmahera/Batavia/Jakarta which (at least since being spotted at Halmahera) had a small crack.[128]

During Orsoy de Flines' remaining days in the Netherlands, the flask had a quiet life at his service flat 'De Schutse' in Bussum, probably representing memories of colonial days gone by, of times when he could relive the days of his expertise, but probably also a certain sense of loss. After Orsoy de Flines died in 1965, the flask entered the Dutch auction world. The prestigious auctioneering firm S. J. Mak van Waay acquired it, and had it bought by another prestigious party, the Rijksmuseum in Amsterdam.[129] Somehow, in the museum, the flask's Netherlands Indies–Chinese connections were further obscured, while its original Chinese roots became emphasised. The catalogue of the Asiatic art collection of the Rijksmuseum from 1985 very briefly describes the object, its acquisition, and its history, and categorised it as part of the china collection. It mentions, 'This flask is known to have come from Halmahera, an island in the Moluccas in the Indonesian archipelago'; yet by 2016, the Rijksmuseum website refrains from referring to this link with Halmahera.[130] Curiously, in 1993 another aspect of the travels of the flask was highlighted, giving it a strong post-colonial blend. Jan Fontein, in the journal *Aziatische Kunst* ('Asiatic art'), describes the object, its acquisition and

[128] Fontein, 'Het verzamelen van Aziatische kunst in de twintigste eeuw', 10–11. Compare with J. van Campen, 'History of the collection', in C. J. A. Jörg and J. van Campen (eds.), *Chinese ceramics in the collection of the Rijksmuseum Amsterdam: the Ming and Qing dynasties* (London: Philip Wilson Publishers, 1997), 21.

[129] 'Appendix: chronological list of acquisitions', in Jörg and Van Campen (eds.), *Chinese ceramics in the collection of the Rijksmuseum Amsterdam*, 25.

[130] Lunsingh Scheurleer (ed.), *Asiatic art in the Rijksmuseum Amsterdam*, 77: www.rijksmuseum.nl/nl/collectie/AK-RBK-1965-87 (accessed 3 November 2016).

its history, and mentions that the previous owner, Orsoy de Flines, was forced to leave Indonesia, whereby the Indonesian authorities breached an earlier agreement that he could stay. But they allowed him to take some pieces of his collection along to the Netherlands. In the Rijksmuseum the flask thus became a symbol of exclusion: not of the Chinese in Indonesia, but of an Indonesian Dutchman who in 1949 chose to stay in the independent country in order to contribute to its development, but a few years later was nonetheless forced to emigrate.[131]

Inaugurating Siva: Who Cares?

Starting at the Siva temple, and via the examples of 'Old Bali' and Chinese *pusaka*, we have showed how disaster, colonial expansion, war, destruction, regime change, and trans-Asian (archaeological) collaboration and competition contributed to heritage formation on location. The colonial state supported archaeological research and care, and helped to musealise Balinese and Chinese antiquities. Moreover, the process of (state-supported) research, collecting, reconstruction, knowledge gathering, and display made it possible for subsequent Japanese and post-colonial Indonesian regimes to take over the business of care, maintenance, and reconstruction of local sites as Indonesian sites. However, the Balinese and Chinese sites and objects of heritage formation that we discussed, bound by their materiality and by their sacredness, were being cared for long before the state and state archaeologists came in, and continued to be so in various ways that did not necessarily address state interests. Our focus on interactions of various forms of knowledge on location make clear that 'heritage formation' was not and is not the exclusive outcome of top-down state-supported care, nor of elitist reconstructive expertise and/or academic knowledge production. And local care, interests, stories, and transnational (in particular trans-Asian) networks matter in processes of heritage formation.

By way of conclusion, let us briefly return to the inauguration of the Siva temple. It shows clearly how, following Anderson's reasoning, colonial state-supported archaeology provided new independent post-colonial states with national historical monuments, national pasts, and tools and structures for national heritage politics. Bosch's decision to legitimise reconstruction-based Indonesian interests in pre-colonial antiquities powerfully impacted post-colonial Indonesian heritage politics. But it remains unclear the extent to which structures of centralisation secured strong state ownership. Despite the nation-building and national-heritage politics that played out at the Siva temple, there were alternative, multi-vocal engagements possible – coming from

[131] Fontein, 'Het verzamelen van Aziatische kunst in de twintigste eeuw', 10–11.

local, national, and transnational perspectives. In that sense, it was indeed, as Soekarno said, not materiality that mattered, but the temple's intangible 'flame' – or the meanings attached to the monument. After speeches by Van Romondt, Yamin, and Soekmono as the first Indonesian head of the Indonesian Archaeological Service, President Soekarno had the final word. Soekarno's speech emphasised the Siva temple as a national monument demonstrating the capacities of the Indonesian people, but that day Dutch archaeologist Bernet Kempers saw in the beautiful silhouette of the Siva temple the new post-colonial Dutch–Indonesian collaboration.[132] And, when night fell, Balinese priests, headed by the Balinese intellectual I Gusti Bagus Sugriwa, gathered with Balinese students to pay tribute to the temple as a sacred site according to Balinese–Hindu rituals.[133]

To further complicate matters, there were also the (individual and institutional) archaeological-cum-diplomatic interests of foreign parties, some based in India and French Indochina, built on 'older' intellectual and cultural connections. The next chapter investigates these complicated matters, focusing on the 1920s and 1930s to follow some of these 'foreign' perspectives across decolonisation, gauge their long-term effect, and extend our mobile analysis of heritage formation beyond Indonesia. This is also why, after a chapter assessing the forces of centralisation in heritage formation, we conclude the book with the same phenomenon, but understood from the perspective of fragility, loss, and anxieties over loss.

[132] Bernet Kempers, *Herstel in eigen waarde,* 169.

[133] For Sugriwa's own report, see Sugriwa, 'Tjandi Prambanan'; see also 'De Prambanan ingewijd', 1121.

7 Fragility, Losing, and Anxieties over Loss: Difficult Pasts in Wider Asian and Global Contexts

> 'Let the Buddha be my refuge.
>
> The spirit of those words has been muffled in mist in this mocking age of unbelief, and the curious crowds gather here to gloat in the gluttony of an irreverent sight.
>
> Man today has no peace – his heart arid with pride. He clamours for an ever-increasing speed in a fury of chase for objects that ceaselessly run, but never reach a meaning.'[1]
>
> 'Dear Rot, it is necessary to discuss diverse matters concerning Borobudur … It is clear that this will be, or already is, a gigantic project, and I wonder if our Indonesian friends are the right ones to direct such an enormous enterprise. I clearly see coming ahead that first the Cadillacs will be bought with the US dollars, and that after that it remains to be seen what will be left for Borobudur.'[2]

Anxiety over loss is an important motive in the politics of cultural heritage formation. Both the decay of a cherished site and emotions surrounding the loss of a (privileged) connection to it can be strong moral devices to motivate people and governments to plan restoration.[3] The long decolonisation of archaeological heritage in Indonesia forms a case in point. W. T van Erp's bitter and cynical

[1] Rabindranath Tagore, 'Boro-Budur' (1927), in *English writings of Tagore,* Vol. II, *Poems* (New Delhi: Atlantic, 2007), 314–315.

[2] John W. T. van Erp to Vincent van Romondt, 3 September 1968, Leiden University Library, Special Collections, KITLV Collections, Collection Vincent Rogers van Romondt, H 1239, inv. nr 26.

[3] This chapter elaborates on two earlier published essays: Marieke Bloembergen and Martijn Eickhoff, 'Save Borobudur! The moral dynamics of heritage formation in Indonesia across orders and borders', in Michael Falser (ed.), *Cultural heritage as civilizing mission: from decay to recovery* (Heidelberg: Springer, 2015), 83–122; Marieke Bloembergen and Martijn Eickhoff, 'Decolonizing Borobudur: moral engagements and the fear of loss. The Netherlands, Japan and (post)colonial heritage politics in Indonesia', in Susan Legêne, Bambang Purwanto, and Henk Schulte Nordholt (eds.), *Sites, bodies and stories: imagining Indonesian history* (Singapore: NUS Press, 2015), 33–66.

remarks denouncing how corrupt private interests profit from collective heritage ideals illustrate how hard it can be to relinquish a cherished object – in this case the majestic eighth-century Buddhist temple Borobudur in Central Java – in the context of decolonisation. His words contrast with those of Indian poet Rabindranath Tagore when he first saw Borobudur in September 1927 and, recognising India, lamented spiritual loss in a disbelieving age.[4]

As the son of the man who led the first restoration of Borobudur, Van Erp Jnr felt great concern about its fate, and shared his doubts with engineer Vincent van Romondt about the Indonesian government and UNESCO campaign to 'Save Borobudur', which involved plans for the dismantling and subsequent rebuilding of the temple. Van Romondt had been technical inspector of the Colonial Archaeological Service in charge of the reconstruction of the Siva temple at Prambanan, and continued under the new Indonesian Archaeological Service, the Dinas Purbakala. In 1954, he became professor at the new faculty of architecture at the Institut Teknologi Bandung where he taught the history of Indonesian architecture and theory of forms. In 1963 he returned to the Netherlands. Apparently, Van Erp Jnr found Van Romondt more competent than his Indonesian successors. His caustic comments reflect a typical paternalistic attitude, but also indicate how a site such as Borobudur can evoke long-term moral engagements from a sense of 'loss'.

This chapter explores how the anxiety over loss influenced cultural heritage dynamics in post-colonial Indonesia. We reveal different attitudes to difficult pasts from the perspective of various interested parties inside and outside Indonesia. Returning to Borobudur, we revisit Dutch, Indonesian, Indian, Japanese, and international heritage engagements in the period from the late 1920s well into the 1980s, and scrutinise post-war UNESCO politics and the Save Borobudur campaign of the 1970s and 1980s. Numerous dynamic processes reveal the fragility of ownership, even with the appropriation of heritage by the colonial and post-colonial state. Decolonisation stimulated strong emotional and moral passions for restoration, but Dutch post-colonial, inter-Asian, and international interests – such as the continuous Indian, and later UNESCO, interests, developing since colonial times – inflect Borobudur's national Indonesian character.

We also examine how and why Japanese interests in Indonesia's major Buddhist site did not start with the Japanese occupation of Indonesia, but built on older individual and private interests dating from at least the second decade of the twentieth century. These Japanese heritage engagements in Indonesia also reveal political, and specifically spiritual-religious motives in Japan-based pan-Asian thinking. In the final part of this chapter, we explore what interventions at Borobudur (taking place in the context of the UNESCO

[4] On the makings and wide reach of this kind of Greater Indian thinking regarding Indonesia, see Bloembergen, 'Borobudur in "the light of Asia"'.

Save Borobudur campaign since the 1960s) reveal about the way Japanese, Dutch, and Indonesian parties dealt with difficult, colonial, and recent violent pasts.

Borobudur in Wider Asian and Globalising World Views

In June 1956 Borobudur featured in a special issue of the *UNESCO Courier* that was dedicated to the theme of 'Buddhist art and culture' on the occasion of the annual Waisek festival celebrating the 2,500-year anniversary of the Buddha's enlightenment. The editors wanted to show 'the great masterpieces of architecture, sculpture, and painting of Buddhist art in Asia', and in line with UNESCO's global educational aims, to provide a 'glimpse of some of the ethical ideas and the message of peace, gentleness and mercy' which Buddhism, 'one of the noblest edifices of thought ever created by the human spirit', had inspired.[5] Borobudur, presented as 'Java's monument to Buddhism', was one of several masterpieces of Buddhist art in Asia that embellished this vision of peace and nobility.[6] A map indicating the peaceful spread of Buddhist culture and art from India via China to Southeast Asia situated Borobudur at the outer borders of a larger Asian Buddhist sphere (Figure 7.1). This map, and the accompanying article on the spread of Buddhist culture, conveyed the concept of a trans-Asian 'Greater Buddhist' and moral framework in which the site of Borobudur, like the other Asian sites discussed in this issue of the *UNESCO Courier*, were to be understood – at least according to the editors.[7] With this popularised and peaceful vision of a Greater Buddhist culture in Asia, UNESCO was pursuing its 1956 Cold War campaign to promote East–West understanding, but was also building on older notions in both 'the East' and 'the West' of a Greater Asian culture.[8]

5 'Editorial', 'Twenty-five centuries of Buddhist art and culture', Special Issue, *UNESCO Courier* 9:6 (June 1956), 2.

6 'Borobudur: "the terraced mountain". Java's monument to Buddhism', 'Twenty-five centuries of Buddhist art and culture', *UNESCO Courier*, 43–45.

7 Anil da Silva Vigier, 'Across the face of Asia', 'Twenty-five centuries of Buddhist art and culture', *UNESCO Courier*, 10–14.

8 Georges Fradier, *East and West: towards mutual understanding?* (Paris: UNESCO, 1959). See also the UNESCO monthly newsletter, *Orient–Occident*, published since 1958, informing its readers on 'UNESCO's major project on mutual appreciation of Eastern and Western cultural values'. On the post-war developmental aims behind UNESCO's cultural programmes in the 1950s, see Laura Elizabeth Wong, 'Relocating East and West: UNESCO's major project on the mutual appreciation of Eastern and Western cultural values', *Journal of World History* 19:3 (September 2008), 349–374; Rheling, 'Universalismen und Partikularismen im Wiederstreit', 3–4, online edn (accessed December 19, 2011). For the continuities of UNESCO's humanitarian ideals of the unity of humankind with nineteenth-century evolutionary thinking, see Glenda Sluga, 'UNESCO and the (one) world of Julian Huxley', *Journal of World History* 21:3 (2010), 393–418.

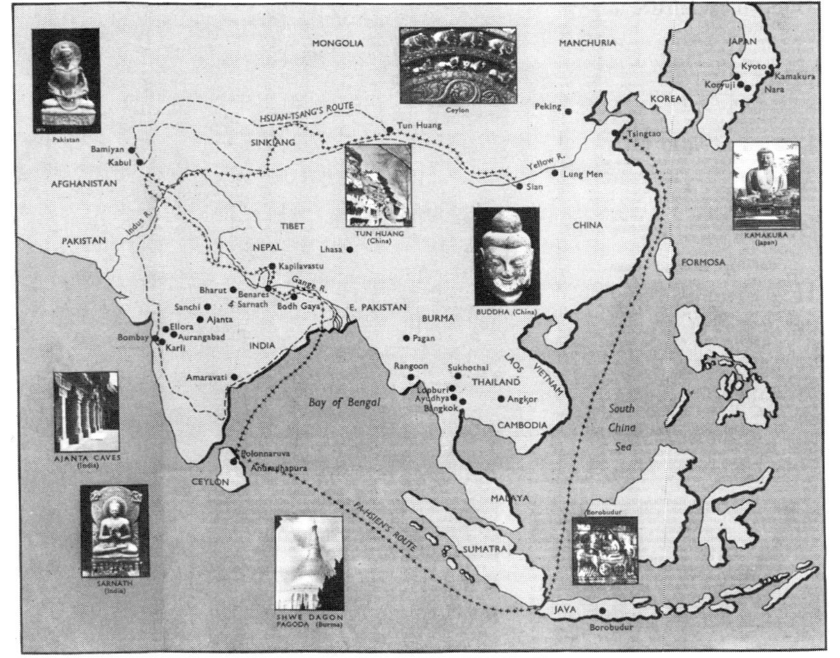

Figure 7.1 *UNESCO* map showing the spread of Buddhist culture and art from India and China to Southeast Asia, 1956.

With their Greater Buddhist Asian perspective, the editors of the *UNESCO Courier* were following the footsteps of the French and Indian scholars who had searched for cultural evidence in Southeast Asia that would confirm their notion of the spread of a benign and higher Indian civilisation, or Greater India. Susan Bayly has examined these (Western, mainly French) scholarly inspirations and the supra-local 'Greater India' practices of the thinkers and political actors who worked within the Calcutta-based Greater India Society (set up in 1926), which upheld this vision and propagated its revival.[9] During the colonial period these Greater Indian visions, and the question of the origin, spread, and nature of the Buddhist and Hindu civilisations in Asia, stimulated archaeological investigations, discussions, and interactions between scholars and the local elites in wider Asia.

Transnational, inter-Asian, and intercolonial scholarly investigation, as well as more general artistic, religious revivalist, philosophical, and theosophical interests in Asia's 'classic' religious antiquities and shrines were lively in the early twentieth century. As we discussed in Chapter 2 with King Chulalongkorn's staged praying at Borobudur in 1896 and the stimulation of theosophical foremen and monks, old Buddhist temple sites were being relocated (or reinvented) on religious and scholarly maps. Scholars, pilgrims, and tourists based inside and outside the colonial empires, as well as royal visitors, foreign political leaders, and local elites (including anti-colonial nationalists), travelled across the borders of colonial empires and independent kingdoms (Siam) in Asia to admire and pay tribute, whether purposefully or in passing, to museums, religious shrines, and monumental buildings that had recently been excavated, reconstructed, or conserved. They also sought to investigate past connections and interactions between Asian peoples or, more pointedly, to identify the Indian influences on local art and architecture on the basis of these material remains.[10] This search for meaning was also, as we argue throughout the book, a matter of giving and exchange – and thus also of losing. Cultural elites and professional scholars, delegates of archaeological

9 Bayly, 'Imagining "Greater India"'; see also Kwa, 'Introduction: visions of early Southeast Asia as Greater India'; Carolien Stolte, 'Orienting India: interwar internationalism in an Asian inflection, 1917–1937', PhD thesis, Leiden University, 2013, chapter 3. More specifically, for the role of Greater India thinking in Indian–Indonesian encounters, see Martin Ramstedt, 'Colonial encounters between India and Indonesia', *South Asian History and Culture* 2:4 (2011), 522–539; Bloembergen, 'Borobudur in "the light of Asia"'.

10 This line of inter-Asian cultural knowledge production and conservation practices needs further investigation. For some historiographic inventories, see J. G. de Casparis, 'Twintig jaar studie van de oudere geschiedenis van Indonesië: 1931–1951', *Oriëntatie: Cultureel Maandblad* 46 (1954), 626–664; Kishor K. Basa, 'Indian writings on early history and archaeology of Southeast Asia: a historiographical analysis', *JRAS* 8:3 (1989), 398–410; Ali, 'Connected histories?' For case studies, see Clémentin-Ojha and Manguin, *A century in Asia*; Jory, 'Thai and Western Buddhist scholarship'; Peleggi, 'Royal antiquarianism'; Ramstedt, 'Colonial encounters'; Bloembergen and Eickhoff, 'Exchange and the protection of Java's antiquities'.

institutions and learned societies, and individual researchers from Asia, Europe, and the United States visited each other at local heritage and research institutions, met at international conferences, and exchanged knowledge in collaboration and competition – thereby creating an intricate network of academic, spiritual, and political interdependencies and reciprocal obligations that could also assimilate the feeling of loss or the sense of losing control.

This Greater India (or Greater Asian) mindset strongly impacted the 'situating' of Borobudur within the geographic and moral imaginations that transgressed the borders of the Netherlands Indies. Thus, four decades after Chulalongkorn, in 1934, Nerada Thera, a Buddhist monk from Sri Lanka active in missionary work in Malaya and Singapore who claimed to have felt the 'pull' of Borobudur for some time, came at the invitation of the Bandung lodge of the Theosophical Society in the Netherlands Indies and famously planted the Bodhi tree at Borobudur that is still central to the Waisek ceremony. As in the case of Chulalongkorn, Dutch archaeologists hosted him when he came to fulfil his Buddhist devotion at the temple, exchanging various forms of knowledge, and important material and non-material gifts.[11]

Rabindranath Tagore's trip to Java in 1927 offers another illustrative case of inter-Asian–European interaction and miscommunication. The internationally famous Indian poet, who was also extremely popular among Javanese and Sumatran nationalists, visited Java (and Bali) in 1927 at the private invitation of the Dutch colonial society, the Bond van Nederlandsch-Indische Kunstkringen (Association of Netherlands Indies Art Circles). This was part of Tagore's three-and-a half-month Southeast Asian tour during which he also visited Singapore, Malaya, and Siam. Although not strictly affiliated to the Greater India Society, Tagore's mindset during this tour was comparable. During a farewell meeting held for him by eminent Calcutta scholars, he mentioned that 'he was going on a pilgrimage to India beyond its modern political boundaries' and that he was eager to find 'what could be seen of the remains of ancient Indian culture'.[12]

According to Arun Das Gupta, who has made a study of Tagore's writings on this trip, Tagore believed that 'he was looking at India when he was walking along the galleries of Borobudur'.[13] While the temple as a whole

[11] On Narada's visit, see Iem Brown, 'Buddhist revival in modern Indonesia', in Martin Ramstedt (ed.), *Hinduism in modern Indonesia: a minority religion between local, national, and global interests* (London: Routledge, 2004), 49–51. On Nerada's gift exchange taking place in Batavia, see Bloembergen, 'Borobudur in "the light of Asia"'.

[12] Anrun Das Gupta, 'Rabindranath Tagore in Indonesian experience in bridge-building', *BKI* 158 (2002), 456. For Tagore's visit to Borobudur, see also Ramstedt, 'Colonial encounters', 527–528.

[13] Das Gupta, 'Rabindranath Tagore', 474.

Figure 7.2 Rabindranath Tagore at Borobudur, 1927.

did not impress him, Tagore was thrilled by what he called the temple's 'soul' and by the spirituality that characterised the time in which it was built (Figure 7.2). Tagore's letters reveal that he took special interest in the Jataka reliefs located at the lower terraces of the temple, which depicted episodes of the Buddha's previous lives. In those, he recognised the 'life of the king and the beggar in their daily appearances' and 'the respect for the life of common man'. He interpreted their message as the victory of the good and 'the liberation from the nodes that tie our lives from all sides'.[14] Borobudur's Jataka reliefs may have even been the main inspiration for the poem Tagore dedicated to the temple, quoted in the quotation at the beginning of this chapter.

Apparently, Tagore also brought with him a wider framework with which to value Borobudur, one that may have gone beyond the borders of Greater India to favour Buddhism and spiritualism in general. In the last verses of the poem about Borobudur, which he wrote while sitting on the porch of the *pasanggrahan* (rest house) facing the temple, Tagore reflected upon Borobudur as 'a gift' in itself to the people ('let the Buddha be my refuge') that offered shelter through the possibility of enlightenment. He suggested that this 'gift' had been disgracefully neglected – sensing thus fragility both of the temple and of humanity's spiritual state – and that it deserved to be restored to regain recognition for its original meaning of 'immeasurable love'. Apart from this poem inspired by the temple, other important exchanges took place between Tagore and his Dutch colonial hosts through Borobudur, exchanges of academic, technical, and spiritual knowledge. Tagore was deeply impressed by the work done by the archaeologists and epigraphists of the Archaeological Service. He apparently remarked about the Dutch archaeologists P. V. van Stein Callenfels and F. D. K. Bosch (then respectively the inspector and head of the Archaeological Service) who accompanied him to and informed him about Borobudur as well as other temples on Java including nearby Prambanan (which was under reconstruction): 'They have dedicated their lives to making the dumb figures speak . . . we must accept them as our Gurus, if we would understand India in its completeness.'[15]

In other words, it was impossible to appreciate Borobudur without understanding its Indian connection – a line of thought that repeatedly returned in the history of Borobudur's transformation into heritage during the colonial and post-colonial era. Note that this line of thought has never caused a serious

[14] Letter from Tagore, 17 November 1927, Leiden University Library, Special Collections, KITLV Collection, KITLV, H 1214. Tagore's four 'Letters from Java' (which included Bali) were published in English in *Visva-Bharati Quarterly* 5:4 (January 1928), 323–328; 6:1 (April 1928), 1–13; 6:2 (July 1928), 169–178; 6:3 (October 1928), 273–280. They were translated into Dutch by one of Tagore's travel companions in Java and Bali, the Dutch Sanskritist and musicologist Arnold A. Bake, and published, in 1929, in the (bilingual: Dutch and Malay) cultural journal *Oedaya* which was set up by the Javanese poet and admirer of Tagore, Noto Soeroto. See Rabindranath Tagore, 'Brieven, geschreven gedurende de Javaansche reis 1', transl. A. A. Bake, *Oedaya* 6:9 (September 1929); 'Brieven, geschreven gedurende de Javaansche reis 2', *Oedaya* 6:10 (October 1929), 133–135; 'Brieven, geschreven gedurende de Javaansche reis 3', *Oedaya* 6:12 (December 1929), 190–193. *Oedaya* also published a Dutch translation (by Noto Soeroto) of Tagore's poem 'To Java': Rabindranath Tagore, 'Aan Java', *Oedaya* 4:11 (November 1927), 138.

[15] Das Gupta, 'Rabindranath Tagore', 474; see also letter by Tagore, 17 November 1927, Leiden University Library, Special Collections, KITLV Collection, KITLV, H 1214.

problem in the question of ownership, a fact indicating that state interests in and state control of the site are strong. However, that is not to say that the state determines everything.

Saving Borobudur: a Modern Indonesian Concern?

The inauguration of the reconstructed Siva temple at Prambanan in December 1953 launched post-independence Indonesian archaeological heritage politics. Apart from pride in the great buildings of the pre-colonial past, the Indonesian Republic had also inherited colonial anxieties over loss, in particular with regard to Borobudur's decay, which had also started to concern the Dutch Colonial Archaeological Service only two decades after Van Erp's major restoration of the temple. In 1946, Soekmono had pronounced Borobudur 'Poesaka Indonesia, poesaka tanah air kita', an heirloom of the young Indonesian republic, in both a spiritual and a material sense, inherited from the ancestors of the Indonesian people.[16] Borobudur's decay – the result of weathering and internal humidity – thus likewise caused concerns during the years of revolution, enough for the republican government to seek a solution. Here again, nationalist concerns proactively included Indian interests. In 1948, just after Indian independence and anticipating old British Indian expertise in temple conservation, the newly founded Dinas Purbakala invited two young Indian experts from the Indian Department of Archaeology to investigate and estimate if, and how urgently, Borobudur should undergo a second restoration.[17] Looking back in his farewell speech at the University of Indonesia in 1990, Dinas Purbakala head Soekmono identified this moment as a major step for what he called typical Indonesian 'rescue archeology'. The fact that the young Indonesian Republic took this step in the midst of armed struggles was, according to him, convincing proof that 'the Indonesian people' even 'under the toughest conditions' would take care of their own cultural heritage.[18]

Even as early as 1955, however, Soekmono approached UNESCO for advice on the weathering of monuments in Java and Bali. This resulted in a diagnosis: as Borobudur is built around a hill, water coming from the inside (effectively

[16] Soekmono, 'Kepentingan leloehoer nenek moyang kita', *Pantja Raja* 1:6 (1946), 149–150. We thank Marijke Klokke for this reference.

[17] K. R. Srinivasan, 'Barabudur. A report on its conditions in 1949. In two parts. Submitted to Government of India, Ministery of Education' (1950), typescript (Leiden University Library); S. Sivaramamurti, *Le stupa du Barabadur* (Paris: Presses universitaires de France, 1961).

[18] R. Soekmono, 'Archeologie zoals die beoefend wordt in Indonesië', Inaugural Lecture, Leiden University, 28 November 1986, 11; R. Soekmono, 'Langkah pemerintah tahun 1948 dalam bidang kepurbakalaan: Landasan untuk pengembangan arkeologi Indonesia', Departure Speech, University of Indonesia, 5 March 1990, 3. Copies of both are available at Leiden University Library.

groundwater) was the main cause of deterioration both through damp and by pushing the walls and bas-reliefs outwards – Belgian conservation expert Paul Coremans called it 'stone cancer' – but immediate action did not follow. Although the political turmoil and the introduction of President Soekarno's Guided Democracy and the subsequent economic decline at the end of the 1950s may explain in part this apparent reluctance to act, it was also a matter of technique and scale. The proposed solution was to dismantle (parts of) the monument in order to insert a modern drainage system. Despite violent political turmoil, Soekmono managed to convince two successive Indonesian regimes to invest in Borobudur. In 1963, the Indonesian government allotted funding for the restoration: bamboo scaffolding arose and work was started on the north-western side of Borobudur. This work was interrupted – but not cancelled – by the pre-empted 1965 communist coup, and the mass killings that followed.[19] Conservation practices on the site apparently survived the violence and even overcame Indonesia's chilly relations with UNESCO after – still under President Soekarno – Indonesia's withdrawal from the United Nations in January 1965, and subsequently from UNESCO in February 1965. This may have been due to the combination of moral motives – conservation was politically useful for (new) regimes in need of legitimation – and technical motives that are involved in heritage formation. After all, one does not stop work in the middle of 'a heart transplant' as Dutch archaeologist Bernet-Kempers put it, and Van Erp Jnr, too, indicated that the job was 'risky'.[20] In this way heritage sites generate moral dynamics that are not necessarily related to state interests.

In July 1966 a new Indonesian regime headed by General Soeharto and proclaiming itself the New Order, cancelled Indonesia's withdrawal from the United Nations, and thus could collaborate again with UNESCO. This occurred in the aftermath of the extremely violent period in Indonesia's history that followed the coup of 30 September 1965, when in a repressive campaign at least 500,000 people were killed and around 1,500,000 others imprisoned (the precise number of victims is uncertain).[21] The New Order, while continuing to repress all political criticism, opened up for international economic investment.

19 For the technical details of the restoration, see I Gusti Nyoman Anom, *The restoration of Borobudur* (Paris: UNESCO, 2005), 57–58. Rumour has it that this early endeavour of conserving the temple was troubled more by illegal sales and financial mismanagement than by political upheaval: (Roger) Yong Djiet Tann to Van Erp Jnr, 5 March 1969, Leiden University Library, Special Collections, KITLV Collection, KITLV, Archive Van Romondt, inv. nr 27.

20 Bernet Kempers to Yudhishthir Raj Isar, Division of Cultural Heritage, UNESCO, 20 March 1977, UNESCO, CLT/CH/80, Campagne de Borobudur – exposition – ceremonie de cloture, 1976–1984.

21 Figures here are based on Adrian Vickers, *A history of modern Indonesia* (Cambridge: Cambridge University Press, 2005). See also John Roosa, *Pretext for mass murder: the September 30th Movement and Suharto's coup d'état in Indonesia* (Madison: University of Wisconsin Press, 2006).

Soekmono's warning that 'Borobudur is in danger' became an important tool for the New Order cultural diplomacy that accompanied the new economic policies.

In August 1967, at the 27th International Congress of Orientalists in Ann Arbor, one of the world's most prestigious academic meetings of orientalists (established in Paris in 1873), Soekmono's warning call about Borobudur's fate triggered worries and moral concerns for Borobudur – anxieties over loss – among the international academic community.[22] In the following year, in the framework of the United Nations Development Programme, two foreign technical experts, the French archaeologist Bernard Philippe Groslier, director of the Conservatoire d'Angkor in Cambodia, and C. Voûte, a Dutch hydrogeologist at the Aerial Service and Earth Sciences in the Netherlands, studied Borobudur on site.[23] This mission was part of an enlargement of the scale and instrumental repertoire of UNESCO's programme for the preservation of cultural heritage, which it had initiated in the 1950s and which was now also aimed at international technical training missions for stone conservation. This was one of thirty-three conservation and restoration missions UNESCO had sent around the world since January 1965, and thus, as a world map in the *UNESCO Courier* of 30 July 1968 indicated, Borobudur became part of another moral and potentially political map: UNESCO's map of world heritage management.[24]

These national and international initiatives relating to Borobudur's fate were all preparatory steps to the resolution, submitted by Indonesia at the 15th session of the General Conference of UNESCO on 30 July 1968 and endorsed by UNESCO's director-general, noting 'the importance of the monument of Borobudur . . . as part of the culture and historical heritage' (without indicating whose) and urging UNESCO 'to consider all effective measures, including an international campaign, to collect funds necessary to restore this artistic heritage'.[25] Taken together, these various preparatory steps – all moral and material investments – had moved Borobudur to the centre of an international web that tied multi-centred moral and economic concerns and obligations (that did not necessarily overlap) and Cold War cultural diplomatic interests to (Indonesian, Dutch, Japanese, and French) colonial legacies. We start with one apparently 'new' perspective which we have not yet discussed: Japanese financial and technical support for the UNESCO-promoted endeavour at

[22] Anom, *The Restoration of Borobudur,* 58; Denis Sinor (ed.), *Proceedings of the 27th International Congress of Orientalists, 13th–19th August 1967* (Wiesbaden: Otto Harrassowitz, 1971), 414–415.

[23] Anom, *The Restoration of Borobudur,* 58.

[24] Hiroshi Daifuku, 'Saving our heritage in stone: a world-wide challenge', *UNESCO Courier* (June 1968), 6.

[25] UNESCO, *Sessions of the General Conference* 1968, 15 C/DR 66, 30 July 1968.

Borobudur was remarkably large. This patronage built on older Japanese interests in fitting this heritage in the context of Japan-based pan-Asian thinking and propaganda going back to the Japanese occupation and the pre-war era.

Japanese Heritage Propaganda and Private Curiosity in Java

A 1943 Japanese newsreel shows the official visit of Field Marshal Hisaichi Terauchi to Borobudur accompanied by military officials. First, they view the so-called unfinished Buddha, posing under the large kenari trees in front of the south-west corner of the temple (where Van Erp had placed this statue, after deciding that it could not have originated from the main *stupa*). Then they visit the temple itself. The final shot shows another of the many Buddha statues, placed in a niche of the temple. Remarkably, the statue is not headless, as many are in the other niches; high commander Hitoshi Imamura was apparently horrified by the headless Buddha statues at Borobudur.[26] We do not know exactly what motivated the Japanese military officials who visited Borobudur in 1942–1943, but considering the wider context, there are some possible clues. What do wartime heritage engagements in Indonesia reveal in the framework of pan-Asianism and Japanese Great East Asian co-prosperity politics after 1900?

In recent years, pan-Asianism as it developed in various locations in Asia has received much scholarly attention.[27] This movement, which also connected with notions of a Greater India, developed conceptualisations of Asia that stressed earlier cultural links between societies in the region, and provided an alternative to processes of state formation there. The Japan-based pan-Asianism around 1900 was also multi-form, with imperialist strains as well as inclusive and egalitarian ideologies of 'fellow Asians' who had been exploited by other cultures. It was only later that it was co-opted for military purposes.[28]

The visit by Japanese officials to Borobudur was not coincidental. Before the occupation, Japanese military, high officials, academics, and artists had already

[26] C. L. Damais to Claire Holt, 27 September 1945, EFEO Jakarta, Letters of C. L. Damais.

[27] For recent overviews on India- and Japan-centred Pan-Asianism, see Stolte and Fischer-Tiné, 'Imagining Asia in India'; Sven Saaler and Christopher W. A. Szpilman (eds.), *Pan-Asianism: a documentary history*, vol. I, *1850–1920*, vol. II, *1920–Present* (Lanham: Rowman & Littlefield, 2011). See also Cemil Aydin, *The politics of anti-Westernism in Asia: visions of world order in pan-Islamic and pan-Asian thought* (New York: Columbia University Press, 2007); Prasenjit Duara, 'Asia redux: conceptualizing a region for our times', *JAS* 69:4 (2010), 963–983; Mark, '"Asia's" transwar lineage'; Katzenstein and Shiraishi (eds.), *Network power*; Sven Saaler, 'Pan-Asianism in Meiji and Taishô Japan: a preliminary framework', working paper (Tokyo: Philipp Franz von Siebold Stiftung, Deutsches Institut für Japanstudien, 2002); Saaler and Koschmann (eds.), *Pan-Asianism in modern Japanese history*.

[28] Saaler, 'Pan-Asianism in Meiji and Taishô Japan', 9; Shunsuke Tsurumi, *An intellectual history of wartime Japan, 1931–1945* (London: Routledge, 1986), 33–34.

shown their interest in Java and in the site in particular. As early as the 1910s Japanese intellectual-politicians such as historian-journalist Yosaburo Takekoshi (visiting Java in 1910) and intellectual propagandist Yusuke Tsurumi (visiting Java in 1917), included Java in their interest in 'Nanshin ron' (the doctrine legitimising Japan's interest in the south) and what they saw as the 'region of the south'.[29] When biologist and historian Marquis Yoshichika Tokugawa, heir of a branch of the Tokugawa family, visited Borobudur on a journey around Java in 1921, he encountered Miura Hidenosoke, a pupil from the Tokyo School of Fine Arts, who had made a thorough study of the temple and of the story of its reliefs published by the Tokyo-based Borobudur Publishing Association in 1925.[30] Enchanted by Borobudur since his first visit in 1918, the spiritual teacher Susume Ijiri preceded him: he too published a short study of Borobudur's reliefs, in 1924,[31] and founded the Borobudur Society in Osaka in 1938. Accordingly, this society attracted leading figures from the literary, academic, financial, and military worlds. The personal mission of Ijiri to spread the spiritual message of 'learning' that he encountered in Borobudur in 1918, like the other individual journeys and travel accounts, may have helped to enlarge the knowledge of Borobudur among higher circles in Osaka.[32] In January 1934, the Japanese general Seishiro Itagaki, who as supreme commander of the Japanese army had led the Japanese occupation of Manchuria, visited Borobudur, during a short stay on Java (on his way to Europe). In October 1935, a group of seventy-eight Japanese, among them professors, students, and journalists, made a four-day trip to Java, during which they too visited Borobudur.[33]

During the occupation, Japan continued some of the important activities of the Dutch Colonial Archaeological Service on Javanese Hindu and Buddhist remains. But they were dependent on Dutch scholars whom they had interned and, in August 1942, as we saw in Chapter 6, chose to release some, including Willem Stutterheim. Stutterheim, who died a month afterward of a brain tumour, left a 'Report on the upkeep and repairs (restoration) of Old Javanese monuments', addressing the problem of restoration during wartime in general, advising the continuation works at the Siva temple alone because (among other reasons) the expertise was still there.[34]

[29] Iguchi, 'Introduction about the author, the book, and the historical background', lvii; Barak Kushner, *The thought war: Japanese imperial propaganda* (Honolulu: University of Hawai'I Press, 2006), 35–38.

[30] Hidenosoke Miura, *Java Busekki Borubudur Kaisetsu* (Tokyo: Tokyo School of Fine Arts, Borobudur Kakōkai, 1925); Tokugawa, *Marquis Tokugawa: Journeys to Java* (Bandung: ITB Press, 2004), 195 and 201.

[31] Susume Ijiri, *Baraboedoer* (Shanghai: Aoki Bunkyō, 1924).

[32] See more on Susume Ijiri below, pp. 250–252.

[33] *De Indische Courant*, 16 January 1934; 14 October 1935.

[34] *OV 1941–1947* (1949), 49–50.

On the local level, archaeological and preservation activities in Java were officially supported by the Japanese administration. However, these activities did not fall under the Japanese Ministry of Foreign Affairs, as they did elsewhere in occupied Asia, which suggests that these were primarily a matter of private and personal interests. This confirms the general interpretation provided by the Japanese historian-archaeologist Sakazume Hideichi that official state co-prosperity archaeology was implemented only in the countries Japan had earlier colonised (Korea, Manchuria, Taiwan). These projects generally stagnated around 1940. In Southeast Asia, archaeological excavations were nonetheless initiated but because of private interests.[35] In addition, we offer an alternative reason for Java, namely, the takeover by the Japanese military regime of the local institutions and administrative structure of heritage politics left by the previous colonial government.[36] The Archaeological Service continued to exist, but was now manned exclusively by Indonesians and under Japanese direction. The service fell under Bunkyo Kyoku (Department of Education) in Djakarta.

As an example of the extent to which private initiatives mattered, in the autumn of 1943 a Japanese civil servant, Yasujiro Furusawa, a scholar of English literature attached to the Japanese military government in Magelang (Central Java, near Borobudur) as officer for cultural affairs, started an archaeological excavation at the southeast corner of Borobudur on his own initiative. During his first visit to the temple, Furusawa had learned about the 'hidden hell scenes' of Borobudur from an old local inhabitant who claimed to have worked for the Van Erp restoration.[37] This triggered his curiosity and, after a failed attempt to excavate at the site, he visited the Architectural Office of the former Dutch colonial Archaeological Service located at Prambanan, where he discovered that in 1890 Dutch engineer J. W. IJzerman had uncovered all 160 hidden reliefs. Moreover, the Javanese photographer Kassian Cephas, attached to the court of the sultan of Yogyakarta, had photographed them all, after which for technical reasons they had been covered again. Furusawa wished to see these reliefs, which, it was known by then, depicted in carved images the content of the Indian text *Karmawibhanggha*, showing the earthly life and the lessons of karma, or the laws of cause and effect. In a second effort, Furusawa excavated two reliefs and a hitherto unknown inscription (Figure 7.3). Assisted, albeit under protest, by Indonesian servants of the office of the Archaeological Service at Prambanan, he arranged for these to remain on display for visitors – and,

35 Hideichi, *Taiheiyou sensou*.

36 The particularities of the administrative structure of heritage politics may also explain the differences between the Japanese heritage activities in the Indonesian archipelago and those in Vichy Indochina.

37 Fontein, *The law of cause and effect in ancient Java*, 8.

Figure 7.3 Excavation of the hidden foot by Furusawa Yasujiro, 1943.

notably, they still are.[38] News and Japanese theorising on the background of the hidden foot featured in the Malay-language propaganda journal *Kita-Sumatoro-Sinbun: Soerat Kabar Harian* in February 1944.[39]

Apart from the archaeological interventions at Borobudur and the Siva temple, there are indications that the Japanese military regime maintained the heritage institutions in Java and that it prompted research and excavation projects related to 'Indonesia' with great interest. (Recall that Furusawa, as the Japanese head of the office in Prambanan, occupied himself with the translation into Japanese of Krom's classic *Inleiding tot de Hindoe-Javaansche geschiedenis*.)[40] In 1942, when the Dutch, Indies-born architect Henri Maclaine Pont was still actively investigating the site of the thirteenth–fourteenth century Hindu–Buddhist Majapahit empire in Trowulan in East Java, the commander of East Java visited the site six times. Imamura himself

[38] *OV 1941–1947* (1949), 22; Soekmono, 'Sedikit riwayat. 50 years archaeological research', in Satyawati Suleiman, Rumbi Mulia, Nies Anggraeni and F. X. Supandi (eds.), *50 Tahun Lembaga Purbakala dan Peninggalan Nasional 1913–1963* (Jakarta: Proyek Pelita Pembinaan Kepurbakalaan dan Peninggalan Nasional, Dept. P & K., 1977), 12; Daigoro Chihara, 'Busseki Borobudōru hinzū Jawa no kenchiku geijutsu', *Hara Shobō* (1969); Hideichi, *Taiheiyou sensou*.

[39] 'Keterangan baroe tentang Borobodoer', *Kita-Sumatoro-Sinbun: Soerat Kabar Harian*, 12 February 1944.

[40] See also Chapter 6, n. 33.

came along as well, personally stressing the importance of these works 'for the development of an Indonesian architecture' – incidentally, the same motive that inspired Maclaine Pont in his lifelong heritage engagements in Trowulan.[41] However, this particular site also provides counter-evidence that economic interests could become more important than heritage concerns. In 1943, the year after Maclaine Pont was interned, the head of the Archaeological Service's Office in Jakarta, Kayashima, ordered the auction of part of his private collection of Majapahit antiquities. Some important pieces were sold and disappeared.[42]

The Hindu–Buddhist material remains in Java were also useful for propaganda aims. A picture in the propaganda journal *Djawa Baroe* shows Heiho recruits (Indonesian auxiliary soldiers) posing before Borobudur.[43] A pamphlet of 1942, distributed in Batavia, spoke about the Asian unity in a distant past when all Asian peoples were one, called Tayio Minzoku (People of the Sun).[44] These people, according to the pamphlet, left many material traces, such as the pyramids in Egypt, the temples in Angkor, the Thaitong temple in West China, and Borobudur. Nowadays, according to the pamphlet, the people of Asia were divided partly as a result of colonialism, but the old grandeur was about to return under Japanese guidance. This is a clear example of how Greater Asian thought – or pan-Asianism – could be given an imperialistic tinge.

Continuities in Japanese Heritage Engagements in Indonesia

The long-term continuities and discontinuities in Japanese heritage engagements in Java seem to be ignored in public, as if today there is no public memory in Japan and Indonesia with regard to the Japanese archaeological intervention during the Japanese occupation. But when we take a closer look, we find traces – in literature, in discussions with archaeologists, and on location. The UNESCO restoration in the 1970s added two reliefs to the two of the hidden foot that Furusawa had uncovered. Moreover, today Borobudur sits in a national park, the PT Taman Wisata Borobudur, a result of the master plan for the post-restoration phase that the Japan International Cooperation Agency

41 Maclaine Pont to Van der Hoop, 28 kujaten 2602 [28 September 1942], ANRI, KBG DIR 1097.

42 BP3, East Java, Trowulan, *Laporan tentang ambruknya museum purbakala di Trowulan* (Lampiran dari laporan tahunan 1966–1967).

43 'Oentoek kemerdekaan jg. penoeh kehormatan', *Djawa Baroe*, 1 June 1945. This picture was also used to provoke anti-Indonesian sentiments, with the description: 'Een kamikaze of zelfmoordbataljon van kinderen van 14–16 jaar, met de Boroboedoer op de achtergrond [A kamikaze or suicide battalion of children aged between 14–16, in front of Borobudur]'. See W. K. H. Feuilletau de Bruyn, *Welk aandeel heeft Dr van Mook gehad in de gezagsschemering in Nederlandsch-Indië?* (The Hague: Van Stockum, 1946).

44 I. J. Brugmans (ed.), *Nederlandsch-Indië onder Japanse bezetting: gegevens en documenten over de jaren 1942–1945* (Franeker: Wever, 1960), 178–179.

(JICA), in collaboration with the Indonesian government, developed during the 1970s. This park hosts a site museum that displays Kassian Cephas' 1890s photographs of the complete series of reliefs of the hidden foot, as well as a brief overview of the history of Borobudur's conservation since its public rediscovery during the British regime in 1814 by Lieutenant Governor-General T. S. Raffles. While Japanese material signs are therefore clearly visible at Borobudur, *in* the Karmawibhanggha museum itself there is also an apparent silence on the subject: there is no mention of the Japanese excavation of the hidden foot during the Pacific War.[45]

Regarding the motif of 'loss', Hideichi offers an intriguing comment on the intervention over the hidden foot (in the study of Japanese archaeology during the Pacific War mentioned above, available only in Japanese). 'Up to today people can visit the part of the hidden foot, as Furusawa had excavated it, and it looks still the same. Nowadays many Japanese people visit Borobudur. In the south-eastern corner, they view both the old and the new hidden foot. Only a few people know that this can be done thanks to a Japanese who was a civil servant there from March 1942 during the Japanese military regime.'[46] Hideichi thus represents the Japanese intervention at Borobudur as a kind of gift, especially to contemporary Japanese visitors to Indonesia.

To what extent can the atmosphere of (or anxiety over) 'loss' due to decolonisation explain the remarkable post-war Japanese engagements in international heritage formation, including in Indonesia, in the context of the UNESCO Save Borobudur campaign? To what extent can we see long-term continuities in the cultural political or idealist framing of these activities?[47] We came across two individuals who may provide some important clues: the spiritual teacher Susume Ijiri (1892–1965) and the architect Daigoro Chihara (1916–1997), a graduate of Kyoto Imperial University (1941). As individuals, they provide motives for heritage engagements with Borobudur for the transformative periods *into* and *out of* the war.

45 This, while a 1970s report of the international technical advisory meeting for the UNESCO Save Borobudur campaign confirms that some parties involved knew that this part of the foot had been uncovered through a Japanese intervention. See 'Verslag van een dienstreis naar Indonesië door A. J. Bernet-Kempers, 13 januari–1 februari 1971', Leiden University Library, Special Collections, KITLV Collection, KITLV, H 1045. Not accidentally, this meeting included Bernet Kempers (former head of the Dutch Colonial Archaeological Service (1946–1949), and of the Indonesian Dinas Purbakala (1950–1954)), and the Japanese architect Daigoro Chihara, who worked in Java during the Japanese occupation. Another Japanese architect, who played a leading role in the development of the JICA plan (1973–1979) and who knew Chihara well, told us that he had 'no idea' of Japanese archaeological activities during the Japanese occupation, nor of the uncovering of Borobudur's hidden foot in wartime: interview, Marieke Bloembergen with Yasuhiro Iwasaki, Jakarta, 26 June 2012.

46 Hideichi, *Taiheiyou sensou*.

47 Compare Aki Toyoyama, 'Perceptions of Buddhist heritage in Japan', in Patrick Daly and Tim Winter (eds.), *Routledge handbook of heritage in Asia* (London and New York: Routledge, 2012), 339–349.

Borobudur completely enchanted Susume Ijiri from his first encounter in 1918. The Dutch Archaeological Service, particularly its head N. J. Krom, guided him to the relevant academic studies and interpretations for his book on the Borobudur's construction and reliefs.[48] But more important to Susume Ijiri was what he saw and felt while contemplating Borobudur. Somewhat akin to the Indian poet Tagore's sentiment a decade later, Susume Ijiri felt the temple was spiritually alive and carried an important moral message to mankind: to live well meant to arrive at the learning, imperfect state of the bodhisattva, which he found symbolised by Borobudur's main *stupa*, and the 'unfinished' Buddha that Van Erp had moved from the *stupa* to the entrance road.[49] Back in Japan, Susume Ijiri started on a personal mission to live according to these 'universal' spiritual and moral lessons, and to disseminate these ideas. Through his lectures at the Borobudur Society, he built a reputation as a Borobudur expert in higher official and military circles; at the same time, Borobudur itself apparently had gained status in Japan. According to family lore, this was why in 1941 one of the influential people who had attended Ijiri's lectures, naval minister and admiral Koshiro Oikawa, invited him to speak at the navy headquarters in Tokyo. There, accordingly, Susume Ijiri advised the admiral to make sure that during the war on Java the Hindu–Buddhist material remains would not be harmed – advice that Oikawa subsequently transmitted to the Japanese military regime in Java.[50]

After the war, the Borobudur Society revived in Himeji, where Susume Ijiri settled. In 1956 he located a 'Borobudur' hill there, mirroring the sacred site in Central Java, and still being honoured by members of the society. Near this hill his son, Masuro Ijiri, set up a museum. One room is dedicated to (the study of) Borobudur, displaying Susume Ijiri's books, drawings, and other Borobudur publications, above all those of Krom, whom father and son Ijiri came to honor greatly.

The engineer Daigoro Chihara personally connects Japan's imperial wartime and post-war interests in Java-based Hindu–Buddhist temple sites. According to his CV, Chihara was posted in occupied Java as 'director' of the ITB.[51]

[48] Ijiri, *Baraboedoer*. In the bibliography of his own magnus opus on Borobudur, Krom describes Ijiri's study as a summary of his own work. See Krom and Van Erp, *Beschrijving van Barabudur, Part II*, 151.

[49] Interview, Marieke Bloembergen and Martijn Eickhoff with Yuko Ijiri, Leiden, 25 April 2012.

[50] This information is partly derived from a reprint of Ijiri's work on Borobudur. See Susume Ijiri, *Barabudur* (Tokyo: Chukko-bunko, 1989). We thank Matty Forrer for leading us to this source, and for a first translation, Leiden, February 2012. It was generously elaborated by Ijiri's son Masuro Ijiri, Himeji, March 2012; and by his granddaughter, Yuko Ijiri, Leiden, 24 May 2012, and in an additional e-mail, 19 June 2012. Photographs of the late 1930s in the museum in Himeji display a close, friendly relationship between Susume Ijiri and Koshiro Oikawa.

[51] International symposium Borobudur, *International symposium on Chandi Borobudur: 'Religious art of Borobudur and its preservation'* (Kyoto: Executive Committee for the International Symposium on Chandi Borobudur etc., 25–27 September 1980), 101.

During that time he got to know Borobudur, visited other regions in Southeast Asia, and began to study the Hindu–Buddhist architecture across the region.[52] After the war he continued his Southeast Asia-based architectural research, which resulted in a PhD in 1967 (from Kyoto University), and in the publication, in 1996, of *Hindu–Buddhist architecture in Southeast Asia*.[53] Chihara looked at Borobudur with a Greater Asia framework in mind.[54] Today Daigoro Chihara is known in expert circles in Japan and Indonesia for his involvement in the UNESCO Save Borobudur campaign. In 1971, at the invitation of UNESCO and the Indonesian government, he became a member of the International Consultative Committee. For a variety of technical reasons and restoration 'keep as found' ethics, this team decided that the hidden foot should retain its surrounding wall, and that a site museum should inform the visitors about it.[55]

Chihara clearly became intrigued by the Japanese archaeological interventions during the war. In the 1980s he investigated the case of Furusawa's excavations at the hidden foot, published on it, and found the photo of Furusawa in action at Borobudur (Figure 7.3).[56] He also explored Susume Ijiri's connections to Borobudur. Intriguingly, he also befriended the Dutch archaeologist August Bernet Kempers.[57] Apparently, to Chihara, Borobudur was not only a fascinating example of Asian art and architecture, but also a means to connect to 'lost' engagements with Borobudur – in the past and in the present. Susume Ijiri and Daigoro Chihara illustrate two closely connected motives in Japan-based interests in Borobudur that guided these men's queries before, during, and after the war – the spiritual motive and its material manifestations. These were motives that made them follow paths on which their knowledge production could provide legitimation for co-prosperity appropriation of of 'overseas' heritage.

Interestingly, both motives – the 'spiritual' and the 'material' – also seem to form the main components of post-war Japanese involvement in international

52 'The achievements of Dr Daigoro Chihara', English summary of the short biography in 'The list of the Dr Daigoro Chihara library' at the Japan Center for International Cooperation in Conservation (JCICC), Tokyo.

53 Daigoro Chihara, *Hindu–Buddhist architecture in Southeast Asia*, transl. from Japanese by Rolf W. Giebel (Leiden: Brill, 1996).

54 On the basis of his library, now kept at the JCICC in Tokyo, we may conclude that he was an eager student of the relevant international scholarly works, including those of Dutch colonial scholars such as Krom, that, typically for the 1920s and 1930s were all – also – dealing with the nature of previous connections and civilisational influencing between mainland and island Asia.

55 'Verslag van een dienstreis naar Indonesië door A. J. Bernet-Kempers, 13 januari–1 februari 1971', Leiden University Library, Special Collections, KITLV Collection, KITLV, H 1045.

56 Diagoro Chihara, 'Borobudur monogatari III: Borobudur to Nihon-jin', *Wafu-Kenchiku* 17 (1983), 126–133.

57 After his return to the Netherlands in 1957, Bernet Kempers became director of the Dutch open-air museum in Arnhem, continuing to be an authority on Indonesian archaeology and conservation politics in Java and Bali, and was deeply engaged with Borobudur's fate.

Asia-based heritage projects, including those in Indonesia. This post-war Japanese involvement with Asia-based heritage politics accorded very well with UNESCO's international politics, also determined by the awareness of cruelties and losses through war, of regaining peace through education and cultural heritage restoration and conservation. Apparently, the Japan–UNESCO 'match' was so effective that Japan has played a key role within UNESCO up to today;[58] Japan was responsible for 22 per cent of UNESCO's 'general budget', and positions itself as the Maecenas of monumental care in post-conflict countries in Southeast Asia.[59] Considering the international and ASEAN (Association of Southeast Asian Nations)-based meetings on heritage politics in Asia, as well as the inter-Asian training programmes in conservation techniques that took place at Borobudur in the 1980s and 1990s, Borobudur may have become instrumental in an 'Asian' way of heritage policies with ambiguous colonial legacies.[60] The framework of the UNESCO-supported restoration interventions at Borobudur may help us view the multiple exchanges, and some of the great losses, that the various parties in this chapter were involved in. In this process, the (old) Dutch care of the temple became almost irrelevant in the light of Greater Asian views, of fresh and acute New Order political and economic interests, and of likewise 'actual' local engagements that all played roles in the efforts to keep or obtain a temple. The process of restoration involving worldwide engagements dramatically changed the outlook of the temple and the ways it became situated in the landscape, silencing difficult pasts and difficult presents.

Reinventing a Temple, Losing Local Horizons, 1970s–1980s

On 10 August 1973, at the inauguration of the immense, expensive, ten-year-long international campaign to safeguard Borobudur which had been

58 This despite the threat by the Japanese Ministry of Foreign Affairs to hold back its funding, temporarily, following a protest against the listing of documents related to the Nanjing massacre of 1937–1938; see www.theguardian.com/world/2016/oct/14/japan-halts-unesco-funding-nanjing-massacre-row; www.reuters.com/article/us-japan-unesco/japan-pays-funds-for-unesco-after-halt-over-nanjing-row-with-china-idUSKBN14B095?il=0</u> (accessed 3 August 2018).

59 Kawada Tsukasa and Nao Hayashi-Denis, 'Cooperation between UNESCO and Japan in the safeguarding of cultural heritage', *Museum International* 56:4 (2004), 32–39. Compare Toyoyama, 'Perceptions of Buddhist heritage in Japan', and Natsuko Agawa, *Heritage conservation and Japan's cultural diplomacy: heritage, identity and national interest* (London: Routledge, 2015). The Asia-based heritage projects in Cambodia, Afghanistan, and Padang undertaken by the international section of Nara National Research Institute for Cultural Properties under the Ministry of Foreign Affairs, are explicitly part of Japanese cultural diplomacy. Information kindly provided by Tomo Ishimura, Nara, 21 March 2012.

60 *Report of the ASEAN meeting of experts for formulating guidelines for archaeological field procedures and techniques: Borobudur* (Jakarta: Directorate General for Culture, Ministry of Education and Culture, 12–19 December 1995); Bloembergen and Eickhoff, 'Save Borobudur!'

co-ordinated and supervised by UNESCO, President Soeharto had the *national* meaning of this enterprise engraved in stone, at Borobudur. In this inscription, Soeharto made the seven-year-old New Order regime the architect of safeguarding Borobudur and of an Indonesian national cultural heritage programme. Ten years later, on 23 February 1983, he announced the completion of this prestigious international collaboration project, echoing Soekarno's 1953 speech at Prambanan: 'With the restoration of Candi Borobudur we have managed to preserve the proof of the greatness of the Indonesian people of the past, the people that gave birth to Indonesian society and the Indonesian people of the present.'[61]

That the restoration of Borobudur was something all Indonesians cared about in the same proposed way is questionable. But one event that broke the spell for a moment took place within two years after the inauguration of the UNESCO restoration. On the night of 20 January 1985, a bomb attack at Borobudur caused damage to nine of Borobudur's seventy-two *stupa*, and international upheaval. In a public statement, Soeharto referred to the then still unidentified perpetrators as 'people that do not feel national pride, because Borobudur is a national monument, even more a monument of the world'.[62] The reasons for the attack, including its presumed religious motivations and the circumstances under which it took place, require further historical investigation.[63] But here we restrict ourselves to the likewise meaningful official public reaction of the Indonesian government. While the attacks sent shockwaves through the UNESCO headquarters in Paris and among its international members, the Indonesian government outwardly appeared to remain calm. By declining any assistance – a gift offered by UNESCO for the necessary restoration works – the government signalled to the international community that Indonesia could handle this problem itself. In the hands of the Indonesian government, the bomb attack was thus transformed from an internal threat into another occasion both to promote the campaigns of national safeguarding that were supported by the general Indonesian public and to avoid international interference in its internal affairs.[64] As remarkable as it may be that Japanese wartime involvement at Borobudur is invisible at the site today, the bomb attack is nowadays part of a completely neutralised and technical display in the Karmawibhangga museum, addressing causes of

[61] Speech, Soeharto, Borobudur, 23 February 1983, UNESCO, CLT/CH/78; 'Pemugaran bukan pekerjaan mewah', *Kedaulatan Rakyat*, 24 February 1983.

[62] 'Ledakan Malam di Borobudur', *Tempo*, 26 January 1985.

[63] On how the Indonesian government used the bomb attack to criminalise certain (Shi'a) Islamic groups, and represented the act itself as coming from 'outside', see Chiara Formichi, 'Violence, sectarianism, and the politics of religion: articulations of anti-Shi'a discourse in Indonesia', *Indonesia* 98 (2014), 9–10.

[64] UNESCO, CLT/CH/79.2. This file contains the international reactions (official and in the press), as well as UNESCO Press review, 25 January 1985.

deterioration and loss of the world's great monuments (weather, disasters, and bomb attacks).[65]

From the Indonesian government's perspective, Borobudur's safeguarding campaign was a highly moral national event. The international dimension of this mammoth project and the worldwide attention that it attracted only emphasised to the world, and thus to the Indonesian public, the prestige of Indonesia and of Soeharto's New Order. But the modern, trans-Asian, and global concern for the temple that pre-dated the New Order would remain strong at the site as well. Indeed, the fledgling UNESCO of the 1950s was built on pre-war, trans-Asian, and colonial engagements with the temple. That it was hard to maintain that the Great Borobudur Restoration was a truly and solely Indonesian investment for the Indonesian people can be seen on the back of yet another memorial stone at Borobudur. It shows the twenty-eight countries and eight private organisations that had also supported Borobudur's gigantic restoration. In 1969 a well-organised national and international propaganda campaign was launched, with official Save Borobudur stamps, cultural lobbyists, stone Buddhas, movies and exhibitions travelling around the world, and through a competition of honour and distinction, many national governments along with foreign private foundations dipped into their purses. While the UNESCO Save Borobudur campaign was clearly an international collaborative project, the contributions of the Netherlands and Japan, the two states that successively colonised the archipelago that now formed the Indonesian Republic, seemed to stand out in size and intensity.

A Japanese Master Plan and Local Agency

In February 1973, a statue of the Buddha travelled from Borobudur to Japan. It was the highlight of a national travelling exhibition that aimed to alert the Japanese public that 'one of the greatest achievements of Buddhist civilisation' was seriously threatened. This Japanese national Save Borobudur campaign was a Japanese success – for material, spiritual, moral, and diplomatic reasons. Japan, in the first preparatory phase of the restoration of Borobudur (1969–1972), contributed $1.8 million, while a private fund, the Commemorative Association of the World Exhibition (Osaka, 1974), would later add another $109,000. In 1973, at the request of the Indonesian government, JICA became responsible for the development of plans for the 'post-restoration' phase, which culminated in a twenty-year master plan for the construction of a Borobudur and Prambanan Archaeological Park. This was to be run by the government-owned PT Taman Wisata (Tourist Park) Borobudur and Prambanan. The master plan involved the development of a zoning system

[65] Site visit by Marieke Bloembergen and Martijn Eickhoff, 28 January 2009.

around Borobudur, marking widening circles around the temple with different levels of restrictions for the public and for local inhabitants. For this, Japan earmarked extra funding that would guarantee Japan's long-term engagement with Borobudur. In its ideal form this master plan – finished on paper in 1979 and enormous in size and ambition – breathed a mixture of 1970s optimism about the possibility of 'making' a better world, notions of (intangible, natural landscape) heritage, national economic entrepreneurship, and the New Order's need for political control.

Japan seemed especially interested in the religious aspect of the monument, for while the Indonesian government sought to emphasise the temple's neutrality, and would categorise it as a dead monument, JICA proposed to re-install Waisek (the Buddhist commemoration of the enlightenment and death of the Buddha, a re-invention in itself) as a regular annual event at Borobudur.[66] Also, anticipating the final phase of the actual restoration of the monument, Japanese parties who were involved in the project organised an international conference in Kyoto, in which Indonesian, Japanese, and Dutch archaeologists and art historians – including Chihara and Bernet Kempers – participated, and that focused on '*religious art* of Borobudur and its preservation' (our emphasis), whereas the Indonesian government wished to emphasise neutrality, making clear to UNESCO's Office of Public Information (OPI) that it considered 'Borobudur ... as a cultural heritage, and not as a place of worship.'[67] One other line of continuity is the master plan's civilising and spiritual mission, which posited that mere preservation of the monuments and their environment was not enough to effectively 'pass on the message of Borobudur and Prambanan' to future generations. Therefore, the monuments should be utilised as cultural and educational assets 'for the purpose of giving people at home and abroad a better understanding and appreciation of their part in Indonesia's

[66] Japan International Cooperation Agency, *The national archaeological parks development project. Borobudur and Prambanan: interim report* (Tokyo: JICA, 1975), 87. Waisek, reintroduced by theosophists at Borobudur in 1932, became a yearly event-cum-national holiday from 1984 onwards. As noted above, according to Article 21 of Law 1992, 5, concerning cultural properties, Borobudur falls under the category of 'dead monument': 'Items of cultural property which at the time of their discovery are no longer used in the manner for which they were originally intended are prohibited from being brought into use again' (Undang-Undang Republik Indonesia nomor 5 tahun 1992 tentang Benda Cagar Budaya, pasal 38). See also *Report of the ASEAN meeting of experts for formulating guidelines for archaeological field procedures and techniques: Borobudur.*

[67] Borobudur – comité executive, Eiji Hattori, OPI/ACP to ADG/PRS via deputy director OPI, 18 May 1982, UNESCO, CLT/CH/ 81. However, the Indonesian government's venture to neutralise Borobudur seems full of contradictions (or leniencies). An indication that the site was not neutral to the government was the offering of a *kerbau* (water buffalo) during the inauguration of the start of the restoration works in August 1973. Information provided by Henri Chambert-Loir (Jakarta, 1 February 2011). The emergence of two Buddhist monasteries was tolerated; one (Theravada) was developed near Mendut in the 1960s, the other (Mahayana), more recently, was near Borobudur.

cultural past'. In that regard, and intriguingly, the master plan also dwelt on a wider Asian concern, with scholarly pan-Asian references, most clearly expressed in the argument for the 'formation of an International Cultural Tourism City' in Central Java around the two monuments of Prambanan and Borobudur. The connection between them was 'Indian culture', 'from which the Hindu Java Culture was born' and which had had

> a great influence on China, Korea, and Japan to the north and the Indochina peninsula and Indonesia to the south, putting down roots there and fusing with indigenous cultures as an initiating element in the formation of the distinct culture of each area. In fact, the capitals of various countries were sister cities within what might be considered a great sphere of Indian cultures.[68]

The master plan declared that this 'treasure house of Hindu Java', once the centre of exchange with India, should 'again become a center for international exchanges for the purpose of conveying an accurate picture of twentieth-century Indonesian culture to international society'.[69]

Following the mechanisms Mauss described, the gift from 'PT Taman Wisata' entailed material investments in this plan by the Indonesian government and its Japanese partner,[70] as well as preservation of the cultural, spiritual heritage of Indonesia, Greater Asia, and humankind. The gift implied something tangible (economic development through cultural tourism) as well as something intangible: 'passing on the message from Prambanan and Borobudur' to Indonesia, wider Asia, and the world. It was, following Mauss, also a matter of creating obligations and of taking. The nationalising of the monument and the intention to turn it into a national sanctuary would entail reducing the space for Buddhist prayer (on the site) to the national holiday Waisek. State appropriation implied a promise to make the site economically and morally advantageous. But – as is always the question in heritage politics – advantageous to whom and in what sense?

It is important to note here that in all of the stages of the conservation programme and in the negotiations for the master plan, various local parties became actively involved in the campaign and, therefore, these local parties were potentially morally supportive (allied) to it as well. At the site, the gigantic operation was hosted and facilitated by the Indonesian Archaeological Service under the ever-energetic Soekmono. It involved staff and students from the Department of Archaeology at Gadjah Mada University in Yogyakarta, from the ITB in Bandung, and from Solo Saraswati University,

[68] Japan International Cooperation Agency, *Borobudur and Prambanan: final report* (Tokyo: JICA, 1979), 10.

[69] Ibid.

[70] These were formalised in 1982 by the Indonesian government and its Japanese partner, with the earmarking of US$ 150,000 to be used in the future maintenance of Borobudur and (among other things) its natural surroundings.

from international parties and trainees, and from an Indonesian–Philippines construction company. Last but not least, local residents around Borobudur (mostly male) found jobs at the restoration works or in a slowly burgeoning tourist industry; the number of tourists at Borobudur increased from about 5,000 a year at the end of the 1960s to more than 60,000 at the end of the 1970s. After conducting interviews at the site in 2011 we realised that the site's transformation had led not only to conflict but also to new engagements with the temple and its academic or archaeological status.[71] At least one man (and father) involved in the restoration project would come home, his son told us, with 'a book about Borobudur' and would narrate to his son the many stories in the reliefs. Another informant, the owner of one of the first hotels near the site, wrote about the temple – for tourists – by gathering information from Buddhist visitors from Italy and Tibet and consulting academic studies. A third became a photographer for the restoration project and still knew the reliefs by heart.[72]

One man from the area, the former air marshal and minister of communications and transport (1968–1973) Boediardjo, was chosen (probably for diplomatic reasons) as the first director of PT Taman Borobudur and Prambanan (1979–1985), and he operated as the recognisable face of an enterprise that envisioned land acquisition and relocation of complete villages.[73] It should be noted that the interests of the Archaeological Service (which fell under the responsibility of the Ministry of Education and Culture) and those of PT Taman Wisata (which fell under the Directorate-General of Tourism, then part of the Ministry of Transport and Communication) did not always overlap, nor would they in the future. But at this early stage the Archaeological Service, represented by Soekmono, and the PT Taman Wisata collaborated in a 'socialisasi' programme that would brief local residents about the plans for the area, and thus about their fate. According to the master plan, 1,330 of these residents would ultimately have to move to make way for the development of the Archaeological Park that now is Taman Wisata.[74]

The relocation programme for the residents and villages around Borobudur, offering to compensate residents for their land and homes, started at the

[71] See Dedi Supriadi Adhuri and Gutomo Bayu Aji, 'The hidden story of Borobudur', *Inside Indonesia* 125 (Jul.–Sep. 2016), www.insideindonesia.org/the-hidden-story-of-borobudur-2 (accessed 14 July 2017).

[72] Interviews, Marieke Bloembergen with Jack Prayono, Borobudur, 26 and 30 January 2011; with Atmojo and Rini, Seganan (near Borobudur), 27 January 2011; with Pak Tomo, Ngaran, 12 May 2012. See Ariswara, *Temples of Java* (Jakarta: Intermasa, 1992 (English, French, and Japanese)); Larissa, *The magnificence of Borobudur* (Jakarta: PT Gramedia Pustaka Utama, 1995 (English, French, and Japanese)).

[73] 'Dari Dukuh yang harus ditinggalkan', *Tempo*, 26 February 1983.

[74] Japan International Cooperation Agency, *Borobudur and Prambanan: Final Report* (Tokyo: JICA, 1979), 24. The picture is of space structure plan of the Borobudur Archaeological Park (zone 1 (sanctuary) and zone 2 (park)), in which the village compartments and market near the temple are already dislocated – as envisioned ibid.

beginning of 1981 and involved the *dusun* (hamlets) Kenayan, Ngaran, Gendingan, Gopolan, and Sabrangrowo. While many residents chose to move to a life that – as they informed the critical journal *Tempo* in 1983 – economically did not differ from their previous life, the inhabitants of Kenayan and Ngaran, the two *dusun* that were located closest to the temple, were unwilling to move.[75] In December 1982, less than two months before the inauguration of the completion of the temple, alarming news reached the headquarters of UNESCO (intriguingly, via Japan) that protest movements against the plans for a 'National Park' were to be expected on the inauguration day. About 100 families living within the 85 hectares around the temple would participate.[76] The protests did occur, but not during the festive and most strategic day of the inauguration. In the end, through a mixture of 'socialisasi' (which in this case meant that members of the Archaeological Service would visit and try to convince them that this was for their own good), a policy of intimidation, and accomplished facts (the relocation of the market, the turning off of the electricity), by 1984 these last hold-outs had to make way.

Looking at this relocation programme from the perspective of 'the gift' (of moral and economic goods plus a fixed price for the land, in return for the obligation to move and engage in traditional village development), for some local residents it was not just a question of having to leave their (supposedly ancestral) land, which had suddenly become much more profitable, but also of drifting away from their social life at the site and their various connections (including spiritual ones) to the temple, and of losing both the ability to enter the site freely and the opportunity to make offers at the nearby Waringin tree on the occasion of marriages or for specific (healing) aims at the main *stupa* of Borobudur. This uneven exchange created, moreover, new obligations (do not scratch or climb on the walls of Borobudur; do not trade on the site; do not build in the zones) and thus new debts to the parties that 'accepted' the exchange (what is in it for us?; what did we, the people of Borobudur, get from it?).

After the protests of the early 1980s, dissatisfaction would revive again in the post-Soeharto era of reformation and democratisation, which coincided with the ending of the first master plan of Borobudur and the formulation of a new one. During the post-Soeharto era the mechanisms of gifts, debts, and interdependencies still seem to function, and the conflicting concerns of the PT Taman Wisata and of the Indonesian Archaeological Research and Conservation Centre at the site, the various interests of multiple groups at

[75] 'Dari Dukuh yang harus ditinggalkan', *Tempo*, 26 February 1983.

[76] Eiji Hattori (Japanese philosopher and staff member of UNESCO) to Thet Tun, December 30, 1982, Paris, UNESCO, BRX/AFE/10 (Indonesia/Borobudur, 1972–1983).

location, of local and international mass tourism, and of (organised) pilgrimages from all over the world, still play their role in the development of the area, as well as in the multiple identifications with the temple.[77]

Dutch Colonial Legacies and Self-Indulgences

In comparison to the contributions of others – Japan, the United States, or India – the Dutch contribution to the Save Borobudur project was relatively modest (US$ 15,000, supplemented by US$ 122,000 dollars from the private foundation Stichting Behoud Borobudur (Foundation to Safeguard Borobudur)) – which were contributed in a bilateral way. However, the Netherlands also played an important role by offering technical assistance with the architectural bureau NEDECO, in charge of the development of the technical operation, and of the supervision of the works (which added US$ 155,000 to the Dutch contributions).[78] This technical 'supervising' gesture seemed typical of a small country that (still) overestimated its international role, a country, moreover, that – despite the recently fully completed decolonisation, at least in Asia, followed by the Indonesian takeover of New Guinea – remained blind to its colonial atavism, a not so subtle paternalistic attitude, precisely when it came to cultural diplomacy.

The Dutch engagements with the Save Borobudur programme paralleled Dutch–Indonesian negotiations about the restitution – 'return' as the Indonesians would phrase it, to the chagrin of the Dutch who spoke of 'transfer'– to Indonesia of some special treasures that were defined as important Indonesian heritage. These negotiations took place within the framework of the Cultural Agreement between the two countries, formalised in 1970. Among the important treasures that would be returned in the end were the fourteenth-century Javanese epic *Nagarakrtagama* (discussed in Chapter 3), parts of the so-called Lombok treasure, and the Prajnaparamita statue, in Indonesia thought to be a deified image of Ken Dedes, the first queen of the Singosari kingdom (East Java) – and in the Netherlands still referred to as 'the Mona Lisa of Java' – of which the Dutch at least understood that this had 'an enormous emotional value for the Indonesians', 'an almost sacred meaning'.[79]

77 For a rather positive evaluation of the local versus global profits in heritage politics at Borobudur, see Heather Black and Geoffrey Wall, 'Global–local relationships in UNESCO World Heritage Sites', in T. C. Chang and K. C. Ho (eds.), *Interconnected worlds: tourism in Southeast Asia* (Oxford: Elsevier Science Ltd, 2001), 128–129.

78 Moreover, since 2008, the Netherlands has again engaged in the preservation of Borobudur in a 'Fit-in-Trust', a technical collaboration project between Indonesia and the Netherlands, co-ordinated by the World Heritage Centre of UNESCO: http://whr.unesco.og/en/news/463 (accessed 9 January 2011).

79 'Verslag van de Nederlandse delegatie betr. de culturele samenwerking tussen Indonesië en Nederland op het terrein van archieven en musea, 10 t/m 22 november 1975, NA, Archieven van

Despite this sign of moral empathy in the process of losing a cherished object through decolonisation, the report of the Dutch mission that visited Indonesia in November 1975 for the final negotiations seemed to have no feeling for the new relations when it formulated conditions in the paternalistic and moralistic way it did: 'It makes no sense to talk about "transfer" (the Indonesian government constantly uses the word "return") of huge numbers of works of art and ethnographic objects, as long as there is no good museum infrastructure.'[80]

This was – necessarily – a slight degree more diplomatic than what others could write privately, as from the embittered heart of Van Erp Jnr, as we saw above. Apart from the lines expressing reservations, and again raising doubts, he asked Van Romondt's opinion of Soekmono – 'as an archaeologist? As an organiser? As a technical expert?' However, he added, perhaps to the honour of his father: 'I also have the impression that our own Colonial Archaeological Service [set up after Van Erp's restoration in 1913] has never really understood the real problem, and let the time and chance to take serious measures pass by.'[81]

The Dutch moral commitment to Borobudur would be symbolically underlined during the journey of Queen Juliana and Prince Bernhard to Indonesia in 1971, when the couple also visited Borobudur (Figure 7.4). They were – as all international guests and technical missions that visited Borobudur – accompanied and informed on the ins and outs of Borobudur by the staff of the Indonesian Archaeological Service and the Archaeology Department of Gadjah Mada University. Prince Bernhard also happened to be the patron of the private lobby in the Netherlands, initiated by the Foundation to Safeguard Borobudur, which was set up in 1968. The purpose of this foundation was well summarised by the popular Dutch daily *De Telegraaf* with the heading 'Nederland moet Borobudur redden' ('The Netherlands is obliged to save Borobudur').[82] It had an office in the Tropenmuseum, the former Colonial Institute, in Amsterdam. Through its royal patron, it acquired an important national and international lobbyist, with Prince Bernhard visiting Indonesia again in early 1973, having a brief talk with President Soeharto on minesweepers and temples, and back home pleading for more investment in Borobudur among his friends in governmental circles.[83]

het ministerie voor Algemeene oorlogvoering van het Koninkrijk (hereafter AOK) en van Algemeene zaken (hereafter AZ): kabinet van de Minister President (hereafter KMP), inv. nr 9221.

80 'Verslag van de Nederlandse delegatie betr. de culturele samenwerking tussen Indonesië en Nederland op het terrein van archieven en musea, 10 t/m 22 november 1975', NA, AOK en AZ: KMP, inv. nr 9221.

81 John W. T. van Erp to Van Romondt, 3 September 1968, Leiden University Library, Special Collections, KITLV Collection, KITLV, Archive Van Romondt, 26.

82 'Nederland moet Borobudur redden', *Telegraaf*, 24 September 1970.

83 J. Dohmen, 'Briefwisseling Bernhard en oud-minister openbaar', *NRC Handelsblad*, 11 August 2005.

Figure 7.4 Queen Juliana and Prince Bernhard pose at Borobudur together with Mrs. Isriati Moenadi and Mr. Moenadi, the governor of Central Java, 1971.

The new Dutch government (late 1973–1977), headed by Social Democrat Joop den Uyl, would decline Prince Bernhard's request. However, the previous prime minister, the Christian Democrat Barend Biesheuvel, who (pending new elections) had been in charge of an interim cabinet in 1973, supported the prince. He made sure that part of the technical and financial aid that the Ministry of Foreign Affairs had intended for Indonesia for 1973/1974 (170 million Dutch guilders) could be reserved for Borobudur. However, writing to Prince Bernard, Biesheuvel emphasised the condition that 'the Indonesian government would indeed have to use that [reserved] amount for Borobudur. I fully agree with you that we have to put an effort into the preservation of this monument. The Dutch government is also of that opinion.'[84]

The crowning achievement of the Dutch official and private contributions to Borobudur was the exhibition 'Borobudur: art and religion of ancient Java' held at the Netherlands' most prestigious museum, the Rijksmuseum, the national museum of Dutch art and history, in Amsterdam.[85] This was another journey of Borobudur's Buddha statues to safeguard their home base – they had visited Japan before, and had also travelled to Belgium, Germany, and France. In the Dutch context, and in this national museum (and notably not the former Colonial Institute, now the Tropical Museum), where they would be positioned in exhibition halls next to those displaying Rembrandt and other masters of the Dutch Golden Age, their visit was very meaningful. They were presented as a special Dutch concern, a precious jewel for which the Dutch Colonial Archaeological Service had done its utmost in the past. In short, because of past relationships and because of the legacy of Van Erp, Borobudur at the Rijksmuseum became Dutch heritage in a mental and moral way. It all pointed to the continued mental identification, or feelings of cultural ties, with (things connected to) the former Dutch colony – and thus to a repressed sense of loss, not because of destruction but as a result of the decolonisation – which still played an important role in the formation of Dutch identity.

If we look at the Dutch role in the restoration of Borobudur in an Indonesian context, however, Prince Bernhard may have overestimated its importance, despite the colonial past and despite valuable Dutch technical expertise delivered in the past and the present (by NEDECO), because 'loss' was real. It was now a long row of international experts, partly recruited from previous prestigious UNESCO heritage operations (such as the Abu Simbel temple in Egypt) or those of the French EFEO conservation enterprise in Cambodia, who took over, creating another colonial legacy.[86] For (most of) those experts the language of the Dutch colonial expertise was a hindrance. Thus, even in the paternalistic, advisory, technical role – which, by the end of the 1960s could be identified as a materialised Dutch colonial legacy – the Dutch input was subordinated to those of other international parties.

For instance, in May 1969, Ms N. Suryanti of the Department of Information in Jakarta gave a causerie at the Indonesian Consulate in Amsterdam on the

84 Prime Minister Barend Biesheuvel to Prince Bernhard, 19 April 1973; see also letter of the succeeding prime minister, Joop den Uyl, to Stichting behoud Borobudur, 20 July 1973, NA, AOK and AZ: KMP, inv. nr 9212.

85 See the show bill kept at Stadsarchief Amsterdam, collection affiches, inv. nr 4985.

86 From France, the architect J. Dumarçay and the archaeologist Bernard Groslier, both previously working at the EFEO in Siem Reap; from Belgium Coremans, G. Lemaire and G. Hyvert. Other technical experts came from countries such as Greece and Italy. The Dutch members of the former colonial archaeological service who have been involved as consultants were Van Romondt and Bernet Kempers.

mystical and cultural value of the temple for the present-day Indonesian people, especially the Javanese, 'who until now were living on the wholesome influence of Borobudur'. This lecture on the history, architecture, and reliefs of the building was entirely based on writings of a French scholar – Bernard Groslier, the former 'chief custodian of monuments of Angkor' at the EFEO in Siem Reap, whom UNESCO had recruited, together with the architect Jacques Dumarçay, as technical experts for the safeguarding project of Borobudur.[87] Dutch experts who had also written influential publications on Borobudur, such as Van Erp, Krom, and Stutterheim, were thus effectively marginalised.

Decolonising Heritage Politics and the Mechanisms of the Gift

Borobudur's post-war outlook has turned out to be strongly connected to the moral and material engagements with the site of the two former colonisers of Indonesia – Japan, creating a long-lasting, almost affectionate, relationship with Borubudur's tangible *and* intangible features, and the Netherlands, connecting forever with self-indulgence – and, notably, by the related initiatives of UNESCO of the 1970s and 1980s, that in an indirect way also reflected trans-Asian/Greater Indian perspectives. By focusing on the mechanisms of exchange, interdependencies, feelings of loss, and acts of giving and sacrifice, in the post-colonial era, we can see a selective 'colonial aphasia' (Ann Stoler's concept) with regard to Japanese wartime heritage engagements in Java.[88] Japanese decolonisation after August 1945 implied that Japanese wartime heritage activities on Java had quickly and completely vanished from sight in Indonesia and in Japan. Yet, the past heritage involvements of the previous colonial regimes (the British and the Dutch) are undisputed and still visible at these sites. This loss of visibility and memory of the Japanese archaeological interventions on Java may be partly explained by the relatively short duration of the Japanese occupation as well as the context of the Pacific War in which Japanese cultural policies took place. These became overshadowed by the consequences of international warfare and wartime economy – also in memory.

[87] An off-print of this lecture can be found in NA, Archive of F. den Hollander, inv. nr 17. The engineer Den Hollander, who between 1918 and 1938 worked for the Dutch East-Indies Staatsspoorwegen (Tram- and Railways Department), became head of the Dutch Railways Company (NS) after the war. He was one of the founders of and fundraisers for Stichting Behoud Borobudur. Apparently he had attended the lecture on Borobudur at the Consulate General of the Indonesian Republic, Amsterdam, on 12 May 1969.

[88] Ann Stoler, 'Colonial aphasia: race and disabled histories in France', *Public Culture* 23:1 (2011), 121–156. On Japanese post-colonial archaeology, compare Koji Mizoguchi, 'The colonial experience of the uncolonized and colonized: the case of East Asia, mainly as seen from Japan', in Jane Lydon and Uzma Z. Rizvi (eds.), *Handbook of postcolonial archaeology* (Walnut Creek: Left Coast Press, 2010), 89.

It may also be why Indonesia today denies agency to the imperialist Japan of the past in the field of cultural politics, whereas it recognises this for the other former colonial regimes. However, this 'forgetting' also seems part of a larger lack of knowledge of Japanese cultural policy in Southeast Asia during the Pacific War, except for Japan's wartime propaganda policy.

The comparison of colonial and post-colonial engagements with Borobudur and other Buddhist and Hindu temple sites in Java, from Dutch, Indonesian, Japanese, and, to a lesser extent, UNESCO perspectives, shows four levels of loss that generated the moral and material commitments to save these sites from decay (or to even reconstruct them). Besides, first, the loss of visibility and, second, the loss of memory, for all parties involved there was, third, the anxiety over the loss of a cherished object of the past. This anxiety was connected to different reasons of appreciation (aesthetic, art-historical, historical, religious, spiritual), and based on different legitimations (the Dutch Empire, the (post-)colonial state, the Indonesian nation, the Japanese Empire, Asian civilisation, universal civilisation, Dutch national identity). On this third level, the act of giving could compensate the anxiety over the loss. The crucial question was, then, who was (mainly) in charge of the material commitment to give and could thus claim moral and material ownership?

Last, but not least, there is the notion of loss in the context of decolonisation. For the Dutch, this meant the painful awareness of losing a privileged connection to the most cherished heritage sites, Borobudur and Prambanan, and of losing the chief responsibility for their maintenance and/or reconstruction; these privileges were now all effectively taken over by the new, independent Indonesian Republic. This awareness emerged only gradually and not fully to Dutch parties. All along, because of past connections and being accustomed to past hierarchies, a paternalistic sense of connection to these particular heritage sites, and commitment to their maintenance, persisted. This attitude characterised Dutch private and governmental involvement in the UNESCO Save Borobudur campaign in the 1970s. In the Japanese case, however, the European decolonisation in Asia, which was partly accelerated through the Pacific War, in the first instance implied gain. War and occupation offered to Japanese private and governmental parties further opportunities to recognise in these sites spiritual messages and/or past Asian connections, and thereby to appropriate these sites. This appropriation also happened by continuing the archaeological activities initiated by the Dutch Colonial Archaeological Service and through undertaking (semi-)new initiatives like the re-uncovering of Borobudur's hidden foot.

Borobudur's conservation history shows that the temple continues to attract the awe, amazement, and moral and economic investment of individual pilgrims and tourists, and of groups of people who do not necessarily have connections to state-supported or international heritage agencies. To this day, moreover, different local, national, and international parties continue to dispute how to take care of Borobudur. This is not (only) because heritage politics and authorised heritage discourses work that way,[89] but also because these sites, through the ongoing moral mechanisms of 'the gift', generate alternative moral engagements and anxieties over loss. They continue to win people to their side from within and from beyond the borders of states and empires. The American actor Richard Gere's 2012 Buddhist pilgrimage to Borobudur (triggering his plans to make a major movie about Raffles and Borobudur – yet to materialise) and the fledgling intergovernmental plans to make Angkor Wat and Borobudur sister sites are telling cases in point.[90] Who knows what all this might imply for the positions of Borobudur and Indonesia in the wider cultural imagination of 'Greater India'.

89 As also argued by Jones, *Culture, power, and authoritarianism in the Indonesian state*.

90 Hangga Brata and Arientha Primanita, 'Actor Richard Gere drawn by karma to Borobudur, planning temple movie', *JakartaGlobe*, 27 June 2011, www.thejakartaglobe.com/indonesia/actor-richard-gere-drawn-by-karma-to-borobudur-planning-temple-movie/449282 (accessed 13 January 2012); Sita W. Dewi, 'Angkor Wat, Borobudur Temple to become sister sites, says official', *Jakarta Post*, 12 January 2012, www.thejakartapost.com/news/2012/01/12/angkor-wat-borobudur-temple-become-sister-sites-says-official.html (accessed 13 January 2012).

Epilogue: Heritage Sites, Difficult Histories, and 'Hidden Forces' in Post-Colonial Indonesia

In her first return to Java after the war, in 1955, the Riga-born globe-travelling art historian Claire Holt (1901–1970) took a photograph of the Great Mosque of Demak in a remarkable situation. In front of the building we see posters of several Indonesian political parties trying to attract the voting public, but the silhouette of the hammer and sickle from the Indonesian communist party PKI draws all attention (Figure 8.1).[1] Holt, who had worked and lived in the Netherlands Indies as researcher on Javanese dance and culture, and as the lover and intellectual soulmate of archaeologist Willem Stutterheim, had returned to the now independent republic as one of the inspirers of Cornell's Southeast Asia Program in the United States, and to gather documentation for a book on art and culture in Indonesia. She took the photo during the campaign for the 1955 general election. As a historical document, it seems typical of the Cornell-based Southeast Asia Program's cultural approach, later personified by Benedict Anderson, a self-proclaimed pupil of Holt. This approach integrated a focus on the political motive in the study of culture in Asia and has been inspiring for this book as well. But the picture is also telling for the fact that Indonesia once had the biggest communist party in Asia, and the combination of Islam and communism was once plausible, going back to the founding of the PKI in colonial times, and the communist revolts in West Java and the west coast of Sumatra in 1926–1927. But after General Soeharto's takeover and the repression and mass killings of 'communists' after 1965, such a juxtaposition seems unthinkable.

Thirty years later the mosque in Demak would again occupy centre-stage, when Soeharto arrived by helicopter amid swirling dust to finalise yet another intrusive restoration, transforming the mosque into national heritage of the New Order regime. Echoing his speech at Borobudur, he quickly and solemnly explained that this restoration was important for Indonesian development[2] and

[1] See Rex Mortimer, 'Class, social cleavage, and Indonesian communism', *Indonesia* 8 (October 1969), between 1 and 2. The original is kept in the Holt Archives of the New York City Library. We thank Roger Knight for leading us to this picture.

[2] 'Presiden Suharto di Demak: Pemugaran Masjid bukan tindakan pemboroson', *Kompas*, 22 March 1987.

Figure 8.1 'Great Mosque of Demak with election posters, 1955'.

took off again before the dust of the *alun alun* had even settled.[3] This moment illustrates how, across violent regime changes and governments, sites can serve national unity, and cover with dust many conflicting histories and memories of pain, violence, and repression.

In this Epilogue, we briefly return to some of the sites that have been central to our book. They help us to reflect further on two problems related to the way people in the past few decades, within and outside Indonesia, have been engaging with Indonesia's seen or unseen pasts. As we have shown throughout this book, heritage sites in the making are part of multiple, ambivalent, and changing relationships, between ruler and ruled, and between insiders and outsiders who see and tell different site-related histories. This does not need to lead to conflicts or contestation of sites, as different engagements and histories can develop in parallel. Sites, however, may disclose historical connections that are unseen at the surface, and that may be painful to, unexpected for, or unwanted by different parties for different reasons, in such a way that heritage politics can become highly problematic within a society. The first of the two problems we focus on concerns the question of how heritage sites can

[3] Information provided to Marieke Bloembergen by Zainal, Demak, 3 February 2011.

be a source not to conceal, but to shed light on, violent and difficult pasts of more recent, post-colonial times, in particular of 1965, and their endurance in the present, even though clear traces may initially seem non-existent. The second problem concerns Indonesian Islam as heritage. Given that Indonesia is inhabited by the world's largest Muslim population, the absence of Indonesian Islam in heritage politics at a global level and, at first sight, also in the Indonesian context, is remarkable. By focusing on what people over time do at sites – the method followed throughout this book – we can come close to understanding the meanings of some 'unseen' and difficult histories regarding Indonesia's recent past, again to different groups. This exercise shows that sites, as places that create obligations, debts, and interdependencies, and precisely because they can hide and reveal historical taboos, also enable people to break silences, when they feel time is there, and when we keep on questioning and exchanging knowledge – despite the petrifying politics of heritage.

The Violence and Power of Heritage Sites

We have discussed the relation between violence and heritage politics extensively for the British and Dutch colonial periods, as well as for the Japanese occupation, the period of revolution and recolonisation war, and, to a certain extent also for New Order Indonesia. But there is more to say about the visibility and invisibility of violent pasts at heritage sites. During our research, we were aware that, although unseen and unspoken, at least at some of the sites we explored, there should be signs of the massive violence related to the pre-empted coup of 1965 that brought General Soeharto to power: inter-civilian mass killings orchestrated by the military and endorsed by many Western countries following the coup, the mass graves, the mass detentions of alleged communists, and the subsequent political repression during Soeharto's New Order regime. Although the Soeharto regime came to an end in 1998, and the movement for democratisation and decentralisation has become stronger, the subsequent governments of the so-called reformation have until now avoided any serious investigation into the massacres. Whereas some small first steps towards reconciliation have been taken, the legacies and sensitivities of this extremely violent period continue to have an impact on Indonesian society.

As all historians and social scientists who have studied Indonesia over the past decades know, it is at once impossible not to notice the deep, bitter impact of this period and extremely difficult for Indonesians to talk about it. Both communism and the anti-communist killings are still taboo and have split Indonesian society ever since into winners and losers, perpetrators and victims or survivors that have been marginalised and stigmatised over generations. We encountered this dynamic ourselves. For instance, while visiting Pulau Kemaro (Kemaro island) near Palembang to see a Chinese temple which contains references to the Srivijaya past,[4] our Chinese informant mentioned 'these are our killing fields', but added immediately: 'do not talk about this'. Being informed about the violent past, induced by a site of mass violence, we learned, at the same time entails being socialised not to discuss this violent past.[5]

Sometimes the local references to the violent past are more explicit and related to the military legitimation of the New Order regime. Visitors to the Majapahit site in Trowulan, whether they use printed or live guides, or follow the marked heritage directions, will easily find one building which, if you stay only a bit longer and check all the details, clearly shows signs of the regime change between 1965 and 1967 – when Soeharto officially took over – and the related repression: the Pendopo Agung. This building, at first sight just a large variant of the Javanese-style *pendopo*, has a special position in the archaeological landscape of the Majapahit site. In front, near the entrance, a massive bust of Gajah Mada attests to that as well. Without a doubt, it portrays Soeharto – but it was a later intervention, installed in 1986 by the military police (Figure 8.2). What we see at the Pendopo Agung, and in subsequent interventions at the site, is the military's effort to revive Majapahit's heroic story and powerful spirit in wood and stone. It became a site for military pilgrimage and *musyawrah* (meeting, assembly) of the military in charge of the rightful development of the people, and to empower those in charge, who were about to make important decisions. Intentionally or not, it functioned to intimidate (parts of) the population.

While archaeologists at the BP3 today do not support the claim, the Pendopo Agung stands as a reconstruction of the Royal Audience Hall of the Majapahit empire and is built on what is said to have been the Audience Hall's original site and the original remains of sixteen pillars. An inscription at the site says the building was planned in 1964, but work officially started on 1 October 1966[6] – exactly one year after the pre-empted coup and subsequent mass killings and intimidation unleashed by the new military regime. The framework in which the building took place was now the twenty-first anniversary of the military unit of East Java, Kodam VIII Brawijaya (later Kodam V), named after the famous Majapahit king. In concept and symbolic signs, the building reflected the nation's origin myth, and the leading role of the military therein. The ground plan, for example, reflected the sacred date of the Indonesian independence proclamation, 17 August 1945, and under the Pendopo pictures display a solemn ceremony taking place in gloomy darkness on 14 December 1966:

4 This visit took place on 27 March 2010. Our informant wishes to remain anonymous.

5 Compare with 'Sebuah kamp di Tengah Sungai', *Liputan Khusus Tempo, Pengakuan Algojo 1965* 1 (7 October 2012), 100.

6 Soeyono Wisnoewhardono, *Petunjuk Singkat. Warisan Majapahit di Trowulan* (Surabaya: Surya Grafika, 1986), 40.

Figure 8.2 The Gadjah Mada statue at the Pendopo Agung in Trowulan, 2009.

we see military officers as members of the 'Keluarga Besar Brawijaya' (the extended Brawijaya family) carry a sacred foundation 'naska' (manuscript) to a temple, where it is signed, apparently to officially inaugurate the Pendopo.[7]

On location, the story goes that it was a *dukun* (local priest) who in the 1960s performed rituals at the site, and based on the remains of four pillars, believed this was where Brawijaya had his Royal Audience Hall and convinced General Widjojo Soejono (of the Brawijaya division),[8] who was ostensibly responsible for the idea to reconstruct the Pendopo. Soejono was also in charge of subsequent interventions, emphasising the creative, sacred power of the site. Eight years later, Soejono installed a commemorative plate for the Brawijaya

7 On the spiritual Javanism among high military from the Brawijaya division and on their changing position, see David Jenkins, *Suharto and his generals: Indonesian military politics 1975–1983* (Ithaca: Cornell University Press, 1984). Compare with *Kologdam VIII/Brawijaya (sejarah Militair)* (Surabaya: Kologdam VIII/ Brawijaya 1977); F. H. Soerodjo et al., *Sejarah panglima Kodam V. Brawijaya V* (Jakarta: Gramedia, 1989), with brief biographies of Soemitro (243–252) and Widjojo Soejono (280–298). See also: Ulf Sundhaussen, *The road to power: Indonesian military politics, 1945–1967* (Kuala Lumpur: Oxford University Press, 1982).

8 Explained to M. Bloembergen during a site visit with Pak Sento, former staff member of the BP3 in Trowulan, 13 June 2012.

division, and planted a holy banyan tree at the site, now one of its most sacred spots. He also installed a huge relief in the back wall of the Pendopo, depicting the scene of Gajah Mada's 'Sumpah Pelapa': after eating a sour fruit, Gajah Mada swore an oath not to eat until he had expanded and united the Majapahit empire. This all celebrated the armed forces and connected their power to Brawijaya's military forces that had once unified and empowered the pre-colonial state of Indonesia. Widjojo Soejono explained that Gajah Mada's oath also entailed the 'development' of society into 'ripeness': 'kita tidak akan istirahat begitu saja sebelum tercapai masyarakat adil dan makmur' ('we will not rest until we succeed in creating a just and prosperous society').[9]

This may all seem like artificial reinventions of traditions, and therefore a superficial form of legitimising the new regime and its most important tool of power. But the site, in this case, mattered: as part of the broader site of the Majapahit empire in itself, and as supposed core of the kingdom's power. If you stay longer at the Majapahit site, you will learn that at other meaningful locations constructions were also added in the transitional years of the 1960s, and during the 1970s and 1980s, through the intervention of the military, either on personal or official initiative, by way of appropriation. Other local (non-military) parties sought authority at the site as well, and interacted. In the early 1960s, around the time when plans for the building of the Pendopo Agung came up, a navy general from Jakarta added a new stone building at the grave of Putri Campa. Among the pilgrims from inside and outside Indonesia that come here for *keramat* are many important army generals.[10] At the site of Siti Inggil, in 1961 a certain Haji Idris 'rediscovered' the grave of Brawijaya and turned it into a site of pilgrimage, which drew President Soekarno, and later Soeharto, to Trowulan.[11]

[9] *Djawa Pos*, 15 January 1976. For the Brawijaya division and the Trisula operation of 1968, see V. Hearman, 'Contesting victimhood in the Indonesian anti-communist violence and its implications for justice for the victims of the 1968 South Blitar Trisula operation', in M. Eickhoff, G. van Klinken and G. Robinson (eds.), *Journal of Genocide Research* 19:3 (2017) (Special Issue, *1965 today: living with the Indonesian massacres)*.

[10] Interview, Marieke Bloembergen with Hartono, an official caretaker of the grave, from the BP3, on location, 11 February 2011. One colleague scholar whom we met in Surabaya, and who taught political science at an Indonesian University in the 1980s and 1990s, explained to us that he had individual army members as students in his classes, who were convinced that they had to carry on the spirit and ends of Gajah Mada to unite Indonesia, and that Gajah Mada's power and spirit is still around at the site of the Pendopo Agung. Personal communication by political scientist Dede Oetomo, Surabaya, 9 February 2011.

[11] Interview, Marieke Bloembergen with Pak Tego, on location, 14 June 2012. The alleged grave of Brawijaya plays a significant role in (stories about) New Order legitimations, as well as individual pilgrims' power seeking; Abu Sidik Wibowo, head of the BP3 in Trowulan, 1963–1973, explored the history of the makings of Siti Inggil, but we could not relocate his writings during several visits to the library of the BP3 in 2011 and 2012. Compare, however, the official site of the Indonesian Ministry of Culture and Tourism, which relates this belief to several 'aliran kepercayaan' (lit. 'belief assocations', an official governmental category used to denote the religious

The military interventions at the site of Majapahit fitted Benedict Anderson's 1973 observation that, of the many 'Mahapahit-style' constructions (which we can still encounter) in East Java, most were built under the auspices of East Java's Brawijaya division.[12] The military constructions and activities at the Majapahit site entailed, moreover, forms of sacralisation. These sites link spiritual power and military authority with a primordial sense of nation. In this sense, sites can be potent and persuasive: they can silence people, but also generate a sense of spiritual and physical power and self-righteousness, and, in that role, they can facilitate legitimising past and present state-supported abuse of power and mass violence.

Archaeology and Violence

There is an intrinsic connection between the professionalisation of archaeology in post-colonial times and violence in Indonesian history. This is important to realise, particularly if we want to understand how and to what extent archaeological sites and archaeology in Indonesia were decolonised, and how Indonesian archaeologists themselves define the colonial dimensions of their research field in the past. First, the revolution and recolonisation war was a formative experience for the first generation of post-colonial Indonesian archaeologists. Second, the violent regime change of 1965 had an important, complex, and multifaceted impact on the professionalisation and modernisation of archaeology and heritage politics in the New Order years.

Regarding the formative experience of decolonisation and concrete Dutch colonial violence, consider R. P. Soejono (1926–2011), who like Soekmono and Satyawati Soeleiman studied ancient history under Bernet Kempers. He had a successful career across regime changes: as an esteemed prehistorian and curator, he worked at the Indonesian Archaeological Service, the National Museum, the Universitas Indonesia in Jakarta, and the Pusat Penelitian dan Pengembangan Arkeologi Nasional (Arkenas, the National Archaeological Research Institute). In 2010, during an interview, he vividly recalled (in Dutch) a personal experience of Dutch violence, which he transformed into Indonesian nationalist heroism. As a freedom fighter during the recolonisation war he had been tortured by Dutch soldiers. During that time, he told us, he dreamt of freedom: 'Yes, I am an extremist, but I can speak Dutch. I want to

groups that are not officially acknowledged as *agama* (religion)). See http://kebudayaan.kemdikbud.go.id/bpcbtrowulan/2014/11/12/situs-siti-inggil/ (accessed 21 February 2016). For another website indicating that this is where Brawijaya is buried, describing the pilgrimages of Presidents Soekarno and Soeharto to this site, see https://id-id.facebook.com/republikceritamisteri/posts/617281468284524 (accessed 21 February 2016).

12 Anderson, 'Cartoons and monuments', 178. For a recent, extensive analysis of the organisation of the New Order's cultural politics in this period, and the role of army leaders therein, see Jones, *Culture, power, and authoritarianism in the Indonesian state*, chapters IV and V.

be free – MERDEKA [freedom] – how happy we would be – MERDEKA.'[13] Soejono claimed that his later activities as a professor in archaeology were directly related to this dream. 'I was a nationalist. I wanted to make the [Indonesian] people happy. Look here [showing us the dissertations he supervised]: these are dissertations written by Indonesians. That is an example of a sense of responsibility for the people. Archaeology is a science – read [the archaeologist V. Gordon] Childe!'[14] Following Childe's reasoning, Soejono asked rhetorically: 'What are the achievements of people? Which were their monuments? How did their societies develop? From the past to the present. That is what archaeology is about. It is not there for tourism.'[15] While Soejono thus made archaeology into a national activity, this does not imply that he distanced himself from the archaeology of colonial times. On the contrary, when asked about this topic, he stated: 'They [the Dutch colonial archaeologists] knew that Indonesia had a great past. We continued on that track.'[16]

The older generation of leading Indonesian archaeologists from the Universitas Gadjah Mada in Yogyakarta (founded in 1949) take comparable positions. They regard the colonial archaeologists as their 'founding fathers'. They often define their relationship to colonial archaeology in terms of family ties.[17] Yet when we asked contemporary Indonesian archaeologists about colonial archaeologists, they tended to honour their academic output and not their colonial mindset. Dutch colonial archaeologists may have been founding fathers, but the real professionalisation of the prehistoric archaeology of Indonesia has taken place only in the post-colonial era, thanks to the support of the Indonesian state and its international partners.[18]

In the early 1970s, the Indonesian government led by General Soeharto promoted archaeology with funding, prestige, and space. Within the framework of New Order economic development, tourism politics, and cultural diplomacy, archaeology situated Indonesia on the international stage, conferred high status on those involved, and presented openings for international collaboration[19] –

[13] Interview, Martijn Eickhoff with R. P. Soejono, Jakarta, 25 February 2010.

[14] Soejono was referring to the Australian archaeologist, philologist, and prehistorian V. Gordon Childe (1892–1952), who was based at British academic institutions; through his works such as *Man makes himself* (1936, reprinted in 1948, 1951, 1966, 1981), *Progress and archaeology* (1944), *New light on the most ancient East* (1952, reprinted in 1964), and *The prehistory of European Society* (1958), Childe inspired a generation of students of archaeology worldwide. He followed a Marxist approach to archaeology and the history of civilisations. For an introduction, see Trigger, *A history of archaeological thought*, 167–174.

[15] Interview, Martijn Eickhoff with R. P. Soejono, Jakarta, 25 February 2010. [16] Ibid.

[17] Interviews, Marieke Bloembergen and Martijn Eickhoff with Inayati Adrisijanti M. Romli, Yogyakarta, 22 January 2010; with Timbul Haryono, Yogyakarta, 21 January 2011.

[18] For the decolonisation of Indonesian archaeology, see Bloembergen and Eickhoff, 'The colonial archaeological hero'.

[19] For an extensive analysis of cultural politics under the Soeharto regime, see Jones, *Culture, power, and authoritarianism in the Indonesian state*; on archaeology during the New Order, see Wood, *Official history in modern Indonesia*.

for example, inter-Asian exchanges, including in the framework of the Bangkok-based Asian Regional Centre for Archaeology and Fine Arts, SPAFA.[20] In the West, the Ford Foundation enabled Indonesian universities to attract foreign (American) teaching staff and provided archaeologists with technical equipment and vehicles, and Majapahit became a laboratory for the new field-school approaches in 'settlement archaeology'.

The regime change of 1965 had a huge impact on intellectual life in general and university life in particular. Recent research has revealed how many (presumed) communist and leftist-minded people in Indonesian higher education between 1965 and 1975 were 'eliminated' by those political and religious coalitions that supported Soeharto. During Soekarno's Guided Democracy policy, campuses had been places that fostered political self-organisation and debate, along the lines of the official Nasakom ideology, which combined nationalism, religion, and communism.[21] This politisation of campus life before 1965 partly explains how, after 1965, many thousands of students, lecturers, and university staff members were declared guilty of being communists, and were imprisoned or murdered.[22] Without becoming explicit, one of the archaeologists we interviewed, and who studied at UGM at that time, explained to us, in guarded terms: 'I had to hide out, it was unsafe, a time in which you had better not show up at university.'[23] During his return travels to Indonesia in the late 1960s, the Dutch prehistorian R. H. van Heekeren witnessed the effects of the purges on his archaeological network. He clearly embarrassed his hosts in Bali when he asked the whereabouts of former research collaborators and colleagues who had gone missing and by talking of communists and 'would-be' communists.[24]

That at least one professional archaeologist had acted on behalf of perpetrators becomes clear from an unsettling news special from NBC (the American National Broadcasting Company), dating from 1967, titled 'Indonesia: a troubled victory'.[25] In this 30-minute documentary, reporter Teddy Yates

[20] 'What Is Spafa', *Southeast Asian Archaeology International Newsletter*, 5 (1994), www.geocities.ws/thai_archaeology/seasia/05/spafa1.html (accessed 2 January 2017). See Bloembergen and Eickhoff, 'Save Borobudur!', 110.

[21] Nasakom is an acronym for *nasionalisme* (nationalism), *agama* (religion), and *komunisme* (communism). The ideology aimed to balance – or to appease – the three main factions in Indonesian politics: the (nationalist) army, Islamic groups, and the communists. See Robert Cribb and Colin Brown, *Modern Indonesia: a history since 1945* (London: Longman, 1995), 82–83.

[22] Abdul Wahid, 'Counterrevolution in a revolutionary campus: how did the "1965 event" affect an Indonesian public university?', in Katherine McGregor, Jess Melvin and Annie Pohlman (eds.), *The Indonesian genocide of 1965: causes, dynamics and legacies* (Cham: Palgrave Macmillan, 2017), 157–178.

[23] Interview, Marieke Bloembergen with I Gusti Ngurah Anom, Saba, 8 June 2012.

[24] R. H. van Heekeren, *De onderste steen boven: belevenissen van een globetrotter* (Assen: Van Gorcum, 1969), 185 and 192.

[25] See www.nbcuniversalarchives.com/nbcuni/clip/51A08495_s01.do (accessed 16 December 2016).

expresses his surprise that, even in the exotic, peaceful paradise island of Bali, there had been mass killings. He meets the Balinese archaeologist Rata, who explains to him, while they walk on a fresh mass grave: 'Yeah, but Bali is now becoming more beautiful without communists, and this is the duty of Balinese people, to clean their own island from the communist influence. This is the holy duty.' Another shot shows a temple where cleansing rituals are held, involving many members of the community, including people taking an oath never to return to communism.

The NBC documentary is remarkable for several reasons. First of all it shows and explicitly names a site of mass violence, a mass grave. In later decades, the existence of places like this would become public secrets, while being concealed by New Order history memory politics that referred to the mass killings only in euphemistic language such as 'crushing communism'.[26] The documentary furthermore leads its audience to believe that the violence was primarily an inter-civilian cultural phenomenon, in the guise of a problem of religion, and caused by tensions between radical believers and atheistic communism. The documentary does not mention any military or Western involvement.[27] Furthermore, the archaeologist gets involved in this way of framing the violence, acting as an acknowledged specialist in local religion, culture, and history, and as an intermediary between the local community and the international audience of NBC. In this way, the kind of community-based archaeology, acquiring the participation of the local population, which had developed in Bali since late colonial times, became genocidal during the Cold War: community archaeology legitimised the violence that was directed against a group of people who, while belonging to the same nation, were considered a threat to the community and to traditional culture as defined by the archaeologist-cum-cultural expert. The NBC documentary demonstrates how, directly after or during the time of the killings, and with the encouragement of an American anti-communist journalist, professional Indonesian archaeology could be used in global anti-communist Cold War propaganda, and to legitimise the New Order regime.

Indonesian Islam in Heritage Formation

Focusing on unseen histories at sites, we have explored the (implicit) absence of Indonesian Islam when it comes to heritage politics in general and

[26] John Roosa, 'The September 30th movement: the aporias of the official narratives', in Douglas Kammen and Katharine McGregor (eds.), *The contours of mass violence in Indonesia 1965–1968* (Honolulu: University of Hawai'i Press, 2012), 32–33 and 44–48.

[27] For a critical analysis of the cultural explanation of the mass violence on Bali, including the alleged willingness of communists to be killed, see Geoffrey Robinson, *The dark side of paradise: political violence in Bali* (Ithaca: Cornell University Press, 1995), 275–280.

worldwide. Outside Indonesia, in the world's prestigious art and civilisation museums, Indonesian Islam is conspicuously absent, even from these museum's 'Islamic art' departments.[28] On the other hand, 'Asian art' collections and displays worldwide feature Java's Hindu–Buddhist material remains, especially Borobudur's Buddha heads. These Buddha statues (continue to) define Indonesia as part of an 'Indianised' world in which the Indonesian archipelago gratefully receives a 'superior' Hindu–Buddhist Indian civilisation from India. Inside Indonesia, particularly in the National Museum, exhibits emphasise Java's Hindu–Buddhist past. Islamic objects are on display but remain marginal. This minimising of Indonesian Islam, as our book shows, reflects specific traditions and priorities of collecting and ways of looking at the region since the nineteenth century. But what does this imply for contemporary heritage politics regarding Islamic sites and objects *in* Indonesia? Is it really the case, as one of our Indonesian students at Gadjah Mada University reasoned, that 'Islam does not need heritage politics because it is around us and part of our lives'?[29]

This remark sheds light on the 1980s Demak mosque's restoration, the second site, after Borobudur, of the New Order's cultural heritage politics programme, which was financed by both national and international funding – in this case the Organization of the Islamic Conference, an umbrella organisation based in Istanbul, which at the time involved Brunei, Saudi Arabia, Turkey, and Egypt. An interdisciplinary team of archaeologists, hydrologists, architects, and others first made an intensive 'feasibility study'.[30] The restoration itself was directed by the (Hindu) Balinese archaeologist I Gusti Gde Anom, who could build on long-term experience with anastylosis-style restoration at Prambanan. The inauguration ceremony at Demak followed the Borobudur model, with a presidential speech and a commemorative stone. Like Borobudur, the mosque of Demak, as Java-style Islamic architecture, has

[28] Bloembergen and Eickhoff, 'Een klein land dat de wereld bestormt', 163–165. In the context of a discussion on the problematic relationship between the study of Islam and Southeast Asian studies, see Chiara Formichi, 'Islamic studies or Asian studies?'

[29] Masterclass, 'Archaeological sites in colonial and postcolonial Indonesia', UGM, Yogyakarta, 17–22 June 2011.

[30] This paragraph dwells on *Report on the feasibility studies for the great mosque of Demak, Central Java Indonesia. Appendix I. Historical background* (Ministry of Education and Culture, Directorate General of Culture, restoration and preservation project of historical and archaeological legacies, Central Java, 1981); *Laporan pemugaran Masjid Agung Demak* (Prambanan: Direkorat Jenderal Kebudayaan, Proyek Pemugaran dan Pemeliharaan Peninggalan Sejarah dan Purbakala Jawa Tenggah, Departemen Pendidikan dan Kebudayaan, 1986); *Laporan evalusasi hasil pemugaran Masjid Agung Demak* (Jakarta: Direktorat Jenderal kebudayaan direktorat perlindungan dan pembinaan peninggalan sejarah dan Purbakala, 1991/1992). It also covers conversations, Marieke Bloembergen with Inajati Adrisijanti, Yogyakarta, 29 December 2011; with Haji Abdul Fatah and other members of the Taq'mir of the mosque of Demak, and Haji Alin Sugianto secretary of the Badan Kesejahteran Masjid Demak, in Demak on 3 and 4 February 2012; and with I Gusti Ngurah Anom, in Saba, 8 June 2012.

several miniature copies – quite a number dating from the colonial times – on display in other museums in Indonesia. Islam thus forms not only part of Indonesians' lived experience but also fits into Indonesian heritage politics and museum culture. And, if you focus on Islam as heritage, or as site of archaeological and historical research, you will find it, although it does not dominate.[31]

The Demak mosque is clearly a 'living monument', not only as a regular mosque for daily prayer for the Demak population, but also – perceived as Java's oldest and most sacred mosque, with holy graves nearby – as a site of pilgrimage, visited by Indonesia's Muslim population outside Demak, and attracting pilgrims from the wider Malay Islamic world. Comparable to the procedure of the 1840s which we analysed in Chapter 1, the 1980s restoration entailed a partial deconstruction and the creation of a temporary stand-in mosque. The state-supported heritage specialists then in charge were aware of the traditions and beliefs connected to the mosque, and took them seriously. They negotiated about differing interests of conservation and beliefs with the religious and administrative authorities in Demak in charge of the maintenance of the mosque.[32] Beliefs regarding the sacredness of the four main pillars and their authenticity, and concerns about the public interest, were being exchanged with technical experts' worries about the sustainability of the mosque's building material and construction. As a result of reciprocal understanding between the various parties, the heritage interventions, although they included a partial renewal of the pillars, did not violate the sacredness of the mosque and its pillars. Purist Islamic views denouncing as heretical the syncretic practice of presenting offerings to pillars or graves, and scholarly views historicising antiquities, may have reinforced each other. Or, to quote the Indonesian archaeologist Inajati Adrisijanti, who at the time was involved in the feasibility

[31] On research into the origin of the Javanese mosque, in colonial and postcolonial times, see Helène Njoto, 'À propos des origins de la mosque Javanase', *BEFEO*, 100 (2014), 1–37. On the Muslim graves near Trowulan, see Damais, 'Etudes javanaises VII'. Damais was introduced to this site by Stutterheim. Compare how historian and Javanologist Ricklefs, following Damais, uses these graves as sources for early Islam, accommodation, and contested identity in times of the *Nagarakrtagama* (which ignores Islam): Ricklefs, *Mystic synthesis in Java*, 12–15. One important Indonesian archaeologist of Islam in Indonesia, one of the few, was Uka Tjandrasasmita (1930–2010). He started as assistant staff member of the Indonesian Archaeological Service (1952–1960), succeeding Soekmono as head from 1960 to 1975, and then became head of the Central BP3 in Jakarta; later on he was affiliated to the State Islamic University of Indonesia. See, among others, Uka Tjandrasasmita, *Arkeologi Islam Nusantara* (Jakarta: Gramedia/EFEO/Sharif Hidayatullah State University, 2009). For recent interest in archaeological sites of Islam as a source for early Islamic history in Indonesia, see www.iseas.edu.sg/centres/nalanda-sriwijaya-centre/item/2540 (accessed 17 August 2016).

[32] The *kyai* (Islamic religious leaders) gathered in the Taq'mir of the mosque, responsible for daily religious affairs of the mosque, and the Badan Kesejahteran Masjid Demak (Service for the Maintenance of the Mosque of Demak, BKM, in charge of the land including the mosque, existing since 1974).

research: 'people believe that the four pillars were built by the Wali Songo. But according to historical and archaeological studies, the Wali Songo did not live in the same time as when the mosque was built.' However, she also saw the usefulness of belief and mythical thinking for heritage politics when she concluded: 'a myth can have the function to maintain buildings'.[33]

Regarding the restoration of Borobudur, Prambanan, and other Hindu–Buddhist sites in Indonesia, initially the authorities, considering these to be dead monuments, took no steps to explore religious sensitivities towards the site on location. But we may wonder why and how in Indonesia a Buddhist and a Hindu shrine remain the most important national monuments without any significant problem – though not everyone in Indonesia approved of the ways the Indonesian government made Borobudur the focus of Indonesian heritage politics.[34] (Chapter 7 discussed the protests against village displacements and local spiritual engagements with the site that differed from the official neutral state policy towards Borobudur as a 'dead' monument.) It is clear that heritage politics regarding Borobudur work out differently for people living *in* Borobudur than for the short term, accidental tourist. The bomb attack of 1987, though alarming, seemed more a symbolic protest against New Order governmental policies to 'neutralise' and co-opt an orthodox Islam than a serious effort to clear away Borobudur. Both the attack and the prosecution of the perpetrators are, in public, reduced to incidents, and obscured by taboos. After all, in Borobudur's site museum, the attack is neutralised as just another technical cause of damage and problem of restoration.

A few recent engagements with the sites of Borobudur and Majapahit reveal what we might call, at first sight, non-Western examples of the post-colonial phenomenon of 'epistemic violence'.[35] Two remarkable publications filled the bestseller tables at Indonesia's main bookstore Gramedia: Fami Basha's *Borobudur dan peninggalan nabi Suleiman* ('Borobudur and the legacy of the prophet Solomon', 2012), and Herman Sinung Junatama's *Majapahit Kerajaan Islam* ('Majapahit, the Islamic kingdom', 2014). The first author, a mathematician, explains the mathematical reasoning of why and how the kingdom of Sheba was located on Java and 'proves' that Borobudur is an Islamic monument. The second author, a philosopher, interprets ancient texts to argue that the Majapahit kingdoms were not Hindu–Buddhist, as is commonly 'believed', but were, in fact, Islamic.[36] The question we have to take

[33] Interview, Marieke Bloembergen with Inajati Adrisijanti, Yogyakarta, 29 December 2011.

[34] Compare with Guha-Thakurta who, with regard to archaeological/religious sites in India, speaks of 'contentious sites' and 'the embattled present': Guha-Thakurta, *Monuments, objects, histories*, 237–303.

[35] For 'epistemic violence' as a typical post-colonial Western act of violence, illustrated in Chapter 3 of this book, see Spivak, 'Can the subaltern speak?'

[36] Fami Basha, *Borobudur dan peninggalan nabi Suleiman* (Jakarta and Zaytuna: Herman Sinung Junatama's, 2012); *Majapahit Kerajaan Islam* (Jakarta: Noura Books, 2014). On the

seriously is whether we should indeed call these two publications, which in many a specialist's eyes contain rather absurd pseudo-scientific interpretations, acts of epistemic violence? Do these two books, with their claim to superior scientific knowledge, violate and marginalise other knowledge systems in relation to these sites? This might be the case, as Basha's book in particular did generate enthusiastic discussions on the internet. But the two studies are also idiosyncratic interpretations only partly based on exchange of knowledge. As such, they are just one of many site-related histories we have studied in this book, in order to gain insight into, and visualise, processes, interactions, and hierarchies of knowledge regimes, and of knowledge production. They do not seem to seriously counter dominant academic interpretations, which happen to coincide with more popular views worldwide, supported by the iconography of the monuments and by tourist guides. They do recall, however, what we discussed in Chapter 4, that when it comes to the imagination, sites can be weak, or even not matter, as long as the story is good. Perhaps the stories of Basha and Junatama are just not good enough, or too far-fetched, compared to the nationalist reinterpretations of the Majapahit site by Yamin, in the Indonesian context.

In the end, the success of Borobudur, Prambanan, and Majapahit as lasting monuments *in* Islamic Indonesia may be partly explained by the 1992 Indonesian heritage law which, as we discussed in the Introduction, officially categorised them as dead monuments: that is, no longer used as they were at the time they were built.[37] This law officially forbade people to use such officially 'religiously dead' sites again for religious purposes, but in practice there has been controlled leniency at these three main sites, as we have shown. Waisek even became a national holiday in the context of the UNESCO Borobudur restoration. The slightly revised law of 2010 formalised this leniency as 'Items of cultural property which at the time of their discovery are no longer used in the manner for which they were originally intended are pemitted to be used for specified needs.'[38] This 'controlled' leniency may have been developed in the context of the economic and cultural-political success, especially of Borobudur, which since at least the 1970s, has drawn Buddhist pilgrims and associations from across the world. But it may just as well be that the government does not have the means or justification to enforce the law literally, as the temples are still kept alive and cared for by Indonesians.

phenomena of such forms of historical fiction projected on sites as ideology, and other efforts to appropriate – in texts – sites of Java's Hindu–Buddhist past as Islamic, see Farabi Fakih, 'Reading ideology in Indonesia today', *BKI* 173:2/3 (2015), 353–354.

37 Article 21 of Law 1992, 5 (Undang-Undang Republik Indonesia nomor 5 tahun 1992 tentang Benda Cagar Budaya, pasal 38).

38 Article 87 of Law 2010, 11 (Undang-Undang Republik Indonesia nomor 11 tahun 2010 tentang Cagar Budaya, pasal 87).

Because they have been relocated, restored, reconstructed, and reintegrated in Islamic society for more than two centuries now, the Hindu–Buddhist sites in Indonesia have become part and parcel of official Indonesian culture, bringing in tourist money, and expressing a grand national past, and awesome religious art and architecture, produced by Indonesians' ancestors. But, as our study has shown, beyond these official and marketing stories, all along, these sites were never dead but very much alive, and came to be even more meaningful precisely because they are 'old' and, in many Indonesians' eyes, are therefore endowed with power. The results have been complex, and indeed also contested, but seem to work. Albeit partially restricted by the (adapted) heritage law, the sites have been reappropriated by Indonesia's (Balinese, Chinese, and revivalist) Hindu and Buddhist populations, as well as by foreign Buddhists. And next to the officially 'living monument' mosque of Demak, the 'dead monuments' of Borobudur and Prambanan also matter to the millions of Indonesians who crowd the sites during Lebaran, Christmas, and other Indonesian national holidays – though perhaps not in the ways imagined by purist archaeologists, art historians, or heritage experts. This is how sites show their potential to move people, and why a history of heritage formation in Asia, despite the petrifying forces of heritage, demonstrates mobility and suggests possibilities for change and inclusion.

Bibliography

Archives

Archiv der Universität Wien, Vienna
Arsip Mankunegaran (Archives of the Mangkunegaran), Solo
  Archives Mangkunegara VII
  Correspondence Mangkunegara VII
Arsip Nasional Republik Indonesia (ANRI)
  Algemeene Secretarie (AS, General Secretary of the Dutch Colonial Gvernment)
  Arsip Keresidenan Semarang (AKS, Residential Archive of Semarang)
  Arsip Keresidenan Yogyakarta (Residential Archive of Yogyakarta)
  Arsip Koninklijk Bataviaasch Genootschap (KBG, Archives of the Royal Batavian Society of Arts and Sciences)
  Arsip Sonobudoyo / Java Instituut
  Arsip Muhammad Yamin
Arsip Pakualaman, Yogyakarta
  Badan Pelestarian Peninggalan Purbakala, Bedulu
  Badan Pelestarian Peninggalan Purbakala, Prambanan
  Badan Pelestarian Peninggalan Purbakala, Trowulan
  Badan Pelestarian Peninggalan Purbakala, Yogyakarta
Beeld en Geluid Institute, Hilversum
  Collection Rijksvoorlichtingsdienst
British Library, London
  India Office Library & Records, Mackenzie Private Collection
Bundesarchiv Berlin
  Ahnenerbe NS
Koninklijk Instituut voor de Tropen (Royal Tropical Institute), Amsterdam
  Photographic Collection
Leiden University Library, Special Collections, KITLV Collections
  Collection A. J. Bernet-Kempers, H 1045
  Collection Indisch Wetenschappelijk Instituut, H 1790
  Collection P. A. J. Moojen, H 1169
  Collection V. R. van Romondt, H 1239
  Collection C. J. van der Vlis, DH 341
Museum Volkenkunde, Leiden
  Sieburgh, H. N., *Beschrijving van Brahmansche Oudheden op het eiland Java*, boek 1

Nationaal Archief (NA, National Archives), The Hague
Archief van F. den Hollander
Archief van het Ministerie voor Algemeene oorlogvoering van het Koninkrijk (AOK)
Archief van het Ministerie van Algemeene zaken
Archief van het Ministerie van Buitenlandse zaken
Archief van het Ministerie van Koloniën (MvK)
National Archives, Bangkok
Nederlands Architectuur Instituut (NAI), Rotterdam
Archive Maclaine Pont, inv. nr MACL 33
Stadsarchief Amsterdam
Collection 1303 (Familie de Flines)
Tobunken-National Research Institute for Cultural Properties, Tokyo
UNESCO Archives, Paris
Victoria and Albert Museum (V&A), London
Registry and Archives (R&A)

Publications

Abdulgani, Roeslan, *Indonesia: unique in contrast, culture and change (country, people transition and future)* (n.p.: Ministry of Information, 1951).

Abdullah, Taufik, *Schools and politics: the Kaum Muda movement in West Sumatra 1927–1933* (Ithaca: ISEAP, 1971).

Adhuri, Dedi Supriadi, and Gutomo Bayu Aji, 'The hidden story of Borobudur', *Inside Indonesia* 125 (Jul.–Sep. 2016), www.insideindonesia.org/the-hidden-story-of-borobudur-2 (accessed 14 July 2017).

Agawa, Natsuko, *Heritage conservation and Japan's cultural diplomacy: heritage, identity and national interest* (London: Routledge, 2015).

Akihary, Huib, *Architectuur en stedebouw in Indonesië: 1870–1970* (Zutphen: Walburg Press, 1990).

Ali, Daud, 'Connected histories? Regional historiography and theories of cultural contact between early South and Southeast Asia', in R. Michael Feener and Terenjit Sevea (eds.), *Islamic connections: Muslim societies in South and Southeast Asia* (Singapore: ISEAS, 2009), 1–24.

Alisjahbana, Takdir, 'Menudju masjarakat dan kebudajaan baru', in Achdiat K. Mihardja (ed.), *Polemik Kebudajaan* (Jakarta: Perpustakaan perguran kementerian P.P.dan K., 1954), 14.

Allen, Charles, *The Buddha and the sahibs: the men who discovered India's lost religion* (London: John Murray, 2002).

Almond, Philip, *The British discovery of Buddhism* (Cambridge: Cambridge University Press, 1988).

Amir, 'Geschiedenis. Datoek Katoemanggoengan en Parapatiëh nan Sabatang', *Jong Sumatra* (September–October 1922), 5–10.

'Iets over de Sumatranen als zeevarend volk', *Gedenk-Nummer van Jong Sumatra. Orgaan van den Jong Sumatranen Bond 1917–1922* (Weltevreden: Jong Sumatranen Bond, 1923), 36–43.

Anderson, Benedict R. O'G., 'Cartoons and monuments: the evolution of political communication under the New Order', in Anderson, *Language and power*, 152–194; first published as B. Anderson, 'Notes on contemporary political communications in Indonesia', *Indonesia* 16 (October 1973), 39–80).

Imagined communities: reflections on the origin and spread of nationalism, revised edn (London and New York: Verso, 1991).

Language and power: exploring political cultures in Indonesia (Ithaca and London: Cornell University Press, 1990).

Anom, I Gusti Nyoman, *The restoration of Borobudur* (Paris: UNESCO, 2005).

App, Urs, *The birth of orientalism* (Philadelphia: University of Pennsylvania Press, 2010).

Appadurai, Arjun, *The social life of things: commodities in cultural perspective* (Cambridge: Cambridge University Press, 1985).

Ariswara, *Temples of Java* (Jakarta: Intermasa, 1992).

Arps, Bernhard, *Tembang in two traditions: performance and interpretation of Javanese literature* (London: School of Oriental and African Studies, 1992).

Aryoshi, Iwao, *Indonesia Kodaishi* (Nara: Tenrikyo-Doyu-Sya, 1985).

Asser, Saskia, '"A capable and experienced photographer": Van Kinsbergen and the artistic traditions of his time', in Theuns-de Boer and Asser (eds.), *Isidore van Kinsbergen*, 86–124.

Astawa, Oka, A. A. Gde, I Made Sutaba, et al., *Pura Samuan Tiga: Bedulu Gianyar* (Bedulu: Pemerintah kabupaten Gianyar dan paruman pura Samuan Tiga, 2006).

Atmosudiro, Sumijati, *Bandung Bandawasa di masa kini; Kisah Balik Megahnya hasil pemugaran Benda Cagar Budaya* (Plaosan: BP3 Wilayah Jawa Tenggah; Kementeri Kebudayaan dan Parawisata, 2003).

Aydin, Cemil, *The politics of anti-Westernism in Asia: visions of world order in pan-Islamic and pan-Asian thought* (New York: Columbia University Press, 2007).

Bakker, Jan Albert, *Megalithic research in the Netherlands, 1547–1911: from 'giant's beds' and 'Pillars of Hercules' to accurate investigations* (Leiden: Sidestone Press, 2010).

'Bangun Mandala majapahit di UGM, Hashim: Keluarga kami keturunan Majapahit', https://news.detik.com/berita/d-2769011/bangun-mandala-majapahit-di-ugm-hashim-keluarga-kami-keturunan-majapahit (accessed 22 May 2017).

Barnard, Timothy P. (ed.), *Contesting Malayness: Malay identity across borders* (Singapore: Singapore University Press, 2004).

Barringer, Tim, 'The South Kensington Museum and the colonial project', in Tim Barringer and Tom Flynn (eds.), *Colonialism and the object: empire, material culture and the museum* (London: Routledge, 1998), 11–28.

Barth, Frederik, et al., *One discipline, four ways: British, German, French, and American Anthropology. The Halle Lectures* (Chicago: University of Chicago Press, 2005).

Basa, Kishor K., 'Indian writings on early history and archaeology of Southeast Asia: a historiographical analysis', *JRAS* 8:3 (1989), 398–410.

Basha, Farmi, *Borobudur dan peninggalan nabi Suleiman* (Jakarta and Zaytuna: Herman Sinung Junatama's, 2012).

Bastin, John S., *The native policies of Sir Stamford Raffles in Java and Sumatra: an economic interpretation* (Oxford: At the Clarendon Press, 1957).

Bastin, John S. and Pauline Rohatgi, *Prints of Southeast Asia in the India Office Library: the East India Company in Malaysia and Indonesia 1786–1824* (London: Her Majesty's Stationery Office, 1979).

Bateson, Gregory, 'An old temple and a new myth', *Djawa* 17 (1937), 291–307.

Bauman, Martin, 'Global Buddhism: developmental periods, regional histories, and a new analytical perspective', *Journal of Global Buddhism* 2 (2001), 1–43.

Bayly, Susan, 'Imagining "Greater India": French and Indian visions of colonialism in the Indic mode', *MAS* 38:3 (2004), 703–744.

Bennett, J., *Crescent moon: Islamic art and civilization in Southeast Asia* (Seattle: University of Washington Press, 2016).

Berg, C. C., 'Arya Tada en de Gajah Madah gelofte', *BKI* 98 (1939), 253–283.

'De evolutie der Javaansche geschiedschrijving', *Mededelingen der Koninklijke Nederlandse Akademie van Wetenschappen, afd. Letterkunde, Nieuwe Reeks* 14:2 (1951).

'De geschiedenis van pril Majapahit I. Het mysterie van de vier dochters van Krtanegara', *Indonesië* 4:6 (1950/1951), 481–520.

'De geschiedenis van pril Majapahit II. Achtergrond en oplossing der pril majapahitsche conflicten', *Indonesië* 5:3 (1951), 193–233.

Javaansche geschiedschrijving, Part IIA of F. W. Stapel (ed.), *Geschiedenis van Nederlandsch-Indië*, 5 vols. (Amsterdam: Joost van den Vondel, 1938–1940), 7–150.

'Javanese historiography: a synopsis of its evolution', in G. E. Hall (ed.), *Historians of South East Asia* (London: Oxford University Press, 1961), 13–23.

'Kartanegara, de miskende empire builder', *Orientatie* (July 1950), 1–32.

'De Sadeng oorlog en de mythe van groot Majapahit', *Indonesië* 5:5 (1952), 385–422.

Bernet Kempers, A. J., *Herstel in eigen waarde: monumentenzorg in Indonesië* (Zutphen: De Walburg Pers, 1978).

Monumental Bali: introduction to Balinese archaeology and guide to the monuments (Singapore: Periplus Editions, 1991).

'Oudheidkundig werk in Indonesië na de oorlog', *Indonesië. Tijdschrift gewijd aan het indonesisch Cultuurgebied* 7 (1954), 481–513.

Bie, C. W. P. de, 'Verslag van de ontgraving der Steenen Kamers in de doesoen Tandjoen Ara, Pasemah-Hoogvlakte', *Tijdschrift voor Indische Taal-, Land- en Volkenkunde* 72 (1932), 626–635.

Black, Heather, and Geoffrey Wall, 'Global–local relationships in UNESCO World Heritage Sites', in T. C. Chang and K. C. Ho (eds.), *Interconnected worlds: tourism in Southeast Asia* (Oxford: Elsevier Science Ltd, 2001), 121–136.

Blackburn, Anne M., 'Buddha-relics in the lives of Southern Asian polities', *Numen* 57 (2010), 318–340.

'Ceylonese Buddhism in colonial Singapore: new ritual spaces and specialists, 1895–1935', Asia Research Institute Working Paper Series 184 (Singapore: Asia Research Institute, National University of Singapore, 2012).

Locations of Buddhism: colonialism and modernity in Sri Lanka (Chicago: Chicago University Press, 2010).

Blagden, Charles O., *Catalogue of manuscripts in European languages belonging to the library of the India Office*, Vol. I, *The Mackenzie Collections*, Part 1, *The 1822 Collection and the Private Collection* (London: Oxford University Press, 1916).

Bloembergen, Marieke, 'Borobudur in "the light of Asia": scholars, pilgrims and knowledge networks of Greater India, 1920s–1970s', in Michael Laffan (ed.), *Belonging across the Bay of Bengal: religious rites, colonial migrations, national rights* (London: Bloomsbury, 2017), 35–56.

Colonial spectacles: the Netherlands and the Dutch East Indies at the World Exhibitions, 1880–1931 (Singapore: Singapore University Press, 2006).

'Local knowledge and the problem of civilization: place, affection and persona in the work of "Indonesianists" Willem F. Stutterheim and Claire Holt in the 1930s', unpublished paper presented at the workshop 'The persona of the orientalist scholar, 1870–1930', Leiden University, 28–29 January 2016.

Bloembergen, Marieke, and Martijn Eickhoff, 'The colonial archaeological hero reconsidered: postcolonial perspectives on the "discovery" of pre-historic Indonesia', in Gisela Eberhardt and Fabian Link (eds.), *Historiographical approaches to past archaeological research* (Berlin: Edition Topoi, 2015), 133–164.

'Conserving the past, mobilizing the Indonesian future: archaeological sites, regime change and heritage politics in Indonesia in the 1950s', *BKI* 167:4 (2011), 405–436.

'Critical heritage studies and the importance of studying histories of heritage formation', *IIAS Newsletter* 70 (2015), 44–47.

'Decolonizing Borobudur: moral engagements and the fear of loss. The Netherlands, Japan and (post)colonial heritage politics in Indonesia', in Susan Legêne, Bambang Purwanto, and Henk Schulte Nordholt (eds.), *Sites, bodies and stories: imagining Indonesian history* (Singapore: NUS Press, 2015), 33–66.

'Exchange and the protection of Java's antiquities: a transnational approach to the problem of heritage in colonial Java', *JAS* 72:4 (2013), 1–24.

'Een klein land dat de wereld bestormt: het nieuwe Rijksmuseum en het Nederlandse koloniale verleden', *BMGN* 129:1 (2014), 156–169.

'Re-embarking for "Banten", the sultanate that never really surrendered', in Marjet Derks, Martijn Eickhoff, Remco Ensel, and Floris Meens (eds.), *What's left behind: the* lieux de mémoire *of Europe beyond Europe* (Nijmegen: Vantilt, 2015), 140–148.

'Save Borobudur! The moral dynamics of heritage formation in Indonesia across orders and borders', in Michael Falser (ed.), *Cultural heritage as civilizing mission: from decay to recovery* (Cham; Heidelberg: Springer, 2015), 83–122.

'A wind of change on Java's ruined temples: archaeological activities, imperial circuits and heritage awareness in Java and the Netherlands (1800–1850)', *BMGN* 128:1 (2013), 81–104.

Bloembergen, Marieke, and Remco Raben, 'Wegen naar het nieuwe Indië, 1890–1950', in Marieke Bloembergen and Remco Raben (eds.), *Het Koloniale beschavingsoffensief: wegen naar het nieuwe Indië, 1890–1950* (Leiden: KITLV Uitgeverij, 2009), 7–24.

Bodden, Michael H., 'Utopia and the shadow of nationalism: the plays of Sanusi Pane 1928–1940', *BKI* 153:3 (1997), 332–355.

Boers, J. W., 'Oud Volksgebruik in het Rijk van Jambi', *Tijdschrift voor Neêrland's Indie* 3:1 (1840), 372–384.

Boneff, Marcel, *Pérégrinations javanaises: les voyages de R. M. A. Purwa Lelana. Une vision de Java au XIXe siècle (c. 1860–1875)* (Paris: Ed. De la Maison des sciences de l'homme, 1986).

'Borobudur: "The terraced Mountain". Java's monument to Buddhism', in 'Twenty-five centuries of Buddhist art and culture', *UNESCO Courier* 9:6 (June 1956), 43–45.

Bosch, F. D. K., 'Iets over Oost-Javaansche kunst en hare verhouding tot de Midden-Javaansche en de Balische', *Wederopbouw* 1 (1918), 52–63.

'"Local genius" en Oudjavaansche Kunst', *Mededelingen der Koninklijke Nederlandse Akademie van Wetenschappen*, Afd. Letterkunde, Nieuwe Reeks 15:1 (1952).

'De ontwikkeling van het Museum-Wezen in Nederlandsch-Indië', *Djawa: Tijdschrift van het Java-Instituut* 15 (1935), 209–221.

'Oudheidkundig Verslag over het eerste en tweede kwartaal van 1927', *OV 1927* (1928), 3–35.

'Oudheidkundig Verslag over het vierde Kwartaal 1920', *OV 1920* (1920).

'Het restaureren van Hindoe-Javaansche bouwwerken', *Djawa* 2 (1922), 1–14.

'Verslag van een reis door Sumatra', *OV 1930* (1931) Bijlage C, 133–157.

Bosch, Frederik D. K., and Charles C. F. M. le Roux, 'Wat te Parijs verloren ging', *Tijdschrift voor Indische Taal-, Land- en Volkenkunde* 71 (1931), 663–683.

Bosnak, Judith E., Frans X. Koot, and Revo A. G. Soekatno, *Op reis met een Javaanse edelman: een levendig portret van koloniaal Java in de negentiende eeuw (1860–1875). De reizen van radèn mas arjo Poerwolelono* (Zutphen: Walburg Pers, 2013).

Boulger, Demetrius C., *The Life of Sir Stamford Raffles* (London: Marshall and Son, 1897).

Brandes, J. L. A., *Beschrijving van Tjandi Singasari; en de Wolkentooneelen van Panataran* ('s-Gravenhage: Nijhoff; Batavia: Albrecht, 1908).

'Bijschrift bij de door den heer Neeb gezonden photo's van Oudheden in het Djambische', *Tijdschrift voor Indische Taal-, Land- en Volkenkunde* 45 (1902), 128–133.

Eenige uiteenzettingen (Batavia: Albrecht & Co., 1902).

Nâgarakrĕtâgama: lofdicht van Prapanjtja op Koning Rasadjanagara, Hajam Wuruk, van Madjapahit, uitgegeven naar het eenige daarvan bekende palmbladhandschrift aangetroffen in de puri te Tjakranagara op Lombok, Batavia, Verhandelingen van het Bataviaasch Genootschap voor Kunsten en Wetenschappen 54:1 (Batavia: Landsdrukkerij; 's-Gravenhage: Nijhoff, 1902).

Pararaton (Ken Arok). Het boek der koningen van Tumapĕl en van Majapahit: uitgegeven en toegelicht, Verhandelingen van het Bataviaasch Genootschap van Kunsten en Wetenschappen 49:1 ('s-Gravenhage: Martinus Nijhoff; Batavia: Albrecht & Co., 1897).

'De waarde van Tjandi Prambanan tegenover de andere oudheden van Java en een hartig woord over de deblayeering', *Tijdschrift voor Indische Taal-, Land- en Volkenkunde* (*TBG*) 47 (1904), 414–432.

Branfoot, Crispin, 'Remaking the past: Tamil sacred landscape and temple renovations', *Bulletin of SOAS* 76:1 (2013), 21–47.

Brata, Hangga, and Arientha Primanita, 'Actor Richard Gere drawn by karma to Borobudur, planning temple movie', *JakartaGlobe*, 27 June 2011, www.thejakartaglobe.com/indonesia/actor-richard-gere-drawn-by-karma-to-borobudur-planning-temple-movie/449282 (accessed 13 January 2012).

Brend, Barbara, *Islamic art* (Cambridge, MA: Harvard University Press, 1991).

Brinkgreve, Francine, 'Balinese chiefs and Dutch dominion', in Endang Sri Hardiati and Pieter Ter Keurs (eds.), *Indonesia: the discovery of the past* (Amsterdam: KIT Publishers, 2005), 122–145.

Brix, Emil (ed.), *Memoria Austria*, vols. I–III (Vienna: Verlag für Geschichte und Politik, 2004–2005).

Broeshart, A. C., J. R. van Diessen, and R. G. Gill, *Surabaya: beeld van een stad* (Purmerend: Asia Maior, 1997).

Brown, Iem, 'Buddhist revival in modern Indonesia', in Martin Ramstedt (ed.), *Hinduism in modern Indonesia: a minority religion between local, national, and global interests* (London: Routledge, 2004), 45–55.

Brugmans, I. J. (ed.), *Nederlandsch-Indië onder Japanse bezetting: gegevens en documenten over de jaren 1942–1945* (Franeker: Wever, 1960).

Bruijn, Jean Victor de, *H. N. Sieburgh en zijn beteekenis voor de Javaansche oudheidkunde* (Leiden: Luctor et Emergo, 1937).

Brumund, Jan F. G., *Bijdragen tot de kennis van het Hindoeïsme op Java*, Verhandelingen van het Bataviaasch Genootschap van Kunsten en Wetenschappen 33 (Batavia: Lange, 1868).

'Iets over stenen voorwerpen van verschillend gebruik uit den Hindoe-tijd op Java gevonden', in *Indiana: verzameling van stukken van onderscheidenen aard, over landen, volken, oudheden en geschiedenis van den Indischen archipel*, 2nd part (Amsterdam: P. N. van Kampen, 1854), 101–114.

Bruyn Kops, G. F. de, *Overzicht van Zuid-Sumatra* (Amsterdam: Zuid-Sumatra Instituut, 1919).

Buddingh, S. A., *Neêrlands-Oost-Indië; Reizen . . . gedaan gedurende het tijdvak van 1852–1857*, 3 vols., 1st edn (Rotterdam, 1859–1861).

Neêrlands-Oost-Indië; Reizen . . . gedaan gedurende het tijdvak van 1852–1857, 3 vols., 2nd edn (Amsterdam: Van Kesteren & Zoon, 1867).

Budiarti, Hari, 'Heirlooms of an archipelago', in Retno Sulistianingsih Sitowati and John N. Miksic (eds.), *Icons of art: National Museum Jakarta* (Jakarta: BAB Publishing, 2006), 129–168.

Byrne, Denis R., *Counterheritage: critical perspectives on heritage conservation in Asia* (New York: Routledge, 2014).

Campbell, Siobhan, 'Early Kamasan art in museum collections', *BKI* 170 (2014), 250–280.

Campen, J. van, 'History of the collection', in C. J. A. Jörg and J. van Campen (eds.), *Chinese ceramics in the collection of the Rijksmuseum Amsterdam: the Ming and Qing dynasties* (London: Philip Wilson Publishers, 1997), 11–23.

Carey, Peter (ed.), *The British in Java, 1811–1816: a Javanese account* (London: Oxford University Press for the British Academy, 1992).

Destiny: the life of Prince Diponegoro of Yogyakarta 1785–1855 (Oxford: Peter Lang, 2014).

The power of prophecy: Prince Dipanagara and the end of an old order in Java, 1785–1855 (Leiden: KITLV Press, 2007).

'The Sepoy conspiracy of 1815 in Java', *BKI* 133:2/3 (1977), 294–322.

Carman, John, *Archaeological resource management: an international perspective* (Cambridge: Cambridge University Press, 2015).

Casparis, Johannes G. de, 'Historical writing on Indonesia (early period)', in Daniel G. E. Hall (ed.), *Historians of South East Asia* (London: Oxford University Press, 1961), 121–164.

Selected inscriptions from the seventh to the ninth century AD II (Bandung: Masa Baru, 1956).

'Twintig jaar studie van de oudere geschiedenis van Indonesië: 1931–1951', *Oriëntatie: Cultureel Maandblad* 46 (1954), 626–664.

Catalogus van eene verzameling van voorwerpen van kunstnijverheid uit de hoofdstad Palembang en de landstreek Pasemah Lebar (Amsterdam: Zuid-Sumatra Instituut, 1922).

Chakrabarty, Dipesh, *Provincializing Europe: post-colonial thought and difference*, revised edn (Princeton: Princeton University Press, 2008).

Chambert-Loir, Henri, 'Saints and ancestors: the cult of Muslim saints in Java', in Henri Chambert-Loir and Anthony Reid (eds.), *The potent dead: ancestors, saints and heroes in contemporary Indonesia* (Crows Nest: Allen & Unwin; Honolulu: University of Hawai'i Press, 2002), 132–141.

Chan, J., et al., 'Heritage beyond the boundaries: a manifesto', *IIAS Newsletter* 69 (2014), 22–23, www.iias.asia/the-newsletter/article/heritage-beyond-boundaries-manifesto (accessed 8 August 2019).

Chihara, Diagoro, 'Borobudur monogatari III: Borobudur to Nihon-jin', *Wafu-Kenchiku* 17 (1983), 126–133.

'Busseki Borobudōru hinzū Jawa no kenchiku geijutsu', *Hara Shobō* (1969).

Hindu–Buddhist architecture in Southeast Asia, transl. from Japanese by Rolf W. Giebel (Leiden: Brill, 1996).

Chijs, J. A. van der, 'Oud-Bantam', *Tijdschrift voor Indische Taal-, Land- en Volkenkunde* 26 (1881), 1–62.

Chulalongkorn, *Itinéraire d'un voyage à Java en 1896*, compiled and edited by Chanatip Kesavadhana (Paris: Association Archipel, 1993).

Chutiwongs, N., 'Çandi Singasari – a recent study', in E. A. Bacus, I. C. Glover and P. D. Sharrock (eds.), *Interpreting Southeast Asia's past: monument, image and text* (Singapore: NUS Press, 2008), 100–121.

Clémentin-Ojha, Catherine, and Pierre-Yves Manguin, *A century in Asia: the history of the École française d'Extrême Orient* (Singapore: Didier-Millet, 2001).

Coedès, George, 'Les inscriptions Malaises de Çrîvijaya', *BEFEO* 30 (1930), 29–80.

'Le Royaume de Çrîvijaya', *BEFEO* 18:6 (1918), 1–36.

Cohen, Matthew, *Inventing the performing arts: modernity and tradition in colonial Indonesia* (Honolulu: University of Hawai'í Press, 2016).

Colombijn, Freek, 'A moving history of Middle Sumatra', *MAS* 39:1 (2005), 1–38.

Conklin, Alice L., *A mission to civilize: the republican idea of empire in France and West Africa, 1895–1930* (Stanford: Stanford University Press, 1997).

Cooper, Frederick, *Colonialism in question: theory, knowledge, history* (Berkeley: University of California Press, 2005).

Cornelissen, C. H., A. L. van Hasselt, and J. F. Snelleman, *Reizen in Midden-Sumatra 1877–1879, door de leden der Sumatra-expeditie, uitgerust door het Aardrijkskundige Genootschap*, part II (Leiden, 1882).

Corner, E. J. H., *The marquis: a tale of Syonan-to* (Kuala Lumpur and Hong Kong: Heinemann Asia, 1981).

'Obituary of Prof. H. Tanakadate', *Nature* 167 (14 April 1951), 586–587.

Coté, Joost, and Hugh O' Neill, *The life and work of Thomas Karsten* (Amsterdam: Architectura & Natura, 2017).

Cox, Laurence, *Buddhism and Ireland: from the Celts to the counter-culture* (Sheffield: Equinox, 2013).

Crawfurd, John, *History of the Indian Archipelago: containing an account of the manners, arts, languages, religions, institutions, and commerce of its inhabitants* (Edinburgh: Constable, 1820).

Creese, Helen, *Bali in the early nineteenth century: the ethnographic accounts of Pierre Dubois*, Verhandelingen van het Koninklijk Instituut voor Taal-, Land- en Volkenkunde 305 (Leiden: Brill/KITLV, 2016).

'Balinese television histories: broadcasting historical discourses in Bali', *Review of Indonesian and Malaysian Affairs* 34 (2000), 11–38.

'In search of Majapahit: the transformation of Balinese identities', Centre of Southeast Asian Studies Working Paper 101 (Clayton, Victoria: Monash University, 1997).

Cribb, Robert, and Colin Brown, *Modern Indonesia: a history since 1945* (London: Longman, 1995).

Daifuku, Hiroshi, 'Saving our heritage in stone: a world-wide challenge', *UNESCO Courier* (June 1968), 4–7.

Daly, Patrick, and Tim Winter, 'Heritage in Asia: converging forces, conflicting values', in Daly and Winter (eds.), *Routledge handbook of heritage in Asia*, 1–35.

(eds.), *Routledge handbook of heritage in Asia* (London and New York: Routledge, 2012).

Damais, Louis Charles, 'Etudes javanaises VII: les tombes musulmanes datées de Tralaya', *BEFEO* 48:2 (1957), 353–416.

Dammerman, Karel W., *Overzicht der Nederlandsch-Indische natuurmonumenten* (Buitenzorg: Nederlandsch-Indische Vereeniging tot Natuurbescherming, 1924).

Daniels, Timothy P., 'Imagining selves and inventing Festival Sriwijaya', *Journal of Southeast Asian Studies* 30:1 (1999), 37–53.

Das Gupta, Arun, 'Rabindranath Tagore in Indonesian experience in bridge-building', *BKI* 158 (2002), 451–477.

Day, Tony, and Will Derks, 'Narrating knowledge: reflections on the encyclopedic impulse in literary texts from Indonesian and Malay worlds', *BKI* 155:3 (1999), 309–341.

Day, Tony, and Craig J. Reynolds, 'Cosmologies, truth regimes and the state in Southeast Asia', *MAS* 34:1 (2000), 1–55.

Dewi, Sita W., 'Angkor Wat, Borobudur Temple to become sister sites, says official', *Jakarta Post*, 12 January 2012, www.thejakartapost.com/news/2012/01/12/angkor-wat-borobudur-temple-become-sister-sites-says-official.html (accessed January 13, 2012).

Díaz-Andreu, Margarita, *A world history of nineteenth-century archaeology: nationalism, colonialism, and the past* (Oxford: Oxford University Press, 2007).

Dirks, Nicolas, 'Guiltless spoliations: picturesque beauty, colonial knowledge, and Colin Mackenzie's survey of India', in Catherine B. Asher and Thomas R. Metcalf (eds.), *Perceptions of South Asia's visual past* (New Delhi: American Institute of Indian Studies, 1994), 211–232.

Djoko, *Trowulan: Bekas ibukota Majapahit* (Jakarta: Balai Poestaka, 1983).

Drewes, G., 'The struggle between Javanism and Islam as illustrated by the Serat Dermagandul', *BKI* 122:3 (1966), 309–365.

Duara, Prasenjit, 'Asia redux: conceptualizing a region for our times', *JAS* 69:4 (2010), 963–983.

Dumoulin, S. J. Heinrich, *Christianity meets Buddhism* (La Salle, IL: Open Court Publishing Company, 1974).

Edwards, Penny, *Cambodge: the cultivation of a nation* (Honolulu: University of Hawai'i Press, 2007).

Eerde, J. C. van, 'Hindu-Javaansche en Balische eeredienst', *BKI* 65 (1911), 1–39.

'Kort Verslag nopens de studiereis van den Directeur der Afdeeling Volkenkunde naar Nederlandsch-Indië (4 April–21 November 1929)', *19e Jaarverslag der Koninklijke Vereeniging 'Koloniaal Instituut'* (1929), 49–60.

Eickhoff, Martijn, 'Archeologisch erfgoed: een onbeheersbaar concept', in Frans Grijzenhout (ed.), *Erfgoed; de geschiedenis van een begrip* (Amsterdam: Amsterdam University Press, 2007), 231–236.

De oorsprong van het 'eigene': Nederlands vroegste verleden, archeologie en nationaal-socialisme (Amsterdam: Uitgeverij Boom, 2003).

Van het land naar de markt: 20 jaar RAAP en de vermaatschappelijking van den Nederlandse archeologie (Amsterdam: RAAP, 2005).

Eickhoff, Martijn, Gerry van Klinken, and Geoffrey Robinson (eds.), *Journal of Genocide Research* 19:3 (2017) (Special Issue, 1965 *today: living with the Indonesian massacres*).

Elson, Robert E., *The idea of Indonesia: a history* (Cambridge: Cambridge University Press, 2008).

Erp, Theodoor van, 'Eenige mededelingen betreffende de beelden en fragmenten van Boroboedoer in 1896 geschonken aan de Koning van Siam', *BKI* 73: 1 (1917), 285–310.

'Hindu-Javaansche beelden, thans te Bangkok', *BKI* 79:1 (1923), 429–518.

'Nog eens de Hindoe-Javaansche beelden in Bangkok', *BKI* 83:1 (1927), 503–513.

Fakih, Farabi, 'Reading ideology in Indonesia today', *BKI* 173:2/3 (2015), 347–363.

Fasseur, C., *Kultuurstelsel en koloniale baten: de Nederlandse exploitatie van Java 1840–1860* (Leiden: Universitaire Pers, 1975).

Ferdinandus, Utama, 'Arca-arca dan Relief pada Masa Hindu Jawa di Museum Bangkok', in Edi Sedyawati, Ingrid H. E. Pojoh, Supratikno Rahardjo and R. Soekmono (eds.), *Monumen: karya persembahan untuk Prof. Dr. R. Soekmono* (Depok: Fakultas Sastra Universitas Indonesia, 1990), 78–101.

Feuilletau de Bruyn, W. K. H., *Welk aandeel heeft Dr van Mook gehad in de gezagsschemering in Nederlandsch-Indië?* (The Hague: Van Stockum, 1946).

Fields, Rick, *How the Swans came to the lake: a narrative history of Buddhism in America*. 3rd edn, revised and updated (Boston and London: Sambbhala, 1992 [1st edn, 1981]).

Finot, Louis, 'Inscriptions du Siam et de la Péninsule malaise (Mission Lunet de Lajonquière)', *Bulletin de la Commission archéologique de l'Indochine* (1910), 147–154.

Fischer, H. W., *Catalogus van 's Rijks Ethnografisch Museum Deel XII Zuid-Sumatra (Sumatra IV)* (Leiden: 's Rijks Ethnografisch Museum, 1918).

Fischer-Tiné, Harald, *Shyamji Krishnavarma: Sanskrit, sociology and anti-imperialism* (New Delhi: Routledge, 2014).

Florida, Nancy, *Writing the past, inscribing the future: history as prophecy in colonial Java* (Durham and London: Duke University Press, 1995).

Fontein, Jan, *The law of cause and effect in ancient Java*, Verhandelingen Afdeling Letterkunde, Nieuwe Reeks Deel 140 (Amsterdam: KNAW, 1989).

'Het verzamelen van Aziatische kunst in de twintigste eeuw', *Aziatische Kunst* 23:3 (1993), 3–17.

Forbes, Henry O., *A naturalist's wanderings in the eastern archipelago: a narrative of travel and exploration from 1878 to 1883* (London: Sampson Low, 1885).

Formichi, Chiara, 'Islamic studies or Asian studies? Islam in Southeast Asia', *Muslim World*, 106 (2016), 696–718.

'Violence, sectarianism, and the politics of religion: articulations of anti-Shi'a discourse in Indonesia', *Indonesia* 98 (2014), 1–28.

Foulcher, Keith, 'Perceptions of modernity and the sense of the past: Indonesian poetry in the 1920s', *Indonesia* 23:2 (1977), 39–58.

Pujangga Baru: literature and nationalism in Indonesia, 1933–1942 (Bedford Park: Flinders University, 1980).

Fox, James J., 'Ziarah visits to the tombs of the wali, the founders of Islam on Java', in M. C. Ricklefs (ed.), *Islam in the Indonesian context* (Clayton: Centre of Southeast Asian Studies, Monash University, 1991), 19–39.

Fradier, Georges, *East and West: towards mutual understanding?* (Paris: UNESCO, 1959).

François, Étienne, and Hagen Schultze (eds.), *Deutsche Erinnerungsorte*, vols. I–III (Munich: Verlag C. H. Beck, 2001–2002).

Friederich, R., 'De Oesana Bali', *Tijdschrift voor Neerland's Indië* 9:3 (1847), 245–373.

Fruin-Mees, W., *Geschiedenis van Java*, 2 vols. (Weltevreden: Commissie voor Volkslectuur, 1919–1920).

Sedjarah tanah Djawah, transl. S. M. Latif, 2 vols. (Weltevreden: Balai Poestaka, 1921–1922).

Galaty, Michael L., and Charles Watkinson, *Archaeology under dictatorship* (New York: Springer, 2004).

Geary, David, 'Rebuilding the navel of the earth: Buddhist pilgrimage and transnational religious networks', *MAS* 48:3 (2013), 645–692.

Giffen, A. E. van, *De Hunebedden in Nederland (met atlas). Deel II* (Utrecht: Oosthoek, 1927).

Gomperts, Amrit, Arnoud Haag, and Peter Carey, 'Mapping Majapahit: Wardenaar's archaeological survey at Trowulan in 1815', *Indonesia* 93:1 (2012), 177–196, 233.

'The sage who divided Java in 1052: Maclaine Pont's excavation of Mpu Bharada's hermitage-cemetery at Lĕmah Tulis in 1925', *BKI* 168:1 (2012), 1–25.

'Stutterheim's enigma: the mystery of his mapping of the Majapahit kraton at Trowulan in 1941', *BKI* 164:4 (2008), 411–430.

Gomperts, A. and M. J. Klokke, 'In memoriam J. G. de Casparis: 31 May 1916–19 June 2002', *BKI* 159 (2003), 471–487.

Goris, R., 'The temple system', in J. L. Swellengrebel (ed.), *Bali: studies in life, thought and ritual* (The Hague and Bandung: W. van Hoeve, 1960), 103–112.

Graaf, H. J. de, and Theodore G. Th. Pigeaud, *De eerste moslimse vorstendommen op Java: studiën over de staatkundige geschiedenis van de 15de en 16de eeuw* ('s-Gravenhage: Nijhoff, 1974).

Groeneboer, Kees, 'Nederlands in den vreemde. Het Algemeen-Nederlands Verbond in Nederlands-Indië 1899–1949', *Neerlandia* 97:4 (1993), 140–144.

Groeneveldt, W. P., and Jan L. A. Brandes, *Catalogus der Archaeologische Verzameling van het Bataviaasch Genootschap van Kunsten en Wetenschappen, met aanteekeningen omtrent de op verschillende voorwerpen voorkomende inscripties en een voorloopigen inventaris der beschreven steenen* (Batavia: Albrecht, 1887).

Groneman, Isaac, *Boeddhistische tempelbouwvallen in de Praga-vallei: de Tjandi's Barabadoer, Mendoet en Pawon* (Semarang: Van Dorp, 1907).

'Een Boeddhistischen-koning op den Borobudoer', *Tijdschrift voor de Indische Taal-, Land- en Volkenkunde* 39 (1897), 367–378.

De Garĕbĕg te Ngajogyåkartå ('s-Gravenhage: Nijhoff, 1895).

Tjandi Parambanan op Midden-Java, na de Ontgraving: met lichtdrukken van Cephas (Leiden: Brill, 1893).

Groot, H., *Van Batavia naar Weltevreden: het Bataviaasch Genootschap van Kunsten en Wetenschappen, 1778–1867* (Leiden: KITLV Uitgeverij, 2009).

Guha-Thakurta, Tapati, *Monuments, objects, histories: institutions of art in colonial and postcolonial India* (New York: Columbia University Press, 2004).

Guillot, Claude, 'Un example d' assimilation à Java: le photograph Kassian Céphas', *Archipel* 22 (1981), 55–73.

Gupta, A., 'The song of the non-aligned world: transnational identities and the reinscription of space in late capitalism', in Steven Vertovec and Robin Cohen (eds.), *Migration, diasporas and transnationalism* (Northampton: Edward Elgar, 1999), 503–519.

Haan, F. de, 'De Historie van een Oudgast', *Tijdschrift voor Indische Taal-, Land- en Volkenkunde* 18 (1901), 195–225.

Hadiwardoyo, Sanento Yuliman, 'Genèse de la peinture indonésienne contemporaine: le rôle de S. Sudjojono', PhD thesis, École des Hautes Études des Sciences Sociales, Paris, 1981.

Halbertsma, Ruurd B., *Scholars, travellers and trade: the pioneer years of the National Museum of Antiquities in Leiden, 1818–1840* (London: Routledge, 2003).

Harper, Tim, and Sunil S. Amrith, 'Sites of Asian interaction: an introduction', in Tim Harper (ed.), *Sites of Asian interaction: ideas, networks and mobility*, Special Issue, *MAS* 46 (2012), 249–257.

Harrison, Rodney, *Heritage: critical approaches* (London and New York: Routledge, 2013).

Hart-van den Muyzenberg, Hanneke J. 't, 'Vogel, Jean Philippe (1871–1958)', in *Biografisch Woordenboek van Nederland*, http://resources.huygens.knaw.nl/bwn1880-2000/lemmata/bwn4/vogel (accessed 24 April 2014).

Haskell, Francis, and Nicholas Penny, *Taste and the antique: the lure of classical sculpture, 1500–1900* (New Haven: Yale University Press, 1981).

Hasselt, A. L. van and J. F. Snelleman, *Reizen in Midden-Sumatra 1877–1879, door de leden der Sumatra-expeditie, uitgerust door het Aardrijkskundige Genootschap*, part I (Leiden, 1881).

Heekeren, R. H. van, *De onderste steen boven: belevenissen van een globetrotter* (Assen: Van Gorcum, 1969).

Hefner, Robert W., *Hindu Javanese: Tengger tradition and Islam* (Princeton: Princeton University Press, 1985).

Heine-Geldern, R. von, 'Prehistoric research in the Netherlands Indies', in Pieter Honig and Frans Verdoorn (eds.), *Science and scientists in the Netherlands Indies* (New York: Board for the Netherlands Indies, Surinam and Curaçao, 1945), 129–167.

Herzfeld, Michael, 'Engagement, gentrification and the neoliberal hijacking of history', *Current Anthropology*, 51:2 (2010), 259–267.

Hideichi, Sakazume, *Taiheiyou sensou to koukogaku* (Tokyo: Yoshikawa Kobundo, 1997).

'De Hindoe-Javaansche monumenten: de arbeid der Restauratiecommissie', *Djawa* 6 (1926), 51–52.

Hitchcock, Michael, Victor King, and Michael Parnwell (eds.), *Heritage tourism in Southeast Asia* (Honolulu: University of Hawai'i Press, 2010).

Ho, Engseng, *The graves of Tarim: genealogy and mobility across the Indian Ocean* (Berkeley: University of California Press, 2006).

Hoëvell, Wolter R. van, *Reis over Java, Madura en Bali in het midden van 1847*, Part I (Amsterdam: P. N. van Kampen, 1849).

Hoijtink, Mirjam, *Exhibiting the past: Caspar Reuvens and the museums of antiquities in Europe, 1800–1840* (Turnhout: Brepols, 2012).

Hoock, Holger, *Empires of the imagination: politics, war, and the arts in the British world, 1750–1850* (London: Profile Books, 2010).

Hoop, A. N. J. Th. à Th. van der, *Catalogus der Praehistorische Verzameling* (Bandoeng: Nix, 1941).

Korte Gids voor de Praehistorische Verzameling van het Koninklijk Bataviaasch Genootschap van Kunsten en Wetenschappen door P. V. van Stein Callenfels, Edition II (Bandoeng: Nix, 1939).

Korte Gids voor de Praehistorische Verzameling van het Koninklijk Bataviaasch Genootschap van Kunsten en Wetenschappen door P. V. van Stein Callenfels, Edition III (Bandoeng: A. C. Nix & Co., 1948).

'De Megalithen', *Jaarboek II Koninklijk Bataviaasch Genootschap van Kunsten en Wetenschappen* (1934), 105–106.

Megalithic remains in South-Sumatra (Zutphen: Thieme, 1932); also published as *Megalitische oudheden in Zuid-Sumatra* (Zutphen: Thieme, 1932).

'De Praehistorie', in Frederik W. Stapel (ed.), *Geschiedenis van Nederlandsch Indië* I (Amsterdam: Joost van den Vondel, 1938), 9–111.

'De praehistorische verzameling', *Jaarboek II Koninklijk Bataviaasch Genootschap van Kunsten en Wetenschappen* (1934), 63–68.

'De praehistorische verzameling', *Jaarboek V Koninklijk Bataviaasch Genootschap van Kunsten en Wetenschappen* (1938), 65–68.

Hooykaas, C., *Surya Sevana: dari pandita untuk pandita dan Umat Hindu*, transl. Swariyati (Surabaya: Paramita, 2004).

Howe, Leo, *Hinduism and hierarchy in Bali* (Oxford: Carey, 2001).

Huyssen van Kattendijke-Frank, Katrientje, *Met prins Hendrik naar de Oost: de reis van W. J. C. Huyssen van Kattendijke naar Nederlands-Indië, 1836–1838* (Zutphen: Walburg Pers, 2004).

Iguchi, Masatoshi, 'Introduction about the author, the book, and the historical background', in Marquis Tokugawa, *Journeys to Java* (Bandung: ITB Press, 2004), xv–lviii.

Ijiri, Susume, *Baraboedoer* (Shanghai: Aoki Bunkyō, 1924).

IJzerman, Jan W., 'Over Boro-boedoer', *TKNAG* Tweede Serie 16 (1899), 307–348, 391.

Ingleson, John (ed.), *Regionalism, subregionalism and APEC* (Clayton: Monash Asia Institute, 1997).

International symposium on Chandi Borobudur: 'Religious art of Borobudur and its preservation' (Kyoto: Executive Committee for the International Symposium on Chandi Borobudur etc., 25–27 September 1980).

Isnenghi, Mario (ed.), *I luoghi della memoria*, vols. I–III (Rome: Laterza, 1996–1997).

J.D.P., 'Journal of an excursion to the native provinces in Java in the year of 1828, during the war with Dipo Negoro', *Journal of the Indian Archipelago and Eastern Asia* 7 (1853), 1–19, 138–157, 225–246, 358–378.

Jaarboek Koninklijk Bataviaasch Genootschap van Kunsten en Wetenschappen I–X (1933–1948/51).

Janse, Maartje, 'Representing distant victims: the emergence of an Ethical Movement in Dutch colonial politics, 1840–1880', *BMGN* 128:1 (2013), 53–80.

Japan International Cooperation Agency, *The national archaeological parks development project. Borobudur and Prambanan: interim report* (Tokyo: JICA, 1975).

Borobudur and Prambanan: final report (Tokyo: JICA, 1979).

Jenkins, David, *Suharto and his generals: Indonesian military politics 1975–1983* (Ithaca: Cornell University Press, 1984).

Jensma, G., and H. de Vries, *Veranderingen in het hoger onderwijs in Nederland tussen 1815 en 1940* (Hilversum: Verloren, 1997).

Jones, Tod, *Culture, power, and authoritarianism in the Indonesian state: cultural policy across the twentieth century to the reform era* (Leiden: Brill, 2013).

Jordaan, Roy, 'Nicolaus Engelhard and Thomas Stanford Raffles: brethren in Javanese antiquities', *Indonesia* 101 (April 2016), 39–66.

Jörg, C. J. A., and J. van Campen (eds.), *Chinese ceramics in the collection of the Rijksmuseum Amsterdam: the Ming and Qing dynasties* (London: Philip Wilson Publishers, 1997).

Jory, Patric, 'Thai and Western Buddhist scholarship in the age of colonialism: King Chulalongkorn redefines the Jatakas', *JAS* 61:3 (2002), 891–918.

Kartomi, Margaret J., 'The paradoxical and nostalgic history of "Gending Sriwijaya" in South Sumatra', *Archipel* 45 (1993), 37–50.

Katzenstein, Peter J., and Takashi Shiraishi (eds.), *Network power: Japan and Asia* (Ithaca and London: Cornell University Press, 1997).

Keboedajaan Timoer, I (Djakarta: Kantor Besar Keimin Bunka Shidosho, Kantor Besar Poesat Kebudajaan, 2603 [1943]).

Keboedajaan Timoer, II (Djakarta: Keimin Bunka Shishodo, 2604 [1944]).

Kemmerling, G., 'De aardbeving van Bali op 21 Jan. 1917', *Jaarboek van het Mijnwezen in Nederlandsch-Indië* 46 (1917), 1–49.

Kern, H., 'I. De eerste zang van den Nāgarakrĕtāgama', *BKI* 61 (1908), 395–403.

'II. Korte geschiedenis van Koning Rājasa in den Nāgarakrĕtāgama', *BKI* 61 (1908), 403–408.

'In memoriam J. L. A. Brandes', *BKI* 59:1 (1906), 1–6.

'Inscriptie van Kota Kapoer', *BKI* 67 (1912), 393–400.

Het oud-javaansche lofdicht Nāgarakṛĕtāgama van Prapañca (1365 AD) ('s-Gravenhage: Nijhoff, 1919).

'Zang V tot XII en XV tot XVII van den Nāgarakrĕtāgama', *BKI* 63 (1910), 337–367.

'Zang XVIII tot XXII van den Nāgarakrĕtāgama', *BKI* 66 (1912), 337–347.

'Zang XXIII tot XXXII van den Nāgarakrĕtāgama', *BKI* 67 (1913), 189–202.

'Zang XXXIII tot XXXVI en XXXVIII, XXXIX, L, LI van den Nāgarakrĕtāgama. *BKI* 67 (1913), 367–382.

'Zang LXXV tot LXXXIII van den Nāgarakrĕtāgama', *BKI* 69 (1914), 33–51.

'Zang LXXXIV tot XCI van den Nāgarakrĕtāgama', *BKI* 69 (1914), 297–313.

Kern, J. H. C., N. Krom and L. F. van Gent, *Het oud-Javaansche lofdicht Nagarakertagama* (Weltevreden: Balai Poestaka, 1922).

Keurs, Pieter ter, 'Collecting in Central and South Sumatra', in Endang Sri Hardiati and Pieter Ter Keurs (eds.), *Indonesia: the discovery of the past* (Amsterdam: KIT Publishers, 2005), 85–89.

Kielstra, E. B., 'Het Bantamsch Sultanaat', *Onze Eeuw* 10 (1916), 84–105.

Kleiweg de Zwaan, Johannes P., *Praehistorie en anthropologie: gids in het Volkenkundig Museum* (Amsterdam: Koninklijke Vereeniging Koloniaal Instituut, 1929).

Knaap, G. J., and Yudhi Soerjoadmodjo, *Cephas, Yogyakarta: photography in service of the sultan* (Leiden: KITLV Press, 1999).

Knebel, J., 'Beschrijving Hindoe-oudheden in de afdeeling Modjokerto der residentie Soerabaja', *ROC 1907* (1909), 12–114.

Koleksi Keramik Museum Nasional (Departemen Kebudayaan dan Pariwisata Direktorat Jenderal Sejarah dan Purbakala Museum Nasional, 2001).

Kologdam VIII/Brawijaya (sejarah Militair) (Surabaya: Kologdam VIII/ Brawijaya, 1977).

Kommers, J. H. M., *Besturen in een onbekende wereld: het Europese binnenlandse bestuur in Nederlands-Indië: 1800–1830. Een antropologische studie* I (Meppel: Krips Repro, 1979).

Koperberg, Samuel, 'Pelukis2 Indonesia', *Mimbar Indonesia* 22 (29 May 1954), 22–24.

Koschmann, J. Victor, 'Asianism's ambivalent legacy', in Peter J. Katzenstein and Takashi Shiraishi (eds.), *Network power: Japan and Asia* (Ithaca and London: Cornell University Press, 1997), 83–103.

Kouznetsova, Seda, 'Colin Mackenzie as collector of Javanese manuscripts and Manuscript BL MSS JAV. 29', *Indonesia and the Malay World* 36:106 (2008), 375–394.

Kreps, C., 'The idea of "pusaka" as an indigenous form of cultural heritage preservation', in Fiona Kerlogue (ed.), *Performing objects: museums, material culture and performance in Southeast Asia* (London: Horniman Museum and Gardens, 2004), 1–14.

Krom, N. J., *Beschrijving van Barabudur, Part I, Archaeologische beschrijving* ('s-Gravenhage: Nijhoff, 1920).

'Engelhard over de Javaansche oudheden', *Bijdragen tot de Taal-, Land- en Volkenkunde van Nederlandsch Indië* 76 (1929), 435–448.

'De heiligdommen van Palembang', *Mededeelingen der Koninklijke Nederlandsche Akademie van Wetenschappen* Nieuwe Reeks I, Afdeeling Letterkunde (1938), 397–423.

Hindoe-Javaansche geschiedenis, 2nd revised edn ('s-Gravenhage: Nijhoff, 1931).

'Het Hindoe-Tijdperk', in Stapel (ed.), *Geschiedenis van Nederlandsch Indië* I, 119–298.

Inleiding tot de Hindoe-Javaansche kunst, I–III ('s-Gravenhage: Nijhoff, 1920; 2nd revised edn, 1923).

Het karmawibhanggha op Borobudur (Amsterdam: KNAW, 1933).

'Kort verslag van een studiereis in Voor- en Achter-Indië. I. Britsch-Indië (eerste reis)', *ROC 1910* (Batavia: Albrecht & Co.; 's-Gravenhage: M. Nijhoff, 1911), 48–55.

'De oudheden van Modjokerto', *Nederlandsch-Indië. Oud en Nieuw* 1 (1916–1917), 99–106.

Pararaton (Ken Arok). Het boek der koningen van Tumapĕl en van Majapahit: uitgegeven en toegelicht door Dr J. L. A. Brandes, Verhandelingen van het Bataviaasch Genootschap van Kunsten en Wetenschappen 62 (2nd edn, edited by N. J. Krom) ('s-Gravenhage: Martinus Nijhoff; Batavia: Albrecht & Co., 1920).

'Het restaureren van oude bouwwerken', *Tijdschrift voor Indische Taal-, Land- en Volkenkunde* (*TBG*), 53 (1911), 1–15.

De Sumatraansche periode der Javaansche geschiedenis. Rede uitgesproken bij zijn ambtsaanvaarding als buitengewoon hoogleraar aan de Rijksuniversiteit te Leiden, op 3 december 1919 (Leiden: Brill, 1919).

'De waardering der Hindoe-Javaansche kunst', *Nederlandsch-Indië. Oud en Nieuw* 8 (1923–1924), 171–178.

Zaman Hindu, Terdjemahan Arif Effendi (Jakarta: Pembangunan, 1954).

Krom, Nicolaas Johannes, and Theodor van Erp, *Beschrijving van Barabudur, Part II, Bouwkundige beschrijving en een aanvulling op deel I door N. J. Krom* (The Hague: Nijhoff, 1931).

Kromo Djojo Adinegoro, 'De begraafplaatsen der oude regenten van Grisee voor, tijdens en na de Compagnies tijd', *Djawa* 5 (1925), 253–254.

'Eene beknopte handleiding voor het onderzoek naar de Hindoe- en Boeddhabeelden ... betrekking hebbend op de beelden in het museum in Modjokerto' (typescript, 1916, KITLV collection [published 1921]).

Eene beknopte handleiding voor het onderzoek naar de Hindoe- en Boeddhabeelden (n.p., 18 February 1921).

'Bijvoegsel over de opmerking aangaande de Lĕbaran, ofwel het Inlandsch nieuw jaar', *OV 1924* (1925), 76–80.

'Eenige opmerkingen aangaande den val van Majapahit', *OV 1915* (1915), 29–32.

'Opmerkingen aangaande de Lebaran of het Zoogenaamd Inlandsch Nieuwjaar', *OV 1923* (1923), 55–60.

Oud Javaansche oorkonden op steen uit de afdeeling Modjokerto, opgehelderd door Raden Adipati Ario Kromodjoio Adi Negoro, Oud regent Modjokerto (n.p., 1921).

Eene schets van de wajang poerwo en naar aanleiding hiervan het een en ander over de wajang gedek – wajang kroetjil, gamelan en gamelan melodieën – krissen en andere wapens (Leiden: Brill, 1913).

Kruyt, A. C., 'Boekbespreking "The children of the sun" by W. J. Perry', *Tijdschrift voor Indische Taal-, Land en Volkenkunde* 64 (1924), 292–299.

Kushner, Barak, *The thought war: Japanese imperial propaganda* (Honolulu: University of Hawai'i Press, 2006).

Kusumujaya, I Made, Aris Soviyani, and Wicaksono Nugroho, *Mengenal kepurbakalaan Majapahit di daerah Trowulan* (Mojokerto: BP3 Jatim, 2000).

Kwa Chong-Guan, 'Introduction: visions of early Southeast Asia as Greater India', in *Visions of Greater India: an anthology from the Journal of the Greater India Society* (Singapore: Manohar, 2013), xv–xlvii.

Laffan, Michael F., *Islamic nationhood and colonial Indonesia: the Umma below the winds* (London: Routledge Curzon, 2003).

Lamster, Johann C., *'Indië', gevende eene beschrijving van de inheemsche bevolking van Nederlandsch-Indië en hare beschaving* (Haarlem: Droste's Cacao- en Chocoladefabrieken, 1928).

Lane, Max, *Unfinished nation: Indonesia before and after Suharto* (London: Verso, 2008).

Laporan evalusasi hasil pemugaran Masjid Agung Demak (Jakarta: Direktorat Jenderal kebudayaan direktorat perlindungan dan pembinaan peninggalan sejarah dan Purbakala, 1991/1992).

Laporan pemugaran Masjid Agung Demak (Prambanan: Direkorat Jenderal Kebudayaan, Proyek Pemugaran dan Pemeliharaan Peninggalan Sejarah dan Purbakala Jawa Tenggah, Departemen Pendidikan dan Kebudayaan, 0000).

Larissa, *The magnificence of Borobudur* (Jakarta: PT Gramedia Pustaka Utama, 1995).

Last, Jef, 'Omzwervingen met de archeologische dienst op Bali', *Cultureel Nieuws Indonesië* (1954), 1037–1146.

Leclerc, Jacques, 'La circonscription: remarques sur l'idéologie du territoire nationale en Indonésie', *Culture et Développement* 7:2 (1975), 283–317; republished in Françoise Cayrac Blanchard, Stéphane Dovert, and Frédéric Durand (eds.), *Indonésie: un demi-siècle de construction nationale* (Paris: Harmattan, 2000), 15–48.

'Sentiment national et revendication territorial en Indonésie', *La Pensée* 169 (1973), 57–69.

Leemans, Conrad, 'H. N. Sieburgh en zijne oudheidkundige onderzoekingen in de binnenlanden van Java', *Algemeene Konst- en Letterbode* 2 (1846), 275–281, 290–295, 306–310.

Leerdam, Ben F. van, 'Architect Henri Maclaine Pont. Een speurtocht naar het wezenlijke van de Javaanse architectuur', PhD thesis, Delft University (Delft: Eburon, 1995).

Legêne, S., 'Powerful ideas: museums, empire utopias and connected worlds', in R. Omar, B. Ndhlovu, L. Gibson and S. Vawda (eds.), *Museums and the idea of historical progress* (Cape Town: IZIKO Museums Publications, 2014), 15–30.

Legêne, Susan, and Henk Schulte Nordholt, 'Introduction: imagining heritage and heritage as imagined history', in Susan Legêne, Bambang Purwanto, and Henk Schulte Nordholt (eds.), *Sites, bodies and stories: imagining Indonesian history* (Singapore: NUS Press, 2015), 1–30.

Lekkerkerker, C., *Bali en Lombok: overzicht der litteratuur omtrent deze eilanden rond 1919* (Rijswijk: Blankwaardt en Schoonhoven, 1920).

Lester, Alan, 'Imperial circuits and networks: geographies of the British Empire', *History Compass* 4:1 (2006), 124–141.

Leur, J. C. van, *Indonesian trade and society: essays in Asian social and economic history* (The Hague and Bandung: Van Hoeve, 1955).

Lévi, Sylvain, *Mahakharmavibhangga: la grande classification des actes* (Paris: Ernest Leroux, 1932).

Locher Scholten, Elsbeth, *Ethiek in fragmenten: vijf studies over koloniaal denken en doen van Nederlanders in de Indische Archipel 1877–1942* (Utrecht: Hes Publishers, 1981).

Sumatran sultanate and the colonial state: Jambi and the rise of Dutch imperialism 1830–1907 (Ithaca: Southeast Asia Program, Cornell University, 2004).

Lopez, Donald S., *Curators of the Buddha: the study of Buddhism under colonialism* (Chicago: University of Chicago Press, 1995).

Lowenthal, David, *The heritage crusade and the spoils of history* (Cambridge: Cambridge University Press, 1998).

'Lukisan Karya Gadjah mada Henk Ngantung', *Sudut Istana*, 14 February 2014, www.presidenri.go.id/index.php/sudutistana/2014/02/13/190.html (accessed 18 July 2014).

Lunsingh Scheurleer, P. (ed.), *Asiatic art in the Rijksmuseum Amsterdam* (Amsterdam: Meulenhoff; Landshoff, 1985).

'Collecting Javanese antiquities: the appropriation of a newly discovered Hindu–Buddhist civilisation', in Pieter ter Keurs (ed.), *Colonial collections revisited* (Leiden: Research School CNWS, 2007), 71–114.

McDaniel, Justin Thomas, *Gathering leaves and lifting words: histories of Buddhist monastic education in Laos and Thailand* (Seattle: University of Washington Press, 2008).

MacGregor, Neil, *A history of the world in 100 objects* (London: Penguin Books, 2012).

Mackenzie, Colin, 'Narrative of a Journey to examine the Remains of an Ancient City and Temples at Brambana in Java', *Verhandelingen van het Bataviaasch Genootschap der Kunsten en Wetenschappen* 7 (1814), ix, 1–53.

Maclaine Pont, Henri, 'Aantekeningen bij het artikel van Dr Van Stein Callenfels: "Bijdragen tot de topografie van Oost-Java in de Middeleeuwen"', *OV 1926* (1927), 88–100.

'Beredeneerde opgave der reisschetsen, gemaakt in mei en juni 1915', *Nederlandsch-Indië Oud en Nieuw* 15:2 (1930), 45–54, 69–87.

'De historische rol van Majapahit', *Djawa* 6 (1926), 1–24.

'Inleiding tot het bezoek aan het emplacement en de bouwvallen van Majapahit', *Djawa* 7 (1927), 171–174.

'Javaansche architectuur', *Djawa* 3 (1923), 112–117, 170.

'Madjapahit: poging tot reconstructie van het Stadsplan, nagezocht op het terrein aan de hand van den Middeleeuwschen dichter Prapanca', *OV 1924* (1925), 36–75, 157–199.

Mythe, overlevering en historisch besef op Java en de merkwaardige ontwikkeling van het Museumwezen in Nederl. Indië (Modjokerto: Oudheidkundige Vereeniging Majapahit, 1936).

'De nieuwe Javaansche bouworden', *Djawa* 4 (1924), 44–73.

Maclaine Pont, Henri, and Frederik D. K. Bosch, 'Beschouwingen over Majapahit', *Indisch Bouwkundig Tijdschrift* 10 (1926), 2–18.

McVey, Ruth T., 'Taman Siswa and the Indonesian National Awakening', *Indonesia* 4 (1967), 128–149.

Maier, Henk, *We are playing relatives: a survey of Malay writing* (Leiden: KITLV Press, 2004).

'We are playing relatives: Riau, the cradle of reality and hybridity', *BKI* 53:4 (1997), 672–698.

Majapahit Kerajaan Islam (Jakarta: Noura Books, 2014).

Mandal, Sumit, 'Popular sites of prayer, transoceanic migration, and cultural diversity: exploring the significance of keramat in Southeast Asia', *MAS* 46:2 (2012), 355–372.

Manguin, Pierre-Yves, 'Welcome to Bumi Sriwijaya or the building of a provincial identity in contemporary Indonesia', in Françoise Cayrac-Blanchard, Stéphane Dovert and Frédéric Durand (eds.), *L'Indonésie, un Demi-Siècle de Construction Nationale* (Paris: L'Harmattan, 2000), 199–214.

Manguin, Pierre-Yves, and Mubin Sheppard (eds.), *Sriwijaya: history, religion and language of an early Malay polity. Collected studies by Goerge Coedès and Louis-Charles Damais* (Kuala Lumpur: Malaysian Branch of the Royal Asiatic Society, 1992), viii–xv.

Marchand, Suzanne L., *German orientalism in the age of empire: religion, race and scholarship* (Cambridge: Cambridge University Press, 2009).

Mark, Ethan, '"Asia's" transwar lineage: nationalism, Marxism, and "Greater Asia" in an Indonesian inflection', *JAS*, 65:3 (2006), 461–493.

Masjid Agung Demak. Sebuah karya besar peninggalan wali. Cikal bakal berdirinya kerajaan Islam (Demak: Pertamina, 2000).

Mauss, Marcel, *The gift: the form and reason for exchange in archaic societies*, transl. W. D. Halls (New York and London: W.W. Norton, 1990).

Mengenal beberapa museum di Bali (Denpasar: Proyek Penegmbengan Permuseuman Bali, Direktorat Jenderal Kebudayaan, Departemen Pendidikan dan Kebudayaan, 1981/1982).

Meskell, Lynn, *A future in ruins: UNESCO, world heritage, and the dream of peace* (Oxford: Oxford University Press, 2018).

'Introduction: archaeology matters', in Lynn Meskell (ed.), *Archaeology under fire: nationalism, politics and heritage in the eastern Mediterranean and Middle East* (London: Routledge, 1998), 1–12.

'Transacting UNESCO world heritage: gifts and exchanges on a global stage', *Social Anthropology/Anthropologie Sociale* 23:1 (2015), 3–21.

Miert, Jacobus J. van, *Een koel hoofd en een warm hart: nationalisme, javanisme en jeugdbeweging in Nederlands-Indië, 1918–1930* (Amsterdam: De Bataafsche Leeuw, 1995).

Miert, Hans van, 'The "land of the future": The Jong Sumatranen Bond (1917–1930) and its image of the nation', *MAS* 30:3 (1996), 591–616.

Miksic, John, *Borobudur: golden tales of the Buddhas* (Boston: Shambhala, 1990).

'Survei permukaan Trowulan dalam rangka IFSA, Juni 1991/Recent research at Trowulan: implications for early urbanizations in Indonesia', in Hasan Muarif Ambary, et al. (eds.), *Pertemuan Ilmiah Arkeologi* (Jakarta: Pusat Penelitian Arkeologi Nasional, 1994), 357–367.

Miller, D. B., 'Hinduism in perspective: Bali and India compared', *Review of Indonesian and Malaysian Affairs* 18 (1984), 36–63.

Miura Hidenosoke, *Java Busekki Borubudur Kaisetsu* (Tokyo: Tokyo School of Fine Arts, Borobudur Kakōkai, 1925).

Mizoguchi, Koji, 'The colonial experience of the uncolonized and colonized: the case of East Asia, mainly as seen from Japan', in Jane Lydon and Uzma Z. Rizvi (eds.), *Handbook of postcolonial archaeology* (Walnut Creek: Left Coast Press, 2010), 81–92.

Moeis, Abdoel, 'Bahaja jang tidak boleh dipandang ketjil', *Neratja*, 4 July 1918.

Moojen, P. A. J., *Bali: verslag en voorstellen aan de regering van Nederlandsch-Indië* (Batavia: Bond van Nederlandsch-Indische Kunstkringen en Nederlandsch-Indisch Heemschut, 1920).

Kunst op Bali: inleidende studie tot de bouwkunst (Den Haag: Adi Poestaka, 1926).

Moro-Abadía, O., 'The history of archaeology as a colonial discourse', *Bulletin of the History of Archaeology* 16:2 (2006), 4–17.

Mortimer, Rex, 'Class, social cleavage, and Indonesian communism', *Indonesia* 8 (October 1969), 1–20.

Mukherjee, Sraman, 'Being and becoming Indian: the nation in archaeology', *South Asian Studies* 26:2 (2010), 219–234.

'Relics in transition: material mediations in changing worlds', *Ars Orientalis* 48 (2018), 20–42.

'Relics, ruins, and temple building: archaeological heritage and the construction of the Dharmarajika Vihara, Calcutta', in Nayanjot Lahiri and Upinder Singh (eds.), *Buddhism in Asia: revival and reinvention* (New Delhi: Manohar, 2016), 147–190.

Muussens, Martha A., 'De restauratiekwestie', *Djawa* 4 (1924), 77–98.

Napitupulu, Intan Mardiana, S. Engelsman and E. W. Veen, 'The director's foreword', in Endang Sri Hardiati and Pieter Ter Keurs (eds.), *Indonesia: the discovery of the past* (Amsterdam: KIT Publishers, 2005), 6.

Neeb, C. J., 'Het een en ander over Hindoe oudheden in het Djambische', *Tijdschrift voor Indische Taal-, Land- en Volkenkunde* 45 (1902), 120–127.

'Nieuwe opnamen, opgravingen, enz.', *OV 1914* (1914).

Nieuwenhuis, A. W., *Körperliche und kulturelle Volksentartung in Gebieten endemischer Malaria* (Leiden: E. J. Brill, 1936).

Njoto, Helène, 'À propos des origins de la mosque Javanase', *BEFEO*, 100 (2014), 1–37.

'L'invention du patrimoine indonésien', in Remy Madinier (ed.), *Indonésie contemporaine* (Paris: Les Indes Savantes, 2016), 416–423.

Noer, Deliar, *The modernist Muslim movement in Indonesia 1900–1942* (Singapore: Oxford University Press, 1973).

Noor, Farish A., *The discursive construction of Southeast Asia in nineteenth-century colonial-capitalist discourse* (Amsterdam: Amsterdam University Press, 2016).

Nora, Pierre (ed.), *Les lieux de mémoire*, vols. I–VII (Paris: Gallimard, 1984–1992).

Noto Soeroto, 'De Boro-Boedoer', *De geur van moeders haarwong* (Amsterdam: S. L. van Looy, 1916), 53–55.

Olthof, Willem L., *Babad Tanah Jawi: de prozaversie van Ngabèhi Kertapradja* (Dordrecht: Floris, 1987).

Orsoy de Flines, E. W. van, *Gids voor de Keramische Verzameling (Uitheemse Keramiek). Koninklijk Bataviaasch Genootschap van Kunsten en Wetenschappen* (Nix: Batavia, 1949).

Guide to the ceramic collection (foreign ceramics) (Djakarta: Museum Pusat Djakarta, 1969).

Guide to the ceramic collection (foreign ceramics) (Jakarta: Museum Pusat Jakarta, 1975).

'De keramische Verzameling 1934', *Jaarboek III Koninklijk Bataviaasch Genootschap van Kunsten en Wetenschappen* (1936), 206–215.

'De keramische Verzameling', *Jaarboek IV Koninklijk Bataviaasch Genootschap van Kunsten en Wetenschappen* (1937), 173–179.

'De keramische Verzameling', *Jaarboek V Koninklijk Bataviaasch Genootschap van Kunsten en Wetenschappen* (1938), 159–166.

'Onderzoek maar en van keramische scherven in de bodem in Noordelijk Midden-Java, 1940–'42', *OV 1941–1947* (1949), 66–84.

'Vroeg Ming en pre-Ming blauw-wit chineesch porselein in Nederlandsch-Indië', *Maandblad voor Beeldende Kunsten* 15 (1938), 262–271, 342–348, 366–371.

Oudheidkundig Verslag (Weltevreden: Albrecht & Co.; 's-Gravenhage: Nijhoff; Bandoeng/Bandung: A. C. Nix & Co., 1912–1950).

'Het Palembangsche Museum', *Djawa. Tijdschrift van het Java-Instituut* 13 (1933), 263–264.

Pané, Sanusi, *Madah Kelana* (Batavia: Balai Poestaka, 1931).

Sandhyakala ning Majapahit (Jakarta: Pustaka Jaya, 1971); reprinted from *Timboel* 7: 1–6 (1932).

Sedjarah Indonesia (Djakarta: Balai Poestaka, 2603 [1943]).

Sedjarah Indonesia, vol. I, 4th edn (Jakarta: Balai Pustaka, 1950).

'Tjandi Mendoet', *Madah Kelana*. 2nd edition (Djakarta: Balai Pustaka, 1957).

Passchier, Cor, *Building in Indonesia, 1600–1960* (Volendam: LM Publishers, 2016).

Patijn, Jacob A. N., 'Over den Boroboedoer', *Tijdschrift van Nederlandsch-Indië* Tweede nieuwe Serie 5 (1901), 386–389.

Peleggi, Maurizio, *Lords of things: the fashioning of the Siamese monarchy's modern image* (Honolulu: University of Hawai'i Press, 2002).

'Royal antiquarianism: European Orientalism and the production of archaeological knowledge in Siam', in Srilata Ravi, Mario Rutten, and Beng-Lan Goh (eds.), *Asia in Europe, Europe in Asia* (Leiden and Singapore: International Institute for Asian Studies, 2004), 133–161.

Pemberton, John, *On the subject of 'Java'* (Ithaca: Cornell University Press, 1994).

Perquin, P. J., 'Oudheidkundig Onderzoek te Palembang', *OV 1928* (1929), Bijlage J, 123–128.

Perry, W. J., *The children of the sun: a study in the early history of civilization* (London: Methuen, 1923).

The Megalithic culture of Indonesia (Manchester: Longmans and Green, 1918).

Perry, Jos, *Ons fatsoen als natie: Victor de Stuers 1843–1916* (Amsterdam: Sun, 2004).

Picard, Michel, *Bali: cultural tourism and touristic culture* (Singapore: Archipelago Press, 1998).

'Balinese religion in search of recognition: from *Agama Hindu Bali* to *Agama Hindu*', *BKI* 167:4 (2011), 482–510.

Pigeaud, Theodore G. Th., *Islamic states in Java 1500–1700: eight Dutch books and articles by H. J. de Graaf*, Verhandelingen van het Koninklijk Instituut voor Taal-, Landen Volkenkunde 70 (The Hague: Nijhoff, 1976).

Java in the fourteenth century: a study in cultural history. The Nāgara-Kĕrtāgama by Rakawi, Prapañca of Majapahit, 1365 AD, vol. I, Javanese texts in transcription, Translation series, Koninklijk Instituut voor Taal-, Land- en Volkenkunde 4:1 (The Hague: Nijhoff, 1960).

Java in the fourteenth century: a study in cultural history. The Nāgara-Kĕrtāgama by Rakawi,Pprapañca of Majapahit, 1365 AD, vol. IV, Commentaries and recapitulation, Translation series, Koninklijk Instituut voor Taal-, Land- en Volkenkunde 4:4 (The Hague: Nijhoff, 1962).

Pocock, J. G. A., *The ancient constitution and the feudal law* (Cambridge: Cambridge University Press, 1987).

Poerbatjaraka, 'Aanteekeningen op de Nagarakretagama', *BKI* 80 (1924), 219.

Poorthuis, Marcel, and Theo Salemink, 'Christelijke omgang met het boeddhisme in Nederland', *Tijdschrift voor Nederlandse Kerkgeschiedenis* 12:4 (2009), 137–150.

Pots, Roel, *Cultuur, koningen en democraten: overheid en cultuur in Nederland* (Nijmegen: Sun, 2000).

'Presiden Suharto di Demak: Pemugaran Masjid bukan tindakan pemboroson', *Kompas*, 22 March 1987.

Prijohoetomo, 'De betekenis van Demak voor den Islam', *Nederlandsch Indië Oud en Nieuw* 13 (1928–1929), 261–265.

Quaritch Wales, H. G., 'Cultural change in Greater India', *JRAS* (1948), 2–32.

Raffles, Thomas S., 'A Discourse delivered at a Meeting of the Society of Arts and Sciences in Batavia, on the Twenty-fourth day of April 1813, being the Anniversary of the Institute', *Verhandelingen van het Bataviaasch Genootschap der Kunsten en Wetenschappen* 7 (1814), 1–34.

The History of Java I–II (London: Black, Parbury and Allen, 1817).

'Raffle's History of Java', *De Curaçaosche Courant*, 16 September 1820.

Ramstedt, Martin, 'Colonial encounters between India and Indonesia', *South Asian History and Culture* 2:4 (2011), 522–539.

Rapport van de commissie in Nederlandsch-Indië voor oudheidkundig onderzoek op Java en Madoera of 1907 (Batavia: Albrecht & Co.; 's-Gravenhage: M. Nijhoff, 1909).

'Ratusan rumah akan jadi kampong Majapahit', *Tempo*, 21 January 2014, www.tempo.co/read/news/2014/01/22/058547182/Ratusan-Rumah-Akan-Jadi-Kampung-Majapahit- (accessed 9 May 2017).

Rawson, Philip S., James R. Brandon, Maung Htin Aung, and José Maceda, 'Southeast Asian arts', *Encyclopaedia Brittanica*, www.britannica.com/EBchecked/topic/556535/Southeast-Asian-arts/29535/Indonesia#toc29539 (accessed 22 April 2014).

Reichle, Natasha, *Violence and serenity: late Buddhist sculpture from Indonesia* (Honolulu: University of Hawai'i Press, 2007).

Reid, Anthony, 'The nationalist quest for an Indonesian past', in Reid and Marr (eds.), *Perceptions of the past*, 281–298.

Southeast Asia in the age of commerce 1450–1680, vol. I, The land below the winds (New Haven: Yale University Press, 1988).

Reid, Anthony, and David Marr (eds.), *Perceptions of the past in Southeast Asia* (Singapore: Heinemann, 1979).

Report of the ASEAN meeting of experts for formulating guidelines for archaeological field procedures and techniques: Borobudur (Jakarta: Directorate General for Culture, Ministry of Education and Culture, 12–19 December 1995).

Report on the feasibility studies for the great mosque of Demak, Central Java Indonesia. Appendix I. Historical background (Ministry of Education and Culture, Directorate General of Culture, restoration and preservation project of historical and archaeological legacies, Central Java, 1981).

Resink, G. J., 'Uit het stof van een beeldenstorm', *Indonesië* 9 (1956), 433–448.

Reuvens, Casper J. C., *Verhandeling over drie groote steenen beelden in den jare 1819 uit Java naar den Nederlanden overgezonden (1824): gedenkschriften in de hedendaagsche talen van der derde klasse van het Koninklijk Nederlandsch Instituut van Wetenschappen, Letterkunde en Schone Kunsten. Deel III* (Amsterdam: Pieper & Ipenbuur, 1826).

Rheling, Andrea, 'Universalismen und Partikularismen im Wiederstreit: Zur Genese des UNESCO-Welterbes', *Zeithistorische Forschungen/ Studies in Contemporary History* 8:3 (2001), 3–4 (accessed 19 December 2011).

Ricci, Ronit, 'Reading a history of writing: heritage, religion and script change in Java', *Itinerario* 39:3 (2015), 419–435.

Ricklefs, Merle, 'A consideration of three versions of the "Babad tanah Djawi", with experts on the fall of Madjapahit', *Bulletin of the School of Oriental and African Studies, University of London* 35:2 (1972), 285–315.

Islamisation and its opponents in Java c. 1930 to the present (Honolulu: University of Hawai'i Press, 2012).

Mystic synthesis in Java: a history of Islamization from the fourteenth to the early ninteenth century (Norwalk: East Bridge, 2006).

Polarising Javanese society: Islamic and other visions, c. 1830–1930 (Leiden: KITLV Press, 2007).

Rigg, Jonathan, 'The Grand Exhibition of Batavia', *Journal of the Indian Archipelago and Eastern Asia* 7 (1853), 261–324.

Robinson, Geoffrey, *The dark side of paradise: political violence in Bali* (Ithaca: Cornell University Press, 1995).

Robson, Stuart O., *Deśawarnana (Nāgarakrtāgama), by Mpu Prapañca*, transl. from the Javanese, Verhandelingen van het Koninklijk Instituut voor Taal-, Land- en Volkenkunde 169 (Leiden: KITLV Press, 1995).

Rodgers, Susan, 'Imagining tradition, imagining modernity: a southern Batak novel from the 1920s', *BKI* 147:2–3 (1991), 273–297.

Römer, L.S.A.M. von, 'Iets over het congres voor de Javaansche cultuurontwikkeling', *Wederopbouw* 1 (1918), 165–197.

Roolvink, Roelof, 'The variant versions of the Malay Annals', in Charles C. Brown and Roelof Roolvink (eds.), *Sejarah Melayu or Malay Annals* (Kuala Lumpur: Oxford University Press, 1970), xv–xxxv.

Roosa, John, *Pretext for mass murder: the September 30th Movement and Suharto's coup d'état in Indonesia* (Madison: University of Wisconsin Press, 2006).

'The September 30th movement: the aporias of the official narratives', in Douglas Kammen and Katharine McGregor (eds.), *The contours of mass violence in Indonesia 1965–1968* (Honolulu: University of Hawai'i Press, 2012), 25–49.

Roosmalen, Pauline van, 'Ontwerpen aan de stad: stedenbouw in Nederlands-Indië en Indonesië, 1905–1950', PhD Thesis, Technical University (Delft: Technische Universiteit, 2008).

Roque, Ricardo, and Kim A. Wagner, 'Introduction: engaging colonial knowledge', in Ricardo Roque and Kim A. Wagner (eds.), *Engaging colonial knowledge: reading European archives in world history* (Basingstoke: Palgrave Macmillan, 2011), 1–32.

Rouffaer, G. P., 'Herdenking aan Dr J. L. A. Brandes' in *Beschrijving van Tjandi Singasari in de residentie Pasoeroean en De wolkentoneelen van Panataran in de residentie Kediri: Archaeologisch onderzoek op Java en Madura II* ('s-Gravenhage: Martinus Nijhoff; Batavia: Albrecht & Co., 1908), i–xlvi.

'Monumentale kunst op Java', *De Gids* 4:9 (1901) part II, 225–252.

Rujivacharakul, Vimalin, 'China and china: an introduction to materiality and a history of collecting', in Vimalin Rujivacharakul (ed.), *Collecting china: the world, China, and a history of collecting* (Newark: University of Delaware Press, 2001), 15–30.

Saaler, Sven, 'Pan-Asianism in Meiji and Taishô Japan: a preliminary framework', working paper (Tokyo: Philipp Franz von Siebold Stiftung, Deutsches Institut für Japanstudien, 2002).

Saaler, Sven, and J. Victor Koschmann (eds.), *Pan-Asianism in modern Japanese history: colonialism, regionalism and borders* (London: Routledge, 2007).

Saaler, Sven and Christopher W. A. Szpilman (eds.), *Pan-Asianism: a documentary history, Volume I 1850–1920; Volume II 1920–Present* (Lanham: Rowman & Littlefield, 2011).

Saleh, Bujung, 'De mythe als opium en zelfkennis als zweep', *Indonesië* 9:6 (1956), 449–452.

Sarasin, Paul, 'Neue lithochrone Funde im Innern von Sumatra', *Verhandelungen der Naturforschenden Gesellschaft in Basel* (1914), 97–111.

Sarasin, Paul, and Fritz Sarasin, *Materialien zur Naturgeschichte von Celebes. 5. Die Toala-Höhlen von Lamongtjong* (Wiesbaden: Kreidel, 1905).

Die Steinzeit auf Ceylon. Ergebnisse naturwissenschaftlicher Forschungen auf Ceylon (Wiesbaden: Kreidel, 1908).

Scalliet, Marie-Odette, 'Natuurtonelen en taferelen van Oost-Indië: Europese schilders in Oost-Indië in de negentiende eeuw', in J. H. van Brakel et al. (eds.), *Indië omlijst: vier eeuwen schilderkunst in Nederlands-Indië* (Amsterdam: KIT; Wijk en Aalburg: Picture Publishers, 1998), 39–89.

Schär, Bernard C., *Tropenliebe: schweizer Naturforscher und niederländischer Imperialismus in Südostasien um 1900* (Frankfurt am Main: Campus, 2015).

Scheltema, J. F., *Monumental Java* (London: Macmillan, 1912).

Schildgen, Brenda Deen, *Heritage or heresy: preservation and destruction of religious art and architecture in Europe* (New York: Palgrave Macmillan, 2008).

Schnitger, Friedrich M., *The Archaeology of Hindoo Sumatra* (Leiden, 1937).

'Gajah Mada', *Nederlandsch-Indië. Oud en Nieuw* 16:10 (1932), 289–294.

Oudheidkundige vondsten in Palembang (Palembang: Ebeling, 1935).

Oudheidkundige vondsten in Palembang, Bijlage A, *Verslag over de gevonden inscriptie's door Dr W. F. Stutterheim* (Palembang: Ebeling, 1935).

Oudheidkundige vondsten in Palembang, Bijlage C (Leiden: Brill, 1936).

Schnitger, Friedrich M., with contributions by C. von Fürer-Haimendorf and G. L. Tichelman and introduction by J. N. Miksic, *Forgotten kingdoms in Sumatra* (Oxford: Oxford University Press, 1989 [1939]).

Schrieke, B. J. O., 'Breuk en continuïteit in de Javaanse geschiedschrijving', in *Gedenkboek uitgegeven ter gelegenheid van het vijf en twintig jarig bestaan van het rechtswetenschappelijk hoger onderwijs in Indonesië op 28 oktober 1948* (Groningen: Wolters, 1949).

Schrikker, Alicia, 'Restoration in Java, a review', *BMGN* 130:4 (2015), 132–144.

Schulte Nordholt, Henk, 'The making of traditional Bali', *History and Anthropology* 8 (1994), 89–127.

'Temple and authority in South Bali, 1900–1980', in H. Geertz (ed.), *State and society in Bali* (Leiden: KITLV, 1994), 137–164.

Scott, Cynthia, 'Sharing the divisions of the colonial past: an assessment of the Netherlands–Indonesia shared cultural heritage project, 2003–2006', *International Journal of Heritage Studies*, 20:2 (2014), 81–195.

'Sebuah kamp di Tengah Sungai', *Liputan Khusus Tempo, Pengakuan Algojo 1965* 1 (7 October 2012), 100.

Sengupta, Indra, 'Code for the colony: John Marshall's *Conservation Manual* and monument preservation between India and Europe', in Michael Falser and Monica Juneja (eds.), *'Archaeolizing' heritage? Transcultural entanglements between local practices and global virtual realities* (Berlin and Heidelberg: Springer Verlag, 2013), 21–37.

'Locating lieux de mémoire: a (post)colonial perspective', in Indra Sengupta (ed.), *Memory, history and colonialism: engaging with Pierre Nora in colonial and postcolonial contexts*, *Bulletin, German Historical Institute London* Suppl. 1 (2009), 1–8.

Sentoso, Soewito, *The Centhini story: the Javanese journey of life* (Singapore: Marshall Cavendish International (Asia) Prive limited, 2006).

Sevea, T., '*Keramats* running amok', in Michael Laffan (ed.), *Belonging across the Bay of Bengal: religious rites, colonial migrations, national rights* (London: Bloomsbury, 2017), 57–72.

Shatanawi, Mirjam, *Islam at the Tropenmuseum* (Arnhem: LM Publishers, 2014).

Shiraishi, Takashi, 'The disputes between Tjipto Mangoenkoesoemo and Soetatmo Soeriokoesoemo: Satria vs. Pandita', *Indonesia* 14 (1981), 93–108.

Silva Vigier, Anil da, 'Across the face of Asia', *UNESCO Courier* 9:6 (1956), 10–14.

Singh, Upinder, *The discovery of ancient India: early archaeologists and the beginnings of archaeology* (Delhi: Permanent Black, 2004).

'Exile and return: the reinvention of Buddhism and Buddhist sites in modern India', *Journal of South Asian Studies* 26:2 (2010), 193–217.

Sinor, Denis (ed.), *Proceedings of the 27th International Congress of Orientalists, 13th–19th August 1967* (Wiesbaden: Otto Harrassowitz, 1971).

Sivaramamurti, S., *Le stupa du Barabadur* (Paris: Presses universitaires de France, 1961).

Sivasundaram, Sujit, 'Buddhist kingship, archaeology and historical narratives in Sri Lanka, 1750–1850', *Past & Present* 197:1 (2007), 111–142.

Skilling, Peter, 'Theravada in history', *Pacific World* 11 (2009), 61–94.

Slametmuljana 'Adakah Prapantja sungguh pudjangga kerato?', *Bahasa dan Budaja* 1:2 (1952), 14–22.

The structure of the national government of Majapahit (Jakarta: Balai Pustaka, 1966).

Sluga, Glenda, 'UNESCO and the (one) world of Julian Huxley', *Journal of World History* 21:3 (2010), 393–418.

Smith, Laurajane, *Uses of heritage* (London and New York: Routledge, 2006).

Smith, Laurajane, and Gary Campbell, '2012 Association of Critical Heritage Studies manifesto', presented at inaugural meeting of Association of Critical Heritage Studies, University of Gothenburg, 2012, www.criticalheritagestudies.org/history/ (accessed 21 August 2017).

Soebardi, 'Santri-religious elements reflected in the book of Tjentini', *BKI* 127 (1971), 331–349.

Soejono, R. P., 'The history of prehistoric research in Indonesia to 1950', *Asian Perspectives* 12 (1969), 69–91.

Soekarno, *Indonesia klaagt aan! Pleitrede voor den Landraad te Bandoeng op 2 December 1930* (Amsterdam: De Arbeiderspers, 1931).

Soekmono, 'Kepentingan leloehoer nenek moyang kita', *Pantja Raja* 1:6 (1946), 149–150.

'Ngajah, Gotong-Rojong di Bali', *Madjalah ilmu-ilmu sastra Indonesia/ Indonesian Journal of Cultural Studies* 3:1 (March 1965), 31–38.

'Sedikit riwayat. 50 years archaeological research', in Satyawati Suleiman, Rumbi Mulia, Nies Anggraeni and F. X. Supandi (eds.), *50 Tahun Lembaga Purbakala dan Peninggalan Nasional 1913–1963* (Jakarta: Proyek Pelita Pembinaan Kepurbakalaan dan Peninggalan Nasional, Dept. P & K., 1977), 1–27.

'Serat Centhini and the rejected Buddha from the main stupa of Borobudur', in Marijke J. Klokke and Karel R. van Kooij (eds.), *Fruits of inspiration: studies in honour of Prof. J. G. de Casparis* (Groningen: Forsten, 2001), 474–485.

Soekmono, R., 'Archeologie zoals die beoefend wordt in Indonesië', inaugural lecture, Leiden University, 28 November 1986.

'Langkah pemerintah tahun 1948 dalam bidang kepurbakalaan: Landasan untuk pengembangan arkeologi Indonesia', departure speech, University of Indonesia, 5 March 1990.

Soemarsono, 'Boekbespreking', *Wederopbouw* 3:4 (1920), 83–87.

Soepprodjo, 'Congres hal kemadjoean bangsa Djawa di Solo', *Oetoesan Hindia*, 3 July 1918.

Soeriokoesoemo, 'Ons derde levensjaar', *Wederopbouw* 3:1 (1920), 1–4.

'Het rijk van Gadjah Mada', *Wederopbouw* 3:1 (1920), 5–7.

Soerodjo, F. H., et al., *Sejarah panglima Kodam V. Brawijaya V* (Jakarta: Gramedia, 1989).

Somers, J. A., *Nederlandsch-Indië: staatkundige ontwikkelingen binnen een koloniale relatie* (Zutphen: Walburg Pers, 2005).

Spanjaard, Helena Geertruida, 'Het ideaal van een moderne Indonesische schilderkunst: de creatie van een nationale culturele identiteit', PhD thesis, Leiden University, 1998.

Spivak, Gayatri Chakravorty, 'Can the subaltern speak?', in Cary Nelson and Lawrence Grossberg (eds.), *Marxism and the interpretation of culture* (Basingstoke: Macmillan Education, 1988), 271–313.

Stapel, F. W. (ed.), *Geschiedenis van Nederlandsch-Indië*, I–V (Amsterdam: Joost van den Vondel, 1938–1940).

Steenis, Cornelis G. G. J. van, *Album van natuurmonumenten in Nederlandsch-Indië, naar photographische opnamen van vele natuurvrienden* (Batavia: Nederlandsch-Indische Vereeniging tot Natuurbescherming, 1937).

Steiger, G. Nye, H. Otley Beyer, and Conrado Benitz, *A history of the Orient* (Boston: Ginn, 1926).

Stein Callenfels, P. V. van, 'Bijdragen tot de topographie van Java in de Middeleeuwen', in *Feestbundel uitgegeven door het Koninklijk Bataviaasch Genootschap van Kunsten en Wetenschappen bij gelegenheid van het 150-jarig bestaan 1778–1928*, vol. II (Weltevreden: Kolff & Co., 1929), 370–392.

'Bijdragen tot de topografie van Oost-Java in de Middeleeuwen II', *OV 1926* (1927), 81–87.

'Het eerste palaeolitische werktuig in den archipel', *OV 1924* (1925), 127–138.

'Historische gegevens uit Balische oorkonden I–III', *OV 1920–1924* (1920–1925).

Korte Gids voor de Praehistorische Verzameling van het Koninklijk Bataviaasch Genootschap van Kunsten en Wetenschappen (Bandoeng: Nix, 1934).

'Naschrift', in H. N. Noosten, L. Kirschner, and J. J. Th. Vos, 'Rhinoscleroom op Bali', *Geneeskundig Tijdschrift voor Nederlandsch-Indië* 74:14 (1934), 835–852.

'De praehistorische verzameling', *Jaarboek I Koninklijk Bataviaasch Genootschap van Kunsten en Wetenschappen* (1933), 205–215.

'Sumatra's beteekenis voor Prehistori en Archaeologie', *Jong Sumatra* 8 (October 1925), 3.

'De vorsten van de Trawoelan. Plaat no. III', *OV 1919* (1919), 22–30.

Stein Callenfels, P. V. van, and L. Van Vuuren, 'Bijdragen tot de topografie van de residentie Soerabaia in de 14de eeuw', *TKNAG* 41:2 (1924), 67–81.

Stengs, Irene, *Worshipping the great moderniser: King Chulalongkorn, patron saint of the Thai middle class* (Singapore: NUS Press, 2009).

Stig Sørensen, Marie Louise, and John Carman, 'Heritage studies: an outline', in Marie Louise Stig Sørensen and John Carman (eds.), *Heritage studies: methods and approaches* (London: Routledge, 2009), 11–28.

Stocking, George W. Jnr, *Objects and others: essays on museums and material culture* (Madison: University of Wisconsin Press, 1985).

Stoler, Ann, 'Colonial aphasia: race and disabled histories in France', *Public Culture* 23:1 (2011), 121–156.

Stolte, Carolien, 'Orienting India: interwar internationalism in an Asian inflection, 1917–1937', PhD thesis, Leiden University, 2013.

Stolte, Carolien, and Harald Fischer-Tiné, 'Imagining Asia in India: nationalism and internationalism (ca. 1905–1940)', *Comparative Studies in Society and History* 54:1 (2012), 65–92.

Strong, John S., *Relics of the Buddha* (Princeton: Princeton University Press, 2004).

Stuart Fox, David J., *Pura Besakih: temple, religion and society in Bali* (Leiden: KITLV, 2002).

Sturler, W. L. de, *Bijdrage tot de kennis en rigtige beoordeling van den zedelijken, maatschappelijken en staatkundigen toestand van het Palembangsche gebied* (Groningen: Oomkens, 1855).

Stutterheim, W. F., 'De archeologische verzameling: lijst van aanwinsten 1935', *Jaarboek III. Koninklijk Bataviaasch Genootschap van Kunsten en Wetenschappen* (1936).

Indian influences in Old-Balinese art (London: India Society, 1935).

Indian influences in the lands of the Pacific, transl. Claire Holt (Weltevreden: G. Kolff & Co., 1929).

A Javanese period in Sumatran history (Surakarta: De Bliksem, 1929).

De kraton van Majapahit, Verhandelingen van het Koninklijk Instituut voor de Taal-, Land- en Volkenkunde van Nederlandsch-Indië 7 ('s-Gravenhage: Nijhoff, 1948).

'De oudheden-collectie van Z. H. Mangkoenagoro VII te Soerakarta', *Djawa* 17 (1937), 1–112.

Oudheden van Bali, vol. I (Singaraja: Kirtya Liefrinck – Van der Tuuk, 1929).

Oudheden van Bali, vol. II, *Platen* (Singaraja: Kirtya Liefrinck – Van der Tuuk, 1930).

'De oudheden van Pedjeng', *Djawa* 17 (1937), 440–441.

'Oudjavaansche kunst', *BKI* 79 (1923), 323–362.

'Rapport van Dr W. F. Stutterheim over een reis naar Bali van 1–10 October 1926', *OV 1926* (1927), 150–155.

'Verslag van den adjunct-oudheidkundige nopens zijn reis naar Bali', *OV 1925* (1926), 90–102.

'Voorlopige inventaris der Oudheden van Bali', *OV 1925* (1926), 150–170.

Subhadradis Diskul, M. C., *History of the Temple of the Emerald Buddha* (Bangkok: Bureau of the Royal Household, 1980).

Sugriwa, I. Gusti Bagus, 'Tjandi Prambanan', *Damai* 17 (January 1954), 5–6, 18.

Sukanti, *Koleksi Arkeologika: Museum Balaputra Dewi* (Palembang, 2010).

Sundhaussen, Ulf, *The road to power: Indonesian military politics, 1945–1967* (Kuala Lumpur: Oxford University Press, 1982).

Supomo, S., 'The image of Majapahit in later Javanese and Indonesian writing', in Reid and Marr (eds.), *Perceptions of the past*, 171–185.

'Tugas penulis babad dan pelaksanaannja', in *Laporan ilmu pengetahuan nasional kedua 1962*, vol. VI (Jakarta: Madjelis Ilmu Pengetahuan Indonesia, 1965), 9–36.

Sutherland, Heather A., *The making of a bureaucratic elite: the colonial transformation of the Javanese priyayi* (Singapore: Heinemann, 1979).

'Pujangga Baru: aspects of Indonesian intellectual life in the 1930s', *Indonesia* 6 (October 1968), 106–127.

'Treacherous translators and improvident paupers: perception and practice in Dutch Makassar, eighteenth and nineteenth centuries', *Journal of the Economic and Social History of the Orient* 53:1–2 (2010), 319–356.

Swanenburg, B. D., *Iwan de Verschikkelijke: leven en werken van Dr P. V. van Stein Callenfels* (Maastricht: Leiter Nypels, 1951).

Swenson, Astrid, and Peter Mandler (eds.), *From plunder to preservation: Britain and the heritage of empire c. 1800–1940* (Oxford: Oxford University Press, 2013).

Sweta, I. Made, 'Babad toea Poelau Bali', *Bhawanagara* 1:1 (1931), 28–30.

Tagore, Rabindranath, 'Aan Java', transl. Noto Soeroto, *Oedaya* 4:11 (November 1927), 138.

'Boro-Budur' (1927), in *English writings of Tagore, Vol. II, Poems* (New Delhi: Atlantic, 2007), 314–315.

'Brieven, geschreven gedurende de Javaansche reis 1–3', transl. A. A. Bake, *Oedaya* 6:9 (September 1929); 6:10 (October 1929), 133–135; 6:12 (December 1929), 190–193.

'Letters from Java', *Visva-Bharati Quarterly* 5:4 (January 1928), 323–328; 6:1 (April 1928), 1–13; 6:2 (July 1928), 169–178; 6:3 (October 1928), 273–280.

Takakusu, Junjirō, *A record of the Buddhist religion as practised in India and the Malay archipelago (AD 671–695) by I-Tsing* (Oxford: Clarendon Press, 1896).

Tanudirjo, Daud Aris, 'Theoretical trends in Indonesian archaeology', in Peter J. Ucko (ed.), *Theory in archaeology: a world perspective* (London: Routledge, 1995), 61–75.

Teeuw, Andries, *Modern Indonesian literature* (The Hague: Nijhoff, 1979).

Theuns-de Boer, Gerda, 'The distribution of Van Kinsbergen's oeuvre: decorative albums, engravings and world exhibitions', in Gerda Theuns-de Boer and Saskia Asser (eds.), *Isidore van Kinsbergen; fotopionier en theatermaker in Nederlands-Indië/photo pioneer and theater maker in the Netherlands Indies* (Leiden: KITLV Press; Amsterdam: Huis Marseille, 2005), 124–142.

Tiffin, Sarah, 'Java's ruined candis and the British picturesque ideal', *Bulletin of SOAS* 72:3 (2009), 525–558.

'Raffles and the barometer of civilisation: images and descriptions of ruined candis in *The History of Java*', *JRAS* Series 3 18:3 (2008), 241–360.

Southeast Asia in ruins: art and empire in the early nineteenth century (Singapore: National University of Singapore Press, Royal Asiatic Society of Great Britain and Ireland, 2016).

Tillema, J. A. C., *Schetsen uit de geschiedenis van de monumentenzorg in Nederland* ('s-Gravenhage: Staatsuitgeverij, 1975).

Tjahjono, Gunawan, *Indonesian heritage-architecture* (Singapore: Archipelago Press, 1998).

Tjandrasasmita, Uka, *Arkeologi Islam Nusantara* (Jakarta: Gramedia/EFEO/Sharif Hidayatullah State University, 2009).

Tollebeek, Jo (ed.), *België, een parcours van herinnering*, vols. I–II (Amsterdam: Bert Bakker, 2008).

Tombrink, E. P., 'Hindoe-Monumenten in de Bovenlanden van Palembang, als bron van geschiedkundig onderzoek', *Tijdschrift voor Indische Taal-, Land- en Volkenkunde* (1870), 1–45.

Toyoyama, Aki, 'Perceptions of Buddhist heritage in Japan', in Patrick Daly and Tim Winter (eds.), *Routledge handbook of heritage in Asia* (London and New York: Routledge, 2012), 339–349.

Trevithick, Alan, 'British archaeologists, Hindu abbots, and Burmese Buddhists: the Mahabodhi temple at Bodh Gaya, 1811–1877', *MAS* 33:3 (1999), 635–656.

The revival of Buddhist pilgrimage at Bodh Gaya (1811–1949): Anagarika Dharmapala and the Mahabodhi temple (Delhi: Motilal Banarsidass, 2006).

Trigger, Bruce G., 'Alternative archaeologies: nationalist, colonialist, imperialist', *Man: the Journal of the Royal Anthropological Institute* 19:3 (1984), 355–370.

A history of archaeological thought (Cambridge: Cambridge University Press, 1989).

Tsuchiya, Kenji, 'Javanology and the age of Ranggawarsita: an introduction to nineteenth-century Javanese culture', in *Reading Southeast Asia* (Ithaca: Cornell University Press, 1990), 75–108.

Tsukasa, Kawada, and Nao Hayashi-Denis, 'Cooperation between UNESCO and Japan in the safeguarding of cultural heritage', *Museum International* 56:4 (2004), 32–39.

Tsurumi, Shunsuke, *An intellectual history of wartime Japan, 1931–1945* (London: Routledge, 1986).

Tuuk, H. N. van der, and J. L. Brandes, 'Transcriptie van vier Oud-Javaansche oorkonden gevonden op het eiland Bali', *Tijdschrift voor Indische Taal-, Land- en Volkenkunde* 30 (1885), 603–607.

'Twenty-five centuries of Buddhist art and culture', Special issue, *UNESCO Courier* 9:6 (June 1956).

Uhlenbeck, Eugenius M., *A critical survey of studies on the languages of Java and Madura* ('s-Gravenhage: Nijhoff, 1964).

Ullmann, L., 'Hindoe-Beelden in de Binnenlanden van Palembang', *Indisch Archief. Tijdschrift voor de Indiën* 1:2 (1850), 493–494.

Valck, F. G., 'Oudheidkunde: gedachten over de Ruïnen van de Hindoesche godsdienst, welke op Java voorkomen', *Tijdschrift voor Neêrland's Indie* 3:1 (1840), 177–203.

Velde, Paul van der, *Een Indische Liefde: P. J. Veth (1814–1895) en de inburgering van Nederlands-Indië* (Amsterdam: Balans, 2000).

Verbeek, R. D. M., *Lijst der voornaamste overblijfselen uit den Hindoetijd op Java met eene oudheidkundige kaart*, Verhandelingen van het Bataviaasch Genootschap van Kunsten en Wetenschappen 46 (Batavia: Landsdrukkerij; 's-Gravenhage: M. Nijhoff, 1891).

'De Oudheden van Madjapahit in 1815 en in 1887, met een kaartje', *Tijdschrift voor Indische Taal-, Land- en Volkenkunde* 33 (1890), 14.

Verslag van de commissie van advies inzake de restauratie der Hindoe-Javaansche monumenten, nopens de reconstructie van de Çiwatempel te Prambanan (Weltevreden: Kolff, 1926).

Veth, D. D., *Midden-Sumatra: reizen en onderzoekingen der Sumatra-expeditie, uitgerust door het Aardrijkskundig Genootschap 1877–1879* (Leiden, 1879).

Vickers, Adrian, *Bali: a Paradise created* (Ringwood, Victoria: Penguin, 1989; 2nd edn, Tokyo: Tuttle Publishing, 2012).

Balinese art: paintings and drawings of Bali, 1800–2010 (Tokyo: Tuttle, 2012).

A history of modern Indonesia (Cambridge: Cambridge University Press, 2005).

Vogel, Jean Ph., 'Het Koninkrijk Çrîvijaya', *BKI* 75 (1919), 626–637.

Vonk, H. W., 'De "batoc tatahan" bij Air Peoar (Pasemah-landen) met naschrift', *Tijdschrift voor Indische Taal-, Land- en Volkenkunde* 74:2 (1934), 296–300.

Vries, Gerrit de, and Dorothee Segaar Höweler, *Henri Maclaine Pont: architect, controleur, archeoloog* (Rotterdam: Stichting Bonas, 2009).

Wahid, Abdul, 'Counterrevolution in a revolutionary campus: how did the "1965 event" affect an Indonesian public university?', in Katherine McGregor, Jess Melvin, and Annie Pohlman (eds.), *The Indonesian genocide of 1965: causes, dynamics and legacies* (Cham: Palgrave Macmillan, 2017), 157–178.

Wassing-Visser, Rita, *Koninklijke geschenken uit Indonesië: historische banden met het Huis Oranje-Nassau (1600–1938)* (Zwolle: Waanders, 1995).

Weatherbee, Donald E., 'Raffles' sources for traditional Javanese historiography and the Mackenzie collection', *Indonesia* 26 (October 1978), 63–93.

Weber, Andreas, *Hybrid ambitions: science, governance, and empire in the career of Caspar G. C. Reinwardt (1773–1854)* (Leiden: Leiden University Press, 2012).

'Sprache im "Zwischenraum": Adriaan David Cornets de Groot (1804–1829) als multilingualer Grenzgänger im zentraljavanischeschen Surakarta', in Mark Häberlein and Alexander Keese (eds.), *Sprachgrenzen – Sprachkontakte – kulturelle Vermittler: Kommunikation zwischen Europäern und Außereuropäern (16.–20. Jahrhundert)* (Stuttgart: Franz Steiner Verlag, 2010), 223–243.

Wentholt, Arnold (ed.), *In kaart gebracht met kapmes en kompas: met het Koninklijk Nederlands Aardrijkskundig Genootschap op expeditie tussen 1873 en 1960* (Heerlen: ABP, 2003).

Wesseling, H.L., *Plaatsen van Herinnering*, vols. I–IV (Amsterdam: Bert Bakker, 2005–2006).

Westenenk, L. C., 'De Hindoe-Javanen in Midden- en Zuid-Sumatra', *Handelingen van het Eerste Congres voor de Taal-, Land en Volkenkunde van Java; Solo, 25 en 26 December 1919* (1921), 1–46.

'De Hindoe-Oudheden in de Pasemah-Hoogvlakte (Residentie Palembang)', *OV 1922* (1922), 31–37.

'Uit het land van Bitterong (Zuid-Sumatra)', *Djawa* 1:1 (1921), 5–11.

'What Is Spafa', *Southeast Asian Archaeology International Newsletter*, 5 (1994), www.geocities.ws/thai_archaeology/seasia/05/spafa1.html (accessed 2 January 2017).

Wiener, Margaret J., *Visible and invisible realms: power, magic and colonial conquest in Bali* (Chicago: University of Chicago Press, 1995).

Wilsen, Frans C., 'Boro Boedoer', *Tijdschrift voor Indische Taal- Land- en Volkenkunde* 1 (1853), 235–303.

Winter, Carel Frederik, 'Oudheidkunde: oorsprong van oudheden te Brambanan', *Tijdschrift voor Neêrlandsch Indië* 2:1 (1839), 469–471.

(transl.), J. J. B. Gaal and T. Roorda (eds.), *Het boek Adji Saka: oude fabelachtige geschiedenis van Java van de regering van vorst Sindoela te Galoeh tot aan de stichting van Madja-Pait door vorst Soesoeroeh* (Amsterdam: Frederick Muller, 1857).

Wirjosuparto, Sutjipto, 'Prapantja sebagai penulis sedjarah', *Peneltian Sedjarah* 1:1 (1960), 15–20.

Wisnoewhardono, Soeyono, *Petunjuk Singkat. Warisan Majapahit di Trowulan* (Surabaya: Surya Grafika, 1986).

Wisseman Christie, Jan, 'Under the volcano: stabilizing the early Javanese state in an unstable environment', in David Henley and Henk Schulte Nordholt (eds.), *Environment, trade and society in Southeast Asia: a* longue durée *perspective* (Leiden: Brill, 2015), 46–61.

Wittgenstein, Ludwig, *Culture and value*, transl. Peter Winch (Chicago: University of Chicago Press, 1984).

Woelders, Michiel Otto, 'Het Sultanaat Palembang 1811–1825', dissertation, Leiden University ('s-Gravenhage: De Nederlandsche Boek- en Steendrukkerij V/H. H. L. Smits, 1975).

Wolff Schoemaker, C. P., *Aesthetiek en oorsprong der Hindoe-kunst op Java* (Semarang: Van Dorp, 1925).

Wong, Laura Elizabeth, 'Relocating East and West: UNESCO's major project on the mutual appreciation of Eastern and Western cultural values', *Journal of World History* 19:3 (September 2008), 349–374.

Wood, Michael, *Official history in modern Indonesia: New Order perceptions and counterviews* (Leiden: Brill, 2005).

Yamin, Muhammad, *6000 Tahun Sang Merah-Putih* (n.p., 1953).

Gadjah Mada: Pahlawan Persatuan Nusantara, 3rd edn (Jakarta: Balai Poestaka, 1948).

Ken Arok dan Ken Dedes: Tjerita Sandiwara jang kedjadian dalam sedjarah Tumapel-Singhasari pada tahun 1227 AD (Jakarta: Balai Pustaka, 1951).

Lukisan sedjarah, jaitu risalah berisi 563 gambar, foto dll., melukisan perdjalanan sedjarah Indonésia dan sedjarah dunia untuk dipergunakan dipelbagai perguruan (Amsterdam: Djamabtan, 1956).

Tatanegara Madjapahit: Risalah Sapta-parwa berisi 7 djilid atau parwa, hasil penelitian ketatanegaraan Indonesia tentang dasar dan bentuk negara Nusantara bernama Madjapahit, 1293–1525, 4 vols. (Jakarta: Prapantja, 1962).

'Tjandi Loro Djonggrang', *Budaya* 12 (1954), 5–10.

Index

1965, 20, 102, 222, 230, 243, 267, 269, 270, 273, 275, 276

Abhakorn, Rujaya, xii
Aceh, 90
Aceh War, 14, 71
Adams, Alexander, 25
Adil, 148
Adinegoro (Raden Toemenggoeng Ario), 54, 58, 59
Adinegoro III, 132
Adinegoro IV, 129, 130, 131, 132, 133, 134, 135, 136, 138, 141
Adiwarna, 29, 30
Adrisijanti, Inajati, x, xii, 278
Agung, Gusti Mangku, xii
Air Poear, 179, 180
Akib, Mohammad, 188
Al Hudayah, Khairani, xii
Algemeen Nederlandsch Verbond. *See* General Dutch Language Association
All Indonesia Youth Congress, 152
Amangkurat I, 25
Amangkurat III, 32
Amir, Mohammad, 190
Amsterdam, 40, 91, 93, 95, 113, 170, 173, 185, 186, 190, 231, 261, 263
Anderson, Benedict, 9, 10, 11, 23, 137, 232, 267, 273
Angkor, 202, 244, 264
Angkor Wat, 1, 249, 266
Anglo-Dutch treaty of 1814, 27, 38
Anom, I. Gusti Ngurah, xii, 101, 277
archaeological resource management, 4
Archaeological Service (Indonesian), 157, 202, 208, 209, 220, 221, 233, 257, 258, 259, 261, 273
Archaeological Service (Oudheidkundige Dienst), 12, 84, 85, 96, 120, 127, 129, 133, 135, 136, 137, 141, 144, 145, 146, 151, 153, 163, 165, 166, 170, 176, 177, 178, 179, 181, 183, 185, 186, 189, 194, 196, 197, 198, 199, 200, 201, 202, 203, 204, 207, 208, 212, 216, 219, 220, 224, 225, 226, 235, 241, 242, 247, 249, 251, 261, 263, 265
Archaeological Society in Yogyakarta, 61, 64, 65, 79, 88, 95, 125, 199
Ardhana, I Ketut, xii
Ardika, I Wayan, xii
Arsip Nasional Republik Indonesia. *See* Indonesian National Archives
Asia Raya, 157
Astawa, Anak Agung Gde Oka, xii
Atmoko, Agus Widi, xii
Aziatische Kunst, 231

Babad Kĕdiri, 121, 122, 123
Badaruddin II, Mahmud (Sultan), 168
Badjang Ratoe, 114, 115, 117
Badung, 197, 210
Balai Pelestarian Peninggalan Purbakala. *See* BP3
Balai Poestaka, 127
Bali, 11, 14, 15, 98, 99, 103, 197, 206, 207, 220–224, 227, 233, 239, 242, 275, 276
Bamian, 5
Banda Aceh, 14
Bandung Bandawasa, 25
Bangkok, 76, 80, 81
Banjumas, 45
Bantam. *See* Banten
Banten, 12, 13, 14, 228
Banyunibo temple. *See* Candi Banyunibo
Banyuwangi, 135
Barisan Pelopor Soerabaia, 206
Basha, Fami, 279, 280
Batavia, 9, 42, 78, 111, 118, 126, 129, 131, 132, 133, 137, 139, 141, 142, 144, 148, 152, 165, 166, 167, 170, 178, 182, 186, 204, 207, 208, 211, 213, 229, 249
Bataviaasch Genootschap van Kunsten en Wetenschappen. *See* Batavian Society of Arts and Sciences

Bataviaasch Museum. *See* Batavian Museum
Batavian Museum (Bataviaasch Museum), 122, 126, 147, 151, 164, 165, 171, 176, 177, 179, 180, 182, 183, 186, 197, 204, 207, 210, 225, 226, 227, 228, 230
Batavian Society of Arts and Sciences (Bataviaasch Genootschap van Kunsten en Wetenschappen), 13, 35, 36, 42, 58, 59, 64, 70, 78, 86, 108, 110, 111, 112, 120, 125, 127, 128, 134, 142, 144, 177, 181, 183, 185, 186, 201, 225
Batenburg, C. J., 169, 173, 176
Batoe Gadjah, 179
Baud, G. L., 50, 51, 52
Baud, Jean Chrétien, 41, 42, 50
Bayly, Susan, 10, 238
Bazuki, xi
Bedulu, 214–220
Berg, Cornelis C., 132, 161, 162, 163
Berlage, H. P., 201, 202
Bernet Kempers, August, 200, 207, 208, 209, 233, 252, 256, 273
Bernhard von Lippe-Biesterfeld (Prince), viii, 92, 261, 262, 263
Bernhardt, Sarah, 73
Beuge, J. A. van, 183
Bhawanagara, 219
Bie, C. W. P. de, 171, 181, 182
Biesheuvel, Barend, 262
Blora, 71, 73
Bodden, Michael H., 151
Bodh Gaya, 1, 3, 61, 76
Boedi Oetomo, 126, 150, 213
Boediardjo, 258
Boemi Segoro, 38, 43
Boonstra, Sadiah, x
Boro Boemen, 38, 43
Borobudur, 1–3, 8, 15, 23, 32, 38, 39, 43, 44, 45–47, 61, 63–68, 69, 76–84, 85, 94, 116, 121, 139, 151, 175, 176, 189, 195, 196, 199, 207, 209, 236–245, 246, 249, 250–255, 256, 257, 258, 259, 262, 264, 277, 279, 280
  Borobudur and Prambanan Archaeological Park, 255, 258
  PT Taman Wisata Borobudur, 249, 255, 257, 258, 259
  restoration, 81, 86, 88, 195, 209, 235, 242, 247, 254, 255, 256, 258, 261, 263, 265, 279, 280
  visit to, 1, 3, 6, 15, 19, 23, 33, 43, 44, 45, 47, 62, 63, 64, 65, 70, 71, 72, 73, 74, 75, 205, 245, 246, 247, 250, 261, 266, 280
Bosch, F. D. K., 85, 141, 145, 146, 147, 148, 151, 170, 176, 177, 178, 185, 186, 200, 201, 202, 212, 232, 241
BP3 (Balai Pelestarian Peninggalan Purbakala), 102, 214, 223, 224, 270
Bramartani, 121
Brandes, Jan Laurens Andries, 98, 108, 124–128, 199, 200, 217
Brawijaya, 102, 122, 123, 124, 128, 133, 148, 271, 272
Brawijaya Division, 102, 270, 271, 273
Brawoe temple. *See* Candi Brawoe
Brebes, 59, 65, 116
Browidjojo, 114
Brummelhuis, Han ten, xii
Brumund, Jan Frederik Gerrit, 97, 107, 108, 136
Buchheim, Eveline, xiii
Buddhism, 1, 5, 19, 62, 63, 75, 76–78, 79, 81, 83, 86, 91, 94, 100, 123, 135, 137, 151, 175, 191, 200, 204, 236, 238, 239, 241, 255, 266, 281
Buddingh, S.A., 59, 60, 116, 173
Bukit Siguntang, 174, 177
Bunkyo Kyoku. *See* Department of Education
Bustaman, Saleh Sharif, 120

Cabolang, 32, 33
Cakra Něgara, 98
Campa, Princess of (Putri Campa), 102
Candi Banyunibo, 204
Candi Borobudur. *See* Borobudur
Candi Brahoe, 128
Candi Brawoe, 114
Candi Kalasan, 30, 79, 175, 176, 189
Candi Lumbung, 43
Candi Mendut, 32, 38, 39, 45, 64, 69, 74, 80, 82, 116, 125, 175, 176, 189, 200
Candi Papak, 44
Candi Pasar, 113
Candi Plaosan, 81, 92, 204
Candi Rimbi, 110
Candi Sari, 28, 79, 89, 90, 91
Candi Sewu, 25, 29, 37, 199
Candi Singasari, 22, 25, 30, 37, 40, 41, 44, 80, 84, 85, 87
Candi Sukuh, 45
Candi Tikus, 135, 138
Canny, Agus, xi
Capellen, G. van der, 38
Carey, Peter, 30, 105, 106
Caron, L. J. J., 216
Casparis, Johannes G. de, 163, 208
Centre for Indonesian Arts (Pusat Kesenian Indonesia), 157

Centre for the Guidance of Popular Culture and Enlightenment (Keimin Bunka Shidosho), 157
Cephas, Kassian, 65, 79, 247, 250
ceramics, 118, 197, 224–230
Chambert-Loir, Henry, xi
Chandra Dewi, Ni Lu Putu, xi
Chihara, Daigoro, 250, 251, 252, 256
Chinese people, 1, 2, 3, 6, 23, 29, 30, 35, 39, 41, 43, 45, 71, 102, 160, 172, 190, 197, 212, 224–230, 231, 232, 270
Christianity, 46, 58, 71, 74, 75
Chulalongkorn, xii, 15, 19, 61, 62, 63, 65, 76, 78–81, 82–89, 92, 95, 199, 238, 239
Citroen, Cosman, 145
Clarke, Stanley, 93
Coedès, Georges, 84, 86, 174, 175, 176, 186, 190
Colijn, H., 71
Colonial Institute (Koloniaal Instituut, Amsterdam), 91, 92, 93, 95, 112, 170, 173, 185, 190, 261, 263
colonial state, 9, 11, 14, 16, 19, 22, 23, 27, 33, 38, 39, 42, 43, 45, 47, 49, 54, 55, 56, 63, 87, 89, 93, 96, 107, 110, 120, 124, 129, 137, 149, 165, 166, 169, 174, 178, 196, 197, 198, 207, 210, 212, 216, 232, 235
colonialism, 6, 10, 13, 14, 37, 89, 95, 116, 138, 168, 184, 191, 198, 213, 232, 249, 260
Committee for Javanese Cultural Development (Comité voor de Javaansche Cultuurontwikkeling), 150
Cooper, Frederick, 9
Coremans, Paul, 243, 263
Cornelius, H. C., 24, 34, 36, 37
Cremer, J. T., 88

Daendels, H. W., 15, 26
Dahlan Mahibat, Ahmad, 192
Daly, Patrick, 17
Damrong Rajanubhap (Prince), 61, 82, 84, 85, 86
Danardono, Donny, xii
Daniell, William, 37
Danuningrat, Ario, 44
Deli, 88
Demak, xi, 22, 54, 55, 56, 59, 60, 69, 102, 111, 113, 116, 124, 132, 148, 159, 188, 267, 277, 278
  Great Mosque of Demak, ix, 15, 16, 19, 22, 23, 47–60, 89, 267, 268, 277, 278, 281
demolition, 15, 51, 52, 53, 55, 57, 87, 89, 91, 179, 181
Denpasar, xii, 210, 214, 223
Department of Education (Bunkyo Kyoku), 204, 247
Department of Education and Culture, 101, 206
Destrika, xi
destruction, 4, 5, 13, 14, 15, 22, 23, 27, 50, 112, 116, 182, 196, 197, 198, 207, 210, 232, 263
Deventer, van (Resident), 111
Dewa, xii
Dharmowijono, Widjajanti, xii
Dhaugkul Singh, 31
Dieng, 45
Dihan, xii
Dinas Purbakala, 207, 235, 242
Dipanagara, 39, 57
Djajadiningrat, Hoesein, 132, 166, 231
Djambi. *See* Jambi
Djawa, 133, 172
Djawa Baroe, 249
Djawatan Purbakala, 207
Djokja. *See* Yogyakarta
Djokjakarta. *See* Yogyakarta
Djoko Dolok. *See* Joko Dolok
Drieënhuizen, Caroline, x
Dumarçay, Jacques, 263, 264
Dutch East India Company (Vereenigde Oostindische Compagnie, VOC), 13, 24, 37, 173, 174
Duti, Mas, xi

earthquakes, 2, 197, 210, 211, 214, 221, 222, 232
Eberhardt, Gisela, xiii
École française d'Extrême-Orient (EFEO), xi, 174, 194, 263, 264
Eerde, J. C. van, 170, 185, 186
EFEO. *See* École française d'Extrême Orient
Engelhard, H. E. D., 169
Engelhard, Nicolaus, 22, 24, 25, 30, 34, 36, 37, 39, 40, 41, 45, 60, 80, 87, 196
Erp, John W. T. van, 235, 243, 261
Erp, Theodoor van, 81, 82, 84, 85, 86, 195, 199, 234, 242, 245, 247, 251, 261, 263, 264

Falser, Michael, xiii
Fatah (Raden), 47
Fatah, Haji Abdul, xi
First World War, 93
Florida, Nancy, 47
Forbes, H. O., 171
Forrer, Kuniko, xiii
Forrer, Matthi, xiii
Friedenthal, Alberto, 76
Friederich, R., 217
Fruin-Mees, W., 127, 131, 151

Furusawa, Yasujiro, 247, 249, 250, 252
Futagami, Yoko, xiii

Gadjah Mada University, 221, 257, 261, 274, 277
Gajah Mada, 129, 150, 151, 152–156, 271, 272
Gebhardt, Andrew, xiii
Geding Soera, 188
Gedung Arca, 223
Gehren, A. H. von, 169
Gending Sriwijaya, 164, 192
General Dutch Language Association (Algemeen Nederlandsch Verbond), 175
Gentengkali, 205
Gere, Richard, 266
Giffen, A. E. van, 171
Gimbirowati, 24, 25
Goenoeng Kidoel, 183
Gomperts, Amrith, 105, 106
graves, 15, 22, 24, 25, 30, 39, 48, 50, 52, 60, 100, 101, 102, 107, 114, 116, 119, 122, 127, 128, 159, 174, 177, 181, 188, 204, 272, 276, 278
Great Mosque of Demak. *See under* Demak
Griffiths, Arlo, xi
Groneman, Isaac, 61, 63, 65, 71, 72, 75, 76, 77, 79, 82, 199
Groslier, Bernard Philippe, 244, 264
Grote Postweg, 26
Gunawan, Bambang, xii
Gunung Agung, 211
Gunung Tidhal, 43

Haag, Arnout, 105, 106
Hakubutukan, 204
Halmahera, 197, 227, 228, 229, 231
Hamengkubuwono II, 24, 30
Hamengkubuwono III, 28
Hamengkubuwono V, 51
Hamengkubuwono VII, 64, 79, 199
Hardiati, Endang Sri, xii
Hartmann, C. L., 43
Haryono, Timbul, xii
Haviz, Abdul, xii
Hayam Wuruk, 97, 103, 150, 162
Hendrik (Prince), 45, 64
heritage awareness, 3, 17, 22, 23, 42, 48, 50, 72, 76, 77, 86, 87, 89, 96, 106, 116, 119, 135, 176, 219, 223, 253, 278
Heyting, L. C., 183, 185, 186
Hideichi, Sakazume, 205, 247, 250
Hindu–Buddhist sites, 5, 14, 15, 16, 18, 20, 22, 23, 25, 28, 30, 34, 43, 45, 62, 63, 64, 77, 78, 79, 81, 89, 96, 102, 139, 151, 158, 169, 194, 195, 198, 199, 201, 202, 203, 213, 235, 238, 246, 249, 251, 265, 279, 281
Hinduism, 31, 96, 100, 121, 122, 135, 136, 147, 149, 157, 169, 174, 196, 200, 201, 204, 211, 217, 233, 238, 257
Ho, Engseng, 10
Hoëvell, Wolter Robert van, 15, 58, 59, 60, 108, 111, 112, 113, 114, 116, 117, 136
Hogendorp, C. S. W. van, 42
Holt, Claire, 267
Hoock, Holger, 27
Hoop, A. N. J. Th. à Th. van der, 170, 178–180, 182–183, 185–186
Horii, Hoko, xiii
Horn, Nico van, xi
Hoven, W., 169
Hurst Boram, A. W., 74

iconoclasm, 5, 41
Ijiri, Masuro, xiii
Ijiri, Susume, xiii, 246, 250, 251, 252
Ijiri, Yuko, xiii
IJzerman, J. W., 65, 88, 90, 91, 247
Indische Courant, 144, 145
Indische Partij, 150
Indonesian National Archives (Arsip Nasional Republik Indonesia), 47
invented traditions, 136, 192
Islam, 3, 5, 12, 13, 16, 20, 46, 47, 48, 49, 51, 57, 69, 70, 91, 100, 102, 111, 112, 120, 121, 122, 135, 148, 149, 150, 159, 174, 179, 211, 267, 269, 276–281
Islamic sites, 10, 14, 16, 18, 23, 47, 48, 100, 107, 127, 188, 277, 279
Isyima, 204
Ita, Mahirta, x
Itagaki, 246
Iwasaki, Yasuhiro, xi

Jacobs, Femke, xiii
Jakarta, xi, 97, 156, 204, 209, 222, 229, 247, 249, 263, 272
Jambi, xii, 164, 165, 167, 169, 175, 178, 192, 224
Jarernparn, Penpan, xii
Java Institute (Yogyakarta), 138, 146, 172, 201
Java War, 3, 19, 23, 39, 41, 43, 54, 56, 103
Javaansche Cultuurcongres, 151
Johnston, Susi, xii
Joko Dolok, 108–111, 119
Jombang, 110, 133
Jonckbloedt, G., 75
Jong Sumatra, 191
Jong Sumatranen Bond, 190, 191
Jourdan, H. G., 106, 107

Juliana (Queen), 92, 97, 261, 262
Junatama, Herman Sinung, 279
Junius, F. J., 169

Kadè, xii
Kadilangu, 48
Kalasan temple. *See* Candi Kalasan
Kalijaga, 48
Kantor Besar Poesat Kebudajaan. *See* Centre for the Guidance of Popular Culture and Enlightenment
Kartodipoera, (Raden Toemenggoeng), 56
Kate, Herman ten, 71
Kayashima, 204, 249
Kedu, 38, 39, 43, 63, 82
Kedukan Bukit, 176
Keimin bunka shidosho. *See* Centre for the Guidance of Popular Culture and Enlightenment
Ken Dedes, 89, 152, 260
Kertanagera, 162
Ketut, Setiawan, xii
Kinosita, R., 204
Kinsbergen, Isidore van, 64
Kirtya Liefrinck Society, 216, 217, 219
Kita-Sumatoro-Sinbun
Soerat Kabar Harian, 248
Klaten, 24
Kleiweg de Zwaan, J. P., 186
Kloeroehang, 104
Kloos, David, xiii
Klungkung, 197, 210
Knebel, J., 117, 128, 141
Kobijitu Kenkyo Sho, 204
Koechling-Schwartz, A., 73
Koenigswald, G. H. R. von, 182
Koloniaal Instituut. *See* Colonial Institute
Koninklijk Bataviaasch Genootschap. *See* Batavian Society of Arts and Sciences
Koninklijk Instituut voor Taal-, Land- en Volkenkunde van Nederlandsch-Indië. *See* Royal Netherlands Institute of Linguistics, Geography and Ethnography of the Netherlands Indies
Koninklijk Nederlandsche Instituut van Wetenschappen, Letterkunde en Schone Kunsten. *See* Royal Dutch Institute of Sciences, Literature and Fine Arts
Koninklijk Nederlandsch Aardrijkskundig Genootschap. *See* Royal Dutch Geographical Society
Koperberg, Sam, 142
Kota Gede, 24
Kremer, J., 75
Krijgsman, C., 207, 220, 221, 223, 224
Krom, Nicolaas J., 130, 131, 135, 136, 137, 145, 162, 163, 175, 176, 189, 191, 200, 204, 248, 251, 264
Kromodjojo Adinegoro III. *See* Adinegoro III
Kromodjojo Adinegoro IV. *See* Adinegoro IV
Krtanagara, 108
Kurniawan, Muhammad, xii
Kusumayuda, 29
Kwartanada, Didi, xi
Kwee Ang Kie, 71

Lamster, J.C., 92
Lara Jonggrang, 25, 25, 29, 33, 198
Larigarde, Francois, xii
Legêne, Susan, x
Lemabang, 188
Lidchi, Henrietta, x
Lie, Ravando, xii
lieux de mémoire, 6, 8, 14
Limburg Stirum, J. P. graaf van, 213
Link, Fabian, xiii
Lombok, 14, 90, 98, 124, 185, 213, 216, 260
looting, 5, 14, 24, 25, 27, 86, 146, 207, 210
Louis Bonaparte, 26, 40
Lumbung temple. *See* Candi Lumbung

Ma Huan, 160
Mackenzie, Colin, 28, 28, 29, 35, 36, 37, 103, 107
Maclaine Pont, Henri, 130, 131, 132, 138–148, 150, 153, 156, 160, 249
Madiun, 71
Madura, 16, 22, 50, 51, 52, 53, 54, 57, 58, 113
Magelang, 38, 39, 43, 44, 68, 69, 71, 72, 73, 74, 75, 79, 82, 247
Majapahit, 19, 28, 45, 47, 58, 97–108, 111–124, 127–150, 156–163, 174, 182, 188, 191, 205, 211, 214, 217, 220, 224, 249, 270–273, 275, 279, 280
Majapahit Society, 141–144, 146
Malang, 22, 40, 141
Mangkubumi, 31
Mangkunegara VII, 45, 92, 196
Manguin, Pierre-Yves, 192
Margana, Sri, x
Marshall, William and Ethel J. Marshall, 75
Marzuki, Sangkot, x
Masanori, xi
Mata Deen, 31
Mataram, 24, 48, 54, 103, 104
Matsui, Akira, xii
Mattjik, (Raden) Hadji, 172

Mauss, Marcel, ix, 6, 78, 95, 100, 105, 257
Mendut temple. *See* Candi Mendut
Meyer, W., 65
Miert, Hans van, 150, 191
Miksic, John, xii, 63, 87, 101
Minto, (Lord), 26, 28
Moechtar, 164, 188
Moeis, Abdoel, 149
Moenaf, 188
Moerdiano, Retno, xi
Moewara Klingi, 172
Mojokerto, 106, 111, 112, 113, 116, 117, 118, 119, 120, 128, 129, 131, 133, 136, 137, 142, 145, 146, 147, 177
Mongkut (King Rama IV), 77, 84
Monnereau, D., 40
Moojen, P. A. J., 150, 212, 213
Moon of Pejeng, 216, 219, 222
mosques, ix, xi, 14, 15, 16, 19, 23, 47–53, 54, 55, 56, 58, 60, 89, 174, 212, 267, 268, 277, 278, 281
  Great Mosque of Demak. *See under* Demak
  Mosque of Banda Aceh, 14
  Mosque of Banten, 12, 13, 14
  Mosque of Palembang, 174
Muara Jambi, xii, 188, 189
Mundardjito, xii, 101
Museum Nasional in Jakarta. *See* National Museum (Jakarta)
Museum of Antiquities (Leiden), 40, 91
Museum Volkenkunde. *See* National Ethnographic Museum (Leiden)
Mysore, 28

Nagarakrtagama, 97, 98, 99, 101, 103, 114, 121, 124, 126, 127, 133, 135, 138, 152, 153, 158, 159, 160, 161, 163, 219, 260
National Ethnographic Museum (Leiden), 40, 210
National Museum (Museum Nasional, Jakarta), 12, 13, 78, 151, 273, 277
National Museum of World Cultures (Leiden), 40, 44, 80
nationalism, 9, 19, 96, 120, 121, 126, 130, 131, 132, 140, 148, 149, 150, 151, 152, 156, 157, 158, 163, 165, 166, 167, 179, 182, 191, 192, 200, 230, 238, 239, 242, 273, 274, 275, 280
NBC (National Broadcasting Company, USA), 275, 276
NEDECO, 260, 263
Neeb, C. J., 165
Nerada Thera, 239
Neratja, 149
Ngabehi Resonegoro, 56
Ngadiredjo, 74
Ngantung, Henk, 156
Nora, Pierre, 8
Novita, Aryandini, xii
Nugroho, Uji, x
Nung Cik A. R., 192
Nunuk, xi
Nurika, xi

Ockers, H. A. J., 180
Oetomo, Dede, xi
Oikawa, Koshiro, 251
Opak, 30
Orsoy de Flines, Egbert van, 197, 225, 226, 227, 228, 229, 230, 231, 232
Oudheidkundige Dienst. *See* Archeological Service

Pacific War, 12, 19, 157, 205, 229, 245, 250, 251, 252, 264, 265
Pakerisan (river), 214, 216, 220, 223
Pakubuwana II, 39
Pakubuwana IV, 24, 31, 32
Pakubuwana V, 32
Pakubuwana VI, 43
Pakubuwana VII, ix, 45, 47, 51, 104
Pakunataningrat I, Abdurrachman, 51
Palembang, xii, 102, 164–180, 186–193
Palembangsch Museum, 167
Palmyra, 5
Pané, Sanusi, 150, 151, 156–159, 160, 162
Panular, Arya (Pangéran), 29
Papak temple. *See* Candi Papak
Pararaton, 121, 126, 133, 135, 138, 152, 158, 161, 162
Pasar temple. *See* Candi Pasar
Pasemah, 165, 167, 169, 170, 171, 173, 178, 179, 180, 181, 183, 184, 187, 192
Patah (Raden), 102, 122, 148
Patram, I Wayan, xii
Pejeng, 214–220
Peleggi, Maurizio, 7, 83
Pelt, C. A., 172
pendopo, 60, 68, 115, 139, 142, 165, 169, 270, 271, 272
Pendopo Agung, 101, 156, 270, 271, 272
Peranakan. *See* Chinese people
Perquin, P. J., 177, 196, 199, 200, 202
Perry, W. J., 171
Pieneman, Nicolaas, 68

pilgrimages, 1, 3, 10, 12, 15, 22, 27, 45, 48, 54, 56, 60, 61, 62, 63, 76, 86, 100, 101, 117, 189, 238, 239, 260, 266, 270, 272, 278, 280
Pitukthanin, Anuk (Pooh), xii
Plaosan temple. *See* Candi Plaosan
Pleret, 24
Pleyte, C. M., 71
Poerbatjaraka, 127, 132, 160, 166, 207
Poerwolelono, 59, 60, 65, 68, 69, 70, 71, 116–118
porcelain. *See* ceramics
Post, Peter, xiii
post-colonial state, 6, 7, 10, 11, 19, 23, 98, 163, 223, 232, 235, 265
Prajnaparamita, 40, 89, 92, 152, 260
Prambanan, ix, 15, 19, 24, 25, 28–30, 32, 33, 36, 37, 43, 45, 48, 63, 64, 79, 80, 84, 85, 86, 87, 139, 194–200, 202, 204, 205, 206, 207, 208, 221, 225, 235, 241, 242, 247, 254, 255, 256, 257, 258, 265, 277, 279, 280, 281
Prang Wedono, (Adipati) Ario. *See* Mangkunegara VII
Prapanca, Mpu, 97, 138, 141, 150, 153, 157, 160, 162, 163
Prayono, Jack, xi
prehistory, 11, 19, 147, 164, 166, 167, 170, 172, 179, 182, 183, 184, 185, 274
Probolinggo, 123, 124
Progo-Brojonolan, 71
PT Taman Borobudur dan Prambanan. *See* Borobudur and Prambanan Archaeological Park
Pujangga Baru, 159
Pulau Kemaro, 269
Puputan, 14, 210
Pura Besakih, 211
oura Penataran Sasih, 216, 219, 222
Purnomo, Pujo, xi
Purwanto, Bambang, x
pusaka, 18, 103, 104, 224, 227, 228, 232
Pusat Kesenian Indonesia. *See* Center for Indonesian Arts
Putri Campa, 100, 128, 272. *See* Campa, Princess of
Putten, Jan van der, xii

Raaf, R. M. E., 79
Raben, Remco, x
Raffles, T. S., 3, 9, 26, 27, 28, 31, 34, 35, 36, 37, 38, 39, 41, 43, 45, 63, 77, 94, 103, 105, 106, 107, 113, 117, 266
Rahardjo, Tjahjono, xii
Raj, Cokorde Gde, xii
Rajasanagara, (King). *See* Hayam Wuruk
Rama IV. *See* Mongkut
Rama VI. *See* Vajiravudh
Rangkuti, Nurhadi, xii
Rasser, W. H., 217
regime change, 4, 5, 10, 12, 18, 19, 23, 26, 33, 112, 203, 220–224, 232
Reid, Anthony, 131
Reinwardt, C. G. C., 40
Rĕksadiwirya, Ky. Ng., 122
religion, 15, 16, 20, 70, 74, 94, 122, 123, 216, 217, 275, 276
restoration, 16, 19, 22, 23, 47–50, 52, 53, 54, 55, 56, 57, 85, 88, 89, 96, 101, 196, 197, 198, 199, 200, 201, 202, 203, 209, 211, 212, 213, 214, 221, 222, 234, 235, 244, 246, 249, 253, 267, 277, 278
restoration of Borobudur. *See* Borobudur: restoration
restoration of Demak Mosque. *See under* Demak
Reuvens, Caspar J. C., 40, 41, 112
Revire, Nicolas, xii
Rhys Davids, T. W., 77
Ricklefs, Merle C., 102, 106, 120, 121, 122, 123
Ridwan, Koriaty, xii
Riggs, John, 118
Rijksmuseum Amsterdam, 84, 231, 232, 263
Rimbi temple. *See* Candi Rimbi
Ripaul Singh, 31
Rizki, xi
Robson, Stuart, 114
Romijn, Peter, x
Romondt, Vincent van, 202, 207, 233, 235, 261
Roock, J. D. de, 178
Rouffaer, G. P., 71
Royal Batavian Society. *See* Batavian Society of Arts and Sciences
Royal Dutch Geographical Society (Koninklijk Nederlandsch Aardrijkskundig Genootschap, KNAG), 164
Royal Dutch Institute of Sciences, Literature and Fine Arts (Koninklijk Nederlandsch Instituut van Wetenschappen), 40
Royal Netherlands Institute of Linguistics, Geography and Ethnography of the Netherlands Indies, 59
Rozak, Abdul, xi

Sakata, Takashi, xiii
Saleh, (Raden), 68

Salis, A. M. T. de, 110
Sancigny, Ernest De, 42
Sanggar Pamalangan, 114
Santikarma, Degung, xii
Sarasin, Fritz, 184
Sarasin, Paul, 184
Sarekat Islam, 149, 150
Sari temple. *See* Candi Sari
Sato, Katsura, xiii
Satyawati Soeryono Soeryo, 209, 273
Save Borobudur campaign, 101, 222, 235, 236, 250, 252, 255, 260, 265
Sawita, Roro, xii
Scheltema, J. F., 87
Scherbatoff, (Prince and Princess), 73
Schneider, H., 228
Schnitger, F. M., 153, 154, 167, 171, 180, 182, 186–190
Schulte Nordholt, Henk, x, xiii
Second World War. *See* Pacific War
Seinendan, 206
Sekh Amongraga, 32
Semarang, xii, 22, 24, 37, 50, 53, 54, 55, 56, 73, 74, 116, 141, 226
Sengupta, Indra, xiii
Sento, xi
Sepoeh, 183
Serat Centhini, 32, 33, 59
Sĕrat Dĕrmagandhul, 121, 122, 123, 124
Serat Rama, 33
Sewu temple. *See* Candi Sewu
Shaeffer, Adolph, 64
shared heritage, 7
Sieburgh, H. N., 1, 2, 3, 43, 44, 45, 64, 108, 110
Simanjuntak, Truman, xi
Singasari, 81, 89, 108, 152, 163
Singasari temple. *See* Candi Singasari
Singen Lor, 54
Siti Inggil, 272
Siva, 194–195, 197, 198–200, 203–209, 221, 226, 232–233, 235, 242, 246, 248
Skilling, Peter, xii
Sloet van der Beele, L. A. J. W. (governor-general), 183
Smith, Laurajane, 17
Snouck Hurgronje, C., 71
Soehamir, 203, 204, 206, 207
Soeharto (Suharto), 97, 102, 156, 222, 243, 254, 255, 259, 261, 267, 269, 270, 272, 274, 275
Soejono, R. P., xii, 273, 274
Soejono, Widjojo, 271, 272
Soekarno (Sukarno), 156, 191, 192, 194, 195, 202, 208, 221, 230, 233, 243, 254, 272, 275
Soekarno, Dhyanti, xi
Soekawati, Tjokorde Gde Raka, 218
Soekmono, 32, 157, 209, 221, 233, 242, 244, 257, 258, 261, 273
Soenario, 132
Soeparno, xi
Soeriokoesoemo, Soetatmo, 150–152, 159, 212, 213
Soetomo, Ariswata, xi
Sommot, (Prince), 61
Sonobudoyo Museum, 146, 147
Sosrodiningrat, ix, 51
Srivijaya, 19, 166, 167, 172, 173, 174, 175, 176, 177, 186, 187, 188, 189, 190–193, 270
SS-Ahnenerbe, 190
Stapel, Frederik Willem, 163, 187
statues, 14, 19, 22, 24–26, 29, 31, 31, 32, 33, 37, 39, 40, 63, 69, 78, 79, 80, 82, 83, 86, 87, 89, 92, 96, 104, 107, 108–111, 114, 116, 119, 129, 135, 136, 137, 147, 151, 152, 154, 156, 159, 169, 170, 172, 177, 179, 189, 201, 207, 214, 215, 219, 260, 271
  Buddha statues, 45, 77, 80, 81, 82, 83, 86, 94, 172, 188, 245, 255, 263, 277
  Ganesha statues, 41, 85
  Joko Dolok statue. *See* Joko Dolok
Stein Callenfels, P. V. van, 84, 85, 143, 175, 183, 184, 185, 186, 188, 217, 241
Steur, Pa and Ma van der, 71, 74, 75
Stichting Behoud Borobudur, 260, 264
Stoler, Ann, 264
Stuers, Victor de, 88
Sturler, W. L. de, 173, 176
Stutterheim, Willem F., 160, 161, 162, 189, 200, 210, 216–220, 222, 224, 246, 264, 267
Suarbhawa, xii
Sucoro, xi
Sugriwa, I. Gusti Bagus, 221, 233
Sukianto, Alin, xi
Sukuh temple. *See* Candi Sukuh
Sultan Mahmud Badaruddin II Museum, 190
Suluk Gatholoco, 121
Sumasĕntika, M., 122
Sumatra, 19, 88, 150, 159, 164–168, 169, 170, 171, 172, 175, 176, 178, 179–193, 267
Sumedi, Tular, x
Sumenep, 50, 51, 54, 57

Sundari, Ekowati, xi
Suntarawanitch, Chalong, xii
Supomo, 131, 159, 162
Surakarta (Solo), ix, 24, 31, 32, 43, 45, 47, 50, 51, 52, 54, 55, 56, 57, 73, 74, 81, 92, 103, 104, 116, 126, 131, 132, 133, 141, 142, 148, 149, 196, 257
Surjadjaja, Claudia, x
Suryanti, N., 263
Sutaba, I Made, xii
Sutherland, Heather, x
Sutopo, Marsia, xi
Swaab, J. L. M., 172
Sweta, I. Made, 219
Switzerland, 184
Syafei, Mohammed, 192
Sysling, Fenneke, x

Tagore, Rabindranath, 235, 239, 240, 241, 251
Takakusu, J., 174
Takekoshi, Yosaburo, 246
Talang Pangeran, 172
Talang Tuwo, 176
Taman Apsari, 110, 111
Tan Jin Sing, 29
Tandjoeng Aro, 181, 182, 184
Tangkilisan, Daniel, xii
Tanudirjo, Daud Aris, x
Tarik, 147
Tashiro, Akiko, xii
Tawang Mangoe, 104
Tego, xi
Tempo, 259
Tengger, 135
Thomassen à Thuessink van der Hoop, A. N. J., 170, 178, 179, 180, 182, 183, 185, 186. *See* Hoop, A. N. .J. Th. à Th. van der
Tidhal, 43
Tikus temple. *See* Candi Tikus
Tjakra Adiningrat, 51
Tjakranegara, 14, 124
Tjokro Negoro, (Toemenggoeng), 73
Tjokro Negoro, Pandji, 110
Tjokroaminoto, Oemar Said, 149
Tjokrosoejoso, Abi Koesno, 149
Tjondro Negoro, 59
Tjondronegoro V. *See* Poerwolelono
Tobler, August, 184
Tombrink, E. P., 169
tourism, 1, 3, 9, 15, 61, 71, 72, 73, 111, 209, 223, 238, 257, 258, 260, 265
Troloyo, 100
Trowulan, 45, 98, 100, 101, 102, 104, 105, 106, 107, 108, 113, 114, 128, 131, 132, 135, 136, 139, 142, 144, 145, 146, 147, 153, 154, 156, 158, 159, 205, 248, 270, 271, 272
Tsurumi, Yusuke, 246

UGM. *See* Gadjah Mada University
Ullmann, S., 169
UNESCO, 1, 5, 7, 15, 17, 20, 101, 194, 209, 214, 222, 235, 236, 237, 238, 242, 243, 244, 249, 250, 252, 253, 254, 255, 256, 259, 263, 264, 265, 280
United Nations Educational, Scientific and Cultural Organization. *See* UNESCO
Universitas Gadjah Mada. *See* Gadjah Mada University
Usana Bali, 217, 220
Uyl, Joop den, 262

Vajiravudh, (King Rama VI), 83
Valck, F. G., 34, 169
Vayyna, Banthe, xi
Verbeek, Rogier D. M., 108, 109, 127, 128
Vereenigde Oostindische Compagnie. *See* Dutch East India Company
Vereeniging Majapahit. *See* Majapahit Society
Victoria and Albert Museum, 93, 94, 95
Vienna, 187, 189
violence, 4, 12, 14, 18, 20, 69, 124, 168, 197, 210, 243, 268, 269, 270, 273, 276, 279
Vlis, C. J. van der, 51, 103
VOC. *See* Dutch East India Company
Vogel, J. Ph., 175
Vogel, Jakob, xiii
Voûte, C., 244

Wali Songo, 47, 116, 279
war, 4, 5, 10, 14, 18, 23, 35, 39, 50, 69, 98, 159, 196, 197, 203, 207, 232, 246, 253, 264, 269, 273
Wardenaar, J. W. B., 105, 107, 108, 109, 110, 112, 113, 114, 117, 128, 141
Waringin Lawang, 113
Warsaw, 189
Wat Bowomiwet, 84
Wat Phra Keo, 83
Wat Rachathiwat, 84
Wayang Limbak, I, 218, 220
Wederopbouw, 126, 149, 151
Wediodiningrat, Radjiman, 150, 202

Westenenk, L. C., 170, 175, 176
Westerkamp, Pim, x
Widodo, xi
Wijayanti, Widya, xii
Wijck, C. H. A. van der, 80, 82
Wilkens, A., 64, 71
Willem I (King), 40, 87, 89
Willems, Erik, x
Wilsen, F. C., 45, 46, 47
Winter, Tim, 17
World War I, 93. *See* First World War
World War II. *See* Pacific War
Worms, Sjir, xiii

Yamin, Muhammad, 150, 151, 152–156, 159, 162, 182, 190, 191, 194, 233, 280
Yanti, xi
Yogyakarta, 24, 27, 28, 29, 30, 31, 34, 35, 50, 51, 52, 53, 54, 55, 56, 57, 64, 69, 73, 80, 82, 88, 103, 104, 125, 126, 131, 132, 133, 141, 142, 148, 150, 201, 204, 207, 208, 247